The
Austrian
Mind

AN
INTELLECTUAL
AND
SOCIAL
HISTORY
1848-1938

Architecture of the 1880's
along Vienna's Ringstrasse, looking across
Parliament toward Town Hall
and the university.

The Austrian Mind

AN INTELLECTUAL AND SOCIAL HISTORY 1848-1938

WILLIAM M. JOHNSTON

UNIVERSITY OF
CALIFORNIA PRESS
BERKELEY   LOS ANGELES   LONDON

University of California Press

Berkeley and Los Angeles, California

University of California Press, Ltd.

London, England

Copyright © 1972 by The Regents of the University of California

First California Paperback Printing 1983

ISBN 0-520-04955-1 (alk. paper)

Library of Congress Catalog Card Number: 75-111418

Designed by Wolfgang Lederer

Printed in the United States of America

5   6   7   8   9

The paper used in this publication meets the minimum
requirements of American National Standard for Information
Sciences—Permanence of Paper for Printed Library Materials,
ANSI Z39.48-1984. ⊚

Magistris,
Amicis,
Discipulisque

Etwas Neues kann man nur finden,
wenn man das Alte kennt.

One can find something new
only if one knows the old

—Jean Gebser
URSPRUNG UND
GEGENWART

Preface

This volume will, I earnestly hope, stimulate—or as the case may be, irritate—future researchers into reexamining the entire range of modern Austrian thought. To facilitate further study I have included biographical sketches together with bibliographies for nearly every major figure discussed. In passing, mention is made of many less conspicuous figures who deserve renewed attention. Throughout, my intention is to open up this long-neglected field, not to foreclose it.

A word about usage is in order. In presenting quotations, I have included in the footnotes—and sometimes in the text—the German original for nearly every passage quoted. Translations are my own except where otherwise noted. Perhaps to the dismay of those who do not read German, I have not translated book titles. The context will, I hope, indicate the subject of such books. I have cited place names by their German equivalents except for standard anglicizations such as Vienna, Prague, or Styria.

A book of this scope distills its author's entire experience. It would be futile to enumerate conversations, lectures, readings, or travels that inspired one passage or another. Yet, I owe a special debt to those Austrian intellectuals who encouraged the enterprise at its inception. During 1966-1967 Professor Werner Haas, now of Ohio State University, stimulated my interest in Austria—with consequences that he little imagined. During the summer of 1967 at Vienna, I was privileged to talk with Professor Franz Theodor Csokor (d. 1969), Professor Friedrich Heer, Professor Ernst Florian Winter, Dr. Viktor Süchy, and Ernst Fischer. At Budapest I conducted memorable interviews with Professor Antal Mádl and Professor Georg Lukács (d. 1971). The views of these scholars broadened and sharpened my own, while inciting me to renewed effort.

During the fall of 1967 I conversed in New York with Professor Ernst Waldinger (d. 1970), and later I corresponded most fruitfully with Professor Ludwig von Bertalanffy, now at the State University of New York at Buffalo. Repeatedly Professor Werner Stark of Fordham University bolstered my enthusiasm with discerning suggestions. Professor Robert A. Kann of Rutgers University offered incisive advice once he had completed his duties as chairman of the Jury for the Austrian History Prize. Finally, each of two unknown readers for the University of California Press left a far-reaching imprint on the book.

All illustrations come from the Bildarchiv of the Österreichische Nationalbibliothek, Vienna.

While preparing the first drafts, I enjoyed invaluable support from the University of Massachusetts Graduate School. A research grant, authorized by Edward C. Moore, then dean of the Graduate School, sustained me when all other sources of financial aid had failed. Throughout, my wife has exemplified, as only she can, the wisdom of George Eliot's statement, "Those who trust us educate us."

W. M. J.

Amherst, Massachusetts

Contents

List of Illustrations

Introduction

OBJECTIVES AND OBSTACLES
OF AUSTRIAN INTELLECTUAL HISTORY

"THE GAY APOCALYPSE"—so Hermann Broch called the period from 1848 to 1918 within the Habsburg Empire and, above all, at Vienna, where old and new attitudes interacted with unequaled fecundity. It was in Austria and its successor states that many, perhaps even most, of the seminal thinkers of the twentieth century emerged: Freud, Brentano, Husserl, Buber, Wittgenstein, Lukács, and countless others. This book investigates why so many innovative thinkers should have inhabited that vanished realm. An arrangement into six themes coordinates sociological analysis with exposition of approximately seventy major thinkers. These individuals have been selected both for the extent of their contributions to academic disciplines and for the vividness with which they illustrate Austrian attitudes.

Part One shows how bureaucracy sustained the Habsburg Empire while inciting economists, legal theorists, and socialists to urge reform. Part Two examines how Vienna's coffeehouses, theaters, and concert halls stimulated creativity together with complacency. Part Three explores the fin-de-siècle world view known as Viennese Impressionism. Interacting with positivistic science, this reverence for the ephemeral inspired such pioneers as Mach, Wittgenstein, Buber, and Freud. Part Four describes the vision of an ordered cosmos which flourished among Germans in Bohemia. Their philosophers cultivated a Leibnizian faith whose eventual collapse haunted Kafka and Mahler. Part Five explains how in Hungary wishful thinking reinforced a political activism rare elsewhere in Habsburg domains. Engagé intellectuals like Lukács and Mannheim systematized the sociology of knowledge, while two other Hungarians, Herzl and Nordau, initiated political Zionism. Part Six investigates certain attitudes that have permeated Austrian thought, such as hostility to technology and delight in polar opposites.

No branch of historical inquiry has been so hampered by conflicting methodologies as has intellectual history. Exponents of one or another approach proceed as if their method excluded or subsumed all others.[1] In an effort to untangle these disputes, I propose to differentiate three disciplines within intellectual history. These I call internal history of ideas, the sociology of thinkers, and the sociology of engagé intellectuals. In order to delineate what I conceive to be an all-inclusive program for intellectual history, I shall explain how these three disciplines relate to one another. All three are implemented in this book.

The first and irreplaceable discipline of intellectual history expounds ideas for their own sake, in isolation from individuals and society. Mathematics and philosophy epitomize the necessity for expositing what a man said while ignoring whatever extrinsic reasons may have impelled him to say it. Among Austrian philosophers, Bolzano and Husserl exemplified a logical rigor that outsoared social limitations. Certain Austrian historians of ideas such as Karl Pribram and Rudolf Eisler conceived categories as timeless entities that constitute a seamless web overarching all ages and milieus. However much Habsburg society may have helped to elicit their Platonism, these scholars rightly insisted that internal history of ideas must precede every other form of intellectual history.

Before one can undertake sociological analysis, it is essential to record not merely what opinions a theorist held, but what arguments he advanced to support them. Accordingly, I have supplied for nearly every major philosopher and social theorist an exposition of his principal theses, together with some analysis of his argumentation. In order to bring out debaters' nuances, I have used comparisons, adducing both allies and adversaries to contrast with a given contention. Wherever possible, I have phrased exposition of each thinker in terms that he himself could have understood. To reconstruct a thinker's lifework requires that the historian should have received formal instruction in each of the disciplines treated. There is no other way to learn how to exegete technical terms, to unravel crucial issues, and to interpret previous masters of a field. In this book, philosophy, theology, political theory, sociology, and history of literature provide the underpinnings upon which my formulations rest.

To expound a thinker's principal arguments does not by itself constitute intellectual history. A second discipline, known loosely as the sociology of knowledge, aims to situate theorists in society. To avoid ambiguities inherent in this term, I shall introduce two new labels, which differentiate the main field from a subdivision of it. However clumsy such new labels may seem, there is no simpler designation of conflicting ways in which thinkers react to society. What I call the sociology of thinkers examines how milieu modifies a person's thought.

A subdivision of this field, which I call sociology of engagé intellectuals, explores how thinkers seek to modify their milieu. The first treats each thinker as a recipient of social influences; the second views him as a disseminator of them. The distinction is crucial because—*pace* Marx—not every thinker plays the second role.

Once a theorist's premises have been exposited, a question arises as to how these may have been shaped by his milieu. Such an inquiry may embark on either of two levels, which following Werner Stark I call micro- and macro-sociology. Micro-sociology of thinkers examines formative influences exercised upon intellectuals by their immediate environment, especially during childhood and youth. The example of parents, schools, and church, and later of military service, profession, and hobbies channels a man's thinking, reinforcing some options and foreclosing others. Early influences leave an indelible imprint precisely because a child cannot choose them; he inherits them. Among impulses that are first inherited only later to be embraced or rejected, religion plays a paramount role. In this book I have emphasized how frequently a vestige of theology persisted beneath seemingly nonreligious creativity.[2] Even the most secularized of Austrian thinkers imbibed during childhood Jewish or Christian attitudes that could not easily be shed.

In contrast with micro-sociology, which scrutinizes one or more milieus within a larger society, macro-sociology investigates attitudes pervading an entire city or nation. Bureaucracy, industrialism, nationalism, and anti-Semitism touched nearly every inhabitant of the Habsburg Empire. More particularly, Freud and Wittgenstein betrayed affinity with such Viennese traditions as aestheticism, the cult of nostalgia, and preference for diagnosis over therapy. To describe Freud's interaction with his society requires first a micro-sociology of the persons and institutions that trained him and then a macro-sociology of Viennese proclivities that at once attracted and repelled him. Often such proclivities have been discerned most keenly by novelists, notably those who like Robert Musil or Joseph Roth also wrote culture criticism. No less revealing is the testimony of memoirs and autobiographies, which chronicle how individuals reacted to successive milieus. It goes without saying that neither micro- nor macro-sociology can succeed unless the thinkers studied have first undergone systematic exposition.[3]

What by rights ought to have remained a subdiscipline of the sociology of thinkers has come to constitute a third branch of intellectual history: the sociology of engagé intellectuals. This is what Mannheim meant by the sociology of knowledge. It is what most political historians envision when they embark upon intellectual history. Decisive debates within this subdiscipline have weighed such questions as whether Rousseau's ideas influenced Robespierre's actions, and whether the Russian intelligentsia could have reformed Imperial Russia without resort to revolution. The sociology of engagé intellectuals presupposes that thinkers yearn above all else to instigate social change. Their customary vehicle for implementing far-reaching change is to formulate dissent into an ideology.[4]

The sociology of engagé intellectuals has gained autonomy from the main discipline chiefly because the former field emerged first. Karl Marx introduced the concept of ideology in order to differentiate the distorted class-consciousness of the bourgeoisie from the objective truth believed to be distilled in socialism. Marx assessed thinkers simply by reckoning whether their premises promoted or impeded proletarian revolution. Although Marx's followers usually excel at sociological analysis, too often they discount or degrade contemplative thought. Some Marxists pontificate that to be worthwhile a thinker must be engagé; anyone else may be dismissed as "decadent" or "aesthetic" or "irrational." In an endeavor to avoid such invective, less vituperative Marxists often impute to a thinker political convictions without first inquiring whether the supposed "fellow traveler" would have acknowledged them. To be sure, a lifetime spent in disdaining politics may constitute a political gesture, as the virulence of Karl Kraus shows. What counts is whether the motive for opting out is ideological, as in the case of Nietzsche or Kraus, or purely disinterested, as in the careers of countless Austrian literati and theorists.

However justified it may be to evaluate a publicist by his flair for mobilizing society to change, such a criterion can only caricature someone who spurns politics. Because Austria, albeit not Hungary, abounded in such adamantly apolitical figures, it is indispensable to segregate Marxist sociology of engagé intellectuals from the more inclusive sociology of thinkers. The former does violence not merely to those who repudiate Marx but even more to those who ignore him. To assume that only by seeking to alter society can a thinker display embeddedness within it, unduly narrows the relevance of sociology for intellectual history. Max Scheler and more recently Werner Stark have redressed this imbalance by differentiating social determination of ideas from Marx's emphasis on the ideological distortion of thought.[5] The dichotomy of Scheler and Stark prompted my distinction between the sociology of thinkers and the sociology of engagé intellectuals. By discriminating these two types of sociology of knowledge, I hope to apply the discipline as equitably to apolitical theorists as to political activists.

My effort to coordinate two varieties of the sociology of knowledge with the history of ideas convinces me that these three disciplines yield uneven results. The sociology of thinkers cannot unveil the mystery of creativity. No matter how beneficent or hostile a milieu, a titan like Husserl will wrestle free to initiate unprecedented visions. Applied to highly contemplative philosophers, micro-sociology discloses more about epigones than about creators. In particular, it can forestall errors of exegesis by clarifying what technical terms meant at a given time within a certain university or church.[6] More broadly, macro-sociology elucidates ways in which a regional tradition such as Bohemian Reform Catholicism fostered adherence to Leibniz. At the opposite extreme, advocates of social change invite sociological analysis. Nearly every ideology incorporates specific grievances that its authors leveled against society. Straddling the middle of the spectrum stand the writers, philosophers, and psychoanalysts associated with Viennese Impressionism. However firmly they may have eschewed politics, these innovators interacted with numerous milieus and traditions, challenging the sociologist to display his panoply of tools. Because the Habsburg Empire harbored such a diversity of milieus, the sociology of thinkers can yield a rich harvest of insights. Polymaths in particular gain in intelligibility from such a study of their background. In an age when intellectual versatility has all but disappeared, it seems pertinent to explore how social conditions promoted a flowering of integrative thinking just two generations ago in Austria-Hungary.

Anyone who has confronted Austrian thought must wonder why so many of its luminaries have fallen into neglect or even disrepute. Innumerable historians and scholars of literature write on things German without differentiating Austria-Hungary from Bismarck's empire. The fundamental cause of this neglect is the disappearance of the Habsburg Empire as a geographic unit. Whereas England, France, Germany, Italy, Russia, and even Poland have survived as familiar entities, Austria-Hungary, if we exclude the Ottoman Empire, is the only Great Power to have fragmented since Sweden was rolled back early in the eighteenth century. How many people remember which parts of Romania, Yugoslavia, Italy, and Poland belonged to the Habsburg monarchy in 1918? Truncated Austria and Hungary can scarcely aspire even to be epigones of these vanished dominions. Circumlocutions such as east central Europe or Danubian history merely veil the dismemberment that area underwent fifty years ago. Although a growing band of historians, both in the United States and Europe, is resurrecting Habsburg studies, their zeal has not yet spurred philosophers or social theorists to inventory the intellectual riches that Austrians have bequeathed us.

Reinforcing the geographic impediment to scholarship stands the plethora of languages once spoken in the Habsburg Empire. Historians who cannot read Czech, Polish, or Magyar shrink from studying Bohemia, Galicia, or Hungary. However laudable in principle, such caution prevents a scholar from discovering that he can interpret the culture of these areas provided he is fluent in German. In Austria-Hungary, German did provide a *lingua franca* for all but the most recalcitrant nationalists. Although I can scarcely decipher Magyar, throughout this book I have stressed Hungarian thinkers who also wrote in German. Even a cursory acquaintance with the literature and customs of Hungary accentuates previously unnoticed features in the culture of Vienna and Prague. Similar scrutiny of Bohemia, even without reading Czech, sheds a provocative light over the rest of the empire. It is high time for scholars to view Vienna as a foil to Prague and Budapest, and no longer simply as a competitor of Paris and Berlin.

Other obstacles discourage the intellectual historian who would study the Habsburg Empire. First, too many English-speaking and French-speaking scholars patronize the German language, interpreting its abstruseness as obfuscation.[7] Second, even among those adept in German, the virtual disappearance of classical education has removed a precondition for understanding men who regarded Latin and Greek as prerequisite to thinking. A facility in juggling ideas, imparted by eight years of translating Latin and five or six years of assimilating Greek, cannot be acquired by easier means. Third, many Jews who might otherwise study Austria-Hungary are repelled by Hitler's persecution of their people. Too often those Jews who do research on the history of the Habsburg Empire either ignore its virtues, or, increasingly, scant its faults. Finally, the splintering of scholarship through specialization has made polymaths seem obsolete, especially in the United States. Today Freud, Neurath, or even Wittgenstein would be patronized as unprofessional, so dazzling was their versatility. Constricted by training and by criteria for advancement, scholars who do examine these men cannot help but interpret them from a parochial point of view. Philosophers consider it demeaning to recall Wittgenstein's antecedents in Vienna, and historians of psychoanalysis forget that Freud's favorite teacher, the physiologist Ernst Brücke, was no less versatile than Freud himself.

More than anything else, a lost breadth of knowledge separates these men from ourselves. In an attempt to bridge that gap, this book will coordinate analysis of social conditions with systematic exposition of thought. By situating thinkers in their respective milieus, I hope to elucidate that Gay Apocalypse, without whose innovations our intellectual lives would be barren indeed.

Part One

HABSBURG BUREAUCRACY: INERTIA VERSUS REFORM

Nicht tödlich, aber unheilbar,
das sind die schlimmsten Krankheiten.

Not fatal, but incurable, these are the
worst diseases.

—MARIE VON EBNER-ESCHENBACH

I

From Baroque to Biedermeier

FROM ORIGINS OF THE HABSBURG EMPIRE
TO BAROQUE FAITH IN PROVIDENCE

BETWEEN 1867 and 1914 the Habsburg Empire presented the anomaly of a dynastic state whose floundering for lack of a purpose was matched by lack of a name. Prior to 1800, the Habsburg dynasty had fulfilled with distinction at least three missions in central and eastern Europe. It had reconverted the South Germans to Roman Catholicism, it had withstood the Ottoman Turks, and it had disseminated Western civilization throughout semi-Oriental lands. Failure to renew any of these missions after 1800 threatened survival at the very time when success at Westernizing subject peoples was turning some of them into bitter opponents. The ensuing six chapters examine how bureaucrats endeavored to sustain, and theorists struggled to reform, the shaky edifice of empire.

A review of the uncertainty surrounding Austria's name permits a survey of the evolution of Habsburg territories. As late as 1800, the dynasty styled itself the House of Habsburg, its ruler being also the Holy Roman Emperor.[1] The Habsburg Empire meant simply those territories belonging to the imperial family. From 1806 until 1867 these territories were called loosely the Austrian Empire, while from 1867 to 1918 they were known as Austria-Hungary. The name "Austria" became appropriate whenever a land or a people had been divided into eastern and western portions. Labels such as Ostrogoth and Austrasia had preceded this usage. Similarly in 1156 the Eastern March on the Danube was elevated into the duchy of Austria (*Herzogtum Österreich*). At that time Emperor Friedrich Barbarossa issued the *Privilegium Minus*, bestowing the title of duke on the Babenberg Margrave, Heinrich II. Since 867 his family had been enlarging the Carolingian March which Emperor Otto I had revived. In 1192 the Babenbergs annexed Styria, soon thereafter establishing in their coat-

of-arms the colors red-white-red, which in 1918 the Austrian Republic
chose for its flag.

The first Habsburg to control Austria was the Holy Roman Emperor
Rudolf I (1273–1291). During the Imperial Interregnum the Bohemian
king Ottokar Premysl had seized the Babenberg duchies of Austria,
Styria, and Carniola (Krain). Having defeated Ottokar at the March-
feld in August, 1278, Rudolf I enfeoffed his son Albrecht with these
lands together with ancestral holdings of the Habsburgs in Swabia.
Known as Fore-Austria (Vorderösterreich), the Swabian possessions
in what is today Baden remained within the empire until 1804. Between 1335 and 1382, the dynasty gained control of Carinthia (Kärn-
ten), Tirol, and Trieste. The largest single acquisition came in 1526
when Lajos II, king of Hungary and Bohemia, died in battle against
the Turks, bequeathing both crowns to Spanish-born Ferdinand I. This
brother of Charles V succeeded as Holy Roman Emperor from 1556
to 1564. While the son of Charles V ruled Spain, Ferdinand I founded
the Austrian Line of Habsburgs, which held the title of Holy Roman
Emperor until 1806 except for a brief hiatus during the 1740's. After
the electors in 1745 had acknowledged as emperor Franz Stephan of
Lorraine, the dynasty styled itself the House of Habsburg-Lorraine.

In 1804, Emperor Franz I (1792–1835) anticipated the dissolution
of the Holy Roman Empire by proclaiming himself Hereditary Emperor of Austria (Erbkaiser Österreichs). Two years later when he
abdicated as Holy Roman Emperor, he substituted his new title. If
Franz had obeyed the rules of heraldry, he would have contented
himself with lesser ancestral titles such as archduke of Austria, king
of Hungary, and king of Bohemia. Not to be outdone by the upstart
Emperor Napoleon, the Austrian conservative renewed his dynasty's
claim to an imperial title. At the same time, he retained the two-headed
eagle which had adorned their coat of arms since the fifteenth century.

Sixty years later when Emperor Franz Joseph granted parity to
Hungary, the empire's western half no longer had a name. Although
conceivably the region might have been called Neustria or simply non-
Hungary, it was labeled "the Kingdoms and Provinces represented in
the Reichsrat." Bureaucrats used the awkward term Cisleithania to designate non-Hungary, while dubbing Hungary Transleithania, on the
grounds that the river Leitha separated the two states. After 1867 the
word Austria survived only in the unofficial phrase Austria-Hungary,
besides designating the archduchies of Upper and Lower Austria.
Strictly speaking, the Kingdoms and Provinces represented in the
Reichsrat enjoyed no simpler name.

The Habsburg Empire established its role as a great power between

1620 and 1720, first by opposing the Protestant Reformation and then
by resisting the Ottoman Turks. Although by 1550 a majority of Germans in Habsburg domains had embraced Protestantism, by 1650 that
religion had been virtually wiped out. The rollback was begun by
missionaries such as the Dutch-born Peter Canisius (1521–1597), who
founded Catholic primary and secondary schools.[2] Teaching orders
such as the Piarists, founded in 1597, collaborated with Benedictines
and Augustinians, to direct most schools until the 1860's. After the
mystical Rudolf II (1576–1612) had appeased the Protestants, in 1612
his successor moved the capital from Prague to Vienna, where from
1619 to 1637 a fanatical Catholic ruled as Emperor Ferdinand II. Not
only did Ferdinand expel Protestants from Styria and Austria, but after
their leaders had been defeated at the White Mountain west of Prague
in 1620, the emperor replaced the Protestant nobility of Bohemia with
Catholics. Ferdinand's rigid adherence to the principle of *cuius regio,
eius religio* unleashed the Thirty Years' War, during which he demonstrated to his Bohemian *condottiere* Albrecht von Wallenstein (1583–
1634) the proverbial ingratitude of the Habsburgs. Only in Hungary
and Transylvania did Protestantism survive, sheltered by the Turks
and by the grand-prince of Transylvania. Owing to Ferdinand II's
enforcement of Catholicism, religious observance in Austria tended to
substitute pomp for zeal.

Thereafter the empire expanded at the expense of the Ottoman
Turks, who in 1683 saw their siege of Vienna come within a hair of
triumph, only to end in a rout.[3] The heroic defense of the imperial
capital dramatized the Habsburgs' mission as the easternmost outpost
of Christendom, after Muslims had captured Central Hungary during
the 1520's. To the dismay of Louis XIV of France, Emperor Leopold I
(1658–1705) organized a crusade that saved his capital. The victory
liberated Central Hungary; Buda fell in 1686 and the following year
the Hungarian diet bestowed the Crown of Saint Stephen on the male
line of the Habsburgs. One hundred fifty years after Lajos II had
perished at Mohács, his successors finally conquered the Hungarian
plain, opening a vast hinterland to German colonists. Prince Eugene
of Savoy (1663–1736) reorganized the Military Frontier, drilling Croatian "Grenzer" troops into the finest in the imperial army, thus securing
the empire against further attack. Once the Turkish menace had receded, the Habsburg Empire could find no purpose of comparable
urgency to replace the negative one of defense.

It was amid the euphoria of Turkish retreat that Austria's Baroque
culture emerged.[4] Ravaged churches, monasteries, and castles were
rebuilt to celebrate release from the incubus. Only after 1683 could

the Viennese occupy their suburbs without fear of marauders; Schönbrunn Palace sprang up outside the city, and Prince Eugene selected
a hill overlooking the whole area for his Belvedere Palace. Emperors
Joseph I (1705–1711) and the Spanish-bred Karl VI (1711–1740) introduced the lavish ritual dear to Baroque monarchs. While emulating
the Escorial at an uncompleted palace at Klosterneuburg, Karl imposed
upon the court the Spanish Court Ceremonial that lasted until 1918.
He enlarged the Spanish Riding School, which had faltered since its
founding during the 1570's. Bred at Lipizza northeast of Trieste until
1918 and thereafter in Styria, the white stallions still execute Baroque
figures.

Baroque attitudes decisively influenced later intellectual achievements by inculcating an interpenetration of religion with worldliness.[5]
Most Austrians have esteemed the created world as God's theater, ruled
by His Providence, where men graduate from service on earth to
salvation beyond. Here below, innumerable polar opposites beset man,
tearing him between love and hate, feast and famine, sanctity and sin.
Not only did such opposites invite allegory in art but their ineluctable
conflict reminded beholders of a need for God to supervise the outcome. Leibniz' monadology rationalized this worship of creation, just
as Haydn's oratorio *The Creation* (1798) celebrated divine wisdom in
designing the whole. At Vienna a colorful exponent of the clash of
opposites was the Augustinian friar, Abraham a Sancta Clara (1644–
1709), who preached fear of death through terrifying similes. In
Austria awareness of polarities has reinforced devotion to the good of
the whole, as men and women have prided themselves on being links
in a hierarchy. Such subservience to the created order has diminished
willingness to assail the status quo.

Joyful acquiescence in all that exists found ritual expression in the
cult of the Eucharist. Habsburg monarchs had long venerated the
sacrament of the altar, first in Spain and then in Austria. Emperors
knelt in the presence of the Host to signify fealty to the heavenly
suzerain, the sole power before whom they trembled.[6] After 1620, the
Virgin Mary received countless pilgrimages, to thank her for having
vanquished Protestantism. As Queen of Heaven, she presided over
joyful worshipers, curbing the wrath of the Old Testament God and
assuring the faithful that death need not be feared.[7] Death itself
seemed part of life, furnishing an additional role that God's servant
undertook at the hands of Providence. The medieval notion of *Me-
mento mori* now inspired a vision of the world as theater of life and
death.

Throughout Habsburg lands Baroque churches were fashioned into earthly paradises, where members of all classes could enjoy luxury otherwise confined to palaces. Stucco workers from Italy, architects from Saxony, painters from Austria, as well as Spanish-Jewish goldsmiths and embroiderers, collaborated to erect hymns in stone to the God of Creation.[8] Reverence for Creation fostered capacity to see God suffusing all things, as if art, like the Eucharist, conveyed a Real Presence. Thus the Baroque instilled faith in cosmic order, which the nineteenth century secularized into myriad forms of aestheticism, positivism, and eventually impressionism.

JOSEPHINISM AS A FOUNT OF
BOTH LIBERALISM AND CONSERVATISM

Following this upsurge of Baroque piety, Habsburg rulers adopted from France and Prussia policies of enlightened absolutism. They endeavored to replace local feudal privilege with centralized administration. Under Maria Theresa (1740–1780) and her son Joseph II (1780–1790), enlightened absolutism crystallized into the movement known as Josephinism, which combined bureaucratization with antipapal reform Catholicism.[9] Growing ever more complex, Josephinism survived well into the nineteenth century, as philosophers, jurists, and bureaucrats implemented its goals in conflicting ways.

Administrative centralization had begun before Maria Theresa, chiefly in the Italian domains of her father, Karl VI (1711–1740).[10] She issued a revised law code and reorganized the administration of Bohemia, attempting even to regulate the gypsies. Under her Saxon-born minister Friedrich Wilhelm Count von Haugwitz (1702–1765), Maria Theresa reorganized state finances in 1749, and separated law courts from the Ministry of Justice. To improve trade, in 1756 she standardized weights and measures, extending the Viennese standard to all of Austria; the metric system would not be introduced until 1872. In 1749 she founded the Haus-, Hof- und Staatsarchiv to assemble royal documents, and in 1773 she followed the example of Portugal and France by expelling the Jesuit order and secularizing its schools. Under the Vienna-born chancellor Wenzel Anton Prince Kaunitz (1711–1794), she conducted an unremitting rivalry with Friedrich II of Prussia, winning Galicia and Bukovina during the 1770's as compensation for loss of Silesia. Besides Kaunitz, the leading exponent of enlightenment at her court was the Moravian-born Jew Josef von Sonnenfels (1732–1817), a professor of statecraft (Staatswissenschaft) who revamped the Austrian penal code, abolishing torture in 1776. As a cameralist, he favored centralizing commerce, improving public health, and increasing population so as to promote prosperity and well-being. Sonnenfels advocated elevating the Burgtheater, founded in 1741, into a forum of national culture, whose glory would enhance that of the dynasty. The flowering of Austrian drama more than fulfilled the Josephinist goal of promoting loyalty to the crown.[11] Maria Theresa also fostered Hungarian literature by founding a Hungarian bodyguard at Vienna in 1760. Led by György Bessenyei (1747–1811), these young noblemen established a literary circle, which aspired to write a national drama for Hungary, modeled on plays by Corneille, Racine, and Voltaire. Although Maria Theresa has been eulogized by many post-1918 writers, her forty-year reign ended in unpopularity. Only later did she come to be regarded as Mother of her Country. Having combined gentleness with vision, she seemed a kind of Queen of Heaven enthroned.

Her son Joseph II, who had grown increasingly restless during his mother's last years, was a bewildering mixture of reason and enthusiasm. His haste in issuing thousands of reform decrees prevented most of them from being effectively executed. One of his most enduring reforms was to forbid nobles to buy the lands of the peasants whom he freed from serfdom. Although his successor reinstated forced labor (*robota*), which lasted until 1848, Joseph's prohibition protected the peasantry from losing their lands down to 1918. In Hungary, where no such provision existed, landless peasants plagued the countryside after 1848, whereas in Austrian territories a class of independent proprietors flourished. A thoroughgoing centralizer, Joseph reduced the number of chief officials serving the crown to four, and refused to be crowned separately in Bohemia and Hungary. In 1781 he imposed censorship of antimonarchical writings, while continuing, as had his mother, to tolerate anticlerical ones.[12]

Joseph introduced his most decisive changes in the field of church-state relations. In the Tolerance Patent of October, 1781, he granted freedom of worship and civil equality to Lutherans, Calvinists, and Greek Orthodox. Protestant churches were, nonetheless, forbidden to erect towers, or to have bells, or entrances on the street. Although Jews were exempted from sumptuary laws, being permitted for the first time to dwell outside the ghetto as well as to conduct commerce and to attend state schools, it was not until 1849 that Austrian Jews received the right to vote and to own land. One month after the Tolerance Edict, in November, 1781, the monarch abolished more than four hundred monasteries that did not engage in education or take care of the sick. This disestablishment of "parasitic" monks angered Trent-born Cardinal Christoph Anton Migazzi, who as archbishop of Vienna from

1757 to 1803 combatted the entire antipapal program. Even a visit to Vienna by Pope Pius VI in 1782 could not stay execution of the edict. Using proceeds from the sale of monastic land, a fund was established to pay local pastors a fee, the so-called *Kongrua*, reimbursing their service as registrars of births, marriages, and deaths. This payment by the state to priests continued until 1938. Scandalized by the frequency of holy days and of pilgrimages, Joseph prohibited most of these as a hindrance to economic productivity. Joseph's fostering of a state church, combined with his persecuting of monks and Jesuits, justifies a narrow definition of the term Josephinism to designate the Austrian compromise between state religion and papal supremacy. Yet like French Jansenism and German Febronianism, Josephinism encompassed far more than an ecclesiastical policy.

Some of Joseph's most beneficial reforms concerned public health. He founded the Landespolizei of Lower Austria to supervise public welfare and to enforce such hygienic measures as the closing in 1783 of mass graves beneath St. Stephen's Cathedral. In 1784 the emperor established the General Hospital at Vienna, followed a year later by the Josephinum to train military surgeons. Joseph was also an enthusiastic naturalist, rearranging the gardens at Schönbrunn and collecting exotic plants and animals. He delighted in serving guests coffee, tea, and sugar grown in his own greenhouses. In architecture Joseph's ideals found expression in the classicism of Johann Ferdinand Hetzendorf von Hohenberg (1732–1816), who designed the park at Schönbrunn to resemble a giant stage crowned by the Gloriette. During the mid-1780's, Hetzendorf furthered Joseph's Enlightenment program by "purifying" the interior of several Gothic churches through the addition of Baroque altars and ornament.

In one of his least successful measures, Joseph, in 1784, proclaimed German the universal language of the empire. His insistence that local languages disappear only guaranteed their survival, goading Czechs, Magyars, and Serbs to resurrect their spoken language as a literary one. In Bohemia and Moravia, the quarrel between German and Czech dragged on until 1918, while after 1867 the Hungarians reversed Josephinism by compelling all citizens to use Magyar. Although linguistic centralization incited such opposition that Leopold II (1790–1792) had to rescind it together with many of his brother's other reforms, Joseph's Enlightenment ideals inspired numerous intellectuals in Bohemia. His anticlerical Catholicism flowered into Bohemian Reform Catholicism, a movement that through several generations sponsored some of the nineteenth century's most original thought. *[Was tun]*

After 1792, Josephinism split into a right wing of administrators and *[Beispiel?]*

a left wing of reformers, spanning a religious-philosophical center. The conservative wing relied upon Emperor Franz I (1792–1835), who perfected his uncle's techniques of centralization so as to thwart followers of Joseph's religious goals as well as exponents of the French Revolution. To quell Freemasonry and suspected Jacobinism, administrators became highly repressive, rallying around what they opposed rather than what they espoused. Admirers of Joseph's rationalistic piety survived mainly in Bohemia, where German and Czech intellectuals cooperated until about 1840. In sum, the unfolding of Josephinism at Vienna, as told by Fritz Valjavec and Ferdinand Maass, stresses repressive bureaucracy, while the flowering of Josephinism in Bohemia, as recounted by Eugen Lemberg and Eduard Winter, features philosophical and literary renaissance. A tragic figure who agonized in his attempts to reconcile administrative Josephinism with its philosophic twin was the dramatist Franz Grillparzer (1791–1872). His patriotic dramas, such as *Ein treuer Diener seines Herrn* (Vienna, 1830), seemed too inflammatory to please the court and too dynamic to win the public.

Joseph left an unmanageable heritage, which conservatives, liberals, and eclectics each claimed. Insisting that reason direct public and religious affairs, he had imported both means and goals of the Enlightenment in a form amenable to all factions. Whereas Franz I and Metternich exploited rational planning to repress rationalism, Reform Catholics such as Bolzano and Kaspar Sternberg labored to harmonize religion with science. Their encyclopedism scandalized scientific positivists no less than Catholic dogmatists. Exponents of Joseph II's theology fell victim to administrators whom he had trained to rule by decree. By 1848, everywhere in the empire liberals were ready to hail Joseph as a precursor whose Tolerance Edict had been nullified by timid successors. Following the March Revolution of 1848, Emperor Franz Joseph (1848–1916) renewed administrative Josephinism, sometimes paying lip service to a liberalism whose premises he never accepted.

BIEDERMEIER CULTURE AS A
SEEDBED OF LATER ATTITUDES

Under Franz I administrative Josephinism fostered political resignation. The emperor himself succumbed to this attitude when in August, 1806, at Napoleon's bidding, he abdicated his title as Holy Roman Emperor, three years later giving his daughter in marriage to the

Corsican and in 1813 hesitating at Metternich's insistence to join the coalition against the beleaguered conqueror. The emperor's subjects felt even more helpless under the regime instituted after 1809 by German-born Klemens Prince von Metternich (1773–1859), whose preeminence lasted through the reign of Franz's half-witted son Ferdinand I (1835–1848). Despite Metternich's skill at diplomacy, he allowed officials to exert a baleful influence on domestic affairs.[13] Josephinist bureaucrats employed censorship, secret police, and red tape to discourage participation in politics. Only in Hungary and Bohemia did widespread desire for political activity survive. Under bureaucratic rule, citizens of Austria continued their habit of carping (Raunzerei) at authority without resisting it, reinforcing a political flaccidity that survives to this day.

The arbitrariness of Metternich's regime gained European-wide notoriety from memoirs by a Byronesque Italian poet, Silvio Pellico (1789–1854). In My Prisons (1832), he described eight years of incarceration in the Spielberg at Brünn. Hostility felt by North Italians toward Austrian occupiers, evoked by Stendhal in The Charterhouse of Parma (1839), infected many Englishmen and Frenchmen. Numerous visitors to Vienna denounced the prevalence of police spies.[14]

Under Metternich, Vienna's traditions of theater, music, and painting produced the culture known as Biedermeier. This epithet derives from the satiric figure of Gottlieb Biedermeier, a Swabian schoolmaster created in 1850 by the Swabian humorist Ludwig Eichrodt. Together with his schoolmate Adolf Kussmaul, Eichrodt modeled Biedermeier on his own teacher Samuel Friedrich Sauter (1766–1846), who had taught in Baden from 1786 to 1841 while writing folk songs and dilettantish verse. This pious village schoolmaster, law-abiding and serene, came to personify the apolitical bourgeois culture of the pre-March period (1815–1848), both in Germany and the Austrian empire. The term Biedermeier was revived in 1906 when devotees of art nouveau staged an exposition of pre-1848 interior decoration, and in 1923 Paul Kluckhohn extended the concept from visual arts to literature.[15]

Although literary scholars now prefer the concept of early realism, the term "Biedermeier" is used in this book to designate both the pre-March period in Austria and the cultural attitudes that it engendered.[16] No other term conveys so well Austria's enduring combination of political resignation with aesthetic delectation and Catholic piety. For Austrians, the years between 1815 and 1848 bear special importance because it was at this time that the empire first contemplated existence independent of Germany. Most subsequent descriptions of Austrian attitudes echo those of Biedermeier publicists. Especially after 1918, the Biedermeier has entranced nostalgic patriots, who see in it a glorious idyll, when Austria combined a lingering tie to Germany with dawning independence. In sociological terms, the Biedermeier represents the waning years of unalloyed preindustrial society. To use a distinction coined by Ferdinand Tönnies in 1887, Biedermeier Austria preserved *Gemeinschaft* society, rural and cohesive, while thereafter her cities began to harbor the anonymous society of industrial capitalism that Tönnies called *Gesellschaft*. Tönnies contended, on the basis of having grown up in rural Schleswig before moving to Berlin, that each type of society implants complex attitudes. Persons dwelling in Gemeinschaft, on the one hand, shun competition in order to practice mutual support and to preserve common beliefs. Gesellschaft, on the other hand, individualizes its members by obliging them to compete; it breeds anxiety by unraveling close-knit bonds. The fact that Gemeinschaft survived in Austria up to 1870, unimpaired except by an occasional overzealous official, beguiled those who had to confront Gesellschaft thereafter. Even at Vienna capitalism awakened nostalgia for Biedermeier security, causing social theorists after 1870 to extol either Gemeinschaft or some compromise version of it.

Although Tönnies' terminology is employed throughout this book, some readers may prefer to substitute Talcott Parsons' pattern variables.[17] According to Parsons, Gemeinschaft society is particularistic and ascriptive. Particularistic means that local rather than universal standards prevail, while ascriptive means that a person is evaluated in terms of who he is, not what he can do. Gesellschaft society is universalistic — uniform standards govern everyone — and achievement-oriented. Not birth but performance determines status. If Parsons' variables are applied to Austria around 1800, it appears that lord and peasant adhered to local standards, and each conformed to an inherited role. Because industrialization lagged in Austria, generalized standards and achievement-orientation never quite erased the particularistic, ascriptive patterns dear to the countryside.

Biedermeier culture encouraged the middle classes to emulate aesthetic pursuits that had earlier attracted the aristocracy. The bourgeoisie fled from politics into artistic activities that a family could share, such as improvising verse, painting, and performing chamber music. The coterie who surrounded Franz Schubert (1797–1828) typified such amateurism, while in his preference for miniature pieces, Schubert filled a need for chamber music in place of symphonies. The amassing of documents in the pursuit of scholarship produced such monuments as an eleven-volume history of the Ottoman Turks by Joseph von Hammer-Purgstall (1774–1856). The extent to which a compiler could ignore politics was demonstrated by a prolific Viennese Orientalist, August Pfizmaier (1808–1887), who first learned of the Franco-Prussian War by reading a Chinese newspaper.

Love of the past promoted the assembling of archives and founding of museums, where local oddities could accumulate. Archduke Johann (1782–1859), a younger son of Leopold II, established such a museum at Graz in 1811, where he combined history and ethnography. In 1829 he further endeared himself to the people of Styria by marrying a postmaster's daughter, a triumph of love over dynastic pride, which sentiment the middle class applauded. Delight in museum curatorship found its poet in Bohemian-born Adalbert Stifter, who in *Der Nachsommer* (Pest, 1857) extolled an aristocratic household dedicated to upholding, as in a museum, eternal laws of nature and art.

The visual arts reflected desire to freeze the present in every sort of memorial. Landscape painting and portraiture flourished, as did sketching wild flowers. The yearning of every bourgeois to be memorialized was answered by lithography, which its Prague-born inventor Alois Senefelder (1771–1834) introduced to Vienna in 1803. Its grand master was Vienna-born Josef Kriehuber (1800–1876), who left more than three thousand lithographs executed with the finesse of an etcher. In prints such as *Matinee bei Liszt* (1846), he worked directly onto stone so as to catch the essence of a moment just as photography was soon to do.

In literature, Biedermeier taste favored what has been called the "little man" *(der kleine Mann)*, typified by Grillparzer's *Der arme Spielmann* (1848) and Stifter's *Kalkstein* (Leipzig, 1853). The long-suffering citizen, usually middle-aged and lower middle class, who accepts his humble lot and believes in Providence, became a folk hero, celebrated later by Ferdinand von Saar and Marie von Ebner-Eschenbach, as well as by dozens of feuilletonists. Epitomizing resignation that citizens felt toward bureaucracy and aristocracy, the little man demonstrated how the lowly could rejoice in God's Creation by obeying His laws. Throughout this book the term "little man" is used to designate intellectuals of lowly origin who displayed inordinate humility in order to disguise creative aspirations.

The lot of the little man was unfortunately all too real. The Biedermeier produced a number of inventors, whose devices the bureaucracy discouraged, only to have them later made famous by others. The Bohemian Josef Ressel (1793–1857) devised a screw propeller at Trieste in 1826, ten years before Ericsson, but was forbidden to experiment with it. As early as 1815 the Austrian tailor Josef Madersperger had invented a sewing machine with a needle hole in the tip. Although by

1840 he had perfected the device, he died penniless because no one would market it. Bureaucratic resistance to innovation plagued other inventors and theorists, not least Gregor Mendel (1822–1884), whose humility caused him to refrain in the 1860's from publicizing his experiments.

The Biedermeier marked the heyday of the theater. In addition to Grillparzer, whose popularity faded after 1830, the *Zauberposse* blossomed in the hands of Ferdinand Raimund (1790–1836), whose fairy plays continued the tradition embodied in *The Magic Flute* (1791). In a more modern vein, Vienna-born Johann Nestroy (1801–1862) perfected a technique of satire through plays on words which frustrated the censor. Biedermeier playwrights revived Baroque attitudes, especially in envisioning the entire world as a theater. In *Der Traum ein Leben* (1831) Grillparzer borrowed from Calderón to evoke a Baroque interpenetration of heaven and earth, of reality and illusion, reminding beholders that hierarchy rules the world. Renunciation sometimes merged into fascination with death; Grillparzer's tragedies depicted death as a great reconciler. The refusal of Austrian intellectuals to propose remedies, which will be called therapeutic nihilism, reinforced Biedermeier resignation.

Austrian Biedermeier values were contrasted with those of Prussia by the Berlin-born Germanist, Walter Brecht (1876–1950), who taught at Vienna from 1913 to 1925.[18] He argued that Austria preserved into the twentieth century attitudes that two centuries before had characterized all of Germany. Particularism, family cohesiveness, and lack of state-consciousness were attributes of Gemeinschaft society, which survived longer in the Habsburg Empire than in Germany. Accompanying ubiquitous bureaucracy was, Brecht added, a willingness to bend rules by overlooking infractions. Inefficiency in enforcing edicts became known as *Schlamperei*, meaning laxity or muddle. In the mind of many Austrians, Schlamperei symbolized the opposite of Prussian efficiency, offering at once a source of strength and weakness. In lower echelons, laxity stemmed from the fact that underlings pitied "little men" like themselves, making them accede to bribes or tales of woe. Among higher officials, a Schlamperei of sorts resulted from persistence of feudal values: etiquette decreed that an official grant the wishes of an archduke or a count. In Parsons' terms, lower officials held particularized standards, while their superiors prized ascription above achievement.

When Viktor Adler called Austria's government *"ein durch Schlamperei gemilderter Absolutismus"* (Absolutism mitigated by Schlamperei), he meant to praise the humanizing impact of anti-Prussian *laissez-vivre*. Similarly, in the "Schema of Prussians and Austrians" which Hugo von Hofmannsthal sketched in 1917, he lauded Austrians for greater diversity, humanity, and tradition.[19] The poet's schema neatly recapitulated Tönnies' dichotomy between Gemeinschaft and Gesellschaft, so convinced was he of Austria's rootedness in preindustrial values. The fact that after 1850 officials at every level felt torn between duty to the state and that to fellow citizens reflected encroachment of Gesellschaft rigor on the spontaneity of the countryside. Although universal standards threatened local custom, Schlamperei persisted, at least until 1938, symbolizing that suspension between old and new which distinguished the Habsburg Empire.

THE INTELLECTUAL PREEMINENCE OF JEWS:
ITS ROOTS IN TRIBAL TRADITION
AND GENTILE REJECTION

Any study of intellectual life in Austria must single out the Jews for special attention. No other ethnic group produced so many thinkers of transcendent originality — theorists such as Freud, Husserl, Kelsen, Wittgenstein, Mahler, not to mention such authors as Schnitzler, Kraus, Broch, and Roth. In addition to these creative geniuses, a disproportionate number of productive thinkers in every field—with the exception of ethnology—were Jewish. In some fields such as psychoanalysis and Austro-Marxism, Jews constituted an overwhelming preponderance. Of course not all seminal thinkers in Austria were Jews. The Catholics Brentano, Mach, and Carl Menger founded schools no less original than those of Jewish invention. Yet the Jewish middle class provided a unique forum for discussion and dissemination of new ideas. Under Moritz Benedikt the *Neue Freie Presse*, like the *Wiener Tagblatt* under Moriz Szeps, promulgated liberal views written largely by Jews for other Jews. Similarly subscribers to smaller journals like Karl Kraus's *Die Fackel* were mainly Jewish. Without this audience avid for witticisms and novelty, Austrian literature might have been as impoverished after 1850 as it has become since 1938.

Many hypotheses seek to explain the intellectual preeminence that Jews displayed both in general and within Austria-Hungary. Such analyses must begin with the question of what constitutes the cohesiveness of Jews. Is it religion, education, mores, race, or some combination of these which has imparted to such dissimilar people a com-

mon identity? To elucidate this riddle, Prague-born Erich Kahler
(1885–1970) has differentiated a tribe, such as the Jews, from a nation,
such as France:

> a *tribe* is an ethnic group that has evolved out of and with its
> proper religion and *before* the development of a world re-
> ligion, or out of its reach. A *nation* is an ethnic group that
> came into being *after* the development and under the aegis of
> a world religion, as did France, England, Russia, and other
> countries.[20]

Owing to their tribal religion, Jews have maintained an archaic kind
of unity that can survive the process known as assimilation. The latter
term denotes two distinct types of behavior: the positive action of
identifying with secular culture and the negative action of divesting
oneself of Jewish ties. For most assimilated Jews to identify with
German-speaking culture meant to abandon religious practice, although anti-Semites would not allow even nonprofessing Jews to forget
their origin. Bound together in what Ben Halpern has called a "community of fate," both believer and nonbeliever have preserved Judaic
traits.[21] We shall examine how certain of these customs and doctrines
fostered intellectual excellence.

At least until 1880 most Jewish boys studied a modicum of Hebrew,
although many quickly forgot the language or ceased religious observance altogether. Training in Hebrew emphasized memorization, while
students of the Talmud learned to sift concrete cases so as to discern
their ethical significance. The facility that resulted has been described
by the Russian-born Jew Immanuel Velikovsky (1895–), who studied
at Vienna with the psychoanalysts Wilhelm Stekel and Alfred Adler
during the early 1930's.[22] Most Jews pray in Hebrew even when they
do not quite understand it, and sometimes they dream in it. Because in
Hebrew, vowels are transcribed not by letters of an alphabet but by
diacritical marks, which are frequently omitted, speakers of that
language encounter infinite opportunities for puns. Any Jew who has
learned to read Hebrew without diacritical marks must have developed
a keen eye for every sort of wordplay. This exercise, Velikovsky
argued, stimulates Jewish wit, schooling Jewish writers to make
associations implausible for gentiles. In addition, the prohibition
against graven images of God obliges Jews to think about Him in
abstractions. Early training in legal and theological niceties imparts
dialectical skill to an extent that only a few Jesuit-trained Catholics
share. Finally, the bizarre names that many Austrian Jews had been

given during the eighteenth century sharpened their awareness of puns. Although preposterous names were not confined to Jews, they became a favorite topic of Jewish jokes. Wilhelm Stekel contended that often a man's name shaped his self-image—*nomen est omen*—as when a clerk called Sicher (Mr. Sure) tried to live up to his name by rehearsing every transaction over and over.[23]

Hermann Broch stressed another aspect of Jewish religious training.[24] The supreme Jewish value, said Broch, is reverence for life; this premise underlies the whole Jewish law, especially regulations concerning kosher food. Such reverence for life makes it difficult for Jews to counter anti-Semites' disdain for it. For a Jew, whatever enhances life is just, and that which curtails it, unjust. Talmudic casuistry teaches boys to weigh how actions may enhance or threaten living beings. Despite a thirst for earthly justice, Jews torment themselves by conceiving God as an infinitely distant being, who can be approached but never reached. It becomes incumbent upon the Jew, said Broch, to pursue God without respite, yet without hope of attainment because no earthly deed can influence the deity. Although such austerity was mitigated by thinkers like Martin Buber, the incorruptibility of the Jewish God helps to explain the demonic energy displayed by men like Broch, Husserl, Herzl, and Kraus. As partisans of justice, they had been taught that no deed of men could appease God.

Skill in language helped to assuage humiliations inflicted upon Jews by gentiles. Wounded self-esteem could be compensated by double-edged jokes that ridicule the tormentor as well as the tormented, often with marked brevity:

Two Strangers Introduce Themselves in a Train Compartment
"Von Bredow—Lieutenant in the Reserve."
"Lilienthal—permanently unfit" *(dauernd untauglich).*[25]

Many jokes twitted the lazy Jew or *Schnorrer* who lived by begging from coreligionists; sometimes he worked harder than did others legitimately employed.[26] Jewish capacity to sublimate humiliation into witticism made language itself a defense against trauma. Linguistic facility, especially an ability to see double meanings, became part of every Jew's psychic armor. This immersion in language may have stimulated philosophers such as Mauthner and Wittgenstein to teach that language is autonomous from experience. Similarly Freud's fascination with slips of the tongue may reflect a deep-set Jewish attitude.

Many Jewish thinkers were motivated by feelings of insecurity. It was a commonplace that Jews excelled at the university because their families exhorted them to study harder in order to overcome prejudice. The Hungarian essayist Emil Reich described how a Jewish mother, unable to identify with the country in which she lives, coddles her child, lavishing upon him love that she cannot give to society. For such a mother, her child was her country.[27] The dream of Freud's mother that her "golden Sigi" would become famous acted as a self-fulfilling prophecy: she did everything possible to further her son's education, even banishing his sister's piano when it annoyed the budding scholar. Freud received additional reinforcement from having seen his father shoved off a sidewalk and humbly accepting the insult. Such meekness spurred Freud to avoid a similar fate by earning gentile respect. In some Jews, disgust at humiliation culminated in self-hatred. Otto Weininger venerated ruthless efficiency, equating Jewish passivity with feminine weakness. In place of the Jewish value of life, he worshiped might, whereas a mild Jewish self-hatred such as Freud's merely stimulated ambition.

Of course not all careers barred Jews. Just as court Jews such as Samson Wertheimer (1658–1724) had once prospered, others became leading bankers of the Continent after 1815. The learned professions of medicine, law, and journalism, and a professorship at a university promised a shortcut out of the ghetto by employing skills for which childhood training predisposed Jews. At age twenty-three Weininger received through *Geschlecht und Charakter* the burst of fame about which Jewish boys dreamed. A novel by Arthur Schnitzler, *Der Weg ins Freie* (Berlin, 1908), probed the insecurity and megalomania that afficted some Jewish intellectuals. Desperate for success, they displayed a willingness to experiment uncommon in others. Having survived for generations in a marginal situation, Jews had less to lose by espousing novelty. Jews who weathered the hard school of anti-Semitism were likely to be very pertinacious indeed.

Catholic artisans who feared economic competition from Jews knew little of the intimacy of Jewish villages. In the *Shtetls* of Bohemia, Moravia, and especially Galicia, a Gemeinschaft ethos flourished into the twentieth century. It was there that Hasidism survived to influence Martin Buber, and it was rural Jews who inspired Herzl to envision agricultural colonies in his Jewish state.[28] Two Jewish writers, Prague-born Leopold Kompert (1822–1886) and Galician-born Karl Emil Franzos (1848–1904), were beloved for portraying humble Jews similar to the "little men" of Saar and Ebner-Eschenbach.[29] Cradled by the Shtetl, Austrian Jews embraced nineteenth-century civilization as new-comers, unleashing energy nurtured by centuries of isolation. Revering his paternal grandfather in Moravia, Freud was one of many who acknowledged a debt to centuries' old wisdom newly released into the urban cauldron.

Jewish intellectuals epitomized the estrangement between writer and society which pervaded Austria after 1800. In Hungary, on the contrary, not only did Jews assimilate more readily, but all writers enjoyed greater adulation. It was in Bohemia that Jews suffered most acutely, wrenched by hostility between Czechs and Germans. Numerous Bohemian Jews converted to Catholicism, among them Gustav Mahler, Hans Kelsen and, for a time, Karl Kraus. Others, among whom was Viktor Adler, adopted Protestantism. In particular, Bohemian Jews tended to sublimate their destiny into some vision of eternity. By inventing a dreamworld, visionaries such as Mahler and Kafka created a tranquillity denied them on earth. Hermann Broch and Stefan Zweig esteemed art as a great equalizer in Viennese society. Although out of delicacy Zweig's father might refuse to dine next to a count, he felt no compunction about sitting next to an archduke at the theater.[30]

For all its democracy in art, Vienna roiled with anti-Semitism, chiefly economic in origin. Once Wilhelm Marr had invented the term anti-Semitism in 1879, it came to denote a movement lacking the religious animus of earlier anti-Judaism (Judenhass). Industrialism had thrust Jews into competition with gentiles, whereas in a rural economy Jews had complemented gentiles. Nobles of Hungary and Poland, who disdained engaging in commerce, had welcomed the services of Jewish moneylenders and merchants. Once this economic complementarity had yielded to competition, the increasing wealth of the Jews, exasperated those artisans, shopkeepers, and peasants who were sinking into poverty. In Austria, as in Germany, industrialization began only after Jews had gained emancipation in 1848, whereas in England and to a lesser extent in France, economic growth had preceded Jewish emergence. Where Jews entered capitalist competition at the same time as everyone else, they became the most conspicuous of nouveaux riches, goading the lower middle class into frustration. Stanislaw Andreski emphasizes that whereas Jews could take pride in strong family solidarity and a tradition of mutual assistance, gentiles of the lower middle class were losing even those reasons for self-respect.[31] They desperately needed a scapegoat.

At Vienna the intrusion of rural Jews exacerbated anti-Semitism. After 1900, Jews and Turks remained the only nationalities whose members regularly wore their national costume on the streets of Vienna. The sight of a kaftan affronted a lower middle class steeped in nostalgia for its own preindustrial roots and nurtured on spectacles like May Day in the Prater. Psychoanalysts Otto Fenichel, Bruno Bettelheim, Rudolph Loewenstein, and others, have postulated that an anti-Semite projects onto Jews certain undesirable qualities that he represses in himself. It seems that lower middle-class Viennese may have projected onto kaftan-wearers of the Judengasse their own yearning for a simpler past.[32]

During 1899 a Jewish scapegoat appeared in the person of a shoemaker's apprentice, Leopold Hilsner. In April of that year he was accused of having murdered a nineteen-year-old seamstress at Polna in southeastern Bohemia. The prosecutor implied that the youth had committed a ritual murder to get Christian blood for matzoh. This apocryphal crime had acquired fresh currency through the efforts of a German-born priest at Prague, August Rohling (1839–1931).[33] His scurrilous *Der Talmudjude: Zur Beherzigung für Juden und Christen aller Stände* (Münster, 1871) popularized the notion of a blood libel which Johann Andreas Eisenmenger (1654–1704) had disseminated in 1700. After a local court had sentenced Hilsner to death on the basis of circumstantial evidence, Tomáš Masaryk in late 1899 published several brochures and articles pleading for a new trial. Although the second trial in November, 1900, avoided any reference to ritual murder, Hilsner was sentenced to life imprisonment. After serving eighteen years, he was pardoned by Emperor Karl. Coinciding with the climax of the Dreyfus Affair, the Polna case intimidated Jews throughout Austria. One university professor, himself a converted Jew, appalled Masaryk by conceding, "You know that I am a Jew myself and I am convinced that this ritual murder business is merely superstition. But this case proves the possible existence of a secret sect which might after all practice ritual murder."[34]

A generation later anti-Semitism was satirized by a Vienna-born Protestant, Hugo Bettauer (1877–1925), in *Die Stadt ohne Juden: Ein Roman von Übermorgen* (Vienna, 1922). In describing how economic life collapses once all Jews have been expelled from the Austrian Republic, this fantasy specifies ways in which Jews stimulate commerce. Christians can no longer consult a Jewish banker about speculating in foreign exchange. Christian women no longer trouble to dress fashionably because they feel no need to compete with Jewish women. Gentile girls tire of drunken boyfriends now that no Jewish suitors ply them with presents. Luxury trades languish; even prostitutes can no longer afford to maintain lovers. A Socialist ally of Karl Kraus, Bettauer was shot in his office on March 10, 1925, by a dental student, who accused the journalist of fomenting sexual promiscuity. Bettauer died sixteen days later, virtually unmourned.

Sympathy for Jews should not be allowed to conceal the achieve-

ments of gentiles. However much Jews in Austria may have imbibed
energy from a rural ancestry, their entry into industrializing society
was but one of many abrasive encounters that Austria fostered. The
Habsburg Empire was par excellence the abode of the stranger, where
clashing nationalities heightened achievement. Czechs, Germans, and
Jews vied in Bohemia; Poles, Germans, Ruthenes, and Jews in Galicia;
Slovaks, Germans, Magyars, and Jews in Slovakia; Romanians, Germans, Magyars, and Jews in Transylvania; Croats, Serbs, Germans,
Magyars, and Jews in the Banat; while at Prague, Budapest, and Vienna
all these peoples unleashed creative ferment. What distinguished the
Jews is that like the Germans, they constituted a ubiquitous element,
dispersed throughout the empire. Again like Germans, Jews were cosmopolitan, possessing kinsmen outside Austria who made them feel
they were members of a larger community. If we ask why the Jews of
Austria should have been more persistently innovative than those of
Germany, the answer lies in Austria's population of rural Jews. In
Germany, as in France, nearly all Jews inhabited an urban ghetto,
where they had lost touch with mysticism and the soil. In Austria
rural Jews entered directly into urban life, further leavening an already heady mixture of races. No one benefited so much from the
variety inherent in Danubian society as the Jews who, more than any
other group of individuals, created the Gay Apocalypse.

2

The Emperor and His Court

 It is a commonplace that the Habsburg Empire was doomed to collapse, if not through war then through natural attrition. The blunder of Count Berchtold, who in July, 1914, chose war only to get a war other than the one he had chosen, seems to typify a regime tottering on its last legs. Against this view, Peter Feldl has argued that the empire succumbed only because in 1917 and 1918 its leaders failed to adapt quickly enough to changing events.[1] Although collapse was not preordained, insists Feldl, policymakers no longer possessed either desire or capacity to prevent it. The emphasis of this book will fall more on forces of stability within the empire than on those of disintegration. Tragically, the very forces that united the empire, such as the tenacity of the emperor and the traditionalism of his officials, in the long run abetted demise. The effete policies of 1917 and 1918 climaxed decades of having evaded hard decisions.

Although today readers salute thinkers who prophesied disaster, empathy with Karl Kraus and Georg Trakl should not hide the fact that before 1914 these Cassandras were tolerated but not believed, in a world confident of survival. Optimists like Ferenc Molnár and Hermann Bahr spoke more congenially to the bourgeois lucky enough to live before the deluge. No one has described this world of security more pointedly than the Vienna-born Jew Stefan Zweig (1881–1942) in *Die Welt von Gestern: Erinnerungen eines Europäers* (Stockholm, 1942). Growing up during the 1880's and 1890's, he rejoiced in a society where prosperous families could contemplate the future with equanimity. Currency was in gold, everyone knew how much he owed or was owed, just as each official and each officer knew in what year he would retire on pension. Zweig's father preferred running a solid business earning assured profits to indulging in speculation; addicted to buying insurance, his motto was "Safety first." The middle classes believed in the tangibility of progress: they had seen the advent of electric lights and also such marvels as plumbing, telephones, and bicycles. Europe was genuinely more advanced, it seemed, than the rest of the world, having remained without prolonged war since 1815.

Although nostalgic wish-fulfillment pervades Zweig's thesis, other observers confirm its gist. The Jewish music critic Max Graf (1873–1958), who was a friend of Freud, recalled the buoyancy that prevailed from 1890 to 1914:

> We who were born in Vienna, and grew up there, had no idea, during the city's brilliant period before the first world war that this epoch was to be the end . . . and still less did we suspect that the Habsburg Monarchy . . . was destined to decline. . . . We enjoyed the splendid city which was so elegantly beautiful, and never thought that the light which shone over it could ever be that of a colorful sunset.[2]

A younger Viennese associate of Freud, Robert Waelder (1900–1967), differentiated between long-run and short-run attitudes:

> There was much pessimism and resignation with regard to the long-term future. But on the other hand there was economic progress and a splendid intellectual and cultural life.[3]

Most intellectuals and ordinary citizens reveled in culture and entertainment, not caring to ponder whether the idyll would last forever.

The nostalgia that caused Zweig and Graf to celebrate prewar stability led other writers to stress forebodings of collapse. Robert Musil in *Der Mann ohne Eigenschaften* (1930–1943) and Joseph Roth in *Radetzkymarsch* (Berlin, 1932) went to the opposite extreme from Zweig, portraying characters gnawed by premonitions. In the case of the Galician Jew Roth (1894–1939), life as an alcoholic, alternating between intoxication and sobering up, may have intensified his awareness of a similar oscillation in prewar Austria. Roth's fatalistic acceptance of disaster scarcely accords with the bravado that many young men of his generation had displayed. As Max Brod remarked, the prewar generation was anything but lost. Despite misgivings, young men had faced World War One with courage and defiance in hope of averting catastrophe.[4] In the arts, expressionists embodied these hopes, aspiring after World War One to erect a society better than the one that had perished.

Dissillusionists like Musil and Roth reinforce the temptation to construe the history of Austria-Hungary as a tale of decay. Recently this view has been espoused by an Italian Germanist, Claudio Magris, in *Der habsburgische Mythos in der österreichischen Literatur* [1963] (Salzburg, 1966). Whereas before 1918 most Austrian writers, says Magris, had dreaded the very thought of imperial collapse, after 1918 they mourned the prewar fragility as if it had embellished a paradise. The myth of Habsburg beneficence beguiled former devotees of Young Vienna like Bahr and Hofmannsthal, who after the war apotheosized the fallen realm. Earlier the Habsburg myth had served Grillparzer and Stifter to mask the decadence and inequities that surrounded them. Although Magris offers many valuable insights, his analysis founders on a failure to define the term myth. By not differentiating between psychoanalytical, Marxian, and literary meanings of the term, he leaves unexplored the extent to which his myth penetrated the populace. Having implied that Austrian writers shunned reality, he does not specify whether it was political, economic, or psychological reality that they evaded. Magris himself seems to shift perspective with the nonchalance of the impressionists whom he deplores.

Magris' portrayal of Austrian illusions about their emperors suffers from significant omissions. Like many other students of Austro-Hungarian intellectual history, Magris ignores Hungary. There dynastic loyalty motivated writers such as Mór Jókai, while after 1918 nostalgia for the Habsburgs animated publicists such as Gyula Szekfü. Magris sees Bohemia as a thorn in the side of Austrian Germans, without recognizing how conflict there between Czech, German, and Jew engendered extraordinary aptitudes, especially among Bohemians who came to Vienna. Even more damaging to the thesis of a Habsburg myth, Magris ignores men who while distrusting the Habsburgs labored to preserve the empire, notably Austro-Marxists like Karl Renner and federalists like Aurel Popovici.

Magris' stress on weaknesses of the empire may stem in part from an Italian perspective. Having suffered Habsburg rule in Venice until 1866 and in Trieste until 1918, Italians, like the Czechs, often delight in blackening Habsburg achievements. Such disparagement reached a peak in Virginio Gayda's prewar indictment of Austria-Hungary, *Modern Austria: Her Racial and Social Problems* [1913] (London, 1915). More mercilessly than Seton-Watson or Wickham Steed, this pro-Czech Italian publicized scandals in every facet of Austrian life. To read his pages, as to read Magris', is to wonder how the Habsburg Empire survived after 1860, let alone 1900. This book will attempt to redress their bias by stressing forces of cohesion rather than of disso-

lution. Like the Jews, Austria-Hungary somehow survived long after
outsiders had given her up.

EMPEROR FRANZ JOSEPH:
BIEDERMEIER MONARCH IN AN INDUSTRIALIZING WORLD

Franz Joseph I, emperor of Austria, king of Hungary, and inheritor of
some twenty other titles, symbolized more than he achieved.[5] Reign-
ing from December, 1848, to November, 1916, longer than any other
European monarch, Franz Joseph became a living embodiment of the
will to survive. Grandson of the Biedermeier emperor Franz I and
nephew of the befuddled Ferdinand I, he perpetuated their adherence
to tradition. Although enjoying a veto over all legislation, he granted
demands for constitutional rule in 1860 and 1867 and permitted universal suffrage in Austria in 1907. Regarding himself as a dynasty
personified, Franz Joseph could still in July, 1914, address a proclamation of war "To My Peoples" (An meine Völker), with stress on the
adjective.
    This "Imperial Hofrat," who toiled eight to ten hours a day signing
documents and holding audiences, commanded wide respect, especially
after 1890. Once he had attained old age, Franz Joseph, like Queen
Victoria, seemed a relic whose very venerability inspired awe. The
emperor's muttonchop whiskers were imitated by many a dignitary.
Countless citizens displayed a portrait of the emperor at home, as if to
remind themselves that they had seen his face presiding over every
schoolroom and military establishment.
    In his personal life, the emperor obeyed an iron regimen, rising
regularly at 5:00 A.M. and retiring no later than 11:00 P.M. His aversion to innovation was epitomized by the Spanish Court Ceremonial.
Having stood stiffly to receive each visitor, he would terminate an
audience by a nod of the head. Visitors were expected to back out of
the room, lest they display a derriere to his Imperial Majesty. The
grand master of the court rather than the emperor decided who should
be granted an audience. At public functions he insisted on being
addressed as "His Apostolic Majesty, our most gracious Emperor and
Lord, Franz Joseph I" (Seine Apostolische Majestät, unser allergnädig-
ster Kaiser und Herr). So punctilious was the emperor in matters of
dress that on his deathbed, anecdote had it, he roused himself to
reprimand the hastily summoned physician: "Go home and dress cor-
rectly." To the end the emperor dined from a table set in the Spanish

manner, with all silverware laid at the right of the plate. When formal dinner was served at Schönbrunn, every guest ceased eating the moment the emperor had finished each course. Because he ate very rapidly, most guests received little or no opportunity to partake of the cuisine Franz Joseph steadfastly resisted technological change. No toilets were installed in the Hofburg until Empress Elisabeth insisted during the 1850's. The Emperor distrusted telephones, trains, and especially automobiles, while electric lights irritated his eyes. Like most aristocrats of his realm, he was very fond of hunting and of mountain climbing, particularly at the resort of Bad Ischl.

The emperor was profoundly influenced by members of his family. His mother, Archduchess Sophie (1805–1872), daughter of King Maximilian I of Bavaria, was extremely ambitious for her son. In 1848 she schemed to bring him to the throne, and in 1854 she arranged his marriage with one of her nieces, Elisabeth (1837–1898). This marriage between first cousins was consummated at Vienna just a few years before Gregor Mendel began his research on genetics at Brünn, seventy-five miles away. Thanks to Archduchess Sophie, marriages of consanguinity, which had debilitated Habsburgs during the seventeenth century and had addled Ferdinand I, continued unabated, helping to cause the instability of Crown Prince Rudolf. Sophie further blighted the marriage by denying the empress control over the imperial household or even over her own children. The unhappy empress solaced herself by riding horseback and by traveling to Hungary, Bavaria, and Corfu. During the 1870's the growing lunacy of her cousin King Ludwig II of Bavaria spurred Elisabeth to roam Europe in quest of an elixir against insanity. So many legends were inspired by the life of Empress Elisabeth, that it is difficult to assess her influence on events. However much Franz Joseph may have loved her, clearly he loved duty, which meant obedience to his mother, more. Elisabeth's chief act of statesmanship was to help persuade the emperor to adopt Deák's Compromise in 1866 and to charm Hungarians into welcoming the emperor in 1867. Had she performed similar service on behalf of the Czechs, she would deserve better of posterity.

Although Elisabeth spent most of her last twenty years abroad, she was in Vienna at the time of Crown Prince Rudolf's suicide, a setback from which she never recovered. Her senseless murder by an Italian anarchist at Geneva on September 10, 1898, caused Franz Joseph unspeakable grief, impelling him to cancel grandiose festivities for his fiftieth jubilee. Her funeral cortege furnished one of the most somber displays of imperial pomp during the entire reign.

Long before Elisabeth's death, the emperor sought respite from his loneliness by taking breakfast in the company of Katharina Schratt (1855-1940), an actress to whom the empress had introduced him in 1886. This one gesture of unbending endeared Franz Joseph to his people.

Next to the empress, the most enigmatic of Franz Joseph's relatives was their only son, Crown Prince Rudolf (1858–1889). They also had two surviving daughters. Rudolf combined the delicate nerves and Madame-Bovary-martyrdom of his mother with his father's sense of duty and devotion to detail. Neglected by his father, Rudolf grew up during the Liberal Auersperg Ministry of the 1870's. Although initially friendly to the Czechs, he came to detest the clerical regime of Taaffe, just as he deplored repressive policies of Kálmán Tisza. Rudolf shared his mother's fondness for Hungarians, speaking their language, in the words of Mór Jókai, like a peasant.[6] An anticlerical, who relished Descartes and Voltaire, Rudolf further differed from his father by admiring France. Only because he feared that Russia would block Austria's advance through the Balkans to Salonica would Rudolf concede the need for an alliance with Prussia.

From 1876 to 1878 the economist Carl Menger traveled with Rudolf as his tutor. While visiting England, they published an anonymous pamphlet, *Der österreichische Adel und sein constitutioneller Beruf* (Munich. 1878), whose authorship was divulged only in 1906. Impressed by the civic responsibility of the British aristocracy, Rudolf and his mentor decried the idleness of younger sons in the Austrian nobility; they lived solely to hunt and to dance. In 1882 Menger introduced Rudolf to a fellow Francophile, Moriz Szeps (1834–1902), editor of the *Neues Wiener Tagblatt*. For six years Szeps and Rudolf corresponded, and from 1883 to 1885 the crown prince contributed anonymous articles to the paper, especially during the Hungarian crisis of August, 1883.[7]

Scholars have never cleared the mystery that shrouded Rudolf's death by suicide at the hunting lodge of Mayerling on January 30, 1889. Berta Szeps, daughter of Moriz, has left a revealing account of Rudolf's motives, reporting that as a youth in Prague the crown prince had fallen in love with a young Jewess, who died of fever after running away from her place of exile in the country.[8] The half-Greek Baroness Mary Vetsera, whom Rudolf met on November 5, 1888, supposedly reminded him of his Jewish sweetheart. His affair with Mary came at a time when strife with Franz Joseph was growing insufferable. Having written to Pope Leo XIII to seek annulment of his unhappy marriage with Princess Stephanie, Rudolf was disgraced when the pope returned the petition directly to Franz Joseph. On the evening the petition came back, Franz Joseph attended a reception held by the new German ambassador; in the receiving line the emperor turned his back just as Rudolf bowed to him. A shudder ran through the room as Rudolf fled. Later that evening, the crown prince told Szeps, "The emperor has openly affronted me. From now on, all ties between us are broken. From now on, I am free!"[9] Berta Szeps contended that Rudolf's suicide was above all a political act, kindled by despair over German Emperor Wilhelm II, who had come to the throne in June, 1888. and whose arrogance revived the chagrin that Rudolf had felt at the time of Königgrätz.[10] Thwarted in politics, in marriage, and as a son, Rudolf shot Mary Vetsera and himself. In order to hide political consequences, the Viennese emphasized the sentimental adventure of this deed. As if public life were an operetta, they found it pleasanter to believe that Rudolf had died for a woman than for his convictions.

Rapport was no better between Franz Joseph and the middle-aged heir presumptive Archduke Franz Ferdinand (1863–1914), who was the eldest son of the emperor's younger brother Archduke Karl Ludwig. Himself heir presumptive for seven years, Karl Ludwig (1833–1896) had indulged in such piety that in 1896 he insisted on drinking from the River Jordan, a deed that cost him his life from intestinal infection. Son of Neapolitan princess Maria Annunziata, Franz Ferdinand undertook a world voyage during 1892–1893. He spent the years 1895 to 1898 convalescing from tuberculosis. In 1900 he contracted a morganatic marriage with Sophie Chotek (1868–1914), after Franz Joseph had extracted a promise that the couple would never seek the throne for any of their children. Although the marriage was serene, both partners seethed at snubs that the grand master of the court, Prince Montenuovo, inflicted on Sophie. Until 1909 a mere princess and thereafter duchess of Hohenberg, she stood lower in rank than some thirty archduchesses, each of whom, no matter how young, marched ahead of her on ceremonial occasions. She knew that she would never become empress, and on state occasions she rode in a separate carriage from her husband. Extremely pious, Sophie converted Franz Ferdinand back to the clerical viewpoint of his father, a stance that together with Latin manners made him unpopular with the masses. Referring to Magyars as Hunnen, he berated Jews of Budapest who assimilated too eagerly, and he deplored the Los-von-Rom movement as being pro-Prussian.

From 1901, Franz Ferdinand took an active role in military affairs, maintaining his own staff at the Belvedere Palace and backing the Protestant General Franz Conrad von Hötzendorf (1852–1925). Franz

Ferdinand urged that Austria-Hungary enter the naval race against Italy, with sailors to be recruited from Croatia. The heir presumptive flaunted hostility to Hungary, where he hoped to see universal suffrage introduced. Allegedly, he desired to unite within the empire Catholic Croats and Orthodox Serbs. Because this prospect had disarmed separatist leaders within the empire, young Serbs had to use desperate measures in order to salvage their dream of a Greater Serbia.

The assassination of Franz Ferdinand and his wife, who had disregarded warnings for their safety because of their rivalry with Franz Joseph, came on Derby Day, the close of the social season in Vienna. Not even news of the murder could silence orchestras in the Prater on this last Sunday in June. Josef Redlich noted in his diary that such nonchalance may have betrayed premonitions that as emperor Franz Ferdinand would have brought even greater disaster than could his death. Redlich reviled the fallen archduke for clerical bigotry, pettiness in money matters, distrust of associates, tastelessness in art-collecting, and bloodthirsty slaughter of wild game.[11] Despite these faults, the murdered man became a martyr thanks partly to disrespect that Prince Montenuovo showered upon him in death. Delays and neglect impeded the coffins at every stage of their journey from Sarajevo via Vienna to burial in the Castle of Artstetten near Pöchlarn on the Danube.[12] This deliberate insult so shocked officials and soldiers who witnessed it that their indignation turned into ill-founded hero-worship for Franz Ferdinand, stiffening determination to avenge his murder at any cost. Preventive war, advocated earlier by his favorites Conrad von Hötzendorf and Count Berchtold, found credence at the very time when caution was most needed. Prince Montenuovo, who in March, 1913, had labored to avert war, helped unwittingly to instigate it sixteen months later.

Franz Joseph's cruelty to his son and to Franz Ferdinand's wife was paralleled by even crasser ingratitude to ministers. He condescended to all ministers, as if it were such a privilege to serve him that no gratitude could be necessary. Shameless self-confidence permitted Franz Joseph in 1906 to accept as trade minister of Hungary, Ferenc Kossuth, a man whose father in 1849 had declared the Habsburg dynasty defunct. In contrast to King Wilhelm I of Prussia, Franz Joseph could not tolerate a minister of first-rate ability. Just when a vigorous reformer required support, the emperor would withdraw it, as he did to Schmerling in 1861, Beust in 1871, Badeni in 1897, and Beck in 1908. In 1854 his refusal to enter the Crimean War outraged Nicholas I of Russia, whose troops had saved the Hungarian crown for Franz Joseph in 1849. Even more heartless was the betrayal in 1866 of the Protestant General Ludwig von Benedek (1804–1881). Against his better judgment, Benedek had consented to take supreme command of the Bohemian campaign. Although as early as July 1 he foresaw the disaster that would come at Königgrätz, his request to be relieved of command was overruled. Following the defeat, Benedek was removed from command and subjected to two-and-one-half months of official inquiry. On November 19, 1866, Archduke Albrecht (1817–1895), the victor at Custozza, forced Benedek to sign a promise never to write or bequeath any material regarding the campaign of 1866. Three weeks later on December 18, 1866, the official *Wiener Zeitung* carried an article sanctioned by Albrecht and Franz Joseph, charging that Benedek's deficiencies had been solely responsible for the disaster at Königgrätz. Muzzled by oath, the reluctant commander could only lick his wounds in silence, while anticlericals rumored that a Jesuit confessor had persuaded Franz Joseph to humiliate the Protestant general.

His faults notwithstanding, Franz Joseph left an imprint on every aspect of life in Austria-Hungary. Beloved by few, hated by few, during his later years he was respected by nearly all as the linchpin that held the empire together. Industrious and unimaginative, he seemed the bureaucrat supreme, who expected that by following routine he could transmit to his successor the territories and privileges he himself had inherited. Loss of Lombardy in 1859 and of Venice in 1866, coupled with definitive extrusion from Germany, made him feel that he had failed in his duty toward the dynasty. In 1870 he remarked half-jokingly, yet bitterly, to Albert Schäffle, "I am an unlucky man."[13] Having surmounted the bereavements of 1889 and 1898, he preserved his dignity to the end.

The aristocrats, bureaucrats, army officers, priests, and professors, whom Franz Joseph patronized as personal servants, functioned as cogs in a system that enshrined its ruler's strengths and weaknesses. His policy of *quieta non movere* reinforced the rigidity and torpor that Franz I and Metternich had embedded in political life. Secrecy shrouded transaction of public business, fomenting rumors of conspiracy and of sentimental adventure to explain even the most routine events. Because ministers were enjoined not to publish memoirs, and as the press remained censored, gossip supplanted factual reporting. In an atmosphere of half-truths, temporizing sustained the empire. Fabian tactics might have succeeded even longer if after decades of hesitation Berchtold and his advisers had not taken a wrong initiative in July, 1914. Having foiled so many innovations in the past, by then the eighty-four-year-old emperor was too old to impose his preference for eleventh-hour compromises.

ARISTOCRACY AND LESSER NOBILITY: PRIVILEGE AS A CHECK ON INNOVATION

The regimen of Franz Joseph contrasted with the frivolity of his court. Good society was divided into two circles, a first society of aristocracy or upper nobility *(Hochadel* or *Aristokratie)* and a second society of lesser nobility *(Briefadel* or *Dienstadel).*[14]

Within the first society, descendants of former sovereign families, whose holdings had been mediatized in 1806, took precedence over those whose ancestors had never ruled a principality of the Holy Roman Empire. Members of the upper nobility bore the title Prince *(Fürst),* Count *(Graf),* or if they belonged to the royal family, Archduke *(Erzherzog).* Lesser nobility, whose families had earned a title by recent service to the crown, comprised in descending order the ranks of *Freiherr, Ritter, Edler,* and the simple *von.* The title *Hofrat* which adorned bureau chiefs in the civil service carried no claim to nobility. Whereas upper nobility were addressed as *"Hochgeboren,"* lower nobility and even commoners were frequently called "Herr Baron" or *"Wohlgeboren."* Members of the two societies mingled only at charity balls during pre-Lent. Further to differentiate the two circles, the *Almanach de Gotha* listed them separately. Officially, all this ended on April 3, 1919, when the Republic of Austria abolished titles of nobility, forbidding the use even of "von" in legal documents, albeit powerless to prevent continued use of titles in society. Two years later the city council of Vienna voted to remove imperial statues and to change street names reminiscent of the empire—an ordinance that was imperfectly carried out.

Members of the lower nobility were not admitted to Franz Joseph's court. According to ancient heraldic practice, to be eligible for court *(hoffähig)* one must possess sixteen quarters of nobility, that is, one must have had sixteen great-great-grandparents all of whom were noble. To enforce this rule, the emperor relied on the incorruptible grand master of the court *(Obersthofmeister),* a position held for many years by Prince Montenuovo (1854–1927), a grandson of Napoleon's widow Marie Louise by Count Adam Neipperg. The grand master of the court stood first in command among the four high officers, ranking above the grand chamberlain, the grand marshal of the court, and the master of the stable. These positions could be held only by men of purest pedigree, who were privileged to direct a dozen lesser officers and hundreds of servants. Not only did Montenuovo torment Franz Ferdinand's wife, but he refused many offers of bribes from financiers who sought admittance to court. Until about 1885 even wives of ministers were excluded from the charmed circle, and then only wives of ministers actually in office could accompany their husbands at court. One advantage of being a military officer was that all officers were hoffähig, a privilege that greatly enhanced prestige. The aristocracy was concentrated in eighty families who had intermarried so often that they constituted one large family. They addressed each other as "Du" and by nicknames, except when speaking to members of the imperial family. From December to May, the families frequented a common round of parties, at which everyone knew details of the others' lives. Swaddled in mutual congratulation and exclusiveness, they understood one another with half-spoken words.

The favorites of court society were archdukes and archduchesses, who in 1884 numbered sixty-six, descended from the sixteen children of Maria Theresa and the seventeen children of Leopold II. Many held high positions in the military, even after the reform of 1868. Nearly all were known to the populace, who cheered their carriages in the same way they applauded actors and actresses. Martin Freud has described how as a child he adored the imperial family:

> We Freud children were all stout royalists . . . [at the Hofburg] we could tell with precision the extent of the passengers' importance by the color of the high wheels and the angle at which the magnificent liveried coachman held his whip.[15]

Members of the imperial family spoke Schönbrunnerdeutsch, a refinement of Viennese dialect. Their speech sufficiently resembled that of cabdrivers so that—at least in print—it was difficult to recognize social class by speech alone.

Within the aristocracy, real and tangible property was entailed: family estates belonged to the eldest son who as ruling prince or count sat in the Herrenhaus, together with bishops and life-members. Deprived by law of Majoratsrechte, younger sons had to fend for themselves, often dwelling under a brother's roof. Entail had originated in the medieval fidei commissum, from which 292 Austrian families still benefited in 1885, amassing enormous wealth before entail was abolished in 1919. Just before World War One, Prince Schwarzenberg controlled the following holdings in southern Bohemia: 7 fidei commissum estates totaling 315,000 acres and 4 freehold estates embracing 45,000 acres, enclosing 12 castles, 95 dairies, 12 breweries, 2 sugar refineries, 22 sawmills, and several graphite mines. Presiding over 73 parishes with 87 churches, he employed 5,000 peasant families and several hundred clerks.[16] In such a menage, personal servants worshiped their masters, expecting in return to be cared for during old age.

From June to October or November, upper nobility forsook Vienna to hunt on country estates. Once a year relatives would gather around their patriarch at family day, when the men would hunt while the ladies planned festivities for the coming season. Hunting captivated the nobility, not least the emperor and his son. In June, 1898, as part of the fiftieth jubilee of Franz Joseph, five thousand hunters from the farthest corners of the empire gathered at Schönbrunn to honor the emperor with a shooting party. During winter, the court riding school attracted equestrians; Austrians and even more Hungarians gloried in the excellence of their Arabian horses and their skill as riders. Franz Joseph prided himself on the Royal Stables, which housed four hundred steeds, nearly all of which were jet black or pure white, in addition to bays that drew the emperor's carriage.

Although some nobles disdained frivolity, exceptions grew fewer as the middle classes gained power. In the anonymous pamphlet of 1878 which Crown Prince Rudolf wrote with Carl Menger, they upbraided the nobility for dissipating themselves in hunting and visiting, while disdaining to participate in politics or even to train for military service now that examinations had made this traditional calling more demanding. Mór Jókai rebuked the nobility for denying assistance to members in trouble: if someone squandered his fortune, friends would ride with him without reproach only to forsake him the moment he was ruined.[17] If nobles enjoyed greater privileges, they also incurred greater risks than ordinary citizens should they fail to keep up appearances.

Not a few of the nobility preferred eccentricity to banality. One such was Vienna-born Princess Pauline Metternich (1836–1921), a granddaughter of the famous diplomat, who married her uncle, Metternich's son. While he was ambassador at Paris from 1859 to 1871, she enlivened social life there, invigorating anti-Prussian circles. After returning to Vienna, she reigned as hostess supreme for more than forty years, organizing innumerable balls, art shows, concerts, and festivals. It was she who in May 1886 instituted the annual competition of flowers (Blumenkorso) to climax the traditional May Day parade of celebrities at the Prater.

Another flamboyant figure—and a favorite target of scandalmongers —was the emperor's nephew, Archduke Otto (1865–1906). This younger brother of Franz Ferdinand had married Maria Josepha, a prim daughter of the king of Saxony, and it was their son Karl (1887–1922) who ruled as Emperor Karl I. Torn between his father's punctilio and his mother's Neapolitan blood, by day Otto was the most fastidious of officers and by night an incurable roué. On one occasion when he and his riding companions glimpsed a funeral cortege across a meadow, they proceeded to jump their horses over the hearse. His most famous prank was to appear before ladies in the lobby of the Hotel Sacher, stark naked except for his officer's sword and cap. After the German-Nationalist deputy Engelbert Pernerstorfer (1850–1918) had presumed to allude to these abuses during a Reichsrat debate on student disorders, he and his wife were assaulted at home by two rowdies.[18] Although Parliament condemned this intimidation of a member—it was the first incident of its kind—police refused to prosecute the bullies. With the years, Otto's syphilis worsened so that he had to wear a leather nose to hide his disfigurement. Disregarding his own affair with an actress, in 1900 Otto deplored Franz Ferdinand's morganatic marriage. When Otto died, the press waxed fulsome in praise of an archduke whom everyone knew to have been a wastrel.

A less privileged eccentric was the Moravian-born Catholic, Count Adalbert Sternberg (1868–1930), a world traveler who spoke six languages, drank to excess, and wrote sarcastic feuilletons. To express disgust at the abolition of titles in Austria and Czechoslovakia, he revised his visiting card:

> Adalbert Sternberg
> Geadelt von Karl dem Grossen 798
> Entadelt von Karl Renner 1918
>
> Adalbert Sternberg
> Ennobled by Charlemagne 798
> Unnobled by Karl Renner 1918.[19]

In his memoirs, *Warum Österreich zugrunde gehen musste* (Vienna, 1927), Sternberg excoriated the immunity of court personages like Archduke Otto, declaring that protection of miscreants had hastened the empire's collapse.

For most aristocrats home away from home was the Hotel Sacher, which Anna Sacher, née Fuchs (1859-1930), took over in 1892 from her deceased husband, Eduard, who had founded it in 1876. Cigar-smoking and *exigeante*, she knew her guests personally. A penniless charmer whom she fancied could receive everything at nominal charge, while a millionaire whom she despised would be turned away. The front dining room, which boasted fabulous cuisine, was reserved for guests of her choosing, while the kitchen regularly fed the indigent. *Chambres separées* upstairs were renowned for sheltering political intrigue and intimate rendezvous. On December 1, 1921, Frau Sacher dispelled a mob of striking workers who had just ransacked three nearby hotels. Cigar in hand and bellowing in Viennese dialect, she persuaded the crowd to disband, thereby sparing portraits of Franz Joseph and Wilhelm II, which adorned the dining room until her death.[20] Max Graf offered a vignette of the society to which Anna Sacher catered:

> I can still see the distinguished Count Berchtold on a summer's day in 1914, standing in the doorway of a Ringstrasse Hotel. He had just signed the declaration of war on Serbia. Now he stood here, slender, laughing ironically, a gold-tipped cigarette in his well-manicured fingers, watching the crowds and conversing with the passersby. Thus cultivated Ringstrasse society entered the world war which disrupted it. It had lived laughing and joking, and laughing and joking it died.[21]

The most damaging of the aristocracy's privileges was power to make or break careers. Because members of court society granted favors to leaders of the bureaucracy, any enterprise required preliminary backing from court if it was to win bureaucratic approval. Through the institution of *Protektion*, archdukes and princes influenced nearly every aspect of public life, tempting the middle classes to curry favor through the back door *(Hintertürl)*. Hanns Sachs has described how the aristocracy exploited their authority, if not with brutality at least with a good deal of "graceful and complacent callousness":

> without any trace of organization or leadership, their amorphous, anonymous, irresponsible power could only work in one way: to inhibit any innovation, to exclude all new forces from cooperation.[22]

Protektion influenced not only university professorships, but all cultural institutions. The opera and the Burgtheater suffered constant interference. In 1900 Schnitzler's *Der grüne Kakadu* was removed from the Burgtheater, ostensibly because the director had lost his "taste" for it, in reality because an archduchess had disapproved its praise of the French Revolution.[23] Two years earlier Katharina Schratt had threatened to terminate her career unless Schnitzler's *Der Schleier der Beatrice* was performed as promised despite its flaunting of free love. Because the emperor would not let her retire during his Jubilee Year, he ordered a role created for her, in which she had to wear a black lace cap befitting a seduced woman who was planning suicide. In 1900 Frau Schratt did quit the Burgtheater when the director refused to accept a French play that she had selected; the director insisted that the figure of Napoleon could not mount that august stage. After her retirement, Franz Joseph never again attended the theater.[24]

The emperor interfered even in administration of justice. When Archduke Ernst died about 1907, he bequeathed his fortune to four children by his morganatic wife. The emperor had the children declared illegitimate, so that the fortune could go to the octogenarian Archduke Rainer. When one of the daughters sued, the case lost at every turn because of influence from court, although some judges resigned rather than yield to pressure.[25] Such abuses notwithstanding, the imperial court did reward individuals deemed worthy. In 1895 the ailing Anton Bruckner received lodgings at the garden of the Upper Belvedere through the patronage of Archduchess Valerie. Numerous painters and sculptors were granted commissions from the court. Although Hans Makart was given a villa at state expense, others, including the vast majority of Jewish artists, were left to fend for themselves.

Despite inequities of Protektion and the frivolity of the nobility, aristocrats injected an irreplaceable independence of spirit into cultural life. As patrons of art, philanthropists like Princess Metternich and Hans Wilczek sponsored enterprises that the state shunned. Intellectuals of the aristocracy like Christian von Ehrenfels and Richard Coudenhove-Kalergi—as well as countless sons of the lower nobility—excelled at philosophy and social theory. One quality that the nobility shared with all classes was love of art and festivals; both at the theater and at the Prater, upper, middle, and lower classes joined in what Hermann Broch called a "style-democracy." Distrusting the state as an abstraction that lacked any ethical goal, members of all classes preferred escapism. The nobility also shared certain of its prejudices with the lower middle classes. Both resented the prosperous middle class and especially the bureaucracy that was recruited from it. Both revered rural society, dreading the achievement-orientation of urban—and Jewish—liberalism. Between them the nobility and the lower middle class conspired to resist innovation, supplanting liberalism with Christian socialism while encouraging the court to uphold the status quo.

3

An Empire of Bureaucrats

UNIFORMITY VERSUS VENALITY
IN AN ANTIQUATED BUREAUCRACY

THE BUREAUCRACY that Maria Theresa and Joseph II had created infiltrated every corner of Austrian life. Ostensibly the administration's
mission was to extend uniformity throughout the empire, Westernizing
the non-German peoples and regimenting everyone to obey edicts of
the crown. Emblems of uniformity blanketed the empire: every court-
house, post office, and railroad station bore a yellow shield emblazoned
with a double-headed black eagle. In Bukovina as in Vienna, railroad
officials wore identical dark blue uniforms and rang identical bells.
Cafés and hotels from Lemberg to Laibach imitated those of Vienna;
tradesmen and fiacre drivers dressed and gesticulated in the same
fashion, so that a traveler could feel no less at home on the Russian
frontier than in the Italian Alps. These shared amenities and customs
resulted from regulations that spanned the empire, creating an apparent unity that tantalized post-1918 romantics.

Despite the veneer of security which it created, the bureaucracy was
more feared than admired. The title Hofrat, which had been introduced in 1765 for high officials, came to symbolize power to dispense
Protektion. After 1850 new titles such as *Ministerialrat* and *Sektionsrat*
proliferated to dignify an expanding officialdom. Franz Joseph exercised veto power over all appointments. Once hired, officials entered a
world of security, in which promotions followed at prescribed intervals
until—usually after thirty years—one could retire on pension, perhaps
to dwell in the "Pensionopolis" of Graz. Many high officials prided
themselves on diligence and impartiality, as attested by memoirs of
Alexander Spitzmüller (1862–1953), the last imperial minister of finance.[1] Another pillar of rectitude was Heinrich Lammasch (1853–
1920), a supporter of the peace movement, who served as the last

Austrian prime minister. Ernst Lothar recalled that as a student he heard Professor Lammasch inveigh against Protektion, insisting that an examining judge must brook no interference, whether from Hofräte, aristocrats, or emperor. On one occasion, when Lothar was handling a case against one of Lammasch's relatives, the old man came to inquire about it, alarming the young judge lest his idolized professor seek to intervene. When Lothar told him that the case would be brought to trial, Lammasch said simply, "Thank you for the information," inspiring Lothar for the first time with pride in his calling.[2]

A more innovative bureaucrat was Emil Steinbach (1846–1907), a Jew who had converted to Catholicism.[3] From within the Department of Justice he supported Taaffe's law of 1883 establishing an inspectorate of trade to prohibit labor on Sundays and to limit working hours for women and adolescents. In 1887 Steinbach devised a program of health and accident insurance for workers which surpassed that of Bismarck, and as finance minister from 1891 to 1893 he supervised reform of the empire's currency. Although his proposal for universal suffrage brought down Taaffe's government, Steinbach had helped to give Austria what in 1891 Viktor Adler called the best social legislation of any country outside of England and Switzerland.[4] Unfortunately, costs imposed by these labor laws tended to place Austrian industry at a disadvantage with that of Germany and even Hungary. In 1904 Steinbach became the second Jew to serve as president of the Supreme Court. Steinbach was one of many officials who came from teaching at the university to ministerial service. Another was the German-born Karl Theodor von Inama-Sternegg (1843–1908), who directed the Central Commission for Statistics from 1884–1908, making the Austrian census of 1890 and 1900 the most detailed in the world. Many economists and jurists pursued such double careers, introducing innovation to government and practical experience to teaching. In 1882 advantages of late industrialization accrued when a German-born official in the Ministry of Trade, Georg Coch (1842–1890), examined techniques of postal savings in England, Belgium, Holland, and France before fashioning such a system for Austria. Exploiting his comparative studies, he devised the first postal check, which was promptly adopted throughout Europe.

Unfortunately, the energy of such innovators could not prevent bureaucracy from fostering inertia more often than advance. This was partly because the government shrouded its affairs in secrecy. Franz Joseph discouraged ministers from writing memoirs, sometimes as in the case of Benedek exacting an oath to prevent it. Not only did the emperor drop ministers at crucial juctures, but frequent changes or infractions of the constitution—in 1848, 1860, 1867, the 1880's, 1897, 1907, and 1914—caused statesmen identified with one system to disappear under the next.[5] Amid general ignorance, the Reichsrat alone offered a forum where bureaucracy could be exposed to public scrutiny by crusading deputies like Engelbert Pernerstorfer. Tension between Reichsrat and ministries culminated in 1897 when the Polish Count Kasimir Badeni (1846–1909) introduced his language ordinances. He had miscalculated by choosing for pro-Czech legislation a year in which the ten-year treaty between Austria and Hungary had to be renewed. Conservatives and German-Nationals united to filibuster against renewal until Badeni would either fall from office or withdraw his proposal to make Czech a language of official business in Bohemia. The filibuster of October, 1897, brought on tactics of obstruction unprecedented in Europe. Every faction stowed away noisemakers such as whistles, sleigh bells, harmonicas, cowbells, trombones, hunting horns, and snare drums, appointing one member to act as bandmaster whenever a speaker was to be drowned out. Mark Twain, who was living in Vienna, left a graphic account of these disturbances, dramatizing a marathon speech that Dr. Otto Lecher, president of the Board of Trade at Brünn, delivered on October 28, 1897 from 8:45 p.m. until 8:45 a.m. the following day.[6] In Moravia and Bohemia, Lecher became a national hero, featured on postal cards and given a tumultuous welcome upon returning to Brünn. Badeni fell a few days later, after he had summoned sixty policemen to clear the Reichsrat of obstructionists. The filibuster attracted so much publicity that the otherwise apolitical Sigmund Freud identified his own habit of seeing patients for eleven hours per day with Dr. Lecher's recordbreaking speech.[7] Although obstructionism had originated among Irish deputies in the British Parliament in 1877, and although in the same year as Dr. Lecher's marathon a Romanian delivered an address of thirty-seven hours at Bucharest, Austria offered the *locus classicus* of a legislature paralyzed by members who flouted their own rules of procedure. This produced the unhappy result that in November, 1897, Franz Joseph invoked Article Fourteen of the Constitutional Law on Parliamentary Representation, which authorized the bureaucracy to govern on an emergency basis *(ausnahmsweise)*. The necessity of circumventing the Reichsrat during most of the next ten years discredited everyone concerned, above all the bureaucracy that incurred blame for every misadventure.

Although the granting of universal male suffrage in 1907 restored parliamentary rule, in March, 1914, Count Stürgkh dissolved the Reichsrat, which was not reconvened until May 30, 1917. Despising Parliament and holding himself responsible solely to the emperor, Prime Minister Stürgkh steered the empire into World War One, whereupon he invoked at once the War Service Act passed in 1913. It authorized censorship of press and mails and universal conscription of persons and property.[8] In contrast with Hungary, Austria waged war by imposing unprecedented secrecy, while a shortage of food, created by devastation of Galicia's wheat and by Hungary's sealing her borders, tempted peasants to sell crops on the black market. Amid famine and rumors of defeat, wartime stringency further demoralized the public.

Prior to 1914 it was the middle class that suffered most from the foot-dragging of a bureaucracy whose motto was "We can wait." Red tape was legendary; at Vienna twenty-seven officials handled each tax payment. About 1905 a train dispatcher, who was being tried for negligence, won acquittal when his lawyer hauled thirty tomes into court, declaring "The regulation my client is accused of breaking is somewhere in these thirty volumes."[9] The state lottery, founded in 1787, was designed to eat up savings of the poor by luring further payments in hope of ever greater winnings. In 1891 Carl Menger denounced his countrymen for lacking initiative, asserting that a café owner's three sons would all open coffeehouses in the same town, while a baker's sons would each establish a bakery. Bribery was rife in certain institutions. At the Landesgericht jail in Vienna, prisoners could satisfy any wish—for books or a mistress—provided they could smuggle in money to bribe the guards.[10] A more subtle abuse was committed by young men who would enter the bureaucracy for a few years so as to groom themselves for private business, where they could exploit familiarity with inner workings of government.

Repeatedly courts and police perpetrated outrages—displaying what Karl Kraus called *Bürokretinismus*. In 1906 at Trieste, an Italian worker, Anton Zamparatti, was imprisoned for lese majesty because he persisted in calling the emperor "king."[11] In 1904 at Leoben, a widow spent five months in jail while authorities investigated charges of witchcraft against her.[12] During 1906 Kraus publicized the case of Regine Riehl, proprietor of a bordello at Vienna, who was sentenced to three-and-one-half years for usury and other maltreatment of her girls.[13] At her trial, police dignitaries testified that subordinates had hesitated to prosecute her because they regularly visited her establishment gratis. Kraus then stated that exposure by the press had forced the police to safeguard the girls against unfair labor practices.

The Viennese press wallowed in venality. Officials played favorites, leaking stories or planting false ones. The "revolver-press" blackmailed prominent persons and businesses by threatening revelations unless compensated. By purchasing newspaper support the Südbahn railroad delayed nationalization until 1923, whereas others like the Nordbahn had been expropriated in 1885 amid rumors of malfeasance.[14] Perhaps the most famous press scandal concerned an article which the German-Nationalist historian, Heinrich Friedjung (1851–1920), a converted Jew, published in the *Neue Freie Presse* of March 25, 1909, accusing a Serb deputy, Supilo, of conspiring with agents in Belgrade.[15] A libel suit against Friedjung in December, 1909, revealed that someone as highly placed as Foreign Minister Aloys Aehrenthal (1854–1912) had supplied the unwitting Friedjung with documents a double agent had forged, possibly with the foreign minister's knowledge. Friedjung's reputation as a historian never recovered from his failure to detect this canard.

Nothing illustrated so well the sloppiness of bureaucracy as the manner in which it handled censorship of the press.[16] Each morning preliminary copies of every paper were rushed to the censor, who might order any story confiscated. In its place would appear an empty space bearing the word *konfisziert*. Because papers were read so hastily, frequently a story confiscated in one paper would be overlooked in another. In such cases, every paper was allowed to reprint the story, citing the unconfiscated version as its source. More reliable was the preventive censorship whereby police officials notified publishers that certain matters ought to be hushed up. The Board of Censors licensed prospective publishers, who until 1894 had to deposit a large bail *(Kaution)* and whose character or political activities might furnish grounds for refusal of a license. Until 1903 a license also was required to sell newspapers, a trade that until then had been limited to a few widely scattered kiosks. Newsboys were not permitted until 1922. In January, 1883, Taaffe, at the instigation of Bismarck, tried to destroy Moriz Szep's *Neues Wiener Tagblatt* by forbidding its sale at kiosks, whereupon Szeps hired vacant rooms and shops with posters advertising sale of the paper.[17] Having barely weathered this persecution, in 1886 Szeps founded the *Wiener Tagblatt* to renew his campaign to woo Austria into friendship with France. Most newspapers were distributed by mail, the chief subscribers being countless coffeehouses, which stocked a complete line of dailies and weeklies. Further to discourage sale of newspapers, a tax on them remained in force until 1898, while semiofficial papers like the *Wiener Zeitung* paid no tax in return for publishing legal notices. Under Friedrich Uhl (1825–1906), the father-in-law of August Strindberg, the *Wiener Zeitung* became a leading vehicle of culture, rivaling the *Neue Freie Presse*.[18]

Books were also subject to confiscation. In 1906 Hermann Bahr's

Wien was seized because Mayor Lueger found it unflattering. A year later Josef Redlich, to whom Bahr had dedicated the book, got the prohibition lifted through interpellation in the Reichsrat. Although during World War One censorship became more stringent under the War Press Office *(Kriegspressequartier)*, many sallies escaped notice because as Kraus put it, "Satires which the censor can understand deserve to be banned." Kraus himself underwent an official inquiry that dragged on so long the empire had collapsed before guilt could be ascertained.

The propensity of bureaucracy to stumble over red tape engendered that "absolutism mitigated by Schlamperei," whose loopholes made life bearable in what might otherwise have been an oppressive state. After 1880 administrators proliferated formalities, which strangled not only innovation but routine as well. Only stagnation could result from the logrolling without policy, which Taaffe called muddling through *(Fortwursteln)*. Through incompetence, the regime elicited the very criticism it strove to silence, goading Kraus to pen some of the most cutting satires of the twentieth century. The unfathomable officials of Kafka's novels and Kraus's essays reflect banalities of Franz Joseph's bureaucracy. Although outwardly a bastion of unity and regimen, Austrian bureaucrats committed blunders that unleashed catastrophe on the rest of Europe.

THE MIXED BLESSING
OF A PEACETIME ARMY

More colorfully than the bureaucracy, military services buttressed the Habsburg Empire. Despite a record of disaster in every major war from 1740 to 1918, no army in Europe was more popular, thanks less to prowess in battle than to omnipresence as pacifier of the realm.[19] Garrisons of imperial and royal *(k. und k.)* troops, carrying the yellow flag with its black eagle throughout rural Bohemia, Galicia, Hungary, and Croatia, dramatized imperial presence to even the most indifferent peoples.

Together with the gendarmerie, which had been founded in 1849, the army acted as an internal police force to quell conflict between nationalities. Because the army might have to put down agitation by Bohemian Sokols or Ruthenians in Bukovina, officials stationed Slav recruits far from their homelands under German officers. The military itself became a melting pot of nationalities, toward which officers and men felt a *"schwarz-gelb"* loyalty transcending national origin. Perhaps the best description of this function of the army is Roth's *Radetzky-marsch*, which celebrated the military as a living bond between emperor and people. Roth's title, taken from the march that Johann Strauss senior wrote to commemorate the restorer of order in 1848, underlined how music united a dozen-odd nationalities in the ranks. The expertise of military bands led Stefan Zweig to quip that the Austro-Hungarian army possessed better bandmasters than generals.

Despite stress on unity between nationalities, the fact that the language of command *(Dienstsprache)* at the rank of major and below was German stirred much discontent. Magyar officers resented having to command other Magyars using a seventy-word German vocabulary. Although the Independence party under Ferenc Kossuth made this a major grievance around 1900, Franz Joseph refused to budge. The emperor prized his army as an instrument of unity, a last remaining link with the past. No less than Emperor Wilhelm, he delighted in attending maneuvers and consulting commanders; the uniform he wore most proudly was that of a field marshal in ceremonial dress.

In addition to defensive and police duties, the army performed ceremonial functions. All officers were hoffähig, and like the aristocracy they addressed each other as "Du." This custom had arisen after 1815 among officers stationed in Italy as a token of solidarity against a hostile populace. As if to compensate for their "hedgehog" haircuts, Austro-Hungarian officers wore colorful uniforms. Tunics of blue or green, over white trousers, which Freud likened to plumage of a parakeet, adorned every ballroom, spurring civilian men to dress with greater flair than elsewhere in Europe. A special favorite with the public was the Hungarian Body Guard, established by Maria Theresa: wearing scarlet uniforms trimmed in silver with a sable cap and mounted on white horses, every day at noon the Guard was changed in the courtyard of the Hofburg, attracting children and passersby. Because the military enjoyed popularity, World War One did not arouse great opposition among civilians, most of whom respected the military almost as much as they venerated the emperor.

Although the Austro-Hungarian army displayed a proud front, it remained in perpetual crisis. Up to 1867, archdukes held the higher staff positions, excluding abler professional officers, and producing inferior commanders-in-chief. Although thorough reform instituted after the defeat of Königgrätz increased professionalism, it also made for routinization; supply services never approached the efficiency attained in the German army. Despite a law of 1868 which established a system of universal military service similar to Prussia's, illiteracy and ill health meant that as few as one-quarter of the peasantry had to serve the three-year term. Still others escaped service by virtue of a treaty of 1870 which exempted any literate male who had spent in the United States the five years required to become a naturalized citizen. This proviso became a powerful incentive to emigration, especially among peasants in Galicia and Hungary.

One of the bluntest critics of the army was the Hungarian publicist Emil Reich, who deemed its greatest flaw lack of a common native language.[20] In spite of the fact that modern campaigns increasingly emphasized initiative by field officers, Austria-Hungary hamstrung line officers by requiring them to communicate in the sacrosanct seventy words of German; this precluded very rapid or complex orders. Although 80 percent of the officers were German, hardly any could speak the tongues of the Hungarian and Slav troops whom they commanded. Not only did the language barrier reduce rapport between officers and men, but it thwarted the purpose of the Maria-Theresa-Order, a decoration the empress had established in 1757 to reward deeds of valor that a soldier performed on his own initiative but without contravening a direct order. Although this highest of decorations did not reward disobedience, it paid homage to military improvisation unthinkable in Prussia. It is doubtful whether the military justice dramatized by Kleist in *Prinz Friedrich von Homburg* (1810) could ever have been meted out in Austria. Although tradition paid lip service to military initiative, Franz Joseph further undermined it when in 1869 he dissolved the Military Frontier in Croatia and the Banat. By consigning to Magyar oppression Croat and Serb soldiers who had fought bravely through almost two hundred years and who had defeated the Italians at Custozza in 1866, the emperor alienated his most loyal troops.

Besides the language barrier, Reich found other causes for total absence of esprit de corps between officers and men. Officers rode to the front in railroad coaches, while enlisted men were transported in cattle cars that bore the words, "For forty men or six horses." While on maneuvers in Moravia as an army doctor in 1886, Sigmund Freud deplored rivalry among officers, writing to Josef Breuer:

> each officer envies his equals in rank, bullies his subordinates and fears his superiors. The higher he rises the more he fears them.[21]

A soldier was trained to dread his superiors more than any foe. Musil described this cult of masochism and sadism in his first novel, *Die Verwirrungen des Zöglings Törless* (Berlin, 1906), where cadets at a

military academy in Galicia conspire to torture a misfit. Indeed the life
of both officers and men was often miserable. Transferred from one
garrison to another, many felt as homeless as itinerant actors. The
rootlessness of military children became proverbial. Military surgeons
were kept in poverty by a regulation that forbade them to treat officers or their families outside the hospital. Although everyone expected surgeons to disregard this rule, no money could be accepted;
the superior of Wilhelm Stekel had collected thirty vases for illicit
house calls.[22] Officers ran deeply into debt, especially in the provinces
where they gambled among companions of their own nationality. In
some regiments, as many as one-half the officers would be having pay
docked to meet debts.[23] An unhappy few, who like Rainer Maria Rilke's
father, had to retire prematurely, never adjusted to civilian life where
they had no superiors to obey.

Hate-love for military service permeated university students, who
under the law of 1868 were allowed to serve one year instead of three.
However much this privilege may have enhanced intellectual excellence, it hurt the army. One-year volunteers (Einjährig-Freiwillige)
spent seven months undergoing purely theoretical training in detach-
ments of their own kind. After just five months of field drill, they were
mustered into the reserve—woefully ill-prepared officers. Needless to
say, intellectuals resented the transition from cafés of the Ringstrasse
to garrison life. In 1894–1895 Hugo von Hofmannsthal found everything at his post in Galicia ugly, muddy, and infinitely depressing.[24]
When World War One came, however, many intellectuals flocked to
the colors. Ludwig Wittgenstein volunteered for the duration in spite
of a hernia. Nurtured on a military ethos during elementary school and
gymnasium, young men went to war dreaming of heroism.[25] In the
Polish novel, Salt of the Earth (1935; English trans., New York, 1941),
Józef Wittlin (1895–), a Jewish friend of Joseph Roth, described
how mobilization into the Austrian army uprooted and gradually educated a forty-year-old Galician railroad worker. The illiterate protagonist surmounted his fear of printed words by dedicating every deed
to the emperor. Not many men of letters detested warfare with the
vehemence of Georg Trakl, Albert Ehrenstein, or Karl Kraus. Those
who did, objected above all to mechanized weapons that killed and
maimed wholesale, making, as Bertha von Suttner had foreseen, a
mockery of honor.

The code of honor (Ehrenkodex), which Schopenhauer called a code
for fools, dogged officers. It acted as a superego requiring them to
settle disputes by dueling. Although the duel had died out in England
before 1850, in Austria-Hungary until 1911 a challenge by one officer

to another imposed a sacred obligation. An officer who declined a challenge would lose his commission, besides being cut dead in good society. Unlike the *Mensur,* which students fought in heavy padding with swords, a military duel required deadly weapons used with intent to kill.[26] Up to 1900 civilian courts in Austria-Hungary refrained from enforcing against officers laws that made dueling punishable by imprisonment. In cases where an officer killed a civilian, Franz Joseph never failed to grant pardon. Although canon law stipulated excommunication for both participants and seconds in a duel, this too was never enforced. After 1900 dueling began to lose prestige, because of several miscarriages of justice.[27] In 1900 two close friends were compelled by fellow officers to carry out a duel proposed in fun; one friend killed the other. In the same year, another officer was degraded for refusing to fight over a trivial insult. In a third case an officer in the reserve felt obliged to issue a challenge in order to preserve his commission. Because reserve officers came under jurisdiction of civilian courts, he was imprisoned, thereby losing his commission.

These inequities prompted Crown Prince Alfonso of Spain to sponsor antidueling leagues, the first of which he founded in Austria in 1901 in order to mobilize support for officers who refused to duel. Already by 1904, the army settled three hundred cases without resort to arms, and even in Hungary and Galicia, where dueling was most popular, public opinion began to deplore it. The outcry was so effective that in 1911 Franz Joseph issued a decree making it no longer mandatory for officers to give and accept challenges and forbidding duels for any but the most serious grounds. Recognized grounds included above all revenge for adultery.

No one has written more searchingly about dueling than Arthur Schnitzler. In his novella *Leutnant Gustl,* which he published in the Christmas issue of the *Neue Freie Presse* in 1900 at the request of his friend Theodor Herzl, Schnitzler unmasked the duplicity of the code of honor. Leutnant Gustl, who is contemplating suicide, meets every threat to his ego—even the most trivial—by wishing to call out his opponent. Within a month Schnitzler, an officer in the reserve, was court-martialed and cashiered for conduct unbecoming an officer. In *Der Sekundant* (1932), Schnitzler described a duel in which an aggrieved husband dies at the hands of a vastly superior marksman. Although Schnitzler recognized that dueling had disappeared in more advanced countries, he had one of his characters praise it as a means of testing an officer's mettle by preparing him to face sudden death. Dueling enforced the military ethos.[28]

Even the code of honor could not counteract the most grievous weakness of the Austro-Hungarian army. Thanks to Schlamperei, enemy agents penetrated military secrets with ease. In 1864 Prussian officers disguised as civilians swarmed over Bohemia, taking jobs in the countryside in order to survey the terrain. Prussian agents purchased defense plans from ill-paid subordinates in the Austrian Defense Ministry, with the result that von Moltke's officers knew the landscape of Bohemia more intimately than the Austrians and learned in advance the disposition of Austrian troops at Königgrätz.[29]

Even more disastrous was the treachery of Colonel Alfred Redl (1864–1913), who in May, 1913, committed suicide after years as chief of Austro-Hungarian espionage.[30] His superiors had just learned that he had sold to the Russians detailed plans of Austrian fortresses in Galicia, having earlier exposed Austria's agents inside Russia. This betrayal had inestimable consequences: fifteen months before war began, Austria had to revise plans for defense of Galicia and for invasion of Serbia. The Austrian General Staff forfeited the trust of the Germans and also that of Franz Ferdinand. Perhaps most disastrous, the Austrian spy network in Russia had been wiped out, so that the General Staff went into the crisis of July, 1914, underestimating both Russian strength and Austria-Hungary's weakness. Conceivably, had it not been for Redl's treachery, Austria-Hungary could have held Galicia in 1914 and conquered Serbia. The government tried to hush up Redl's misdeeds, only to have a Prague-born Socialist crime reporter, Egon Erwin Kisch, divulge the facts—to universal consternation.

Austria-Hungary maintained a peacetime army, which resisted innovation with Biedermeier tenacity. In 1911 the General Staff rejected as unworkable the invention of a tank by Gunther Burstyn (1879–1945). What might this device not have achieved on the plains of Galicia? Similarly, Moritz Auffenberg-Komarów (1852–1928), who won the sole victory in Galicia during September, 1914, was court-martialed in 1915 for allegedly having disregarded regulations while minister of war in 1912.[31] Although he won acquittal, the army lost one of its best commanders and one of its few innovators.

For all its failings as a military machine, the Austro-Hungarian army served as a pillar of empire. During the 1920's, not a few civilians missed seeing bright uniforms enlivening the streets of Vienna. The army embellished social life, pacified outlying provinces, and furnished soldiers of disparate nationality a focus for patriotism. Thanks to an unwieldly code of honor, refusal to innovate, and pride in the face of disaster, the military reflected the regime that it served. Like Emperor Franz Joseph, the k. und k. army was more respected than feared, more popular than effective. Together with the Habsburg bureaucracy, it helped to supply to the Danube Basin a unity that since 1918 the region has sorely lacked.

A STATE CHURCH GALLS ANTICLERICALS

A third bulwark of tradition in Austria was the Roman Catholic church.[32] With thirty-one million Catholics and another five million Uniates out of a population of forty-six million in 1905, Habsburg lands constituted the largest Catholic realm in Europe. Yet by 1875 Italy had four times more parish priests per capita, while France and Germany had one and one-half times as many.[33] Under Franz Joseph, dispute over church policy centered around the Concordat of November, 1855, which had placed all marriages under the jurisdiction of canon law and had given the church supervision over elementary schools. After the liberal Auersperg Ministry had modified the Concordat with its laws of May, 1868, the Concordat was declared lapsed by Austria on July 30, 1870, on the grounds that the Declaration of Papal Infallibility had altered the character of the contracting party of 1855. In May, 1874, the Concordat was formally replaced by legislation that granted the Roman Catholic church a privileged but not monopolistic status.

Although at first the episcopate, inspired by Pope Pius IX's condemnation of the "abominable laws," refused to accept them, in due course the hierarchy conformed to what was in fact a favorable arrangement. The most renowned opponent was the bishop of Linz, Franz Josef Rudigier (1811-1884), who had been religious preceptor to young Franz Joseph. After the emperor had signed the new School and Marriage Law, Bishop Rudigier warned his former pupil that he would have to answer for this act in heaven. When the bishop instructed parish priests to preach disregard of the laws, he was sentenced to fourteen days in jail, only to be pardoned by the emperor.

The May laws of 1868, which were confirmed in 1874, restricted canon law to marriage between Catholics, while withdrawing marriage disputes from ecclesiastical courts. Although nearly all elementary schools were placed under state direction, the state paid priests to dispense religious instruction in the schools. The new laws did not alter the arrangement whereby, since 1781, the state had reimbursed parish priests for their services as registrars of births, marriages, and deaths. Parish priests continued to be appointed by local secular authorities, while bishops were appointed by the emperor and confirmed by the Holy See. Until 1918 all bishops sat in the upper house of the Reichsrat, and in 1900 as many as twenty priests were serving in the lower house. State financing of the church continued through-out the 1920's and was reconfirmed by the Concordat that Dollfuss signed with Cardinal Pacelli in 1933. The Concordat of that year fell into ill repute mainly because it brought marriages between Catholics once more under the jurisdiction of ecclesiastical courts.

Every year the interdependence of church and state was celebrated in the Corpus Christi procession *(Fronleichnam)*, staged on the Thursday following Trinity Sunday. After Luther had denounced this *fête-Dieu*, it became a focus of Counter-Reformation piety, renewing the Habsburgs' ancestral veneration of the Eucharist. The Socialist Julius Braunthal (1891–) recalled how the procession flattered Viennese love of spectacle:

> The pageantry was opened by imperial troops in battle-dress, as if they had to force the way for the representatives of the Church who followed them. Behind the troops walked monks and friars, the Franciscans and the Capuchins, the Domini-cans, the Augustinians and Carmelites, reciting the rosary; then came white-clad girls and young men, carrying a forest of colorful church flags and standards with votive pictures and sacred images; then came the choristers and choirboys, singing the litany; then came the high dignitaries of the Church, the prelates and deacons in purple and ermine, and bishops carrying crosiers; and then the cardinal-archbishop in his mitre, with the sacred vessels in his hands, walking be-neath a canopy, surrounded by choirboys swinging the censer. Then followed the old Emperor, bareheaded, flanked by the Spanish Guard carrying halberds; and behind him the im-perial Court; then the nobility and the generals, and behind them marched more imperial troops in battledress. This was the order of that magnificent pageantry; it reflected somehow the actual power relations between Church and State.[34]

Karl Lueger had modified Corpus Christi Day into a demonstration of the power of the Christian Socialist party, so that the Corpus Christi procession counteracted the May Day parade that Socialists staged at the Prater from 1890 on. Until old age forced Franz Joseph to with-draw about 1912, he took part in this procession every year, as well as in a tableau on Maundy Thursday, when he washed the feet of twelve paupers in order to pay obeisance to the Eucharist. Three days before Easter this pageant was enacted—as late as 1910—before an invited audience in the Hofburg, where the emperor waited on table for twelve indigents and then knelt at their feet while priests went through the motions of pouring water. An even more moving ritual of abasement before the church climaxed the funeral of an emperor. When the body was brought to the Capuchin Church for interment, the prior would open the gate and ask, "Who are you that seek entry here?" The grand master of the court would reply, "I am His Majesty, the Emperor of Austria, King of Hungary." The prior would rejoin, "I do not know him. Who seeks entry here?" The reply came: "I am Emperor Franz Joseph, Apostolic King of Hungary, King of Bohemia, Dalmatia, Croatia, Slavonia, Galicia, Lodomeria, Illyria, Jerusalem, Archduke of Austria, Grand-Prince of Transylvania, Grand Duke of Tuscany and Krakow, Duke of Lorraine, Salzburg, Styria, Carinthia, and Carniola." The prior would insist, "I do not know him. Who seeks entry here?" This time the grand master would kneel, saying, "I am a man, who begs God's mercy." "Then, enter."[35]

The masses practiced a piety less august than this. Most worshipers were women, who paid special devotion to the Virgin Mary. The cult of the Virgin had been popularized by the Moravian-born priest Klemens Maria Hofbauer (1751–1820), who led the Redemptorist Order in Vienna from 1808 until his death. Not only did he attract intellectuals like Friedrich Schlegel, Adam Müller, Zacharias· Werner, and Anton Günther, but he revolutionized techniques of evangelizing, exploiting the press and visits to parishioners in order to infuse emotion into Josephinist piety. Hofbauer, who was canonized in 1909, had won such a following among the middle and lower classes that his funeral attracted thousands to St. Stephen's Cathedral. The throng demanded that the main door be opened to receive this lowly priest whose order had not yet been recognized in Austria.

The Catholic church fostered several varieties of social thought in Austria. Chief among these was the Christian socialism disseminated by Karl Baron von Vogelsang (1818-1890).[36] During the 1880's his writings paved the way for Karl Lueger's founding of the Christian Socialist party and for renewal of organicist theory. Having converted to Catholicism at Innsbruck in 1850, the Prussian-born Vogelsang moved to Pressburg in 1859 to become tutor to the sons of the widowed Princess von Liechtenstein. For a time he traveled with her sons, while his own efforts as a landowner near Vienna ended in bankruptcy. In 1875 Count Leo Thun invited Vogelsang to Vienna to edit the Catholic daily Vaterland, into which Vogelsang threw himself totally. He wrote several thousand articles for it before his death in a traffic accident in 1890. Several of his associates, including his pupil Prince Alois von Liechtenstein (1846–1920), participated in seven years of discussion that preceded Pope Leo XIII's proclamation of *De rerum novarum* on May 15, 1891. Portions of its text appear to be borrowings from Vogelsang.[37] In France René de la Tour du Pin (1834–1924) owed his corporatist theory to the Austrian.

Vogelsang brought both Prussian assiduity and the zeal of a convert to preaching that Justice, Love, and Solidarity must be the foundations of Catholic social thought. He wanted Christian ethics to replace capitalist competition, whose evils were only compounded by the quack remedies of state socialism and Marxism. In contrast with all these systems, Vogelsang sought not to increase productivity or to expand political rights, but to restore the hierarchical structure of medieval society. Echoing the predilection of Adam Müller for the family, Vogelsang desired every business firm to become an industrial family *(industrielle Familie)*, in which workers and owners would share management. Each firm or family would belong to a regional body known as a branch corporation *(Branchencorporation)*, consisting of firms in its locality. These branch corporations would send delegates to the Industrial Chamber *(Industriekammer)*, where workers and owners would legislate economic policy for each industry. Artisans would be required to join a guild, which would fix the number of masters and apprentices. This medieval institution would shield its members from the perils of individualism.

Catholic socialism, even with less nostalgia, could not have stemmed the rise of anticlericalism. Austrian writers had never depicted the clergy with sympathy. One of very few attractive priests adorns Adalbert Stifter's novella *Kalkstein*, first published under the title *Der arme Wohltäter* (1848). Stifter depicted the pastor of Kar as a little man who in a spirit of Bohemian Josephinism deprives himself for the good of the community. His humility and resignation resemble that of the Bohemian protagonist in Ferdinand von Saar's *Innocens* (Heidelberg, 1866), who lamented the decline of genuine fervor. In 1870 Ludwig Anzengruber (1839–1889) contrasted a Josephinist priest with a feudal aristocrat in *Der Pfarrer von Kirchfeld*, a play that won enormous popularity among opponents of the Declaration of Papal Infallibility.

In the forefront of anticlericals, Social Democrats and free-thinkers denounced the control that the church retained over marriage and primary education. Catholics who married outside their faith were faced with so many impediments, that in 1914 an estimated one million common-law marriages existed in Austria-Hungary. Between August and October, 1914, as war threatened to leave common-law wives bereft, 115,000 of these marriages were legalized in Vienna alone, with another 37,000 in Budapest, and 26,000 in Prague.[38] One source of popularity for the Los-von-Rom movement was the wish of some Catholics to marry while retaining freedom to divorce; after a Protestant marriage, they would resume Catholic worship. One Protestant pastor who about 1890 refused to accept such hypocritical conversions was rebuked by his fellow pastors as a bigot.[39] Even crueler than prohibition of divorce was a law that forbade former priests to marry on the ground that priestly vows were irrevocable. As an ex-priest, Franz Brentano found it necessary in 1880 to marry in Saxony, after having resigned his professorship at Vienna. Egregious persecution hounded one Knaus, who after eleven years as a priest, in 1870 converted to Protestantism. He married nine years later, and he and his wife lived unmolested for another eleven years before someone brought suit to have the marriage annulled. On July 2, 1891 the Supreme Court of Austria confirmed the annulment, declaring that once Knaus had submitted to the statutes of the Church he was forever bound by them. The court proclaimed that public order gained when the state upheld canon law.[40]

Anticlericalism wracked universities, culminating in 1908 in transfer of a professor of canon law, Ludwig Wahrmund (1860–1932). Son of the director of the Vienna Oriental Academy, this Catholic professor at Innsbruck denounced in 1908 Karl Lueger's threat of November, 1907, to catholicize the universities. In an address to the sixth Katholikentag, a gathering of clergy and laymen assembled to counter the Los-von-Rom movement, the mayor had declared, "I hope that we also conquer back those universities which our church had founded."[41] Wahrmund's rejoinder, *Katholische Weltanschauung und freie Wissenschaft* (1908) stressed contradictions between church doctrine and the "well-established, even proven convictions of the historical, physical, and philosophical sciences." Not only did the public prosecutor of Vienna confiscate the pamphlet, but the Papal Nuncio demanded Wahrmund's ouster. The *Neue Freie Presse* escalated the conflict by inciting anticlerical students to threaten a general academic strike if Wahrmund, who had taken a brief vacation, should not be reinstated. Catholic students retaliated against the Jewish press by seizing the University of Graz on May 16, 1908, necessitating its closing for the summer. When Wahrmund returned from his trip to resume lecturing at Innsbruck that university had to close to prevent further agitation. After Franz Joseph had rebuked the minister of education, Wahrmund was persuaded to accept a call that autumn to the German University at Prague; he eventually became an agnostic.

This case helped to inspire Schnitzler's play *Professor Bernhardi*

(1912), which portrayed a priest too self-serving to state his convictions to his superiors and a minister of education who cloaked ambition in concern for the good of the whole. The play revolved around the Jewish chief of a private clinic—not unlike that run by Schnitzler's own father—who restrained a priest from delivering extreme unction to a girl who was hallucinating in ecstasy. Professor Bernhardi went to prison rather than accede to a compromise proposed by anti-Semites in the Reichsrat. This dramatization of Protektion obscured the fact that the clergy were openly divided in their attitude toward anti-Semitism. After 1850, parish clergy, who were recruited from the lower middle class, often scandalized the episcopacy by preaching anti-Semitism. Joseph Deckert (1843–1901), the son of a shoemaker who became a priest in the Vienna suburbs, several times landed in court for vilifying Jews.[42] Fanning memories of the Tisza-Eszlár trial of 1882, he charged that Jews murdered Christian children; he carried anti-Protestant polemics to the point of postulating Luther's suicide.

Another source of anticlericalism was hostility toward Protestantism which clerics had inherited from the Counter-Reformation policies of Ferdinand II (1619–1637). Joseph II's Edict of Toleration did not protect Lutheran sectarians in the Zillertal, a region that had fallen to Austria only in 1816. In 1837 the archbishop of Salzburg required them to choose between Catholicism and emigration. A similar travesty of justice befell the Lutheran Konrad Deubler (1814–1884), who in 1854 was sentenced to the Spielberg at Brünn for having written a defense of David Friedrich Strauss.[43] Exploiting earthy means to counter Protestantism, Passau-born Jesuit Heinrich Abel (1843–1926) served as a priest in Vienna from 1891 until 1926. An avid supporter of Lueger, he branded the Los-von-Rom movement as a Los-von-Gott movement and revived pilgrimages to Klosterneuburg and Mariazell. Bluntly appealing to workingmen, he delivered in Viennese dialect sermons so full of vulgarity that women were forbidden to attend. On one occasion, he bodily removed an intruding woman. By steadfastly refusing to take confession from women, he counteracted other priests who were known to flout the vow of chastity.[44]

After 1866, Protestantism served to disguise German national sentiment.[45] Initiated in 1898 by the Vienna-born anti-Semite Georg von Schönerer (1842–1921), the Los-von-Rom movement protested against the state church while offering a rehearsal for eventual union of Cisleithania with the German Empire. In Styria the Los-von-Rom movement attracted Germans who disliked their Croatian priests, while in Bohemia it expressed hostility alternatively to Habsburg hegemony and to Czech resurgence. Many Czechs simply left the church altogether, deeming it an instrument of Habsburg rule, so that the Czechoslovak Republic found Catholicism discredited while Hussite-tinged Protestantism recouped. In Austria, Christian socialism blunted the Los-von-Rom movement. Although he did not perceptibly weaken the church, Schönerer's success in branding the Roman Catholic church an enemy of Germans predisposed some Catholics to accept Hitler's anticlericalism.

Whether Protestant, Jewish, or free-thinking, Austrian anticlericals deplored papal intervention in Habsburg affairs. Pope Leo XIII (1878–1903) tried to induce the empire to renounce the Triple Alliance so as to weaken united Italy. After 1880 the pontiff openly supported Slav minorities against Hungary, sending Jesuit missionaries to encourage them, and in 1886 and again in 1893 he condemned the laws that permitted civil marriage and lay education. Despite these affronts, Franz Joseph retained sufficient respect for the pontiff to decline repaying a state visit by his ally the king of Italy, while the pontiff aided the emperor by returning to him Crown Prince Rudolf's request for annulment of his marriage. Nevertheless, Franz Joseph was so exasperated by the anti-Magyar policy of Leo XIII that in the conclave of 1903 Cardinal Puzyna made it known that His Apostolic Majesty would deem it an unfriendly act to have Leo's secretary of state, Cardinal Rampolla, elected pope.[46] The cardinals heeded this veto.

Leo XIII had drawn the hostility of Socialists through his encyclical *Quod apostolicis numeris* of December 28, 1878, which anathematized the "pestilence" of socialism. For decades, even after *De rerum novarum* had attenuated the condemnation, his words thundered from Austrian pulpits:

> Firmly united in a criminal association . . . seized by the savage greed for wealth . . . they [Socialists and Communists] propagate their monstrous ideas among the multitude.[47]

Having thrown down the gauntlet, the pope faced adamant counterpropaganda, through which Socialists wooed workers away from the church. The Christian socialism of Vogelsang and Lueger only intensified the struggle, creating by the 1920's an unbridgeable gulf between the secular left and the clerical right. As a result, by 1950 less than 20 percent of Vienna's Catholics regularly attended Sunday mass.[48] In other Catholic countries such as Italy and France, the identification of the church with the status quo forced progressives to become secular, whereas in England and the United States the clergy joined in promoting social reform. Religious polarization of politics caused both sides to waste in polemics energy that they could better have spent resisting common foes such as economic stagnation and incipient dictatorship. Although the church remained a bulwark of Franz Joseph's regime, hostility to clerical influence crystallized into a major feature of the First Republic. While nostalgic writers like Bahr, Roth, Hofmannsthal, and Schaukal celebrated the Catholic pageantry of old Austria, the Socialist government of Vienna secured the allegiance of the masses by executing secular reforms. A state church proved to be its own worst enemy, once industrialism had eroded the age-old piety of the countryside.

THE MUNICIPAL SOCIALISM OF KARL LUEGER

In 1849 Count Stadion had granted governmental autonomy to all municipalities in the Habsburg Empire. Although thereafter Vienna enjoyed self-government, repeatedly the emperor intervened in its affairs; he insisted that his imperial, capital, and residence city (*Reichs-, Haupt- und Residenzstadt*) be ruled in a manner becoming to it. In 1857 the emperor authorized demolition of the seventeenth-century fortifications that separated the core city from the suburbs. Competition to fill this zone, won by Ludwig Förster's plan for the Ringstrasse, was administered by an imperial commission rather than by the city.

From 1850 onward, Vienna underwent rapid growth, expanding in 1890 to incorporate suburbs across the Danube and along the Vienna woods. A municipal constitution of 1850 established a city council (Gemeinderat) to be elected by tax-paying citizens divided into three classes; in 1885 the minimum taxation for suffrage was lowered to five gulden, excluding the indigent until universal suffrage came in 1907. After 1890 the unwieldy city council of 138 members was directed by twenty-five of its members, known as the Stadtrat, who together with the mayor ran the city.

As mayor of Vienna from 1897 to 1910, Karl Lueger (1844–1910) so dominated public life that next to Franz Joseph he was the city's best known citizen.[49] As son of the concierge at the Technische Hochschule, Lueger had learned firsthand the tribulations of the lower middle class. A sickly child, he did not learn to speak until he was four years old; his mother had nursed him so devotedly that he never married, residing instead with two sisters. As a day student at the Theresianum, Lueger acquired polished manners that later helped him mediate between classes. He was so outraged by the defeat of Königgrätz and the compromise with Hungary that he never ceased to wage anti-Magyar propaganda. Having taken a doctorate of law in 1866, during the 1870's he worked as a Liberal lawyer, spending countless evenings in suburban beerhouses, where he perfected his oratorical skill among "his" people. Although he had entered the city council in 1875 still a Liberal, over the next decade Lueger broke with liberalism; by the time he entered the Reichsrat in 1885 he was denouncing international capitalism as a Jewish monopoly. After being briefly an ally of Georg von Schönerer, he became in 1888 a friend of the Catholic Socialist Karl von Vogelsang, whose doctrines Lueger incorporated into the Christian Social party (Christlichsoziale Partei) founded in 1893.

In 1895 the Christian Socialist majority of the city council elected Lueger mayor, only to have the appointment vetoed by Franz Joseph, who did not wish his capital governed by a demagogue who denounced Jews and Magyars. At the urging of the Statthalter of Lower Austria, Count Erich von Kielmansegg (1847–1923), who had arranged the expansion of the city in 1890, the emperor dissolved the city council and ruled the capital for two years through a board of commissioners. Four times Lueger was elected mayor until in April, 1897, Franz Joseph bowed to the inevitable, having been alarmed during the Corpus Christi procession of 1896 that Lueger had received almost more applause than the emperor himself. As a result of his prodigious affability, "der schöne Karl" reigned for thirteen years as uncrowned king of Vienna, applauded wherever he went. He carried a full work load despite worsening diabetes, which caused his death in March, 1910. His funeral was reputed to have been the largest that the city had yet seen.

Lueger represented above all the lower middle classes, who were suffering from industrialization. He implemented municipal socialism, on the premise that small proprietors and shopkeepers needed to be protected from monopoly entrepreneurs. Without raising taxes, he municipalized the gasworks in 1899, electrified the streetcars in 1902, introduced electric street lighting, and built a municipal slaughterhouse and public market. After requests for loans to finance the gasworks were refused by Jewish banks of Vienna, Lueger secured funds from the Deutsche Bank of Berlin. He expanded municipal services begun under Cajetan Felder (1814–1894), who as Liberal mayor between 1868 and 1878 had commissioned the new Town Hall (Rathaus), the Central Market, the Stadtpark, and in 1874 the Central Cemetery.[50] Although between 1868 and 1875 geologist Eduard Suess (1831–1914) had supervised regulation of the Danube to prevent a flood such as that of February, 1862, from recurring, the river sometimes overflowed its widened banks. To supplement the aqueduct of 1873, which Suess

had engineered to bring water from the nearby Höllental, Lueger inaugurated a second aqueduct stretching more than 150 miles into
Styria.

Lueger differed from Felder by sponsoring institutions designed to
help the lower middle classes. While expanding the Central Cemetery,
he bought out two funeral companies that had charged extortionist
rates. New schoolhouses were built and underfed children were supplied food free of charge. In 1904 Lueger opened a poorhouse at Lainz,
near Schönbrunn, followed by a new hospital for the indigent. To
beautify the city, parks were doubled, a beach was opened on the
Danube, and flower boxes adorned lampposts. To help beleaguered
city dwellers, Lueger placed under municipal control a savings bank, a
life insurance company, and an old-age pension fund, opening also a
housing agency as well as a registry for servants. Of less universal
appeal was his insistence on reintroducing crucifixes and religious
instruction into the schools; this only antagonized anticlericals, notably
those on the *Neue Freie Presse,* whose reporters Lueger sometimes
barred from meetings of the city council.

It was Lueger who pioneered the municipal socialism that Social
Democrats expanded during the 1920's. Although Lueger's moderniz-
ing of Vienna is sometimes compared to slum-clearing carried out by
Joseph Chamberlain while mayor of Birmingham during 1875–1876,
the Christian Socialist made no effort to remove slums, a task that had
to await the Social Democrats. Lueger also encouraged the entrenched
Austrian habit of placing funds in insurance rather than in more risky
ventures.

The most controversial feature of Lueger's politics was anti-Semitism. He denounced Jewish capital in order to win support from
artisans, who were losing business to foreign manufacturers of commodities such as toys, fans, and leather goods. Small producers had
never recovered many of the customers lost to Berlin after the crash
of 1873. Even without that debacle, Vienna would have suffered economic backwardness. In order to aid shopkeepers, the city prohibited
department stores until about 1900. Because the law required most
shops to sell a very narrow specialty such as music paper or gloves, the
business cycle victimized merchants, who blamed hard times on Jewish
financiers. As late as the turn of the century, nearly all clothes were
sewn by hand; during 1894 the first factory-made shoes from America
created a sensation, and the first bread factory did not come until the
following year.[51] Conservative consumers meant that modern contriv-
ances were introduced very slowly. In 1890 drinking water was still
hauled to suburbs in barrels. In 1900 telephones and elevators were

rare, while refrigerators and fixed bathtubs remained unknown, as did central heating and payments by check. Government offices disdained the typewriter until after 1918.

Lueger battened on the fears of his constituents. Although Lueger's anti-Semitism waned in his later years, and he always had Jewish friends—witness his saying "Wer a Jud is, bestimm' i' " "It is I who decide who is a Jew"—he continued to contribute articles to the Wiener Volkszeitung edited by the scurrilous Bohemian deputy Karl Wolf (1862–1941). Perhaps unwittingly Lueger lent respectability to anti-Semitic violence, which during 1905 culminated in riots where German-National students blocked the door of the university to Jewish students. Artur Schnabel could remember being warned during the 1890's that young hoodlums scoured the streets looking for Jewish children to bully.[52]

Lueger exploited every form of sociability. By 1904 he had attended fourteen hundred golden wedding anniversaries as well as countless christenings and weddings, where he would be the most honored guest. Frequently he visited sickbeds, and like Freud, he relished the four-handed card game Tarock. Having consorted with voters in beerhalls and coffeehouses, this tribune of the people did not scorn them once he had risen to high office. Given the economic backwardness of Austria, Lueger appears to have sponsored more forward-looking programs than regressive ones. Where he particularly anticipated twentieth-century politicians was in his skill at mobilizing the masses through propaganda. This master of public relations was saluted by Hitler as a man who had taught him how to flatter an urban populace. By pandering to aestheticism and economic insecurity, Lueger personified the Imperial City at the height of its Gay Apocalypse.

SCHOOLS AND UNIVERSITIES:
IMMERSION IN TRADITION AS TRAINING FOR GENIUS

After 1850 the Habsburg Empire boasted an excellent system of schools and universities.[53] Elementary schools (Volksschulen), taught until 1850 mostly by priests, prepared Christian and Jew alike to enter either gymnasium or Oberrealschule. Gymnasien led in turn to the examination known as the Matura, called in Germany the Abitur, which entitled its recipient to enter any university in Germany or Austria-Hungary. The empire ran full-fledged universities at Vienna, Graz, Innsbruck, Prague, Krakow, Lemberg, Budapest, Klausenburg, and Agram. There were also engineering colleges (Technische Hochschulen) at Vienna, Graz, Prague, Brünn, Budapest, and elsewhere, as well as specialty schools in the applied arts, agriculture, and the like, preparation for which was gained at an Oberrealschule. After completion of elementary school less ambitious students attended one of the Bürgerschulen established in 1869 as terminal institutions preparing for practical life. In the previous year the Pädagogium had been founded at Vienna to train teachers for these nonacademic schools.

During the 1850's the educational system was overhauled by the Bohemian-born Count Leo Thun (1811–1888), an exponent of Bohemian Catholicism who commissioned two Herbartians, Franz Exner and Hermann Bonitz, to draft a reform based on German and French models.[54] Stress fell no longer on religion or obedience to the state, but on training students to engage in research at the university. In 1850 gymnasium was lengthened from six to eight years, and instead of teaching all subjects, instructors now presented their specialty. Natural science was introduced, and the younger, livelier teachers taught the upper grades, where according to Josef Breuer, "criticism and contradiction were encouraged rather than suppressed."[55] The first gymnasium to be reformed was the Akademisches Gymnasium, attended by among others Breuer, Arthur Schnitzler, Hugo von Hofmannsthal, Hans Kelsen, and Ludwig von Mises. Less secular and hence more popular among the nobility was the Schottengymnasium, attended by Eugen von Böhm-Bawerk, Friedrich von Wieser, and Jews such as Heinrich Friedjung and Otto Weininger. The Benedictines who taught there, including the distinguished historian and abbot Ernest Hauswirth (1818–1901), did not foster clericalism, any more than they did at Kremsmünster, where during the 1820's Adalbert Stifter had studied Kant and various Josephinist writers. In an atmosphere full of respect for learning, students who stood first in their class like Sigmund Freud and Otto Weininger were honored as *Musterschüler*, although like everywhere else many prodigies burned out young.

More punctilious than gymnasien were Ritterakademien, of which the most prestigious was the Theresianum, which Maria Theresa had founded in 1746 to occupy a former pleasure palace, conducted at first by Jesuits and then until the late 1850's by Piarist fathers. Designed to train sons of the aristocracy and upper bourgeoisie for military and political careers, the Theresianum graduated Field Marshal Radetzky, the Croat General Josef Jellačić, Prime Minister Hohenwart, and later Joseph Schumpeter and Richard Coudenhove-Kalergi. As in other gymnasien, alumni of the Theresianum continued throughout their careers to address each other as "Du," even when one was a prime minister and the other a lowly clerk.

As late as 1914 the curriculum at gymnasium required eight years of Latin, studied six hours per week except for two years of eight hours per week, as well as five or six years of Greek at five hours per week. In better gymnasien like the Schottengymnasium, the Greek course culminated in the reading of Aristotle. By obliging teen-agers to read authors whose experience far surpassed their own, gymnasium prepared its most able graduates to manipulate abstractions. A thinker who had digested Sophocles at age eighteen would not hesitate later to formulate his own maxims. Although the Bonitz-Exner reforms had diminished systematic memorization, up to 1918 and beyond pupils learned passages by rote. This exercise implanted a remarkable knowledge of ancient literature and mythology in minds as disparate as those of Freud and Spann, Riegl and Kraus. Besides promoting mastery of syntax, drill in translating ancient texts facilitated impromptu speaking, a skill that requires translating thoughts instantly into words. Political speeches and university lectures abounded in allusions to Greek and Roman authors, instilling in every student awareness that he was participating in an enterprise begun millenia ago by sages whom he could not hope to equal.

Veneration of tradition was reinforced by Catholic priests who continued to teach primary school until after 1918. Piarist fathers, members of a teaching order established in 1597, shared the openness of Bohemian Josephinism, teaching Jews without any effort to convert them. At Prague, the Piarist elementary school was preferred by Jewish families because of the excellence of its instruction; its pupils included Fritz Mauthner, Egon Erwin Kisch, and Hans Kohn.[56] Like many other Jews, Arthur Schnitzler was attracted by priest-teachers, and even Freud, who deplored clericalism in education, confessed that as a student he had regarded his teachers as father figures.[57] During the liberal Auersperg era, Jews at gymnasium were accorded instruction in their own religion, with results more farcical than effective.[58] During the mid-1880's the Reichsrat enacted a law that required the principal of each school to be of the same religion as the majority of his students, thus barring Jews from assuming this post. Although persons "of Mosaic descent" like Wilhelm Jerusalem were allowed to teach, they could not aspire to preeminence.

Discipline at gymnasium was stern and fear of failure keen. In Die Traumdeutung (Vienna, 1900), Freud probed what he called examination-dreams and Matura-dreams in which years later an adult would imagine that he had failed his Matura—usually in his strongest subject.[59] By reenacting anxiety felt before the dies irae, the dreamer could, said Freud, summon confidence for new trials, rejoicing in the fact that in a hierarchical society to have passed the Matura meant lasting distinction. The oral examination at the Matura also accustomed students to *ex tempore* delivery before superiors, rehearsing a technique that every professional would need in dealing with bureaucrats and colleagues. Although gymnasium benefited those who survived it, after 1880 it no longer fully suited the needs of the empire. Friedrich Jodl complained that none of his students at university knew how to read English or French, and he lamented that six years of Greek had left Thucydides unread.[60] Lawyers versed only in German and Latin were, he warned, ill equipped to administer Bohemia or Carniola; in refusing to teach Czech, German-speaking faculty at gymnasien in Bohemia truckled to prejudice. In Hungary, gymnasien demanded mastery of Magyar, excluding by this expedient all but a handful of subject peoples. By 1918 Slovakia and Transylvania lacked any middle class apart from Magyars and Germans.

Once a student had entered university, he became a privileged personage, entitled after 1870 to reduced military service and welcome to compete for higher positions in the state service. University professors were themselves bureaucrats, personal servants of the emperor who could veto any appointment. Because the Ministry of Education exercised such firm control over faculty appointments, Protektion ran rampant. Houston Stewart Chamberlain told of a chemist at the University of Vienna who advised him to marry the daughter of a professor, and preferably of a Hofrat, if he desired to advance. Following years of waiting, this chemist had received a professorship three months after he had married a professor's daughter.[61] The best known of these cases concerned the maneuvering required to get Freud a position as Professor Extraordinarius, a post far less prestigious than that of Ordinarius, which Freud never held. Whereas an Ordinarius enjoyed privileges comparable to those of a bureau chief, an Extraordinarius was a glorified docent. Even so, in Freud's case, three years of petitions gained nothing; neither did special pleading by Elise Gomperz, wife of the renowned philosopher Theodor Gomperz. Early in 1902 another of Freud's patients, Baronin Marie Ferstel, pledged to deliver to Minister of Education Wilhelm von Hartel a picture for the Modern Gallery that he planned to open in 1903. Freud received his professorship a few weeks later, although the promised picture, Böcklin's *Die Burgruine*, was never donated.[62] As we shall see, most able researchers knew how to secure appointment, so that faculties, especially at Vienna, Graz, and Prague, abounded in professors of creative genius—as well as in mediocrities. As a special honor, highly productive scholars, whether gentile or Jew, might be awarded life tenure in the Herrenhaus. This honor went to such scientists as Ernst

Brücke, a teacher of Freud, and the plant physiologist Julius von
Wiesner, a Jewish mentor of Houston Stewart Chamberlain. In 1901
Ernst Mach accepted membership in the Herrenhaus but declined a
title of nobility on the grounds that it was unbecoming to a man of
science. The most pretentious forum of the academic establishment
was the Academy of Sciences, founded in 1847 with aid from Metternich.[63] Divided into separate branches for philosophical-historical
studies and for mathematical-natural sciences, the academy tended to
favor, at least in the humanities, Biedermeier accumulations of data
rather than path-breaking research. With the caution characteristic of
such bodies, the academy refused membership to countless innovators,
while honoring more than a few nonentities.

Routinely, university professors of economics and law served as
high officials, just as they frequently engaged in journalism. In their
capacity as bureaucrats, professors served above all to administer examinations for the doctorate, which certified that a candidate was
ready to enter a profession. The *Rigorosum* consisted of an oral
examination, in which four professors questioned the candidate, each
for fifteen minutes. More fearsome even than the Matura, this oral
examination abetted both Protektion and persecution. Ernst Lothar
recalled the sarcasm of Edmund Bernatzik, a professor of Constitutional Law at Vienna, who told the son of Statthalter Kielmansegg, "I
cannot prevent your becoming Statthalter, but I shall delay it."[64] On
another occasion after a student had missed the first question, Bernatzik rose to leave. When the student retorted, "I have paid my examination fee for the whole fifteen minutes," the professor resumed his
seat, arising after a quarter of an hour with the words, "Thank you,
Herr Kandidat. Your fifteen minutes of silence have elapsed to the
second."[65] Oskar Kraus suffered more insidious persecution when the
dean of the Law Faculty at Prague refused to pass his habilitation.
After other professors had protested, Dean Horaz Krasnopolski told
them to choose between him and Kraus.[66] Later the Faculty of Philosophy exercised special dispensation to promote Kraus to docent.

For conscientious students the schedule at the University of Vienna
imposed hardship. Around 1900 lectures began regularly at 7:00 A.M.
—there was one even at 6:15 A.M.—continuing until 8:00 P.M.[67] Those
students who had to work for a living put in a grueling day, which
effectively excluded them from student clubs. Penniless students from
the country encountered an ostracism such as Jakob Julius David
described in his novel *Am Wege sterben* (Berlin, 1900). Except in
medicine and economics, Vienna attracted relatively few foreign students. Women gained entry to the Philosophical Faculty at Vienna

only in 1897. Three years later the Medical Faculty was opened to women over the opposition of the entire university when the emperor decreed that the Muslim women of Bosnia deserved female physicians. In resisting this innovation, the dean of the faculty told its leading advocate, the Hungarian-born anatomist Emil Zuckerkandl (1849-1910), that he ought to know better than most that women's brains are less developed than those of men.[68]

Although we shall discuss the Medical Faculty later, we mention here an attitude that prevailed around 1850 known as therapeutic nihilism. In medicine this phrase denoted systematic refusal to prescribe remedies for fear of perpetuating quack cures. Passive therapy, which had arisen around 1800, flourished at Vienna up to 1870 and despite vigorous opposition never quite disappeared. Although originally therapeutic nihilism had presupposed that nature's healing powers would suffice, in its extreme form this doctrine encouraged neglect of patients and indifference to human life. Outside the Medical Faculty a conviction that no remedy could relieve suffering or forestall decline infected such thinkers as Karl Kraus, Otto Weininger, and Albert Ehrenstein. They preserved therapeutic nihilism as a major trend in Viennese thought long after it had waned at the Medical Faculty.

In 1884 the University of Vienna moved into a massive neo-Renaissance building on the Ringstrasse, next to the Town Hall and not far from Parliament. This juxtaposition reminded students that they were part of the cultural complex that bourgeois Vienna had erected since 1860 to celebrate its worship of arts and learning. Proximity to civic buildings prompted students to stage increasingly violent political demonstrations as in 1897 and in 1905, when anti-Semitic students rioted in front of the university in an effort to bar Jewish students.[69] Student politics centered in clubs or *Burschenschaften*, which after 1870 practiced dueling with swords. Although, student fencers, unlike participants in military pistol duels, wore face masks and heavy padding, their affairs of honor carried political overtones. After 1870 German-National sympathizers had popularized dueling both at Prague and Vienna as a token of sympathy with the German Empire.[70] In 1888 the Jewish fraternity Kadimah, founded at Vienna in 1882, adopted dueling in order to defend Jewish honor against German challenges. German nationalists expressed anti-Czech sentiments by singing the "Wacht am Rhein" during lectures by the art historian Franz Wickhoff in order to intimidate his Czech assistant Max Dvořák.[71] Such unseemly activities notwithstanding, Burschenschaften performed a cathartic function by staging drinking binges *(Kneipen)* and facilitating liaisons with *süsse Mädel* ("sweet girls"). As Arthur Koestler put it, the student clubs exerted a civilizing influence during years of emotional seasickness: in a taboo-ridden civilization they "took the edge off the highbrow's traditional *nostalgie de la boue*."[72] Although girls might suffer from sexual repression, men did not; thanks to the cameraderie of the *Kneipe*, students and young professionals found it easier to endure authoritarian professors and bureaucrats. For those lucky enough to possess a moderate income, student years could be remembered as a kind of Gemeinschaft idyll in an otherwise unpermissive society.

Because by 1910 the University of Vienna admitted only six thousand students, half of them in law, public-spirited educators took the initiative to organize adult education. The guiding spirit of the *Volksbildungsbewegung* was a docent in ancient history, Ludo Moritz Hartmann (1865–1924), a nonprofessing Jew whose father had been the Bohemian poet Moritz Hartmann (1821–1872).[73] A student of Theodor Mommsen, the younger Hartmann helped in 1900 to found the Vienna Volksheim, which offered evening courses for workingmen. During the same year the Jewish journalist Moriz Szeps began to publish a weekly journal *Wissen für Alle*, which digested contemporary knowledge for working people.[74] In 1897 the province of Lower Austria had founded the Urania at Vienna, as a center for adult education. Encouraged by such professors as Friedrich Jodl, these institutions, which after 1918 were administered by the Socialist city council, made Vienna a leader in educating the masses.

Although universities might expend every effort to promote research, the Habsburg Empire enjoyed an unenviable record of ignoring gifted inventors. We have already mentioned the cases of the Biedermeier inventors Josef Ressel, whose screw propeller was rejected, and Josef Madersperger, whose sewing machine got no support. After 1870 Gregor Mendel's refusal to persevere against opposition of a Swiss botanist renewed this syndrome. Another decisive innovator who left his greatest discovery unexploited was the German Jew Siegfried Marcus (1831–1898), who from 1852 ran a workshop at Vienna. In 1864 he built an internal combustion engine, replete with electric ignition and water-cooling, perfecting his automobile in 1875 to include hydraulic brakes. Although he drove through Vienna, this otherwise successful inventor failed to recognize that this was his greatest brainchild. Russian-born Wilhelm Kress (1836–1913), active at Vienna since 1873, came close to launching the first engine-powered aircraft; in 1901 his "flying dragon" failed to take off because he allowed too little runway for an engine that was heavier than he had requested.[75]

Despite bureaucratic inertia, after 1850 the Habsburg Empire excelled at producing new ideas, no less in technology and medicine, than in the humanities and social theory. Austrian inventors displayed the same ingenuity and perseverance that characterized such pioneers of new world views as Ernst Mach, Edmund Husserl, Sigmund Freud, Otto Neurath, and Ludwig Wittgenstein. Like so many others, they profited from training in ancient classics, from drill in oral delivery, and from confronting past achievements. Through teachers as diverse as priest and Jew, philologue and historian, young men acquired an intellectual apparatus that enabled the gifted to interpret their crazy-quilt environment. Precisely because it transmitted traditional skills, Austrian education equipped its alumni to supplant what they had inherited.

TWILIGHT AT VIENNA:
INTELLECTUAL INNOVATION AMID ECONOMIC RUIN

The bureaucracy of Austria faltered in late 1918, leaving Vienna prey to famine and unemployment, while the empire disintegrated into six nation-states, including the three Slav states of Poland, Czechoslovakia, and Yugoslavia. None of the successor states suffered so grievously as Austria, left with a capital of two million ruling a nation of seven million. Former officials of the empire flocked to Vienna, where into the early 1920's, famine, inflation, lack of fuel, and an epidemic of influenza caused unparalleled misery. Housewives cut trees in the Vienna woods, and the winter of 1921–1922 was so severe that the University of Vienna had to close because its roof had not been repaired since 1914.

Monuments of Habsburg rule became reminders of desolation.[76] Furnishings of the Hofburg were sold at auction, the proceeds going to buy food, and its halls were rented for private parties, while Schönbrunn Palace served as an orphanage. When an American corporation offered in 1919 to supply food in exchange for the emperor's Gobelin tapestries, public protest prevented the transaction. Peasants smuggled black-market goods into the city, continuing a trade begun during the war. Ersatz coffee made of barley accompanied bread that caused dysentery. The influenza epidemic killed thousands, including Freud's daughter Sophie and the painter Egon Schiele. Others like the art historian Max Dvořák died from aftereffects of famine. To acquire foreign exchange, many Viennese sold jewelry to foreigners, who haunted hotel corridors in their sack of the city. It was in this atmosphere that Alban Berg wrote his opera *Wozzeck* (1917–1921). During these bleak years Police Commissioner Schober quipped, "If I close the Vienna cafés tomorrow, there will be a revolution on the following day."[77] So ended the prewar era of security. The inflation of 1924, which followed that of Weimar Germany, wiped out savings of any rentiers or bourgeois who had not put their savings into Swiss francs. Young men, brought up to believe in insurance and stable values, saw their families impoverished by the government's debasing of the currency. Such young men would welcome desperate expedients.

For Austria, hope of economic recovery was precluded by the Treaty of Saint-Germain, which had been dictated largely out of Allied fear of Bolshevik coups. The Austrian delegation to the Peace Conference, led by Karl Renner, brought trunks full of documents to justify its plea that Austria be united with Germany. The trunks were never opened. Instead delegates were confined to their hotel, prevented by barbed wire from visiting Paris or even the adjoining forest.[78] Unlike the Germans, the Austrians were permitted to plead their case in the press, employing as a mediator with the British their compatriot Rudolf Karl von Slatin (1857–1932), who had served under Gordon Pasha in Egypt. Ignoring these efforts, in June, 1919, the Allies summoned the delegates to receive a copy of the treaty. This the Austrians signed on September 10, 1919, pledging to keep their country independent. Karl Kraus's imprecation, *Vae victoribus,* proved only too prophetic.

The next fifteen years fanned rivalry between Socialists who controlled Vienna and Christian Socialists who dominated the countryside. In 1919 the provinces blocked a Socialist draft constitution, and by threatening to withhold food, forced Vienna to accept Hans Kelsen's federal constitution of 1920. In 1921 the Catholic majority elevated Vienna into a separate province so that it could not outvote rural areas of Lower Austria. During the early 1920's Schlamperei reigned supreme at Vienna. Railroad ticket offices were open only a few hours a day, necessitating queuing up for sometimes three or four hours. In 1922 the Ministry of Finance was still collecting the income tax of 1920 and had not yet assessed that of 1921. Such inefficiencies galled all the more because in 1919 the coalition government had hired every German employee of the railroad and post office whom successor states had fired. Although this fattened the payroll, overstaffing caused service to deteriorate. To replace initiative formerly exercised by the crown, the Main Committee of the Nationalrat convened leaders of both parties in closed session to iron out legislation acceptable to both sides.[79] This anticipated *in camera* the Grand Coalition that prevailed after 1945.

The Social Democratic government of Vienna administered a mas-

sive building program.[80] A tax on private property devised by Hugo
Breitner (1873–1946) financed seventy-five thousand housing units
between 1919 and 1934, although hardly any slums were razed. The
Tenant Protection Law of 1917 remained in force, keeping rents so
low that private capital lacked incentive to build. Apartment complexes, whose residents had to belong to the Social Democratic party,
dotted previously conservative districts, guaranteeing a Socialist majority for years to come. In a novel crammed with minutiae, *Wohn-
ungen* (Munich, 1969), Vienna-born Wolfgang Georg Fischer (1933–)
has contrasted the new factuality *(Neue Sachlichkeit)* of these dwellings with the plushness of older flats on the Ringstrasse. The municipality also erected garden towns for pensioned civil servants and
wounded veterans, besides sponsoring clubs where Social Democrats
could engage in sports, learn languages, or receive family counseling.
For many, the Social Democratic party had supplanted the church.

Although Vienna's Socialists became increasingly bourgeois, clericals
in the provinces convinced peasants that "Red Vienna" harbored a
dictatorship of the proletariat. This rang true only to the extent that
confiscatory taxation and street demonstrations intimidated the bourgeoisie, albeit without toppling them. Tension deepened following
events of July 15, 1927, when State Police under Johannes Schober
(1874–1932) shot eighty-seven rioters who had stormed and burned
the Palace of Justice. The debacle that ensued in February, 1934, we
shall discuss in connection with Otto Bauer.

During the 1920's and 1930's, intellectual life was dominated by
men who had grown up under the empire. Many of them deemed the
Habsburg monarchy a lost paradise, whose luster brightened as time
passed. Other thinkers of the 1920's such as Hans Kelsen, Otto Bauer,
Moritz Schlick, and Otto Neurath, fortified positivism with values un-
shaken by World War One. They boasted a self-confidence left over
from the era of security. In 1938 the last vestiges of cosmopolitanism
perished as Jews were decimated, saddling their successors with a
corrosive guilt. No doubt it is revulsion at the events of 1938 which has
prevented so many young Austrians from confronting their nation's
intellectual giants. Since 1945 the provinces have persisted in exalting
Alpine folklore above their Habsburg inheritance.[81] Since 1938, in
the realm of ideas the Viennese truism that the past excels the present
has proved only too apt. Still more tragic, no other forum for debate
has emerged to replace what Hitler destroyed. The demise of intellectual Vienna is a major reason why post-1945 Europe has produced so
few innovative thinkers. Epigones of Freud, Neurath, Wittgenstein,
Buber, and Kelsen only commemorate all that has vanished.

4

Economists as Bureaucrats

KARL PRIBRAM'S TERMINOLOGY FOR THE
TRANSITION FROM FEUDALISM TO CAPITALISM

THE PROBLEM that more than any other traverses Austrian social thought since 1848 is the transition from rural feudal society to urban industrial society. This is what Ferdinand Tönnies meant by his distinction between Gemeinschaft and Gesellschaft. None other than Freud echoed this dichotomy between a rural society of face-to-face intimacy and an urban society of atomistic individuals. In a letter of 1883 to his fiancée, Freud described how peasants differ from bourgeois like himself:

> The rabble lives to the full while we deprive ourselves. . . .
> Thus our striving is more concerned with avoiding pain than
> with creating enjoyment. . . . Such people have more feeling
> of community than we do: it is only they who are alive in
> the way in which one life is the continuation of the next,
> whereas for each of us the world vanishes with his death.[1]

Gesellschaft preaches self-denial, imposing an asceticism which for the sake of long-run achievement stifles spontaneity. This is what Max Weber in 1904 called the Protestant work ethic. As capitalist, achievement-oriented society emerged in Austria, it found champions among economists, jurists, and Socialists. The next three chapters examine how such theorists responded to the change from rural to industrial society.

The Austrian theorist who did most to clarify the terminology applied to this transition was Karl Pribram (1877–). Born and educated in Prague, Pribram studied under Georg Jellinek in Heidelberg before becoming a docent in economics at Vienna from 1907 to 1921. Thereafter he taught at Geneva and Frankfurt, settling in the United States in 1934. In *Die Entstehung der individualistischen Sozialphilosophie* (Leipzig, 1912), Pribram traced two world views, which he called individualism and universalism, from the early Middle Ages to Adam Smith. Individualism, on the one hand, which had originated in medieval nominalism, reveres empirical reason in the manner of the Enlightenment, seeking to verify truth by formulating and testing hypotheses. Universalism, on the other hand, named for the Aristotelian realism of Aquinas, posits eternal, extramental truths, whose validity defies testing. An individualist uncovers truth, while a universalist undergoes it. Pribram argued that the capitalist economics of Adam Smith reflected individualism, while the anticapitalistic collectivism of Adam Müller bespoke Romantic universalism. When applied to society, universalism engenders a vision of the whole to be studied by intuition. Individualism, on the contrary, investigates hypotheses that limit reason to formulating conditions under which causal relationships may be tested. Hegel and Marx fused the minutiae of individualism with the grandeur of organicism to yield dialectical reason, a tool which in Pribram's view has both the faults and virtues of its components.

As one who respected universalism no less than individualism, Pribram applied his dichotomy to intellectual life at Vienna:

> The intellectual classes of Vienna had established the only outpost of nominalistic reasoning east of the Rhine. Vienna's scientific, philosophical, literary, and artistic achievements . . . were attributable to the influence of that reasoning. This nominalistic attitude contrasted sharply with a semi-universalistic trend, the heritage of the dynastic tradition, which was fostered by the nobility and the Catholic clergy and which found its adherents particularly among the lower middle class.[2]

Here Pribram contrasts the liberalism of Carl Menger with the Christian socialism of Vogelsang. Pribram could have cited numerous individuals to document the affinity between Viennese middle classes and empirical thinkers in England and France. The friendship of Theodor Gomperz with John Stuart Mill, Fritz Mauthner's devotion to Bacon and Hume, Josef Popper-Lynkeus' reverence for Voltaire, and Freud's sympathy with French and British psychiatry show how nominalistic reasoning inspired Jews of Vienna and Bohemia. It was they who furnished the luminaries of Austro-Marxism and philosophy of language. In addition, students of Brentano cultivated British philosophy: disquisitions by Alexius Meinong on Hume and Anton Marty on Locke parallel the veneration that Friedrich Jodl and Moritz Schlick harbored for the Scottish skeptic.

Pribram has been largely forgotten. It was Spann who made famous the distinction between individualism and universalism, the dichotomy itself having been advanced before 1900 by Gustav Ratzenhofer in his distinction between individualism and socialism. Like Ratzenhofer and Spann, Pribram believed that polar opposites would suffice to classify every system of social thought. Extrapolating from the *Methodenstreit* of 1882 between Carl Menger's empiricism and Gustav Schmoller's historicism, Pribram applied polar opposites to the history of social theory in exhaustive detail.[3] What Pribram dubbed universalism corresponds to the realism of Herbartians who "believe that reason can discover the substance of things and teach the real laws underlying the cause of real events."[4]

In what follows, the terms holism, organicism, feudalism, ascription, and particularism are used interchangeably to denote Gemeinschaft mentality. The terms individualism, nominalism, empiricism, industrialism, capitalism, and achievement-orientation designate Gesellschaft values. It seems appropriate to begin a survey of social theory in Austria with its most nominalistic school, that of marginal analysis founded by the economist Carl Menger.

CARL MENGER'S PSYCHOLOGICAL THEORY
OF ECONOMIC NEEDS

The Austrian School of Economics was inaugurated by Carl Menger (1840–1921), who served from 1876 to 1878 as tutor to Crown Prince Rudolf.[5] Son of a Catholic landowner in Galicia who died when his son was eight, Menger studied law at Prague and Vienna before entering the civil service. In 1871 he published his path-breaking *Grundsätze der Volkswirtschaftslehre*, which earned him a position as docent and in 1873 a professorship at Vienna. He taught there until the late 1890's, when he retired prematurely, much to the regret of students. Menger was revered for the clarity of his lectures, copies of which circulated as late as the 1920's. His sole avocation was fishing, which he pursued every Sunday with consummate skill. Together with his brother Anton, he amassed a library of more than twenty thousand volumes, which reposes today in the Commercial College of Tokyo. As tutor to the crown prince, Menger indoctrinated him in liberalism before introducing him to the journalist Moriz Szeps.

After 1880, Menger no longer felt impelled to elaborate his economic theory. Leaving this task to students, he waged a *Methodenstreit* against the Swabian historicist, Gustav Schmoller (1838–1917), a clash that climaxed in 1882. It was Menger who applied the term *Historismus* to characterize his opponent's aversion to theory. To employ Pribram's terms, Menger defended nominalism against organicism. Schmoller contended that because economics has no eternal laws, it can be studied only one society at a time. Menger, however, postulated a mechanism that pervades every society. Although their polemic polarized the issue for twenty years—helping Pribram to arrive at his categories—in the end Max Weber fused the two approaches into his concept of ideal type. Weber formulated what Friedrich von Wieser called "idealizing assumptions" to classify the data of past cultures. Thus Menger's models could be used to guide Schmoller's historicist reconstructing of the past.[6]

Menger's great innovation concerned the theory of value. Contrary to medieval scholastics and even to Adam Smith, Menger held that value resides not in some quality inherent in a good, but rather in human wants. Because it is human beings who assign value to goods, to understand the process of valuation necessitates studying men's desires. Menger began by defining goods as commodities or activities that can satisfy a recognized human want *(Bedarf)*. A good is an economic good only when need for it exceeds supply. Menger next differentiated between goods of the first order, which satisfy a want directly, and goods of a higher order, which serve in manufacturing goods of the first order. Menger postulated that desire for first-order goods is the sole spring of what he called *Güterqualität*. It follows that goods of a higher order derive value solely from the anticipated value of the first-order goods in whose manufacture they serve. To compare values of first-order goods, Menger devised a table of marginal utilities. His schema indicates the decline in satisfaction experienced as a supply of goods gradually increases. Across the top of a chart, Menger listed ten different goods, labeled I, II to IX, X. In each column, he designated degrees of satisfaction that decrease on a scale of ten as the supply of each good increases:

Different Goods

	I	II	III	IV	V	VI	VII	VIII	IX	X
Degree of	10	9	8	7	6	5	4	3	2	1
satisfaction as	9	8	7	6	5	4	3	2	1	
supply increases	8	7	6	5						
	7	6	5	4						

According to the chart, the first unit of good III, say motor transport, yields roughly the same amount of satisfaction as the third unit of good I, such as staple food. Good X is so expendable that its first unit is no more valued than the tenth unit of good I. A second unit of good X would be valueless. Menger contended that men conduct economic behavior by setting priorities on wants. Each consumer selects which wants to leave unappeased and which to indulge; valuation results from discriminating among felt needs. Menger insisted that numerals on his chart were merely suggestive, since each consumer sets different priorities. Prices arise from aggregate demand created by consumers of first-order goods and by the ensuing needs of manufacturers.

Menger published his marginal theory in the same year that William Stanley Jevons (1835–1882), working independently, announced a similar hypothesis in his *Theory of Political Economy* (1871). This was followed three years later by a more sophisticated analysis from a French-born Swiss, Léon Walras, in *Éléments d'économie politique pure* (1874). Outside of Austria, the mathematical finesse of Walras soon outstripped Menger, while in England Jevons' utilitarian calculus had to buck the Smith-Ricardo tradition. Menger was fortunate in being able to fill a vacuum of theory which prevailed among German-speaking economists. His opposition came not from rival theorists but from historicists' objections to theorizing as such. Of the three joint discoverers, Menger was the least mathematical and the most psychological. He was interested less in mechanisms of price fluctuation than in the psychology of how desires influence ratios of exchange. Insisting that utilities cannot be measured, he dismissed as a fiction the equilibrium equations of Walras. All three men presupposed a static economy in which behavior of individuals parallels that of the whole.

No one has been able to ascertain the formative influences on Menger. Oskar Kraus claimed to have detected a parallel between Menger and Aristotle's *Topics*, as interpreted by Brentano, without being able to show that Menger had read either work.[7] In his quest for laws, conceivably Menger was influenced by Herbartians such as Robert Zimmermann, who discerned formal regularities in social life. Menger's *Grundsätze* preceded by three years Brentano's *Psychologie vom empirischen Standpunkt*, whose concept of value as a mode of intentionality parallels Menger's conception of want. Christian von Ehrenfels endeavored to synthesize the two approaches in his *System der Werttheorie* (1897–1898). Menger also showed affinity with Mach's principle of economy: although both men sought to explain phenomena by generating a minimum of hypotheses, Menger had greater respect for theory as such. In Austria, no other branch of social thought attracted so many adherents of hypothetical reasoning as did marginal economics.

FRIEDRICH VON WIESER AS
ADVOCATE OF A MIXED ECONOMY

The man who did most to systematize Menger's theory was Friedrich von Wieser (1851–1926).[8] Born in Vienna the son of an army quartermaster who was ennobled in 1859, Wieser studied law there under Lorenz von Stein. Through reading Spencer and Tolstoy's *War and Peace*, he was weaned away from the "great man" theory of history to the analysis of anonymous social forces. Although he read Menger's *Grundsätze* in 1872, he did not attend his lectures. Together with his classmate from the Schottengymnasium Eugen von Böhm-Bawerk (1851–1914), Wieser studied at Heidelberg, Leipzig, and Jena from 1875 to 1877. At Heidelberg in 1876, he wrote a seminar paper for Karl Knies on the concept of alternative cost, arguing that cost measures what might have been produced with the same raw materials. After returning to Vienna, Wieser showed his papers to Menger, who encouraged the aspiring bureaucrat to habilitate in economics. From 1884 to 1903 he served as a professor of economics at the German University in Prague; thereafter he succeeded to Menger's chair at Vienna, serving as minister of trade in 1917–1918. Although he was a close friend of Carl Menger, he did not become his mentor's son-in-law, as is sometimes reported. Instead in 1886 he married the daughter of a German architect in Prague.

Wieser coined two terms that became slogans of the Austrian school. In *Über den Ursprung und die Hauptgesetze des wirtschaftlichen Werthes* (Vienna, 1884), he introduced the terms marginal utility *(Grenznutz)* and imputation *(Zurechnung)*. He was the first Austrian economist to study allocation of resources as well as the structure of a free enterprise economy, thus fulfilling Menger's promise that all topics of economics could be subsumed under the roof of marginal utility. Similar rigor was demonstrated by another professor of economics at Prague, Emil Sax (1845–1927), who applied Menger's insights to administrative law and to transportation. Although Wieser possessed more mathematical ability than either Menger or Böhm-Bawerk, like them he used mathematics sparingly, preferring illustrations drawn from Robinson Crusoe.

In contrast with Menger's individualism, Wieser favored social economics in the tradition of eighteenth-century cameralism. In his

Theorie der gesellschaftlichen Wirtschaft (Tübingen, 1914), a treatise commissioned by Max Weber, he portrayed marginal economics as a middle way between the ideologies of Ricardo's classical school and of the Socialists. To elude those who exploit economic theory as a means to power, Wieser championed a mixed economy. In the same book, he advocated use of "idealizing assumptions" that "eliminate whatever may be subordinate, accidental, or individual."[9] He proposed a psychological theory that would uncover "in the conscious of every economically active human being a wealth of experiences which are common to all."[10] This postulate accorded with a conviction derived from the Second Epilogue (1869) to Tolstoy's *War and Peace* that events proceed from masses of men obeying natural laws. Opposing the utopianism of Theodor Hertzka's *Freiland,* during the 1890's Wieser taught a seminar to refute it. In his last book, *Das Gesetz der Macht* (Vienna, 1926), he examined the role of elites, arguing, *pace* Gumplowicz, that voluntary compliance with law must eventually supersede rule of force.

Although, like his student Schumpeter, Wieser revered the Habsburg monarchy, he did not allow nostalgia to hide its faults. His *Österreichs Ende* (Vienna, 1919), based in part on experience as minister of trade during 1917–1918, ranks as one of the soberest analyses of that debacle to be written so close in time to the event. Through his·imposing personality, Wieser helped to groom two generations of Austrian economists. Together with his brother-in-law Böhm-Bawerk, he shouldered the task of refining and disseminating Menger's discovery. Like Schumpeter and the Austro-Marxists, Wieser united breadth of vision with meticulous scholarship, interweaving economics with sociology and political theory. Schumpeter deemed Wieser the Austrian economist to espouse views nearest his own. Neither a progenitor nor an epigone, Wieser played the mediator, resembling Julius von Schlosser in art history and Rudolf Eisler in philosophy. Good bureaucrat that he was, he exerted a largely anonymous influence.

JOSEPH SCHUMPETER: DISINHERITED HEIR OF THE HABSBURG EMPIRE

After the death of Eugen von Böhm-Bawerk in 1914, the Austrian economist best known in the United States became Joseph Schumpeter (1883–1950).[11] Although as a professor of economics at Harvard University from 1932 to 1950 he exercised wide influence—greater than that of fellow refugees Ludwig von Mises or Friedrich von Hayek—his career was anything but happy. Schumpeter was born at Triesch, Moravia. His father, a wealthy textile entrepreneur, died when his son was four. After his mother had moved to Vienna, in 1893 she married the military commandant of the city, Sigismund von Kéler. From 1893 to 1901, Joseph attended the Theresianum as a day student, where as a bourgeois arriviste he acquired a taste for things aristocratic. After taking his doctorate at Vienna under Wieser and Böhm-Bawerk in 1906, the next year he married an Englishwoman, from whom he separated after a few months, although unable because of his Catholicism to dissolve the marriage until 1920. After two years in Cairo, he earned his habilitation at Vienna in 1909, followed by two lonely years at Czernowitz. As a professor at Graz from 1911 to 1921, he frequently commuted to Vienna, striving in vain during World War One to negotiate a separate peace through English friends. In 1919 he emulated Böhm-Bawerk by becoming minister of finance in the coalition government, where his advocacy of a mixed economy estranged both Socialists and clericals. During the early 1920's he served as president of the Biedermannbank at Vienna; when it failed in 1924, after exhausting his personal fortune, he went deeply into debt to pay off its creditors, going far beyond what the law required. Schumpeter's marriage in 1925 to Annie Riesinger, a protegée of his mother, ended with her death in childbirth, followed soon thereafter by that of his mother. From 1924 to 1932, Schumpeter taught public finance at Bonn, departing thence to become a professor of economics at Harvard University. Exile to the United States marked a final break with the Europe of his youth. Even as a young man he had been consumed by work; as a refugee, he remained isolated to the end, working feverishly amid reminiscences of a world he had lost.

In the United States, Schumpeter is best remembered for *Capitalism, Socialism, and Democracy* (New York, 1942; 3d ed., 1949). This work foresaw a drift into socialism because entrepreneurs have lost the capacity to innovate, which had sustained capitalism. Part of this thesis Schumpeter had advanced already in *Die Theorie der wirtschaftlichen Entwicklung* (Leipzig, 1911; 2d ed., 1926), based on lectures at Czernowitz. Postulating that an economy constitutes an uninterrupted flow of goods and services, he adapted Walras' equations to describe shifting equilibrium positions. Once the motor of innovation stalls, the whole system stagnates. On a visit to England during 1906, he had glorified that country's free-wheeling entrepreneurs, while blaming Austria's bureaucracy for snarling her economy in red tape. After he had insisted in 1919 that taxes, not income from nationalized industries, should finance economic recovery, his awareness that entrepreneurs were losing nerve was sharpened by the failure of his bank during the inflation of 1924.

Schumpeter's virtuosity is best demonstrated by his posthumous *History of Economic Analysis* (New York, 1954). This unfinished magnum opus proliferates insights into every aspect of social theory since the Middle Ages. Its wealth of *aperçus* reflects what Gottfried Haberler has called Schumpeter's *l'art pour l'art* delight in discussion:

> The great wealth of ideas which constantly streamed through his mind, and his acute awareness of all sides of every question, and of the limitations of each standpoint and method, made it very hard for him to present his views on any subject neatly and systematically.[12]

A nonpareil historian, Schumpeter envisioned complexities and obstacles too vividly to be able to remedy them.

Sharing Wieser's horror of ideology, Schumpeter swam against the tide during both World Wars, opposing Austria's cause in the First and America's in the Second. Throughout, he remained bewitched by the world of his youth, doting over years at the Theresianum, at Graz, and as minister of finance. He even sentimentalized the Oriental atmosphere of Czernowitz, which he had loathed. While esteeming entrepreneurs, Schumpeter rejoiced that aristocracy can foster disinterestedness such as a bourgeoisie can never match. In a sketch of Böhm-Bawerk written in 1925, Schumpeter extolled the Habsburg Empire:

> No one can mistake what Austria in that period [1890 to 1914] accomplished in every realm of public life, in spite of difficulties which seem hardly believable to the distant observer. How thoroughly and successfully the pre-conditions for a powerful and effective state were created in every branch of public administration, especially in that of public finance.[13]

Schumpeter never achieved his potential. Like another student of Böhm-Bawerk, Otto Bauer, with whom he collaborated in the coalition ministry of 1919, Schumpeter felt the collapse of 1918 as an amputation. Both men never adjusted to the loss of the empire. If it had survived, they might have worked together, counteracting each other's vagaries to construct lasting reforms. For them after 1920, futility dispelled the confidence that Austria had once instilled in its elite.

AFFINITIES BETWEEN THE AUSTRIAN SCHOOL
OF ECONOMICS AND JOSEPHINIST BUREAUCRACY

The Austrian School of Economics consisted of Carl Menger, his students, and his students' students *(Enkelschüler)*. They displayed greater unity than the Vienna School of Art History or Brentano and his students. The Austrian economists operated at a high level of abstraction, preferring examples drawn from preindustrial economies like that attributed to Robinson Crusoe. They all endorsed Menger's postulate that generalizations or idealizing assumptions are indispensable for organizing the data of social behavior. Except for Schumpeter and Mises, these theorists slighted mathematics. The school divided in evaluating socialism: Menger, Böhm-Bawerk, and Mises regarded any tincture of socialism as distorting the free-market economy, while somewhat halfheartedly Wieser and Schumpeter advocated a mixed economy.

One of the most trenchant appraisals of the Austrian school came from an associate of Lenin, Nikolai Bukharin (1887–1938), who studied economics at Vienna from 1912 to 1914 before being interned as a Russian spy in August, 1914. During the winter of 1912–1913, he helped Stalin to write his *Nationalitätenfrage und Sozialdemokratie* (Berlin, 1913), a polemic against Karl Renner and Otto Bauer. At the same time, Bukharin was preparing his *Economic Theory of the Leisure Class* [1919] (New York, 1927), which probed sociological roots of Böhm-Bawerk's critique of Marx. The Austrian school, Bukharin argued, epitomized the interests of rentiers, who like the aristocracy of eighteenth-century France comprised a parasitical class conscious of impending demise. Because they did not have to labor, rentiers flaunted the psychology of consumers, which Menger elevated into marginal economics. Enjoying moderate affluence, they dismissed concern for the poor as indecent and threatening. Dreading the future, they cultivated epicureanism and coffeehouse aestheticism. Their ideology was unhistorical and undynamic; because change could only injure them, rentiers shunned thinking about it, indulging what Lukács called reified class-consciousness.

This analysis, however ingenious, reflected as much the days that Bukharin had spent in coffeehouses as hours listening to economists lecture. He imputed to professors attitudes that characterized young dandies of the Ringstrasse. These idle sons of parvenu fathers did lead parasitical lives, luxuriating in consumption and prizing individualism. Votaries of *carpe diem* in Schnitzler's *Der Weg ins Freie* evade the future with the insouciance of an overrefined and dying elite. What Bukharin calls fear of change, I have labeled resignation and, in extreme form, therapeutic nihilism. It seems more plausible, however, to identify the Austrian school with the standpoint not of rentiers but of bureaucrats. Financially and socially secure, professor-officials forged techniques whereby to regulate economic life impartially. As employees of the state and servants of the emperor, they stood above the fray, free to expound a standpoint abstracted from class. Austrian economists extended Josephinist impartiality toward class to the prosperity of post-1860 capitalism.

Berlin-born Emil Kauder (1901-) has propounded a different thesis to account for anti-interventionism preferred by the Austrian school.[14] Kauder postulates a parallel between the economists' belief in abstract regularities and the faith of Bohemian Reform Catholics in natural order. For Bolzano and Stifter, as for Menger and Böhm-Bawerk, the task of statesman and scholar alike was to sustain eternal verities embodied in society's hierarchy. Böhm-Bawerk rejected Marx, says Kauder, because Marx urges man to play the sorcerer's apprentice; to overturn natural order for fragmentary goals is to sacrifice stability for a will-of-the-wisp. Kauder detects an analogy between Wieser's advocacy in *Das Gesetz der Macht* (1926) of charity as the highest good and Stifter's "gentle law" *(sanfte Gesetz)*: both seek to maximize human potential at all levels without dismantling hierarchy. Austrian economists experienced aesthetic joy in beholding natural law guide the economy, just as Stifter and Bolzano cherished God's work in nature and society. For the invisible hand of Adam Smith, the economists substituted a Leibnizian premise of harmony between created nature and social law. No one carried faith in an invisible order underlying the market economy farther than Ludwig von Mises, who insisted that any meddling with the market can only disrupt it. Schumpeter, by way of exception, infused into this static vision British enthusiasm for accelerating change. Unless entrepreneurs initiate quantum leaps in technology and in commercial practice, stagnation ensues.

For all its appeal, Kauder's thesis remains difficult to substantiate. If Menger, Wieser, and Böhm-Bawerk had imbibed the Leibnizian vision, from whom did they absorb it? Was it perhaps from Herbartian textbooks used at gymnasium during the 1850's and 1860's? Did economists knowingly adopt a philosophy that inculcated belief in an inviolable order uniting nature and society? Anyone who wishes to assert an upserge of Herbartian thought in economics confronts a dearth of evidence. Although there appears to exist a parallel between economists' faith in natural law and Herbart's doctrine of realia, direct influence cannot be documented. It seems likely, nevertheless, that economists adapted noninterventionism from the impartiality tradition- al in Josephinist bureaucracy. Although many a model official had never pondered Herbart, some may have fortified their ideal by study- ing a philosophy that embodied it. Once the Leibnizian vision had become institutionalized, its tenets, however watered down, impinged upon every bureaucrat.

5
Legal Theorists

AUTHORITY OF THE STATE CHALLENGED
AND ABETTED BY THEORISTS OF LAW

IN THE FIELD of legal theory, Karl Pribram's dichotomy between individualism and universalism fits less aptly than in economics. Trained to
sympathize with both points of view, jurists debated issues that span
the gap between nominalism and organicism. One theorist, Eugen
Ehrlich, who tried to build a sociology of law on the distinction between Gemeinschaft and Gesellschaft, floundered in the attempt.

More crucial to understanding legal theory in Austria is the empire's
system of courts, which in essentials duplicated that of Imperial Germany. In important ways, continental judicial systems differed from
those of Anglo-Saxon common law.[1] In cases of civil suit, continental
law, based on ancient Roman law, provides a hearing before three
judges; a civil dispute never goes to a jury. In criminal prosecution, the
state is not itself a party that must prove allegations before an impartial
judge. Instead, examining judges (Untersuchungsrichter) gather evidence. adhering slavishly to elaborate rules of procedure, before chan-
neling testimony to a jury. As delegates of the state, both examining
judges and trial judges must abstain from controversy: their task is
to enforce rules of procedure that, it is assumed, guarantee fairness to
the accused. The state itself cannot be arraigned under these rules
because it created them. Indeed, the state, modeled on that of Rome,
heeds a "public" law distinct from that which regulates citizens. Separation of private law from public law exalts the state as benevolent
protector of private rights, especially of property, at the same time
exempting bureaucracy from redress by private citizens.

In Germany and Austria-Hungary, not only did Roman law elevate
judges into a sacrosanct position, but it instilled belief in the infallibility of the state. As arbiter above the law, the state alone wielded
power to curb its own authority; this authority was never attenuated,

as it was in Great Britain, by an obligation to do battle against citizens in a courtroom. In contrast to the Anglo-Saxon adversary system, continental law enlists attorneys as colleagues of judges, with whom they collaborate to enforce the rules. Professors, in turn, play a major role by revising and codifying statutes, a task that in Great Britain and the United States falls mainly to legislators. In the Habsburg Empire, judges presided as Josephinist bureaucrats, who exercised the royal function of dispensing justice. Appointees of the emperor, judges arbitrated human destinies, ensconced above the partisanship of civilian life.

Within a highly centralized system, codified by reforms of Maria Theresa and Joseph II, the crux of legal theory was to define the limits of state authority. On the one hand, legal dogmatists like Rudolf von Jhering insisted that the state alone enjoys competence to delimit its own authority, a privilege that Georg Jellinek called *Kompetenz-Kompetenz*.[2] Backing state supremacy, on the other hand, was Hans Gross, who perfected techniques of investigating and prosecuting crime. More blatant still was the legal positivism of the early Kelsen, who simply equated the state with law. Assailing the status quo, other jurists forged theories to weaken or decentralize the state. In the Habsburg Empire, the conflict of nationalities, abuses of Protektion and Schlamperei, and sheer diversity spurred jurists to champion alternatives. Critics included Eugen Ehrlich, who esteemed folkways of Gemeinschaft society as a superior source of law; Anton Menger, who advocated community socialism; and Karl Renner, who with Marxist tools unmasked private law as a delegation of state power to property owners. First, critics of the state are considered—reserving Renner for the chapter on Austro-Marxists—and then Gross and Kelsen as advocates of state supremacy.

EUGEN EHRLICH AS CHAMPION
OF LOCAL CUSTOM

The theorist who most systematically applied to law the dichotomy between Gemeinschaft and Gesellschaft was Eugen Ehrlich (1862–1922).[3] Born and educated at Czernowitz, this Jewish lawyer knew at first hand the Gemeinschaft society of Bukovina. Having taken a doctorate in law at Vienna in 1886, he remained there as an official, before Anton Menger encouraged him to earn a habilitation in 1894. At about this time Ehrlich converted to Catholicism. From 1895 to 1897 he was docent in Roman law at Vienna, and from 1897 to 1918 he served as a professor of law in his native Czernowitz, presiding as university rector during 1906–1907.

Lying just twenty miles from Russia, Czernowitz afforded a living laboratory for comparative law, where daily life followed ethnic codes unknown in Austrian courts. Here Ehrlich founded an Institute for Research on Legal Data (*Rechtstatsachenforschung*), which collated customs of the ten-odd races who inhabited the region. In 1918 annexation of Bukovina by Romania unnerved Ehrlich. Rather than lecture in Romanian, he withdrew to Bucharest and thence to Vienna, where he died of diabetes.

Ehrlich used acquaintance with folkways in Bukovina to differentiate three types of law. First, living law (*das lebende Recht*) includes traditional regularities that guide daily behavior among Gemeinschaft peoples. Second, the inner order of associations (*die innere Ordnung der Verbände* or *gesellschaftliches Recht*) constitutes mores and folkways from which living law emerges. Gemeinschaft society manifests this spontaneous order through family, church, and manor, while in Gesellschaft society, the order of associations governs clubs, corporations, labor unions, and political parties. Third, decisional law (*Entscheidungsnormen*) encompasses rules of law enforced by courts. Ehrlich glorified living law, urging that decisional law incorporate it. Decisional law he subdivided into state law or legislation (*staatliches Recht*) and juristic law or court decisions (*Juristenrecht*). Although the latter approximates living law better than the former, both stem from officials who lack contact with living law. All too often, jurists deduce decisions from statutes without consulting either equity or local custom.

Against legal dogmatists, Ehrlich espoused free lawmaking (*freie Rechtsfindung*), imploring judges to studing living law in their locality before issuing decisions. Free law construed all statutes as if they embodied stopgap rules (*jus dispositivum*), that is, rules to govern eventualities that contracting parties or legislators did not foresee. By broadening the concept of unforeseen circumstances, Ehrlich hoped to expand the applicability of living law. In this, Ehrlich won support from Roscoe Pound (1870–1964), who sponsored an English translation of the Austrian's major treastise, *Grundlegung der Soziologie des Rechts* (Munich, 1913).[4] In June, 1914, Pound had arranged for Ehrlich to deliver the Lowell Institute Lectures at Boston that year, only to have outbreak of war cancel the trip. It is curious that Ehrlich, who championed customary law, should have been admired by a jurist whose social engineering would overturn American custom.

As a historian of Roman law, Ehrlich contended that the so-called logic of law, which furnished a hermeneutic for statutes, constituted an ideology to exalt the state. The axiom that judges must enforce abstract rules, even where these flout equity, arose after northern and central European states had absorbed Roman law during the Renaissance. The fiction that law serves the state was a ploy invented by Roman emperors to foil sympathy that republican lawyers had felt for living law. Ehrlich assailed a corollary that defined law as a monistic system, a seamless web without contradiction. Modeled on the deductive rationalism of Kant and Hegel, this straitjacket abetted what Ehrlich dubbed the jurisprudence of concepts *(Begriffsjuriprudenz)*. By stigmatizing contradictions, conceptual jurisprudence scuttled equity in order to aggrandize the state.

As a pioneering effort, Ehrlich's sociology of law succeeded better at criticism than construction. He overstated the distinction between living law of Gemeinschaft and state-made law of Gesellschaft. He deemed living law born of folkways more equitable and more enforcible than state-made law. By apotheosizing local custom, Ehrlich overlooked need for an apparatus to resolve conflicts between local laws. Beyond that, living law lacks capacity to evolve as industrialism encroaches upon it. In glorifying the self-regulating life of the countryside, replete with feuds and ordeals, Ehrlich disregarded the need of capitalist society for generalized, easily revised rules. As society democratizes, all classes expect the state to arbitrate disputes, and associations must open themselves to public inspection. Resisting this transformation, Ehrlich perpetuated the particularism of his province, where antipathy to distant Vienna still flourished.

Rivaling Schumpeter, Ehrlich proved an expert historian, who excelled at collating Roman, British, and continental law. Reading twelve languages and traveling widely, he insisted that dissemination to the Continent of English speech would not alter either society or law. The structure of families, corporations, ownership, and rights emanated from society, not from lawyers. Here Ehrlich converged with Marxist jurisprudence, which holds that economic and social forces mold law, not vice versa. Although Ehrlich paralleled Austro-Marxists in reviling the state, he did not develop sociology of law into sociology of knowledge. By hypothesis, living law eludes theorists; it must be experienced, Ehrlich insisted, just as Wittgenstein held that the mystical can be felt but not verbalized. Less artfully than such a critic of abstraction in philosophy, Ehrlich decried empty formulas on the bench. Yet one-sided analysis did not impair Ehrlich's skill as a compiler. His institute assembled data on customs in Bukovina with Biedermeier delight in minutiae. The more Bukovina lagged behind western provinces of Austria, the more Ehrlich exploited the gap in order to remind advanced regions of their own past.

ANTON MENGER:
UTOPIAN CRITIC OF PRIVATE LAW

Anton Menger (1841–1906), albeit less acclaimed than his economist brother Carl, crusaded for reform of private law.[5] Sharing his brother's commitment to nominalistic reason, Anton pressed demands for rational behavior to utopian lengths. Brought up a strict Catholic, he was ejected from gymnasium at Tetschen for insubordination, whereupon he apprenticed himself to a mechanic. After finally earning a Matura at Krakow, he used winnings from a lottery to earn a doctorate in law at Vienna in 1865. In 1872 he won habilitation in civil procedure, serving at Vienna from 1875 to 1899 as professor of this subject. Disdaining etiquette, he dressed in old clothes and mountain boots. Every afternoon during the 1880's and 1890's, he conversed with his brother Carl at a coffeehouse opposite the university. Despite their differences, the two theorists patronized their elder brother Max (1838–1911), who for more than thirty years served as a liberal deputy in the Reichsrat. In contrast to the dispassionate Carl, Anton burned with zeal for social justice. Having learned Polish as a youth, he aided Polish students, especially Jews. His chief disciple was a Romanian Jew, Karl Grünberg (1861–1940), who in 1924 founded the Institut für Sozialforschung at Frankfurt. As an amateur mathematician, Menger espoused unbridled rationalism, discounting any but cerebral motives for conduct. After retirement, the bachelor, an invalid, lived in Nice, Abbazia, and Rome, tended by a faithful female companion.

In his *Neue Staatslehre* (Jena, 1903), Anton Menger proposed a system of community socialism resembling that of Hertzka's *Freiland*. He argued that ownership by communes would increase workers' capacity to consume. Anathematizing the culture-state (*Kulturstaat*) of liberal individualism as perpetuating the right of parasites to receive income without work, he advocated a work-state (*Arbeitsstaat*) to benefit the working classes. Without invoking Marx, he analyzed regimes according to the classes that they serve. First, a monarch seeks power and pomp; second, nobility and higher clergy strive for preferment; third, the bourgeoisie cherishes above all material goods and intellectual opportunity; while fourth, unpropertied classes have no choice but to demand fundamentals such as bodily security and family solidarity. Like the Austro-Marxists, Menger attributed to the working classes superior morality. They represent an enclave of preindustrial integrity amidst capitalist rapacity.

As a professor of law, Menger pilloried private law for safeguarding the interests of the possessing classes. In *Das Recht auf den vollen Arbeitsertrag in geschichtlicher Darstellung* (Stuttgart, 1886; 4th ed., 1910), Menger inveighed against disparities in protection which a supposedly impartial law accords to rich and poor. Laws penalizing illegitimacy sanction the infidelities of the wealthy by saddling lower-class mistresses with the offspring. To accelerate transition to his work-state, Menger advocated curtailing rentier income. Wealth was being squandered on culture centers of the Ringstrasse, while the poor were denied rights to live, work, and procreate.

Menger united tenets of individualism with values cherished by organicists. Postulating that self-interest motivates conduct, he insisted even more strenuously than his brother Carl that people tend to calculate rationally. The act of weighing satisfactions, which Carl Menger ascribed to economic decisions, his brother Anton discerned in all behavior. Although Anton backed the plea of Socialists for society to safeguard the poor and weak, his distrust for an overly centralized state stopped short of anarchism. The utopias of Godwin, Proudhon, and Kropotkin he deprecated for jettisoning the exercise of power.

As consultant on the German Civil Code of 1896, Anton Menger urged that the poor receive safeguards. He excoriated the right of an employer to punish employees, contending that this made the former judge in his own case, empowered to deprive his adversary of livelihood. By demanding that judges decide each case however equity required without heeding statutes, Menger anticipated the free-law movement of Ehrlich. The latter esteemed Menger as a friend who had foreshadowed his own sociology of law, although the latter professed scant sympathy for Ehrlich's equation of folkways with law. In unmasking private law as a privilege seized by possessing classes, Menger anticipated a major thesis of Renner's critique of private law, albeit without Marxist overtones.

Thanks to his asceticism and rationalism, Menger injected unwonted moral fervor into the Vienna Faculty of Law. Although he was too idiosyncratic to found a school, his kindness to students won devotion. His closest affinity lay with Josef Popper-Lynkeus and Theodor Hertzka: with them he shared compassion for the dispossessed, exalting the right to live above the right to own. He shared their bewilderment as to why people should ridicule his proposals. Anton Menger was that rarity among social theorists, a utopian who taught law. By flaunting eccentricity within a bastion of conformity such as a Faculty of Law, he proved that Vienna had room for utopians. Around 1900,

no city—with the possible exception of Paris—fostered so many out-
landish schemes as did the Habsburg capital, partly because piecemeal
reform was so hopelessly obstructed.

HANS GROSS: PIONEER OF
SCIENTIFIC CRIME DETECTION

Remembered even less than Eugen Ehrlich or Anton Menger is Hans
Gross (1847–1915), the creator of modern crime detection.[6] The innovations of this criminologist have been more widely, albeit unknow-
ingly, implemented than those of any other Austrian social thinker.
Born and educated in Graz, this methodical Catholic revolutionized
techniques of crime detection and prosecution. Thanks to a Vienna-
born theorist Franz von Liszt (1851–1919) Gross's approach was early
incorporated into penology and penal law. From 1869 to 1897, he
worked in Styria as an examining judge, traveling widely and sifting
evidence from thousands of cases. Holders of this post were expected
to perform functions of detective, district attorney, and judge, all with
a minimum of equipment and training. Having had this job thrust upon
him at age twenty-two, Gross forged rules-of-thumb to guide investigators. He was scandalized by the neglect of police work in rural
areas, where retired soldiers provided only desultory enforcement.
Haphazard centralized law, such as Ehrlich praised, goaded Gross to
the opposite extreme of codifying police procedures. Although he never
earned habilitation, from 1897 to 1902 he served as a professor of penal
law at Czernowitz, from 1902 to 1905 at Prague, and thereafter at
Graz, where in 1912 he founded an Institute of Criminalistics. Graduates disseminated laboratory methods of crime detection throughout
Europe.

Gross summarized his experience in the two-volume *Handbuch für
Untersuchungsrichter* (Munich, 1893; 6th ed., 1914), which was widely
translated. The third edition of 1898 coined the term criminalistics
(Kriminalistik) to designate scientific crime detection. Combining two
disciplines, later differentiated into phenomenology of crime and police
science, the treatise investigated the motivation, tactics, and technology
of criminals. Exploiting his own experience, Gross explained how to
read footprints and to translate argot, as well as to decipher the sign
language *(Zinken)* used by illiterates. He devoted one chapter to
expounding the uncanny skills of gypsies. By offering a compendium of
case histories, Gross's treatise resembled that by his friend Richard
Krafft-Ebing (1840–1902), director of the Graz Insane Asylum, who assembled cases on sexual deviance in *Psychopathia sexualis: Eine*

klinisch-forensische Studie (Stuttgart, 1886; 12th ed., 1902). No sooner had Wilhelm Roentgen discovered X rays at Würzburg in 1895 than Gross began to apply them to crime detection. Having collected instruments of crime throughout his career, Gross preserved these memorabilia in a museum attached to his institute. During the 1920's his collection of murder weapons, passkeys, and forgeries trained Vienna's police, as well as Johann Schober's state police, to become Europe's most advanced.[7] One of Gross's Students, Adolf Lenz (1868–1959), enlarged his master's research, instituting the discipline of criminal biology.

Gross abetted the bureaucratic state by insisting that it investigate crimes thoroughly and swiftly. Although he had begun his career in countryside resembling that of Ehrlich's Bukovina, Gross wanted outlying regions to undergo central authority. Unlike Ehrlich, the Graz detective favored bureaucracy, instilling Gesellschaft values where Schlamperei had prevailed. Gross pursued this goal with the pertinacity and humility of a character created by Saar or Ebner-Eschenbach, penning case histories that read like *Heimat-Literatur* for Styria. With Biedermeier meticulousness, he equaled and surpassed the exploits of the legendary Sherlock Holmes, reading footprints, deciphering bloodstains, and vindicating implausible hypotheses. Not long before a Marxist analyst of cinema Béla Balázs would declare the detective to be the romantic hero of the bourgeoisie, Austria produced a real-life figure to epitomize this ideal. Gross was that anomaly in the Habsburg Empire, an innovator who earned official recognition and with it opportunity to disseminate his inventions.

HANS KELSEN'S PURE THEORY OF LAW: THE POLITICAL IMPOTENCE OF THEORETICAL RIGOR

The most influential of Austrian jurists in the twentieth century has been Hans Kelsen (1881–).[8] Born at Prague of Jewish parents, in 1883 Kelsen moved to Vienna, where he attended the Akademisches Gymnasium. At the University of Vienna, Otto Weininger awakened his interest in philosophy. In 1905 Kelsen wrote a dissertation under the redoubtable Edmund Bernatzik on Dante's *De Monarchia*. Next he studied under Jellinek at Heidelberg and Gerhard Anschütz at Berlin before becoming a docent at Vienna in 1911, where his friends included Bohemian-born historian of Greek social theory Adolf Menzel (1857–1938). From 1917 to 1929 Kelsen served as a professor of constitutional law at Vienna, drafting at the request of Renner the federal constitution adopted in 1920 and serving thereafter as adviser to the

Supreme Court.[9] From 1929 to 1933 Kelsen taught at Cologne and then at Geneva and Prague before coming to the United States in 1938. After lecturing at Harvard for two years, he taught from 1942 to 1952 at the University of California at Berkeley, where he has subsequently lived. One of the most rigorous, yet wide-ranging minds in twentieth-century social theory, Kelsen has combined systematic virtuosity with vast learning in the manner of his friends Othmar Spann and Otto Bauer.

In his first major work, *Hauptprobleme der Staatsrechtslehre* (Tübingen, 1911), Kelsen proved himself a relentless dualist. Isolating Is from Ought, nature from spirit, body from soul, and reality from value, Kelsen opened his treatise with a Humean declaration that no Ought can be derived from any Is. Not yet acquainted with the Marburg neo-Kantian Hermann Cohen (1842–1918), Kelsen relied above all on Schleiermacher, Simmel, and Windelband to expound dualism. Only after reviewers noted resemblances did Kelsen use the older Jewish scholar's arguments to buttress his own. He dubbed his system pure theory of law *(reine Rechtslehre)*, as distinct from pure law *(reines Recht)*; a German jurist Karl Magnus Bergbohm (1849–1927) had introduced the latter term to designate a disguised natural law.[10] Kelsen assailed the foundation of natural law which underlay the Austrian civil code compiled between 1713 and 1811. Although his critique recalled John Austin's attack on Blackstone, Kelsen did not explore affinities with the English positivist until the late 1920's.[11]

Pure theory of law expunged from jurisprudence any social science except law. This self-enclosed system enshrined a dichotomy between legal fact and legal norm, the latter being a rule that the former is presumed to embody. Norms constitute Weberian ideal types to which actual laws conform. Because there exists no standard of justice beyond norms decreed by a given state, the state coincides with law. No matter what norms a state may adopt, its choice cannot be impugned by sociology, philosophy, or psychology. Although he was an arch-dualist in epistemology, Kelsen imposed relentless monism upon jurisprudence. To elucidate imputation *(Zurechnung)* of responsibility, Kelsen differentiated a person's legal will from psychological will. The state holds each person responsible for any acts within its code of law, imputing to an individual's legal will intentions that he otherwise might disavow.

To discredit natural law jurisprudence, Kelsen explained how monarchical apologists who glorified duties had spawned revolutionaries like Thomas Paine who trumpeted natural rights. Kelsen unmasked both schools as having championed class ideologies that shrouded absolutism behind theological categories. After 1800, bourgeois liberals had expounded empirical legal science to keep pace with positivism in natural science.[12] In the manner of Mannheim, Kelsen emphasized a distinction between past-oriented ideologies and future-oriented utopias. In dissecting Marx and Lenin, he lamented that Ferdinand Lassalle (1825–1864) had perished in a duel before he could formulate democratic socialism.[13] In his *Allgemeine Staatslehre* (Berlin, 1925), which he modeled on Jellinek's treatise of that name, Kelsen expressed exasperation with socialism—and with Ehrlich—by banishing sociology altogether from jurisprudence, retracting an earlier half-hearted approval of it.

Kelsen's use of norms to explicate rules of law may have derived in part from confusions that affected Habsburg law. In order to differentiate overlapping jurisdictions, Austro-Hungarian law invited the postulate of an *Urnorm*. There existed so many levels of jurisdiction, descending from *k. und k.* ministries down through Austrian ministries and those of individual crownlands to municipalities, that endless conflicts ensued. To disentangle levels and accretions, it was essential to propound ideal types. As a further debt to Austria, Kelsen's jurisprudence, shorn of social science and ideology, flourished as a corrective in a nation where professors of law could implement their theories. Desire to expunge extraneous influence was less likely among Anglo-Americans, where judges, not professors, fashion law.

After 1930, Kelsen became increasingly fascinated by Plato, whose dualism between Is and Ought paralleled his own. In a series of essays, the jurist expounded Plato's disjunction between good and evil, the one and the many, form and content, while defending a Kantian version of the Greek's epistemology.[14] Influenced by his friend Freud, Kelsen unmasked homosexuality behind Plato's derogation of women and his indoctrination of boys into a higher world.[15] Kelsen argued, *pace* Viennese impressionists, that mind transcends a flux of sensations; serenely it excogitates norms or ideal types that subsist outside society, invulnerable to empirical critique. Unable to conceal admiration for Plato's epistemology, Kelsen nevertheless sided with the Sophists in branding Plato's social theory anti-democratic; the *Republic*, said the jurist purveyed an ideology of absolutism. Attacking Othmar Spann while anticipating the anti-Platonic polemic of Karl Popper, Kelsen praised relativism as the world view of democracy.[16]

After 1930, Kelsen diverged from earlier legal positivists like Austin to embrace internationalist jurisprudence. Disregarding his own contempt for ideology, he espoused an ideology of internationalism, contending that only international law can impart homogeneity and continuity to national systems. International law caps a pyramid of norms, which Kelsen's Vienna-born disciple Adolf Merkl (1890–) formulated into what he called dynamic pluralism. International law, said Kelsen, climaxes an all-embracing system, which reprobates war not as a crime against nature but merely as an infraction of norms. By scuttling extralegal criteria, Kelsen had landed in a thoroughgoing relativism, which obliged him to accept nazism as a different but equal system of norms. After coming to the United States, Kelsen evolved from monism toward Anglo-Saxon pragmatism.

Kelsen stands as heir to a tradition within Austrian jurisprudence, which running through Josef Unger, Adolf Menzel, and Georg Jellinek united legal positivism with philosophical dualism, the whole enlivened by vast erudition. Like Pribram, Kelsen invited misinterpretation by waging polemics against both right and left. After 1930, his internationalist ideology recalled the pre-1914 world of security, as if the whole globe, like Austria-Hungary, acknowledged a single framework of norms. By scrutinizing the span of Western history in order to elucidate contemporary events, Kelsen revived the encyclopedism of prewar scholars such as Jellinek and Wieser. His recognition of timeless categories affiliated him, however remotely, with the Leibnizian vision of Bohemia. Against a welter of ideologies and maneuvers prevailing here below, Kelsen counterposed seamless unity in a higher world of norms. With the abandon of a deontologist who proclaims, "Let justice be done though the heavens may fall," he made law master in its own house, a science in its own right. A disillusioned Platonist who turned positivist, he demanded conceptual consistency, not, to be sure, between fields of knowledge, as had Leibniz, but merely within each field. By transferring to his own specialty the Leibnizian quest for internal consistency and overarching unity, he paralleled members of the Vienna Circle who elevated logic into a self-contained science while jettisoning whatever did not fit their premises.

As with Schumpeter and Bauer, pathos surrounds this rigorist who demarcated law from other disciplines. By combining immersion in tradition with desire to surpass it, Kelsen shared the ambivalence of conservative revolutionaries such as Kraus and Wittgenstein. Like them, the more he enriched social theory, the more he exemplified the impotence of Austrian scholars to salvage their world. It was as if Kelsen expected imperial bureaucracy to enforce benevolent norms forever, liberating jurists to design edifices of thought. Even participation in drafting and implementing the Constitution of the First Republic cannot exculpate Kelsen from the charge of therapeutic nihilism; together with other democrats he fled Fascist onslaught. Unrivaled at juggling ideas, theorists like Kelsen could not safeguard conditions that made theorizing possible.

6

Austro-Marxists

VIKTOR ADLER:
ORGANIZER OF AUSTRIAN SOCIALISM

THE SOCIAL DEMOCRATIC party of Austria attracted some of the keenest minds to espouse socialism anywhere. After the party had been organized by Viktor Adler in 1888, it nurtured a bevy of young theorists who between 1900 and 1905 began to call themselves Austro-Marxists.[1] Led by Otto Bauer, Karl Renner, and Max Adler, they proposed reforming the empire in *Marxstudien,* which Max Adler edited from 1904 to 1922, and in Otto Bauer's periodical *Der Kampf* (1907–1934; repr. Vienna, 1969). Despite the originality of their views, especially as to means of reconciling nationalities and on the need to improve workers' education, the Austro-Marxists have never received the attention they deserve. In 1913 Stalin pilloried them as fellow travelers of the bourgeoisie, and after 1918 their repudiation of terrorism ostracized them from the Communist International. Their intense intellectuality, combined with eagerness to emend the existing order, provoked enemies on both right and left. Their eclipse parallels that of the empire whose proclivity to compromise they shared too well.

The father of socialism in Austria was Viktor Adler (1852–1918).[2] This Prague-born Jew became an ardent German-National student in Vienna. An ally of Heinrich Friedjung and Engelbert Pernerstorfer, during the early 1870's he helped organize a pan-German league of university students. In debate against Sigmund Freud, Adler was maltreated by his combative opponent.[3] Oddly enough, during the 1880's Adler inhabited the ground-floor flat at Berggasse 19, which from 1892 to 1908 Freud used as an office. As a student of medicine, Adler was befriended by the cerebral anatomist Theodor Meynert; exuding concern for patients, Adler excoriated the therapeutic nihilism that made physicians prefer autopsies to cures. In 1878 Adler and his father were baptized Protestants. To the end, Adler harbored Jewish self-hatred, depising the majority of Jews as uncouth and dreaming that socialism would accelerate assimilation.

In 1885 Adler joined the Socialist party after his application to become inspector of trade under the law of 1883 had been rebuffed. Between 1887 and 1889, he spent many months in jail for efforts to organize a unified Social Democratic party, a goal that he achieved at the party congress of Hainfeld in December, 1888. Thereafter, he enjoyed relative immunity from the Anarchist Law of 1886, becoming a stout defender of the Habsburg Empire. In 1889 he declared at Paris: "Except for France and England, Austria has perhaps the most liberal laws in all Europe, so much so that it resembles a republic which has a monarch in place of a president at its head."[4] From 1905 to 1918 Adler served as a deputy in the Reichsrat, where in 1907 Socialist deputies took the lead in enacting universal suffrage. On November 28, 1905, Adler had organized a general strike to show sympathy with the Russian revolution and to demand universal suffrage. The march of 250,000 workers impelled the government, at the urging of Emil Steinbach, to grant this demand which led in 1907 to the election of eighty-seven Social Democratic deputies. Earlier, in 1890 Adler had shown his skill as an organizer by inaugurating Socialist May Day on the Prater to demand an eight-hour working day. The choice of May 1 had been made by the Second International at Paris in 1889 so as to coincide with an American rally already scheduled for that day. Thereafter Adler made this annual parade of workers on the Prater Hauptallee an event to compete with the Blumencorso that Princess Metternich had revived in 1886.

Under Adler's leadership, the Social Democratic Workers party (SDAP) of Austria represented above all Sudeten Germans who had flocked to Vienna. Although many of its leaders were Jewish, they tended to share Adler's anti-Semitism.[5] Middle-class Jews gravitated to the party out of sympathy for laborers, whose exclusion from society seemed to mirror their own. Engelbert Pernerstorfer, a German nationalist Catholic with whom Adler attended the Schottengymnasium, became infected by his friend's anti-Semitism after joining the Socialist party in 1896. Viktor Adler's achievement was to unite the radical and moderate factions of the Social Democratic party, insisting that unity in tactics take precedence over doctrinal unanimity. Under Adler, the SDAP competed fiercely with Karl Lueger's Christian Socialist party. Strife came to a head on February 11, 1913, when Vienna-born Socialist deputy Franz Schuhmeier (1864–1913) was assassinated in the Northwest Railroad Station of Vienna. The assassin was Paul Kun-

schak, brother of Christian Socialist deputy Leopold Kunschak; allegedly the murderer sought to avenge himself on the Socialist party for
unspecified grievances. As a spellbinding orator, admired by Lueger,
Schuhmeier had led the fight for universal suffrage while opposing
clerical control of schools. His murder so shocked Adler and his followers that 250,000 mourners joined the cortege for Schuhmeier, more
even than had marched after Lueger three years before.

Resort to violence entered the Socialist camp in the person of Adler's son, Friedrich Adler (1879–1960). Having studied under Ernst
Mach, he achieved worldwide notoriety by assassinating on October
21, 1916, Prime Minister Count Karl Stürgkh (1859–1916), who since
March, 1914, had governed Austria without convening the Reichsrat.
At his trial in May, 1917, Friedrich Adler delivered such a ringing indictment of wartime tyranny that his execution was postponed. Eventually Emperor Karl pardoned him.[6]

A number of foreign Socialists were influenced by Austro-Marxism
before and after World War One. While living in Vienna from 1911 to
1914, Leon Trotsky met nearly every Saturday evening at the Café
Central with Karl Renner, Otto Bauer, and Max Adler. After 1917
Trotsky deplored their repudiation of Bolshevism. Josip Broz, later
Marshal Tito (1892–), had been taken prisoner in 1915 by the Russians while a member of the Austro-Hungarian army. After conversion
to communism in Russia, he worked at an auto factory in Wiener
Neustadt while endeavoring to organize the Communist party in Yugoslavia. During 1923 the Italian Marxist Antonio Gramsci (1891–1937)
lived in Vienna, where his friends included Victor Serge.[7] Although
Vienna attracted non-German Marxists, for years it repelled the most
famous of all Austrian Socialists, Prague-born Karl Kautsky (1854–
1938). As described in his *Erinnerungen und Erörterungen* (The
Hague, 1960), this son of a Czech painter and an Austrian actress
lived in Vienna from 1863 to 1880, where his father Jan Kautsky
(1827–1896) directed a studio for theater sets. Having been converted
to socialism by the Paris Commune of 1871, Karl studied at the University of Vienna, before departing in 1880 for Switzerland and Germany. As editor of *Die Neue Zeit* from 1883 to 1917, he deplored the
moderation of Viktor Adler and of later Austro-Marxists. After his retirement, Kautsky lived quietly in Vienna from 1924 to 1938.

The chief failing of Austrian socialism under Viktor Adler was a
tendency to ignore the misery of the masses. The SDAP proved so
loyal to Franz Joseph that it recruited an elite among labor while ignoring the nameless many. Gifted men from the working class had to

endure a succession of debilitating jobs such as the poet Alfons Petzold described in his autobiography, *Das rauhe Leben: Der Roman eines Menschen* (Berlin, 1920). At Vienna it was not uncommon for the poor, many of them Czech, to live six or eight persons to a room, while thousands even less fortunate merely rented a bed—they were known as *Bettgeher*—subsisting on bread and coffee and often succumbing to tuberculosis. It was in such quarters that cholera broke out during the Exposition of 1873. The flophouses of Vienna, which helped to sour Hitler, found too few critics among Social Democratic leaders; the slums of Ottakring and Brigittenau, where working girls sold themselves to the first comer, were not improved until after World War One.

Despite neglect of fundamental reform, Austrian Socialists cultivated an almost religious sense of mission. Younger intellectuals chose to believe that ideas could better society and that the empire could be rebuilt from within. Quasi-religious zeal fostered among Socialists a sense of brotherhood that the state church no longer inspired. In rivalry with the Christian Socialist party, Social Democrats displayed, especially after 1918, more concern for the welfare of individuals. By assailing clerical control of schools as well as impediments to divorce, Socialists dangled reforms of wide appeal. At the time of his death, November 11, 1918, Adler had so united the Social Democratic party that for eighteen months it could share rule with the Christian Socialists, as well as govern Vienna for the next sixteen years. The experience of having been elected to power steered the Austro-Marxists to theorize in directions even more democratic than those known under Viktor Adler.

TACTICAL BLUNDERS BY A
THEORETICIAN: OTTO BAUER

Otto Bauer (1881–1938) possessed one of the keenest intellects of all Austrian social theorists.[8] In a society that produced skillful orators and writers in abundance, Bauer was one of the most talented. Born at Vienna of a wealthy Jewish manufacturing family from Bohemia, the young prodigy wrote at age nine a drama in five acts, *Napoleon's End.* Like Freud, he was *Primus* in his class at gymnasium, going on to earn his doctorate in law with distinction, while studying under Böhm-Bawerk. From 1907 to 1914 he served as secretary of the Social Democratic party, impressing everyone with his capacity to impose order on experience. Julius Braunthal recalled the charisma of the twenty-six-year-old party secretary:

> What amazed me most when I listened to his speeches was his wonderful brain. He did not use notes, and he never paused in his speech—facts and thoughts flowed in a ceaseless stream, well ordered, well proportioned, imprinting the contours and even many of the details of the problem under discussion upon the memory of his audience.[9]

.In *Die Nationalitätenfrage und die Sozialdemokratie* (Vienna, 1907), Bauer reopened in masterful fashion a question canvassed earlier by Renner. In August, 1914, on the second day of hostilities, he volunteered for military service, fighting as a lieutenant in Galicia, where in November, 1914, the Russians took him prisoner because he had advanced too hastily. After experiencing the Russian revolution while in prison camp, he became so radical that the Russians allowed him to return to Austria in September, 1917. Struggling to reunite the Social Democratic party that Friedrich Adler had split asunder, Bauer became in October, 1918, Viktor Adler's subaltern as foreign minister in the provisional government, assuming full duties after Adler's death on November 11, 1918.[10] As foreign minister until July 26, 1919, Bauer advocated *Anschluss* with Germany—ignoring the warnings of a Vienna-born colleague, Rudolf Hilferding (1877–1941), who having lived in Berlin since 1907 feared that Austria's Catholics would dilute the energy of Germany's Protestants. After the collapse of the postwar coalition, Bauer labored from 1920 to 1934 as the leading tactician of the Social Democratic party, a role in which his theoretical acumen could not serve to best advantage.

In *Die Nationalitätenfrage*, Bauer marshaled exceptional historical learning to show that within Austria-Hungary what Friedrich Engels had called nations without history represented the proletariat, while the Germans and Hungarians represented middle-class capitalists. Himself a firm nationalist, Bauer interpreted Austria-Hungary's national struggles as disguised class conflicts. He advanced this thesis again in *Die österreichische Revolution* (Vienna, 1923), asserting that oppression of the Czechs had made fission of the empire inevitable. Emphasizing that the Socialists alone had foreseen the collapse of 1918, Bauer explained how foresight had won them a place in the coalition government. In an incisive survey of European thought since Occam, "Das Weltbild des Kapitalismus" (1924),[11] Bauer ascribed the triumph of mathematical science to the middle class, while interpreting Darwin as a bourgeois who had projected onto nature the struggle for existence which afflicted capitalist society.

After 1920, Bauer proved himself more adept at juggling ideas than at directing action. In June, 1920, over protests from Karl Renner, Bauer led the Socialists out of the coalition to begin fourteen years of opposition to Seipel's Christian Socialists. Although the official head of the SDPO remained Karl Seitz (1869-1950), who served as mayor of Vienna from 1923 to 1934, it was Bauer who decreed root-and-branch opposition to the Christian Socialists, not realizing that thereby he would only strengthen his opponents while enfeebling the state. Acting as if the emperor were still on the throne to guarantee stability, Bauer renewed pre-1914 tactics of obstruction, making Chancellor Seipel ever more anti-Socialist.[12] Until the burning of the Palace of Justice on July 15, 1927, Bauer insisted that Socialists could win support through progressive legislation. Although many laws of 1918 and 1919 merely perpetuated wartime measures, they did promote a high level of education so as to train cadres badly needed by industry. An eight-hour workday, paid vacations, public health resorts, resettlement of peasants, and orderly labor negotiations were undeniable achievements.[13] The success of these reforms was overshadowed by bitter polemics between right and left, which prevented Seipel and Bauer from cooperating to protect the state against the extreme right. Unlike Renner, Bauer was not one of those who foresaw the Fascist menace.

Meanwhile Austro-Marxists had been waging a battle on their left flank to prevent Bolshevists from bolting the SDPO. Although unity was preserved, it came at the price of ideological vapidity, producing that immobility common to Popular Fronts and Grand Coalitions. By 1933 the Social Democratic party under Bauer's leadership had lost its nerve, so that when Dollfuss suspended the Nationalrat on March 17, 1933, Bauer to his everlasting regret let slip the one opportunity legally to resist this infraction of the constitution. The denouement came in February, 1934, when Dollfuss, who hated Bauer for having called him a scoundrel *(Schuft)* in Parliament, profited from the riots at Paris on February 6, 1934, to destroy democratic institutions in Austria. Having borrowed foreign exchange from France in 1933, Dollfuss had promised French Premier Daladier to safeguard Austrian democracy, but when Daladier fell, Dollfuss felt free to ignore this pledge.

The tragic miscalculations of February 12, 1934, revealed to what extent Bauer could falter as an administrator. On the evening of February 11, he met contacts at a movie house, while without his knowledge workers at Linz were organizing a general strike. On the morning of February 12, the electrical workers of Vienna struck, an act that constituted an agreed upon signal for a general strike. Unfortunately, they did so before the SDPO had printed posters announcing the strike. Once loss of electric power had halted the presses, many workers never heard about the strike, while others fought a pitched battle against overzealous government troops. During the siege of the apartment complex known as Karl-Marx-Hof, dedicated resisters were slaughtered because the few Socialist leaders who had access to caches of arms had been arrested in advance. Bauer fled to Brünn, as Dollfuss outlawed the Socialist party, ushering in four years of underground resistance.[14] Stephen Spender elegized the bombardment of Karl-Marx-Hof in *Vienna* (New York, 1935).

Like Schumpeter and Josef Redlich, Bauer never accommodated himself to the demise of the Habsburg Empire. During the 1920's he preferred exchanging polemics with Seipel to assessing international realities. The fact that an illegitimate son of peasants could become prime minister, as did Dollfuss, offended Bauer's sense of propriety. A theoretician, he respected individuals too highly to run a party efficiently, never regimenting ideology and devoting more energy to refuting Lenin than to forestalling Hitler. In his love for debate, Bauer embodied the Schlamperei of Imperial Austria, convinced that somehow bureaucracy would sustain the state while educated men discoursed.

Like other Austro-Marxists, Bauer exalted individuality. For him as for Neurath, class struggle meant above all an instrument for liberating individuals so that they could cultivate leisured pursuits once reserved to the wealthy. Bauer believed so ardently that socialism must use constitutional means that he failed to withstand emerging enemies of democracy. Such naiveté was another legacy of the prewar empire, where tradition had safeguarded dissent. Down to 1934 Bauer prolonged prewar crusades against church and aristocracy, when he should have joined these erstwhile enemies to repel fascism. Few blunders have been so costly.

KARL RENNER:
THE AUSTRO-MARXIST AS CONCILIATOR

The stature of Karl Renner (1870–1950) as theorist has been obscured by his tenure as president of the Second Republic from 1945 to 1950.[15] He was in fact the only Austro-Marxist leader to survive World War Two. As the eighteenth child of Catholic peasants in Southern Moravia who suffered during the depression of the 1870's, he always showed greater readiness to cooperate with the bourgeoisie than did the more affluent Viktor Adler or the pugnacious Otto Bauer. After studying under Wilhelm Jerusalem at gymnasium in Nikolsburg, in 1898 Renner took a doctorate in law at Vienna, where his teachers included the Menger brothers. From 1896 to 1932 he served as librarian of Parliament, using its resources for his own research. As a friend of Viktor Adler, he was elected to the Reichsrat in 1907, serving in the lower house until 1934, while pleading vainly in 1920 that the Grand Coalition be continued.

As a theorist, Renner contributed to Marxist discussion of nationalities and of jurisprudence. In 1899 he published under the pseudonym Synopticus his *Staat und Nation*, which advanced the first of many proposals to prevent national conflicts from fragmenting the Social Democratic party. Renner made himself heir of the federalist scheme put forward by the Hungarian-born Jewish physician Adolf Fischhof (1816–1893) in *Österreich und die Bürgschaften seines Bestandes: Politische Studie* (Vienna, 1869). Imbued with Hungarian utopianism and influenced by Swiss methods of arbitrating differences among nationalities, the Sage of Emmersdorf had sought unsuccessfully during the 1870's to mediate between the Old Czechs under Rieger and the Liberal Auersperg Ministry.[16] Renner's program anticipated that endorsed by the Brünn conference of the SDAP in September, 1899.[17] Renner called for division of the empire into national units *(Kreise)*, each of which would tax its own members in order to administer schools and cultural institutions. Each citizen would choose membership in a nation, reviving the medieval practice whereby a person could elect which law to acknowledge. In mixed areas, national minorities would be protected by an Imperial Parliament, which would retain control over foreign, military, and fiscal affairs. German would be a language of convenience *(Vermittlungssprache)*, not a language of state.

By urging that the state withdraw from cultural affairs, the Socialists opposed the principle of· *cuius regio, eius lingua*, which the Badeni Ordinances had vainly sought to mitigate. In defending cultural federalism, Renner argued that the nobility favored historic provinces, and the bourgeoisie championed a centralized state in order better to exploit labor, while it was the proletariat that desired national-cultural autonomy. Like Bauer after him, Renner rejected the demand of Jews for cultural autonomy; they were to remain a religious not a national group. Despite Renner's pleas, the Brünn program failed to unite the Social Democratic party, which after 1900 split along national lines, as the proletariat of each nationality cooperated with its own bourgeoisie in an effort to block the bureaucracy from circumventing Parliament under Article Fourteen.

Another federalist recipe to counter the constitutional impasse was offered by the Hungarian-born Romanian Aurel Popovici (1863–1917), whose *Die Vereinigten Staaten von Gross-Österreich: Politische Studien zur Lösung der nationalen Fragen und staatsrechtlichen Krisen in Österreich-Ungarn* (Leipzig, 1906) advocated the establishment of fifteen territorial states, including cession of the Burgenland to Austria. In Renner's view, the Romanian's scheme would perpetuate tyranny over minorities; no geographic gerrymandering could achieve that "democratic Switzerland with a monarchical base" of which the Austro-Marxist dreamed. In his reverence for the principle of nationality, Renner revived the romanticism of Eötvös and Palacký. Although he conceded that within the state class-conflicts might rage, he believed, like the Old Czechs, that inside each nation such quarrels cease. Because nationality was a sacred trust with which the state had no right to interfere, Marxism should keep silent where culture was involved.

Renner elaborated his critique of the state into one of the most penetrating Marxist analyses of continental law. *Die soziale Funktion der Rechtsinstitute,* published in the inaugural volume of *Marxstudien* (Vienna, 1904), launched Marxist sociology of law.[18] Writing under the pseudonym of Joseph Karner, Renner expanded Rudolf von Jhering's view that law results from conflicts among competing social groups. Just as Jhering had drafted *Der Kampf um's Recht* (Vienna, 1872) after witnessing struggles over the Hohenwart proposals for Czech autonomy, so Renner formulated his analysis after growing up amid Czech-German conflicts in Moravia. As a Marxist, Renner differentiated social changes from revisions of law, arguing that because the former precede the latter legal devices cannot prevent social change, although they can delay or accelerate it. The separation between private and public law is, Renner held, a creation of capitalism, whereby the state enforces the interests of the middle class. The right of private property presupposes more than a mere title to dispose of goods: the sanctity of property delegates sovereignty to the bourgeoisie, entitling it to exploit persons who lack property. Whereas Gumplowicz saw the right of property as a weapon in a struggle for survival, Renner interpreted it as an obsolescent bastion of class struggle. Surveying modes of property since the Middle Ages, Renner showed that legal ownership no longer necessarily conveys physical control, which has devolved upon managers through legal fictions, which he called connecting institutions *(Konnexinstitute).* In studying the managerial class, Renner was the first to argue that expropriation would merely deprive paper owners of rights that are in fact exercised by agents; such managers would retain their authority even under state ownership.

After 1920, Renner suffered from the same malaise as Bauer. As chancellor of the coalition government of 1918 to 1920, he had conducted the peace delegation to its barbed-wire enclosure at Saint-Germain, where the Anschluss was forever forbidden. When Bauer led the Socialists into opposition, Renner withdrew from leadership of the party, although he did serve from 1930 to 1933 as president of the Nationalrat. More conciliatory than Bauer, this Marxist turned Socialist might well have fared better as party leader. For Renner, the pathos of the empire's collapse was symbolized by loss of a farm in Moravia which he and his sister had owned jointly. In order to keep the farm, she had been obliged to become a Czech citizen, while in order to remain chancellor of Austria, he—the critic of private ownership—had had to give up the farm. How could one feel loyal, he asked, to a country that exacted such sacrifices of its citizens?[19]

An amateur poet, in 1919 Renner wrote the national anthem of the First Republic, which Wilhelm Kienzl set to music. To console himself after 1934, he composed a philosophical epic, which was published posthumously as *Das Weltbild der Moderne* (Vienna, 1954). Modeled on Lucretius' *De rerum natura* and dedicated to Investigators of Nature *(Naturforscher)*, this four-hundred-page treatise in verse unfolded the teachings of astronomy, chemistry, and atomic physics, through an astonishing variety of stanza forms. Evincing partiality for astronomy and for the ancient Greeks, Renner wrote verse, which while sometimes turgid and mostly epigonal, nevertheless throbs with faith. Reading like a didactic poem that Mach or Boltzmann might have written, amid Nazi occupation the epic praised modern science as a citadel of truth. Renner's poem is one of the forgotten monuments of Austrian internal emigration.

Renner's eclipse as a social theorist after 1920 does not lessen his prewar achievement. Renner opened new perspectives in analysis both of national conflict and of private law, all the while disowning his innovations under a variety of pseudonyms lest he lose his coveted post as parliamentary librarian. His willingness to cooperate with Christian Socialists inspired the moderation of Austria's Social Democrats after 1945, making him an early advocate of coexistence between East and West. Few thinkers embodied so attractively the Austrian propensity for molding opposites into a living whole as this peasant proprietor who turned Marxist, only later to regret being deprived by treaty of the family farm. He was the very example of what Lenin would call petit-bourgeois contradictions.

MAX ADLER'S SYNTHESIS
OF KANT AND MARX

The third leading theorist of Austro-Marxism besides Bauer and Renner was Max Adler (1873–1937).[20] Born in Vienna of Jewish parents—he was not related to either Viktor Adler or Alfred Adler—he took his law degree there in 1896 before entering the practice of law. A scholar rather than a politician, Adler edited *Marxstudien* from 1904 to 1922, at the same time contributing many articles to *Der Kampf*. In 1907 he cofounded the Vienna Sociological Society together with Renner, Rudolf Eisler, Josef Redlich, Wilhelm Jersualem, and Rudolf Goldscheid. While representing Floridsdorf in the Nationalrat from 1920 to 1923, he took a habilitation at the University of Vienna, where he served from 1920 until 1937 as an *ausserordentlicher* professor of sociology. Although after 1934 he was permitted to continue teaching, he was forbidden to treat any but historical topics. Unable to lecture or publish on Marxism, he left a sizable *Nachlass* that has recently been published.[21] Adler's fellow professors included the Vienna-born empirical sociologist Paul Lazarsfeld (1901–) as well as the social psychologists Karl Bühler (1879–1963) and his wife Charlotte Bühler (1893–).[22] After coming to the United States, these pioneers of statistical research eclipsed the Austro-Marxists, by elaborating a positivism that Adler found one-sided. Although Adler could not know it, the future of sociology lay with the empiricists rather than with the Austro-Marxist fusion of Kant and Marx.

Adler published his first major work, *Kausalität und Teleologie im Streite um die Wissenschaft,* in the same volume of *Marxstudien* (1904) as Renner's *Rechtsinstitute*. Here Adler expounded the pair of polar opposites on which his lifework is built: mechanistic causation versus holistic purpose. This same dichotomy pervades the thought of Karl Pribram and Hans Kelsen. The Austro-Marxist posited a parallelism between Kant's concept of mind and Marx's concept of society. According to what Adler called the social a priori, mind is embedded in society, so that neither can be understood without the other. A person's mind begins as a product of social conditioning, only later to acquire individual traits. Neither natural science grounded in causation nor *Geisteswissenschaft* based on purpose will suffice to interpret the social a priori. What is needed is a science examining what Adler called socialized existence *(Vergesellschaftetes Dasein)*. Although mind remains free to choose among the givens offered by society, environment narrows options for knowledge and action, just as Kant's categories restrict the possibilities of thought.

Like other synthesizers such as Bauer and Mannheim, Adler had to face enemies on both right and left. He repudiated the historical materialism of Kautsky and Lenin for presupposing a fatalism that degrades man into a tool of economic forces. He assailed the neo-Kantianism of Rickert and Cohen as an empty formalism, which divorced schemas of values from life. The notion of propositions-in-themselves espoused by Husserl and Lask, Adler rejected for ignoring man's socialized existence. He attacked the neo-Romantic universalism of Othmar Spann for reifying life's supraindividual element, that is the social a priori, into a doctrine of God's Providence. Finally he rejected the positivism of Gumplowicz which interpreted social facts solely in the light of causality rather than purpose.

His sharpest polemic Adler reserved for Lenin and Kautsky, who allegedly had falsified Marx by identifying his philosophy with materialism. The Austro-Marxist insisted that nowhere did Marx define human sensations and thoughts as products of matter. Rather, Marx's metaphor of mental superstructure topping a material substructure presupposes the independence of mind from matter. To explain why Marx had adopted the term materialism, Adler cited three ways in which this label had helped to refute speculative idealism.[23] First, Marx used materialism as a synonym for positivism so as to exclude metaphysical locutions like God, soul, and immortality. Second, materialism presupposes a reality independent of consciousness; and third, it implies that Marx built his case on facts whereas Hegel had rested his on ideas. For Marx as for Feuerbach, the adjective material *(materiell)* provided a synonym for real *(wirklich)*. By expounding dialectical materialism, Marx could correct the simplistic doctrine of Holbach, Moleschott, and Büchner that man is a machine determined exclusively by processes of physics and physiology. Man lives, Marx said, in a dialectic between mind and matter, between self and society. Lenin misinterpreted his mentor in averring that mind emerges from matter; for Marx had insisted that mind exists independently from the beginning.

Adler found corroboration for what today would be called humanist Marxism in the *Kritik der Hegelschen Rechtsphilosophie*, which Marx had published in the *Deutsch-Französische Jahrbücher* of 1844. Franz Mehring had reprinted the essay in 1902.[24] More than twenty years before Marx's Paris manuscripts were published at Moscow in 1932,

Adler, even earlier than Georg Lukács, divined a Kantian-Hegelian motif in the early Marx. Unlike Lukács, Adler never doubted that this Kantian Marx was the authentic one. Adler used Kant to exegete the early Marx in the way that Lukács later used Hegel; Ernst Bloch, Old Testament chiliasm; and Karl Korsch, syndicalism. Although unlike these precursors of Marxist humanism Adler did not seek to unleash violent revolution, neither did he flatter bourgeois society, asserting more intransigently even than Bauer the autonomy of the Social Democratic party. When during the mid-1920's Adler advocated dictatorship of the proletariat, he intended not to vindicate Stalin but to proclaim a new, more individualistic type of Socialist man.

What separates Adler from post-1945 Marxism is his indifference to the concept of alienation *(Entfremdung)*. Far from lamenting that laborers are divided within themselves and from one another by having repugnant ends foisted upon them, Adler urged individuals embedded in society to extricate part of themselves from it. What neo-Marxists deplore as alienation, Adler sought to remedy by abetting individuation, for like Kant, he esteemed creative unity of personality as man's highest goal. Individuals achieve this unity by cooperating with society so as to grasp existing options as well as to create new ones. By failing to anticipate the invective against depersonalization that has prevailed since 1945, Adler assured his own eclipse. Like Bauer, he was so rooted in the security of Habsburg bureaucracy—where professors, bureaucrats, and journalists interchanged roles—he could not imagine a society where nearly all intellectuals feel homeless. At Vienna, even by 1934, specialization had not yet engendered that alienation which in the words of Alasdair MacIntyre splits life into rival and competing spheres, each with its own set of norms and each claiming its own deforming sovereignty.[25] In synthesizing individualism with socialism, Adler exploited the symbiosis of Gemeinschaft and Gesellschaft which lingered in Vienna longer than in perhaps any other metropolis.

Now that this equilibrium has vanished, Adler seems a continuator of the utopian faith that animated Anton Menger. A "little man" imbued with faith in his own vision, Max Adler was one of those Austrian innovators whose insights tell us more about his society than ours. What is trenchant in his works, others have said more cogently, and what no longer convinces seems merely quaint. Such is the verdict that most Marxists—and most sociologists—would pronounce not only on Adler but on the movement that he served.

Part Two

AESTHETICISM AT VIENNA

Ein Mann mit grossen Ideen
  ist ein unbequemer Nachbar.

A man with grand ideas
  is a disquieting neighbor.

—MARIE VON EBNER-ESCHENBACH

7

Phaeacians and Feuilletonists

SOCIABILITY AND SEX
UNDER THE SWAY OF AESTHETICISM

Vienna was more than capital of the Habsburg Empire; it was a state of mind. Two attitudes interacted in the outlook of most Viennese: lighthearted enjoyment of the arts, or aestheticism, and indifference to political and social reform, or therapeutic nihilism. The next four chapters examine how these expectations by the public influenced Vienna's writers, musicians, and painters.

As Schiller put it in a famous *Xenie* of 1797:

> Donau in O . . .
> Mich umwohnet mit glänzendem Aug das Volk der Phaiaken;
> Immer ists Sonntag, es dreht immer am Herd sich der Spiess.

> The Danube in Austria
> Around me lives with gleaming eye the people of the Phaeacians;
> Everyday is Sunday, everyday the spit turns on the hearth.

The German poet popularized the notion that Austrians were modern Phaeacians, who rivaled the people described in Books Five and Six of the *Odyssey* through love of festivity, food, and leisure. The term Phaeacianism *(Phäakentum)* will be employed to designate that preference for merrymaking and make-believe that the Biedermeier enshrined. More narrowly Phaeacianism characterized consumers of art, while aestheticism animated producers of it. Phaeacianism abetted creativity, owing to economic conditions that C. A. Macartney explained:

when money can be acquired with ease in small quantities,
but only with difficulty in large, it attains its highest state of
semi-invisibility. A servant and not a master, it promotes ur-
bane manners and the humanities.[1]

For the upper bourgeoisie, financial security between 1867 and 1914
prompted pursuit of pleasure for its own sake. Among people loath to
make decisions, spectacle and amusement gladdened daily life. Before
the crash of 1873, even the stock market seemed to offer a new form
of stage magic. Phaeacianism invited therapeutic nihilism, as Ringstrasse dandies savored the essays of Schopenhauer. Militantly apolitical, aesthetes extolled the "willless perception" of art as a haven
from strife.[2]

In such a milieu, sociability became an art, flourishing among both
nobility and bourgeoisie. Under the guise of *Gemütlichkeit*, the Viennese cultivated ability to put people at ease by evincing pleasure in
enjoyment of others. Polite concern for the well-being of others fostered
a mood of merriment which Arthur Koestler has described:

> [The nouveaux riches of the 1920's possessed] . . . the unique
> Viennese art of being not only rich but actually enjoying it.
> They had the courteous gaiety and amused self-mockery and
> warm malice and flickering erotic spark [of prewar Vienna].[3]

This gaiety required incessant playacting. Everyone from porter and
streetcar conductor to count and emperor delighted in impersonation
and witty repartee, turning each social transaction into a smoothly
played scene. Although foreigners sometimes belittled Viennese polite-
ness as pretense, participants understood that no scene, however well
acted, could produce lasting results. Instead of seeking changes, skill in
acting relieved frustration by aestheticizing it. Amiability channeled
into dramatics involved no downright lying; rather as Hanns Sachs
said, there prevailed "a general insincerity with comparatively little
hypocrisy."[4]

In a society where appearances counted so heavily, it was imperative for aspiring bourgeois to make the correct impression. Martin
Freud has described how more importance was ascribed to how im-
peccably a doctor dressed than to how well he practiced his craft.[5] A
physician was expected to drive a pair-drawn fiacre rather than the
one-horse *Einspänner*. If a doctor entered with less than the required
pomp, patients would feel their vanity so wounded that he could not
hope to cure them. Conspicuous consumption also governed the prac

tice of tipping. Aristocrats were expected to pay more for every service. If a bourgeois wished to cut a figure above his class, the easiest way was to overtip with *nobel* ostentation. Noting that every person in service demanded a tip, including elevator operators and restaurant cashiers, Karl Kraus quipped that when he arrived in heaven, he expected the angel who opened his coffin to extend a palm.

In families of breeding, strict etiquette regulated visits. It was customary for a doorman to ring once to signify male visitors, twice for ladies, and three times for an archduke or cardinal. In Vienna all houses great and small stood open all day, often with no concierge in attendance. Promptly at 10:00 P.M., however, the front gate would be locked; anyone returning thereafter had to pay the porter *(Hausmeister)* ten kreutzers. In order to avoid the *Sperrkreuzer*, it was customary, except during Fasching, for public functions to end shortly after 9:00 P.M. Thus members of Vienna's best families bowed to the tyranny of their concierges, while the less privileged might haunt streets and cafés until any hour.[6]

Etiquette gradually relaxed as the nineteenth century wore on. To kiss the hand remained a sign of respect that gentlemen paid to ladies, and even today one may say "Küss die Hand" as a greeting. Yet the era was past when the mother of Count Hans Wilczek was so scandalized to see Field Marshall Radetzky kiss the hand of Fanny Elssler at a military parade that she barred her house to him.[7] By 1900 married women were smoking freely, although usually only at home. In 1885 it was considered bad form *(mauvais genre)* for girls to smoke cigarettes; by 1905 they were smoking cigars in public.

Indeed, Vienna became renowned for its glamorous and—thanks to descriptions by Schnitzler and Freud—neurotic women. Attitudes toward sex reflected the duplicity natural in a society that reverences tradition. While daughters fumbled in sexual ignorance, fathers urged sons to initiate themselves with some süsses Mädel, a custom that Nestroy satirized in *Das Mädl aus der Vorstadt* (Vienna, 1845). Girls of good family were so sheltered that they seldom left the house without a chaperon *(Promeneuse)*, who in wealthy families would be a French or English lady hired to converse in those languages. Puzzled by sexuality, girls gushed with curiosity and yearning; they would blush when greeted by a man. In *Das Konzert* (Berlin, 1909), Hermann Bahr portrayed skittish girls who indulged a crush on their music teacher, overwhelmed by curiosity about something called love. They released libido in the only way their station in life permitted. On a dance floor, young ladies in hoffähig circles huddled like deer, dressed exclusively in white. Because an unmarried woman of thirty labored under the same rules as a girl of fifteen, an old maid of good family might take refuge as a nun or else join a secular order. As a *Stiftsfrau* she bore the title Frau instead of Fräulein, while remaining free to marry.

Young men enjoyed far greater freedom. They were encouraged to grow a beard and even to frequent the demimonde, although its existence was ignored in polite society just as, in the words of Zweig, sewers remain hidden from pedestrians. Some fathers would have the family physician warn a son about venereal disease, while others would hire a comely Czech maid to initiate their son without his resorting to a "raffinierte Person."[8] When a little older, a young man would seek a liaison with a süsses Mädel, who might be a shopgirl, typist, washerwoman, or dressmaker's employee. As described in Schnitzler's *Anatol* (Berlin, 1893), she would be flirtatious but well behaved, loving for love's sake without hope of permanent attachment.[9] It was not uncommon for a gentleman to pursue a pretty woman on the street in the ritual known as *Nachsteigen*. Martin Freud recounted an incident that illustrates the cult of the süsses Mädel. One morning during his year of military service, he informed his landlady that he expected a lady to visit him that afternoon. Before he could explain that he wished to have coffee served, the landlady offered, "Very well, Mr. One-Year-Volunteer, I shall change the bed-sheets and pillow."[10]

However much women may have suffered from deficient education about sex, prudery did not prevent them from becoming arbiters of taste. At least as conspicuously as Paris during the eighteenth century, Vienna during the nineteenth feminized culture. Lou Andreas-Salomé remarked that Viennese intellectuals gained geniality by constantly consorting with women; comforted by süsse Mädel, writers in Vienna displayed less pettiness toward one another than did literati of Paris or Berlin.[11] Salons organized by women inspired musicians, painters, and writers to their best efforts. Women lionized favorites, making Makart the most idolized painter of the century. Saar, Wolf, Mahler, and Klimt were but a few of the creators who owed their perseverance to protection by society women. The flowing curves preferred by artists of the Viennese Secession and by Josef Hoffmann's Wiener Werkstätte catered to feminine taste while flattering women's figures. Even traits of Viennese impressionism—changeability, passivity, fascination with latent meanings—are qualities that men have traditionally identified with women.

In its attitude toward women and sex, Vienna combined extremes. While some fathers were introducing their daughters into lives of prostitution—witness the case of Mizzi Veith in 1907—most girls lan-

guished from sexual repression.[12] The preoccupation of Freud, Schnitzler, and Weininger with sexuality arose in a society of libertine men
and repressed women, where hand-kissing chivalry veiled male indulgence. For most men and for a few emancipated women, sex offered
another outlet for aesthetic dalliance.

CONVERSATION TRIUMPHANT IN COFFEEHOUSE
AND FEUILLETON

Throughout the Habsburg Empire, the coffeehouse flourished as a
cultural institution, a kind of public salon where men and women of
all classes gathered to read, brood, or converse. Although citizens of
Budapest and Prague frequented the coffeehouse no less than the
people of Vienna, it was the Imperial City that made the institution
famous.[13] It came to epitomize the aestheticism of Young Vienna,
whose writers gathered first at the Café Griensteidl and then at the
Central. So dependent were Schnitzler, Bahr, Altenberg, Hofmannsthal,
Brahms, Wolf, Hanslick, and numerous others on daily encounters, that
when the Griensteidl was demolished in 1897 Kraus wrote caustically
in Die demolierte Literatur (Vienna, 1897) that the school of Hermann
Bahr would soon expire for lack of a foyer.[14] Instead literati repaired
to the Café Central, while during the 1920's they preferred the Herren-
hof.

Intellectuals of Young Vienna came mostly from nouveau riche
families. For them aestheticism meant above all escaping idleness
through conversation, dilettantism, and occasional writing. Dabbling at
art made time pass agreeably without exacting any commitment to
larger issues. In Der Weg ins Freie, Schnitzler portrayed a group of
aesthetes, surrounding the musician Georg von Wergenthin, who
exudes coffeehouse nonchalance. Living for the moment, he is correct
and charming, yet totally self-centered and indecisive, forever pro-
crastinating and squandering opportunities, like a masculine süsses
Mädel. Wergenthin and his companions typify the impracticality of
Young Vienna; in hundreds of coffeehouses, intellectuals would converse for hours without seeking to alter reality. Their whims were
embodied by a girl in Prague who recited pages from Kierkegaard in
hopes of winning an admirer.[15] It was to such idlers that Count Berchtold referred when warned in 1914 that war with Russia might provoke revolution there. "Who is supposed to make that revolution?" he
asked. "Herr Trotsky in the Café Central?"

Hermann Bahr (1863–1934), a Catholic born in Linz, was the

Bahr as
catalyst

weathervane of coffeehouse intellectuals.[16] Having journeyed through France and Spain, he returned to Vienna in 1889 bearing the gospel of French symbolism. As dramatist and critic, Bahr showed an uncanny flair for assimilating and advocating every new current. A quintessential impressionist, he displayed exceptional powers of appreciation and a capacity to highlight the work of others. Ever hungry for something new, he typified the gossip of coffeehouses, anticipating like a seismograph the next turn in public taste. He ran the gamut from symbolism to the Secession, expressionism, neo-baroque, and Austrian patriotism. His reviews of drama and of painters glorified the artist rather than the work, while juxtaposing innumerable antitheses. Frequently chided for a lability that precluded moral integrity, Bahr was one of those Viennese who, in the phrase of Kürnberger, could not say no.

A second writer even more addicted to the coffeehouse was Peter Altenberg (1859–1919), a Jew born in Vienna as Richard Engländer. One day in 1893, his writing was discovered by Schnitzler and his companions at the Café Central.[17] Kraus staunchly defended Altenberg's sketches of Viennese life, which epitomize impressionism. Vignettes of rootless persons in cafés illustrate the symbiosis of impressionism with a metropolis. Encounters are fleeting; life consists of glimpses and of conversations overheard; experience occurs *in mediis rebus,* where nothing is undertaken and nothing completed. Altenberg's fragments reflected his existence as a *clochard* or *Schnorrer,* the eternal Bohemian who spent each day strolling from one café to another. Like Joseph Roth he was always drunk and was known to every policeman as a harmless devotee of *carpe diem.* Eschewing the Satanism of Paris fin de siècle, Altenberg distilled the benevolent aestheticism of Vienna in hymns to the passing scene.

The coffeehouse afforded much besides conversation. Most persons relied upon their café to furnish daily papers, which could be bought only at widely scattered kiosks. For some *Stammgäste,* the coffeehouse provided a place to receive mail and laundry or to change clothes. Games of cards and chess abounded. It was customary to hold election campaign meetings at a café or restaurant, where the voters could eat and drink before listening to the candidate. It was at such meetings that Lueger sparkled. Many a book was written in a café; at student haunts, the headwaiter could direct clientele to tables where a given specialty was being discussed.

Corresponding to the cameraderie of the coffeehouse was the literary genre known as the Viennese feuilleton. The term had been introduced at Paris about 1800 by drama critic Julien-Louis Geoffroy (1743–1814) to denote the detachable lower portion of a newspaper's front page. Whereas in Germany articles *unter dem Strich* usually concerned culture rather than politics, at Vienna, the feuilleton developed into a chatty essay on any topic, written to match the verve and sparkle of conversation. As sprightly and evanescent as coffee-house banter, after 1848 the feuilleton furnished a model of wit and good taste, catering to a demand both for novelty and nostalgia.[18] One feuilletonist has described the genre as the art of writing something out of nothing, a skill that can be neither described nor defined without producing a feuilleton.

A precursor of the Ringstrasse feuilletonist was the gentle Budapest-born Jew Moritz Saphir (1795–1858), who from 1838 to 1858 edited the *Humorist* in Vienna. His sketches of Biedermeier manners exude mock pathos, not unlike that of the Berlin humorist Adolf Glassbrenner (1810–1876). After 1848 the humorous fragment emphasized local color as in the genre pictures of Vienna-born Friedrich Schlögl (1821–1892) and of the Swabian Ludwig Speidel (1830–1906). A mordant variation came from Vienna-born Ferdinand Kürnberger (1821–1879), who like Kraus castigated the mores and sloppy language of his contemporaries.[19] In travelogues and genre scenes from Viennese life, these writers expressed nostalgia for pre-1848 Vienna. Another master of the form was the Viennese Jew Daniel Spitzer (1835–1893), who from 1865 to 1891 wrote his "Wiener Spaziergänge" for the *Neue Freie Presse*, recording the foibles and spoliation of the city.[20] Two other Viennese, who wrote for the *Neues Wiener Tagblatt*, Vinzenz Chiavacci (1847–1916) and Eduard Pötzl (1851–1914), renewed Nestroy's use of dialect and sarcasm.[21]

Many scholars deprecate the feuilleton as a symptom of decadence, ascribing its popularity to what Hermann Broch called the "vacuum of values." Claudio Magris contends that the writing of fragments paralyzed the will and fomented dilettantism. A more sympathetic judgment would emphasize the role of improvisation in the composition of feuilletons. The genre renewed Biedermeier delight in penning occasional verse and in improvising music. Because the feuilleton required impromptu writing, it allowed Hungarians to exploit their skill at extemporizing. The success of Budapest-born writers like Saphir, Herzl, Nordau, and Salten represented a flowering of Hungarian improvisation in the German-speaking world.

The feuilleton provided a natural medium for Viennese impressionism. Many of the innovations that Arthur Schnitzler (1862–1931) brought to the novella resemble techniques of the feuilleton. His interior monologues, narrated in the third person in *Ein Abschied* (1895) and in the first person in *Leutnant Gustl*, can be read as spoken feuilletons, in which the protagonist muses on his past the way Spitzer or Speidel reflect on that of Vienna. Immersed in a conflict between past and present, Schnitzler's characters revive slumbering memories so as to illuminate some dilemma. Both Schnitzler's interior monologues and the feuilleton presupposed remembering by free association. Both called for a genteel conversation held before an indulgent audience, in Schnitzler's case an audience of one. When Freud wrote in 1896 that neurotics grow sick on reminiscences, he could have been describing both Schnitzler's characters and the Viennese feuilleton.

The harshest critic of the feuilleton was Kraus, who saw it as the apotheosis of Schlamperei in writing. Arguing that the subjectivism of feuilletons had infected the entire press, Kraus indicted journalists for hastening the decline of the bourgeois world. Either they could choose to cultivate the language of Goethe, Jean Paul, and Nestroy, or they would drown in a feuilletonistic sea of half poetry and half lies. Before he began publishing *Die Fackel* in 1899, Kraus spurned an offer to succeed Spitzer as feuilleton editor of the *Neue Freie Presse*, a position that went to Herzl, who used it to aid friends such as Schnitzler and Zweig. In the essay, "Heine und die Folgen" (Vienna, 1910), Kraus singled out Heine as founder of the unholy style— breezy, superficial, and popular—which had driven out classic style.[22] Paradoxically, Kraus revered the writing of Jean Paul, who was in many ways the first feuilletonist. As we shall see, Kraus's philosophy of language emerged as a critique of the feuilleton, which he believed travestied the identity between language and ethics.

"Herodotus was the feuilletonist of antiquity—was he also bourgeois?" So begins a defense of the feuilleton which Joseph Roth published in July, 1921, to refute the charge that it was an indolent genre for women and children.[23] As if rebuking Kraus, Roth applauded Heine's descriptions of Paris as more ethical than a boring tome of statistics which a pedant might have written. As devil's advocate, Roth indulged in outrageous puns and exaggerations, parodying the style that ostensibly he was defending. Through his virtuosity he exemplified another advantage of the feuilleton; it provided training ground for debaters, allowing conversationalists who enjoyed defending the indefensible to do so in print. As a platform for outrageous opinions, it served to satirize propriety in a society ruled by etiquette.

During the 1920's and 1930's the feuilleton enjoyed a renaissance. In *Das grosse Bestiarium der Literatur* (Munich, 1920; 2d ed., Berlin, 1924) Vienna-born Franz Blei classified German men of letters as bizarre species of birds and animals. A Kafka was a rarely seen moonblue mouse, a Hofmannsthal was a gazelle-like, slender-legged creature bred of D'Annunzio and Swinburne, while Schnitzler was a racehorse beloved by women for his melancholy fire. At Munich, Roda

Roda, in reality a Hungarian-born cavalry officer named Friedrich
Rosenfeld (1872–1945), published in *Simplicissimus* such comic masterpieces as the story of a polar bear at Schönbrunn zoo who became
an official of Franz Joseph's court.[24] Another practitioner was the
Budapest-born Jew Felix Salten (1869–1945), born Siegmund Salz-
mann, who achieved worldwide renown for his empathy with forest
animals in *Bambi: Eine Lebensgeschichte aus dem Walde* (Berlin,
1923).

The most ambitious of late feuilletonists was a Vienna-born Jew,
Egon Friedell (1878–1938), born Egon Friedmann, who shone both as
an actor and as a writer.[25] Having dedicated to Kuno Fischer a doctoral
dissertation in 1904 on Novalis' universal science, eight years later
Friedell published a lengthy feuilleton about his friend Peter Altenberg. *Ecce Poeta* (Berlin, 1912) portrayed the Viennese fragmentist as
a walking kaleidoscope of world views. Like Altenberg, Friedell himself personified Viennese impressionism. Having translated Carlyle's *On
Heroes, Hero Worship and the Heroic in History* in 1914, Friedell
saluted the Scotsman's notion that heroes are people who master
everyday reality dutifully and without fanfare. The cabaret performer
continued to dabble at every field of knowledge before beginning
secretly to write his three-volume *Kulturgeschichte der Neuzeit:
Die Krisis der europäischen Seele von der schwarzen Pest bis zum
ersten Weltkrieg* (Munich, 1927–1931; repr. 1965), which he dedicated to Max Reinhardt. Inspired by H. G. Wells' *Outline of History*
(1920), the aesthete-scholar produced a gigantic feuilleton, full of
striking chapter titles, memorable anecdotes, and exotic cross-refer-
ences. As befits a feuilleton, the work reeks of prejudice: the baptized
Jew assailed Freud and preferred France to Germany. In order to
discredit the Jewish doctrine of Providence, Friedell exalted Plato
and Gnostics like Marcion in an unfinished work, *Kulturgeschichte
des Altertums: Leben und Legende der vorchristlichen Seele* (Zürich
and London, 1936–1949). Deploring mechanization, this admirer of
Hans Christian Andersen contended that industrialism had debased
reality, causing art to commit suicide. Manifesting rare capacity for
concentration, Friedell cultivated the ideal of the universal man.
Convinced that history yields whatever meaning an artist may impute
to it, he scattered insights appropriate to a survey course in intellectual
history. Witty and original, sometimes frivolous but more often profound, his aperçus offer an unending source of provocative error.[26]

However much critics may belittle popularization, masters of the
feuilleton like Friedell have demonstrated its strengths more than its
weaknesses. The feuilleton enchanted several generations of cultured
men and women, who had ample leisure, did not demand practical

proposals, and savored improvisation. In Vienna the feuilleton appealed to the same impulses as the operetta and the coffeehouse, bridging classes and differences of opinion by providing music in words to lull a people who feared moral issues. Because the feuilleton embodied Phaeacianism, it outraged zealots like Karl Kraus, while furnishing a source of innovation for impressionists like Schnitzler. Together the coffeehouse and the feuilleton supplied an atmosphere that conduced to innovations in thought. Although Freud claimed to detest the din of coffeehouses, it was in a café at Bellevue overlooking Vienna that on July 24, 1895, he first analyzed one of his own dreams as wish-fulfillment.[27] Although Freud, like Kraus, transcended the mores of his environment, he could not have exerted such wide influence if he had not found disciples with a gift for popularizing. The Vienna that Freud deplored furnished him followers like Fritz Wittels and Theodor Reik whose feuilletons disseminated Freud's message to a different audience than he would have reached on his own.

HATE-LOVE BETWEEN ARTISTS AND PUBLIC

Saturated in the arts, the Viennese public forced artists to vie for its favor. Audiences were so *au courant* of theater and opera that composers and writers felt intimidated by the attention showered on a lucky few. This patronage fomented hate-love for the city in men as different as Beethoven and Karl Kraus, whose anxiety was expressed with rueful insight by Grillparzer in his poem "Abschied von Wien (am 27. August 1847)":

> Schön bist du, doch gefährlich auch.
> Dem Schüler wie dem Meister,
> Entnervend weht dein Sommerhauch,
> Du Capua der Geister.
>
> .   .   .   .
>
> Weithin Musik, wie wenn im Baum
> Der Vögel Chor erwachte,
> Man spricht nicht, denkt wohl etwa kaum
> Und fühlt das Halbgedachte.
>
> .   .   .   .
>
> Doch weil, von so viel Schönheit voll,
> Wir nur zu atmen brauchen,
> Vergisst man, was zum Herzen quoll,
> Auch wieder auszuhauchen.

Farewell From Vienna (on August 27, 1847)

Beautiful art thou; but dangerous too,
To the pupil as the master,
Enervating wafts thy summer breeze
Thou Capua of minds.
. . . .
Everywhere music, as if a choir of birds
Had awakened in a tree.
One does not speak, he scarcely thinks,
And feels what has been half-thought.
. . . .
Yet because filled with so much beauty
We merely have to breathe,
One forgets to exhale
What has poured into the heart.

The institution that epitomized intimacy between artist and audience
was the Burgtheater, which Maria Theresa had founded in 1741. Promoted by Josef von Sonnenfels, it offered the most sophisticated performances in a city where everyone enjoyed acting out his libido and
aggressions.[28] Each actor and singer was known to everyone and expected to have his autograph solicited on the street. In theaters,
claques abounded, as dramatized in Schnitzler's novella Der Ehrentag
(1897). Students congregated in the so-called fourth gallery, showering
their favorites with applause and roses. When the old Hofburgtheater
closed down after a performance of Goethe's Iphigenie auf Tauris on
October 12, 1888, the audience ripped splinters from its stage, exhibiting them proudly for decades.[29] At the death of a renowned actor the
city went into mourning; his loss was bemoaned even by those who
had never seen him perform. Performers like Adolf von Sonnenthal
(1834–1909), Alexander Girardi (1850–1918), and Josef Kainz (1858–
1910) vied with Lueger for popularity. The repertoire of each theater
provided a prime topic in every salon, and any new author who had a
play accepted at the Burgtheater was lionized. Although the public
might feel indifferent to politics and nonchalant about morals, it demanded the utmost from each actor and musician, exercising a surveillance that guaranteed attention to detail. The Burgtheater also furnished a school of good manners, where young people might observe
how to behave in a salon.[30] As if to underline its veneration of art, since
1778 the Burgtheater has disdained curtain calls. At the opera, as at
other theaters, bedlam broke loose at the stage door after every per-

formance, the highest honor coming when fans would unhitch horses to delay a star's departure.

Although this art-steeped public prided itself on being the most fastidious in the world, its smugness unnerved some of the artists who wrote for it. Schnitzler analyzed this hate-love for Vienna in *Der Weg ins Freie* where Heinrich Bermann, an aspiring Jewish dramatist, cannot live with and cannot live without this tormenting city. Similar exasperation was voiced by Hermann Bahr in 1905:

> I often say to myself, I say to myself daily:
> No, one can no longer live in Vienna. Away! Here there are not a dozen men who perceive half-way in a European manner. And behind them is just nothing, chaos. But then Klimt paints a new picture, Roller does *Tristan* or *Fidelio* in a novel way, Mahler conducts, Mildenburg sings. And then I say to myself: Yet nowhere else could I live as in Vienna, really live the life I wish.[31]

True to his theater mania, in 1909 the volatile Bahr married the singer Anna Mildenburg whom he had mentioned as one of the redeeming features of the city.

An additional burden for Viennese writers was the local dialect; they were obliged to speak one language with tradesmen and another in salons. Josef Weinheber (1892–1945), a formalist poet from the lower middle class, complained that he was forced to think in two languages, Viennese and High German. He observed that Nestroy's highest achievement had been to

> confront Viennese with the High German which at that time still sounded very foreign and stilted and so seek his comic effects out of a linguistic tension, which is truly a work of genius because it has its roots right in the language.[32]

Similarly Kraus reprobated all vernaculars as vehicles of sloppiness. No one agonized so much over the gap between literary German and spoken Viennese as Hofmannsthal who after surmounting his crisis in 1902 endeavored to reproduce living language rather than evoke the esoteric usage of a Stefan George. In 1927 Hofmannsthal lamented concerning the German language:

> we have a very lofty poetic language and very charming and expressive popular dialects. . . . What we lack is the

intermediate language, not too high, not too low, in which social contact between segments of people takes place.[33]

In no German-speaking city was lack of an intermediate speech so salient as in Vienna. The fact that every Viennese writer spoke the local patois invited idiosyncrasies of usage. Frequent diminutives and the substitution of "I should like" *(möchte)* for other modal auxiliaries domesticated reality in the way that children do.[34] It was as if each speaker stood on friendly terms with the objects he addressed: he possessed his own little house with a tiny door and a cosy bed. The world itself seemed to dwindle to manageable proportions. By substituting "I should like" for "I would" or "I could," the Viennese stressed the optative mood, coloring every statement with a wish and making every intention an occasion for narcissism. Members of any social class could affect a lower-class accent, so that *Schönbrunnerdeutsch* seemed a refined version of Cockney: in dialogue such as that written by Altenberg or Schnitzler class distinctions vanished. Nothing has so reinforced solidarity within the metropolis as the persistence of Viennese dialect after 1900, preserving particularistic manners in industrial society. Toward foreigners patois represents a defense, while against North Germans it guarantees insularity. Dialect has encouraged the Viennese to regard their city as a privileged stage in the theater of the world, where rituals survive to edify visitors with a Baroque multiplicity.

8

Musicians and Music Critics

WALTZ AND OPERETTA:
FRIVOLITY AS A POLITICAL WEAPON

AFTER 1840 the waltz made Vienna a center of the world's most elegant dance music, just as around 1800 the works of Mozart and Haydn had won the rest of Europe to Viennese symphonic music. Since World War Two, the waltz, together with Austrian pastry, has become identified with a sentimentality that American Yiddish calls schmaltz. Featuring languorous melodies and saccharine lyrics, countless songs of Vienna ooze nostalgia for some bygone spot or event. Epitomizing this mood of daydreaming is the most famous of these songs, "Wien, Du Stadt meiner Träume," written and composed in 1913 by a Viennese feuilletonist and bureaucrat, Rudolf Sieczynski (1879–1952). Possessing ancestors who included Poles, Italians, French, and Germans, he personified the varied provenance of Viennese manners and music alike.

The waltz celebrated much more than nostalgia. It had evolved from the village *Ländler*, which in turn had derived from yodeling; this consists of singing an arpeggio on the dominant chord.[1] In the hands of Josef Lanner (1801–1843) and Johann Strauss senior (1804–1849) the tempo became livelier than the slow circle-dance of the Ländler, in which pronounced pauses marked the dancers' halt. The waltz filled these pauses with whirling movements, creating a hymn to motion which has been damned as well as praised. Silesian-born Heinrich Laube (1806–1884), who later directed the Burgtheater from 1849 to 1867, expressed shock in 1833 at the melodies of Johann Strauss the elder:

> African and hot-blooded, crazy with life . . . restless, unbeautiful, passionate . . . he . . . exorcises the wicked devils from our bodies. . . . typically African too is the way he conducts

his dances; his own limbs no longer belong to him when the
thunderstorm of his waltz is let loose . . . he is a man who
could do a great deal of harm if he were to fiddle Rousseau
ideas; in one single night, the Viennese went with him
through the entire *Contrat Social*.[2]

In actuality, far from fomenting revolution, the waltz may have helped
to forestall it, lulling the Viennese while Strauss's musicians fiddled.
Beloved equally at the Hofburg and at the lowliest public hall, the
dance appeared anything but erotic because whirling couples had to
lean away from each other in order to keep balance. There was something intoxicating, nevertheless, about whirling uninterrupted for minutes on end, often in the arms of a stranger. As Ferdinand von Saar
described in *Marianne* (1874), a waltz could melt years of repression,
fanning flirtation into passion. Through rapid motion, this dance seemed to make time stop, symbolizing a preference for vivacity amid suspended animation.

After 1850, the dancing public craved fresh melodies to enliven
their innumerable balls, especially during the pre-Lent season. No one
fulfilled this desire so well as the "Waltz-King" Johann Strauss junior
(1825–1899), whose life mirrored the Phaeacian Vienna he loved.[3]
Thrice married, given to attacks of depression and transports of creative frenzy, Strauss displayed his eccentricities. More than anything
else he dreaded losing a melody before he could write it down; one
tune that he had jotted onto a bedsheet was lost in the laundry.[4] Like
Freud, he dreaded traveling by train, and he used to work late at
night, pausing to pen endearments to his wife.

Johann Strauss the younger perfected the orchestral waltz, elevating
a small form into a decorative masterpiece. Evincing improvisatory
genius reminiscent of the feuilleton, Strauss turned after 1870 to operetta, which he modeled on the *opéra comique* of the German-born
Jew Jacques Offenbach. In 1856 Nestroy had pirated the first of sixty-
five Offenbach operettas to be presented at Vienna. Strauss's *Die
Fledermaus* (1874), adapted from a play *Doktor Vespe* (1843) written by Leipzig-born Roderich Bendix (1811–1873), created a new
genre that flattered the sensibilities of Ringstrasse Vienna. The libretto
by Max Steiner portrayed aristocrats, businessmen, and servants min-
gling in an atmosphere of levity calculated to mask the disappoint-
ments of the liberal era. Besides reconciling class divisions, the operetta satirized bureaucracy for its good-hearted Schlamperei. Above all,
the operetta exuded narcissistic love for Vienna, using dialect and
Hungarian accents to display a wealth of social types. Although ill-

received at first, *Die Fledermaus* quickly caught on, following as it did the catastrophes of 1873, during which the World Exposition had been blighted by a stock market crash and a cholera epidemic. After a visit to Hungary in 1882, Strauss strove to promote reconciliation between Magyar and German in the *Zigeunerbaron* (1885), which he based on a novella by Jókai.

Although Strauss is remembered as the grand master of Viennese operetta, mediocre librettists caused him to produce far more failures than successes. Such light operas as Friedrich von Flotow's *Marta* (1847) and Franz von Suppé's *Die schöne Galathee* (1865) preceded Strauss. After 1880, smash successes were scored in Vienna by *Der Bettelstudent* (1882), in which Vienna-born Karl Millöcker (1842–1899) spoofed Polish conspirators; by the Tirolean *Vogelhändler* (1891) of Karl Zeller (1842–1898); and by the comic *Der Opernball* (1898) of Richard Heuberger (1850–1914). Hungarian-born Franz Lehár (1870–1948) was fortunate to enlist Heuberger's librettist, Viktor Léon (1858–1940), to collaborate on the world-renowned spoof of Balkan politics, *Die lustige Witwe* (1905). After 1920, Viennese-style operetta was made popular in the United States by the compositions of Hungarian-born Sigmund Romberg (1887–1951) and Prague-born Rudolf Friml (1879–). Although today such works seem contrived, they resound with melodies and sentiments worthy of pre-1914 Vienna, albeit lacking the local color of Strauss or Lehár. Just as operetta catered to the style-democracy of Ringstrasse Vienna, plays like those by Ferenc Molnár and Hermann Bahr flattered a society that wanted to believe—at least on stage—in harmony between the classes. Comparable to operettas without music, Molnár's *Liliom* (1909) or Bahr's *Das Konzert* (1909) presented an idyll of class solidarity which Hungarian-born Ödön von Horváth (1901–1938) shattered in caustic plays like *Geschichten aus dem Wiener Wald* (1931).

Up to and even after 1918, the world of frivolity portrayed in operetta achieved reality during the pre-Lent Fasching season.[5] As many as fifty balls would occur during a single evening, reaching their climax between one and five A.M. At most of them, a man might dance with any of the ladies, signifying his wish by presenting her with a rose. Often she would be masked, and during a dance conversation was taboo. By going to several balls in one evening, a boulevardier could waltz with countless partners from good society, all of whom would cut him dead the next day. While some balls were organized by aristocrats like Pauline Metternich to promote charity or art, the lower middle class sponsored its own affairs, which were thronged by gallants in search of a süsses Mädel. In the suburbs, buxom washerwomen staged Fasching balls, which swarmed with officers and aristocrats. Year-round dalliance flourished at the Wurstel-Prater, where any evening a liaison could be had for the asking. Expanded during the World Exposition of 1873, the Prater grew to boast such marvels as the giant Ferris wheel, erected in 1897, and the largest roller coaster in Europe, opened in 1909. It was as though the Viennese wished to confine technological advance to an amusement park.[6]

Masked balls fostered a spirit of evanescence, in which any stranger could dance with ladies of society provided he demanded no tie more permanent. By enacting the unity of classes which the operetta celebrated, such balls helped to keep the Viennese young and buoyant. During the rest of the year, most festivities remained private, consisting often of dinner at home. Friday was the evening of elegance, when gala performances at the theater allowed everyone to show off manners and dress. Except during Fasching, tourists found Vienna dull because conviviality blossomed in private rather than at nightclubs.

After 1890, sporting events began to vie with theater and dancing as pastimes of the lower middle class. Since then, Sunday afternoon soccer matches have been wildly supported, supplying since 1920 an outlet for energies that had flowed into May Day on the Prater. After 1890 the bicycle enabled young people to take excursions in the country, just as skiing began to attract the hardy. Although skiing did not become a mass sport until after 1945, its basic techniques were perfected in Austria by Moravian-born Matthias Zdarsky (1856–1940), who invented the slalom in 1905, and by Arlberg-born Hannes Schneider (1890–1955), who popularized the stem-christy after 1920. Both men adapted rudiments that Norwegians had introduced about 1870.

Through sports, dancing, theater, and concert-going, the Viennese cultivated a conviviality that fostered nostalgia for Gemeinschaft society. Aestheticism healed what politics abraded, uniting Jew and gentile, cabby and lord, beggar and emperor in common veneration for the arts. What Broch called the style-democracy of Vienna shone forth with special splendor during the May Days at the Prater. There on the Hauptallee of the Nobel Prater, aristocrats, actors, politicians, and businessmen drove between rows of cheering citizens. As late as 1910 the poor and the unemployed vied to behold their idols, participating in a popular festival like that which Wagner staged in Act Three of *Die Meistersinger*. Those who wonder why Vienna did not explode under racial and bureaucratic tensions should ponder this spectacle of all classes joining to celebrate ties that bound them. In an annual outpouring, arts sustained politics in a way that Wagner could only dream. Although eventually aestheticism undermined Vienna's will to survive, for decades love of art curbed strife while heightening city pride. After an evening at the theater or May Day in the Prater, a Viennese might with equanimity regard his city as the pivot of the universe. Where else did appearance so beguilingly sweeten reality?

EDUARD HANSLICK: A FORMALIST AESTHETIC FROM AN ARBITER OF MUSICAL TASTE

Vienna's favorite entertainment was undoubtedly music. In homes music-making was so popular that a law forbade playing an instrument after 11:00 P.M. Many families staged musicales on Sunday afternoon inviting young musicians to perform. These circles preferred Brahms to Wagner, because chamber music suited the intimate atmosphere Aristocratic families deemed it a matter of course to assist young musicians. The Galician Jew Arthur Schnabel (1882–1951) studied piano at Vienna from 1891 to 1898 under three renowned teachers, one of whom was Paderewski's master Theodor Leschetizky (1830–1915). For eight years Schnabel's expenses were paid by three aristocratic benefactors, who never met either the boy or his family; they preferred to deliver a monthly allowance through a lawyer.[7] Although Schnabel attended school for only a few months, authorities never objected.

Piano repertoire favored florid bravura pieces: Mozart's concertos remained almost unknown and Beethoven's concertos were considered too easy for a virtuoso. The quality of orchestral playing reached extraordinary heights. The Vienna Opera House employed a double set of instrumentalists, numbering almost two hundred. Because they were not overworked, these musicians were able to fulfill the demanding expectations of their public. Since 1842 ten times a year on Sunday at noon, instrumentalists of the opera offered a subscription concert under the name of the Wiener Philharmoniker. Rehearsed to perfection by Hungarian-born Hans Richter and his successor Gustav Mahler, members of the philharmonic, many of whom were renowned quartet players, were greeted by strangers on the street as if they were soloists.

From 1860 to about 1900 the most feared personage in the musical life of Vienna was Eduard Hanslick (1825–1904). Today he is remembered above all for having belittled Wagner, Bruckner, and Hugo Wolf.[8] Hanslick built his prestige on feuilletons that appeared in the *Neue Freie Presse*, two to five days after the concerts in question Hanslick had been born in Prague of a Czech father and a Jewish mother, his father having used lottery winnings in order to marry one of his music pupils. Eduard studied law and music at Vienna, earning a doctorate in law in 1849, a year after he had begun publishing music criticism. From 1855 to 1904 he published biweekly articles in the *Neue Freie Presse.* In 1855 he was appointed docent in music and in 1861 professor of the aesthetics and history of music at the University of Vienna. Using a piano that he had installed in the classroom, for forty years Hanslick discoursed on fundamentals of musical taste in what was probably the first course anywhere in music appreciation.

Hanslick indulged to the full the tastes and foibles of cultivated Vienna. He dressed like a dandy, took snuff, courted the ladies while telling the latest anecdotes, and delighted in playing Strauss waltzes. Whenever his vanity was piqued, charm turned to sarcasm. Preferring Italian opera and French orchestral music, Hanslick nurtured implacable hostility to Wagner, whom he accused of debasing music. In 1862 the critic attended a gathering at which Wagner read the libretto for *Die Meistersinger:* in that early version the philistine Beckmesser was named Veit Hanslick.

Hanslick's aversion to Wagner derived from a Herbartian aesthetic that the critic had presented in *Vom Musikalisch-Schönens Ein Beitrag zur Revision der Ästhetik der Tonkunst* (Leipzig, 1854). Rejecting every sort of program music, Hanslick postulated that music consists of "sounding forms set into motion" *(tönend bewegte Formen),* whose interrelations engender impressions of beauty. Composers are impelled not by emotion but by an inward singing, which discloses formal relationships inexpressible in any other medium. Tension, such as that generated by Wagner's chromaticism, stems not from any intrinsic emotion like love or grief, but from experiencing the integration and disintegration of musical forms. Hanslick drew the corollary that in a lied the text makes no difference; a performer can interchange texts without harming the music. The critic rejoiced that motivational qualities, such as the Greeks had attributed to the martial Phrygian mode and the erotic Doric, had disappeared for good. Although Hanslick enjoyed the marches and waltzes of the Strauss family, presumably he did so on strictly formalistic grounds.

Because Hanslick's credo emancipates a composer from extramusical scruples, his victims such as Wagner, Bruckner, and Wolf, might have invoked his doctrine to justify their experiments in creating form. As a classicist, Hanslick detested music that stirs emotional depths, elevating serenity above expressiveness.[9] True to the aestheticism of Ringstrasse Vienna, he wanted to enjoy music without being overwhelmed by it. His aesthetic has undergone a renaissance in the work of Suzanne K. Langer, who studied at Vienna during the early 1920's. Endorsing Hanslick's equation between the form of music and its content, she concedes that his rejection of musical onomatopoeia anticipated her view of music as "unconsummated symbol."[10]

With the encouragement of the surgeon Theodor Billroth, Hanslick grew to esteem the music of the North German Johannes Brahms (1833–1897). After he settled at Vienna in 1862, Brahms used to premiere his chamber music in Billroth's apartment. The world-renowned surgeon wrote a treatise on musical aptitude, which Hanslick published posthumously, as *Wer ist musikalisch?* (Leipzig, 1894). Brahms became an eccentric during his later years, appearing in public with an assistant Max Kalbeck, whose multivolume biography of the master wits dubbed "Brahms Stillleben," in allusion to Brehm's *Tierleben.* Hanslick saw in his friend's music a fulfillment of his own Herbartian ideals.

Hanslick's successor at the University of Vienna was a Moravian-born Jew Guido Adler (1855–1941) who revolutionized modern musicology.[11] After taking a doctorate in law at Vienna in 1878, Adler, his admiration for Wagner notwithstanding, was encouraged by Hanslick to study under Bruckner. After earning a habilitation at Vienna, Adler served as a professor of musicology at Prague from 1885 to 1898 and then at Vienna until 1927. There he founded the Vienna School of Music History, which in at least two respects resembled the Vienna School of Art History. First, Adler studied composers in the context of their society, albeit not in relation to other arts. Second, in the manner of connoisseurs such as Wickhoff and Schlosser, Adler coupled performance of music with music history, insisting that a musicologist must know the concert practice of his own day in order to interpret that of the past. In his two-volume *Handbuch der Musikgeschichte* (Frankfurt, 1924; 2d ed., Berlin, 1930), Adler elaborated a periodization of musical styles which still prevails, emphasizing the notion of a common practice period from 1600 to about 1880. However much Adler revered the Viennese classical school of Mozart, Haydn, and Beethoven, he deplored Hanslick's prejudice against moderns, organizing concerts in behalf of his close friends Mahler and Schönberg. Adler elevated the discipline that Hanslick had founded into a seminal school of Viennese scholarship.

FOUR PERSECUTED INNOVATORS:
BRUCKNER, WOLF, MAHLER, SCHÖNBERG

All four of the most inventive Austrian composers active between 1880 and 1938 suffered obloquy from Hanslick. The first of these martyrs, and probably the most idiosyncratic, was Anton Bruckner (1824–1896), a pious peasant from Upper Austria.[12] From 1845 to 1855 he taught organ at St. Florian Monastery, before serving from 1855 to 1866 as organist at the Cathedral of Linz. After meeting Wagner in 1865, he began the first of nine symphonies, which Hanslick disparaged while applauding the composer's mastery of the organ. Bruckner moved to Vienna in 1869 and taught composition in private as well as at the university. As a docent from 1875 to 1892, he astonished students by addressing them as Brothers Gaudeamus, by wearing peasant costume, and by kneeling to pray when he heard the Angelus. After his Seventh Symphony had won world renown following its premiere at Leipzig in 1884, Bruckner found growing approval at Vienna. In 1891 to the consternation of Hanslick, Bruckner became the first composer to receive an honorary doctorate from the University of Vienna; critics routinely had received such degrees. In July, 1895, thanks to protection by the emperor's daughter, Archduchess Valerie, the ailing musician occupied a ground-floor apartment at the Upper Belvedere, where he enjoyed the gardens until his death sixteen months later.

Christian von Ehrenfels, who studied composition under Bruckner from 1880 to 1882, recounted his teacher's naiveté. Once Ehrenfels arrived to find the master reading Schiller's *Wallenstein*. Pacing up and down, he queried the student, "It is really true that Wallenstein wanted to betray the Emperor?"[13] With his unkempt clothes and peasant accent, Bruckner became a laughingstock on the Ringstrasse. In order to infuse unworldliness into music, Bruckner revived the sacred music of the Baroque, recalling the period before Mozart, Haydn, Beethoven, and Schubert had modeled the mass on secular compositions. Exuding simple faith in God and Providence, Bruckner seemed the very opposite of the tormented Mahler, who was so aggrieved by cruelty in God's Creation that he longed for life after death. Hanslick dismissed as Wagnerian Bruckner's effort to compose sacred music, while his adagios bored an aristocracy that preferred Strauss. However keenly Bruckner may have regretted neglect of his symphonies, as an organist he succeeded beyond his dreams. Hailed as the finest virtuoso of his time and feted by the emperor, he has been honored by a plaque at the Church of Maria Treu, which records that when Bruckner passed his Matura in organ-playing on November 19, 1861, one of his examiners declared, *"Er hätte uns prüfen sollen"* (He should have examined us).

A second Catholic composer whom most Viennese ignored was Hugo Wolf (1860–1903).[14] Son of a Slovene mother and a German father, who had a talent for music which never was fulfilled as he had inherited a leather business, Hugo studied at a convent school in Carinthia before enrolling at the Vienna Conservatory in 1875. Around 1880, Wolf so revered Kleist that he carried *Penthesilea* as a breviary in the vain hope of setting it to music. An admirer of Bruckner, Wolf was forced to subsist as a critic, writing for the *Wiener Salonblatt* from 1884 to 1887, where he parodied Hanslick while defending Wagner. Because he had dared to mock Hanslick and Brahms, the press ignored publication in 1888 of fifty-three Mörike songs. Gradually he won a select following, including Hermann Bahr and the feminist Rosa Mayreder, whom he met at the Café Griensteidl. From 1887 love for a married woman, Melanie Köchert, instilled selfless devotion to his art. He earned a meager living by giving music lessons, including among his pupils the children of Freud's colleague Josef Breuer.

Like Bruckner, Wolf was a "little man" persecuted for his talent. A strict Catholic upbringing could not shield him from the heady atmosphere of the Café Griensteidl, whose luminaries he blithely assailed. His benefactress remained Rosa Mayreder, who in 1895 persuaded him to compose a score for her libretto *Der Corregidor*. She has described how fussy the tiny man was. Since even the ticking of a watch could unnerve him, he forbade anyone to enter when he was composing. As a guest in the Mayreder house, he was fascinated to hear Lou Andreas-Salomé reminiscing about Nietzsche, although she in turn proved an unmusical listener. When told that a friend held him dearer as a person than for his music, the composer protested, "My works, my music —for these he must care above all—compared to them my person is entirely secondary."[15] Such was the self-effacement of the man who signed letters to Frau Mayreder, "Your poor little Wolf" (*Dein armer Wölfling*)—an allusion to Siegmund in *Die Walküre*. Having contracted syphilis at age seventeen, Wolf succumbed to paralysis briefly in 1898 and definitively in 1902. One day some friends discovered him declaiming on the steps of the Opera House, shouting that he was its new director awaiting an audience with the emperor. Pretending to oblige him, they escorted the megalomaniac to an insane asylum where he died a few months later. His funeral took place on February 19, 1903; since this happened to be Mardi Gras, his mourners had to penetrate throngs of jesters.

Wolf composed lieder so readily that even his opera *Der Corregidor* resembled a cycle of songs. He favored texts by Spanish and Italian poets whose Catholic stoicism paralleled his own. In contrast with Schubert, Schumann, Loewe, and Brahms, Wolf perfected the declamatory song, which subordinates piano accompaniment to the text. Wolf would abandon himself to a poem, prostrating himself before its meaning. Such subservience resembled the ethos of Hofmannsthal, Schnitzler, and Altenberg who devoted themselves to unfolding impressions of the moment. Like the Protean Bahr, Wolf dissolved his own ego in order to convey the message of someone else's verse. Too empathetic to create a new entity in the manner of Schubert or Schumann, he preferred to accentuate words that already existed; Wolf enhanced each text instead of obscuring it. By joining Biedermeier love of minutiae with impressionistic capacity to deny self, he carried to excess a negative capability such as enabled other Viennese impressionists to formulate an all-embracing world view.

Outwardly more successful while inwardly no less tormented was the Bohemian-born Jew, Gustav Mahler (1860–1911).[16] Son of a distiller near Iglau, Mahler grew up afflicted by tragedy. He was the eldest of twelve children, nine of whom died before reaching maturity. Five of these deaths blighted Gustav's childhood, while one brother committed suicide later. His mother died when Mahler was an adolescent, succumbing to the same heart ailment that would claim his life. An early admirer of Schopenhauer and Nietzsche, he studied composition under Bruckner from 1875 to 1878. During the next twenty years, he conducted at Leipzig, Budapest, and Hamburg, while composing each summer. In 1897 Mahler succeeded Hans Richter as head conductor and music director of the Vienna Court Opera, accepting on condition that no one at court interfere with his stewardship. By then he had converted to Catholicism and was spending summers among aristocrats in the Salzkammergut.

At Vienna, the conductor moved in a circle that included Adolf Loos, Gustav Klimt, and Berta Szeps. It was she who in 1902 introduced him to a comely pianist, Alma Schindler (1879–1964), daughter of the landscape painter Emil Jakob Schindler (1842–1892). Within weeks, the two musicians were married in the Karlskirche, beginning a stormy marriage that launched Alma Mahler-Werfel's career as muse successively to Ossip Gabrilowitsch, Oskar Kokoschka, Walter Gropius, Franz Werfel, and the aged Gerhart Hauptmann. Mahler, unfortunately, could not help remaining extremely puritanical, having adored first his mother and then his sister. The death of the Mahlers' daughter in 1907 agonized the composer, intensifying his fascination with death and his preoccupation with the world to come. As music director of the opera, Mahler terrorized performers with his perfectionism, executing reforms in the spirit of his putative comment, "Tradition is *Schlamperei.*" At the Opera House, Mahler was the first conductor in a century to stand rather than to sit. Together with Arthur Nikisch, he pioneered techniques of expressive conducting, using both hands to shape each phrase. He had lifted performances of the ensemble to an unexcelled level when in 1907 tactlessness forced him to resign. After serving for two years as conductor at the Metropolitan Opera in New York, in 1910 he completed his ninth symphony followed by *Das Lied von der Erde*, which he did not live to hear performed.

Like Gustav Meyrink and Paul Kornfeld, he was a genuine Marcionist who awaited redemption from earthly torment only in a world to come. Mahler portrayed the joys of resurrection in his Fourth and Eighth Symphonies (1901 and 1910). As if to dispute Darwin, he confessed that cruelty in nature bewildered him: he impugned God for having permitted malice. To his protégé Bruno Walter, Mahler confided that he feared people might commit suicide after hearing the finale of *Das Lied von der Erde*. On August 26, 1910, the composer consulted Sigmund Freud while on a visit to Leiden. Freud concluded that Mahler desired his wife to be as infirm as his mother had been. The psychoanalyst noted that Mahler evinced an overwhelming need for order.[17] Mahler also suffered the uneasiness of an uprooted Jew. His widow recalled his lamenting,

> I am thrice homeless. As a native of Bohemia in Austria, as an Austrian among Germans, and as a Jew throughout the whole world. Everywhere an intruder, never welcomed.[18]

Mahler combined qualities of both impressionism and expressionism. Parodies of familiar melodies reveal Mahler's affinity with Jewish ironists who, as Kurt List puts it, "never make a definitely traditional or a grandiose statement without taking it back the next moment."[19] Mahler's musical citations resembled pastiches by his fellow Bohemian Jew Kraus, with whom the composer shared fanatical dedication to work and contempt for Viennese sloppiness. Plagiarism of motifs anticipated a technique that composers for motion pictures have perpetuated. Above all, Mahler incarnated a cult of communion with the dead, which as we shall see prevailed among impressionists of Young Vienna.

Together with Mahler, Arnold Schönberg (1874–1951) is hailed today as one of the decisive innovators of the twentieth century.[20] Born in Vienna of middle-class Jewish parents and raised a Catholic, Schönberg converted to Protestantism in 1902, only to be received back into Judaism in 1935. The young man displayed talent both as a painter and a writer while studying composition under his friend Alexander von Zemlinsky (1872–1942), whose sister he married in 1901. After striving restlessly from 1903 to 1911, Schönberg felt obliged to seek recognition away from Vienna. The reception that the public there accorded Schönberg's early works has become a legend, propagated by those who assert the banality of Viennese taste. One wag quipped that the Viennese greeted Schönberg's music the way ladies at a ball might have derided the misogynist Weininger. In 1900 two Schönberg songs met laughing and hissing. In 1911 the premiere of an atonal orchestral piece incited a riot to which an ambulance had to be sent. In 1912 at a performance of works by Alban Berg, a Schönberg adherent slapped a detractor, unwittingly terminating the concert. During 1908 and 1909 Schönberg submitted to every newspaper in Vienna an open letter defending his music; only his friend Kraus consented to publish it.[21]

Together with two Vienna-born pupils, Anton von Webern (1883–1945) and Alban Berg (1885–1935), Schönberg unleashed a revolution in music. The twelve-tone system, which after many years of experimentation he perfected around 1920, landed him in controversy with an isolated composer Josef Matthias Hauer (1883–1959). The latter has been portrayed in Otto Stoessl's novel, *Sonnenmelodie: Eine Lebensgeschichte* (Stuttgart, 1923). A quintessential "little man," Hauer claimed his "tropos" had been plagiarized in Schönberg's tone row. Unlike his would-be rival, Schönberg abounded in dialectical talent, mastering contrapuntal devices such as the canons and mirror canons of *Pierrot Lunaire* (1912). Tone rows place a composer under limitations similar to those championed by Loos and Kraus, who like their friend heeded an imperious will to form.

In the preface to the *Harmonielehre* (1911), a work dedicated to Kraus, Schönberg praised Maeterlinck, Strindberg, and Weininger as precursors who had sought purity through self-imposed limitations. The aphoristic style of the *Gurrelieder* (1911) bore affinity with the fragments written by Altenberg, Schaukal, and Wittgenstein. In their severity Schönberg's tiny pieces contrast with the monumentality of symphonies by Bruckner and Mahler; even Wolf's lieder seem grandiloquent by comparison. In the visual arts, Schönberg's quest for purity found a counterpart in the crusade of Loos and Schiele to strip away the ornament that camouflaged Ringstrasse buildings and the canvases of Makart and Klimt. Schönberg expounded his penchant for form in a speech of 1913 commemorating Mahler:

> When we have taken the pieces apart, we usually are no longer able to put them back together properly, and we have lost what we had before: the whole with all its details and its soul.[22]

Here the composer espoused what was best in Austrian thought, a passion for grasping things whole.

Rejection of sloppiness and sentimentality goaded this classicist to innovations now universally accepted. In his opera *Moses und Aaron* (1932), Schönberg portrayed how a creative genius Moses found in his worldly brother a deputy who could sway the recalcitrant.[23] Lest we castigate those Viennese who railed in 1910, we should remember that they helped to stimulate Schönberg's inventiveness. By apotheosizing popularizers and mediators, the Viennese cultivated a tradition that spurred Schönberg to defiance. A prophet, if he is to be without honor, must have an audience worthy of his spite. This the Phaeacians of Vienna provided in full measure.

9
Devotees of the Visual Arts

HANS MAKART: CULTURE-HERO
OF A DECORATIVE ERA

Although Austria never produced painters to match her composers, a number of painters became highly successful. Even more unerringly than musicians, artists embodied the taste of Vienna. During the Biedermeier, Friedrich von Amerling (1803–1887) and Ferdinand Waldmüller (1793–1865) had created Ingres-like portraits to fill the desire aroused in Austrian aristocrats by the visit of Thomas Lawrence to the Congress of Vienna. Waldmüller helped to make landscape painting a mode of escape from the industrializing city. Through genre pictures, Joseph Danhauser (1805–1845) contributed to designing the decor of heavy furniture and drapery known as Viennese Biedermeier. Still another representative of this period was the extraordinarily long-lived Rudolf von Alt (1812–1905), who painted the buildings of Vienna in painstaking detail. As an old man he became an unwitting pioneer of pointillism when he resorted to juxtaposing dots because he could no longer make brushstrokes.

The painter who incarnated Viennese aestheticism better perhaps than any other man was Hans Makart (1840–1884).[1] Born in Salzburg the son of an inspector at Mirabell Castle. Makart studied at Munich under the historicizing painter Karl Theodor von Piloty. After four years' apprenticeship in England, France, and Italy, in 1869 Makart accepted a call to Vienna, encouraged by Count Hans Wilczek. The emperor furnished the painter a villa at the Art Foundry *(Kunsterzgiesserei)* located behind the Karlskirche. Replete with tapestries, Venetian glass, plants, and Greek statues, every day aftr 4:00 P.M. the studio opened to the public offering a mecca for dilettantes, tourists, and society ladies. There Makart would advise ladies on their toilette, popularizing the Makart-hat, Makart-collar, and Makart bouquet of dried leaves and fruits.

Between 1869 and 1884 Makart achieved a feat unique in the nineteenth century: as a painter he became the cynosure of a metropolis. Like Johann Strauss, he catered to the Phaeacianism of a public that yearned to forget military defeat and the crash of 1873, as well as the censoriousness of Archduchess Sophie, who had died the year before. Whereas she had required ballet dancers to wear dresses below the knee, Makart invited the public to revel in nudes. Although most of his nudes were posed by professional models, art dealers boasted that some society ladies had consented to model au naturel. The eagerness of a few ladies to flaunt this feat accented the duplicity that in Vienna governed matters of sex.[2] Such rumors titillated a public that applauded salacious works such as Adolf Wilbrandt's drama *Arria und Messalina* (1874) or Robert Hamerling's novel *Aspasia* (1876). One giant canvas by Makart, *Charles V's Entry into Antwerp*, attracted 34,000 visitors during early 1878. His acceptability in good society diminished after his marriage in 1881 to a ballet dancer. Previously he had staged balls for the court and received the French Legion of Honor. In 1884 he died after four days in an asylum, succumbing like Lenau and Nietzsche to paralysis caused by syphilis. Makart received a princely funeral, the most elaborate yet given in Vienna to a non-noble, not again to be equaled until the death of Lueger.

Makart enjoyed greater prestige and wealth than any painter since Rubens, with whom he identified. Emulating Rubens and Veronese, he excelled at tapestry-like canvases designed to embellish spacious halls. At the peak of his career he supervised a pageant to celebrate the twenty-fifth wedding anniversary of Franz Joseph and Elisabeth on April 27, 1879. The Makart Festival Parade *(Festzug)* marked a pinnacle of self-congratulation for Ringstrasse Vienna, abounding in the historical decoration of which the city was so fond. Costumes of the sixteenth century flattered the city's image of itself as home of a new Renaissance. For five hours, up to a million spectators watched a sunlit procession wind along the Ringstrasse. Makart based forty-three groups of tradesmen and artisans on Act Three of *Die Meistersinger* by his friend Richard Wagner. Makart outfitted the painters in seventeenth-century dress, imitating what he had witnessed during the Rubens Tercentenary at Antwerp two years before. Having proven himself during rehearsals a tireless organizer as well as an expert tailor, on the great day Makart paraded in black silk on a white horse, bowing ostentatiously to applause.[3]

By matching in theatricality the city that worshiped him, Makart fulfilled its stereotype of creative genius. Good-looking, taciturn, and incredibly spendthrift, he basked in the attention showered upon him. He gloried in painting before an audience of select guests, and at his studio he kept a contingency fund that friends could use without asking. Makart was above all a decorator: his canvases resembled stage pieces in which spectators could look for well-known faces as they would in the Prater. As if aping architects of the Ringstrasse, he rearranged familiar elements without adding new ones; his style offered a colorful version of Biedermeier passion for historical collecting. Because of careless draftsmanship that admirers ascribed to haste, Makart attracted vitriolic critics. The classicist painter Anselm von Feuerbach (1829–1880), a nephew of Ludwig Feuerbach, ridiculed Makart while serving as a professor at the Vienna Academy of Fine Arts from 1873 to 1876. Berating his rival for lack of training in anatomy, drawing, and coloration, Feuerbach dubbed Makart a tailor, who painted clothes into which no person could fit. In his novella *Der Hellene* (1904), Ferdinand von Saar repeated these strictures, which by then had effaced Makart's merits.

Makart gave his name to the 1870's in Vienna and personified that city's Phaeacianism in both its sunny and sinister aspects. Feted to satiety, he produced paintings so deficient in basic technique that however he may have excelled at reviving the past, he bequeathed little for posterity to admire. Makart's success resembled that of a comet; a worshiper of color, fame, and voluptuous women, he died syphilitic and ignored.

AESTHETICISM CONFRONTS MODERNITY:
KLIMT, SCHIELE, AND KOKOSCHKA

Makart's glory all but eclipsed several more innovative painters, notably Vienna-born Anton Romako (1832–1889).[4] Descended from generations of Czech cabinetmakers named Hromadko, Romako studied at Vienna under Waldmüller and Carl Rahl before going to Italy and Spain, where he came under the influence of Goya's works. He returned to Vienna after his wife had left him, having lived in Rome from 1857 to 1876, only to find that Makart had preempted the major commissions. His isolation was so complete that death from natural causes was rumored to be a suicide. A master of rapid brushwork, Romako eked out a livelihood doing psychological portraits that anticipated those of Kokoschka. His most famous work, *Tegetthoff in der Seeschlacht bei Lissa* (1880), captured the intensity of battle with unprecedented vividness. By combining desire to freeze the momentary with baroque delight in tempestuous movement, he fashioned works more enduring than the color extravaganzas of Makart.

Greater success was enjoyed by Gustav Klimt (1862–1918), who began as a fresco painter in the style of Makart.[5] Born in Baumgarten near Vienna, the son of a goldsmith, Klimt applied his father's trade to creating gold-laden canvases, whose decorative motifs evoke the entire history of art. During the mid-1880's he worked with his brother Ernst on Makart-like murals for theaters at Karlsbad, Fiume, and Budapest, as well as in the Burgtheater at Vienna. Having abandoned architectural painting after the death of his brother in 1892, Klimt submerged for five years, nurturing himself on Whistler, Beardsley, and Munch. In 1897 he reemerged to lead the Viennese Secession, a group of artists who spurned the official painters' association to promote art nouveau—in German it was known as *Jugendstil*. Their gallery erected in 1898 across from the Akademie der bildenden Künste by Josef Maria Olbrich (1867–1908) championed avant-garde painting.

Klimt made more than a few innovations in painting. He was the first modern to employ square canvas, a shape that heightened the hieratic effect of gold backgrounds. His lavish application of gold leaf anticipated the collage, and concurrently with the pointillists, Klimt favored tiny flecks of color to create mosaiclike surfaces. More subtly than Makart, this eclectic could combine in a single canvas hieroglyphs from Egypt, spirals from Mycenae, and floral patterns from Ravenna. By integrating such diverse constituents, the artist seemed to vindicate the thesis of Alois Riegl that decorative motifs enjoy greater longevity than do pictorial devices. Evincing a pronounced will to form, Klimt's later landscapes unfold expanses of carpetlike grass and water devoid of human presence. Even more compelling are portraits of women, whose quizzical faces and sinuous figures anticipated the image of the vamp made popular during the 1920's.

Although his opulent canvases were always popular with women of the upper middle class, Klimt outraged their husbands. Commissioned to paint murals of Philosophy, Medicine, and Jurisprudence for the Aula of the University, he exhibited *Philosophy* during March, 1900, provoking a scandal that attracted 34,000 onlookers in two months. Its emaciated nudes aroused eighty-odd professors to sign a petition demanding that it never be mounted in the university, whereupon Klimt returned his fee while refusing to exhibit the other two murals. Unfortunately, these gigantic masterpieces were destroyed at Immendorf Castle, which the Nazis burned in 1945. Unlike Makart, whose allegorical figures Klimt revived, the younger artist was reviled for nudes that seemed too graphic without historical settings to transfigure them.

Klimt was a supreme aesthete, who as a bachelor enjoyed nude models, without, however, succumbing to Makart's excesses. In adopting linear and floral patterns from art nouveau, Klimt embraced a movement that sought to make life conform to art. His paintings convey the static atmosphere of a daydream, unruffled by any call to action; in erotic canvases he depicted society ladies trifling with sexuality. In contrast with the passionate embraces of Schiele's couples, Klimt's women seem detached, as if harboring the malice of Judith. Resembling the hesitant protagonists in Hofmannsthal's *Der Tor und der Tod* (1893) or Leopold von Andrian-Werburg's *Der Garten der Erkenntnis* (Berlin, 1895), Klimt's figures inhabit a sensual daydream, enwrapped in plants, which shield them from the fecundity of nature. Unable to invest libido in the external world, the nonheroes beloved by Young Vienna wished nature to imitate art. Owing partly to Klimt, art nouveau lingered longer there than elsewhere, because historicizing tradition ostracized French Impressionists. Like Schnitzler, Klimt exposed the erotic depths beneath Viennese Phaeaceanism, using stylistic devices adapted from the arch-Phaeacean Makart, just as Schnitzler borrowed devices from the feuilleton. Born during the same year, these impressionists modified genres beloved by Viennese in order to expose the underside of their compatriots' lives.

A painter even more obsessed by the erotic was Egon Schiele (1890–1918), whom critics, such as Otto Benesch, believe might have become one of the twentieth century's towering artists.[6] Born in Tulln, near Vienna, Schiele was a prodigious draftsman from infancy, sketching on tablecloths the way Strauss composed on bedsheets. Best known for his drawings, Schiele would make dozens of sketches from a model, never using an eraser; he added color later. When Toulouse-Lautrec was first exhibited at Vienna in 1909, his proletarian women fascinated Schiele, who began to portray embracing couples with the ardor of a voyeur. In 1912 he was sentenced to twenty-four days in jail for having made pornographic drawings of schoolgirls; his studio had been raided and one of his sketches burned by the examining judge. Although Klimt protected the prodigy, whom he met in 1907, Schiele's nudes caricatured the society ladies whom the older painter flattered. Contrasted with the hieratic repose of Klimt's figures, Schiele's, in the words of his friend Benesch, breathe "an outward striving, an outpouring into the universe," as well as readiness for sexual surrender.[7]

The young prodigy died of influenza on October 31, 1918, just three days after his wife had succumbed to the disease. Alfred Werner laments that death cut Schiele off just as he was mastering techniques adapted from Klimt, Munch, Toulouse-Lautrec, and van Gogh. Other critics contend that despite mastery of line, his neglect of color would have prevented him from ever outgrowing the crowded space dear to the mannerists Makart and Klimt. Geno Baro dismisses Schiele as less innovative that Klimt, suggesting that the younger man merely exploited the linear conventions of art nouveau to perform a lewd gesture. Schiele won more success than a Vienna-born contemporary, Richard Gerstl (1883–1908), a friend of Schönberg and Berg, who committed suicide after painting a number of garish canvases. The *fauve* Gerstl had tried to combine Edvard Munch and van Gogh in a clash of colors. Solipsistic and prematurely old, both youths made of every canvas a self-portrait. Whereas Gerstl suffered total neglect, Schiele began to sell paintings after 1914, only to have his name fade during the 1920's. Both painters' preoccupation with sexuality reflected the prevaricating morality that tainted the Vienna of Freud and Archduke Otto.

Among the least known of Austrian painters are three pioneers of nonrepresentational painting, all of whom worked abroad. The Czech Frank Kupka (1871–1957) lived in Paris from 1895 to 1957, after working briefly at Vienna. His *Amorpha: Fugue à deux couleurs* (1911–1912) has been called the first totally abstract canvas. It was paralleled by works of Moravian-born Adolf Hölzel (1853–1934), who first studied at Vienna before settling in Stuttgart from 1906 to 1918. Independently of Kandinsky, he created between 1912 and 1914 his *Abstractions I* and *II*. Still more radical was the constructivism of the Hungarian László Moholy-Nagy (1895–1946), who taught at the Bauhaus from 1923 to 1928, anticipating the mobile as well as recent techniques of instruction in visual design. To explain such wealth of innovation, Wladyslaw Tatarkiewiecz suggests that three schools of Austrian philosophy may have helped unwittingly to vindicate abstraction in art.[8] First, Husserl and Meinong taught the autonomy of logical abstractions; second, Ehrenfels through his concept of Gestalt held that forms are more general and permanent than their content; and third, the Vienna Circle segregated facts from hypotheses—the latter can explain but never duplicate facts. Such affinities notwithstanding, scarcely any artists appear to have cultivated contact with philosophers.

One Austrian painter, Oskar Kokoschka (1886–), has won in ample measure the fame denied to his compatriots.[9] Born in Lower Austria where his mother was vacationing, this son of a Czech goldsmith dwelt at Vienna until 1910. In 1909 his introspective portraits created a scandal when they were exhibited together with works by Schiele and van Gogh. In portraits that may have been modeled on Mycenaean masks, Kokoschka modified the quasi-pointillist technique of his teacher Klimt in order to expose duplicity.

As pitilessly as Kraus, to whom Loos introduced Kokoschka, the painter unmasked moral turpitude. In his expressionist play, *Mörder, Hoffnung der Frauen* (1907), set in antiquity and dedicated to Loos, the artist succumbed to therapeutic nihilism. Of this play, which in 1919 Paul Hindemith made into an opera, Kokoschka later declared: "I felt quite intensely and suddenly as if man were stricken with an incurable disease."[10] Kokoschka had to emigrate to receive recognition, after Franz Ferdinand stated in 1911 that the artist deserved to have every bone in his body broken (*"Dem Kerl sollte man die Knochen im Leibe zerbrechen"*). As late as 1918, preference for historical painting prevented Vienna from fostering an avant-garde group like the Brücke in Dresden or Blaue Reiter in Munich. True to Austrian proclivities, Kokoschka's art is, in the view of Alfred Werner, basically theatrical; his sitters, or "victims" as he called them, gesticulate like actors. Using the ferocious brushstrokes of Romako and the florid colors of Prandtauer, Kokoschka flaunted Baroque love of wide spaces that flow together like music.

Because he is so well-known, Kokoschka has reinforced the legend of Austrian decadence. His exposure of corrupt bourgeois, his abject dependence on Alma Mahler-Werfel, and his aversion to modernity are thought by many to epitomize Austrian attitudes. He is, to be sure, an unrepentant therapeutic nihilist, and his double gifts as painter and writer place him in the company of such other Austrians as Schönberg, Stifter, Brücke, and Billroth. His acquiescence in the dry rot of Western civilization contrasts with efforts by numerous reformers and Socialists to salvage something from the wreckage. Aestheticism, which led Kokoschka to despair of civilization, provoked others to demand reform.

RINGSTRASSE ARCHITECTURE AND ITS CRITICS: SITTE, WAGNER, AND LOOS

Although Habsburg Vienna never equaled Munich or Paris in the quality of its painting or sculpture, it did attract wide attention for buildings erected after 1850. A so-called Ringstrasse-style emerged after Franz Joseph had ordered abolition of the city ramparts in 1857. Plans for using the immense tracts girdling the inner city were thrown open to competition, won in 1859 by German-born Ludwig Förster (1787–1863). His proposal called for a boulevard, or Ringstrasse, to be adorned by cultural and public buildings, which would be financed by selling the rest of the land to private developers.[11] Between 1860 and 1890, twelve major public buildings were erected along the Ringstrasse at no cost to the taxpayer. All the buildings were adapted to previous styles, so that Vienna became a museum of historical architecture.[12]

The first building in Ringstrasse-style had preceded the opening of the boulevard by ten years. Following an attempt by a Hungarian tailor János Libényi to stab Franz Joseph on February 18, 1853, which the emperor's collar button thwarted, the Votivkirche, designed by Vienna-born Heinrich Ferstel (1828–1885), was begun in 1854 and completed for the Makart-Festival of 1879 in partial imitation of the Cologne Cathedral.[13] Next to be erected in fifteenth-century Italian style was the Opera House, designed by Ferstel's teachers, Vienna-born Eduard Van der Nüll (1812–1868), and Budapest-born August Siccard von Siccardsburg (1813–1868). Dubbed the "Königgrätz of Architecture," the building occasioned the suicide of Van der Nüll when the emperor inadvertently assented to criticism that the front steps were too low.[14] Parliáment, fashioned in classical Greek style by the Dane Theophil von Hansen (1813–1891), held its first session in December, 1883. The Town Hall, in Belgian Gothic, by the Swabian Friedrich von Schmidt (1825–1891), opened in 1884. In 1885 the new university opened, designed in severe Italian Renaissance style by Ferstel to gather under one roof the Faculties of Law and Philosophy which had been dispersed since 1848.

In 1888 there opened opposite the Town Hall the new Burgtheater that Hamburg-born Gottfried Semper (1803–1879) and Vienna-born Karl von Hasenauer (1833–1894) had designed in a style described variously as florid Renaissance and Parisian theater. Its acoustics had to be revamped in 1897. Semper and Hasenauer were responsible also for the two Court Museums, whose Italian Renaissance exteriors were completed by 1881, although the Art History Museum did not open to the public until 1891. In addition, Semper drafted a plan for expanding the Hofburg in German Renaissance style, connecting it to the two museums in a giant court like that of the Louvre. This plan, which was left unexecuted, would have created at the center of the Ringstrasse a huge *Zwinger* such as Semper had completed for the kings of Saxony in Dresden during the 1840's.

Except for the Parliament and the Opera House, Ringstrasse buildings lacked monumentality. They were modeled on tiny shrines, whose delicacy palled when enlarged. Built to please a bourgeoisie that had never cultivated a style of its own, these buildings copied old facades, indicating function through historical allusion. A Greek Parliament bespoke the cradle of democracy, a Belgian town hall signified municipal glory, while Italian Renaissance embellished theatrical and academic pursuits. The architects' immersion in the past perpetuated

Biedermeier passion for amassing details. Like Makart, Vienna's architects were decorators, who rearranged existing elements without creating new ones. They preferred to glorify past masters rather than to supplant them. This historicizing impulse culminated in the Art History Museum, whose ornate decor subverted the purpose of the building. Ceiling paintings by Makart and Munkácsy were dwarfed by black pillars. In the galleries green walls flattered the gold frames but stifled the canvases, which were further overwhelmed by busts above every door. Ten years of highly publicized toil had produced an insult to functionality.

From its inception the Ringstrasse had invited criticism as well as adulation. Opponents helped to pioneer modern city planning by advocating a variety of alternatives to the broad spaces created by Förster's plan. A romantic among city planners was the Catholic architect Camillo Sitte (1843–1903).[15] Born in Vienna the son of a Bohemian stonemason who had turned architect, Sitte absorbed artisan values while growing up in a house on the Piaristenplatz, known today as the Jodok-Fink-Platz. By the time he entered the university in 1863, he had already learned to venerate town squares as the touchstone of urban design. In order to train himself as a draftsman, Sitte studied anatomy and the physiology of vision for three semesters at the Medical Faculty. He also worked under Ferstel and the art historian Eitelberger, who awakened Sitte's interest in the applied arts. After teaching at Salzburg from 1875 to 1883, for the remainder of his life Sitte taught draftsmanship and practiced architecture in Vienna.

Modesty did not prevent Sitte from winning worldwide renown for a treatise on city planning, *Der Städtebau nach seinen künstlerischen Grundsätzen* (Vienna, 1889). Extolling medieval towns like Rothenburg and Siena, Sitte advocated gently curving streets that would open unexpected vistas on residential squares. The grid plans of engineers and geometers he anathematized as destructive of man's contact with nature. Sitte deplored the empty space around free-standing buildings like Ferstel's Votivkirche, urging that a colonnade be erected in front to connect it with adjoining buildings. Similarly, he proposed placing low houses in front of the Rathaus so as to link it with surrounding structures.

Rooted in the artisan class, Sitte paralleled the aesthetic of Viennese impressionism. Delighting in shifting perspectives and unexpected vistas, he tried to make the city conform to Mach's postulate that experience consists in an ordered sequence of impressions. The task of a city planner is to vary impressions for pedestrians and fiacre passengers proceeding through gently winding streets. When examining Greek and medieval towns, Sitte discerned a creative will to form such as the art historian Alois Riegl held underlies all art. Like Riegl, Sitte postulated that all cities can be compared according to a systematic aesthetic. Above all, Sitte embodied Viennese aestheticism by blithely disregarding functional problems. As if he were a stage designer, a city planner should aim to please the eye of the beholder, not to facilitate commerce. Sitte seemed to wish to turn cities into backdrops for romantic opera.

Having started from a similar aestheticism, Vienna-born Otto Wagner (1841–1918) developed toward functionalism.[16] The son of a Catholic notary, he studied under Van der Nüll and Siccardsburg before becoming a successful designer of villas for the upper middle class. After winning a competition for design of the Vienna underground in 1894, Wagner became a professor of architecture at the Academy of Fine Arts, where he advocated antihistoricist innovations. He led in bringing to Vienna the art nouveau architecture of Van de Velde.

Although he had always preferred flat surfaces albeit with fantastic ornament, Wagner was slow to fulfill his own precepts. His Kirche Am Steinhof, built between 1905 and 1907 as part of an insane asylum, renewed many motifs of art nouveau, as did his stations for the underground. His Postal Savings Bank of 1906 introduced a more utilitarian style, which he carried over into many unrealized projects, some on the grandest scale.[17]

In *Moderne Architektur* (Vienna, 1896), which Wagner wrote for his students, he criticized the Ringstrasse in the name of functional simplicity. He repudiated palace style for railway stations on the grounds that something impractical cannot be beautiful. In *Die Grossstadt: Eine Studie* (Vienna, 1911), Wagner analyzed the rebuilding of Vienna to date, contending that sixty years of planning had produced only two successful plans: Semper's outer Burgplatz and the Schwarzenberg Platz. More aware of economic exigencies than Sitte, Wagner recognized that in an industrial city competition for space precluded both extensive parks and winding streets. In order to save time for commuters, he advocated that blocklike tenements of many stories be arrayed around an air center *(Luftzentrum)*, which would house government buildings, shops, and recreation facilities. Abandoning decorative screens, Wagner wanted to expose hurried urban life, while removing slums. Envisioning more than he could hope to achieve, Otto Wagner, like Popper-Lynkeus and Theodor Hertzka, proved himself a genuine utopian. Less attached to the past than Sitte, he built for all social classes, recognizing that the engineer, not the decorator must plan cities of the future.

An even more uncompromising opponent of decoration was Wag-

ner's disciple Adolf Loos (1870–1933).[18] The son of a German stonemason in Brünn, Loos studied at Vienna before sojourning with relatives in the United States from 1893 to 1897. Entranced with the
functional, Loos returned to Vienna to inveigh against art nouveau.
An intimate of Altenberg, Loos also remained a lifelong friend of
Kraus, who often quoted the architect in *Die Fackel*. Loos's conversion
to Catholicism prompted Kraus's own, and although later the two
friends quarreled on the subject of religion and World War One, together they despised pretense and duplicity. Both admired crisp, clear
style in writing as well as in architecture; Loos carried contempt to
the point of writing German, like Stefan George, without capitalizing
nouns. As an architect, Loos anticipated Wagner's later utilitarian style.
Already in the 1890's Loos insisted that designers reveal rather than
hide beams of a building.

Between 1897 and 1900, Loos penned essays later collected to form
Ins Leere gesprochen (Vienna, 1921).[19] With the sympathy of a stonemason's son for artisans, he urged that class to repudiate art nouveau.
Tools such as the locomotive and the bicycle scorn ornament, Loos
argued; only primitive peoples relish tattoos. Loos hailed the plumber
as a revolutionary who would erode tradition. Contemporary dress he
condemned as outmoded: military uniforms were as ill suited to railroad travel as costumes of Louis XIV would have been. In "Ornament
and Crime" (1908), the purist censured fancy clothes as demeaning:

> . . . modern man uses his clothes like a mask. His individuality
> is so strong that he does not need to express it any longer by
> his clothing. Lack of ornament is a sign of spiritual strength.[20]

Like Schönberg and Kraus, Loos wanted to reduce art to fundamentals.

THE VIENNA SCHOOL OF ART HISTORY

The University of Vienna fostered a distinctive approach to the study
of art history. By undertaking the study of various arts in relation to
one another, art historians harnessed the aestheticism of their city.[21]
Precursors of the Vienna School included the founder of the Museum
for Applied Art, Rudolf Eitelberger von Edelberg (1817–1885), who
strove to better the craftsmanship of artisans.[22] One of his students,
Moriz Thausing (1838–1884),[23] a Bohemain Jew, introduced to Vienna
the technique of attribution perfected by the Italian senator Giovanni
Morelli (1816–1891). Bourgeois collectors of paintings demanded a

more reliable method of verifying the authenticity of canvases, a task that the medically trained Morelli performed by scrutinizing minute details such as a nose, ears, and feet.[24]

The founder of the Vienna School of Art History was Franz Wickhoff (1853–1909).[25] Born in Steyr, he studied Greek archaeology under Alexander Conze (1831–1914), a student of Semper, and diplomatics under the founder of the Institute for Research in Austrian History, Theodor von Sickel (1826–1908). Under the influence of Thausing, Wickhoff united connoisseurship with archaeology and philosophy to achieve a precision of observation analogous to that demanded by giants of the Vienna Medical School. He was the first member of the Vienna School to assert the interdependence of culture, arguing that Christian painting of the second and third centuries had derived from pagan wall painting and relief sculpture. Even more revolutionary was his insistence, similar to that of Guido Adler, that every period of art was equally worthy of study. Discarding the Renaissance canon that had belittled late Roman art, he compared it with contemporary French impressionism. A champion of Klimt and of functional architecture, Wickhoff was also an amateur painter and poet, completing Goethe's *Pandora* in a fashion that won critical acclaim. Because of the exceptional breadth of his training, Wickhoff dared to break with tradition, combining connoisseurship with historical accuracy, and opening whole epochs for further study.

Wickhoff's principles were sharpened by his younger colleague, Alois Riegl (1858–1905).[26] Having grown up in Zablotow, Galicia, where his father was an official in the tobacco administration, Riegl took his Matura at Kremsmünster in 1874. After his father's death in 1873, a guardian insisted that Riegl study law for two years before he could enter Theodor von Sickel's Institute, where he acquired thorough training in paleography. Riegl also studied under Robert Zimmermann, whose formalism encouraged strict objectivity in the study of art. Becoming an art historian, he served from 1887 to 1898 as curator of textiles at Eitelberger's Museum of Art and Industry, earning a habilitation in 1889 and becoming Ordinarius at the university in 1897. In 1901 he was appointed head of the Art Conservation Commission. Infusing objectivity into conservation, Riegl halted demolition of Baroque buildings and launched the twenty-one volume *Österreichische Kunst-Topographie* (Vienna, 1907–1927), to survey what remained. Although ill with cancer and growing deaf, Riegl labored right up to his death.

In *Stilfragen: Grundlegungen zu einer Geschichte der Ornamentik* (Berlin, 1893) and in *Spätrömische Kunstindustrie nach den Funden in Österreich-Ungarn* (Vienna, 1910), Riegl used knowledge of late

Roman textiles to dispute the aesthetic materialism of Gottfried Semper. To refute that architect's preoccupation with materials as a determinant of style, Riegl coined the term art-will *(Kunstwollen)*, or artistic intention, to designate the autonomous life of forms. Like Hanslick, Riegl contended that changes of form are caused not by extraneous forces in society but by impulses within forms themselves. It was unfortunate that in order to stress the autonomy of forms, Riegl introduced the term "will," which mistakenly suggests conscious volition by artists. Although Riegl wrote too early to know of Freud, the misleading term art-will was borrowed by later theorists of the unconscious such as Wilhelm Worringer and Oswald Spengler.

Under the influence of Zimmermann, Riegl introduced a pair of polar opposites even more comprehensive than those made famous by Heinrich Wölfflin. To differentiate the art of Egypt and Greece from later painting, Riegl distinguished between haptic and optic styles. This polarity was corroborated by the fact that primitive peoples cannot recognize an image in a photograph; they grasp images only in three dimensions. Haptic art creates sculpturesque images, detached, as in ancient Egypt, from surrounding space. Such statues convey permanence by highlighting contours and eschewing shadows. Optic art portrays space in two dimensions through chiaroscuro, jagged contours, and impressionistic play-of-light. Riegl held that an alternating rhythm has prevailed between the two styles. Once the haptic art of the Greeks had given way to the optic art of late Rome, haptic style predominated during the Renaissance, as well as in neoclassicism and in postimpressionism, while optic style held sway during the Baroque and in impressionism. Fascinated by formalism, Riegl, like the Swiss Wölfflin, ignored human passions, contending that the ideal judge of early art would be someone who had never seen subsequent works. These two scholars removed the barrier between major and minor arts, as well as that between classic and decadent styles. In the words of Edgar Wind, we owe it to them that "we no longer judge one style by the canons of another."[27]

After the premature deaths of Wickhoff and Riegl, the leadership of the Vienna School fell to the Czech Max Dvořák (1874–1921).[28] The son of the curator at Raudnitz Castle outside Prague, the Catholic Dvořák became the favorite student of Wickhoff, who was horrified to hear German students hiss their Czech lecturer. Appointed Extraordinarius in 1906, Dvořák prepared his lectures with exceptional thoroughness, adhering until 1914 to the formalism to Riegl. To Dvořák World War One portended the demise of materialistic culture; he predicted that from it would issue a new spiritualism, typified by the expressionism of Kokoschka. After the war, Dvořák harried himself to

death struggling to preserve Austria's monuments. His untimely demise
left the Vienna School fragmented between followers of the connoisseur Julius von Schlosser (1866–1938), an admirer of Croce, and the
archaeologist turned Orientalist, Josef Strzygowski (1862–1941), who
postulated continuity between Central Asian and North European styles
while belittling Mediterranean art.[29]

Dvořák is remembered above all for his post-1914 program, inspired
by Dilthey, of integrating art history with the history of ideas. In
essays collected under a title proposed by Felix Horb, *Kunstgeschichte
als Geistesgeschichte* (Vienna, 1923), the Czech scholar examined
interrelations between literature and art, including parallels between
El Greco and Counter-Reformation theology, as well as between Goya
and contemporaries such as Goethe, Leopardi, and Hölderlin. For a
time Dvořák's postulate of parallels between visual art and intellectual
currents promised to revolutionize the study of art history. Imaginative
students like Hans Tietze, Frigyes Antal, Dagobert Frey, Otto Benesch,
and Arnold Hauser explored affinities between art and literature.
Without necessarily claiming causal connection, they supposed that at
any given moment similar problems in different media were solved in
similar ways. For Dvořák each art monument and each literary work
constitutes an element in the mosaic that forms the zeitgeist; each
contributes to the whole without necessarily shaping others. This logic
of wholes, reminiscent of Ehrenfels' notion of Gestalt, was elaborated
with consummate skill by Strzygowski in *Die Krisis der Geisteswissenschaften* (Vienna, 1923), and by Dagobert Frey in *Gotik und Renaissance als Grundlage der modernen Weltanschauung* (Augsburg, 1929).
A student of Schlosser, Hans Sedlmayr (1896–), used Gestalt psychology to formulate a characterology of artistic form,[30] while a Vienna-
born archaeologist, Guido Kaschnitz von Weinberg (1890–1958) employed Husserl's categories to refine those of Riegl.[31]

The dangers of Dvořák's method emerged in his "Idealismus und
Naturalismus in der gotischen Skulptur und Malerei" [1918], written
between 1915 and 1917.[32] Using a pair of polar opposites introduced
by Konrad Lange (1855–1921) in *Das Wesen der Kunst* (1901), Dvořák
interpreted the Middle Ages from 500 to 1100 as the high point of
otherworldly idealism. Between 1150 and 1500 the empirical spirit of
naturalism vied with idealism, ending in decisive victory for the former; the last traces of idealism flickered out in El Greco and Cervantes.
After 1600 natural science gradually destroyed the canon of naturalism, forcing artists during the nineteenth century either to forge their
own standards or to acknowledge enslaving rules. Idealism began to
reemerge, said Dvořák, in impressionism and above all in expressionism, so that in "Über El Greco und den Manierismus" [1922] Dvořák

could forecast a rebirth of spiritual values.[33] Dvořák honored impressionist and expressionist scholars for challenging specialization. By integrating philosophy with poetry, history with sociology, and fine arts with psychology, Dilthey, Worringer, and Spengler embraced the whole man.

Because Dvořák had spent twenty years making formalistic analyses before he ventured into cultural history, his fusion of art history with the history of ideas was firmly anchored in connoisseurship. Yet no amount of caution could prevent his method from being excessively a priori. Arguing in a circle from literature to art and vice versa, he could discern what he pleased in one medium and project it into another. At his best, Dvořák revived the preference of Bohemian Reform Catholicism for wholes, identifying idealism with attention to the whole and naturalism with empirical analysis of parts. Here he resembled Othmar Spann, whose concept of universalism corresponded to Dvořák's idealism, while Spann's notion of individualism corresponded to the Czech's naturalism. Just as Spann nurtured nostalgia for preindustrial society, so Dvořák embodied an expressionist desire to revive the emotional spontaneity that he attributed to the Middle Ages. Although today such hopes appear naive, Dvořák ignited numerous students with his enthusiasm and helpfulness.

The Vienna School of Art History exploited commonplaces of Viennese aestheticism in order to dispel preconceptions that had hampered their discipline. Eager to compare visual art with literature, the Viennese scholars presupposed in all cultures the kind of cross-fertilization between genres which distinguished their own city. Among its authors, Saar, Hofmannsthal, and Schnitzler esteemed the work of Klimt and Wagner as paralleling their own. The intoxication of the Viennese public with Makart and the Secession suggested that in other ages consumers of art may have interacted with artists in a similar way. Paradoxically, it was a city steeped in tradition that led scholars to discard the Renaissance canon in order to study little-known periods such as late Rome and neglected media such as textiles and intaglios. Through Dvořák, the school reached beyond Herbartian formalism toward Hegelian encyclopedism. By fusing art history with the history of ideas, Dvořák projected Viennese assumptions onto other cultures, where often these applied imperfectly. Like the musicologist Guido Adler, who united the best of Hanslick's formalism with historical scholarship, Dvořák buttressed the formalism of Riegl with historical expertise, posing problems of methodology which have yet to be resolved.[34] Although expressionist visions endeared Dvořák to contemporaries, his prophecies have discredited him among successors, who wish that he had wielded his learning more judiciously.

Critics of Aestheticism

ROSA MAYREDER: CONNOISSEUR OF WOMAN'S ROLE

Although love of the arts consoled many Viennese, it drove others to defiance. Now forgotten, Rosa Mayreder (1858–1938) combated therapeutic nihilism by campaigning to improve woman's lot.[1] She ranks as one of the sanest interpreters in her generation, and indeed in any generation, of the role of woman in modern society. The daughter of a wealthy Viennese hotelier, F. Obermayr, she grew up in a large upper-middle-class family, where a girl's education was devoted exclusively to the art of cultivating beauty. She was obliged to wear a corset at age twelve, to don shoes that shrank the feet, and to avoid gymnastics for fear of enlarging her hands. It was argued that study would make a girl bald and spoil her figure. Young Rosa pleaded for an education, but to no avail, while her father had to pull strings to get her brother through school. Outraged by favoritism shown her brothers, she resolved to expand the opportunities available to young women. A painter of talent, she moved in the same artistic circles as Berta Szeps and Alma Mahler-Werfel. Here she met, and in 1881 married, the architect Karl Mayreder, in whose firm Adolf Loos later served, and who together with Otto Wagner developed between 1893 and 1895 a prizewinning plan for completing the Ringstrasse. Encouraged by her husband, in 1893 Rosa founded the General Austrian Women's Association (*Allgemeiner Österreichischer Frauenverein*). As we have mentioned, she protected Hugo Wolf, sheltering him from critics and stimulating him in 1895 to set to music her libretto, *Der Corregidor*, which she had adapted from the *Three-Cornered Hat* (1874) by Pedro de Alarcón.

Mayreder displayed exceptional grasp of the woman problem in *Zur Kritik der Weiblichkeit* (Jena, 1905), which won acclaim in English translation under the title *A Survey of the Woman Problem* (London, 1912). Unlike most feminists, Mayreder deplored allowing the accident of sex to mold every attitude. The goal of life, Mayreder insisted, is to cultivate aspects of personality that both sexes share, such as intelligence, charity, and aestheticism. Coining neologisms as cacophonous as those of Weininger, she differentiated four ways an individual can relate to sexuality. First, the acratic person, or sex-patriot, indulges unmitigated sexuality, becoming wholly male like Don Juan or wholly female like Messalina; such expenditure of sexual energy Mayreder labeled centrifugal. Second, the iliastric person strives to attain sexlessness through asceticism, conserving sexual energy in the manner of Christian and Buddhist monks so as to achieve centripetal sexuality. Third, a dyscratic person is one who can achieve neither of the preceding extremes. Unable to accommodate sexuality to other activities, he founders in whatever he undertakes. Psychoanalysis would deem him neurotic. Fourth, a synthetic person overcomes conflict between centrifugal and centripetal sexuality. Two synthetic persons who marry learn to share intellect and emotion without sacrificing sexual fulfillment.

Mayreder did not allow quest for harmony between the sexes to preclude backing women's demands for greater rights. She attributed the woman's movement to industrialization, which was causing the business cycle to impinge on every homemaker. As shopkeepers were forced out of business and workers laid off, housewives demanded to understand the forces that so disrupted homes. A second factor in promoting feminism had been athletics, especially the bicycle, which by requiring rapid movements undermined the older ideal of feminine grace. Mayreder contended that the bicycle, in use since 1890, had done more for women's emancipation and for comradeship between the sexes than had the entire feminist movement.[2] Mayreder's approval of sport as an alternative to corsets was shared by many doctors; during the early 1880's Freud had to prescribe pills to cure his sedentary fiancée of the then common anemia (chlorosis).[3]

In an essay of 1913 on "Sex and Culture," Mayreder formulated her conception of woman's duty.[4] Citing Houston Stewart Chamberlain's distinction between external civilization (Zivilisation) and inward culture (Kultur), Mayreder held that the responsibilities of motherhood must keep a woman sexbound, while a man's freedom to transcend sex permits him to build the external order of civilization. But because man lacks inner restraints imposed by nature, woman must serve as the "measure of all things." She has a cultural mission to prevent man from losing himself in external activity. If she fails to act as a cultural brake, externality will reign, spreading cruelty and neglect of emotion. To illustrate masculine thinking unleavened by female compassion, Mayreder cited Weininger's contention that women possess no soul, a doctrine that the church had rejected about A.D. 900. To refute Weininger, she pressed to absurdity his notion that every cell bears sexual characteristics: if so, the strongest woman would be weaker than the scrawniest man. To document the futility of men's pretentions to understand women without having consulted them, Mayreder listed some qualities that men have attributed to the opposite sex:

> There is Lotze saying that the "female hates analysis" and therefore cannot distinguish the true from the false. There is Lafitte saying that "the female prefers analysis." There is Kingsley calling her "the only true missionary of civilization," and Pope calling her a rake at heart; Havelock Ellis saying that she cannot work under pressure, and Von Horn saying that in the fulfilling of heavy requirements she puts a man to shame; M. de Lambert that she plays with love, Krafft-Ebing that her heart is toward Monogamy; . . . Lombroso that there is "a half-criminaloid being even in the normal woman"; Bachhofen that "Law is innate in women."[5]

These fatuities constitute, said Mayreder, a subjective fetish that men have devised to flatter themselves. Men's image of an "eternal feminine" is pure wish-fulfillment.

In exposing abuses of sexuality, Mayreder paralleled Krafft-Ebing and Freud, whose *Drei Abhandlungen zur Sexualtheorie* (Vienna, 1905) she reviewed favorably in 1906. Disputing the patriarchal psychoanalyst, she implored men and women to cooperate as equals in nurturing nonsexual aspects of personality. By being moderate, she proved more persuasive than the sexual utopian Ehrenfels or the antisexual fanatic Weininger. By insisting that individuals can fulfill themselves by merging into a larger unit—the couple—she implemented the faith of Bohemian Reform Catholicism that the good of the whole conditions that of its members. Mayreder epitomized her own ideal of woman as measure of all things, acting as balancewheel for Quixotes like Ehrenfels and Wolf. Although her equanimity may seem bland now that many of her crusades are won, Rosa Mayreder incarnated what was best in the woman-steeped aestheticism of Vienna.

OTTO WEININGER: EARNESTNESS DEBASED INTO MISOGYNY AND JEWISH SELF-HATRED

The most searing indictment of Viennese aestheticism—and of its women—came from Otto Weininger (1880–1903).[6] Ravaged by an overactive conscience, he committed suicide less than a year after achieving instant fame through an expanded version of his doctoral dissertation, *Geschlecht und Charakter: Eine prinzipielle Untersuchung* (Vienna, 1903). Probably no other dissertation has gone through so many editions—nearly thirty by 1940—nor stirred so much controversy, as this diatribe against women and Jews.

Otto was the son of a gifted, if censorious Jewish father, the goldsmith Leopold Weininger (1854–1922), who had married a woman of inferior talent. Young Otto grew up with two sisters and a brother, admiring his father's self-taught mastery of languages, his skill as a goldsmith, his love of Wagner, and his anti-Semitism. Despising his mother's lack of schooling, Otto allowed disappointed oedipal feelings to degenerate into rabid antifeminism. While attending the Schottengymnasium, he learned to read Latin and Greek as well as to speak French, English, Italian, Spanish, and Norwegian. Encouraged by coffeehouse friends such as Oskar Ewald, Emil Lucka, and Hermann Swoboda, Otto preened as a dandy while doing his schoolwork heedless of his teachers. From 1898 to 1902, he studied at the University of Vienna under Friedrich Jodl (1849–1914), for whom he wrote a dissertation entitled "Eros und Psyche." Since Jodl deemed Weininger personally repugnant and had found the dissertation to abound in extravagances and crudities, he was astonished to see its success as a book under the title of *Geschlecht und Charakter*.[7] Whereas the dissertation had remained self-consciously scientific, the expanded version smacked of wish-fulfillment in its speculations about Jews and women. During the summer of 1902 Weininger had converted to Protestantism. After traveling through Germany to Norway in 1902, he toured Italy the following summer, penning aphorisms that appeared posthumously as *Über die letzten Dinge* (Vienna, 1904). Upon returning to Vienna in September, 1903, he fell prey to deepening despondency that, on October 3, prompted him to rent a room in the house where Beethoven had died. There he shot himself in the chest after sending his brother and father letters announcing this intention. The suicide provoked polemics in which Kraus, Strindberg, and other admirers defended his reputation against the clerical press. Weininger's friends also rebutted the German characterologist Paul Möbius (1854–1906), who accused the deceased of having plagiarized his *Über den physiologischen Schwachsinn des Weibes* (Leipzig, 1901).

In *Geschlecht und Charakter*, Weininger distorted a useful hypothesis into monomania. He postulated that all human behavior can be explained in terms of male and female protoplasm constituting each person. Contending that every cell of every organism possesses sexuality, he coined several terms to designate various types of protoplasm. Idioplasm is sexually undifferentiated, arrhenoplasm is male protoplasm, while thelyplasm is female cellular tissue. Using algebraic formulas, he demonstrated how varying proportions of arrhenoplasm and thelyplasm could elucidate such topics as the psychology of genius, physiognomy, theory of memory, prostitution, anti-Semitism, and theory of race. In an ever-widening series of concentric rings, these inquiries rotate around the obsession that male and female are irreconcilably hostile. In breadth of interests, Weininger caricatured the encyclopedism that the Herbartians had popularized in Vienna, unfurling an impressive array of authorities that included Plato, Aristotle, Kant, Spencer, Schopenhauer, and Darwin. Exuding a cockiness reminiscent of his idol Houston Stewart Chamberlain, the young man claimed to have unraveled puzzles that had baffled scholars for millennia.

Although Weininger concealed it, he had derived his postulate of ubiquitous bisexuality from none other than Freud. In October, 1900, Weininger's friend Hermann Swoboda, a patient of Freud, talked with the psychoanalyst about the bisexual disposition of every person. Having gleaned this notion from Swoboda, Weininger inflated it into a treatise which in the fall of 1901 he submitted to Freud for appraisal. Freud admonished Weininger, "You have opened the castle with a stolen key."[8] During 1904 and 1905 Freud's former confidant Wilhelm Fliess accused the psychoanalyst of having divulged not merely his own but Fliess's insights to Weininger and Swoboda. In a letter of January 12, 1906, to Kraus, in which Freud disparaged Weininger, the psychoanalyst acknowledged that his patient Swoboda had disclosed certain Freudian ideas to the young prodigy.[9]

Weininger ranks as one of the most petulant of misogynists. He simply equated sexuality with woman, who contaminates man in the paroxysm of orgasm. He diagnosed hysteria as a malady peculiar to woman, caused by conflict between her exclusively sexual nature and the ideal of chastity, which men foist upon her. As if parodying male stereotypes about women, Weininger pontificated that women are free to choose between motherhood and prostitution; *tertium non datur*. Since the former merely disguises the latter, the only way for men to elude earthbound women is to cease procreation.

Misogyny afflicted several other Austro-Hungarian authors, many of them Jewish. Joseph Roth portrayed women as temptresses who seduce men from duty, smothering capacity for higher things by inviting self-indulgence. Kafka read Weininger with sympathy, although it is difficult to disentangle in Kafka's wraithlike women Weininger's influence from that of Strindberg.[10] During his youth, Broch esteemed Weininger's austere morality and relentless use of polar opposites, while Kraus deemed the young man a frustrated poet. Having read Weininger with avidity, Ferdinand Ebner declared that Jodl's student had carried secular idealism to its logical conclusion: Weininger had exposed the antifeminism and anti-Semitism that lurked behind the dream of spirit *(Geist)* dear to idealists.[11] The opposite obsession gripped Schiele, who painted the female body ad nauseam, envisioning woman not as a vampire, but as a partner in the ecstasy of procreation. Both men suffered, in the words of Alfred Werner, the *tristitia* of young men, who cannot reconcile instinct to duty.[12] For Weininger, woman played the roles of Judith and Salome, which art nouveau had celebrated; she could never be *alma Venus* or *Maria redemptrix*, much less Rosa Mayreder's synthetic person. During the 1920's Weininger's theory that sexuality pervades protoplasm was rehabilitated by a Tiroleanborn Jew, Eugen Steinach (1862–1944). This endocrinologist at Prague and Vienna introduced a technique of rejuvenation by implanting sex hormones. Freud himself underwent a Steinach operation in November, 1923, in vain hopes of arresting his cancer.

In the expanded version of his dissertation, Weininger coupled Jews with women. Endorsing the formula of Chamberlain that Jews constitute not a race but a mental attitude, Weininger cited Jewish anti-Semitism to corroborate Jews' innate inferiority. Since Jews like women lack an ego together with its sense of self-esteem, they must be amoral and lascivious; in a word, they are pimps.[13] As materialists incapable of piety, lacking even that faith in men which sustains women, Jews excel above all as research chemists whose solvents corrode idealism. Flaunting Jewish self-hatred, Weininger dismissed Zionism as self-defeating: only as an individual can a Jew cease to be Jewish. Despising in himself feminine traits he reviled in others, Weininger resembled the hero of Ferdinand Bronner's novel *Schmilz* (Vienna, 1905), a Jew who joined an anti-Semitic fraternity in order to appease self-hatred. Partly because of a Latin complexion, Weininger forfeited the kind of adulation accorded a fellow Viennese Jewish anti-Semite, Arthur Trebitsch (1880–1927), whose blond good looks made him the center of a cult.[14]

Such vagaries notwithstanding, Weininger embodied something pure and edifying. Even Freud conceded that the young man had about him a touch of genius.[15] Swoboda praised his friend's super-Kantian pursuit of law in defiance of earthly imperfection. Never having outgrown adolescent appetite for immaculate justice, Weininger could not stomach a universe whose evils no one had plumbed. During midnight walks, he lamented:

Schauder

Allmählich kehr ich heim an diese Stätte
Mit müden Sinnen, schlaff und ohne Kraft;
Wie jeder andere ist der Tag verronnen.
Der Mond ist da, soll trösten für die Sonnen.

Des Winters schweigend' mitleidslose Kälte,
Der Himmel starr in seinem Leichentuch:
Es schneit in meinem Herzen, seine Sehnsucht
Erfrieret langsam vor des Lebens Zucht.

Shivering

Slowly my steps turn homeward to this place,
With weary soul, abject and powerless.
Like any other this day's course has run;
The moon is there, as solace for the sun.

Wrapped in the winter's mute, unpitying cold,
The sky is stiff and stark within its shroud.
With deeper winter, snow falls in my heart,
Where longing freezes ere life's growth can start.[16]

Here he voiced that fascination with death which animated many writers of Young Vienna. In a world throbbing with women and sex, he found peace only in the grave.

More conspicuously than other impressionists, Weininger epitomized therapeutic nihilism. Scorning study of society and politics, he so withdrew into contemplation of the human predicament that he forsook all desire to remedy it. Like giants of the Vienna Medical School, he preferred postmortem diagnosis to timely therapy, sacrificing the patient for truth. In this moralist, diagnosis engendered self-paralysis, making him no less narcissistic than the aesthetes whom he disdained. Weininger lived and died a quintessential prodigy, a youth who amassed knowledge so feverishly that he never developed roots. Despising the ballrooms and brothels of pleasure-loving Vienna, he epitomized the obsession of young Jews to exalt themselves through intellectual prowess. Whereas Freud, Schnitzler, and Herzl channeled their ambition into lasting achievements, Weininger flowered too early and too intensely. More poignantly than perhaps any other individual, he embodied the promise and the peril of Viennese intellectuality.

Part Three

POSITIVISM
AND
IMPRESSIONISM:
AN UNLIKELY
SYMBIOSIS

Alles Wissen geht aus einem Zweifel hervor
und endigt in einem Glauben.

All knowledge proceeds from doubt
and ends in faith.

—MARIE VON EBNER-ESCHENBACH

Fascination with Death

DEATH AS BULWARK AGAINST CHANGE

THE VARIOUS ATTITUDES that characterized Austrian thought—aestheticism, therapeutic nihilism, impressionism—were all part of the national attitude toward death. Analysis of Austria's accommodation with death will elucidate the interaction between positivism and impressionism which inspired so many innovative theorists. In contrast with Hungarians, who dreamed of political action, Austrians cultivated a Baroque vision of death as the fulfillment of life. No one expressed this better than Mozart in a letter to his father of April 4, 1787:

> As death, when we consider it closely, is the true goal of our existence, I have formed during the last few years such close relations with this best and truest friend of mankind, that his image is not only no longer terrifying to me, but is indeed very soothing and consoling! And I thank my God for graciously granting me the opportunity (you know what I mean) of learning that death is the key to our true happiness. I never lie down at night without reflecting that—young as I am—I may not live to see another day. Yet no one of all my acquaintances could say that in company I am morose or disgruntled. For this blessing I daily thank my Creator and wish with all my heart that each one of my fellow-creatures could enjoy it.[1]

Comparable jubilation pervades the *Requiem* mass that Mozart composed on his deathbed. In the novella *Mozart auf der Reise nach Prag* (Stuttgart, 1856) Eduard Mörike portrayed the beleaguered composer weighing his blessings and his woes. The story was a favorite of Ludwig Wittgenstein. Having been introduced to the Freemasons by Joseph Haydn in 1785, Mozart had learned from them to regard death as a friend and consoler. The Freemasons preached a conviction held by most Austrians: death constitutes part of life. It discloses the hidden side of experience, embodying the quintessence, as Hermann Bahr said, of everything that we have not known here:

> I am fond of death. Not as a saviour, for I do not suffer from life, but as consummator. It will bring me everything which I still lack. Then the seed of my life will germinate for the first time. Death takes nothing from me, yet gives me so much. . . . [I await death] with a nervous joy, as we children used to await the *Christkindl;* we sat in the dark while through a crack in the door broke a ray of welcome light.[2]

This joyful affirmation that death consummates something already good has been voiced with varying nuances by writers from Feuchtersleben and Stifter to Werfel and Broch. Broch reiterated Mozart's message that death offers an unfailing goad to creativity:

> At the side of the truly religious man and of the poet death is always standing, admonishing him to endow life with the utmost possible meaning, lest it have been lived in vain.[3]

In daily life, reverence for death occasioned a complex ritual of mourning. When the husband of Maria Theresa died on August 18, 1765, she went into lifelong mourning, performing with royal flourish a ceremonial that all Austrians cherished. Having replaced her hair with a wig, she converted the death chamber into a chapel; she herself moved to the third floor of the Hofburg, where she resided for fifteen years in rooms hung with black silk. Thereafter she spent the eighteenth day of each month secluded in prayer, as she did the entire month of August. Maria Theresa surrendered herself to cultivating the memory of her spouse, as if he were merely away on a journey.[4]

Among royalty and populace alike, the cult of the dead entailed intimate veneration of the corpse. Saar described in *Innocens* (1866) how beholding a laid-out corpse had taught the protagonist resignation; in *Ein Abschied,* Schnitzler evoked a similar scene. Zweig detected in the Viennese custom of staging magnificent funerals—known as having a "beautiful corpse" *(schöne Leich')*—a symptom of aestheticism.[5] Although showmanship pervaded Viennese funerals, the ceremonial presupposed a loftier conviction than mere love of pomp. Well into the twentieth century, Austrian Catholics believed that the dead live on in the soul of their relatives and friends. Grillparzer's *Die Ahn-frau* (1818) dramatized the legend of the "poor soul" that wanders on earth until it has been avenged. This doctrine received heterodox formulation in a tract by the Silesian-born philosopher, Gustav Theo-dor Fechner (1801–1887). Written under a pseudonym, his *Das Büch-lein vom Leben und Tod* (Leipzig, 1836; 2d ed., 1866), circulated widely in Austria. This pastor's son infused Romantic nature-philoso-phy into Christian doctrine, arguing that immortality consists in the ongoing impact that a person exerts on the souls of his survivors. Just as Christ lives in the Church, the dead remain suffused in the living, playing on their souls as on a lute. Richard Coudenhove-Kalergi ex-pressed this more concretely when he described how the death of his father had molded the twelve-year-old boy:

> I did not know then that it is the living that are lost to us so often. The dead stay with us, always. For, strangely enough, the profound influence of my father on my further evolution was partly due to his early death. In the depth of my heart I wanted to continue his fragmentary life and to complete it as well as I could.[6]

No less than Mozart and Broch, Coudenhove-Kalergi revered the life-giving power of the dead.

An explanation for the appeal of the "beautiful corpse" appears in a neglected theory by Auguste Comte (1798–1857) concerning fetish-ism.[7] The later Comte contended that God's majesty tends to over-power a worshiper unless some more accessible symbol can focus adoration. Comte specified that a fetish should serve the following functions: first, to remind a worshiper of God's will within every object; second, to spring spontaneously into every mind; third, to connect maturity with infancy; fourth, to give coherence and plausibility to one's act of submission; and fifth, to show that love is the desirable synthesis of all human activity. In the Austrian ceremonial of death, the corpse of the beloved served as such a Comtean fetish. The laid-out corpse embodied God's will on earth, it appealed to universal emotions, it linked all phases of human life, it focused awe on a con-crete object, and it demonstrated the power of love to transcend space and time. This sort of fetish casts its spell most conspicuously in the crypt of Vienna's Capuchin Church (*Kapuzinergruft*), where since 1633 deceased Habsburg rulers have lain in bronze caskets, some on a dais, some at floor level. In the crypt a visitor—even today—cannot help but tremble before the dead, as they molder side by side in sarcophagi sculpted with emblems of life yet enveloped in an odor of dust. These caskets perpetuate the pathos of a funeral, incarnating homage to the monarchy and to its departed servants of God.[8]

The Austrian ceremonial of death dispelled black arts: voodoo, necrophilia, and necromancy bored a people who welcomed life without fearing death. There was little need to placate spirits through condign means where funerals were so festive and mourning so public, linking each person with his ancestors and with *Lares* of his city. Yet after 1880 as religious zeal began to wane, a vogue of spiritualism swept Vienna. None other than Crown Prince Rudolf deigned to unmask as a charlatan one medium who employed an apparatus of deceit as elaborate as that in Schiller's *Der Geisterseher* (1788).[9] As a further detriment, fascination with death sometimes prompted wistfulness and fatigue, especially among the lower classes. The little men portrayed by Saar and Ebner-Eschenbach frequently viewed death as release from an uncomprehending world. Crowning a lifetime of humble satisfactions, death loomed as the one grand event. Still another abuse marred the pompous funerals of which the Viennese were so fond. The city was tempted to wait until after a gifted man had died before it honored him. After Grillparzer had succumbed in January, 1872, all Vienna vied to heap his corpse with wreaths, hastening to atone for years of near oblivion that the author's retirement had brought upon himself. All too often, as Ferdinand Kürnberger pointed out, the Viennese preferred, like Byzantines, to erect statues to a genius safely dead, rather than to fete him while he remained alive to plague them.[10]

Exaggerated reverence for the dead encouraged indifference to the living. During the mid-nineteenth century Vienna's physicians seemed to prize the results of postmortem autopsies more highly than saving a patient. Worship of the dead reinforced that preference for things past which permeated Viennese taste. The collector's zeal of the Biedermeier, the historicizing architecture of the Ringstrasse, the idyll of the operetta offered respite from life by substituting timeless communion with past or imagined utopias. Aesthetic rituals meant in the nineteenth century what ruins, skulls, and tombs, had meant to the seventeenth: too often Austrians preferred communing with the dead to succoring the living. Hostility to change was enshrined in countless ceremonies and monuments, as if music and stone could abort the future. When Georg Lukács in 1922 diagnosed the world view of the bourgeoisie as "thinglike," because that class regards the world as unchanging and unchangeable, he may have had Vienna in mind. Extolling the past while revering death, most Viennese indulged a self-satisfaction which however beguiling was incapable of self-renewal.

DEATH AS SYMBOL OF EPHEMERALITY

Viennese literati who around 1900 frequented coffeehouses and wrote feuilletons shared a preoccupation with evanescence, especially with its definitive form—death. Fascination with the transitory justifies classifying writers such as Hofmannsthal, Schnitzler, Beer-Hofmann, Schaukal, and Altenberg under the rubric of impressionism. Of many attempts to define this attitude, the best comes from a Hungarian-born art historian, Arnold Hauser (1892–), who has construed impressionism as an urban art that "describes the changeability, the nervous rhythm, the sudden, sharp, but always ephemeral impressions of city life."[11] Impressionism entails "an acquiescence in the role of the spectator . . . a standpoint of aloofness, a waiting, non-involvement—in short, the aesthetic attitude purely and simply." "It will consider chance the principle of all being, and the truth of the moment as invalidating all other truth."[12] For the impressionist, nature undergoes a process of growth and more particularly of decay. Small wonder that Hermann Bahr hailed Vienna-born Ferdinand von Saar (1833–1906) as progenitor of Young Vienna. Habitués of the Café Griensteidl recognized in Saar's little men and *ratés* forebodings of their own disenchantment and plasticity.

Fascinated by decay, these unemployed sons of the upper and middle classes carried Baroque reverence for death to unheard-of extremes. To them death promised release from ennui; in a world gone stale, it alone remained a mighty unknown. By committing suicide, Weininger enacted what countless others dreamed of doing. In *Der Tor und der Tod*, Hofmannsthal portrayed a young aesthete who wearied of life after having tasted its variegated surfaces. Contemplation of death formed the reverse side of Viennese Phaeacianism. What Marcionism meant to Prague and political involvement to Budapest, musing on death meant to Viennese impressionists.

No one invoked the omnipresence of death in life so poignantly as the Brünn-born dandy Richard Schaukal (1874–1942), who resided at Vienna from 1903. Relishing the ubiquity of death, this Catholic extolled the funeral ceremonial whereby men acclimate themselves to the Great Order:

> Is not death in life, is he not in the middle of it, sitting in us, around us, breathing on us, is he not our friend and companion? . . . All men live in the great shadow of death who comes from God and who ought to be as familiar to them as the fragrance of the flowers by their window, as the breath in their mouth.[13]

Elsewhere he describes the pettiness that besets a young aesthete as he stands beside the bier of a friend, who had expired without settling a bet on a cigar case.[14]

A more sinister view of funerals was taken by the Vienna-born Jew Albert Ehrenstein (1886–1950). An admirer of Karl Kraus, he shared Kraus's anti-Semitism and therapeutic nihilism, approximating Marcionism as closely as any Viennese could. His first and best-known work, a short novel *Tubutsch* (Vienna, 1911), illustrated with twelve drawings by Kokoschka, described a rich Viennese who for all his wealth laments possessing nothing but his name. Tubutsch concludes his memoirs by likening death to a fiacre driver who is forbidden to speak with the passengers or even to indicate the destination. In the novella *Begräbnis* (1912), Ehrenstein depicted a Jewish funeral at Floridsdorf, where instead of exhibiting grief bourgeois participants resent having their routine disrupted.[15] They dress so elegantly that the narrator decides not to attend his own funeral. In case he should tell a bad joke or wear an inappropriate suit, his mourners would never forgive him. This macabre satire of the punctilio that sometimes displaces grief at funerals veiled the self-disgust of Ehrenstein, who after 1920 took spiritual flight from "Barbaropa" to immerse himself in Chinese culture.

A more positive valuation of death sustained another Vienna-born Jew, Richard Beer-Hofmann (1866–1945).[16] In *Der Tod Georgs* (Berlin, 1900), the lingering death of a young professor prompts his friend Paul to confront his own futility. Full of hymns to nature, this third-person interior monologue describes Paul's growth toward acknowledging unity with past generations. Joseph Roth (1894–1939) depicted a similar process in *Radetzkymarsch*, where the death in a duel of a Jewish friend, Dr. Demant, deepens the narrator's affection for his ancestors. Later Roth evokes the death agony of Jacques the self-effacing manservant of Land-Captain von Trotta. Jacques is a little man in the tradition of Ebner-Eschenbach's *Ein Spätgeborener* (1875), who dies ever ready to serve. His decease crushes the Land-Captain, who sees a last link with the past severed. In the semifeudal society celebrated by Roth, death cemented the bond between generations: "Everything which grew needed much time to grow and everything which perished needed a long time to be forgotten."[17]

A parallel to these Austrian students of death was the Trieste-born Italian writer Italo Svevo (1861–1928).[18] Son of an Austrian father and an Italian-Jewish mother, Svevo, whose given name was Ettore Schmitz, studied for five years at Würzburg before settling at Trieste from 1878 to 1928. After his father had gone bankrupt, he was forced to work as a bank clerk from 1879 to 1897, living thereafter as an independent writer. In 1907 Svevo took English lessons from James Joyce. Like other intellectuals of Trieste, Svevo felt hate-love both for Austria and for the bourgeois culture that he saw dissolving around him; affinity with Austria encouraged him to write a pidgin-Italian that has been acclaimed more abroad than in Italy. Having been influenced as a young man by Schopenhauer, in *Una Vita* (1893) he portrayed a bank employee Alfons Nitti, for whom suicide offers a welcome release. In what might be called "Portrait of the Artist as an Old Man," *Seniltà* (1898) depicted another little man who feels prematurely old. Both tales employed a stream-of-consciousness technique similar to that of Schnitzler. After 1900, Svevo was influenced first by Weininger and then decisively by Freud, who is scrutinized in *La Coscienza di Zeno* (1923). Following his father's death, Zeno cultivates an inner life, whose naiveté caricatures psychoanalysis as well as Austrian soldiers. Although Svevo became well-known during the 1920's owing to James Joyce's endorsement, his roots in Austria have been largely ignored.

The most celebrated of these poets of death—and the typical impressionist—was the Vienna-born Jewish doctor, Arthur Schnitzler (1862–1931). Son of a Hungarian-born laryngologist, young Schnitzler grew up a dandy in Ringstrasse Vienna. He revealed his vagaries as an apprentice to his father in recently published memoirs, *Jugend in Wien: Eine Autobiographie* (Vienna, 1968), written between 1915 and 1918. There he described how differently death appears in the dissecting room and at the bedside of a patient:

> At the head of a death-bed, even when it was someone unknown who had just died, death always stands there to a certain extent as an uncannily great phenomenon; while in the morgue, stripped of his terror, he moves as a kind of pedantic master, whom the student believes himself allowed to mock.[19]

In numerous novellas, Schnitzler explored how death assuages the wounds of the living. In *Ein Abschied,* a young gallant learns that his mistress lies dying in the house of her husband. Guilty and confused, he poses as a friend in order to interrogate the doctor, and when finally he sees her corpse, he imagines her reproaching him for concealing his love. The novella evokes a kaleidoscope of shifting moods through a third-person interior monologue, culminating when the protagonist skulks from the funeral ashamed of his duplicity. In *Die Toten schweigen* (1897), an adulterous wife escapes from a fiacre accident in which her lover is killed. She flees the scene through the nocturnal fog, slinking home where she knows she will confess all to her husband. Through recognizing that she lacks the spine to summon the police, she steels herself to conciliate her spouse. In *Der Ehrentag*, Schnitzler portrayed a little man who has spent a career playing bit parts at the Burgtheater. When a lover of the prima donna organizes a claque to honor this nonenity, unaccustomed applause drives him to suicide, whereupon the actress severs relations with the stunt's instigator. She recognizes that she had cherished the modest actor more than the coffeehouse suitor. Most touching of all is *Der Tod des Junggesellen* (1907), in which a bachelor dies, having left instructions that three friends are to be delivered sealed documents upon his decease. After exchanging condolences, the three friends open the envelopes to learn that the bachelor had committed adultery with each of their wives. Although none tells the others, each resolves to forgive his wife, bowing in reverence before death, the great reconciler. In each of these tales Schnitzler emphasizes the moment of insight, which transfigures a person by unleashing a logjam of repressed conflicts. Experiencing what Joyce called an epiphany, the personages undergo a liberating insight to climax slowly unraveled torment. Death heals by imparting liberation to the living in the manner of psychoanalysis. .Startled by the death of a friend, characters in these novellas attain that wisdom of old age, which in the aphorism of Marie von Ebner-Eschenbach, cannot bear to be cruel to what one must leave ere long.

Although Schnitzler's affinity with Freud will be explored later, his epitomizing of Viennese impressionism deserves mention here. To refer to Arnold Hauser's definition, Schnitzler brooded on "the coincidence of the near and the far, the strangeness of the nearest, most everyday things, the feeling of being for ever separated from the world."[20] The eternal spectator, Schnitzler possessed Protean ability to get inside another person's skin. His characters indulge Viennese capacity for playacting, in which they parade grievances while others profess to be moved. In an interview that Schnitzler granted to George Sylvester Viereck during the mid-1920's, the dramatist formulated impressionist mentality into a credo: "Life always creates new wonders. Everything changes. Everything is new. Every hour gives birth to a new world."[21] Schnitzler avowed a need for variety so urgent that he always wrote two plays at once and invariably read several books simultaneously. He confessed a craving to see the familiar from ever new points of view:

When nature repeats herself, we recognize her infinite variety. When a poet repeats himself, we say he is growing stale. There is nothing to justify this conclusion. The poet, like nature, seeks perfection by experimenting with the same material.[22]

Anticipating Hauser's stress on the impressionists' quest for change, in 1909 Ernst Bertram (1884–1957), a German disciple of Stefan George, described the literature of Young Vienna as schizophrenic.[23] These aesthetes were so labile, Bertram declared, that, as in the acting of Eleonora Duse, each mood of theirs would vanish before it could be glimpsed. Groping to chain Proteus, artists endeavored to arrest the moment, whether in pictures by Romako, novellas by Schaukal, feuilletons by Altenberg, verse by Hofmannsthal, or essays by Bahr.[24] Schnitzler conceded to Viereck a sense of frustration at life's elusiveness:

we do not think in words nor in pictures, but in something we cannot grasp. If we could grasp it, we would have a world language. . . . The musician speaks a universal language. Emotion is universal. Thought is individual and untranslatable.[25]

Revering emotion as more contagious than language, Schnitzler sought to expose a latent world behind the manifest one. No less than Freud, Schnitzler believed that every impression imparted at once knowledge and illusion, arguing that words can echo but never truly convey the substratum of experience. Hence the paradox—seen also in Svevo and Schaukal—that the familiar seems strange and the remote, ordinary. For Viennese impressionists, death afforded a supreme arbiter to symbolize at once the latent content of life—the unconscious and emotions that words cannot transmit. In Schnitzler's novellas only the death of a friend exerts impact enough to shatter pretenses of everyday life. For the impressionist, every moment meant a little dying, and a rebirth.

Openness to vicissitudes and to multiplicity helps to explain the originality of thinkers like Freud, Schnitzler, and even Mayreder, who endeavored to piece together experience into an impressionist mosaic. The lability that Schnitzler discerned in all experience has long been hailed as a feminine trait. The skill of Schnitzler, Bahr, and Hofmannsthal—as well as Freud—in portraying women came as no accident: it was a mainspring of their sensitivity. Critics like Bertram who deem

Viennese impressionists passive and feminine recognize what was at once a strength and a weakness. Some like Ehrenstein squandered themselves in therapeutic nihilism, while others like Schaukal and Hofmannsthal embraced tradition. All of them constructed countless pairs of polar opposites, interweaving the fleeting and the permanent, the present and the past, the manifest and the latent. Creators as disparate as Freud and Bahr, Mayreder and Weininger, Musil and Kassner, Buber and Broch excogitated binary pairs and spawned neologisms to express them.

By fostering openness to new perspectives and inviting attention to previously overlooked facts, impressionism enhanced Viennese creativity. In the keenest minds like Mach and Freud, it tempered positivism by instilling a tentative approach to system-building, whereby basic premises were never regarded as irrefragable. This blend of impressionism with positivism meant that Freud would welcome new insights only so long as they did not topple, as did those of Alfred Adler and Jung, still shaky foundations. Through an uneasy alliance of impressionism with laboratory-trained caution, Freud built the most enduring monument of the Gay Apocalypse, clothing insights of an artist in dogmatic utterances of a scientist.

DEATH AS REFUGE:
SUICIDES BY AUSTRIAN INTELLECTUALS

Between 1860 and 1938 an astonishing number of Austrian intellectuals committed suicide. Crown Prince Rudolf was but the best known of a dozen prominent men who chose to terminate unbearable anguish. While his death in January, 1889, publicized the Habsburg Empire as a center for suicide, numerous novellas about it underline the prevalence of this phenomenon. J. J. David in *Ein Poet?* (1892), Svevo in *Una Vita*, Schnitzler in *Der Ehrentag*, Saar in *Ausser Dienst* (1904), and Ebner-Eschenbach in *Das tägliche Leben* (1910) portrayed suicide sympathetically. Almost two dozen cases of suicide are reviewed here, recounting the demise of certain figures discussed elsewhere in the book.[26]

Three eminent men of letters and two scholars of international repute committed suicide at least partly to extinguish the pain of incurable illness. On January 28, 1868, Adalbert Stifter died, two days after he had slashed his throat so as to escape from cancer of the liver. The harmony-loving novelist, who had affirmed Leibnizian faith in Providence, proved no match for the agony meted out to him. On July 24,

1906, Ferdinand von Saar shot himself at Vienna, suffering from an incurable intestinal ailment and appalled by new currents in literature. Twenty-two years earlier almost to the day, Saar's wife had killed herself. A somewhat different case concerned the dramatist Ferdinand Raimund (1790–1836), who shot himself after being bitten by his dog. As if to symbolize the futility of a Biedermeier "little man," Raimund convinced himself—wrongly as it turned out—that the dog was rabid. Like Stifter and Saar, he suffered despondency because his works went unappreciated.

Two further cases of suicide, induced by illness, coming within three years of each other, caused greater consternation. The Vienna physicist Ludwig Boltzmann, a popular lecturer and assiduous researcher, stunned the learned world by committing suicide on September 5, 1906, at Duino near Trieste. Raised a pious Catholic, Boltzmann had fallen prey to depression after a festive banquet celebrating his sixtieth birthday. Overworked from years in the laboratory and irritated by acute nearsightedness, he feared that he had lost his creativity. Worsening attacks of angina pectoris triggered his totally unexpected act. Widely mourned as the first physicist, if not the first natural scientist, to take his own life, Boltzmann's death scandalized his colleagues into supposing that he must have been temporarily deranged. As if to reassure academic Europe, one necrologist quoted Boltzmann as having averred several years earlier, "Only a person not in his senses (nicht bei Sinnen) can take his own life."[27]

The Galician-born Jewish social theorist Ludwig Gumplowicz created a somewhat milder sensation when he and his invalid wife took poison on August 20, 1909. Known as a rigorous theorist of group conflict, the Graz Professor was a buoyant man, who for decades had nursed an ailing wife. After accidentally biting off part of his tongue in 1907, he had incurred cancer by 1909. Rather than allow himself to waste away before his wife's helpless eyes, Gumplowicz and his wife elected self-inflicted euthanasia. Unlike Boltzmann, the seventy-year-old scholar shouldered his lot with stoic calm, unaffected by the suicide twelve years before of his son Maximilian Ernst Gumplowicz (1864–1897). In contrast with the qualms of Boltzmann and Gumplowicz stands the fortitude of Sigmund Freud, who from 1923 to 1939 withstood excruciating pain from cancer of the palate. If anyone had cause to flee from pain, it was he; in defiance of it, he wrote a half-dozen books while living to be eighty-three.

More symptomatic of conditions in Austria were suicides prompted by conflict between inner conviction and outer circumstances. As we have mentioned, in April, 1868, one of the two designers of the new

Opera House, Eduard Van der Null hanged himself over a cavil that Franz Joseph had let slip about the otherwise magnificent structure, into which the architect had poured his life's work. His inseparable companion and collaborator, August Siccard von Siccardsburg, died two months later of a heart attack brought on by grief. The emperor was so appalled by the consequences of his remark—made inadvertently to an adjutant—that for nearly fifty years thereafter he never voiced opinions in public, uttering instead a phrase that became proverbial, "*Es war sehr schön, es hat mich sehr gefreut.*" "It was very beautiful, I enjoyed it very much."[28]

Another Biedermeier tragedy involved the inventor Franz von Uchatius (1811–1881), who had labored twenty years to perfect an alloy called steel-bronze. Manufactured after 1874 by the Skoda works at Pilsen, it gave Austria the sturdiest cannon in Europe. Embittered by years of bureaucratic opposition and disappointed by a recent failure of his alloy when tested in coastal guns, Uchatius killed himself in June, 1881. An autopsy revealed that he was also suffering from incipient cancer of the stomach. His suicide notwithstanding, he was buried, like Crown Prince Rudolf eight years later, with full military and ecclesiastical honors.

Suicide played a crucial role in furthering the career of Sigmund Freud. On September 13, Nathan Weiss (1851–1883), a promising Jewish neurologist, hanged himself in a public bath at Vienna, ten days after returning from a disastrous honeymoon for which he had sacrificed everything. Because Weiss's death opened a vacancy in neurology at the Medical Faculty, Freud decided to launch a career in this field; he explained the suicide to his fiancée as resulting from Jewish self-hatred.[29] A year later the Jewish art historian Moriz Thausing (1838–1884) drowned himself in the Moldau, exhausted from increasing irritability and overwork. As in the case of Boltzmann, perfectionism finally overpowered him. A year after that the Moravian-born poet Alfred Meissner, an advocate of friendship between Czechs and Germans, was hounded into cutting his throat at Bregenz after the Prague-born epigone Franz Hedrich (1823–1895) had for twenty years accused him of plagiarism. Fourteen years later Hungarian literary critic Jenö Péterfy (1850–1899), a connoisseur of Plato, Aristotle, and Dante, committed suicide to quell perfectionist qualms that had long tormented him.

After 1900, several Austrian thinkers in their twenties took their own lives. The most renowned was, of course, Otto Weininger, who shot himself in a room rented in the house where Beethoven had died. While critics mocked his death as an object-lesson in the dangers of nihilism, his friends saluted him for heeding his own principles. We mention again the son of Ludwig Gumplowicz, Maximilian, a promising scholar of Polish literature, who in 1897 shot himself while imprisoned for lese majesty. He despaired of ever being able to better the world. In April, 1908, the Vienna-born expressionist painter Richard Gerstl killed himself because the Viennese ignored his talent. Two years later at Berlin, Prague-born Jewish chemist Max Steiner (1884–1910) poisoned himself, after writing several well-received treatises on free thought and Darwinism. A Jewish anti-Semite, whose hunger for perfection resembled Weininger's, Steiner had embraced Catholicism the year before.[30] In November, 1914, Georg Trakl, already an alcoholic and narcotics addict, died in a Krakow hospital, evidently from an overdose of drugs. It is not known whether the visionary poet, unnerved by suffering he had witnessed as a medic on the Galician front, took his own life by design or by accident.[31] Around 1900, at least three young men who later achieved fame tried unsuccessfully to kill themselves. About 1895, Bohemian-born Alfred Kubin (1877–1959), addicted to drink and hypnotism, tried to shoot himself on the grave of his mother, and in 1903, Alban Berg (1885–1935) attempted suicide after an unhappy love affair. Suffering increasingly from syphilitic paralysis, in October, 1898, Hugo Wolf tried to kill himself shortly after being released from an insane asylum.

Suicide occurred so frequently among persons under thirty that members of the Vienna Psychoanalytical Society, led by Alfred Adler, devoted a symposium to the topic in early 1910. In particular they probed suicides by gymnasium students such as Marie von Ebner-Eschenbach had sketched in *Der Vorzugsschüler* (1900). Wilhelm Stekel and Isidor Sadger argued that suicide originates in desire to expiate sexual guilt, especially that stemming from masturbation, while Adler saw in adolescent suicide an escape from uncompensated feelings of inferiority. Stekel went so far as to declare:

> No one kills himself who has never wanted to kill another or at least wished the death of another. We psychoanalysts know how powerful a role this flirtation with the idea of death, of the nearest relatives as well as of more distant persons, plays in the development of a neurosis.[32]

As chairman of the symposium, Freud expressed disappointment at the result, observing that the participants had offered no explanation as to what process destroys the instinct for self-preservation.[33] In 1910 Freud was not ready to postulate any sort of death instinct.

Within five years after 1918 two suicides occurred inside the psychoanalytical movement, prompting *Schadenfreude* among its critics. In

March, 1919, a Slovakian-born Jew Victor Tausk (1879–1919) killed himself after writing several seminal papers on the mechanism of psychosis.[34] Recently divorced, he had had an affair in 1913 with Lou Andreas-Salomé, and during the war he had spent four grueling years as a military doctor. Exhausted by the war and deeming himself a failure, Tausk wrote farewell notes to Freud, to Frau Andreas-Salomé, and to the fiancée whom he had planned to marry eight days later. Vienna-born Herbert Silberer (1882–1923), a close friend of Wilhelm Stekel, hanged himself from the window of his room, despondent that his studies of mythology and symbolism had been repudiated by Freud's circle.

Between 1920 and 1937 there occurred three Hungarian suicides of note. The jurist Felix Somló (1873–1920) ended his life at Klausenburg out of disgust at the cession of his university to the Romanian state. In 1937 two Hungarian poets killed themselves: the proletarian Attila József (1905–1937), destined to become a Marxist hero after 1945, threw himself under a train, while the languid Szeged-born lyric poet Gyula Juhász (1883–1937) succeeded in ending his misery after eleven previous attempts had failed.[35]

Enlarging the list of young Austrians who killed themselves were the children of four prominent writers. Besides Maximilian Gumplowicz, a son of Ernst Mach, Heinrich, took his own life in 1894 after completing studies at Göttingen. The father never recovered from the blow, which may have helped to induce a stroke four years later. In July, 1928, the daughter of Arthur Schnitzler, Lilli, died of blood poisoning after slashing her wrists, prompting her father to recall to Alma Mahler-Werfel how in 1907 he had seen Gustav Mahler stricken by grief over the death of his infant daughter.[36] In July, 1929, the twenty-six-year-old son of Hugo von Hofmannsthal, Franz, shot himself in his parents' house at Rodaun. Two days later the father, who for three years had suffered from acute arteriosclerosis, succumbed to a heart attack as he was about to depart for his son's funeral. The older Hofmannsthal was buried in the same grave with his son, clad in the habit of the Tertiary Franciscan Order. The inability of these children of famous fathers to endure life under the shadow of greatness bears tragic witness to destructive forces that harassed the Habsburg Empire perhaps more relentlessly than elsewhere.

A distinctive type of suicide in which Austrian intellectuals led the rest of Europe was that induced in Jews by the Nazis. On March 16, 1938, Egon Friedell leaped to his death from an apartment window as storm troopers ascended the staircase. The Brünn-born physician and semi-Marcionist writer, Ernst Weiss (1882 or 1884–1940), killed himself at Paris, as did Wilhelm Stekel (1868–1940) while suffering from diabetes at London. Two years later Stefan Zweig, (1881–1942) together with his second wife, shot himself near Rio de Janeiro, declaring that he was too old to accommodate to a fresh environment.[37] A Vienna-born historian of science Edgar Zilsel (1891–1944) killed himself in New York, partly out of despair at his inability to adapt to the new world.

Additional evidence that suicide was accepted as a matter of course in Austria appears from two false reports. In March, 1889, the painter Anton Romako died suddenly of natural causes. Coming on the heels of Crown Prince Rudolf's deed, Romako's death was rumored to have been a self-inflicted escape from poverty and isolation. The Vienna-born novelist Otto Stoessl (1875–1936), who delighted in tales of neglected artists, speculated about Romako's alleged suicide in a novella *Der einzige Kenner* (1932). Because Romako had been so self-effacing, years elapsed before the public knew that he had not taken his own life.[38] Still more symptomatic of Austrian flirtation with death was a rumor that Theodor Herzl had died a suicide.[39] This canard is true only in the sense that Herzl had worked himself to death while promoting Zionism. On June 3, 1904, he was brought in a state of collapse to the Lower Austrian resort of Edlach, where he contracted pneumonia on July 1. He spent his last day, July 3, awaiting the arrival of his mother from Vienna; she reached his bedside a few hours before he expired in the presence of his doctor. Since Herzl's biographers disdain to discuss rumors of his suicide, their source has yet to be traced. Probing their origin might shed light on Austrian attitudes toward Zionism.

It is difficult to assess the two dozen suicides enumerated here, not to speak of the attempted suicides, rumored ones, or those induced by Nazis. The eight or so gifted young men who after 1890 opted out of life were abandoning a society that tormented countless others. Indeed, the roster of anguished geniuses who might have committed suicide but did not is even longer: Gustav Mahler, Hugo von Hofmannsthal, Oskar Kokoschka, Egon Schiele, Albert Ehrenstein, Ludwig Wittgenstein, and Otto Rank somehow surmounted their qualms without seeking death. In an atmosphere heavy with Protektion and duplicity, desperate intellectuals preferred suicide to twilight existence in an insane asylum. Except for the Hungarians János Bolyai, István Széchenyi, and Nikolaus Lenau, all of whom languished under psychiatric detention, the Habsburg Empire produced hardly any cases of prolonged insanity to compare with Germans like Hölderlin, Robert Schumann, Nietzsche, or Oskar Panizza, not to mention the Frenchmen Gérard de Nerval and Paul Verlaine. Could it be that the Baroque ceremonial of death, and its successor the impressionist cult of evanescence, made suicide seem attractive and even natural to certain Austrians? Power-less to deter even devout men like Stifter, Roman Catholic scruples may even have invited suicide in a culture that esteemed death as an undisclosed side of life. Among those contemplating the act, a con-viction that death heals those left alive may have allayed fear of public opinion. The relative absence of suicides among Hungarian intellectu-als before 1920 suggests that their immersion in politics militated against suicide. Less alienated and more committed to political reform, Hungarian intellectuals welcomed neither impressionism nor prema-ture death.

As shown by Weininger, proclivity to suicide could spring from therapeutic nihilism. The Vienna-born Hungarian Karl Polanyi (1886–1964) expounded this correlation in an article of 1954 on *Hamlet*. The brother of Michael Polanyi recounted that while serving in the Austro-Hungarian cavalry during World War One he read that play twenty times. In the figure of Hamlet he saw epitomized an attitude that afflicted many of his contemporaries; like the Prince of Denmark they could not decide to live.

> If challenged to choose between life and death, he [Hamlet or the Austrian] would be undone, since he cannot deliber-ately choose life.[40]

Willing to exist only so long as he could avoid choosing between life and death, the Austrian let life degenerate into a missed opportunity. Such hesitancy constituted the reverse side of Viennese impression-ism; this world view so cherished evanescence that it could not es-pouse survival. Declining to commit themselves to life, impressionists either embraced therapeutic nihilism in the manner of Weininger and Ehrenstein, or else condoned it with the scruples of Schnitzler, Hof-mannsthal, and Bahr. Even before 1900 these resolutely apolitical thinkers refused to combat the violence that was engulfing politics under the lash of irredentists and anti-Semites. Anticipating the par-alysis of the Vienna Circle during the 1930's, impressionists could propound no rational argument for expunging brutality. Having opted out of politics, aesthetes of Young Vienna predisposed their successors to acquiesce in the demise of their world. Ferdinand Kürnberger once called the Viennese a people who could not say no. By refusing to say no to violence and to death, the Viennese of 1900 cultivated an openness that made them pioneers of modernity. Yet flaccidity ex-cluded them from reaping any fruits: having compromised with death, impressionists and their progeny unwittingly abetted its perpetrators.

Philosophers of Science

ERNST MACH'S REDUCTION OF PHILOSOPHY
AND PSYCHOLOGY TO PHYSICS

B Y SHUNNING metaphysics while cultivating manysidedness, positivism at Vienna resembled impressionism. Interacting like "feuding brothers," these mentalities sustained numerous philosophers of science, philosophers of language, and psychoanalysts. This chapter examines how hostility to metaphysics inspired the physicists-turned-philosophers who abounded at Vienna. Of these the most famous was Ernst Mach (1838–1916), one of Austria's most resourceful and influential thinkers.[1] After having met Mach at Prague in late November, 1882, forty-year-old William James wrote to his wife, "I don't think anyone ever gave me so strong an impression of pure intellectual genius."[2]

Born at Turas near Brünn, Mach owed his independence of mind in part to the fact that until age fifteen he was tutored at home by his father. A landowner and teacher who sympathized with the rebels of 1848, his father urged Mach to emulate heroes of Greek and Latin literature. Although young Mach took his Matura at Krems in 1855, he had already deviated into free thought. He studied mathematics and physics at Vienna under the German Johannes von Ettingshausen (1796–1878), earning a doctorate in 1860 and a habilitation in 1861. Soon thereafter he met Josef Popper-Lynkeus, who became a lifelong friend. For several years Mach gave private lessons on the psychophysics of Fechner before becoming a professor of mathematics at Graz from 1864 to 1867. There he became a close friend of the economist Emanuel Herrmann (1839–1902), who in 1869 put the world in his debt by inventing the postal card. Mach's most fruitful years were spent as a professor of experimental physics at Prague from 1867 to 1895. During 1879–1880, he served as rector of the university, opposing vigorously its division into German and Czech faculties. After this reform had been enacted, Mach refused reelection as rector, likening the riots of Czechs against Germans to wars of religion in the seventeenth century. In 1895 Mach accepted a call to fill a new chair at Vienna in the history and theory of inductive sciences, a post that Theodor Gomperz at the urging of his son Heinrich had helped to found. A year later he was joined at Vienna by his Prague colleague, Friedrich Jodl.

Mach was able to complete only three years of teaching at Vienna before a stroke that occurred in a railroad car in 1898 paralyzed his right side, forcing him to resign from the university in 1901. Although at that time he declined a title of nobility, he did accept membership in the Herrenhaus. Thereafter he lived in retirement at Vienna, so crippled that he was unable to play his beloved piano and organ. The suicide of his son Heinrich in 1894 remained an inconsolable loss, for which his eldest son Ludwig tried to compensate through assiduous care and assistance in the laboratory. Mach died in 1916 near Munich, where he had gone so as to be near Ludwig. Despite the acerbity of his views, Mach was an extremely kind man, unfailingly generous to opponents and students alike.

Since World War Two, Mach's name has become known as a term used to designate the velocity of supersonic aircraft. Technically, Mach number indicates the ratio between airflow velocity and the speed of sound. It was a Swiss physicist, Jakob Ackeret (1898–), who in the late 1920's suggested the concept of Mach number as a way of honoring the Austrian's pioneering studies of airflow made at Prague during the late 1860's. Using the slit-technique of diffraction that the German Toepler had devised in 1864, Mach made photographs of bullets in flight. In *Optisch-akustische Versuche* (1872), he reported that bullets exceeding the speed of sound cause not one but two shock waves: a headwave of gas constricted in front and a tail wave created by a vacuum to the rear. He discovered further that two reports accompany the discharge of a firearm: a report of the shot *(Knall des Geschosses)* follows the projectile, while the thunder of the firearm *(Donner des Geschützes)* occurs at the aperture of the barrel. These analyses were confirmed by photographing cannon fired in 1889 at the naval base of Pola and at the Krupp factory at Meppen.[3] It remained for Ackeret forty years later to apply Mach's ballistic findings to the aerodynamics of aircraft.

In his own time, Mach was renowned for a monistic philosophy of science, which came to be identified with the empirio-criticism of Richard Avenarius (1843–1896) at Zürich.[4] Although Mach first read Avenarius only in 1883, he later credited this positivist with having helped to win acceptance for his own position. Mach disdained his reputation among professional philosophers, desiring instead the esteem of natural scientists. Like his friend Popper-Lynkeus, Mach revered the Enlightenment for having exposed misapplication of concepts like God, nature, and soul. Against such fictions, Mach invoked as his maxim the principle of economy enshrined in Occam's razor: the best theory is that which employs a minimum of variables. Following the commandment of Wilhelm Ostwald that "Thou shalt make unto thee no mental image or likeness whatsoever," Mach insisted that in physics measurement should replace pictorialization. Hypotheses like that of the ether or of atomic theory he deprecated as metaphysical constructs that multiplied entities needlessly. Henri Becquerel's discovery in 1896 of radioactivity came too late to shake Mach's skepticism about the atom. Similarly, he impugned Einstein's theory of special relativity, partly on the grounds that it presupposes the extramental existence of natural laws. Only late in life did Mach acknowledge that his own rejection of absolute time as an abstraction had stimulated Einstein.[5]

Philipp Frank (1884–1966), a Prague-born Jew who studied physics in Vienna before succeeding Einstein as professor of physics at Prague from 1912 to 1939, cited an aphorism by Goethe to characterize Mach's position:

Die Konstanz der Phänomene ist allein bedeutend; was wir dabei denken, ist ganz einerlei.

The constancy of phenomena alone is important; what we think about them is immaterial.[6]

Frank specified that Mach's distrust of theory was useful only in order to defend the edifice of physics against attack from other disciplines. Within physics, however, phenomenalism tended to stifle constructive hypotheses. At a time when most physicists prided themselves on penetrating nature's ultimate secrets, Mach delighted in recalling previous errors. He documented his skepticism toward theory by chronicling the evolution of hypotheses in mechanics, acoustics, optics, and the theory of heat. Through exposing the blunders of previous researchers, Mach hoped to show the artificiality of even his own formulations. Together with Pierre Duhem, he became an unwitting pioneer of the history of science.

After assuming his new chair in Vienna, Mach increasingly pursued historical studies. In his inaugural lecture he professed to be exploring relations between physics, psychology, and epistemology. The task of philosophy he defined as the critical extension, interworking, and unification of individual sciences, an enterprise in which Otto Neurath was to follow him.[7] In *Erkenntnis und Irrtum: Skizzen zur Psychologie der Forschung* (Leipzig, 1905; 5th ed., 1926), Mach showed affinity with Wilhelm Jerusalem's pragmatistic sociology of knowing. Rejecting altogether Kant's a priori theory of number, Mach argued that our system of integers had arisen to fill an economic need for simple notation and rapid calculation.

Mach's hostility to theory in physics was reinforced by research in psychology. He had been one of the first to exploit methods proposed by Gustav Fechner in his two-volume *Elemente der Psychophysik* (Leipzig, 1860). By measuring stimuli this pastor's son had tried to establish the theological dogma of interdependence between body and soul. Discarding Fechner's metaphysics, in 1860 Mach had begun to test the law formulated in 1834 by Ernst Heinrich Weber (1795-1878) that the intensity of sensation varies directly as the intensity of its stimulus. During 1863 Mach reported his results in a series of lectures.[8] In his *Beiträge zur Analyse der Empfindungen* (Jena, 1886; 2d ed., 1900),[9] Mach recapitulated all empirical research on sensation in order to vindicate his doctrine that sensations *(Empfindungen)* are the sole elements of experience. The ego Mach dismissed as a useless hypothesis. Consciousness consists of sensations coming in an orderly, continuous flow, while memory involves reawakening a previous constellation of sensations. Although our sensory apparatus necessarily distorts what it perceives, we lack any means of differentiating impressions from reality. Abandoning any distinction between reality and appearance, Mach left man awash in a sea of appearances. He claimed that he had espoused this doctrine just two or three years after reading, in his father's library, at age fifteen, Kant's *Prolegomena to Any Future Metaphysic*. Like Meinong, he proliferated the chemical metaphors dear to nineteenth-century empiricism, ascribing to the psyche elements and complexes that to us seem needless hypotheses.

Besides research on airflow, Mach made an epochal discovery in psychology. Working simultaneously with, albeit independently of, Freud's mentor Josef Breuer, Mach discovered the function of the semicircular canals in the inner ear. In *Grundlinien der Lehre von den Bewegungsempfindungen* (Leipzig, 1875), Mach reported having confirmed a suggestion made by F. Goltz in 1870 that the labyrinthine canals are sense organs of equilibrium.[10] Mach had demonstrated that during movements of the head fluid in the canals lags so as to activate nerves. Breuer took a neurological approach, showing that when the canals are removed, dizziness cannot be induced, and that during rapid motion of the head, eyes make a reflex movement in the opposite direction. Mach and Breuer each displayed their customary generosity by crediting the other for what was in fact a duplicate discovery.

Through his philosophy and even more through his psychology, Mach exerted wide influence. Among philosophers, he helped to provoke Mauthner's critique of language, and Husserl was prodded during the 1890's by opposing Mach's psychologism.

Stöhr and Wahle elaborated Mach's rejection of ego into a doctrine that the psyche consists of isolated sequences of events. Mach's reductionist psychology also found acclaim among impressionists of Young Vienna. In his *Dialog vom Tragischen* (Berlin, 1904), Bahr used Mach's notion of the irrecoverable ego *(das unrettbare Ich)* to justify the subjectivity of fellow writers, predicting that critics would hail Mach's world view as the "philosophy of impressionism."[11] Young Hugo von Hofmannsthal (1874–1929), who heard Mach lecture in 1897, displayed remarkable affinities with him. In his *Chandosbrief* (1902), Hofmannsthal lamented the loss of an Archimedean point, which would enable one to discriminate appearance from reality. The poet felt adrift in a flux of sensations, which without being true or false merge into external reality. Gotthart Wunberg has pointed out that both Mach and Hofmannsthal borrowed the terminology of Fechner, for whom the words mind, soul, and consciousness *(Geist, Seele,* and *Bewusstsein)* were interchangeable.[12] This vocabulary presupposed a process of depersonalization in which soul flows into body and body into the external world, demolishing all verities built on a Platonic dualism of mind and matter. It was Mach's fusion of mind with matter which Broch denounced as the death-knell of Platonism.

Several interpreters of Viennese impressionism have argued, like Bahr, that Mach's psychology of sensations epitomized that movement.[13] If impressionism means reducing any higher world to a flux of sensations, then the reductionism of Mach, and even more that of Wahle, incarnates impressionism. The definition of Hauser is, however, more comprehensive: impressionism was not primarily a philosophy but an aesthetic attitude that reveled in constant shifts of perspective. Its fascination with evanescence unmasked latent substrata beneath manifest variety, so that impressionism tended to be antisystematic and antimetaphysical, eschewing monism no less than dualism. The malleability of impressionism Mach echoed when he chided Richard Hönigswald for squeezing the master's thought into a Procrustean bed: "Once more, there is no such thing as the 'philosophy of Mach.'"[14] Through his antidogmatism, Mach attracted young Austrian thinkers like Hofmannsthal, Hönigswald, Rudolf Holzapfel, Emil Lucka, and Musil, who held little in common except an impressionist's openness to disparate points of view.[15] Although like Schnitzler and Schaukal, Mach engaged in introspection—his stroke of 1898 impelled him to a lengthy interior monologue[16]—he did not countenance their flirtation with death. To him degeneration was a curse, not a harbinger. Mach, like Freud, coupled impressionism with the older positivism, combining belief in the play of appearances with faith in a bedrock of monism. Although he insisted that experience resolves into a flux of sensations, Mach, unlike Bahr, remained convinced that at bottom rules of reason prevail.

The breadth of Mach's following may be judged from his influence on Russian Marxism. Alexander Bogdanov (1883–1928) and Anatoly Lunacharsky (1875–1933) espoused the empirio-criticism of Avenarius and Mach in order to revise Marx's materialism.[17] Lenin published a celebrated diatribe against their revisionism in *Materialism and Empirio-criticism* (St. Petersburg, 1908), a polemic of which Mach took little note. The Machist heresy revived when Friedrich Adler, Viktor's son, wrote a treatise on Mach while imprisoned for the assassination of Prime Minister Stürgkh.[18]

Since Herbartianism waned around 1880, few Austrian philosophers have influenced so many fields as Mach. Only Brentano, Husserl and, perhaps, Neurath rivaled him in this respect. United by little except interest in empirical psychology, Brentano and Mach between them swept Herbartianism from the field. Mach went on to subvert all attempts at metaphysics including those of Brentano. Like his colleague Boltzmann, Mach subordinated philosophy to physics. That is one reason why the ex-physicists who comprised the Vienna Circle named their group the Ernst Mach Society.

LUDWIG BOLTZMANN ON THE
COMPLEMENTARITY OF CONTRADICTORY HYPOTHESES

Mach shared his role as popularizer of empiricist monism with the physicist Ludwig Boltzmann (1844–1906).[19] The son of a tax official at Vienna, Boltzmann was raised a devout Catholic in Salzburg and Linz. While still in gymnasium, he amassed universal learning, collecting butterflies and plants on the side. He earned a doctorate in physics at Vienna after three years of study under Josef Stefan (1835–1893) and the eccentric Hungarian-born mathematician Josef Petzval. After taking a habilitation in 1867, Boltzmann became a professor of mathematical physics at Graz from 1869 to 1873. He served there also from 1876 to 1890, following three years as a professor of mathematics at

Vienna. At Graz he was dean of the faculty in 1878 and rector of the university in 1887.

Although the laboratory remained his first love, worsening near-sightedness forced him to pursue more bookish tasks. From 1890 to 1894 he taught at Munich; from 1894 to 1900 he served as Stefan's successor at Vienna; and from 1900 to 1902 he lectured at Leipzig, where stage fright compelled him to return to Vienna as Mach's successor. Boltzmann lectured to 600 students before whom he invited Friedrich Jodl to debate. In these unprecedented sessions, the skeptic Boltzmann demolished the ethical idealism of the grandiloquent Jodl. This event may have deepened the animosity that one student of Boltzmann, Hermann Broch, felt against his teacher. Other students included Vienna-born Lise Meitner (1878–1968), who in 1906 was among the first women to earn a doctorate at Vienna.

In September, 1906, at age sixty-two, Boltzmann committed suicide at Duino, impelled by angina pectoris and by fears that his mental powers were fading.

In physics, Boltzmann extended the research of Stefan, who had helped to introduce James Maxwell's theory of gases to the Continent. In 1871 Boltzmann refined the kinetic theory of gases by using a method of statistical mechanics that a fellow student of Stefan, Bohemian-born Josef Loschmidt (1821–1895), had devised. In 1861 the self-effacing Loschmidt had anticipated the discovery of the benzine ring made four years later by Kekulé. In 1873 through experiments on gases, Boltzmann verified Maxwell's electromagnetic theory of light. The Austrian became best known for having confirmed, in 1884, the law first stated by Stefan five years before that the heat radiation of a cooling body varies as the fourth power of its absolute temperature. In his later years, Boltzmann argued that thermodynamics reflects atomic phenomena, inciting Mach and Ostwald to polemics whose intensity so depressed their victim that they may have contributed to his suicide.

As a philosopher, Boltzmann asserted the arbitrariness of all hypotheses, a view that startled Newtonian physicists. Rather than retreat into Mach's phenomenalism, he argued that several contradictory theories may be equally correct. He tried to resolve controversies, such as those between atomism and Kirchhoff's deductive use of differential equations, by contending that both approaches involve arbitrary mental constructs. Although all such constructs distort some of the facts, they complement rather than exclude one another. Boltzmann agreed with Mach that no construct can show exactly what a continuum is or how a particle behaves. Similarly, there may coexist different representations of the world, each accounting for all the facts;

such world hypotheses are complementary rather than antagonistic.[20]

Above all, Boltzmann owed his skepticism to virtuosity as a mathematician. Although he commanded a fine literary style, his writings abounded in equations and diagrams. So skilled was he in formulating alternative mathematical constructs, that he came to regard philosophy as analogous to mathematics. Here he embodied the cross-fertilization between physics and philosophy which later characterized the Vienna Circle. Boltzmann also anticipated the complementarity principle of Niels Bohr, which holds that contradictory hypotheses may be used to explain different aspects of a single phenomenon. Less contentious than Mach and less corrosive than Stöhr or Wahle, Boltzmann in his eagerness to reconcile alternative hypotheses approximated the syncretism of Rudolf Eisler. Irenicism made the physicist's suicide all the more of a shock. Hailing him as a votary of science, his erstwhile rival Ostwald pronounced Boltzmann a martyr who had burned himself out in research. Although most of his contributions were too technical to be widely appreciated, he demonstrated the kind of insight an expert mathematician could bring to philosophy. In so doing he became a hero to the Vienna Circle and a bugbear to Platonists like Broch.

MORITZ SCHLICK AS PRIME MOVER
AND CRITIC OF THE VIENNA CIRCLE

The guiding spirit of the Vienna Circle was Moritz Schlick (1882–1936), a Berlin-born Protestant descendant of the publicist Ernst Moritz Arndt. Best known for an epistemology that differentiated knowledge (*Erkenntnis*) from experience (*Erlebnis*), Schlick's system of ethics was more idiosyncratic.[21] From 1900 to 1904, he studied physics under Max Planck at Berlin; his dissertation concerned equations to chart refraction of light. Having been habilitated at Rostock in 1911, he served there as a docent and professor of philosophy until 1921. In 1922 he left a newly won appointment at Kiel to accept an invitation from mathematician Hans Hahn (1879–1934) to fill the chair left vacant by Mach and Boltzmann. While teaching at Vienna from late 1922 until 1936, Schlick disseminated neopositivist philosophy, declining in 1929 a call to the University of Bonn. He also served as a visiting professor at Stanford in 1929 and at the University of California at Berkeley during 1931-1932. On June 22, 1936, Schlick was shot to death as he mounted the steps of the University of Vienna on his way to deliver the final lecture in his course on philosophy of physics. The assassin was a student whose thesis in ethics Schlick had refused to pass and who for several years had harassed the professor. Although the slayer had been twice interned for symptoms of paranoia, he was permitted, like the killer of Hugo Bettauer, to plead political motives for a crime that some Austro-Fascists applauded. After being sentenced to ten years' imprisonment, the murderer was pardoned by the Nazis in 1938.

In 1924, with encouragement from Herbert Feigl and Friedrich Waismann, Schlick founded an informal Thursday evening discussion group for philosophers and scientists.[22] In October, 1928, the twenty-odd members organized the Ernst Mach Society, which at Otto Neurath's suggestion soon became known as the Vienna Circle (Wiener Kreis). In 1929 the society sponsored at Prague the first of several international congresses, as well as beginning in 1930 to publish the journal Erkenntnis as a successor to Hans Vaihinger's Annalen der Philosophie. Besides Schlick, luminaries of the Vienna Circle were the Vienna-born Jew Neurath and the German Protestant Rudolf Carnap. Other members included Jodl's student Viktor Kraft (1880–), the Prague physicist Philipp Frank (1884–1966), the historian of science Edgar Zilsel (1891–1944), and as visitors the psychoanalyst Heinz Hartmann (1894–1970), the jurist Felix Kaufmann (1895–1949), and the methodologist Karl Popper (1902–). Mathematicians included besides Hans Hahn, Brünn-born Kurt Gödel (1906–) and Karl Menger (1902–). All members of the circle had received training in modern logic and either mathematics or physics. Hoping to introduce greater rigor into Mach's phenomenalism, they adopted as a working basis Wittgenstein's Tractatus Logico-philosophicus (1921), which defended the axiom of Frege, Whitehead, and Russell that statements of logic can be reduced to mathematical formulas. Even before Gödel's proof of 1931 set obstacles in this path, the group had split into two wings. A radical faction led by Hahn, Neurath, and Carnap espoused physicalism, the view that truth can be measured solely by the logical coherence of statements. A moderate group led by Schlick and Feigl insisted that in addition to the formal truth of the physicalists there exists the material truth of observation. Through students like Albert E. Blumberg, Max Black, and Willard Van Orman Quine as well as Schlick's lectures in California, the Vienna Circle began to attract Americans even before the Dollfuss regime sent most of the group's leaders into exile. It was in the United States that the term "logical positivism" emerged to replace Schlick's label of consistent empiricism (konsequenter Empirismus).[23]

Had it not been for Schlick's affability and patience, the Vienna Circle could not have surmounted its factionalism. Both Schlick and

Carnap deplored Neurath's involvement in Viennese politics. Neurath in turn rebuked Hahn for attending spiritualistic seances, where the latter aspired to introduce rigorous methods of experiment. Although Carnap too pursued parapsychology, Wittgenstein pronounced this to be utter nonsense. While dwelling at Vienna from 1926 to 1929, Wittgenstein found Neurath and Carnap increasingly incompatible, so that by 1928 he confined contact to Schlick, Feigl, and Waismann. Schlick never abandoned the doctrine of his *Allgemeine Erkenntnis-lehre* (Berlin, 1918; 2d ed., 1925), in which, following Alois Riehl, he saluted Hume's skepticism as the climax of epistemology.

Schlick's philosophy is not coextensive with that of the Vienna Circle. In ethics, he opposed the physicalism of Neurath as well as the antimetaphysics of Wittgenstein. In *Lebensweisheit: Versuch einer Glückseligkeitslehre* (Munich, 1908), Schlick had propounded an ethics of youthfulness, derived from Nietzsche, John Ruskin, and Jean-Marie Guyau. He enlarged his plea for self-fulfillment in *Fragen der Ethik* (Vienna, 1930). Throughout Schlick disputed the axiology of Brentano, which postulates absolute moral values. In equating values with feelings of pleasure, Schlick defended neoutilitarianism with a subtlety of psychology rare in any philosopher. People hesitate to acknowledge pleasure as the sole standard of value, said Schlick, because teachers have indoctrinated them to regard the word "pleasure" as itself unpleasant. Anticipating the later Karl Mannheim, Schlick exhorted elementary schools to safeguard social and personal happiness. In rebuking teachers who make pleasant things reprehensible, Schlick paralleled antiauthoritarians such as Mayreder and Popper-Lynkeus. Far from being a hedonist, Schlick praised pain: in order to experience the sublimest pleasures, argued Schlick, the soul must first undergo torment. During pain, hope provides pleasure by dangling the idea of an agreeable future, prodding us to seek relief. Schlick equated human fulfillment with ecstasy: joy and sorrow activate man's whole nature into a convulsion through which "the *whole* person is affected to a depth which few impressions can reach."[24] Because this churning of the depths arises more readily from pain than from enjoyment, aversion to pain stimulates growth more effectively than does quest for pleasure. In a doctrine almost identical with that of Stöhr, Schlick contended that the advance of civilization can be gauged by the extent to which pain has ceased to be indispensable for eliciting pleasure. Schlick expected that gradually civilization would outgrow reliance on suffering.

Schlick elucidated the problem of freedom of the will by demonstrating that concepts pertaining to nature have been erroneously applied to the psyche. He drew up a schema to differentiate the two realms:

Nature	Society
Natural Law	Law of the State
Determinism (Causality)	Coercion
Universal Validity	Necessity (Duty)
Indeterminism (Chance)	Freedom
No Cause	No Compulsion[25]

Each column constitutes a chain of concepts any of which entails the others. In disputes over freedom of the will philosophers have transposed terms from the two columns, confusing indeterminism with freedom from coercion and universal validity with duty. Criticizing Greek jurisprudence based on laws of nature, Hans Kelsen likewise urged moderns to disentangle the two realms that the Greeks had conflated. We must recognize that although natural laws determine behavior, they do not coerce us. Conversely, duty to obey the state rests not on natural law but on the state's power to coerce compliance.

Schlick's most distinctive ethical doctrine was to glorify rejuvenation (Verjüngung). His maxim was: "Preserve the spirit of youth, for it is the meaning of life."[26] Citing Schiller's Letters on Aesthetic Education (1794), Schlick equated youthfulness with play, that is, with ability to relish activity for its own sake heedless of extraneous needs. Genius always throbs with childlikeness (Kindlichkeit), as does any genuine enthusiasm. Spontaneity alone imparts meaning to live. Anticipating demands advanced by young people during the 1960's, Schlick advocated building a society that would maximize in every sphere opportunities for youth. Criticism of coercive education entails combating coercion in any guise.

Emil Utitz (1883–1957), a Prague-born aesthetician trained by Anton Marty, detected in Schlick's ethics traits of expressionism.[27] Having sundered knowledge from experience, Schlick stipulated that ethics concerns not the former, only the latter. Although experience is held to be ineffable, ethics undertakes to communicate about it. It was Schlick's insistence on communicating about the incommunicable which Utitz deemed expressionistic. His skepticism about metaphysics notwithstanding, Schlick held that a man's art and metaphysics unmask the psyche. They express what pleasure a thinker prizes and what pain he dreads. Far from abolishing metaphysics, said Utitz, Schlick would use it to diagnose a soul, much as fellow expressionist Spengler used it to characterize civilizations.

Other members of the Vienna Circle have decried Schlick's ethics of youthfulness as incompatible with Humean skepticism. From his posthumously published aphorisms, one can imagine how Schlick would have deplored the preciosity of some of his self-styled disciples:

> Ein Denker, der *nur* Philosoph ist, kann kein *grosser* Philosoph sein.
> Der ist kein Philosoph, der so handelt, als ob alle Menschen Philosophen wären.
> "Im Mann ist mehr Kind als im Jüngling," sagt Nietzsche. Das erklärt die Misere der Flegeljahre.
> Der Forscher bleibt jung, weil er ewig *Neues* sucht.[28]

> A thinker who is nothing but a philosopher cannot be a great philosopher.
> He is no philosopher who behaves as if all men were philosophers.
> "In an adult man there is more of the child than in a youth," says Nietzsche. This explains the misery of adolescence.
> The researcher remains young because he always seeks the novel.

Schlick would have shuddered to see how logical positivists belittle earlier philosophers. By esteeming life above theory, the founder of the Vienna Circle deviated from most of his colleagues. Neurath, the most energetic thinker of the group, saw his exuberance eclipse Schlick's meticulousness. Curiously, Neurath, who abounded in the youthfulness dear to Schlick, supplanted the latter by converting to physicalism Carnap, who before coming to Vienna in 1926 had endorsed the more eclectic views of Schlick. Slain by a crazed youth, the champion of youthfulness has been forgotten; votaries of spontaneity would profit by emulating his erudition.

THE ECLIPSE OF A
UNIVERSAL MAN: OTTO NEURATH

Otto Neurath (1882–1945) was one of the neglected geniuses of the twentieth century. He made innovations in so many fields that even admirers have lost count of his accomplishments. In no small measure, Neurath owed his versatility to his father, Wilhelm Neurath (1840–1901).[29] A Jew born near Pressburg, the elder Neurath took a doctorate in philosophy at Vienna. After earning a second doctorate in

Staatswissenschaften at Tübingen, he served as a docent at the Technische Hochschule in Vienna and after 1889 as a professor at the Hochschule für Bodenkultur. Between 1878 and 1901 this Hungarian intellectual published twenty books analyzing the social problem. Espousing an ethical idealism similar to that of Friedrich Jodl and Wilhelm Jerusalem, the elder Neurath glorified work as the activity that elevates man above the animals. In his *Volkswirtschaftliche und sozialphilosophische Essays* (Vienna, 1880), he hailed historians both as prophets who pass judgment on the past and as reformers who benefit from millenia of experience. Imbued with the crusading zeal of other Hungarian Jews like Hertzka and Nordau, Wilhelm Neurath preached progressivism to the uneducated, lest proletarians flounder amid the plethora of modern philosophies. Proclaiming that *"Mensch sein, heisst ein Kämpfer sein"* (To be a man is to be a fighter), he embodied Hungarian activism as a check on Vienna's therapeutic nihilism.

Born at Vienna, Otto Neurath absorbed his father's encyclopedic learning and reforming zeal.[30] He studied at Vienna and Heidelberg before taking a doctorate at Berlin in 1906. While studying mathematics there, he edited the little known *Faust* (1839) by Ludwig Hermann Wolfram (1807–1852).[31] As a docent at Heidelberg, Neurath met Max Weber, who influenced his interpretation of ancient economies. Around 1910 he collaborated with Olga Hahn on papers in mathematical logic, and as a professor at the Commercial College in Vienna, he examined the impact of Ruthenes on relations between Russia and Austria-Hungary.[32] In prewar articles on the economics of warfare, he pioneered graphic methods of presenting statistics, anticipating his invention of isotypes ten year later.[33] During World War One, he analyzed wartime economics, while also publishing essays on the history of optics and on medieval theology.[34] It was characteristic of Neurath that he urged students to switch careers every five years.

In 1919 as a consultant to the Bavarian government, Neurath urged, a la Emil Steinbach, that wartime production boards be continued so as to regulate the economy without expropriation. This scheme Lujo Brentano likened to the regimentation of Egypt's pharaohs. Neurath persisted in his project even after Communists had seized power on April 7, 1919. Following their overthrow, he was arrested as a revolutionary, only to be acquitted on the strength of testimony by Max Weber and Ernst Niekisch.[35] While awaiting trial, Neurath wrote *Anti-Spengler* (Munich, 1921), which upheld progressivism against the German pessimist.

Upon returning to Vienna, Neurath initiated his most influential project. In 1923 he founded a Social and Economic Museum (*Gesell-*

schafts - und Wirtschaftsmuseum), located in City Hall and designed to inform the public about Socialist policies. In order to enliven statistics, Neurath devised pictographs—he called them isotypes—which personify integers by means of gaily colored little men, houses, boats, and so forth. Together with his staff, Neurath generated more than two thousand isotypes, for which he foresaw unlimited uses. Above all, he desired to apply them to communication between nations and to instructing the illiterate.[36] By 1940 isotypes had been widely adopted, and by 1950 they were so popular that few people remember their origin in Socialist Vienna. Used today in publishing, advertising, museums, and tourism, this visual alphabet fulfilled Neurath's father's dream of helping plain people to understand their environment.

A friend of Otto Bauer and Max Adler, after 1925 Neurath dedicated himself above all to the Vienna Circle. Having persuaded Carnap to espouse physicalism, Neurath urged that the new philosophy be harnessed to unify science through a universal jargon. In 1934 he transferred his museum to the Mundaneum Institute at the Hague, whence he escaped in 1940 by open motorboat to England. He finished his career at Oxford, editing the *Encyclopedia of Unified Science,* promoting isotypes, and designing new buildings for the bombed town of Bilston.

Neurath was a huge, jolly man, known for kindness to friend and foe alike. He used to sign letters with an isotype of an elephant, drawn to be either buoyant or depressed as the moment warranted. A persuasive speaker and tireless organizer, after 1920 Neurath devoted himself to building bridges between disciplines, classes, and nations. He echoed his father's ideals when he wrote:

> As soon as all men can participate in a common culture and the canyon between the educated and the uneducated is bridged, life will be more fully understood and lived.[37]

Few have done so much to promote an ecumenical spirit and to dismantle boundaries as this human dynamo who died before his causes had gained wide backing.

Early training in mathematics under Gregory Itelson at Berlin made Neurath sympathetic to a mathematical model of truth. For him a proposition has meaning only if it stipulates means for its own verification. He based the epistemology known as physicalism on the notion of protocol sentences. These sentences resemble the minutes *(Protokoll)* of a meeting, recording that an individual "i" at time "t" and place "p" perceived such-and-such. This data equips a second person to verify what was perceived, and to invalidate the report if false. Unified science would consist of a system of noncontradictory protocol sentences, linked by statements of laws. Each fresh sentence must be either integrated into the system or discarded. Insisting that language be intersubjective, Neurath proclaimed that metaphysics cannot satisfy this criterion. In order to shun nonsense, one must keep silent about metaphysics, all the while recognizing, *pace* Mauthner, that one is being silent about something that does not exist. Neurath contended that Schlick's ethics of pleasure and pain concealed a metaphysic, as did the logical atomism of Wittgenstein's *Tractatus*.[38]

Although Neurath's involvement in Socialist politics dismayed Carnap and Schlick, it was he who held the Vienna Circle together after Schlick's death. With Philipp Frank and Charles Morris, he edited the *Encyclopedia of Unified Science* as successor to *Erkenntnis*. He viewed the *Encyclopedia* as a clearinghouse for creating a universal jargon, which in the manner of Leibniz's *mathesis universalis*—and of French structuralism—would permit specialists to coordinate premises and findings.[39] Amid galloping industrialization, the world, Neurath believed, could not spurn his program of building bridges between disciplines.

Perhaps the most startling fact about Neurath is his eclipse after 1945. No thinker discussed in this book was more sympathetic to technology nor more in tune with the post-1945 world than this jack-of-all-trades. Had he lived ten years longer, he might have become a culture hero. His father's zeal for uplifting the masses he implemented through visual education, heeding the maxim that the best teacher knows what to omit. Since World War Two, museums of history and civics such as Neurath pioneered at Vienna have dotted the globe, flourishing especially in Eastern Europe where they dispense propaganda as well as data. In scope of interests, Neurath knew no rival in this century. Who else conducted original research in physics, mathematics, logic, economics, sociology, ancient history, political theory, history of German literature, architecture, and graphics? Among Austrian polymaths not even Ernst Brücke could match this diversity. Together with Richard Coudenhove-Kalergi, Neurath worked for world unification, making Vienna during the 1920's a center for ecumenical enterprises that took wing twenty years later. Like Herzl, Neurath was a practical utopian who sowed for others to reap. It is infamous that he who so enhanced adult education should be ignored, a victim of the specialization that his encyclopedism mocked. No other member of the Vienna Circle so outstripped the group's achievements; no other incarnated so boldly the Austrian talent for integrative thinking.

Philosophers of Language

MEMBERS of the Vienna Circle were not the only Austrian philosophers to reject metaphysics. A differently based critique of traditional philosophy emerged among philosophers of language. One of them, Ludwig Wittgenstein, counts among the most influential thinkers discussed in this book, while two others, Adolf Stöhr and Richard Wahle, are among the least known. These men propounded several types of linguistic philosophy, each of which vindicated Nietzsche's dictum, "I fear that we do not get rid of God because we still believe in grammar."[1]

Fritz Mauthner (1849–1923) was the first Austrian—and perhaps the first thinker anywhere—to jettison metaphysics through a merciless analysis of language.[2] Born in Horzitz, Bohemia, of Jewish parents and raised in Prague, Mauthner took a degree in law there before embarking upon a career as an independent writer and journalist. In Prague he was profoundly influenced by Ernst Mach, whom he heard lecture in 1872; Mauthner was also impressed by the mysticism of Johann Heinrich Löwe (1808–1892), a disciple of Günther and Baader, and by the Catholic Herbartian Wilhelm Volkmann. Mauthner found Hermann von Leonhardi incomprehensible.

From 1876 to 1905 Mauthner lived in Berlin, where he earned fame through writing parodies, such as his two-volume *Nach berühmten Mustern: Parodistische Studien* (Bern, 1878–1880). Historical novels, such as *Der neue Ahasver: Roman aus Jung-Berlin* (Dresden, 1882) and *Xanthippe* (Dresden, 1884), confirmed his skill as a satirist. While serving as editor of the *Berliner Tagblatt*, Mauthner wrote essays criticising the assumption that language can denote concepts. From 1905 to 1907 he lived in Freiburg, and from 1907 to 1923 he occupied a house on Lake Constance where poetess Annette von Droste-Hülshoff had once dwelt. At Berlin Mauthner influenced the Jewish syndicalist Gustav Landauer (1870–1919).[3] In *Skepsis und Mystik: Versuch im Anschluss an Mauthners Sprachkritik* (Berlin, 1903), the German-born Landauer transmuted Mauthner's mysticism of silence into an ethic of action, which stimulated Martin Buber and Max Brod.

Like his fellow Bohemian Jew, Popper-Lynkeus, Mauthner displayed exceptional independence of thought. As nonacademic philosophers the two shared an aversion felt by Schopenhauer, Kierkegaard, Nietzsche, Eduard von Hartmann, and Eugen Dühring toward professors. In Mauthner, awareness of the artificiality of language had arisen during his youth as a Jew in Bohemia, where he had been taught not one but three languages as if each had been the idiom of his ancestors: German, Czech, and Hebrew. Early immersion in three tongues had made him question the reliability of any of them as an instrument of thought. In contrast to Johannes Urzidil, Mauthner deplored the "paper German" spoken in Prague: its vaunted purity cloaked isolation from vivifying dialects. Sharing the revulsion of Rilke at pidgin-Czech *(Kuchelböhmisch)* and at the debased Yiddish of Bohemia, Mauthner, like Bolzano, pleaded in vain for Bohemian Germans to master Czech. Mauthner had been converted into a German nationalist by seeing Prussian wounded after Königgrätz. During the mid-1870's, having shed what little remained of Jewish identity, he exchanged Bohemia's racial strife for the comfort of Bismarck's empire.

Because of his proficiency as a parodist, Mauthner early gained freedom from the fetish of words. In 1922 he wrote that his concept of word-superstition *(Wortaberglaube)* owed its genesis to four influences sustained during the early 1870's. First, Bismarck's deeds had freed Mauthner from the word-superstition that paralyzes politics and law. Second, Nietzsche's *Vom Nutzen und Nachteil der Historie für das Leben* (Leipzig, 1873) had unmasked word-superstition in history. Third, diatribes against Schiller by the Saxon dramatist and Shakespeare-worshiper Otto Ludwig (1813–1865) had liberated Mauthner from the magic of rhetoric. Fourth, Ernst Mach's monism had emancipated him from blind acceptance of theory in natural science. Mauthner regarded his critique of the idols of speech as a culmination both of medieval nominalism and of British skepticism, especially that of Bacon and Hume.

In the three-volume *Beiträge zu einer Kritik der Sprache* (Leipzig, 1901–1903; 3d ed., 1923; repr. Hildesheim, 1967), Mauthner argued that language cannot convey the content of thought because to verbalize destroys the uniqueness of what is thought. In the paraphrase of Gershon Weiler, Mauthner contended:

> My momentary experience is unique, therefore it has no name at the instant, and at the moment I name it, I put it into the stock of my memories and the uniqueness has gone. So experience is always one step ahead of language.[4]

Reality can only be lived; it cannot be embalmed in words. Any effort to translate experience into words propagates empty phrases, which bemuse neophytes without enlightening the initiate. To check word-superstition, Mauthner exhorted thinkers to silence. They should cease asking questions, because answers will only multiply webs of words. Mauthner differed from Wittgenstein in holding that there exists no meta-language in which to define the limits of the sayable. Language lacks what in jurisprudence Georg Jellinek would call *Kompetenz-Kompetenz*, namely capacity to demarcate its own authority. Because language cannot transcend itself in order to assess its own competence, resolute thinkers must renounce speech.

Like many other perfectionists, Mauthner disregarded his own counsel. This rhetorician extolled mystic silence in the four volumes of *Der Atheismus und seine Geschichte im Abendlande* (Stuttgart, 1920–1923; repr. Hildesheim, 1963). In expounding "mysticism without God" (*gottlose Mystik*), he insisted that words like *Gott* or *Gottheit* carry no evidence for the existence of any such entity. Espousing negative theology, Mauthner championed the concept of Tao, nameless and without properties. It could be replaced, he opined, by the neutral syllable "das." Influenced by Meister Eckhart, Mauthner elaborated a critique of language into the staunchest negative theology of the twentieth century. Substituting Tao for Eckhart's hidden god, Mauthner bordered on the gnosis of the Moravian mystic Eugen Heinrich Schmitt. Despite affinities with the Marcionism of Kafka, Mauthner believed that experience can be mastered, however solipsistically. From within the prison of ego, each individual can watch life pulse by, while to send signals from one prison to another entails distortion. To construct these signals into a system of philosophy is sheer folly.

Preaching a therapeutic nihilism worthy of Weininger, Mauthner advocated the self-immolation of thought. We have already mentioned the resemblance between Mauthner's injunction to silence and the pronouncement of Schnitzler that "we do not think in words nor in pictures, but in something that we cannot grasp."[5] Like Viennese impressionists, Mauthner postulated a current of emotion underlying

End of Tractatus

a film of words, which by themselves cannot convey the flux beneath. By intimating the ineffable, Mauthner, like other impressionists, contradicted his own premise, for in strict logic he ought to have kept silent about his silence. One of the few thinkers to heed this inference was Hofmannsthal in his *Chandosbrief*, in which for a few months the poet forswore writing.[6] Other philosophers of language, Stöhr, Kraus, and Wittgenstein, combined love of the medium with more adequate analysis of its limits. Speaking with the nostalgia of an exile about a realm that he had abjured, Mauthner, like another rootless Jew of Bohemia, Gustav Mahler, longed to see God face to face. For both of them, language screened a reality that they could not doubt.

ADOLF STÖHR'S CRITIQUE OF LANGUAGE-SHAPED PHILOSOPHY

One of the least known of Austrian thinkers is the Catholic analyst of language, Adolf Stöhr (1855–1921).[7] Born in St. Pölten, this admirer of Mach studied law, philosophy, and plant physiology at Vienna before turning to philosophy. There he served as a docent in philosophy from 1885 to 1901 and as a professor from 1901–1921, directing the psychological laboratory at the Volksuniversität at a time when the University of Vienna still lacked one. Disdaining colleagues, Stöhr pursued a lonely path in psychology and critique of metaphysics, opposing above all Brentano. His chief disciple is the Vienna-born historian of Greek philosophy, Felix Cleve (1890–), who from 1923 to 1938 served as humanities editor of the *Neue Freie Presse*. The Budapest-born novelist, Erwin Guido Kolbenheyer (1878–1962), an admirer of Paracelsus and later of the Nazis, took a doctorate under Stöhr in 1904, writing a dissertation on visual perception of space.

Stöhr published his most original insights in his *Lehrbuch der Logik in psychologisierender Darstellung* (Leipzig, 1910) and *Psychologie* (Vienna, 1917; 2d ed., 1922). Here he summarized several decades of research during which he had applied Mach's monism to the logic of names and to depth perception.[8] In *Umriss einer Theorie der Namen* (Leipzig, 1889), Stöhr defended psychologistic logic, arguing that the distinction between subject and object derives from language rather than experience. Unlike Mach, he believed that the atomic hypothesis could be useful. Coining terms as cacophonous as those of Weininger or Mayreder, Stöhr distinguished three types of contemplative philosophy. First, theorogonous thought aspires merely to behold; it indulges in wonder without ulterior motive in order to construct an architecturally satisfying picture of the world. Second, glossogonous thought equates linguistic expressions with truth, spawning what Stöhr called glossomorphic or language-shaped philosophy. Stöhr's second category suffers the meretriciousness that Mauthner attributed to all philosophy. Third, pathogonous thought desires knowledge not for its own sake but in order to reduce suffering.

Even more than Schlick, Stöhr exalted the phenomenon of suffering. On this foundation he erected a late-Biedermeier social ethics, which he called biotics. Biotics pursues two paths: its negative task is to teach each individual to diminish suffering, while its positive function is to promote enjoyment. More broadly, communal biotics, or ethics, elevates diminution of suffering into a common goal, while culture is that aspect of communal biotics in which people share enjoyment. Religion, Stöhr noted, can be both negative and positive, belonging partly to ethics and partly to culture. Whereas medicine serves solely to alleviate suffering, the arts belong to both realms; as a Viennese, Stöhr knew that theater can sooth pain as well as impart pleasure. Stöhr eschewed therapeutic nihilism, insisting that pain be eased before enjoyment can thrive. Negative biotics falls into four spheres according to the source of suffering: pain can spring from nonhuman nature, man's own nature, fellow men, or superhuman powers. Pathogonous philosophy aims above all to assuage pain inflicted by superhuman forces such as fate and accidents of birth. It lacks, however, the disinterested majesty of theorogonous contemplation.

In ethics, no less than in psychology, Stöhr lamented the necessity of using metaphors:

> Psychology is under the unpleasant necessity of using for the labelling and treatment of its subject matter a figurative language, which did not develop for such purposes. Language is originally an expression for action and suffering.[9]

As in the case of Mauthner, distrust of metaphors did not deter Stöhr from writing a five-hundred page book about them. In his critique of glossomorphic philosophizing, Stöhr joined company with Mauthner and Wittgenstein:

> In fact the history of logic and a large part of the history of philosophy is the history of wrestling with glossomorphy and metaphors. It is the history of the struggle of developing thinking against the reigning figures of speech.[10]

One of the most egregious examples of glossomorphic thought Stöhr took to be Parmenides' elevation of the empty copula "to be" into a metaphysics of being. In Arabic or Chinese, Stöhr retorted, a philosophy based on the copula could scarcely have arisen. Stöhr classified language-shaped philosophers according to root metaphors, distinguishing verb philosophies from noun philosophies.[11] While castigating metaphysics, Stöhr offered provocative exegeses of historical figures, as when he argued in a lecture of 1916 that Heraclitus had formulated his position in order to refute that of Zoroaster.[12]

In unmasking metaphysical language, Stöhr, like Wittgenstein, may have been influenced by the gulf at Vienna between high German and local vernacular. Although professors usually required students to speak high German, both had to use Viennese dialect if they wished to converse with ordinary citizens. In this bifurcated linguistic culture, students discovered that no single idiom suited all purposes of living and thinking. Like the clash among Czech, German, and Yiddish at Prague, the ubiquity of two dialects at Vienna could only invite skepticism toward the monopoly advocated by professors.

Stöhr has exerted so little influence that it is difficult to assess his significance. Although Mach respected this colleague, an unwieldly terminology and stubborn independence discredited Stöhr in the eyes of others. Wahle pursued a similar path even more relentlessly, proclaiming that not merely most but that all metaphysics is specious. Surprisingly, Stöhr condemned as unscientific the dialogical philosophy proposed by Ferdinand Ebner.[13] Evincing a resigned acquiescence in the inevitability of suffering, Stöhr anticipated not only the philosophy but also the compassion of Wittgenstein, who seems to have ignored his predecessor. Stöhr's inventiveness notwithstanding, the role of prompting Wittgenstein's critique of language fell not to him but to Kraus.

RICHARD WAHLE: THERAPEUTIC NIHILISM DIRECTED AGAINST HERBARTIAN PHRASES

The most caustic of these naysayers was Richard Wahle (1857–1935), a Jewish disciple of Mach who dismissed as rubbish all modern metaphysics except that of Spinoza.[14] Born at Vienna, he took a doctorate in philosophy there in 1882, earning a habilitation three years later. During the early 1880's, he was a friend of Freud, his brother being the Fritz Wahle from whom Freud courted away Anna Bernays. Schnitzler could recall waging a political debate with Richard in 1879.[15] From 1885 to 1895, Wahle served with Stöhr as a docent at Vienna before becoming a professor at Czernowitz from 1895 to 1917.

specious

From 1919 to 1933 he lectured once again at Vienna. Although Wahle kept aloof even more than Stöhr, during the early 1890's he influenced young Heinrich Gomperz (1873–1942), who in turn persuaded his father Theodor to have Mach installed at Vienna.

In early works, Wahle reduced psychology to physiology more relentlessly than either Mach or Stöhr. Under the impact of Theodor Meynert, Wahle argued that experience comprises discrete events (*Vorkommnisse*), which memory classifies artificially in order to impose meretricious order upon unknowable reality. In *Das Ganze der Philosophie und ihr Ende* (Vienna, 1894; 2d ed., 1896) and *Über den Mechanismus des geistigen Lebens* (Vienna, 1896)—each volume exceeds five hundred pages—Wahle paralleled the impressionist psychology of Schnitzler and young Hofmannsthal. Had they read his treatises, writers of Young Vienna might have embraced his disintegration of metaphysics even more readily than that of Mach. Wahle hailed Spinoza as his chief ally in expounding reductionist psychology. The Dutch Jew, he said, had rejected acts of will and judgment while endorsing association of ideas.[16] Wahle despised, however, neo-Romantic disciples of Spinoza like Schelling, together with the latter's followers, Hartmann and Theodor Lipps. He branded as corrupt the notion of an unconscious, whether formulated by Schellingians or by psychoanalysts.[17]

As befitted one who deplored Herbartianism, Wahle, like Stöhr, differentiated speculation from formalistic rehashing of concepts. Since Spinoza, nearly all philosophizing has consisted of reworking wornout concepts, an abuse that Wahle dubbed philosophical *Klatsch*. Metaphysics has known two periods of sustained creativity, in Greece from Hesiod up to, but not including, Aristotle and again in early Christian Europe. Because both these awakenings had sprung from religion, the rise of natural science precluded any third flowering such as Brentano envisioned.

In *Die Tragikomödie der Weisheit: Die Ergebnisse und die Geschichte des Philosophierens: Ein Lesebuch* (Vienna, 1915; 2d ed., 1925), Wahle voiced therapeutic nihilism, while examining the history of philosophy from the sixth-century poet Pherecydes to Hartmann, Lotze, and Avenarius. He disparaged modern philosophers of every camp:

> One must say that Kant left the theory of knowledge in a desolate state of total confusion.

> Thus we have examined the doctrines of Herbart rather thoroughly—a bundle of interesting errors, and yet he was one of the best men!

In philosophy manifestly every possible category is exhausted and now any effort to overlook or surpass agnosticism can be easily recognized as nonsense.[18]

Formulating a critique of language less systematic than that of Mauthner, Wahle inveighed against repetitiousness and abstractness:

> the full word is not distinguished from the empty one, and under the guise of the abstract any imprecision, error, or lie, and every crafty phrase can be disseminated.[19]

Here Wahle vented the scorn of a master stylist, who desired to discredit opponents. Although for more than thirty years he served as docent and professor, he disdained footnotes or index. Cultivating an acidulous style more suited to a feuilleton than a treatise, he patronized Aristotle as a Biedermeier observer and compiler, while branding Hegel a sleight-of-hand artist and Fechner a potpourri.

A sort of virulent Egon Friedell, Wahle assailed Western history with aplomb, displaying an arrogance more usual in the self-educated than in academic thinkers. He matched Weininger and Ehrenstein in utter despair at offering remedies. Together with them, he exemplified the vacuum of values which others denounced without being able to fill. Austria produced no more disconsolate mourner of Western civilization than this disenchanted Viennese Jew. If he swept philosophical language into his indictment, this resulted in part from a surfeit of Herbartianism. If ever a philosophy deserved the charge of mouthing empty concepts, it was the watered down psychology and metaphysics purveyed by Austria's gymnasien after 1850. By intoning a program of reworking concepts, Herbartians exasperated budding positivists. Born between 1849 and 1857, Mauthner, Stöhr, Wahle, and Freud belonged to a Herbartian-trained generation that renounced phrasemaking, leaving it for men born twenty years later to examine language with greater sympathy.

KARL KRAUS'S IDOLATRY OF LANGUAGE: THE CURSE OF A PHOTOGRAPHIC MEMORY

Although the Jewish satirist Karl Kraus (1874–1936) was not primarily a philosopher, his Nestroy-like manipulation of language made him a precursor of Wittgenstein.[20] Born in Bohemia of wealthy parents and raised in Vienna, Kraus had sought unsuccessfully to become an actor.

He wrote nothing but occasional pieces, working all night on copy for *Die Fackel*, which he had founded in 1899 and which from 1911 to 1936 he wrote entirely by himself. Although he promised his ten thousand subscribers "at least four issues per year," annually he churned out hundreds of pages at sporadic intervals. After 1910 he presented more than seven-hundred solo recitations, traveling frequently to Prague and Berlin. Encouraged by Adolf Loos, Kraus was baptized a Catholic in April, 1911, remaining in the church until 1923. An adamant moralist, Kraus was incapable of formulating a position except to denounce specific abuses. A venal journalist, a judicial scandal, a sloppy treatise, a senseless war would rouse him to fury. His satires presuppose a distinctive attitude toward language, which is consistent enough to be called a philosophy of language.

Kraus equated language both with reality and with morality:

> Constrained by my literal interpretation of language, which presupposes, so to speak, a preestablished harmony of languages and of the spheres, I experience art as being above understanding, but not below it.[21]

Language substitutes for God, especially the vengeful God of the Old Testament. Morality and politics must be judged not by their own standards but only insofar as language mirrors them. Kraus pilloried the feuilleton and the entire press for scuttling syntax and for spawning neologisms—vices shared by expressionist poets. A return to the virile usage of Goethe, Jean Paul, and Nestroy would, Kraus believed, rid politics of prevarication.

Kraus's idolatry of language sprang from a photographic memory. He claimed that he could remember every occurrence undergone since age two, and he was such an uncanny mimic that those who heard him recite Nestroy or Shakespeare deemed his the definitive interpretation of *every* role. If Kraus had left a legacy of phonograph records instead of books, he would, suggests Willy Haas, rank as one of the greatest of actors. So accurate was Kraus's recall of quotations that he endured a kind of permanent anamnesis: "Much of what I experience for the first time I can already remember."[22] Small wonder that Kraus excelled at weaving quotations into sardonic prose. One third of his "mammoth-drama," *Die letzten Tage der Menschheit* (Vienna, 1922), consisted of excerpts from the daily press. Similarly his conviction that linguistic usage reflects morality stemmed from a tyrannical memory for words. Like that other superb listener, Freud, Kraus averred that

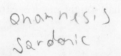

anamnesis
Sardonic

every slip of the tongue—or increasingly, even a printer's error—betrayed some deeper intention. Whatever Kraus's mind recorded, he interpreted with unrelenting literalness, as if the speaker had meant exactly what his words said. Kraus could not stomach anyone who lacked command of words.

That Kraus regarded memory as a mixed blessing is amply illustrated by the poem, "Return into Time" [Rückkehr in die Zeit]:

> Mein Zeiger ist zurückgewendet,
> nie ist Gewesnes mir vollendet
> und anders steh' ich in der Zeit.
> In welche Zukunft ich auch schweife
> und was ich immer erst ergreife,
> es wird mir zur Vergangenheit.
>
> .   .   .   .
>
> Ich bin mein treuester Begleiter
> und lebe das Gelebte weiter,
> und Neues kann mir nicht geschehn.
> Von einem Urbild war gesegnet,
> was mir zum erstenmal begegnet,
> und ist mir wie ein Wiedersehn.[23]

> My watch is turned backward,
> Never is what's past over for me
> And I stand differently in time.
> Whatever future I may reach
> And whatever I grasp for the first time
> Becomes for me the past.
>
> .   .   .   .
>
> I am my own truest companion
> I relive what I have lived before,
> And nothing new can happen to me.
> What I encounter for the first time
> Has been blessed with a primal form
> And is to me like a second meeting.

Kraus yearned to experience something genuinely new, unsullied by memory. Overwhelmed by a sense of déjà vu, he juggled an unending supply of Platonic models, which he used to classify and judge whatever might occur. Imprisoned by what his mind had etched upon it, he flailed at solecisms and disharmonies of contemporary speech, which he could not avoid assimilating. This satirist suffered the agony of a musician blessed with perfect pitch, yet fated to spend a lifetime listening to the tone-deaf.

Kraus excelled at weaving other men's words into pastiches that unmasked vulgarity more mercilessly than any invective. As collected in *Beim Wort genommen* (Munich, 1955), his own telegram-like aphorisms, resembling those of Nietzsche, constitute scintillating montages. Kraus's technique of collating quotations represented a kind of refined Dada, epitomizing Viennese propensity for decorating by means of rearrangement. Inundated by print, he found no haven; disdaining such nonverbal art-forms as cinema, dance, or mime, he relaxed only by reading aloud. Through his worship of language, Kraus exalted Viennese aestheticism: for him words were the supreme, nay the only reality. No Mauthnerian God lurked behind them, no Wahle-like psychic events underlay them. As if parodying the self-effacing devotion of a Hugo Wolf, Kraus heeded feuilletonists solely in order to caricature them. Feigning objectivity toward Viennese impressionism, he extolled some of its virtuosos like Altenberg while mocking others like Bahr. In repudiating the conviction of Mauthner and Schnitzler that no language can convey the uniqueness of thought, Kraus proclaimed himself an anti-impressionist, who revered the classicist's equation of language with thought.

Like Weininger, whom he esteemed, Kraus denounced faults that he himself shared. Decrying Viennese aestheticism as a late-Romantic flight into illusion, he eschewed ballroom and idyll in favor of dissecting a moribund—perhaps even dead—culture. Both Weininger and Kraus declaimed as if they were reporting a postmortem examination on their own era: Kraus executed an autopsy on Austria-Hungary, Weininger on sexuality. If Weininger embodied the ne plus ultra of therapeutic nihilism, Kraus fell not far behind. While censuring feuilletonists for constructing aesthetic paradises, he himself took refuge in a fortress of solipsism. What pained him was not to see other people suffer but to witness how the press exploited it. Although Haas exaggerates in dubbing Kraus an apostle of destruction, he rightly stresses that this verbal Daumier delighted in discomfiting victims by mimicking the bestial in them.[24] Among medical men, therapeutic nihilism originally meant faith in the healing powers of nature; illness should be left to run its course lest an ignorant physician wreak more harm than good. The renegade Jews Kraus and Weininger disdained such faith in the recuperative force of nature; no lapse of time could redress the abuses for which they berated contemporaries. His petulance aside, Kraus anticipated, thanks to remorseless literalism, Witt-

Emperor Franz Joseph marching in the Corpus Christi procession
at Vienna in 1909. This annual event celebrated
the alliance of throne and altar.

Scavenging in the Vienna Woods during the winter
of 1918-1919. With the dissolution of its empire, Vienna had
lost its economic *raison d'être*.

Karl Lueger being adulated in the Volksprater in 1905.
This watercolor by Wilhelm Gause epitomizes the ·
mayor's exploitation of aestheticism.

Young Czechs obstructing the Reichsrat in 1900.
From 1897 to 1907 German and Czech deputies vied in
paralyzing the Austrian lower house.

The studio of Hans Makart as painted by Rudolf Alt
in 1884. As style setter for Vienna during the 1870's,
Markart made his studio a mecca for society.

The Café Griensteidl as pictured by Rudolf Völkel shortly
before it was demolished in 1897. Among the writers who frequented
the café, Peter Altenberg appears seated at the far right.

Ernst Mach

Franz Brentano

Moritz Schlick

Robert Zimmermann

Josef Popper-Lynkeus

Adolf Loos

Fritz Mauthner

Christian von Ehrenfels

Friedrich von Wieser

Carl Menger

Othmar Spann

Hans Kelsen

Max Adler

Viktor Adler

Otto Bauer

Anton Menger

Rosa Mayreder

Hermann Broch

genstein's philosophy of language. Wittgenstein felt no less revulsed by the culture that had begot them both.

THE PERFECTIONISM OF LUDWIG WITTGENSTEIN: UTOPIAN AND THERAPEUTIC NIHILIST AT ONCE

Ludwig Wittgenstein (1889–1951) embodied many of the contradictions of his native Vienna.[25] He renounced the mores of the upper middle class into which he had been born, dispersing an immense inheritance almost as soon as he had received it. Reportedly he never wore a necktie after age twenty-three. At least five times he changed careers, more out of moral quandary than desire; Ludwig worked as an engineer, philosopher, schoolteacher, gardener, architect, professor of philosophy, and during wartime as a hospital orderly and laboratory technician. Although while living in England from 1929 to 1951 he refused to publish any of his voluminous writings, subsequently he has surpassed all other Austrian philosophers of this century in posthumous fame.

Much of this innovator's originality, not to say eccentricity, derived from his German-born Jewish father, Karl Wittgenstein (1847–1913).[26] Having been expelled from the Akademisches Gymnasium for repeated pranks, at age eighteen, Karl ran away to New York, returning to Austria two years later. Early he distinguished himself as an industrial engineer and then as an entrepreneur, during the 1880's securing for his firms in Bohemia a monopoly on manufacture of railroad track. As chief of a giant consortium, the elder Wittgenstein became one of the wealthiest men in Austria, retiring in 1898 to live as a grand seigneur, entertaining lavishly, and traveling around the world. A man of charm and perspicacity, Karl Wittgenstein died after years of painful illness, having seen three sons predecease him. A liberal who wrote on economics in the *Neue Freie Presse*, through overpowering energy he instilled in his children respect for authority, so that his son branded social revolution as immoral. Ludwig also inherited the musical gifts of his parents, who counted Brahms among their friends. Throughout his life the philosopher used to whistle through entire concertos; Schubert was his favorite composer.

As the youngest of five brothers and three sisters, Ludwig was educated at home until age fourteen. After his brother Paul, a pianist, had lost an arm during World War One, Ravel, among other composers, wrote for him a piano concerto for left hand. In his own way, Ludwig demonstrated comparable will power. While growing up in the liberal home of his parents, he had been most unhappy. Having a Jewish father, who had been baptized a Protestant, and a Catholic mother, Ludwig was raised a Catholic. As in the case of another illustrious half-Jew, Michel de Montaigne, such a congeries of parental religions may have implanted precocious skepticism. Early in life Wittgenstein repudiated the meliorism of his entrepreneur father, insisting in the words of Nestroy that "Progress is characterized by the fact that it appears much greater than it really is."[27] Those who hail Wittgenstein for having inaugurated a giant advance in philosophy forget how persistently he belittled such claims. During adulthood, Wittgenstein played the aristocrat raté, unshakeable in cultivating his own vision and in pursuing his own style of life. Although he abjured Western philosophy much as he had his father's success, Wittgenstein did so with the grace of one born to riches who has tasted what he renounces.

As a boy, Wittgenstein had been fascinated by machinery, fabricating a sewing machine and nurturing hopes of studying physics under Boltzmann, only to have these plans crushed by the latter's suicide. After two years in Berlin, from 1908 to 1911 he studied aeronautics at Manchester, experimenting with kite-flying and with jet propulsion. In January, 1912, Wittgenstein entered Cambridge to study under Bertrand Russell and G. E. Moore. There he stayed until mid-1913, declining in January, 1913, to return to Vienna for his father's funeral. That summer he visited Norway with his friend David Pinsent, to whom the Tractatus is dedicated. In October, 1913, Wittgenstein settled alone on a fjord at Skjolden, northeast of Bergen, where he began chronicling the thoughts that comprise the Tractatus. Having earlier esteemed writings by Weininger and Kraus, the hermit arranged to have Die Fackel dispatched to his hideaway in Norway.[28]

In 1914 Wittgenstein followed advice from Kraus as to how best he might divest himself of the fortune that he had just inherited. Kraus recommended that the editor of Der Brenner, Ludwig Ficker (1880–1967), be appointed to distribute a sum of 100,000 crowns among deserving contributors to that journal. During July, 1914, the twenty-five-year-old Maecenas wrote to Ficker, who selected Rilke and Georg Trakl to receive 20,000 crowns each.[29] News of this windfall prompted the drug-ridden Trakl to vomit. Wittgenstein himself did not fancy expressionist poetry, branding the works of Albert Ehrenstein "Hundedreck"; he preferred elegies and epigrams by Goethe and Mörike.[30] Once the war had begun, Wittgenstein showed all the more chivalry in striving to succor Trakl. After collapsing as a medic on the Galician front, the poet was confined to a hospital at Krakow, where in September, 1914, Ficker visited him. Wittgenstein, who was serving in Galicia as a volunteer, journeyed to Krakow at Ficker's request and reached there three days too late to save the invalid, who on November 4, 1914, had died of heart failure, brought on by an overdose of cocaine.[31]

For the duration of war, the volunteer Wittgenstein alternated service at the front with training and furloughs. During 1916 he spent several months at Olmütz, where Adolf Loos gave him an introduction to architect Paul Engelmann (1891–1965). By this time, as Engelmann later recalled, Wittgenstein was devouring Tolstoy's tales and reciting *The Brothers Karamazov*.[32] During a furlough at Vienna in August, 1918, he found time to complete the *Tractatus* before joining the Italian front, where in November he was taken prisoner. While interned at Monte Cassino until August, 1919, he read Augustine's *Confessions* as well as the Gospels. After being released, he hastened back to Vienna to enroll in teacher-training school. Having donated the residue of his fortune in keeping with Tolstoy's self-effacing Christianity, from 1920 to 1926 Wittgenstein labored as an elementary schoolteacher in Lower Austria, working two years each at Trattenbach, Puchberg-am-Schneeberg, and Otterthal. To facilitate teaching, he prepared a *Wörterbuch für Volksschulen* (Vienna, 1926), which the Ministry of Education sanctioned for classroom use. Its relevance to his philosophy has yet to be assessed. During the summer of 1920 the budding teacher toiled as a gardener at Klosterneuburg, and six years later he served as gardener's assistant to monks at Hütteldorf near Vienna. From 1926 to late 1928, he dwelt at Vienna, designing a house at Kundmanngasse 19 for his sister Mrs. Margarethe Stonborough. The amateur architect employed materials favored by Loos, setting a horizontal roof atop three stories of concrete, glass, and steel. The interior featured stone floors, metal doors, and white walls from which all ornament was banished.

In January, 1929, Wittgenstein accepted an invitation from Bertrand Russell and G. E. Moore to take a Fellowship at Trinity College, Cambridge. In 1935, the emigré visited the Soviet Union, soon renouncing plans to settle there; instead he withdrew for almost a year to his hut in Norway. In 1937 Wittgenstein returned to Cambridge, succeeding two years later to Moore's chair, while residing at Trinity College. During World War Two the Tolstoyan impulse spurred Wittgenstein to serve as a hospital orderly in London and later as a medical technician at Newcastle. After the war, he interrupted teaching from 1947 to 1949 to sojourn in Ireland. At Trinity College, Wittgenstein inspired a legend. Uncouth attire, a cluttered room, delight in cowboy stories, and a habit of discussing philosophy with the chambermaid set this bachelor apart. Although he declined to publish, he attracted a coterie of disciples, who since his death in April, 1951, have made his influence paramount in British academic philosophy.

Wittgenstein differentiated sharply between the philosophy of logical atomism, which he published in the *Tractatus Logico-philosophicus* (1921; repr., London, 1922), and the critique of language that he expounded at Cambridge from 1929 onward, published posthumously as *Philosophical Investigations* (London, 1953).[33] During both periods, he recorded thoughts in clipped sentences and paragraphs, which later he would array into sequences. After he had assembled the *Tractatus* in August, 1918, out of notebooks written from 1912 on, he ordered the notebooks destroyed. Through inadvertence, two of them survived at Gmunden, to be published as *Notebooks 1914–1916* (Oxford, 1961). The *Tractatus* aimed to investigate conditions that Russell had stipulated for a logically perfect language. His epigraph Wittgenstein took from Kürnberger:

> und alles, was man weiss, nicht bloss rauschen und brausen gehört hat, lässt sich in drei Worten sagen.

> everything which one knows, and has not merely heard ringing and resounding, can be said in three words.

It may have been with this phrase in mind that Wittgenstein coined the oft-quoted formula:

> Was sich überhaupt sagen lässt, lässt sich klar sagen; und wovon man nicht reden kann, darüber muss man schweigen.

> Whatever can be said can be said clearly, and that of which one cannot speak, one must be silent about.[34]

Unlike Mauthner, whose injunction to silence annuls methodology, Wittgenstein affirmed that language can delimit the sayable. Rather than muzzle philosophy, the early Wittgenstein rejected Kraus's equation of language with reality and morality. Kraus's equation, said Wittgenstein, covers only statements in mathematics and physics. Elsewhere language distorts reality. In the final pages of the *Tractatus*, Wittgenstein nevertheless agreed with Kraus in declaring that "Ethics and aesthetics are one."[35] Just as Kraus arranged excerpts into a pastiche, his admirer constructed passages from notebooks into intricately numbered paragraphs, whose digits designate relationships to the whole.

While Wittgenstein was teaching elementary school, the *Tractatus* captivated Hahn and Schlick, who chose it as a working text for the Vienna Circle, persisting even after its author had disavowed their exegesis of it. By 1926, when he first met Schlick, Wittgenstein prized in his own treatise above all the gnomic allusions to ethics and the mystical, whereas the neopositivists hailed the work as a death blow to metaphysics. During 1927 and 1928, Wittgenstein feuded with his self-styled disciples. Carnap deemed him morbidly sensitive to criticism, while he alarmed both Carnap and Neurath by belittling mathematics and avowing that religion would after all survive. Wittgenstein rebuked the physicalists' efforts to excogitate an artificial language, insisting that to be meaningful, language must exploit, as in poetry, accretions of daily usage. Neurath disdained such truckling to tradition. During these years, Schlick's assistant Waismann was drafting a book to popularize Wittgenstein's views. These altered so rapidly that several times Wittgenstein exacted revisions of the manuscript, only to refuse after 1929 to sanction its publication at all.[36]

After Wittgenstein had emigrated to Cambridge in January, 1929, he passed with flying colors an examination for the doctor's degree that Russell and Moore administered on June 6, 1929. In discussions with Frank Ramsey (1903–1930), who had visited his idol in Austria, Wittgenstein evolved toward a critique of language which he broached in lectures between 1930 and 1933.[37] The new approach consisted in reinstating Kraus's equation of language with reality. Wittgenstein contended that philosophers had intended each utterance to bear scrutiny such as Kraus visited on everyone. Following Kraus, Wittgenstein named his new discipline not criticism of language (*Sprachkritik*), as Mauthner did, but doctrine of language (*Sprachlehre*), a term that Kraus had launched in *Die Fackel* of June, 1921.[38] Although Wittgenstein endeavored to purge language so that meaningful philosophy might resume, he never fulfilled this aim to his satisfaction.

Wittgenstein's later philosophy may have derived impetus from a lecture delivered at Vienna during March, 1928, by the Dutch mathematician Jan Brouwer (1881–1966). After Feigl and Waismann had persuaded Wittgenstein to attend the lecture, that very evening the amateur architect resumed philosophizing.[39] In espousing constructivism, Brouwer deemed the criterion of mathematical truth to be the limit of what mind can construct, according to rules that the mind itself decrees. Such construction is a natural activity of man: no mathematical proposition can be true "unless we can in a nonmiraculous way *know* it to be true."[40] Similarly, the later Wittgenstein interpreted language as a mental construct, limited by rules and their corollaries. Once mind has generated this tool, mind is confined by it, without, however, being, as in Kant, limited by innate filters. Language resolves into a network of games, whose rules a philosopher can explore but never surmount. Games devised by early philosophers shackle modern practitioners, who diagnose handicaps that they cannot escape.

By asserting that language cannot altogether purge itself of mental cramps, Wittgenstein appeared a therapeutic nihilist in the manner of his mentor Schopenhauer.[41] Yet this Austrian lacked the pervasive pessimism of a Vienna-born Jewish follower, Friedrich Waismann (1896–1959), who in the words of Stuart Hampshire indulged:

> A luxuriance in pessimism and passivity, and in the ineffectiveness of reason; a wry sentimentality, a cultivation of mystery, and the sense of belonging to a dying elite, who congratulated themselves on their philosophy, which they know will not save them from being swept away by the violence that is to come.[42]

However aptly this description may fit certain Viennese Jews such as Friedell and Zweig, it ignores the moral integrity of others like Wittgenstein and Broch. Although in assailing philosophy Wittgenstein may have been a therapeutic nihilist, in implementing philanthropy he remained a utopian.

While at Cambridge, Wittgenstein bewailed the lack of genuine puzzlement which plagued British teachers of philosophy. So certain was Wittgenstein that philosophy precludes improvement that he sought to dissuade students from pursuing it as a career. Averse to professional philosophers, he preferred to read cowboy stories and to quote remarks by his chambermaid. Not one to browse widely, Wittgenstein read beloved works over and over, favoring Rabindranath Tagore's play *The King of the Dark Chamber* (1914; German ed., 1919) and Wilhelm Busch's fantasy of a boy's dreams, *Eduards Traum* (Munich, 1891). Wittgenstein also adored the impish girl, Figura Leu, who enlivens Keller's *Der Landvogt von Greifensee* (Stuttgart, 1878), another work that extols childhood.[43] While speaking, Wittgenstein gesticulated vigorously, as if to vindicate belief, *pace* Kraus, that nonverbal communication ranks in importance with verbal.[44] A fan of adventure stories, Wittgenstein relished motion pictures, especially silent pictures that ended happily so that as in Tagore an audience could indulge its dreams.[45] Although Wittgenstein agreed with Freud that art triggers wish-fulfillment, he pronounced the founder of psychoanalysis, whom he first read in 1919, to be more clever than wise.[46]

Besides Kraus and Mauthner, the closest parallel that Austrian thought offers to Wittgenstein may well be the protagonist of Hof-

indomitable

mannsthal's play, *Der Schwierige* (Berlin 1921). Hofmannsthal portrayed Heinz Karl Bühl as a disillusioned Viennese aristocrat, whose laconic utterances belittle the babble of associates. Although Bühl's taciturnity recalled the crisis of the *Chandosbrief*, in this play written during 1916, Hofmannsthal depicted silence not as replacing language but as delimiting it: like pauses in music, silence punctuates. The indomitable Bühl haunts the outskirts of society, speaking his native tongue as if it were foreign in order to eschew the jargon of a fading aristocracy. Like Wittgenstein secreted in his hut, Bühl becomes a pure contemplative, practicing to the letter and without regret the injunction, "That of which one cannot speak, one must be silent about."

For all his similarity to Kraus, Wittgenstein remained the more practical of the two. The younger man respected service to humanity, working as a teacher, architect, and hospital orderly. Kraus's literary taste favored Lichtenberg, Goethe, Jean Paul, Nestroy, and Offenbach, while Wittgenstein esteemed Augustine, Lichtenberg, Schopenhauer, Keller, and Tolstoy. The two rigorists embodied the same paradox as Loos and Schönberg. To vindicate classical taste, these renegades unleashed a conservative counterrevolution so drastic as to threaten their own values. Kraus excoriated impressionism and expressionism in literature, Schönberg deplored excesses of late Romantic music, Loos denounced appliqué ornament in Ringstrasse architecture, and the later Wittgenstein unmasked self-deception in logicians, who in zeal to supplant metaphysics snarl themselves in language.

Dispensing the rueful wisdom of the self-exiled, Wittgenstein propounded with the clarity of a classicist doubts about the very possibility of logical clarity. He keenly regretted that defects of language make metaphysics impossible. Shunning the desperation of Wahle and displaying greater finesse than Stöhr, he argued that although conventional philosophy has played itself out, much remains for commentators to unscramble. Through illustrations and aphorisms worthy of Kraus, Wittgenstein disentangled Western philosophy. By espousing the highest standard of rigor, he discerned Schlamperei in other thinkers' coherence, just as Kraus detected turpitude where others saw merely dalliance. Moral energy, which transplanted his father's dynamism to the world of ideas, made Ludwig Wittgenstein a luminary of twentieth-century thought, who brought to England a campaign that certain Viennese were waging against laxity. Bold and incorruptible, he cultivated a perfectionism that in other Austrian thinkers too often became either therapeutic nihilism or utopianism. No less than Weininger, Broch, and Kraus, Wittgenstein combined both impulses. So enamored was he of perfection that he built a tool for toppling his own ideal.

14

Philosophers of Dialogue

MARTIN BUBER: FROM AESTHETIC MYSTICISM
TO I-THOU RELATIONSHIP

In the preceding chapter, several varieties of philosophy of language
were surveyed: Mauthner's injunction to silence, the discrediting of
metaphysics in Stöhr and Wahle, Kraus's equation of language with
truth, and Wittgenstein's analysis of limits of language. Patently no
topic has so fascinated twentieth-century philosophers as that of language. A shift of attention from content of an utterance to its form
was pioneered in large part by thinkers raised in Vienna and Prague.
It has been suggested previously how the collision of languages and
dialects in those cities helped to intensify skepticism about metaphysics. It remains to consider two Austrian thinkers, Buber and Ebner,
who studied language in order to revivify rather than to abolish metaphysics.

Although Martin Buber (1878–1965) spent his mature years in Germany and Israel, his roots lay in Austria.[1] A Jew born in Vienna, he
was only two years old when his parents were divorced, whereupon he
dwelt from 1880 to 1892 in Lemberg at the home of his grandfather
Salomon Buber (1827–1906). Director of two banks and head of the
Jewish community in Lemberg, this adept of the Jewish Enlightenment
(Haskala) spoke flawless Hebrew and edited texts of the Midrash. He
infused in Martin a passion for philology. During summers spent near
Sadagora in Bukovina, the boy met Hasids, whose "wonder rabbi" had
lived in regal splendor.[2] Here Martin encountered a tradition that
after 1904 he would make peculiarly his own. Although from 1892 to
1896 he attended a Polish-speaking gymnasium in Lemberg, he espoused German rather than Slavic culture.

In 1896 Buber matriculated at the University of Vienna, where his
dissertation directors included Friedrich Jodl and Laurenz Müllner in
philosophy, and Franz Wickhoff and Alois Riegl in art history. Exploit-

ing a flair for learning derived from his grandfather, Buber became an arch-impressionist. In order to imbibe as many disciplines as possible, he enrolled at Leipzig to hear Wilhelm Wundt as well as at Berlin to hear Simmel and Dilthey. The young aesthete also attended Mach's lectures at Vienna, and in 1897 he published in the Polish *Weekly Review (Przegląd tygodniowy)* articles assessing his fellow impressionists Altenberg, Schnitzler, and Hofmannsthal. After reading Herzl's *Judenstaat* when it appeared in 1896, for six years Buber agitated in vain to persuade Zionists to promote Jewish learning. During 1899 in Berlin, he began to study Meister Eckhart and Jakob Böhme, a pursuit that Mauthner's disciple Gustav Landauer encouraged. Having sampled nearly every branch of contemporary culture, in 1904 Buber abandoned partisan activity in order to devote himself to translating texts of Hasidism.

For the next eight years, Buber reevaluated and reviewed Hasidic doctrines. Like Weininger and Broch, Buber dichotomized experience, thereby emulating Marcionist friends at Prague who sequestered man from God. For them, as for the young Buber, only an elite can experience God, achieving already on earth that mystical communion Mauthner and Landauer extolled. In the finely chiseled writings in *Daniel: Gespräche von der Verwirklichung* (Leipzig, 1913), Buber reemphasized age-old polarities, such as God and man, soul and senses, poet and prophet, to preach spiritual rebirth. In the manner of Böhme, he urged artists to descend into the abyss *(Abgrund)* of uncertainty in order to confront the cosmos. Gradually during World War One, Buber transformed panentheistic mysticism into a philosophy of dialogue, which he expounded in *Ich und Du* (Leipzig, 1923). He had exchanged Hasidism for evangelism partly under the influence of Franz Rosenzweig (1886–1929), a German-born Jewish student of Friedrich Meinecke. Having rediscovered God through a baptized Jewish friend, Eugen Rosenstock-Huessy (1888–), Rosenzweig hailed Judaism and Christianity as equally authentic manifestations of religious truth.[3]

In *Ich und Du,* Buber recast polarities that he had expounded in *Daniel.* Borrowing primary words *(Grundworte)* coined by Ludwig Feuerbach, he divided experience into I-Thou and I-It relationships. The first presupposes two mutually aware selves who interact, while the second degrades self into a thing. Although I-Thou intimacy may accompany love or friendship, Buber meant it to culminate in rapport between man and God. Far from being an object or a set of rules, God beckons to man, eager to listen. Communion between man and God entails dialogue, not abasement of slave to master. Whereas *Daniel* celebrated ascent toward God, *Ich und Du* replaced self-centered worship with veneration of the other. After 1916, ecstasy gave way to encounter, experience *(Erlebnis)* became event, and actualizing God *(Verwirklichung Gottes)* became preparing the world for God to inhabit. While preaching personalism, Buber epitomized that reverence for life which Broch identified with Judaism. Each person must cherish every other as a potential partner in dialogue, lonely and labile like himself. Reality dwells not within the psyche, but between psyches and even more between each psyche and God. Just as Othmar Spann considered mental life to emerge from pairings such as parent and child, teacher and student, writer and reader, Buber celebrated symbiosis between speaker and hearer. He agreed with Freud that psychiatrist and patient form a society of two where defenses dissolve. Buber resembled Rank in promoting spontaneity as the fount of vitality, and like Wolf he knew how to prostrate himself in order to exalt another.

Buber practiced irenicism even more resolutely than Coudenhove-Kalergi or Popper-Lynkeus. Conciliating warring brothers by demonstrating their interdependence, he endeavored to end contention without igniting fresh strife. After settling in Israel in 1938, he befriended Arabs, repudiating attempts to dislodge them. By losing himself in I-Thou relationships, Buber—utopian that he was—forfeited ability to manipulate I-It relations. Too self-sacrificing to outmaneuver adversaries, he showed others how to heal wounds that they could not prevent.

As with Husserl, it is difficult to specify how Austria influenced the mature Buber. As a Viennese impressionist he had spent a disaffected youth, goaded like Rank and Weininger by omnivorous curiosity. Whereas they had been fascinated by death, he sought God through the polar opposites postulated by Hasidism and Taoism. Yearning to restore wholeness to a bifurcated world, until World War One Buber flirted with God-drunk Marcionism. Just as Max Dvořák discerned rebirth issuing from that cataclysm, Buber emulated Franz Rosenzweig by allowing catastrophe to repristinate faith. The later Buber resembled activist utopians like Herzl and Hertzka, promising fulfillment, albeit no repose, to worshipers who attain I-Thou communion with God. Having supplanted elitist mysticism with democratic dialogue, Buber embraced the world with an ebullience that mocked therapeutic nihilists like Weininger and Kraus.

Since the 1920's, Buber's personalism has consoled two generations that have exchanged certainties for despondency. After World War Two, existentialists appropriated the I-Thou relation, exhorting individuals to titillate their sensibilities while forsaking society. More recently, Buber's message has invigorated such movements as group therapy, Christian ecumenism, and sensitivity training between races. Buber has buttressed a conviction that even where ideologies clash, individuals can understand one another; I-Thou dialogue has taught skeptics once again to hope.

THE PNEUMATOLOGY OF FERDINAND EBNER: THE PRIORITY OF SPEAKING OVER WRITING

Much less well known than Buber is his Catholic counterpart, Ferdinand Ebner (1882–1931).[4] Independently of Buber and Feuerbach, during 1916 he discovered the I-Thou relation. Born in Wiener Neustadt, and never leaving Lower Austria, Ebner was a "little man," whose life reads like a story by Saar or Ebner-Eschenbach. After his father died in 1904, Ebner felt burdened by memories of his father, who had attended mass daily but whose gauche manner had imbued his son with hate-love for the church. After completing teacher-training school, where to his everlasting regret he learned no Greek, Ebner served from 1902 to 1912 as a primary schoolteacher at Waldegg near Wiener Neustadt. In 1912 he transferred to Gablitz nearer Vienna, so that he could visit libraries and friends in the metropolis. Chronic tuberculosis precluded Ebner from military service, forcing him to retire from teaching in 1923. From 1900 to 1924 his dearest friend was Luise Karpischek, ten years his senior, with whom he corresponded at length, especially after 1912. He dared not marry Luise for fear that as his wife she would cease to be his muse. In October, 1923, he married a fellow teacher at Gablitz, Maria Mizera, who for some years had been nursing him. Besides Adolf Loos and Hermann Swoboda, a close friend until 1920 was the composer Josef Maria Hauer (1883–1959), also born in Wiener Neustadt. Ebner was an enthusiastic pianist, who enjoyed playing Bach and Mozart.

Between 1902 and 1907 admiration for Shakespeare and Dostoevski led Ebner to compose poems including one on Golgotha. In 1907, Weininger's *Geschlecht und Charakter* attracted Ebner to philosophy, an interest he pursued by reading Pascal, Bergson, Freud, and countless others and by friendship with Weininger's associate Swoboda. In 1912 Ebner wrote a four-hundred-page Bergsonian treatise, *Ethik und Leben: Fragmente einer Metaphysik der individuellen Existenz*, which he ne 'r published. Besides writing to Luise Karpischek, Ebner kept a diary and took lengthy notes on what he read, from which one can reconstruct the unfolding of his ideas. During World War One, the

Bible, Kierkegaard's *Fear and Trembling*, and commentaries by Johann Georg Hamann caused Ebner to become an anguished Catholic. Insights garnered between 1916 and 1918 he formulated in *Das Wort und die geistigen Realitäten*, which in 1919 a Viennese publisher declined after Stöhr had ridiculed it. The free-thinker Stöhr branded Ebner's theology of language unscientific. Disconcerted, Ebner submitted his manuscript to a Swabian Kierkegaard scholar, Theodor Haecker (1879–1945), who forwarded it to Ludwig Ficker. Not only did Ficker publish the book in 1921, but he signed Ebner as a contributor to *Der Brenner*. Thereafter the schoolteacher refused to write for any other journal. Throughout the 1920's he grappled with anticlericalism, overcoming it only on his deathbed.

In *Das Wort und die geistigen Realitäten*, Ebner contrasted what he called isolation of the I *(Icheinsamkeit)* with the relation of I-Thou. Loneliness of the ego can be assuaged only by experiencing a Thou through the medium of speech:

> The Word is the vehicle of the relation between I and Thou,
> that is at bottom of the relation between man and God.
> In this relation man has his whole spiritual life.[5]

Ebner insisted that he had met this conception only in Chapter 1 of the Gospel According to St. John, and in Hamann's exegesis of it. Only later did Haecker alert Ebner to Feuerbach's notion of I-It.[6] For Ebner, isolation of the I occurs most readily in aestheticism, in which an I worships beauty in place of a person. Whether in art, literature, religion, or philosophy, a lonely I soliloquizes, like Otto Weininger, unable to achieve genuine communication. Speculative philosophy is a dream, perpetuated by what Ebner dubbed the "cramp of idealism." Isolation of the I had unhinged Nietzsche, and threatened Kraus, whom Ebner heard recite in October, 1918. Repudiating Weininger's dichotomy between man as spirit and woman as nature, Ebner excluded from I and Thou any distinction of sex. By magnifying isolation of the I, Weininger had demonstrated, said his critic, that idealism entails anti-Semitism and antifeminism; in order to persuade the I to repulse any Thou, idealism belittles Jews and women. Mauthner's injunction to silence describes those who practice isolation of the I; for them language blocks communication instead of abetting it.

Egress from the cul-de-sac of ego-isolation comes through recognizing that God created man's capacity to speak. Because to communicate presupposes God's creation of the speaking faculty, the primordial mode of communion runs between man and God. Thanks to God's gift, man can implore the Creator as an eternal Thou, who is ever ready to lift man from loneliness. Adapting the pneumatology of Hamann, Ebner elaborated an ethic of heeding God. The decision of faith necessitates practicing God's word; Christians must not merely hear God's command, but do it. Unless one cultivates reverence for a Thou, language becomes as self-defeating as Mauthner had said. Dogma severs contact with God by congealing the living word. Likening dogma to rigor mortis, Ebner complained that bureaucracy in the church impales Christians between rules and faith. Obliged as a teacher to march in Corpus Christi processions that sanctified alliance of throne and altar, Ebner loathed seeing an iron cross awarded aviators or a jewelled cross adorning knights of a lay order. Like Haecker, this antinomian decried use of the cross to bless weapons, castigating the church for affiliating itself with ego-centered society.

As with Kierkegaard, neurotic perfectionism impelled Ebner to demand from the church a spotless purity. Like Weininger, the teacher endured fits of depression, whose onset he could predict by using Swoboda's theory of periodicity. He attempted suicide during March and again in May of 1923, desperate over his inability to join the church. In the Foreword to *Das Wort und die geistigen Realitäten*, he disclosed pathetic self-doubts about his book, reprinting in full Stöhr's diatribe. Ebner lamented that his book's greatest fault was that his father, to whose memory he dedicated it, could not have understood it. Less cosmopolitan than Buber, Ebner had achieved insight into I-Thou above all by writing to Luise Karpischek. After he had been corresponding with her for five years, for him "Thou" overflowed with significance: writing to his "Thou" constituted communion. By refusing to marry Luise, Ebner emulated the bachelor Grillparzer, who had practiced similar estrangement from his "eternal bride." By wavering toward Luise, Ebner taunted the bureaucracy of the church.

Although Ebner lacked the prophetic grandeur of Buber, the schoolteacher's pneumatology has infiltrated Roman Catholic apologetics. Hailed as a Catholic Kierkegaard, Ebner has helped to rehabilitate anticlerical theology. Like other arguments for existence of God, Ebner's pneumatological one is circular. He could no more deduce God from human speech than Mauthner could from silence. Ebner asserted that written language is inferior to speaking. Differentiating two senses of the German word *Sprache*—language and speech—Ebner insisted that only words uttered heart-to-heart make sense. Extolling face-to-face communication, Ebner championed rural society, while deploring the ego-isolation engendered by metropolises. Radiating nostalgia, Ebner was another Austrian conservative who around 1900 revived preindustrial values.

What Ebner offers is not cogent reasoning but exhortation. Exuding the humility of a "little man," he epitomized the kind of sincerity for which Klemens Hofbauer was canonized in 1909. Yearning to vindicate God, Ebner extolled human speech as evidence of His wisdom, just as Leibnizians had seen divinity suffusing creation. More trenchantly than most critics of dogma, Ebner elucidated why speculative theology founders. Without embracing the negative theology of Mauthner or the aesthetic mysticism of early Buber, Ebner hemmed in reason so that the heart could speak. Deploring ego-bound rationality in the church, Ebner envisioned a utopia linking man with God. More persuasively than the Platonist Broch or the Romantic Spann, these two seekers, Buber and Ebner, renewed a primordial vision of human experience. Like Kraus and Loos, from whom they differed so much, Buber and Ebner executed a conservative revolution in order to rejuvenate faith.

15

Freud and Medicine

A SKETCH OF FREUD'S CAREER

SIGMUND FREUD has become a father-figure to contemporary man. To probe the roots of his ideas is to expose one's own consciousness, and to criticize him is to slay the father. This journey into self-knowledge is both aided and impeded by the vast literature, primary and secondary, by and about Freud and his followers.[1] Nearly everyone has read part of this literature and no one all of it. This chapter, rather than attempting a systematic survey of Freud's life and teachings, examines his ambivalence toward certain Viennese attitudes such as therapeutic nihilism, aestheticism, reverence for death, and Protektion. These traditions permit study of psychoanalysis without reopening internecine quarrels between Freudians, Adlerians, Rankians, and others. It will be assumed that although Freud may have overgeneralized his findings, they pertained accurately to himself and to many of his patients. However dogmatic he may have been toward dissidents, the father of psychoanalysis did possess knowledge of himself.

We begin with a brief resumé of his career.[2] Sigismund Freud (1856–1939) was born on May 6 in Freiberg (Pribor), a rural town in northeastern Moravia south of Ostrau. His father was a Galician-born Jewish wool merchant, Jakob Freud (1815–1896), whose second wife, Galician-born Amalie Nathanson (1835–1930), bore him eight children between 1856 and 1866. Two half brothers born during the 1830's from Jakob's first marriage were old enough to be uncles to young Sigismund, rivaling Jakob's five brothers. In October, 1859, Jakob Freud and family departed the town of declining handweavers for Leipzig, moving thence to Vienna early the next year. There Freud dwelt until June, 1938. Following predictions at his birth that "golden Sigi" would accomplish great things, the young man attended the Sperlgymnasium from 1865 to 1873, where for the last six years he stood first in his class.

In October, 1873, Freud entered the Medical Faculty at Vienna, having been wooed from a career of law by hearing Goethe's fragment "Die Natur" (1783) recited at a lecture earlier that year. In 1878 Sigismund changed his name to Sigmund. Freud did not receive his medical degree until March, 1881, having delayed it in order to work as a research assistant in the physiological laboratory of Ernst Brücke from 1876 to 1882. At Brücke's urging the would-be physiologist switched to general practice with stress on neurology, becoming in September, 1885, docent in neuropathology. That year Freud won a travel stipend for study at Paris under Charcot, and in September, 1886, he fulfilled a dream of four years by marrying Martha Bernays (1861–1951) of Hamburg. In October, 1883, her brother Eli had married Freud's sister Anna (1858–1951), the couple coming to the United States in 1892, where their son Edward L. Bernays (1891–) started, after World War One, the new field of public relations. Freud's marriage proved extremely happy, producing six children and furnishing Freud the emotional outlet he needed. He and his wife resided first in the *Sühnhaus* that Franz Joseph had ordered built on the site of the Ringtheater. The latter had burned on December 8, 1881, during a performance that Freud and his sister Anna had almost attended.[3] In 1891 the Freuds moved to a second-story flat at Berggasse 19, which they occupied until 1938. After some years as a factory, the apartment has, at long last, been restored as a museum.

The book that established Freud's originality was *Die Traumdeutung*. Its publication inaugurated forty years of elaborating and disseminating the theories of psychotherapy, which in February, 1896, Freud had dubbed psychoanalysis *(Psychoanalyse)*. Although in 1902 he became an extraordinary professor at the Medical School, he propagated his school of psychotherapy entirely outside the university. Ever eager to vindicate his brainchild, Freud consulted with patients for as long as twelve hours a day; then he sat writing until as late as three o'clock in the morning. Although he abhorred journeys by train, Freud toured extensively in Germany and Italy, besides attending psychoanalytic congresses at Budapest, the Hague, and London.[4] In 1909 Freud visited the United States to lecture at Clark University in Worcester, Massachusetts, where he garnered an unfavorable impression of America. The psychoanalyst blamed a barbecue prepared by William James for inducing chronic digestive trouble.[5]

After 1923 a stout constitution enabled Freud to withstand sixteen years of excruciating pain from cancer of the palate. Besides braving thirty-three operations under local anaesthesia, every day for all those years a gaping hole in his mouth was scraped so as to accommodate

an ill-fitting prosthesis. He claimed that his indifference to pain stemmed from grief felt over the death in June, 1923, of his four-year-old
grandson Heinz Rudolf. The boy's mother, Freud's daughter Sophie,
had died of influenzal pneumonia three years before.[6] After March,
1938, friends persuaded the octogenarian to quit Nazi-occupied Vienna
for London. There his daughter Anna and Ernest Jones had prepared
a dwelling in a nation that the old man had always esteemed. After
selling most of his library to a dealer—who transferred it to the New
York Psychiatric Institute—on June 4, 1938, Freud forsook the city he
had both hated and loved. To it he owed more than he cared to admit.

THERAPEUTIC NIHILISM IN THE
MEDICAL FACULTY AT VIENNA

Throughout this book therapeutic nihilism has been mentioned as
characteristic of Viennese life. Otto Weininger, Richard Wahle, Karl
Kraus, and Ludwig Wittgenstein embodied the conviction that diseases of society or language defy curing. Outspoken opponents of this
refusal to propose solutions included Bertha von Suttner, Rosa Mayreder, Josef Popper-Lynkeus, Theodor Herzl, and Otto Neurath. Although the concept of therapeutic nihilism has been applied to philosophers and social thinkers, the term is a medical one, having arisen
during the early nineteenth century in the Medical Faculty at Vienna.
As shall be seen, fascination with diagnosis and neglect of therapy still
characterized the Medical Faculty when Freud underwent training;
like many other Viennese physicians of the late nineteenth century,
Freud went through a period of therapeutic nihilism, after which he
cultivated profound compassion for patients.

The founder of the Vienna Medical Faculty was Gerhard van
Swieten (1700–1772), whom Maria Theresa summoned to Vienna in
1745.[7] This disciple of the Dutch physician Hermann Boerhave (1668–
1738) expounded the empiricism of his teacher, who through slow
accumulation of observations had aimed to discredit quack practices.
Van Swieten's followers revived Hippocrates' doctrine of the healing
power of nature in order to diminish the frequency of blood letting. A
Dutch obstetrician Johann Lukas Boër (1751–1835), whom Joseph II
brought to Vienna in 1780, discarded use of artificial aids during childbirth. Coining the slogan, "We should never manage as if nature had
given up her work of parturition," he advocated so-called expectant
therapy. His procedure of waiting for nature to effect recovery became
standard at the General Hospital (Allgemeines Krankenhaus), which

Joseph II had founded in 1784, partly in imitation of hospitals organized in France by his sister Marie Antoinette. Replacing the Great Poor House (Grossarmenhaus), which had housed five thousand patients and indigents around five courtyards, the new hospital enclosed three large courtyards and three small ones, sprawling like a huge barracks on the outskirts of the city. Its buildings are still in use. The following year the emperor founded the Josephinum to train military surgeons; unlike the hospital, it was discontinued in 1872.

That expectant therapy need not neglect patients was shown by Johann Peter Frank (1745–1821), who reorganized the General Hospital between 1795 and 1805. In his six-volume treatise, *System einer vollständigen medizinischen Polizei* (Mannheim, Tübingen, Vienna, and Leipzig, 1779–1819), Frank founded the science of public health. "Medical police" would constitute a branch of cameralistic public law, designed to regulate life from birth to death. The Josephinist bureaucracy would promote births and safeguard health with a view to enhancing the nation's prosperity. Although he cared more for the good of the state than for the good of the individual, he advocated treating the insane as patients rather than prisoners.[8]

During the first quarter of the nineteenth century, the champion of expectant therapy was a Graz-born surgeon, Vinzenz von Kern (1760–1829), who as a professor at Vienna from 1805 to 1829 revolutionized treatment of wounds. Deprecating use of ointments and of pressure, he dressed wounds in loose, water-soaked bandages so that nature could exert her healing powers. By 1850 skepticism toward traditional therapy had so taken root that the only medicament used in the General Hospital was cherry brandy. For fear of distorting symptoms, doctors refused to prescribe any remedies.

This attitude reached a peak of intensity under Königgrätz-born anatomist Carl von Rokitansky (1804–1878). As a professor at Vienna from 1844, Rokitansky reportedly performed more than 85,000 autopsies, forging pathological anatomy into the first reliable tool of diagnosis to supplant Hippocrates' doctrine of signs (semiotics). Pilsen-born Josef Skoda (1805–1881), an uncle of the arms manufacturer Emil von Skoda, codified results of Rokitansky's postmortem examinations so as to found modern diagnostics. He revived the now ubiquitous method of chest percussion which a forgotten Graz-born physician, Leopold von Auenbrugger (1722–1809) had devised at Vienna in 1761. Sharing the limelight with Rokitansky and Skoda was Josef Hyrtl (1810–1894), who as a professor at Vienna from 1845 perfected the techniques of anatomy; his laboratory shipped specimens throughout the world.

All these men were dedicated to their science. Their quest for empirical truth represented a positivist backlash against romantic medicine. The combative Rokitansky disdained the role of a self-effacing scientist. As a member of the Herrenhaus, he led the fight to have compulsory teaching of Catholic religion removed from the schools, applauding suspension of the Concordat in 1868. Henry Ingersoll Bowditch recalled how formidable the anatomist had appeared in 1859:

> Nevertheless he has the true working head of a German—a more learned head than any I have seen—a head to be looked at; a massive skull with a quiet, dull eye, but indicating solid strength of intellect.[9]

Rokitansky's indifference to therapy echoed the theory of human nature, which he expounded in *Die Solidarität alles Thierlebens* (Vienna, 1869). Protoplasm at every level of existence is hungry, said Rokitansky, necessitating each organism to be aggressive so as to stamp out rivals. Because of the aggressiveness of the protoplasm in him, man cannot help resorting to lies, deceit, and duplicity, failings that only the state can curb. Individuals are doomed to wage a Darwinian struggle for freedom, a contest that guarantees progress in science while inflicting much suffering. Rokitansky's debt to Bohemian Reform Catholicism was obvious when he asserted that only sympathy between men can overcome the suffering inherent in life. Preaching a Biedermeier faith in harmony between man and God, the anatomist urged men to imitate Christ's model of enduring pain. Hobbesian and Leibnizian at once, Rokitansky interpreted Darwin's struggle for existence as evidence that harmony pervades the universe. It was owing to sublime faith in the order of nature that this Bohemian could endorse expectant therapy to the exclusion of pharmacology.

However much Rokitansky and Skoda may have countenanced therapeutic nihilism, it was some of their students, especially Joseph Dietl (1804–1878), who distorted skepticism toward nostrums into the doctrine that to do nothing must be the best treatment. Whereas earlier physicians had indiscriminately prescribed leeches and old-wives' potions without making a diagnosis, Rokitansky and Skoda insisted that diagnosis come first. Therapeutic nihilism was reinforced by Rokitansky's lack of success as a surgeon as well as by his students' exposure in the dissecting room to organs so misshapen as to preclude hope either of prevention or cure. A Heidelberg-trained therapist, Adolf Kussmaul (1822–1902), who later played a role in coining the name "Biedermeier," was so horrified by the indifference of teachers to pa-

tients that in 1847 he wrote a poem satirizing Viennese professors
for allowing a patient to die while they debated the diagnosis.[10] At
least one Vienna-born physician, Ernst von Feuchtersleben (1806–
1849), labored in vain to stem overspecialization in medicine by reviving the ancient art of healing. In *Zur Diätetik der Seele* (Vienna,
1838) this disciple of Kant and Goethe pleaded for self-healing through
self-mastery. It was a more cold-blooded self-mastery that impelled
the Vienna anatomists to launch modern medicine. By sweeping away
the *post hoc, ergo propter hoc* fallacies that had vitiated earlier therapy, they enabled the next generation to implement empirical pharmacology.

Vienna's most notorious case of therapeutic nihilism concerned the
Budapest-born obstetrician Ignác Semmelweis (1818–1865).[11] At the
General Hospital in 1847, he discovered that childbed fever resulted
when doctors coming directly from the dissecting room introduced
bacteria into a mother's womb. Although by compelling doctors to
rinse their hands in chloride of lime before touching patients, Semmelweis reduced mortality sharply, the leader of his clinic, Johann Klein
(1788–1856), remained unimpressed. Despite support from Rokitansky
and Skoda, Semmelweis was demoted in 1848, allegedly for sympathiz-
ing with the revolution. Inasmuch as he was not, as is sometimes
claimed, Jewish, it seems that he fell victim not to anti-Semitism, but
to therapeutic nihilism, whose adherents deemed his concern for the
patient unbecoming to a professional. In Budapest from 1849 to 1865,
he spoiled his career by assailing distinguished physicians who refused to adopt prophylaxis. A victim of chronic meningitis, Semmelweis
died at the Döbling Sanatorium a few years before his book of 1861
on childbed fever won universal acceptance. Once Lister had introduced carbolic acid in 1865, antisepsis spread rapidly, being introduced
into Austria by a Bohemian-born surgeon and poet, Eduard Albert
(1841–1900). In the early days, carbolic spray often damaged the
skin of surgeons. Such an allergy prodded Adolf Lorenz (1854–1946),
a student of Albert, to devise a technique of "bloodless" surgery, which
eventually permitted correction of clubfeet.

Not all leaders of the Vienna Medical School scoffed at therapy as
did Rokitansky, Skoda, and Hyrtl. Bohemian-born Johann von Oppolzer (1808–1871) excelled at diagnostics, inspiring such pupils as
Freud's friends Josef Breuer and Rudolf Chrobak. Brünn-born Ferdinand von Hebra (1816–1880), a companion of Semmelweis, systematized dermatology, classifying diseases and devising water-bed therapy. Another Moravian, Leopold von Dittel (1815–1898) founded
modern urology. The man who did most to counteract therapeutic

therapy vs diagnosis

nihilism was a Prussian, Hermann Nothnagel (1841–1905), who as a
professor at Vienna from 1882 to 1905 perfected use of blood pressure
in diagnosis. He was beloved for willingness to visit patients. Perhaps
the most celebrated of Viennese doctors was the German-born surgeon, Theodor Billroth (1829–1894), an amateur musician whose
friends included Brahms and Hanslick. Having invented an anaesthesia
of ether and chloroform, Billroth pioneered such operations as resec-
tioning the stomach and removing the larynx. Billroth reflected the
predilection of Viennese physicians for treatment by surgery. Reliance
on excising a diseased part accorded with stress on pathological
anatomy and skepticism toward drugs. Adamant about postoperative
care, Billroth innovated by improving the training of nurses.

In the field of ophthalmology, a Bohemian, Ferdinand von Arlt
(1812–1887), discovered the cause of nearsightedness, and in 1854 a
Vienna-born eye surgeon Eduard Jäger von Jaxtthal (1818–1884)
introduced eye charts to standardize prescriptions for eyeglasses. The
preponderance of Bohemians among these pioneers demonstrates further the excellence of education available during Bohemia's Catholic
Enlightenment. Whereas in Vienna, religion had been separated from
natural science, in Bohemia the two were pursued in tandem, helping
to groom such giants of the Vienna Medical School as Rokitansky,
Skoda, Oppolzer, Hebra, Dittel, and Arlt.

The Bohemian origin of its luminaries notwithstanding, Vienna
reigned as medical capital of the Habsburg Empire, becoming in the
phrase of Rudolf Virchow, the Mecca of Medicine. The city's preeminence increased as patients from all over the empire flocked there to
be treated. A profusion of clinical evidence, including the rarest
maladies, encouraged Vienna's physicians to exploit observation as a
tool for exploding medical myths. As Fritz Wittels put it, heroes of the
Vienna Medical School displayed

> the fighting spirit, the lust to destroy, sublimated into the fight
> for truth, without which nothing constructive succeeds.[12]

Owing to Rokitansky and Skoda, for decades lectures were devoted
exclusively to diagnosis, not therapy. Students learned by performing
postmortem examinations followed by the critical discussion known as
epikrisis.

Preoccupation with postmortem diagnosis engendered scandalous
conditions at the General Hospital.[13] In 1898, fifty years after Semmelweis' discoveries, nurses helped spread an epidemic through the hospital. This came eleven years after the deputy Engelbert Pernerstorfer

had denounced in the Reichsrat criminal neglect of patients by doctors and nurses alike. Although the director of the hospital resigned, no lasting precautions ensued. Nurses remained abysmally untrained, being recruited from parlormaids and washerwomen unfit for employment elsewhere. Some doctors preferred that nurses remain ignorant lest they countermand orders. Although nurses worked twenty-four hours at a stint, they received so little pay that they had to vend coffee and demand tips for their services. A patient who spurned the coffee would be ignored, and nearly all patients had to administer their own medicine. One nurse, who had worked twelve years at the General Hospital, was convicted for thefts committed throughout her tenure. Even at private sanatoriums, Catholic sisters, albeit kind and honest, lacked qualifications; some received no more than three hours per week of free time. It was in an effort to forestall abuses like these that in 1882 Theodor Billroth and Hans Wilczek founded the Rudolfiner-haus in which girls of good family were trained as nurses.

The poor dreaded entering the hospital, fearing that they would never leave. In a custom still prevalent, patients had to pay in advance. Incoming patients were examined in droves, and every patient who died underwent autopsy. In 1898, C. O'Conor-Eccles recounted the following vignette:

> A doctor who visited the hospital told me he saw a party of students sounding a woman who was dying of pleurisy or pneumonia, in order that they might each hear the crepitation in her lungs as her last moments approached. She expired before they left the ward. He said something about treatment in another case to the professor who was lecturing these young men. The reply was, "Treatment, treatment, that is nothing; it is the diagnosis that we want."[14]

The indifference to human life, which as late as 1900 afflicted the General Hospital, both contradicted and reinforced other Viennese attitudes. The Catholic tradition of charity, which Klemens Maria Hofbauer had revived, was engulfed by the positivism of postmortem examiners. Sympathy for the little man, was not, until after 1900, a consideration of the Medical Faculty. At the General Hospital, the impartiality of Josephinist bureaucracy became impartiality toward death: not even the rich could obtain competent nurses. Disease comprised part of life: the task of doctors was not to eradicate it but merely to understand it. Refusal by nineteenth-century physicians to intervene in natural processes paralleled the reluctance of many

Austrians to participate in politics. Likewise the preference of Carl Menger and Ludwig von Mises for an unimpeded market economy seemed to corroborate the medical dictum, "The essential is to do no harm" *(Primum est non nocere)*. Predilection for scrutiny without remedy afflicted philosophers no less than social theorists. In his diatribe against woman's bestiality, Weininger played variations on Rokitansky's faith that nature favors the strong. After decades of resisting therapeutic nihilism in psychotherapy, even Freud came full circle by postulating a death wish: nature inscrutably condemns some beings to destruction, let doctors do what they may.

FREUD'S MENTORS TURNED RIVALS:
BRÜCKE, MEYNERT, KRAFFT-EBING, BREUER, AND FLIESS

Psychoanalysis marked a triumph over the therapeutic nihilism that had persisted longer in psychiatry than in other branches of medicine. From 1784 to 1869 most psychiatric patients at Vienna were relegated to a prisonlike Fool's Tower *(Narrenturm)* behind the General Hospital. More fortunate patients such as István Széchenyi resided at the Döbling Sanatorium, whose medical personnel sought to comfort rather than cure them. Spurning pleas by Feuchtersleben, physicians trained in anatomy ignored neurotic patients, on whom postmortem analysis could reveal nothing. Sometimes neurasthenia was diagnosed as brain tumor or meningitis. Although kindly doctors might prescribe warm baths, mild electric shocks, and other placebos, prior to Freud no one supposed that emotional disorders might have a purely psychic origin.

It was from medical teachers rather than from philosophers or literati that Freud imbibed the attitudes that enabled him to inaugurate psychoanalysis. At the Medical Faculty, he had been ambivalent toward the practice of medicine, later acquiring sufficient faith in his mission to enable him to found a school. Having studied at the height of Billroth's exploits, he came to regard psychiatric therapy as a kind of surgery that cuts away psychic foreign bodies so as to permit scars to heal without exciting defenses.[15] It is worthwhile to examine in detail the attitudes that five teachers and colleagues imparted to Freud between 1875 and 1900, equipping him to synthesize and transcend their insights.

Among Freud's teachers none exerted such decisive influence upon him as the Berlin-born physiologist, Ernst Wilhelm Brücke (1819–1892).[16] This Protestant polymath had studied at Berlin under the embryologist Johannes Müller (1801–1858), who had inculcated a conviction that empirical physiology must vanquish romantic medicine. Other students of Müller such as Rudolf Virchow, Hermann Helmholtz, and Emil du Bois-Reymond disseminated the faith of their master, which Brücke brought to Vienna in 1849. As a researcher *(Famulus)* from 1876 to 1882 at Brücke's physiological laboratory, Freud drilled himself in the art of detailed observation. Working in a converted rifle factory, Freud learned to detect and avoid spurious effects that an observer may inject into microscopic specimens. Rather than tamper with specimens, the young physiologist learned that embryology requires description, not experimentation, just as diagnosis results from postmortem examination, not therapy. Robert R. Holt, who has applied insights of his Budapest-born teacher David Rapoport (1911–1960), points out that Freud's reliance on the concept of force derived from years spent with Brücke. For Brücke, as for Helmholtz, real causes were denoted by the concept of force. Freud's cathexes, drives, tensions, repressions, and the constancy principle all presuppose discharge of energy. Like Herbart and Brücke, he conceived the nervous system as a passive system that seeks to dissipate energies thrust upon it from outside. Having already been exposed to Herbart's psychology of forces through a gymnasium textbook by Gustav Adolf Lindner, Freud found in Brücke empirical confirmation of the philosopher's premises.

Although most biographers concede that Freud revered Brücke, they tend to limit the latter's influence to his scientific exploits, overlooking the fact that this Prussian was one of the most versatile scholars of the nineteenth century. Brücke, whose interests closely paralleled those of Freud, extolled the city where he dwelt from 1849 to 1892, calling it the "metropolis of East Germanic culture."

As a friend of the art historian Eitelberger, the physiologist studied Italian art, writing several papers on Michelangelo, who was also to become a favorite of Freud's. In *Bruchstücke aus der Theorie der bildenden Künste* (Leipzig, 1877), Brücke analyzed the optics of perspective and chiaroscuro, having earlier discussed the use of color in the applied arts.[17] Not only did he serve as a curator of Eitelberger's Museum of Art and Industry but in order to paint for recreation, he traveled to Italy every summer.

In the year of Freud's birth, Brücke had devised one of the earliest phonetic alphabets.[18] This amazing scholar also wrote a treatise on the physiological basis of German versification, as well as on the structure of Hindi.

In politics, Brücke was an anticlerical, resembling Virchow who in 1873 applied the term *Kulturkampf* to Bismarck's policy. Although

Brücke declined to use the title granted him in 1872, after 1879 he sat in the Herrenhaus, opposing reestablishment of confessional schools. In 1879 he had the distinction of becoming the first Protestant to preside as rector of the University of Vienna. From 1882 to 1885 he served as vice-president of the Academy of Sciences. Most surprising of all, the fearsome examiner, who used to flunk students who missed the first question of an oral examination, published at age seventy-three a primer on child care. In *Wie behütet man Leben und Gesundheit seiner Kinder* (Vienna, 1892) Brücke expounded his own experience as father and grandfather, prompted in part by inextinguishable grief for his son Hans, who had died in 1872 after contracting diphtheria from a patient.

Prone as he was to hero worship, the young Freud could not have failed to admire the versatility of such a teacher. Brücke knew Freud well enough to advise him in 1882 to enter general practice because he lacked funds for a career of research, and in 1885 Brücke warmly recommended Freud for a travel stipend to study under Charcot in Paris. Like Brücke, Freud considered it a matter of course to combine natural science with study of art and literature. Both men felt special affinity for Italy as well as for the sculpture of Michelangelo, and both were anticlericals. Freud, however, evinced less interest in politics, just as Brücke lacked Freud's psychological insight. The adulation that learned Vienna showered on Brücke could only have encouraged his ambitious student to cultivate a similar range of interests.

The psychiatrist whom as a student Freud most admired was Dresden-born Theodor Meynert (1833–1892), who taught at the Vienna Medical Faculty from 1858 to 1892.[19] Theodor studied at Vienna under Rokitansky, as well as under the Herbartian anatomist of the brain Maximilian Leidesdorf (1816–1889), a converted Jew whom Freud met in 1885.[20] A hard-driving scientist who also published poetry, Meynert revolutionized the study of the brain's gross anatomy, working in a cluttered laboratory where his children played. In his *Psychiatrie* (Vienna, 1884), Meynert sought to localize functions of the forebrain so as to propound a more "natural" classification of nervous disorders. This taxonomy he tested during ten years of research at the State Insane Asylum, which handled more than twelve hundred patients per year. Although Meynert sometimes tried to reason with incurable lunatics, on the whole he remained cool and distant toward them.[21] "Treatment of the soul" he disdained, on grounds that this entails "more than we can accomplish and transcends the bounds of accurate scientific investigation."[22]

Having worked in Meynert's clinic from April 1 to October 1, 1883, Freud respected his teacher as the "most brilliant genius he had ever encountered."[23] In his *Entwurf einer Psychologie* (1895), Freud restated Meynert's postulate of a primary and secondary ego. Primary ego is that part of mental life which is genetically early and unconscious; it arises with an infant's awareness of separation between his body and the environment. Secondary ego is the controlling agent of perception, in which beloved persons may be included. Meynert's distinction between a socialized upper cortex and a primitive lower cortex derived from Herbart.[24]

Relations between Meynert and Freud cooled when, with Krafft-Ebing, Meynert disparaged experiments with cocaine which Freud was conducting on neurotics between 1884 and 1887.[25] These experiments, which resulted in addiction of several patients, branded Freud as a fanatic who lacked positivistic restraint. This judgment was corroborated by the young physician's enthusiasm for hypnosis and for French psychiatry, especially that of Charcot. Meynert dismissed resort to hypnotism as pure charlatanry. In his book of 1891 on aphasia, Freud criticized Meynert's cortical anatomy, after Meynert had repudiated Freud's postulate, borrowed in 1886 from Charcot, of masculine hysteria. Reminding Freud that the term hysteria derived from the Greek word for uterus, directors of clinics had closed their doors when the young upstart dared to diagnose hysteria in men. In *Die Traumdeutung*, Freud recalled that Meynert once confessed to having inhaled chloroform as a youth. More surprisingly, when Freud visited his dying teacher, the latter conceded, "You know, I was always one of the best cases of masculine hysteria."[26] By typifying therapeutic nihilism, Meynert provided a foil against which the younger man could react. Misled by a passion for taxonomy, the authoritarian Meynert exemplified the obstacles awaiting anyone who would apply Brücke's method to psychiatry.

Next to Meynert, the most renowned psychiatrist in Vienna was another German, Richard von Krafft-Ebing (1840–1902).[27] A Catholic born in Mannheim, he had studied at Heidelberg and then practiced in Baden-Baden before coming to Graz in 1873. From 1873 to 1889 he served there as director of the Public Insane Asylum, working with Hans Gross before going to Vienna in 1889. He had treated Crown Prince Rudolf, and just before Ludwig II of Bavaria drowned on June 13, 1886, Krafft-Ebing had warned the king's personal physician to beware of his patient's homicidal tendencies. Krafft-Ebing was the first to investigate how syphilis causes paralysis, advancing his hypothesis during the decade when Makart and Nietzsche succumbed to the same syndrome that had felled the poet Lenau during the 1840's. Definitive proof of the connection between syphilis and paresis came in 1895 from Krafft-Ebing's Bohemian-born assistant, Josef Adolf Hirschl (1865–1914).

Krafft-Ebing published a slim volume in Latin entitled *Psychopathia sexualis: Eine klinisch-forensische Studie* (Stuttgart, 1886). The work was quickly translated into seven languages and eventually enlarged to three times its original length, reaching its twelfth edition in 1902 and seventeenth in 1924. Partly under the influence of Hans Gross, most of the studies were drawn from courtroom cases, each carefully classified and the whole preceded by an introduction expounding the relation of sex to art, religion, and married life. Krafft-Ebing never disguised his disapproval of sexual deviance. With an intransigence reinforced by duty as an expert witness in courts of law, he espoused Roman Catholic faith in the teleology of sex, contending that its only natural function is to propagate the species.

Krafft-Ebing coined the term masochism to complement that of sadism, basing the neologism on writings by Lemberg-born Leopold von Sacher-Masoch (1836–1895).[28] Son of a German father named Sacher and a Ruthenian mother named Masoch, Leopold had grown up near Lemberg, adoring a Ruthenian nurse. He had been unnerved by the rebellion of 1846, when he had seen peasant women terrorize the countryside. During famine mothers had even devoured their children.[29] After his father was transferred to Prague in 1848, Leopold adopted the German language without shedding Ruthenian traits. When his father became police director at Graz in 1853, the son enrolled at the university there, earning a habilitation in history four years later. In 1873 when Krafft-Ebing arrived in Graz, tales still circulated of Sacher-Masoch's liaison with one Anna von Kottowitz, whose caprices had fixated her lover during the early 1860's. Influenced by Turgenev, Sacher-Masoch described in his first novel, *Eine galizische Geschichte 1846* (Schaffhausen, 1858), the Polish rebellion that had terrified him. Increasingly thereafter his stories dramatized sexual struggles where women taunt men. In the novellas of *Das Vermächtnis Kains* (Stuttgart, 1870) the tormented author unfolded a synthesis of Schopenhauer and Darwin, in which each protagonist tries like Cain to enslave his brother. In one of these stories, *Venus im Pelze*, Sacher-Masoch described his own relationship at Baden bei Wien with Baroness Fanny Pistor, with whom in December, 1869, he had signed a contract to submit for six months to being her slave. After marriage in 1873 to Graz-born Angelika Rümelin (1845–post–1906), Sacher-Masoch sank further into sexual vagaries, eventually deserting his wife to work as an editor at Budapest, Leipzig, and after 1885 at Paris, where his novellas captivated readers of *La Revue des deux mondes.*

Esteemed by Saar for vivid narrative, Sacher-Masoch catered to the same circles as Makart. *Die Messalinen Wiens: Geschichten aus der guten Gesellschaft* (Leipzig, 1874) celebrated a licentiousness that the death of Archduchess Sophie and the depression of 1873 had unleashed. In *Psychopathia sexualis*, Krafft-Ebing hailed the neurotic writer as a discoverer, rather than a victim of masochism, although the psychiatrist knew the latter also to be true. Nordau challenged Krafft-Ebing's choice of Masoch's name to supplant the older term for love of pain, algolagnia. Writers like Rousseau in his *Confessions*, said Nordau, as well as Balzac in his *Parents Pauvres I. La cousine Bette* (1846) had depicted weak men who yearn to be dominated by women, not to mention viragoes portrayed by Wagner, Ibsen, Zola, and Dostoevski.[30] Having learned from mutual friends of Sacher-Masoch's deviance, Krafft-Ebing unwittingly foisted upon the unhappy writer a notoriety that has eclipsed his literary merits.

Although Krafft-Ebing's *Psychopathia sexualis* indicated rather than provoked a growing preoccupation with sex, it formulated tantalizing anticipations of psychoanalysis. Krafft-Ebing saluted sublimation in both art and religion:

> What other foundation is there for the plastic arts of poetry? From (sensual) love arises that warmth of fancy which alone can inspire the creative mind, and the fire of sensual feeling kindles and preserves the glow and fervor of art.[31]

Religion, he contended, burns similar energies and produces similar effects to those generated by sex. Both enflame imagination, proffering gratification far in excess of what empirical evidence suggests. Sexual experience "promises a boon which far surpasses all other conceivable pleasures, and faith has in store a bliss that endures forever."[32] Because of their exaggerated intensity, sex and religion often reinforce each other by elevating submission into rapture. This can prompt not only the self-flagellation of religious masochism, but an impulse to chastize others through religious sadism. No less than Freud, Krafft-Ebing was fascinated by hypnotism. At a séance about 1890, he hypnotized a medium, whereupon the medium extracted a watch from the pocket of the actor Alexander Girardi. Billroth promptly denounced his medical colleague as a swindler.[33]

Whatever the similarities between them, Krafft-Ebing earned Freud's lasting hostility by deprecating Freud's first paper on infantile sexuality. At a meeting of the Vienna Society for Psychiatry and Neurology, chaired by Krafft-Ebing on May 2, 1896, Freud argued that premature sexual experience underlies all cases of hysteria.[34] In formulating this seduction theory, Freud had mistakenly believed patients' recollections of having undergone sexual intercourse with parents and other relatives. He did not yet recognize that such fantasies conceal an unfulfilled wish. When Krafft-Ebing pronounced the hypothesis to be a scientific fairy tale *(Märchen)*, Freud refused to deliver another paper in public until 1904—although by September, 1897, he too doubted the veracity of his patients' tales.[35] Freud's pique did not hinder Krafft-Ebing from backing his colleague's application for a professorship both in 1897 and 1902. Although the older man never enunciated a theory of personality, his compilation of sexual data greatly enriched Freud's psychopathology.

A physician who after 1880 offered Freud much needed ego support was Josef Breuer (1842–1925).[36] Born in Vienna the son of a Jewish teacher of religion, Breuer attended the Akademisches Gymnasium before studying medicine at Vienna from 1859 to 1867. For four years he served as assistant to the therapist Johann von Oppolzer, whose death in 1871 caused Breuer to decline a position as a docent in order to become a practicing physician. One of the most trusted doctors in Vienna, Breuer served as personal physician to colleagues such as Brücke, Billroth, and Chrobak, as well as to Brentano. Having won fame in 1868 for a paper on the role of the vagus nerve in regulating breathing, in 1873 the physiologist duplicated the discovery by Ernst Mach that the semicircular canals of the inner ear control the body's equilibrium. Imbued with unfailing modesty, Breuer always felt that the learned world overestimated his achievements. For more than twenty-five years he corresponded with Marie von Ebner-Eschenbach, whose gentle compassion matched his own. Breuer's quiet resignation, resembling the description of a character in her *Ein Spätgeborener*, at first helped and then infuriated the ambitious Freud, who scolded his mentor for lacking courage to exploit discoveries. After the two men had met in the late 1870's, Breuer became a father figure to the young researcher, helping him to transfer in 1882 from physiology to general practice and thence to psychotherapy. Although like everyone else, Breuer disapproved of Freud's attempt to treat neurosis with cocaine, the older man did not discourage his protegé.

Breuer's preeminent significance, for Freud and thus for posterity, was his discovery in 1881 of the so-called talking cure, whose details he disclosed to Freud in late 1882. From December, 1880, to June, 1882, Breuer had treated for hysteria a Vienna-born Jewish girl, Bertha

Pappenheim (1859–1936), whom he dubbed "Anna O."[37] Raised in
Vienna the daughter of puritanical Jews from Frankfurt, Bertha became bedridden in December, 1880, while nursing her adored father,
who died the following April. Her symptoms included somnambulism,
paralysis of three limbs, and a phantom pregnancy, all of which alternated with periods of lucidity. After she had moved in June, 1881, to
the countryside outside Vienna, Breuer visited her to find that after
she had described a symptom it would vanish. Conversing exclusively
in English—she professed to have forgotten German—Miss Pappenheim
labeled her talking out *(Aussprechen)* of symptoms as the "talking
cure *(Redecur)* or "chimney sweeping" *(Kaminfegen)*. Under hypnosis
she recalled how she had repressed emotions while standing at her
father's sickbed; by recollecting these forgotten feelings, she could
dispel the hysteric symptoms into which repression had converted
them. After months of narrating each symptom, by June, 1882, Miss
Pappenheim was able to depart Vienna quite restored. In 1889 she
settled in Frankfurt, where from 1890 to 1936 she directed an orphanage and home for unwed mothers. She also translated from the Talmud
and published journals of travels.[38] Refusing thereafter even to mention her experience with Breuer, she adamantly opposed allowing girls
in her charge to undergo psychoanalysis. It was Breuer, through his
contacts with this young woman, who initiated the practice of listening
for hundreds of hours to a single patient. Although as a noninterfering
observer Breuer perpetuated the positivism of Brücke and Mach, he
lavished on a patient compassion that those therapeutic nihilists lacked,
and that Freud would display in abundance.

Miss Pappenheim's outpourings so dislocated Breuer that after 1882
he refused to risk repeating the ordeal, referring all such cases to
Freud. While ruminating on the case of Bertha Pappenheim, Freud
experimented first with cocaine and then with hypnosis. After 1890,
Freud began to substitute for hypnosis free association on the couch,
implementing a hint he had heard from Hippolyte Bernheim (1840–
1919) at Nancy in 1889. Having used hypnosis to trigger acting out or
abreacting *(Abreagieren)* of repressed conflicts, Freud became convinced that repression *(Verdrängung)* holds the key to neurosis.[39] In
Studien über Hysterie (Vienna, 1895), Breuer and Freud collaborated
to work out implications of the older man's serendipity. In a letter of
November, 1907, to August Forel, Breuer insisted that it was he who,
in conjunction with Miss Pappenheim, had discovered that neurotic
symptoms serve to hide unconscious conflicts and that when the conflicts reach consciousness, symptoms subside.[40] Breuer confessed that
after 1895 he had lacked incentive to pursue the matter. George H.

Pollock has suggested that Breuer's aversion to a sexual theory of neurosis may have stemmed from childhood trauma, his mother having died during childbirth when he was three years old.[41] Repressed memories of this disaster may have hindered the otherwise exemplary physician from applying to himself and to others his observations of Bertha Pappenheim.

In 1887 Breuer sent to Freud a Pomeranian-born Jewish physiologist, Wilhelm Fliess (1858–1928), who was studying briefly at Vienna.[42] Upon Fliess's return to Berlin, the two younger men corresponded; after 1893 they became close friends. It was in letters to Fliess, as well as in conversations with him, that between 1895 and 1899 Freud unfolded results of his self-analysis, which the death of his father in October 1896 had helped to provoke. A proponent of romantic *Naturphilosophie,* Fliess used numbers to elaborate a pansexual theory of behavior, based on the rhythm of the menstrual cycle.[43] Despite mounting incompatibility, Fliess furnished Freud a much needed audience of one during a time when the budding psychoanalyst had few colleagues at Vienna. Lacking Fliess's facility with numbers, Freud later disapproved attempts to quantify the intensity of emotional charges. It was under Fliess's tutelage that in 1895 Freud wrote his *Entwurf einer Psychologie,* which outlined an a priori neuropsychology of both normal and abnormal behavior.[44] After *Die Traumdeutung* had appeared in late 1899, Freud cooled toward Fliess, breaking with him in 1902. Having never quite accepted Fliess's theory of periods, Freud repudiated it after a former patient, Hermann Swoboda, began in 1904 to teach Fliess's doctrines. It was Swoboda who in 1900 had transmitted Freud's insights to Otto Weininger.

Prior to falling out with him, Fliess shielded Freud from positivism and nepotism in the Vienna Medical Faculty. By bolstering the hypothesis that psychic disorders have a mental rather than a physical origin, Fliess liberated Freud for the great discoveries of self-analysis. Foiled in seeking promotion beyond the post of docent, Freud found in Fliess solace from the obscurantism of men like Meynert and Krafft-Ebing. In order to cure his own anxiety neurosis by unraveling puzzles about psychotherapy which Breuer had posed, Freud made himself an internal emigré. Although—or perhaps because—he felt hate-love for his teachers at Vienna, he could not have succeeded without them. Once he had achieved a breakthrough, he indulged in Viennese aestheticism as freely as the painter Brücke or the poet Meynert. The father of psychoanalysis owed an even weightier debt to the self-effacing Breuer for having sustained him through years of groping.

16

Freud and Vienna

FREUD'S HATE-LOVE FOR VIENNA:
AFFINITIES BETWEEN PSYCHOANALYSIS AND ITS MILIEU

FREUD PROFESSED HATE-LOVE not only toward the medical profession of Vienna, but toward the city itself. Ernest Jones has cataloged Freud's railings against Vienna,[1] but these were balanced by an interview Freud granted a young admirer in late November, 1918. Ernst Lothar, who had submitted to Freud a laudatory essay on psychoanalysis, sought an interview in order to console himself over collapse of Austria-Hungary. Freud told Lothar:

> Like you I feel an unrestrained affection for Vienna and Austria, although perhaps unlike you, I know her abysses.[2]

Thereupon the psychoanalyst pulled from his desk a memorandum that he had written on November 11, 1918:

> Austria-Hungary is no more. I do not want to live anywhere else. For me emigration is out of the question. I shall live on with the torso and imagine that it is the whole.[3]

For all his protestations of scorn, Freud could not bear to leave the city where he had dwelt since age four. He endured that ambivalence toward Vienna which afflicted so many of her most gifted thinkers, including such other Jews as Loos, Wittgenstein, and Mahler. If one tries to imagine some other city in which Freud might have prospered, one realizes that none other could have offered such provocative colleagues from whom to have patients referred and against whom to react. Although Prague no less than Vienna might have prompted Freud to combine study of medicine with pursuit of the humanities,

interdisciplinary

racial strife there would surely have exacerbated his insecurity as a Jew.

Freud's psychotherapy mirrors the fact that Vienna was a stronghold of memory. In Vienna everyone exemplified what in 1895 Freud ascribed to hysterics: they suffer largely from reminiscences.[4] In this citadel of memory, Freud exploited Breuer's discovery that reliving a trauma could dispel its symptoms. By discharging repressed memories through verbalizing them, engaging as it were in a feuilleton à deux, a neurotic could liberate himself from his past. Having discerned by 1893 that neurotic symptoms arise as a defense against unwanted memories, Freud confessed rather sheepishly that case histories of his patients read like novellas.[5] To a neurotic, indulgence in memory brought both curse and cure, just as remembering both burdened and benefited Vienna's creators.

In formulating his notion of the unconscious, Freud drew upon commonplaces of Habsburg bureaucracy.[6] Rules of decorum were incarnated by the emperor, whose portrait loomed in school and office. When Freud spoke of father-figures, he could have had in mind this macrocosmic father, whose deportment both the ambitious and the lethargic emulated. Secretiveness blanketed public life, prompting a search for latent meanings behind every event. Whatever seemed inexplicable was attributed to conspirators, whether they be Jews, Czechs, Social Democrats, Protestants, or journalists. Canards acted as defense mechanisms, equipping the unconscious to explain what reason could not.

Such duplicity aggravated the mechanisms of neurosis which Freud was seeking. When he spoke of superego censoring id, he knew what press censorship meant: a story would be missing from the front page, unleashing a fresh spate of rumors. Helpless—Freud would say castrated—before the bureaucracy, the populace indulged fantasies that belittled the omnipotent personages who manipulated them. Most Austrians harbored feelings of paranoia toward the state, exacerbating tensions and causing the violence that erupted during the Badeni debates.[7] If aggression could swamp the Reichsrat, how could a psychotherapist banish it from the consulting room? Incursions of id into politics reflected infantile traits which abounded in Viennese speech. Persons who substituted "I should like" for "I could" or "I would," displaced facts with wishes. Friedrich Hacker has called Freud's ego a "Hofrat of appeasement" (Beschwichtigungs-Hofrat), which mediates between frustrated impulses and decorum.[8]

In a society, where every occurrence evoked a wish or an aversion and where every brush with officialdom ended in subterfuge, it was natural to postulate a zone of repressed memories to explain duplicity. Although Austria did not necessarily produce more neurotics than elsewhere, it fostered conditions that helped Freud to uncover the mechanism of neurosis. A public life veiled in dissimulation paralleled the repression that Freud discerned in individuals. In his schema of neurosis we see Habsburg society writ small.

Court preciosity found an equivalent in every bourgeois household, where girls were so sheltered from the facts of sexuality that many marriages foundered in frigidity. In sex-starved young women, neuroses were commonplace: Schnitzler and Bahr portrayed their discomfiture, while Mayreder and Ehrenfels decried it.

Freud acknowledged that as early as 1880 he had suspected the sexual origin of hysteria. About 1880, Breuer divulged that secrets of the marriage bed underlay one patient's neurosis, and in 1885 Charcot declared of certain hysterics, "C'est toujours la chose génitale, toujours . . . toujours . . . toujours."[9] In 1886 Freud's friend Rudolf Chrobak referred to Freud a woman who, after eighteen years of marriage, was still a virgin. The gynecologist commented that the sole effective prescription for her ailment—the male sex organ—could not be administered by a physician. Freud himself was so devoid of humor where sex was concerned, that Breuer's remark of 1880 shocked him.

Freud had many Viennese tastes and habits; although atypically he demanded that guests be punctual, he was a genial host who put strangers at ease. He used his piercing eyes, gestures, and facial expressions to punctuate his speech; in a city of actors, he too knew how to dramatize.

As in many Viennese homes, Freud's waiting room was laid with thick oriental rugs, and on the walls hung reproductions of Rembrandt's *Anatomy Lesson* and Johann Heinrich Füssli's *Nightmare*.[10] In his office stood cabinets filled with objets d'art from ancient Greece and Egypt as well as life-sized casts of Egyptian bas-reliefs. In the manner of Franz Joseph, Freud conducted massive correspondence entirely by hand, disdaining typewriter and secretary. He enjoyed walking the Ringstrasse, for years taking midday constitutionals around its entire circumference, striding at a pace that must have startled the leisurely.

Freud confessed to Max Eastman in 1926, "Politically I am just nothing."[11] He did not register to vote at Vienna until 1908, and he accepted World War One with resignation. An arch-privatist, he despaired of changing social or political conditions, incarnating that withdrawal into the arts and sciences which had sustained Vienna since about 1800. Freud epitomized the political apathy that Karl Kraus despised.

Freud detested music while at work, and at leisure he was neither a gourmet nor a theatergoer. After 1890, he found diversion by playing Tarock every Saturday evening at the home of a Moravian-born ophthalmologist Leopold Königstein (1850-1924). Like his mother, Freud played the four-handed game so ardently that his daughter could recall three things he insisted his children know: how to recognize wild flowers, how to find mushrooms, and how to play Tarock.[12] Some reasons why this game should have captivated Freud may be gleaned from Mór Jókai's account of it:

> The Tarock-player must not only study his cards, but also the faces of his adversaries. He must be Lavater and Tartuffe in one; he must be a general who develops at every moment a fresh plan of campaign, and a Bosco, who can, from the first card that is played, divine the whole situation; he must, however, be generous, and sacrifice himself for the sake of the general good.[13]

Such a game would fascinate a man of quick intellect, astute at detecting intentions and devising countermoves. The proviso that on occasion a Tarock player has to place the common good ahead of his own corresponds to the Leibnizian vision of harmony. Each player belongs to a larger whole, whose welfare incorporates his own. Hermann Bahr may have had this in mind when he declared that Tarock was the only avocation that permeated all classes of Austrian society, noting that Viktor Adler and Engelbert Pernerstorfer—he might have added Karl Lueger—were addicted to it.[14]

Nothing illustrates so well Freud's symbiosis with Viennese culture as the resemblance between his insights and those reached independently by Arthur Schnitzler.[15] Although the two Jewish physicians never met, Freud several times remarked on their affinities. In 1905 he noted that Schnitzler in a one-act play *Paracelsus* (Berlin, 1899) had described a patient's resistance to being cured.[16] In May, 1922, Freud wrote to Schnitzler that he had avoided an encounter for fear of meeting his double *(Doppelgänger)*:

> So I have formed the impression that you know through intuition—or rather through detailed self-observation—everything that I have discovered by laborious work on other people.[17]

A few years later in his interview with George Sylvester Viereck, Schnitzler acknowledged being Freud's psychic twin, commenting that he had invented many of his plots during dreams.[18]

Son of a distinguished laryngologist, Schnitzler practiced hypnotism at the same time as Freud, both men having studied under Hippolyte Bernheim at Nancy. In an early novella, *Der Sohn* (1893), Schnitzler portrayed a neurotic son who after having slain his mother dispelled repressed hatreds by confessing the crime. Albeit less systematically than Freud, Schnitzler recognized that neurotic individuals achieve self-awareness once they are forced to relive their traumas. In interior monologues which resemble feuilletons, Schnitzler depicted free association circling around a neurotic's obsession. Freud's patients, like Schnitzler's characters, wallowed in the subjective world of Viennese speech, undergoing that hate-love that Vienna evoked in most of her creators. In *Der Weg ins Freie*, the musician Georg von Wergenthin feels ambivalent not only toward his mistress, who bears him a stillborn child, but toward Vienna, whose distractions cripple his creativity. This dilettante eventually finds a "path into the open" as assistant conductor elsewhere, reflecting Schnitzler's own feelings toward the city that alternately cheered and jeered his plays.

Freud and Schnitzler shared numerous traits of Viennese aestheticism. Extreme individualists, both men dismissed politics as debasing. Both loved to escape the city into the countryside, yet neither could dwell anywhere but in Vienna. Both were observant travelers, assimilating new impressions with avidity. Although each was fascinated by neurosis, neither identified with neurotics. Freud, like Schnitzler, believed that work and love could elevate everyday life by inculcating involvement in larger issues.

Besides Schnitzler, another arch-impressionist Hermann Bahr displayed prescience with regard to the unconscious. In describing what he called the decompositive psychology of Maurice Barrès, Bahr in 1891 could have been delineating psychoanalysis:

> The new [psychology] will seek the basic elements [of feelings], the beginnings in the darknesses of the soul, before they have come into the clear light: this whole tedious, involved, chaotically entangled process of the feelings, which in the end tosses their complex facts in the form of simple conclusions over the threshold of consciousness.[19]

Although Bahr lacked the perseverance to pursue this insight, it reveals the extent to which impressionism postulated latent contents beneath a changing surface. Popper-Lynkeus applied the same insight to dreams in his sketch "Träumen als Wachen" (1899).

A no less striking anticipation of psychoanalysis appears in a novella by Ferdinand Kürnberger (1821-1879). Years after Kürnberger had visited Széchenyi at the Döbling Sanatorium, the journalist interpreted the effects of repressed guilt in *Die Last des Schweigens: Eine Seelenstudie* (1866). After long silence, a Hungarian landowner voluntarily confesses having committed a murder. What he regrets is not the crime, but the necessity to avoid boasting about it. Kürnberger enunciates a law of contrariety which he says rules psychic life: unconsciously a person who has succeeded yearns to be punished, just as one who has failed craves a reward. Similarly Freud's hypothesis of a duel between Eros and Thanatos presupposes in each person's unconscious an oscillation between irreconcilable impulses.

Impressionist writings circled around the themes of love and death with regularity. Schnitzler, for example, "zeroed in" on a central event, elucidating experience as a ring of concentric circles surrounding a focal phenomenon. In dialogue, free association peeled away layers of memory to unmask an obsession at the core—Eros and Thanatos. Capacity to see life through the spectacles of obsession marked a number of other thinkers described in this book: Mach reduced experience to a flux of sensations, Kraus identified behavior with language, Kelsen equated law with the will of the state, Weininger bifurcated nature into male and female, and Freud traced neurosis to infantile sex trauma. Ability to envision experience in terms of a theme with variations gave coherence to the manifold insights of impressionism. Each of these thinkers coupled the inquisitiveness of impressionism with the rigor of positivism, bracing the openness of Bahr with the solidity of Helmholtz. Because Freud prosecuted this fusion of art and science more vigorously than anyone else, his remains the most acclaimed achievement of the Gay Apocalypse.

FREUD'S ATTITUDE TOWARD
RELIGION AND DEATH

Many scholars have contended that Freud—his anticlericalism notwithstanding—was profoundly religious. Although Freud regarded himself as religiously unmusical, Fritz Wittels and David Bakan among others have argued that his zeal bordered on the mystical. To be sure, at least until 1914, Freud believed in an invisible order underlying the chaos of emotion, postulating that exposure of latent conflicts would disperse

them. Although this faith may have been engendered by study of
Herbartian philosophy at gymnasium, it seems more probable—given
Freud's aversion to philosophy—that his world view crystallized in
Brücke's laboratory. Freud held the faith of a positivist, tinctured with
the skeptical open-mindedness of impressionism.

By age ten, he had shed whatever vestiges of supernatural belief he
might have acquired as a child. Throughout his life, he despised the
Catholic church for nurturing forces which stifled him: Schlamperei,
Protektion, anti-Semitism, and hostility to innovation. His favorite reading included *Don Quixote, Paradise Lost, Tom Jones,* and *Tristram
Shandy,* works that portray conflict between Christian asceticism and
pagan license.[20] In November, 1907, Freud endorsed a hypothesis advanced by Fritz Wittels that the Roman Catholic church could undergo renewal during the sixteenth century chiefly because syphilis had
reimposed an ethic of sexual continence. Freud sharpened his ethical
anticlericalism with the acid of medical training, affirming:

> the Catholic Church was at the brink of dissolution at the
> time of the Renaissance; it was saved by two factors: syphilis
> and Luther.[21]

A harsher indictment of the Counter-Reformation could scarcely be
imagined. Wittels had argued in a paper presented to the Vienna
Psychoanalytical Society that transmission of syphilis to Europe by
Columbus' sailors had quashed the Renaissance's glorying in sex.[22]
By making promiscuity its own punishment, syphilis strangled Renaissance sensualism, imbuing the Counter-Reformation with a revitalized
sense of sin. This thesis had been advanced in more scabrous form by
an arch-anticlerical, Oskar Panizza (1853-1921), a Franconian physician, who spent his last eighteen years in an insane asylum at Bayreuth. His play *Das Liebeskonzil: Eine Himmeltragödie* (Zürich,
1895) depicted a conspiracy between God and the devil to resuscitate
the church by introducing syphilis.[23] Coming after parodies of Luther
in *Die unbefleckte Empfängnis der Päpste* (Zürich, 1893) and *Der
teutsche Michel und der römische Papst* (Leipzig, 1894), the play
landed Panizza in jail at Munich for blasphemy, a setback from which
he never recovered. Almost offhandedly, Freud cited Panizza's play to
substantiate Wittels' thesis, nonchalantly endorsing a speculative, not
to say scurrilous, hypothesis. The plea in *Die Zukunft einer Religion*
(1927) for lay education seems banal by comparison.

Like many anticlericals, Freud venerated Greek and Roman antiquity. Trips to Rome in 1901 and to Athens in 1904 fulfilled deeply
felt childhood wishes. Every year he discussed his treasured objets

d'art with a Vienna-born Jewish archaeologist, Emanuel Loewy (1857-1938), an authority on Greek art who dwelt at Rome from 1889 to 1915 before becoming a professor at Vienna. There his students included two Vienna-born art historians who later applied psychoanalysis to art, the polymath Ernst Kris (1900-1957) and the iconographer Ernst Gombrich (1909–).[24] As a would-be archaeologist, in 1895 Freud could identify probing a patient's unconscious with excavating buried cities.[25] His yearning to reconstitute the past epitomized the curatorship dear to Viennese architects. He also held the conviction that every childhood experience slumbers in the mind, whose recesses resemble museums, where nothing is forgotten and nothing destroyed.

Freud felt special fascination for Greek mythology: in *Die Traumdeutung* he celebrated Sophocles' fate-tragedy of King Oedipus, which in 1910 inspired the term "Oedipus complex."[26] As it happened, in 1873 Freud had translated a passage from this play during his Matura examination. In 1911 he popularized Paul Näcke's coinage of narcissism, and after 1920 he exploited a Greek polarity that Richard Schaukal had dramatized in a collection of novellas entitled *Eros Thanatos* (Vienna, 1906). Like Goethe and Schiller, Freud manipulated these mythical figures to personify his own ideas, projecting onto the Greeks emotions that he could not feel for Christian heroes.[27]

Besides personages from Greek mythology, Freud glorified giants from the Jewish past. At gymnasium he had respected the Semitic leader Hannibal who outwitted the Roman legions, seeing in him a precursor of the Jewish ministers in Auersperg's cabinet whom his father told him to emulate.[28] At Hamburg in July, 1882, where Freud was courting his fiancée, he conversed with a sixty-four-year-old Jewish stationer discussing Jewish rituals in the disinterested spirit of Lessing's Nathan.[29] At Rome in September, 1901, he stood transfixed before the Moses of Michelangelo, culling impressions that shaped his *Der Moses des Michelangelo* (1914). His last work was *Der Mann Moses und die monotheistische Religion* (1939), which advanced the hazardous thesis that Moses had been an Egyptian who divulged mysteries of his court to the Jews. In 1790 Schiller had unfolded a similar hypothesis in *Die Sendung Moses*, to which Freud did not refer, although he may have read the essay earlier and then half-remembered its contents.[30]

Freud's hostility toward the Catholic church makes it difficult to assess his no less pronounced ambivalence toward Judaism. Some Jewish scholars have purported to see in Freud's fascination with Moses a trace of Hebrew values however deeply repressed. David Bakan goes so far as to compare Freud's attitude toward sex with that permeating the Zohar.[31] With greater caution, Ernst Simon, a student of Buber, sees in Freud a nonpracticing Jew, who, nevertheless, displayed such ancestral traits as affinity with the oral lore of the Talmud.[32] Others contend that Freud's patriarchal values, including his deprecation of women, reflected Jewish upbringing.[33] All of these hypotheses suffer from the defect that the supposed Jewish traits were no less Austro-Hungarian. In the Habsburg Empire, one did not have to be Jewish to explain behavior in terms of "the personal," that is, sexual adventure, or to possess Gemeinschaft facility at oral communication, or to play the patriarch toward sons and women alike.

Although it seems more plausible to say that Freud was intensely Austro-Hungarian than that he was intensely Jewish, he did affiliate with certain Jewish values. Around 1910, he warned Max Graf not to deny his son the benefits of Jewish education:

> If you do not let your son grow up a Jew, you will deprive
> him of those sources of energy which cannot be replaced by
> anything else.[34]

Like many other assimilated Jews, Freud cherished his heritage as a spur to creativity. Speaking in May, 1926, before the B'nai B'rith lodge of Vienna, where since the 1890's he had attended semimonthly meetings, Freud extolled Judaism for liberating him from prejudice and for teaching him to persevere.[35] Although he disparaged Jewish mysticism and worship, Freud prized Jewish jokes, especially those featuring puns; when he analyzed himself during the late 1890's he traced many associations in his dreams to plays on words.[36] Structuralist interpreters such as Jacques Lacan (1901–) take comfort in Freud's preoccupation with Jewish witticisms, which permute familiar notions according to established patterns. In its deciphering of dream-language, *Die Traumdeutung* is said to have anticipated categories that Ferdinand de Saussure would soon elaborate within structural linguistics. According to Lacan, Freud detected rules of transformation by observing how the unconscious manipulates signifiers quite heedless of the object they conventionally signify.[37] Freud could foreshadow linguistic structuralism because no less than Mauthner and Wittgenstein he knew how to disentangle terms from their conventional denotations.

Patrick Gordon Walker has pointed out a little-noticed connection between Judaism and psychoanalysis.[38] He argues that Freud's theory of the psyche reflects a recently emerged Gesellschaft society in which rational ego challenges tradition-bound superego. Before psychoanalysis can be accepted, achievement-oriented values must have taken deep root. It was chiefly among Jews, suggests Gordon Walker, that disciplined emotional life had flourished long enough to permit psychic depths to be probed. This hypothesis would help to explain why urban

Jews espoused Freud's theories so readily, while other Austrians spurned them. Among non-Jewish Austrians, irrational convictions ran so deep that most individuals could not endure Freud's exposure of the fanaticism within.

Freud exhibited another interest that may have stemmed in part from the collision between feudalism and industrialism. The sensitivity of Viennese impressionists to evanescence and death reflected fear that the old order soon would perish. Preoccupation with death disguised mourning for preindustrial values. Like the intellectuals of Young Vienna, Freud had long brooded about death. Suzanne Bernfeld suggests that for him archaeology substituted for an afterlife a third kind of museumlike existence, which is neither life nor death.[39] World War One provoked Freud into reassessing prevailing attitudes toward death. In "Zeitgemässes über Krieg und Tod" (1915), Freud contended that when faced with death contemporary man resembles primitive man:

> Our unconscious is just as unreceptive to the idea of our own death, just as desirous of murder toward a stranger, and just as divided (ambivalent) toward a beloved as the man of the primitive times.[40]

Just as a primitive blames himself for the death of a relative because unconsciously he wished that death, during mourning a modern berates himself for having survived a beloved.

Five years later Freud propounded a death instinct in order to explain why some neurotics refuse to be cured. In *Jenseits des Lustprinzips* (1920), Freud postulated a death-instinct *(Todestrieb)*, which in every individual vies with the will to live *(Lebenstrieb)* and eventually triumphs. In 1923 he elaborated this dichotomy into a distinction between Ego *(Ich)* and Id *(Es)*, borrowing the term Id from the Berlin pioneer of psychosomatic medicine, Georg Groddeck (1866–1934), whose *Über das Es* (1920) had taken it from Ludwig Klages.[41] The latter had exploited a passage by Nietzsche in *Jenseits von Gut und Böse: Vorspiel einer Philosophie der Zukunft* (Leipzig, 1886):

> It thinks; but it is, to put it mildly, only an assumption, an assertion and above all no immediate certainty that this I is the famous old Ego.[42]

In *Das Ich und das Es* (1923), Freud forsook equating the unconscious with the life-instinct; now he postulated that the unconscious harbors self-destructive forces, while ego safeguards life. Freud insisted that this revision derived from neither World War One nor from grief at the loss of his daughter Sophie in January, 1920, and still less from his cancer, which commenced in 1923. Rather he recognized in certain neurotics a suicidal drive that no ingenuity could thwart. Conceding their invincible resistance, Freud embraced a limited therapeutic nihilism, concluding that sometimes neither nature nor therapy can foil the will to die.

Franz Alexander has likened the ensuing controversy between Freud and Wilhelm Reich concerning the death-instinct to debates over whether external or internal forces destroyed the Habsburg Empire.[43] Although no historian could doubt that in politics both factors had operated, psychoanalysts futilely isolated one or the other. The Galician-born Jew, Wilhelm Reich (1897–1957), whose mother had committed suicide, contended that self-destructiveness results solely from dread of punishment, never, as Freud had suggested, from desire for it.[44] This Marxist physician posited that fear of adult cruelty impels children to develop "character armor," which stiffens muscles and numbs kinesthesia. Since the late 1930's, the British schoolmaster A. S. Neill has implemented Reich's anarchism, fostering spontaneity by banning parental authority. In the United States, Erich Fromm, Herbert Marcuse, Norman O. Brown, and Paul Goodman have rekindled Reich's advocacy of libido-saturated culture. Reich championed unsullied Gemeinschaft, defying Freud's premise that repression sustains society. The aging Freud had espoused Josephinism, reasserting faith in institutions that constrain, lest permissiveness subvert civilization.

The subtlest interpretation of the death instinct came from Anton Ehrenzweig (1908–1966), a Vienna-born lawyer who after 1938 taught painting in London. There, for over twenty years, he expounded a psychology of creativity, which he summarized in *The Hidden Order of Art: A Study in the Psychology of Artistic Imagination* (London, 1967).[45] Broadening research by Freud, Rank, and Kelsen, Ehrenzweig postulated that creativity entails a rhythm akin to that of birth and death. During creative surrender, ego dissolves in its depths, so that subliminal forces may restructure it. Temporary decomposition of ego, which Ehrenzweig labeled dedifferentiation, generates so called poemagogic images, which help ego to endure dismemberment. Likening these to hypnagogic images that Herbert Silberer had detected while falling asleep, Ehrenzweig equated the death instinct with capacity for dedifferentiation. In order to surrender to powers of the deep, ego identifies with a "dying god," who like Dionysius and Orpheus is mangled by worshipers before being scattered and then reconstituted.

In analyzing the myth of the death of the hero and the birth trauma, Otto Rank had singled out poemagogic images. These dramatize a duel

between superego and ego in which at length ego throttles its tormentor, shattering the boundary between external and internal worlds.
During the manic phase of creativity, an artist, emulating Goethe's
Homunculus, identifies with the womb that bears him.[46] Affinity between genius and childhood springs from a creative person's capacity
to undergo dedifferentiation and redifferentiation. As Lombroso and
Stekel had recognized, creativity mimics symptoms of neurosis when
the ego trembles before its imminent destruction.

While Freud deemed the Doppelgänger a symbol of immortality,
Ehrenzweig construed it as an image of the dying god, or dedifferenti-
ated ego.[47] For Ehrenzweig, as for Schnitzler and Bahr, death provides
a simulacrum of creativity; it is the dark underside of life, which every
artist, like a Baroque saint, must conquer. Whereas for the later Freud,
the death instinct entailed therapeutic nihilism, for Ehrenzweig it renewed Leibnizian faith in a oneness underlying life and death. As a
late impressionist, Ehrenzweig distilled fruits of the Gay Apocalypse
into a vision of rebirth.

CAUSES OF VIENNESE RESISTANCE
TO PSYCHOANALYSIS

Having stressed affinities between Freud and Viennese culture, we
must explain why so few intellectuals there welcomed his theories. To
a degree, Freud disdained honor in his own country. In order to prevent medical professionals from monopolizing psychoanalysis, he
groomed handpicked associates, building a separate organization to
transmit his insights to posterity. He expected psychoanalysis to fare
better in Hungary, Germany, and Great Britain than in Austria. After
1896, he eschewed academic medicine, teaching two hours per week
while working eighteen hours a day on his own concerns. Inhabiting a
world where Protektion prevailed, Freud would not truckle to powerful professors, who must have found his cockiness an all too familiar
sign of cultism. The fact that nine-tenths of his adherents were Jews
intensified separatism, inviting rumors that Freud ran another Jewish
outfit like the Social Democratic party or Zionism.

Whatever else may have isolated Freud in Vienna, it was not his
scrutiny of sex. In a city where Sacher-Masoch, Krafft-Ebing, and
Weininger were read with nonchalance, Freud's pansexualism hardly
shocked anyone. Rather he crystallized a preoccupation with sex which
several disparate movements had awakened. Birth control, campaigns
against venereal disease, study of sexual symbolism in folklore, emanci-

pation of women, and critique of hypocritical morality had exposed the centrality of sex.[48] What irked other psychotherapists was Freud's insistence that neurosis has a psychic rather than a physical etiology. In place of electrotherapy and warm baths, Freud listened to patients hours on end, probing confessions to learn how and when symptoms had commenced. By affirming that long hours of talk could unravel most hysteria, Freud combatted the therapeutic nihilism that had plagued Viennese psychiatry. Among physicians who venerated post-mortem examinations and deemed surgery the surest cure, Freud's faith in talk rankled. He felt more at home with writers and archaeologists, who at least were fellow artists in words.[49]

Freud's exclusiveness had the disadvantage of severing adherents from contact with other Viennese schools. Heinz Hartmann (1894–1970) was the only Freudian to frequent the Vienna Circle, as Ernst Kris did with the Vienna School of Art History. Although during the 1920's Alfred -Adler collaborated with Austro-Marxists, he had long since renounced Freud. The founder of psychoanalysis deprecated cross-fertilizing psychology with philosophy, as Brentano and Mach had urged a generation before. For fear of succumbing to false leads, Freud preferred to keep tight rein on his coterie.

At Vienna Freud provoked relentless opposition in Kraus, Friedell, and the Catholic anthropologist Wilhelm Schmidt (1868–1954). Of these Kraus was by far the most caustic. Until Wittels delivered a paper defaming his onetime friend in January, 1910, the author of *Die Fackel* had respected Freud. Not only did Wittels charge that anti-Semitic envy of the *Neue Freie Presse* had prompted Kraus's vendetta against journalists, but in the novel *Ezechiel der Zugereiste* (Berlin, 1910), he caricatured Kraus as a muckraker who penned vapidities for a Viennese sheet called the *Riesenmaul*. Kraus responded by inveighing against psychoanalysis in aphorisms of *Nachts* (Leipzig, 1918). When Kraus declared that "Psychoanalysis is the mental illness for which it claims to be a cure," he could have been unmasking any ideology; his stricture applies more aptly to fascism or Leninism than to even the most doctrinaire psychoanalyst.[50] Joining countless others, Kraus censured the notion of an unconscious for sanctioning irrational impulses:

> According to the latest research, the subconscious appears to be a kind of ghetto for thoughts. Today many people feel homesick.[51]

He ridiculed any psychology that anatomizes the lightning-quick processes of thought: "Psychology is an auto-bus which accompanies an air-plane."[52] With more venom than insight, Kraus belittled what he could not understand, incensed that anyone should seek to alleviate insanity.

A no less flamboyant anti-Freudian was Friedell, who berated Freud for bolstering irrationalism with tools of rationalism.[53] Like Kraus, Friedell discerned only one side of Freud's equilibrium between reason and instinct.[54] Misunderstandings abounded because Freud disdained to debate critics. Writing always for a friendly audience, he would not stoop to popularize or extenuate, thus relegating public relations to improvisers like Stekel and Wittels, whom he rightly distrusted.

World War One prepared a wider audience to acknowledge Freud's discoveries. Not only did the war unmask self-destructive forces in European civilization, but it worsened anxiety by undermining the authority of father-figures. Long years after Budapest-born Franz Alexander (1891–1964) had espoused psychoanalysis, his father Bernhard Alexander (1850–1927), a Kantian philosopher at Budapest, repudiated Freud's doctrines. Shortly before he died, Bernhard, in his own words, overcame two thousand years of Western civilization to entertain the concept of an unconscious.[55]

In a society as prone to narcissism as Vienna's, it was small wonder that educated men hesitated to recognize Freud's perspicacity. For them, light of reason was too recent to imperil it by granting Freud's assertions. In a city that could not stomach a Schönberg or a Kokoschka, Freud's defiance met similar neglect. He perfected an impressionist's secretiveness, sheltering himself from self-deluding critics whose motives he recognized better than they. Psychoanalysis emerged as a latent work of genius in a city too entranced by surface delights to heed rumblings below.

17

Freud and His Followers

FREUD AS PATRIARCH: PATRON OF
ORTHODOXY AND TARGET OF DISSENT

LIKE ROKITANSKY AND SKODA sixty years before, Freud displayed the perseverance and messianic zeal required to institutionalize his doctrines in a school.[1] Yet he distrusted medical professionals so heartily that he established his school outside of the Medical Faculty. Some of Freud's followers like Ferenczi or Stekel entertained higher hopes for psychoanalysis than did the master himself, who especially after 1920 despaired of eradicating aggression in society. Ambitious to launch a science that would liberate mankind, Freudians resembled followers of Claude-Henri de Saint-Simon a century before, as well as contemporaries like Neurath and Mannheim.

No feature of Freud's career has been so widely deplored as his suppression of dissent. Visitors to the Vienna Psychoanalytical Society complained that orthodoxy was enforced in an atmosphere of almost religious exaltation.[2] Heretics like Vienna-born Herbert Silberer (1882–1923), whose concept of hypnagogic images helped to inspire Ehrenzweig, were alternately applauded or hissed depending on what certain lackeys thought Freud preferred.[3] Such dogmatism reflected Freud's authority as a father-figure in a society partial to patriarchs. Modeling themselves on the emperor, bureaucrats played the omniscient protector, as did professors, physicians, priests, army officers, and even artists like Makart. Although Jewish families honored the paterfamilias more than most, a father did not have to be Jewish to be authoritarian. Freud's denigration of women as castrated men derived from patriarchal assumptions that Rosa Mayreder discerned in society at large.[4] The demise of such patriarchs was explored by a Vienna-born Jewish Freudian, Paul Federn (1871–1950), in *Zur Psychologie der Revolution: Die vaterlose Gesellschaft* (Vienna, 1919). He elucidated Marxist revolutions of 1918 and 1919 by arguing that sons who had endured four years in trenches no longer trusted fathers to govern. In *Radetzkymarsch* Joseph Roth dramatized the disintegration of a son's confidence in his father's values, while Bertha von Suttner and Rosa Mayreder had long impugned the stewardship of fathers.

In this atmosphere, Freud's disciples formed a kind of extended family, feeling at once reverential and recalcitrant before an exigent genius who desired above all to safeguard his invention for posterity. From schisms emerged lonely prophets such as Silberer and Stekel, as well as organizers such as Jung and Adler. After 1910, Freud brooded like Laius, beleaguered by ungrateful sons who sought to pilfer renown by adulterating his discovery. Not infrequently creative pupils harbor hate-love toward a revered teacher; the more they esteem a mentor, the more they resent his failure to impart basic insights that must be garnered elsewhere. Such resentments motivated the ambivalence of Husserl toward Brentano, Schumpeter toward Böhm-Bawerk and, of course, Freud toward Brücke and Breuer. It was inevitable that Freud, who had attracted so many gifted students, should gall fellow innovators such as Adler, Jung, Stekel, and Rank. In place of originality, Freud required that associates supply reassurance and act as a sounding-board for ideas—two luxuries not available at the university. Pre-1905 struggles against Protektion and anti-Semitism had left Freud anxious to vindicate his doctrine. So as not to contaminate psychoanalysis with alien elements, Freud who was himself a victim of Protektion, practiced it upon his followers.

Robert R. Holt has found in Freud an agglutinative principle of revision, whereby he would welcome any supplement to psychoanalysis provided this did not upset basic premises.[5] With an impressionist's fondness for fluctuating viewpoints, Freud never quite decided which tenets had been proven and which not. Like Mach, he would use hyperbole to announce a hypothesis before undertaking to qualify it. Because his system had shaky foundations, Freud abhorred letting others tamper with it. The social activism of Adler menaced the master's privacy, as did the proselytizing and scurrility of Stekel. A stickler for etiquette, Freud deplored the latter's lack of manners as well as his glee in exposing secrets of the couch. Another reason for dissension was that Freud advanced ploddingly. Most conspicuously he neglected the theory of the ego in order to probe that of instincts. This left a vacuum that Adler filled, chiding Freud for overlooking what had merely been postponed.

Freud attracted a number of scholars who specialized in interpreting

literature and art, notably during the years before ample case histories
had accumulated. The little-known Jewish doctor, Isidor Sadger (1867–
ca. 1940), an uncle of Fritz Wittels, wrote pathographies modeled on
those of Paul Möbius. The bumptious Stekel, a Jew from Bukovina,
employed psychoanalysis to buttress the thesis of Lombroso that genius
entails neurosis.[6] Stekel's companion Silberer correlated alchemy with
dreams, insisting that for each person symbols speak a different language.[7] Freud preferred pathographies by Vienna-born Eduard Hitschmann (1871–1957), a physician who wrote fastidious analyses of
Schopenhauer, Samuel Johnson, and Franz Schubert.[8] A Jewish music
critic, Max Graf (1873–1958), who frequented Freud's Wednesday
evening sessions for several years up to 1910, expounded a psychology
of musical creativity in *Die innere Werkstatt des Musikers* (Stuttgart,
1910). Graf argued that a classicist controls his unconscious while a
romantic surrenders to this remnant of the child in himself.[9] Several
times we have mentioned Sadger's nephew, Fritz Wittels (1880–1950),
who was a friend of Popper-Lynkeus. This Vienna-born Jewish feuilletonist broke with Karl Kraus in 1909 and then with Freud in 1910. He
rejoined the circle in 1925 after writing a fanciful biography of Freud.[10]
His essays, which applied psychoanalysis to rulers and revolutionaries,
read like the work of a pro-Freudian Egon Friedell, witty but capricious.[11]

The most intensely Viennese of aesthetic Freudians was Hanns
Sachs (1881–1947).[12] A wealthy Jew born at Vienna, who had aspired
to become a writer, Sachs so dreaded publicity that he secreted his
private affairs even from Freud and Rank. Ernest Jones reported that
this bon vivant cultivated narcissistic love of whatever city he inhabited. Whether it be Vienna, Berlin, or Boston, Sachs extolled his as
the most agreeable city in the world. Having inherited German-National sympathies from his father, who had practiced law in Bohemia,
Sachs became an impressionist, fascinated by the contrast between
latent and manifest. He argued that every artist, like a Josephinist
bureaucrat, vanishes behind his work, into which he pours frustrated
daydreams. Sachs hailed dreams for liberating men, not ensnaring
them. Grillparzer, he opined, had daydreamed about living a life of
obscurity such as he depicted in *Der arme Spielmann* (1848)–so had
Sachs!–while Dostoevski had exorcised hatred of his father by ap-
portioning it among the four brothers Karamazov, murderers all.[13]
Through literature, such fantasies acquire a form that channels wish-
fulfillment not only for an author but for the public. To expound his
psychology of art, in 1912 Sachs collaborated with Otto Rank to found
the periodical *Imago*. Its title came from a novel that the Swiss devotee

of myth Carl Spitteler (1845–1924) had published in 1906, narrating how an artist prefers the image of his beloved to her reality.

Sachs attributed aestheticism to Greeks and Romans in order to explain their failure to perfect technology.[14] Hellenic deities enshrined narcissistic reverence for the human body; the body was so cherished that machines loomed as competitors to it. Only after Christianity had exalted soul above body could machines supplant slave labor. As befitted an adept of daydreaming, Sachs saluted motion pictures: cinema, he declared, reproduces the language of dreams better than any other medium, purveying a kind of popularization that does not deprive the few in order to enlighten the many:

> This perfect mixture, blending together the dramatic and epic element with the visual and kinetic, has never been achieved before, except in the dream.[15]

A gentle would-be artist, Sachs fulfilled the constructive potential of Viennese aestheticism. Eager to welcome the new, he extrapolated his own narcissism into a psychology of creativity.

BOURGEOIS PSYCHOTHERAPY:
ALFRED ADLER'S SELF-FULFILLING PROPHECIES

The most renowned Freudian dissidents were a Swiss pastor's son, Carl Gustav Jung (1875–1961), and a Viennese Jew, Alfred Adler (1870–1937). Jung revived Romantic nature-philosophy, while Adler synthesized Nietzsche, Darwin, and socialism to produce the most bourgeois of all schools of psychoanalysis.[16] Like Lueger and Rank, Adler—he was no relative of other Adlers mentioned in this book—had to surmount a plethora of childhood ailments. The third of seven children of an assimilated Jewish merchant from the Burgenland, Adler suffered so severely from rickets that he could not walk until age four, and he was twice run over by a carriage. Frequent choking spasms engendered fear of death, for which the boy compensated by singing and growing flowers. At Schönbrunn, five-year-old Alfred dallied in the flowerbeds so shamelessly that groundkeepers ejected him. After taking a medical degree in 1895 at Vienna, Adler practiced medicine on the Praterstrasse, where he had circus performers among his patients. Their hypertrophied muscles appeared to compensate for earlier weakness.

Adler studied psychiatry under Meynert and Krafft-Ebing. He heard

Freud lecture in 1899, but did not enter into discussion with him until 1901. During the fall of 1902 Adler joined as a charter member Wednesday evening gatherings at Freud's flat. In *Studie über Minderwertigkeit von Organen* (Vienna, 1907), he argued that children with inferior physiques compensate weaknesses, as had he himself, by exaggerating strengths. Will to survive impels each child to assert himself against stronger parents. Adler regarded sex as one among several weapons that express a child's will to power. Several years of rivalry with Freud preceded a break between the two men in 1911, sealed by Adler's treatise *Über den nervösen Charakter* (Wiesbaden, 1912). Borrowing Hans Vaihinger's theory of fictions, Adler interpreted neurosis not as unconscious repression but as a deliberate ruse whereby one evades some overwhelming task. Without presuming to judge the book's merits, Julius Wagner-Jauregg (1857–1940) rejected it as a Habilitationsschrift on the grounds that depth psychology is no science. After Adler in 1912 dubbed his therapy Individual Psychology and soon thereafter launched a journal, he further imitated Freud by hectoring his own adherents.

Four years as an army doctor alerted Adler to what he called social interest *(Gemeinschaftsgefühl)*, that is, willingness to sacrifice personal gain for the good of one's group. In treating malingering soldiers, Adler noted that they lack sense for the good of the whole, indifferent to the fact that cowardice obliges someone else to fight in their place. Study of malingerers corroborated insights Adler had gained from Marx, as mediated by his Russian-born wife, Raïssa Epstein Adler (1873–1962). Having defied his wife to applaud Austria's entry into World War One, Adler eventually denounced the war. Begun in 1897, their marriage suffered not only from her homesickness for Russia but from friction between her revolutionary Marxism and his Austro-Marxism. Adler was the only member of Freud's early circle to join the Social Democratic party. In March, 1909, he expounded, under influence of his friend Leon Trotsky, what was probably the earliest synthesis of Marx with Freud.[17] Contending that Marx had recognized the primacy of instinct, Adler insisted that this precursor of Freud had taught the proletariat to detect defense mechanisms of the bourgeoisie.

Adler greeted the Austrian Republic as an opportunity to promote psychic hygiene. Otto Glöckel (1874–1935), director of Vienna's schools, urged Adler to found child-guidance clinics in elementary schools as well as to instruct teachers in child psychiatry. The Moravian-born Jewish anatomist, Julius Tandler (1869–1936), who labored to dispel what remained of therapeutic nihilism in medicine, backed the program as commissioner of health for Vienna. Relinquishing further service to Socialist Vienna, by 1932 Adler sought wider renown by transferring his career to Great Britain and the United States. He died in 1937 at Glasgow while on a lecture tour. Buoyancy and fierce temper marked this self-made man, who felt no shame in manipulating Protektion or in relishing its fruits.

In place of Freud's preoccupation with a patient's past, Adler substituted a future-oriented environment psychology. Life-style crystallizes around a person's goals, which seek to compensate childhood defects. If a child's urge to surmount weakness is thwarted, he will wreak destruction against others or himself. Everyone must excel at some endeavor if ego is to stabilize; once stabilized, it can set itself practicable goals. Mistaken life-styles a therapist redirects by showing his patients how social interest can channel otherwise frustrated impulses. Chiding Freud for determinism and pansexualism, Adler claimed to dislodge neurosis by awakening willpower. Such voluntarism Freud dismissed as Couéism, suggesting that it purveyed wish-fulfillment to the lower middle class.

Freud's sarcasm aside, Adler's emphasis on compensation elucidates both capitalism and socialism. He argued that under capitalism struggle for survival goads children to overcompensate in order to compete. In a similar way, Marxists exploit overcompensation in order to exhort revolutionaries to surmount the powerlessness they feel before possessing classes. Himself a bourgeois, Adler hailed Malthus' notion that the niggardliness of nature obliges men to overcome shortages through toil. Under the rubric of social interest, this psychoanalyst praised the goal of Gemeinschaft solidarity, which both Christian Socialists and Marxists were seeking. Adler distrusted feminism, however, denouncing what he called masculine protest in certain women, who compensate for feeling inferior to men by becoming viragoes.

Adler was quintessentially Viennese. Offspring of urbanized culture, he acknowledged the ubiquity of conflict, while striving to fuse individualism with socialism. Although far more political than Freud, Adler was by comparison a philistine; his psychology of creativity seems puerile next to that of Freud or Rank. Adler excelled, nevertheless, at elucidating adult life under capitalism. Repudiating therapeutic nihilism, he injected into psychoanalysis a zeal for curing. His conviction that therapy can be shortened anticipated many schools, notably the group therapy of Romanian-born Jacob Levy Moreno (1892–), who fashioned psychodrama to relieve neurosis. Reveling in coffee-houses and music, both of which irked Freud, Adler did more to promote psychoanalysis at Vienna than did Freud himself. Even Friedell esteemed Adler. More ambitious than Breuer, Adler displayed the same common sense and zeal to cure, together with tireless energy and boundless self-confidence. Whereas Freud expended energy founding a new science, Adler worked to relieve suffering. If psychotherapy entails self-fulfilling prophecy, Adler enacted his own recipe to perfection, molding childhood traumas into a life-style that both suited his native city and gratified his own need for adulation.

OTTO RANK: FROM AESTHETICISM TO
SELF-CREATION IN PSYCHOTHERAPY

Otto Rank (1884–1939) possessed one of the sharpest minds to serve psychoanalysis.[18] In facility he matched Bauer or Kelsen, while in insight he came close to rivaling Freud himself. Born in Vienna, son of a drunken father and shrewish mother, this Jewish prodigy trained himself to become Freud's most perceptive critic, propounding a psychology of creativity whose relevance for technological society has yet to be hailed. Having suffered like Alfred Adler from rickets, rheumatism, and dread of death, at age fifteen, Otto Rank Rosenfeld (he shortened his name in 1909) found wish-fulfillment by frequenting theaters every night for three years. While he attended technical high school, he was inspired by the example of Schopenhauer and Nietzsche to amass tremendous knowledge of literature which he used as a refuge from misery at home.[19] When Rank consulted Alfred Adler for lung trouble contracted while working in a glassblowing plant, the youth's erudition so impressed Adler that in 1905 he introduced his patient to Freud. He venerated Freud as an ego-ideal. From 1906 to 1914 Rank labored as paid secretary of the Vienna Psychoanalytical Society, keeping minutes of its Wednesday evening sessions. Freud and Adler persuaded their protegé to complete gymnasium and to enter the university, where during hours left from writing three other books he earned a doctorate in 1912 with a dissertation on the Lohengrin Saga. None of his colleagues understood how Freud's secretary found time to read and write as voluminously as his mentor.

From 1916 until 1918 Rank edited a military propaganda sheet in Galicia, *Die Krakauer Zeitung*. Having returned to Vienna, the newly married Rank resumed intimacy with Freud until 1924; he was one of six upon whom the master bestowed medals at The Hague in September, 1920. At New York in 1924, amid worsening strife with Ernest Jones, Rank championed his own doctrine of a birth trauma in order to criticize Freud. There ensued two years of alternating rapprochement and disillusionment between father-figure and heir apparent, until after 1926 Rank felt sufficiently liberated to formulate a far-reaching critique of Freud. His emancipation inspired a new psychotherapy, which was not, as Freud supposed, merely a concession to American haste.

From 1905 on, Rank surpassed everyone else, including Sachs, Silberer, and Hitschmann, in applying psychoanalysis to literature. Subsequently only Ehrenzweig has equaled him—and this by building on his foundation. In *Der Künstler* (Leipzig, 1907), Rank revised the thesis of Lombroso and Stekel that genius entails neurosis. Although artists often endure qualms similar to those of neurotics, these stem from sensitivity heightened by overactive drives. In *Der Mythus von der Geburt des Helden* (Leipzig, 1909), a work that influenced Joseph Campbell, Rank expounded an image in comparative mythology that anticipated his later notion of a birth trauma.

His most learned treatise, drafted in 1906 but not published until 1912, was *Das Inzestmotiv in Dichtung und Sage* (Leipzig, 1912), which Rank dedicated to Freud. Through seven hundred pages, he surveyed portrayals, taken mostly from German literature, of love between parents and children or between siblings. Having—to his everlasting regret—experienced sexual initiation at age seven, Rank declared precocity to result from premature puberty. Whereas at first Rank deemed creativity merely a by-product of sexuality, later he praised sublimation as a means of surmounting sexual deficiencies.

In *Das Trauma der Geburt und seine Bedeutung für die Psychoanalyse* (Leipzig, 1924), a work that Freud first extolled and then impugned, Rank likened the symbiosis of psychoanalyst and patient to dependence of a fetus in the womb. Since psychotherapy essays to dispel conflicts precipitated by ejection from this cradle, cure must of necessity resemble rebirth. Having launched these ideas just as he was weaning himself from Freud's tutelage, Rank consummated his own rebirth by fleeing to New York and Paris, where he fashioned a new approach to psychotherapy. Deploring the anathema on fantasy which Freud pronounced in *Die Zukunft einer Illusion* (1927), Rank believed that capacity to proliferate and sustain illusions is indispensable to man. Industrial society errs in deeming rationality the criterion of health; as a Josephinist, Freud had overlooked that rationalized life can itself engender neurosis. Achievement-oriented individuals are fragmented by loss of shared faith such as Gemeinschaft had abetted. By repressing this loss, victims only aggravate its consequences:

> The only remedy is an acceptance of the fundamental irrationality of the human being . . . a real allowance of primi-

tivity's dynamic functioning in human behavior, which would
not be lifelike without it.[20]

During the 1930's Rank argued that frustration of yearning for
illusion whets longing for definitive solutions such as those of totalitarianism. Assailing Freud's rationalism, Rank reinterpreted Oedipus as
a symbol of intellect, which must perish as soon as it learns its past.
Prone to self-criticism, Rank voiced Austrian faith in the redeeming
power of pain:

> We are born in pain and we should accept life-pain as un-
> avoidable—indeed a necessary part of earthly existence, not
> merely the price we have to pay for pleasure.[21]

No less than Buber and Ebner, he glorified interdependence between
I and Thou. An I should nourish itself in a Thou, whether it be

> the individual Thou, or the inspirational Thou of the leader,
> or the symbiotic fusion of another civilization.[22]

Diligent observer that he was, Rank could praise embeddedness in
society without scanting its dangers.

Freud's ratiocentric values Rank attributed to Jewish reverence for
patriarchs. Whereas Weininger had likened Jewish feelings of inferiority to those of women, Freud, said Rank, had projected onto women a
Jewish mentality of the enslaved, the inferior, and the castrated.[23]
Adler in turn tossed inferiority back onto the man, whereupon Jung
proceeded to denigrate psychoanalysis as a Jewish racial myth, replacing it with a racial psychology of his own. In revering the patriarch,
Freud had repudiated as incestuous a child's clinging to its mother,
who, Rank specified, embodies what a child is, while a father represents what a child must become. A child ought to repulse his father's
truckling to ideology, said Rank, because vitality arises not from a
father's preaching of conformity but from a mother's coddling of illusion. In his post-1926 therapy, Rank feared that psychoanalysis would
inhibit patients instead of liberating them from society. Therapy requires
spontaneity; during self-creation a patient apotheosizes his therapist
into a private savior, who helps unleash fantasies. In our lonely epoch,
Rank would have everyone be his own poet. He exhorted artists to
resist conformity by renewing illusions that positivism has banished.

Bred like other aesthetes of Young Vienna on self-induced illusions, in later years Rank elevated aestheticism into an antidote for anomie. He lamented that psychoanalysis had become an ideology that reified predilections of its founder. Indoctrination in positivism under Brücke, reinforced by solicitude for posterity, impelled the later Freud to deify reason while deprecating passion as Schlamperei. More systematically than Sachs, Rank championed the artist in Freud against the scientist, resisting as well the physician in Adler and the visionary in Jung. Voicing Freud's poetic nature, Rank transformed psychoanalysis into a corrective for consumer society. Together with Schlick, this scion of the Gay Apocalypse anticipated demands of post-1960 youth for self-creation.

Part Four

BOHEMIAN REFORM CATHOLICISM

Schaffen führt zum Glauben an einen Schöpfer.

To create leads to belief in a Creator.

—MARIE VON EBNER-ESCHENBACH

Marcionists at Prague

INTERNECINE STRIFE BETWEEN
CZECH AND GERMAN IN BOHEMIA

BETWEEN 1848 AND 1918 two historic processes collided in the Habsburg Empire. One was the transition from an agrarian to industrial economy, spearheaded by Bohemia, Vienna, and Budapest. The other was the awakening of subject peoples (*Bedientenvölker*) to demand a voice in affairs.

The remainder of this book examines how intellectuals in two disparate regions of the empire—Bohemia and Hungary—reacted to national strife. In discussing Bohemia, concentration is on German-speaking philosophers, who sought to evade the onslaught of Czech nationalism by propounding a Leibnizian vision of reconciliation. As members of a minority people, German intellectuals from Bohemia tended to shun politics, while the resurgent Czechs pursued activism.

Within the Austrian half of the Dual Monarchy, the conflict of nationalities raged most intensely in Bohemia. It was here that demand for federal government grew strongest. The Czechs had supported the abortive October Diploma of 1860, which would have established federalism on a feudal basis, and in 1871 they almost received federal autonomy under a plan proposed by Heinrich Clam-Martinic (1826–1887) and supported by Prime Minister Karl Hohenwart (1824–1899). Most of the authority of the central parliament, the Reichsrat, would have been delegated to local diets. At the last minute the Hohenwart proposal failed when German nationals and Hungarian leaders united against it.

After Hohenwart's resignation had sealed the marriage of convenience between German and Magyar, the Czechs continued until 1879 to boycott the Reichsrat, a protest they had begun in 1863. During the 1870's the Liberal Auersperg Ministry subjected Prague to military government, as Statthalter General Alexander von Koller (1813–1890) tried Czech journalists before German juries and restricted public meetings. Under the premiership of Count Eduard Taaffe (1833–1895), Czechs received palliatives in return for supporting the government in the Reichsrat. A Czech university was opened at Prague in 1882, Czech gymnasien were established, and Czech administrative posts became available. In 1890 when Taaffe proposed dividing Bohemia into Czech and German regions, the Young Czechs balked, insisting on control of the whole.

Hostility between Czechs and Germans sharpened competition between their languages.[1] Up to about 1840, a Swiss kind of amity known as Bohemism had prevailed between the two groups. On the German side, thinkers like Bernard Bolzano as well as poets like Karl Egon Ebert (1801–1882), Moritz Hartmann (1821–1872), and Alfred Meissner (1822–1885) worked for reconciliation, a dream that was dashed by Windischgrätz's bloody suppression of Czech rebels at Prague in June, 1848. Earlier that April the Old Czechs, led by František Palacký (1798–1876) and his son-in-law Franz Ladislaus Rieger (1818–1903), had declined an invitation to attend the Frankfurt Parliament. In a famous phrase, Palacký proclaimed that if the Austrian Empire had not already existed, it would be necessary to create it. This so-called Austroslavism preached cultural nationalism: the Old Czechs promoted the revival of the Czech language begun by scholars such as the German Piarist Felix Dobner (1719–1790), a onetime Jesuit Josef Dobrovský (1753–1829) and a gymnasium teacher Josef Jungmann (1773–1847). Implementing the vision of Herder, the Old Czechs founded in 1818 the Bohemian National Museum, whose journal Palacký edited after 1827. In his five-volume *Geschichte Böhmens* (1836–1867), Palacký stressed continuity with aspirations of the Hussites. The Czechs, he contended, were the only people in Europe who had been reconverted to Roman Catholicism by force of arms.

After 1860 young Czechs vented growing impatience at Palacký's failures. Fritz Mauthner remarked that Schiller's Centenary in 1859 was the last public occasion when sympathy united Czechs and Germans at Prague. To solidify national sentiment, Czechs pursued gymnastics in the Sokol movement founded in 1863 by Miroslav Tyrš (1832–1884). A gigantic celebration accompanied the laying of the cornerstone for a Czech National Theater at Prague in 1868. Financed by nationwide subscription, the building opened in 1881, only to be burned to the ground two months later through a roofer's carelessness. Although some Germans contributed toward the rebuilding, Young Czechs never forgave what they mistakenly regarded as an act of sabotage. When the next year Taaffe established a Czech university at Prague, this concession came too late to silence demands of more than twenty years' standing. In 1863 the Technische Hochschule had been divided into Czech and German branches, which in 1869 became separate institutions, and in 1866 Rieger had advocated such an "utraquist" solution for the Karl-Ferdinand University. Separation of the two faculties caused financial hardship for professors in the German branch because the majority of students attended the Czech university. In 1898 celebration of the university's 550th anniversary foundered in rioting between Czech and German students.

Nothing divided the two people so bitterly as the language question. After about 1880, the Germans of Prague refused to master Czech, preferring to speak pidgin Czech (*Kuchelböhmisch*), in which badly pronounced words were fitted into German syntax. Arnold Pick, director of the provincial insane asylum in Prague during the 1880's, had difficulty finding assistants who could speak sufficient Czech to interview patients.[2] The quarrel extended even to Vienna, where in 1883 the Czech community requested from the city council funds to build an elementary school. When the rector of the University of Vienna endorsed this proposal, he was forced to resign; as consolation he received a vote of thanks from the Czech University at Prague, worded not in the hated German, but in French.[3]

In 1897 antipathy mounted thanks to language ordinances that Count Badeni had proposed. These measures, which would have required all officials in Bohemia to become bilingual, favored the Czechs, who alone had bothered to learn both languages. We have already described how the ensuing debate paralyzed the Reichsrat, forcing Badeni to capitulate to obstructionists.[4] Although martial law once again quieted Prague, soon German street names began to disappear, and German actors walked in fear of their lives. Wagner was performed less often than Verdi, and riots proliferated outside the German theater. Some Czechs stuck fingers in their ears whenever a German addressed them.[5] Moravia spared itself such animosity by reaching a compromise in 1905. There Germans and Czechs continued the custom of exchanging children so as to facilitate learning a second language.[6]

In Prague, German was spoken by such a tiny minority that the language lost contact with daily life. Rainer Maria Rilke complained that he was obliged to speak either pidgin Czech or pidgin German. Fritz Mauthner traced his interest in the philosophy of language to the coexistence at Prague of German, Czech, and Yiddish, lamenting that each language debased the others. Willy Haas stated that officials spoke a "completely denaturalized, sterile, and grotesque k.u.k. Czech-German," while nobles spoke French and servants Czech. Johannes

Urzidil, on the contrary, lauded Prague German for being purified by isolation, arguing that salons of the Bohemian capital spoke flawless High German.[7] Bohemian Germans showed their political frustration not only in joining the German-National movement of Georg von Schönerer, but in a schismatic Socialist group—the German Workers' party *(Deutsche Arbeiterpartei)*—which in 1904 split off from Czech Socialists.[8] After 1918 it called itself the German National Socialist Workers party (Deutsche Nationalsozialistische Arbeiterpartei or DNSAP). In 1902 a Moravian-born publicist, Franz Jesser (1869–1949), coined the term "Sudeten German" to designate Germans of Bohemia, Moravia, and Austrian Silesia; through this label he hoped to bolster their opposition to Czech insurgence.

Czech banks counterattacked by sponsoring Czech ownership of German businesses. As soon as a Czech bought German property, signs changed into Czech. Czechs endeavored to halt intermarriage with Germans, and they shuttled orphans to underpopulated districts so as to keep Czech schools operating. In the countryside, the Children's Bureau alleviated poverty and alcoholism that had afflicted peasants for generations. Mothers were schooled in hygiene, physical exercise was stressed in elementary school, and fathers of illegitimate children were ostracized.[9] Czech officials labored to train effective citizens, free from ills such as Marie von Ebner-Eschenbach dramatized in her novel *Das Gemeindekind* (Berlin, 1887). A Prague-born anarchist, Jaroslav Hašek (1883–1923), personified anti-German measures in the protagonist of *Der brave Soldat Schwejk* (Prague, 1921). The "officially certified idiot" Schwejk typified untutored cunning with which Czechs thwarted Josephinist bureaucracy, exacerbating Schlamperei through passive resistance.

After 1918, the Czechoslovak Republic revenged centuries of German hegemony by demolishing monuments to German heroes and by fostering massive defection from the Roman Catholic church.[10] Although the German minority of three million retained their university as well as many gymnasien, they complained bitterly of oppression. Slovaks passed directly from Hungarian to Czech rule, because the Magyars had trained no cadres. President Tomáš Masaryk resided at the Hradschin Palace, continuing the teetotaling regimen that he had imposed upon himself during the 1870's. Although under Foreign Minister Eduard Beneš (1884–1948) Czechoslovakia labored to unify the Danube valley, the Little Entente with Yugoslavia and Romania could not foil Hitler, whose audacity confirmed the wisdom of Palacký. If the Habsburg Empire could have been reinvented, the Third Reich might never have begun.

Despite tragic divisions, up to 1918 Bohemia and Moravia launched an astonishing quota of seminal thinkers, most of whom settled in Vienna. One need only mention the Jews Sigmund Freud, Edmund Husserl, Karl Kraus, Viktor Adler, Josef Popper-Lynkeus, Gustav Mahler, Adolf Loos, and Hans Kelsen, as well as the Catholics Robert Zimmermann, Eugen von Böhm-Bawerk, Bertha von Suttner, and Joseph Schumpeter to illustrate how Bohemia and Moravia enriched the intellectual life of Vienna. In connection with Bernard Bolzano we shall discuss how Bohemian Reform Catholicism kept philosophic Josephinism alive well after 1850, instilling concern for the good of the whole and helping to make Bohemia and Moravia into a seedbed of thinkers unsurpassed in Europe.

VISIONS OF WORLD DESTRUCTION
AMONG PRAGUE GERMANS

Prague, the "Golden City," "City of a Hundred Spires," which the world traveler Alexander von Humboldt deemed the most beautiful inland city he had ever seen, was a hotbed of Czech resistance to German rule. No other provincial capital in the empire harbored such implacable strife between German, Slav, and Jew as did what Max Brod dubbed the polemical city. Unlike Slavs in other Habsburg domains, as early as 1830 Czechs boasted middle-class leaders in Palacký and Rieger, who exhorted the emperor to restore to Bohemia her medieval autonomy.

What distinguished Prague from other cities in Austria-Hungary was a propensity of her writers to excogitate visions of world destruction. Not inappropriately, it was in Hradschin Castle that hapless Ferdinand I had taken refuge; dwelling there from 1848 to 1875, he puttered at botany and heraldry, while below him the city seethed with unrest and disease. Until 1781, Prague Jews had resided perforce in the ghetto, which in 1852 the city incorporated as one of five boroughs, changing the name from Judenstadt to Josephstadt.[11] After 1895, city fathers razed the ghetto, behind whose seven gates crime and poverty festered; by then less than one-fifth of its residents were Jews. As late as 1880, Prague endured year-round epidemics of typhoid and smallpox, for which authorities maintained a separate hospital. Because there existed no pure water, everyone boiled or used bottled water. Until after 1890, public transportation was lamentable, one-horse carriages being the sole public conveyance, which also served to haul the sick.[12] During early September, 1890, devastation struck, as the usually gentle Moldau rampaged, driving forty thousand persons from their homes and toppling three spans of the five-centuries-old Karlsbrücke. Soldiers distributed bread to replace foodstuffs inundated in warehouses.[13]

Germans and Jews suffered far more acutely from rivalry with Czechs. Although neither Germans nor Czechs approved the status quo, Germans dreaded the future, fearing that Czechs would overwhelm them. German intellectuals began to project racial strife onto the cosmos, envisioning a civil war fought in heaven between a beneficent and a malevolent god. Poets and philosophers refurbished Gnostic cosmology, as if to concede that only an apocalypse could reverse the tide that was running against them. The gnosis that flourished at Prague between 1890 and 1930 resembled a Christian heresy known as Marcionism.[14] Preaching in Anatolia and Rome, Marcion (ca. 85–ca. 155) had taught that the Creator God of the Jews was an evil demiurge, whose Creation had trapped men until Christ came to deliver them. Representing the supreme, benevolent God, Christ preached a gospel of love which if heeded would abolish the tyranny imposed by a capricious creator. Marcion reprobated Jewish law, promising redemption after death from the despotism of the Creator. Hostility to law and yearning for a remote salvation characterize the Gnostics of Prague. Kafka pictured law as a barrier to salvation, as if Austrian regulations perpetuated statutes of a Marcionistic demiurge. Franz Werfel's quest for a gospel of love in a vindictive world, Gustav Meyrink's fantasies about capricious laws of nature, Rilke's vision of disembodied angels who enjoy rather than regret freedom from the body, and Mahler's yearning, expressed in his Third Symphony, for a heaven free of carnivors, reflected Marcionistic longing for a world liberated from its cruel creator. Max Brod praised the astrological studies of Emperor Rudolf II, just as Meyrink revived the sixteenth-century legend of the golem. The cosmic dualism of Marcion was formulated into a full-blown cosmology by Christian von Ehrenfels, who taught at Prague from 1895 to 1929. Gnostic critiques of Providence rejected Leibnizian faith in harmony between God and his creation, which had sustained Bohemia up to and after 1850. As we shall see, the Leibnizian theodicy of Bolzano and Herbart so pervaded Bohemia that its collapse after 1860 engendered not indifference but antinomianism, turning gradually into gnosticism.

It was Jewish writers who espoused Marcionism most fervently. Born in Prague between 1878 and 1890, Paul Adler, Franz Kafka, Max Brod, Paul Kornfeld, and Franz Werfel grew up during the height of conflict between Czech and German. Although as Jews they identified with German culture, they comprised a minority within a minority, insulted by both sides. The little-known dramatist Paul Adler (1878–1946) was a polymath who had studied mathematics, medicine, law, and theology, acquiring ideal intellectual equipment with which to indict God. An admirer of Ghandhi, he evaded military service during World War One by hiding near Dresden, where he wrote threnodies on civilization, *Nämlich* (Hellerau, 1915) and *Die Zauberflöte* (Hellerau, 1916).[15] In the former, a schizoid violinist voices his quarrel with God by imagining conversations with Socrates. The latter offered an expressionistic version of Imre Madách's *The Tragedy of Man*, in which Adler used characters from Mozart's opera to reenact the holocaust of Western civilization. Earlier he had signified disgust at Habsburg bureaucracy by resigning his position as a judge because the law required him to pronounce judgment against a poor widow.

Similar dread of law motivated Franz Kafka (1883–1924), whose writings, thanks to Max Brod's preservation of the manuscripts, have made Prague Marcionism into a commonplace of modernity. Kafka carried Marcionism to the extreme of canceling hope of redemption even after death. Not only is the present world mired in bureaucracy, but a heavenly bureaucracy forecloses hope of rescue. Commentators have noted a parallel between the ritualistic procedures of the insurance firm in which Kafka worked and the inscrutable behavior of his bureaucrats. Josephinistic procedures, which had been devised to guarantee impartiality, Kafka inverted to symbolize caprice. He described life as a ritual whose duties remain unknown to participants. Kafka outdid Marcion by contending that any gospel of hope was merely another delusion invented by an inscrutable demiurge.

For Max Brod (1884–1968), Marcionism marked a passing phase of ethical indifferentism based on admiration for Schopenhauer and Flaubert. In his novel *Schloss Nornepygge: Der Roman des Indifferenten* (Berlin, 1908), he depicted an aesthete unconcerned by events around him. Under the influence of Felix Weltsch (1884–1964) and of a blind Prague-born Jewish poet Oskar Baum (1883–1941), after 1910 Brod espoused activism.[16] Later, the serenity of Baum and the holism of Weltsch renewed the Leibnizian tradition.

Next to Kafka and Adler, the most despairing of Prague Jews was Paul Kornfeld (1889–1942). To preach the occultism of Swedenborg and Strindberg, Kornfeld's expressionistic tragedy *Himmel und Hölle* (Berlin, 1919) depicted the imprisonment in a castle of a countess who eventually strangles her daughter. This visionary is best known for an antinaturalist manifesto, "Der beseelte und der psychologische Mensch" (Berlin, 1918), in which like Buber he proclaimed ecstasy and denounced conformity. The soul is ethereal and incorruptible, while character is mechanical and sordid, pandering to the laws of this world. In 1920 Kornfeld entreated God to overturn the rules which he had created:

> I am tired of the primeval rules and laws, of all causes and reasons, and I pray for a miracle amid trumpet calls and thunder and lightning.[17]

Unlike Buber, Kornfeld despaired of ever seeing soul vanquish character except by suspension of natural law.

Several Sudeten Jews have testified to the peasant values that they imbibed from Czech nurses. Prague-born Hans Kohn (1891–1971) praised his childhood cook in moving terms:

> In my life since I have found many "educated" persons much less intelligent and far less ethical than Marie. She taught me not to overestimate the effects of literacy.[18]

As an infant in Freiberg, Moravia, Freud had been cared for by a Czech nurse, who carried him into all five churches of the village and may well have told him about Easter, helping to give him a constructive attitude toward death after his younger brother Julius had died when Freud was nineteen months old.[19] Franz Werfel (1890–1945) has written a hymn to such a sustaining Czech nurse in *Barbara, oder die Frömmigkeit* (Vienna, 1929). Although the protagonist seldom sees his nurse after he has matured, the memory of her presence accompanies him through World War One and the collapse of the empire, imbuing him with faith in redemption. She represents the nourishing love of a preindustrial society, where mutual help has not yet been supplanted by the competitiveness of urban capitalism.

> In Barbara one could behold a woman of the twelfth or thirteenth century. At least for Ferdinand she is painted on a gold-background. Even today it seems to him as if the animality of his early childhood was suffused with sanctity.[20]

Werfel's Prague-born friend, the Jewish essayist Willy Haas (1891–), while admiring Czech women like Barbara, warned that some of them, such as Kafka's adored Milena Jesenská (1896–1944), radiated a matriarchal paganism more insidious even than that of Lou Andreas-Salomé.[21]

Buoyed by a religiosity gained from the early Buber, Werfel avoided the antinomian despair of Adler, Kafka, or Kornfeld. Although he grew increasingly sympathetic to Catholicism, a dualistic theology precluded Werfel from joining the church. He differentiated between isochronic eternity, which offers a timeless compresence of past and future, and heterochronic time, which unfolds in sequence. By seeking to escape from heterochronic time into eternity, Werfel reflected Marcion's impatience with laws of the demiurge. In *Zwischen Oben und Unten* (Stockholm, 1946), he interpreted mind's ability to experience separated events simultaneously as a token of God's grace. Novels such as *Barbara, oder die Frömmigkeit* and *Stern der Ungeborenen: Ein Reiseroman* (Stockholm, 1946) celebrated the capacity of memory to distill in one instant experiences of a whole life.

Although not all Prague Jews embraced Marcionism—witness Oskar Baum—and not all Austrian Marcionists came from Bohemia—witness Albert Ehrenstein—no other city incited so many caustic indictments of creation. The gnosticism of Prague contrasted with the this-worldly involvement of Hungarian intellectuals and the aestheticism of Vienna. Although writers of Young Vienna flirted with death, they never formulated a cosmology to justify their lassitude. Whereas Viennese were merely cloyed, Germans and especially Jews in Prague struggled against mounting odds to preserve their culture. Theirs was a siege mentality: Marcionism expressed the desperation of a beleaguered minority that yearned to silence its tormentor.

The Leibnizian Vision
of Harmony

BERNARD BOLZANO ON THE
UNASSAILABLE OBJECTIVITY OF PROPOSITIONS

THE PROGENITOR of philosophy in Austria, and especially in Bohemia, was the Saxon Gottfried Wilhelm Leibniz (1646–1716), who spent two years in Vienna from 1712 to 1714 as a favorite of Prince Eugene. It was there that he wrote his *Monadologie* and *Principes de la nature et de la grâce* (1718). Alternately a mathematician, physicist, historian, engineer, and philosopher, this universal man approached controversy in a conciliatory spirit: "I have found that most sects are right in a good part of what they affirm, but not so much in what they deny."[1] After 1800 Leibniz' encyclopedic interests, his concern for the good of the whole, and his ecumenical spirit were rejuvenated in Bohemian Reform Catholicism.

Leibniz conceived the universe as being peopled by hierarchy upon hierarchy of sentient beings known as monads. Because each was self-sustaining yet interconnected with the rest, Leibniz could combine the advantages of pluralism and monism. He asserted that harmony suffuses the entire universe: God has so arranged the self-regulating monads that they function in preestablished harmony. Man is a privileged monad, who dwells in equilibrium between God and nature. Delighting in the balance of forces that he contemplates, a reflective person has every reason to rejoice in Creation. Leibniz had defended free will against Spinoza, whose monism was revived after 1800 by the young Schelling. Leibniz in turn found followers in Bolzano, Herbart, and their disciples, who invoked Leibniz in order to refute Kant and his successors.

The most able exponent of Leibnizian philosophy was Bohemian-born Bernard Bolzano (1781–1848), a logician and theologian of exceptional originality.[2] Not only did he help to renew Leibniz around 1820, but when his works were rediscovered after 1880, these encouraged Husserl to espouse antipsychologism. Bolzano was the son of an Italian art dealer from Lake Como and a German mother from Prague, a woman of rare piety. He grew up in the Josephinist atmosphere of Prague, where a lay Catholic professor of philosophy, Karl Heinrich Seibt (1735–1806), had introduced writers of the German Enlightenment like Gottsched, Gellert, Baumgarten, and Wolff. At the Piaristengymnasium, Bolzano had encountered these rationalists even before Seibt's lectures at the university drew his attention to Kant. There he spent more than a year mastering Kant's *Critiques*, at the same time developing skill at mathematics. By 1805 the young prodigy had not yet chosen between teaching mathematics or philosophy; he was also drawn to the priesthood. The announcement in 1805 that a chair of religion was being established at the Philosophical Faculty in Prague provided Bolzano an opportunity to combine these three callings. In February, 1805, he began lectures in mathematics, and in April of that year he was ordained before taking a post as chaplain to students. Bolzano was a brilliant, dedicated teacher, whose weekly sermons to students (*Erbauungsreden*) won wide following. Popularity with students caused him to antagonize anti-Josephinist conservatives like Jakob Frint (1766–1834), who founded the Frintaneum at Vienna. After years of intrigue, Frint, who resented Bolzano's refusal to use the older man's textbook, succeeded in having the lecturer dismissed by Emperor Franz in December, 1819. Bolzano was blamed for unrest that had arisen in the Seminary at Leitmeritz, where one of his students, Michael Josef Fesl (1788–1863), was teaching. Although an effort to convict Bolzano of heresy resulted in acquittal in December, 1825, he never again held a teaching position.

For ten years after his dismissal, Bolzano dwelt with his brother Johann at Prague. After the death of his mother in 1821, the philosopher-priest spent summers from 1824 to 1830 on the estate of a benefactress, Lady Joseph Hoffmann, at Tiechobus, south of Prague. From 1830 to 1841, he lived there year-round, cared for by Lady Hoffmann, and upon her death from cancer in 1842, he returned to his brother's quarters at Prague. Although Bolzano remained under constant police surveillance, he completed between 1820 and 1830 his master work in four volumes, the *Wissenschaftslehre*. After years of effort, he succeeded in having it published during 1837 at Sulzbach in Bavaria, thanks to the intercession of Fesl and of another former student,

Vinzenz Fiebrich (1797–1842). Fiebrich had studied under Bolzano from 1813 to 1815 before joining the Viennese police. By 1835 Fiebrich had risen to be High Commissioner of Police (Oberkommissar), a position that he used to protect both Bolzano and Fesl.[3] A gentle man who needed encouragement to work, Bolzano conducted lively correspondence with many friends and former students, including Fesl, the Vienna-born Herbartian Franz Exner (1802–1853), and the priest Franz Přihonský (1788–1859), who edited his posthumous writings. Other friends at Prague included the influential school principal Franz Schneider and the gymnasium teacher Johann August Zimmermann, the father of Robert Zimmermann. As a friend of the Czech grammarians Dobrovský and Šafařík, Bolzano belonged to the Bohemist party, which sought to promote harmony between Germans and Czechs. During 1816 Bolzano lectured at Prague, urging Czech and German to learn each other's language so that they need no longer gesticulate at each other like wild animals.[4]

Bolzano stands out above all for his logic, particularly for the doctrine of propositions-in-themselves. He was a Platonic realist who taught the intrinsic subsistence (Ansichsein) of ideal entities. In the Wissenschaftslehre, he distinguished among presentations-in-themselves (Vorstellungen an sich), propositions-in-themselves (Sätze an sich), and truths-in-themselves (Wahrheiten an sich). Each of these entities an sich exists independently of any mind. Presentations Bolzano defined as elements out of which propositions are built, and a truth is simply a true proposition. Bolzano insisted that every proposition-in-itself enjoys existence, whether true or not, and irrespective of whether any mind has ever conceived it. Even God need not have conceived such a proposition for it to exist outside of time and space. Each proposition-in-itself may take the form of a proposition expressed in words (ausgesprochen) and/or conceived (gedacht). The same distinction applies to presentations and to truths, which may or may not be expressed in words and may or may not be conceived. The distinction between expressing propositions and conceiving them sought to emphasize that propositions-in-themselves exist prior to language and prior to any mind's act of thinking. Bolzano insisted that propositions-in-themselves must be differentiated from words that denote them and from subjective acts that conceive them. Bolzano's view of logic had been anticipated most precisely by the Berlin physicist Johann Heinrich Lambert (1728–1777), who in his Neues Organon (1764) expounded the a priori character of mathematical truth. It was he who introduced the term phenomenology (Phänomenologie) to designate the study of appearances as distinct from the study of terms (*Semiotik*).[5]

Bolzano's lofty, otherworldly conception of propositions-in-themselves did not prevent him from taking a lowly view of man's intellectual capacities. In sermons he warned that the wisest course in theology is to admit that dogma may err because our finite nature precludes both omniscience and infallibility.[6] In ethics, Bolzano reflected Leibniz' concern for the good of the whole. Bolzano's ethical maxim was:

> Always choose from among the actions possible to you those which, when all the consequences are weighed, will best promote the good of the whole, no matter in which parts.[7]

In practice, this maxim enjoined quietism as the likeliest way to avoid injuring the whole through partisan action. As in the case of his fellow Josephinists Stifter and Grillparzer, Bolzano's zeal for the good of the whole of society invited resignation toward improving any of its parts. This reflects Bolzano's postulate that it is good-in-itself to contemplate truths-in-themselves. To penetrate the architecture of the universe makes us wiser and better without our needing to change it. In political theory, Bolzano analyzed the state-in-itself, which he postulated to be the best state imaginable, without querying whether it could ever be put into practice.[8] He sketched a model of perfection, less in order to measure existing imperfections than to venerate the beauty of the model. Few thinkers have been so dedicated to articulating ideal entities without regard to worldly applications.

For all his brilliance, Bolzano forfeited recognition during his lifetime, as his disciples were forced to adopt a Herbartian facade. In the 1880's Franz Brentano—conceivably under the stimulus of Robert Zimmermann—called attention to Bolzano's logic, arousing the interest of Edmund Husserl, who in turn stirred that of Melchior Palágyi and Hugo Bergmann.[9] Bolzano's eclipse and rediscovery bears comparison with that of Gregor Mendel whose discovery about 1860 of the laws of genetics was recognized only in 1900. Bolzano asserted once and for all the unassailable objectivity of logical propositions. Each proposition-in-itself enjoys the autonomy of a Leibnizian monad, unaltered by men's efforts to express it or think it. This notion that there exists a heaven of ideas, some of which come to be thought by man while others never enter a human mind, is one of the fundamental achievements of Austrian philosophy. In asserting the invincible integrity of ideas, safe from all human meddling, Bolzano forged a most powerful weapon against censorship of ideas. No human error or policy can unseat the truth or modify its character. Like an impregnable fortress, propositions-in-themselves subsist through eternity, consoling thinkers who penetrate their majesty and assuring Bolzano a monument that has outlasted persecution by his enemies.

REFORM CATHOLICISM IN BOHEMIA
RENEWS THE LEIBNIZIAN VISION

During the first half of the nineteenth century, Bolzano and his fellow Catholics sponsored a movement of philosophic Josephinism unique to Bohemia. Their efforts to found schools, to teach rationalistic theology, and to promote harmony between Czechs and Germans influenced thinkers like Adalbert Stifter and Anton Günther, as well as a host of Herbartian philosophers. This Josephinism also fostered the romantic program of Czech-German cooperation known as Bohemism.[10]

In contrast to Austria proper and to Hungary, under Mettėrnich Catholicism played a progressive role in Bohemia. Because values of the Enlightenment flourished inside the church, anticlericalism remained at a minimum, with the result that religious romanticism could emerge as a fruit of the Enlightenment instead of as a protest against it. Reform Catholics steered a middle course, opposing both Ultramontanism and state centralism. Expanding research by Eugen Lemberg, Christoph Thienen-Adlerflycht has compared the ideal of Bohemian leaders to that of Justus Möser: local administrators should make gradual improvements according to "local reason" without having a blueprint imposed from above. In order to promote a Herderian ideal of slow evolution, the church led in founding elementary schools, above all in the northern diocese of Leitmeritz. These schools combined practical training with humanistic culture so as to avoid a one-sided emphasis on theory such as observers detected at the University of Berlin. Urging students to seek social reform, Bohemian teachers instilled a desire to participate in politics. The generation of Czechs whom these schools molded grew up to lead the campaign for autonomy after 1860.

Bohemian intellectuals thronged to Leibniz' doctrine of cosmic harmony. In contrast to the mystics and censors of Metternich's Vienna, they did not believe it hubris to seek unity between science and religion. The older Goethe found friends in Bohemia like Count Kaspar

Sternberg (1761–1838), who endorsed the doctrine of harmony between microcosm and macrocosm at a time when intellectuals in Germany did not. In *Innocens* (1866), Saar portrayed such a Bohemian priest who studies nature in a Goethian spirit. Bohemians rejected Kant for having exempted morals from control by theology. They welcomed Herder's concept of historical evolution not only because it foretold Slavic renaissance but also because it prompted change within the Catholic church. The most enduring monument of Bohemian humanism was the reform of Austrian education executed during the 1850's by Bolzano's friend Count Leo Thun. Sweeping away the confessional bias of Metternich's era, this devout Catholic introduced humanistic and scientific training into both secondary schools and university. On the Leibnizian premise that religion and science cannot contradict each other, Thun ventured to teach students how to think for themselves, thereby giving rebirth to Austrian scholarship.

In Bohemia itself, however, the Leibnizian vision lost ground. After 1850 it began to founder amid growing strife between Czechs and Germans. The opposite doctrine of Marcionism gained ground among thinkers increasingly disenchanted with philosophic Josephinism and with Bohemism. The state church came to personify not cosmic order but Habsburg tyranny, impelling many Czechs to embrace free thought or to convert to Protestantism. Caught between two hostile blocs, the Jews of Bohemia took refuge in anti-Leibnizian visions of world overthrow. In the land where Leibniz' doctrine had flourished longest, eventually it was rejected with greatest vehemence.

Adalbert Stifter (1805–1868), born in Southern Bohemia, fused values of reform Catholicism with those of Goethe. The aristocratic scientist-artist of *Der Nachsommer* (Pest, 1857) was modeled on a Bohemian-born engineer, Andreas von Baumgartner (1793–1865), who directed Austria's first telegraph system and railroads. Stifter's novel of medieval Bohemia, *Witiko* (Pest, 1865–1867), celebrated those who subserve the good of the whole. Based on Palacký's history and Herder's notion of a Gemeinschaft society among Slavs, the novel impugned the worship of art which seduces men from practical affairs. Stifter's conviction that Christian love provides the sole basis of social good recalls Bolzano's ethic. For these Bohemian contemplatives, education must touch heart as well as head, an ideal that Thun tried to carry out at the Ministry of Education.

A utopian exponent of Leibnizian optimism was German-born Hermann Freiherr von Leonhardi (1809–1875), who served as a professor of philosophy at Prague from 1849 to 1875. He was son-in-law and disciple of a Thuringian visionary, Karl Christian Friedrich Krause (1781–1832), who coined the term "panentheism" after having revived the sophiology of Jan Comenius. Renewing the ecumenical zeal of Krause, Leonhardi taught that men are all members of one another. To promote the cause of European confederation, he organized in 1868 at Prague the first International Congress of Philosophy whose political aims anticipated those of Bertha von Suttner and Richard Coudenhove-Kalergi.[11]

One of the most idiosyncratic of Reform Catholics was the Bohemian theologian Anton Günther (1783–1863), who studied under Bolzano before going to Vienna in 1819.[12] After some years of working with Klemens Hofbauer, Günther was ordained priest in 1820, only to serve as a book censor from 1828 to 1848. After three decades of controversy, in 1857 the pope placed all of Günther's writings on the index, forcing the latter to acknowledge his errors. These were alleged to consist of opposing neo-Thomism and of separating soul from spirit. As part of a campaign against speculative idealism, Günther assailed Christian theodicy for having perpetuated the basic error of pagan philosophy, namely the doctrine of God's immanence in nature. Whereas pantheism pertained to the era of original sin, when nature had enslaved man, salvation substitutes God's spirit for man's. This abolishes the doctrine of *analogia entis*, which postulates similarity between natural man and God. If it be true that creator and creature share one substance, Günther asked, how could sin and evil exist? God would then be creator of evil, standing in opposition to himself. In order to salvage the goodness of God, Günther propounded a radical dualism in anthropology. Born a natural soul, divorced from God, man must entreat God so as to receive His Spirit. If every heresy consists in exaggerating some portion of theological truth, Günther overstated the gap between God and man, mainly because he resented the denial of this gap in Hegel and Schelling.

As a polemicist, Günther hurt his cause through a feuilletonistic style modeled on that of Jean Paul. One of the most piquant stylists ever to write theology, Günther so inflated his formulations that even Bolzano found both style and content repugnant. Günther marked a first break with the Leibnizian vision of harmony; by positing a gulf between man and God, he verged toward Marcionism. His dualism in anthropology was renewed by the Catholic sociologist Ernst Karl Winter (1895–1959), who insisted that society and theology constitute separate spheres. If Günther had not been a priest, said Winter, he might have founded an influential school of philosophy. Penalized for his boldness, Günther was an example of why innovators like Franz Brentano found it necessary to leave the church.

THE APPEAL OF
JOHANN FRIEDRICH HERBART IN AUSTRIA

The philosopher who was most widely taught in Austria between 1820 and 1880 never set foot in that country. He was the German realist, Johann Friedrich Herbart (1776–1841), admired by Reform Catholics and secular pedagogues alike.[13] Born in Lower Saxony, this Protestant studied under Fichte at Jena before working from 1797 to 1800 as a family tutor in Bern, where he met Pestalozzi. After serving from 1802 to 1809 as professor of philosophy at Göttingen, he organized a seminar for gymnasium teachers at Königsberg, where he endeavored from 1809 to 1832 to train teachers to participate in Wilhelm von Humboldt's reform of Prussian education. He returned thereafter to his chair at Göttingen.

Herbart excelled at clear exposition and lucid division of his subject, such as Jesuit philosophers had perfected since the sixteenth century. He espoused moderate realism, opposing the speculative idealism of his teacher Fichte as well as that of Schelling. Herbart divided philosophy into four parts: logic, metaphysics, psychology, and practical sciences. Metaphysics examines the origin of ideas, while psychology demonstrates how they are developed and combined. A true scholastic, he subdivided metaphysics into four parts: method, ontology, synechiology (study of continuous phenomena like space and time), and eidolology (study of the possibility of knowledge). In ontology, Herbart defined being as a plurality of realia (*Realen*), which are absolutely simple. Entirely without parts, each reale is immutably identical with itself. The universe resolves not into Spinoza's monistic *natura sive deus*, but into Leibniz' infinity of self-sufficient monads. Herbart differed from Leibniz in that he held with Kant that we cannot know the essential qualities of realia. Yet we can, *pace* Kant, know beyond all doubt the fact of their existence, which we deduce from the aggregate realia presented to us in consciousness. The categories of space, time, motion, and unity derive from such aggregate realia. Herbart rejected both Descartes' innate ideas and Kant's concepts a priori.

Herbart won acclaim for his psychology. The soul, or self is, he said, a reale, tied to a cluster of realia known as the body. Like other realia, each of these strives to persist against perturbations (Störungen) that buffet it. The mind acts like a seismograph to record acts of self-preservation by the self. These self-preserving acts generate presentations (Vorstellungen) to resist foreign realia that impinge on the self. Once generated, presentations become indestructible atoms of the soul. They persist beneath what Herbart called the threshhold (Schwelle) of consciousness, where they vie against one another in an effort to invade consciousness. He coined the term repression (Verdrängung) to designate the force that counteracts their drive (Trieb) toward the surface. Fascinated by the theory of harmony in music, Herbart devised an elaborate calculus for quantifying the strength and weakness of presentations. Like Freud, who borrowed several of these terms, Herbart failed to specify operations to verify his quantifications. In one of his most influential coinages, he modified Leibniz' term "apperception" to denote assimilation of new presentations by old ones of a similar kind. This notion underlay a pedagogy that prized teaching by means of association rather than by rote. For Herbart, presentation constituted the basic phenomenon of mental life. By classifying types of feeling and willing according to the object presented in each act, he opposed voluntarists like Schopenhauer and emotionalists like Carus as well as intellectualists like Kant and Fichte. His mediating position endeared him to experimentalists such as Fechner and Wundt, who exploited his concept of apperception.

In his 350-page Lehrbuch zur Einleitung in die Philosophie (Hamburg, 1813; 5th ed., 1883), Herbart surveyed all fields of philosophy, first unraveling problems of each field as a whole and then explaining each subdivision. Under the head of general problems of metaphysics, he discussed skepticism, change, absolute being, absolute qualities, and Kant's methodology. Under each of these topics, he discriminated the principal points of view expressed to date, supplying in each case what he called a reworking of the concepts (Bearbeitung der Begriffe). This dissecting of options advocated by past philosophers became a major endeavor of Herbart's disciples. He saw his own metaphysics as lying midway between the mysticism of Plotinus and Hegel on the one hand and the empiricism of Locke on the other. In knowledge of past philosophers, Herbart nearly matched Hegel, whose agility at juggling concepts he also shared. Although he surpassed Hegel as a psychologist and as a methodologist of empirical science, Herbart lacked any overarching vision of historical development. Rather, he espoused a classicist's view of static harmony, while Hegel indulged Romantic fascination with intellectual and social change.

In aesthetics Herbart taught thoroughgoing formalism: beauty consists in formal relations between parts of an object. Interrelations of parts awaken pleasing or displeasing presentations, irrespective of content. Herbart opposed Hegel's view that beauty entails harmony between form and content. As we have seen, Hanslick exploited Herbart's formalism to belittle program music. Herbart himself was an accomplished musician: he played piano, composed, and discoursed on the theory of harmony. Apparently study of harmonic ratios inspired his calculus for measuring strength and weakness of psychic drives. At a time when Schopenhauer saw music as objectifying not ideas but will, Herbart interpreted art in Leibnizian fashion. Ratios between harmonious sounds constitute realia that mirror workings of the mind. For Herbart, harmony objectifies interplay of presentations, while for Schopenhauer it apotheosizes that instinct for self-preservation which pervades the universe.[14]

In Germany, and to a somewhat lesser extent in Austria, Herbart won renown above all for a pedagogy that generalized principles of Johann Heinrich Pestalozzi (1746–1827). Inspired by this Swiss disciple of Rousseau, Herbart disseminated the ideals of Goethe's humanism under the guise of a psychology of learning. Herbart differed from earlier pedagogues by insisting that intellect and character should be developed concurrently. Like Goethe and Schiller, he based ethics as well as pedagogy on self-fulfillment. Morality consists in the experience of freedom guided by duty, a condition made possible by a well-trained conscience. Will must be trained to desire what is good. Toward this end, Herbart sought to instill two formal ideas. First, a pupil is taught to heed the idea of inner freedom, which urges him to act in accordance with his conscience. Second, the idea of the efficiency of the will develops a will that is strong, concentrated, and consistent with the ethical order of the world. This ethical order Herbart defined according to three concrete ideas. First, the idea of benevolence requires that each person desire the good for others as if for himself; second, the idea of justice aims to prevent strife by awakening a person's natural displeasure at contention; and third, the idea of equity seeks to redress relations among wills that have been altered for good or bad. Here Herbart implemented Leibniz' principle of maximizing the good of the whole, while paying greater heed to relations among the parts than did Bolzano.

Herbart shared with Goethe and Hegel antipathy toward revolution. Perhaps because his pedagogy had abetted Prussian reform, it tended to train docile, law-abiding citizens who relished work while despising unrest. By affirming a static world view, Herbart's pedagogy buttressed semifeudal Austrian society that dreaded change. After 1848, Herbartians supplanted priest- and police-ridden education by inculcating moral and intellectual discipline while minimizing political or theological bias. Steering between the Scylla of Romanticism and the Charybdis of clericalism, Herbart distilled the best in Weimar classicism.

Herbart's most celebrated followers in Austria were reformers of education. The reform of gymnasien and universities was organized in the early 1850's by two disciples of Bolzano, Count Leo Thun and Franz Exner, as well as by the Thuringian classical philologist Hermann Bonitz (1814–1888). All these men embraced Herbart's philosophy as a stalking horse for convictions derived from Bolzano. After 1850 the University of Prague became a stronghold of Herbartian thought. Three Bohemian-born psychologists at Prague, František Čupr (1821–1882), Wilhelm Fridolin Volkmann (1822–1877), and Gustav Adolf Lindner (1828–1887), who was a student of Franz Exner, wrote textbooks on empirical psychology, which were used throughout Austria. Freud studied Lindner's textbook during his final year at gymnasium.

Apart from professional philosophers, a late recrudescence of Herbart's monadology appeared in a posthumous treatise by the novelist Robert Hamerling (1830–1889). In his two-volume *Die Atomistik des Willens: Beiträge zur Kritik der modernen Erkenntnis* (Hamburg, 1891), Hamerling postulated a radical pluralism, whereby the universe consists of myriad independent entities called atoms. These atoms, which are equivalent to Leibniz' monads and Herbart's realia, exist independently not only of thought but of each other. Like an updated Herbart, Hamerling opposed the voluntarism of Schopenhauer and of neo-Kantians, as well as the monism of Haeckel.[15]

Herbart owed much of his appeal in Austria to the ease with which his philosophy could be accommodated by Catholics, for whom his very omissions became advantages. In taking a neutral view of theology, he was not self-consciously Protestant like Kant, Schelling, or Hegel, and his lack of a progressivist philosophy of history also seemed a merit. On the positive side, by steering a middle course between idealism and empiricism, he appeared to parallel the *via media* of Aquinas. In addition, Herbart's reworking of concepts through reclassification matched the practice of Catholic apologists. The German realist analyzed the gamut of philosophical options with the detachment of an apologetic theologian appraising his tools. Finally, Herbart's concept of realia renewed the Leibnizian belief that the universe consists in hierarchies of indestructible monads, culminating in God as the *reale realissimum*. It was above all Herbart's affinity with Leibniz which made him appeal to disciples of Bolzano.

Among secular thinkers, Herbart's presuppositions evoked wide sympathy in Austria. His practice of reworking concepts corresponded to the historicizing attitude of post-1800 Vienna. His postulate of a reservoir of philosophical options flattered Vienna's image of itself as sustainer and refiner of traditions, where old elements might intermingle without disruption by new ones. Through his pedagogy, Herbart aimed to teach men to understand what is already known, rather than to goad them into making discoveries. He trained connoisseurs, not creators, just as in philosophy he fostered scholars of the subject, not creative geniuses. As in the historicizing architecture of post-1860 Vienna, Herbart's reworking of concepts presupposed that there is nothing new under the sun. Architects like Ferstel and Schmidt were Herbartians who worked in stone. Finally there existed affinity between the metaphysical neutrality of Herbart and the impartiality of Josephinist civil servants, who were administering a codified heritage within a static universe. Thun was permitted to enact his reform of education only after he had persuaded opponents that it would fortify perennial values. To secular Josephinists, Herbart seemed to be saying *plus ça change, plus c'est la même chose.* Imbued with such resistance to change, Herbartians could hardly be expected to have revolutionized Austrian philosophy. Inventiveness had to wait until after 1870 when there emerged refractory geniuses like Brentano, Mach, and Mauthner.

In defending the status quo, Austrian Herbartians indulged paranoic hostility to Kant and Hegel, as if the police measures of Metternich's era had infected philosophers. The placing of Kant's *Critique of Pure Reason* on the papal Index in 1827 had extinguished any chance of his being heeded in Austria. Robert Zimmermann stood alone in recalling that Herbart had regarded himself as a modified Kantian of the year 1828.[16] A conspiracy of silence stifled the pioneering Kantianism of Carl Sigmund Barach (1834–1885), who as a docent at Vienna had dared in 1858 to advocate a systematic return to Kant in his *Die gegenwärtige Aufgabe der Philosophie: Aus der bisherigen Stellung der Philosophie zum Leben und den Forderungen des Lebens entwickelt* (Vienna, 1858). This treatise was the first in the German language to propose reviving Kant's *Critique of Pure Reason*, preceding by seven years Otto Liebmann's seminal work, *Kant und die Epigonen: Eine kritische Abhandlung* (Stuttgart, 1865). Forgotten for having done too early what made Liebmann famous, the anti-Hegelian Barach retreated into historical studies of obscure skeptics like Philippe Huet.[17]

Especially after 1848, Herbartians at Vienna and Prague persecuted followers of Hegel quite shamelessly. Bolzano's friend Franz Exner had published in 1842 a blistering critique of the psychology of

Hegel's students Karl Rosenkranz, Karl Ludwig Michelet, and Johann Eduard Erdmann. His *Die Psychologie der Hegelschen Schule* (Leipzig, 1842) launched a bitter polemic, followed in 1850 by bitter controversy. A Czech priest and student of Exner, Augustin Smetana (1814–1851), was excommunicated for having dared to combine Hegel and Schelling in his *Die Bedeutung des gegenwärtigen Zeitalters* (Prague, 1848) and *Die Katastrophe und der Ausgang der Geschichte der Philosophie* (Hamburg, 1850). Smetana argued that it was the Slavs who must carry German philosophy to completion. His tale of his excommunication indicted clerical and bureaucratic oppression.[18]

The next year, another Czech Catholic Hegelian at Prague fell victim to repression. Ignác Hanuš (1812–1869), also a pupil of Exner, lost his professorship at Prague, partly because he had exposited orthodox Hegelianism in several textbooks and even more because he sympathized with Czech nationalism. A different punishment was accorded the most prolific of Bohemian Hegelians, Gustav Biedermann (1815–1890), who practiced medicine at Tetschen, near the border of Saxony. The Hegelian treatises that he published from 1860 to 1890 were simply ignored. Having begun as a disciple of Alexander von Humboldt's *Kosmos* (1845–1862), Biedermann wrote nearly a dozen volumes paraphrasing Hegel, with only occasional cavils at the master's identification of logic with grammar. In works like *Philosophie des Geistes* (Prague, 1886) and *Religionsphilosophie* (Prague, 1887), he divided every chapter into three parts, each of which contained three subsections. Although few Hegelians have parroted the master so slavishly, not many have been so utterly neglected.

The works of Smetaná and Hanuš only further convinced authorities that Hegel was dangerous to the Catholic faith—one of the few points on which they agreed with Günther. Equally unwelcome was the Hegelians' use of historical dialectic to defend Slav nationalism. Compared to such incitements, the humanism of Herbart seemed safe indeed. It reinvigorated the apolitical, nonsectarian classicism of the late Goethe, while inculcating a Biedermeier spirit of resignation.

ROBERT ZIMMERMANN'S
ALL-EMBRACING THEORY OF THE ARTS

Several times Robert Zimmermann (1824–1898) has been mentioned as a faithful interpreter of Herbart. This most gifted of Austrian Herbartians served from 1861 to 1895 as a professor of philosophy at Vienna, where he exerted a wide influence on ethics and aesthetics. Son of a Catholic gymnasium teacher at Prague, Johann August Zimmermann (1793–1869), Robert grew up under the tutelage of his father's close friend Bolzano, who dubbed the young man his darling boy (*Herzensjunge*).[19] In hope of training a successor, from 1843 on Bolzano initiated Zimmermann into his unpublished mathematical writings, which the youth absorbed with facility but without genuine understanding. In the mid-1840's both the younger and the older Zimmermann scandalized Bolzano by joining the German nationalist movement. Robert voiced his hostility to the rising cultural nationalism of the Czechs in a poem that circulated throughout Prague:

> Czech oder Deutscher, heisst es, nimm Partei!
> Wohl könnten beide friedlich sich vertragen,
> Wollt ihr es nicht, wohlan!
> So will ich mich zu deutschen Brüdern schlagen.[20]

> Whether Czech or German, the word is
>   Choose your Party!
> Both could easily get along in peace,
> But if you do not wish that, so be it.
> Thus I shall side with my German brothers.

From 1844 to 1848 Robert Zimmermann studied at Vienna, where his father had settled in 1844 to work with Franz Exner on the educational reform that Leo Thun later enacted. As a student of astronomy, young Zimmerman moved away from the influence of Bolzano. After taking a doctorate in that subject at Vienna in 1846, he turned from study of celestial laws to examine their earthly counterparts in Leibniz and Herbart. Despite having written in 1848 an inflammatory poem, "To Those Who Fell in March" (*An die Märzgefallenen*), he won his habilitation in philosophy at Vienna in the following year. As a professor at Olmütz and then at Prague from 1852 to 1861, he wrote papers that portrayed Leibniz as a precursor of Bolzano, Herbart, and Lessing. By the mid-1850's he had undertaken to rework Herbart's aesthetics into a comprehensive system. Herbart provided a framework within which the former astronomer could expound belief in immutable laws. In 1861 Zimmermann became an Ordinarius of philosophy at Vienna, the first philosopher to benefit from the constitution of that year which eased restrictions on teaching and publishing. As a stout advocate of academic freedom, Zimmermann allied himself with the art historian Rudolf Eitelberger, even winning the admiration of Friedrich Jodl. In 1874 Zimmermann was active in securing the call to Vienna of Brentano, remaining after the latter's resignation in 1880 the only full professor of philosophy at Vienna until 1896. In 1886 he served as rector of the university, and in 1890 he joined his student, Moravian-born Emil Reich (1864–1937), a devotee of Schopenhauer, in founding the Grillparzer Society. From 1870 to 1898 Zimmermann wrote for the London *Athenaeum* an annual survey of German publications. Written in English, these essays offered a thorough and perceptive chronicle of new works in literature and philosophy. In contrast to most other scholars, Zimmermann included all of Austria-Hungary within the purview of "German" letters.[21]

Having known Eduard Hanslick as a young man in Prague, Zimmermann reviewed enthusiastically the latter's *Vom Musikalisch-Schönen.* The philosopher joined the music critic in condemning Hegel for confusing art history with aesthetics. Whereas art history studies the influence of society on artists, aesthetics explain why a work of art is beautiful. In his two-volume work, *Aesthetik* (Vienna, 1858–1865; repr., 1968), Zimmermann espoused Hanslick's formalism. Beauty resides in the interrelations of forms, which as such possess absolute value. Zimmermann's *Aesthetik*, which he dedicated to Bolzano's friend M. J. Fesl, presented the first systematic history of aesthetic theory. The last one-eighth is devoted to Herbart.

Zimmermann's most startling doctrine is his interpretation of every human activity as embodying one of three types of art. First, the art of self-education *(Bildungskunst)* generates beautiful ideas and good impulses in oneself. Second, the art of images *(Bildekunst)* involves instilling such ideas and impulses in other people. Beginning with pedagogy, it ascends to social philosophy and statecraft *(Staatskunst)*. Third, the formulative arts *(bildende Kunst)* consist in discovering and "re-creating" ideas in matter. The discovery of ideas in matter includes the natural sciences and technology, while their re-creation encompasses the fine arts. With encyclopedic sweep reminiscent of Aristotle, Zimmermann envisioned all mental and practical activity as subdivisions of a single gigantic pursuit known as art. Beginning with *Aesthetik* and culminating in *Anthroposophie* (Vienna, 1882), Zimmermann endeavored to assert continuity between knowledge, practical life, and fine art. Together with Hamerling's *Atomistik*, *Anthroposophie* ranks as one of the last great treatises of the Leibnizian tradition. It found a continuator in Rudolf Steiner (1861–1925), who saw in his teacher Zimmermann a model of Goethe's manysidedness.[22] It was from Zimmermann that Steiner borrowed the term Anthroposophy to designate his own philosophy.

Toward that other model of manysidedness, Hegel, Zimmermann evinced the hostility customary among Herbartians. This found expression in a running polemic against the Swabian Friedrich Theodor Vischer (1807–1887), who championed Hegel's aesthetics against formalism. It was against Zimmermann that Vischer's son Robert Vischer (1846–1933) formulated in 1872 the concept of empathy *(Einfühlung)*, which after 1890 became a hallmark of neo-idealist aesthetics. To Vischer's surprise, in 1873 Zimmermann reviewed his work favorably, later integrating it into his *Anthroposophie*.[23] Apart from Steiner, Zimmermann exerted his most lasting impact on the art historian Alois Riegl, who exploited his teacher's formalism as a weapon with which to attack the art-materialism of Gottfried Semper.[24] Riegl also elevated Zimmermann's Herbartian distinction between tactile and optic art into the polar opposites haptic and optic.

In the fine arts, Zimmermann endorsed neoclassicism, applauding Carl Rahl's epigonal fresco, *The Judgment of Paris* (1861), as well as the Nazarene works of Bohemian-born Josef von Führich (1800–1876). Zimmermann condemned romanticism for introducing into art emotions that spoil the formal beauty of classical works. An artist should excel by exercising ingenuity within the rules of his medium, not by awakening pathological feelings in the beholder. Indulging neoclassical desire for rules to govern art, Zimmermann praised Gottsched's defense of French baroque theater and Schiller's drama of ideas. After 1870 Zimmermann turned increasingly to the history of philosophy, publishing lucid monographs on Herbart, Kant, Hume, Comte, and Samuel Clarke in the *Sitzungsberichte* of the Vienna Academy of Sciences. Having earlier pioneered the history of aesthetics, he continued to excel at clear exposition both of logical subtleties and of historical background. He also asserted Austria's claim to philosophical preeminence by rehabilitating Bolzano and Karl Leonhard Reinhold.[25]

For thirty-five years a professor at Vienna, Zimmermann stood after 1860 as consummate representative of the Leibnizian world view in Austria. His faith in an objective world order, his hostility to subjectivism, and his indifference to progressivism made him an epigone of Bolzano and Herbart in an age when new currents had all but swept away the Leibnizian vision. Like Herbart, Zimmermann demonstrated how perseverance and ingenuity can sustain a superannuated philosophy. Zimmermann did for Viennese philosophy what Rudolf von Alt was doing for painting and Johannes Brahms, with more distinction, for music. These men provided a living link with the past, epitomizing in their person currents against which inventive youth could rebel.

Franz Brentano
and His Followers

FRANZ BRENTANO'S RENEWAL OF PSYCHOLOGY
AND ETHICS THROUGH THE DOCTRINE OF INTENTIONALITY

INNOVATIONS by Franz Brentano (1838–1917) both revised and reinforced the Leibnizian tradition. Teaching at Vienna, this German-born
Catholic helped to inaugurate several major streams of modern philosophy. Among these, Husserl's phenomenology, Meinong's theory of
objects, and Ehrenfels' Gestalt theory showed affinities with Bolzano.
Brentano himself went through three phases: a youth of Catholic neo-
scholasticism, a middle period of quasi-Aristotelian realism, and a later
period of empiricism. Throughout, he embodied values of Bohemian
Reform Catholicism.

Born on the Rhine near Koblenz, Franz Brentano was the son of a
physician, Christian Brentano. His uncle was the Romantic poet Clemens Maria Brentano, and his aunt, Bettina von Arnim.[1] Franz's brother,
Lujo Brentano (1844–1931), became one of Germany's leading advocates of state insurance for workers. Destined for the priesthood, young
Franz enjoyed the finest possible education, living for a time in Berlin
with his uncle the jurist Friedrich von Savigny. In Munich in 1856 he
heard lectures by the Catholic philosopher of history Ernst von
Lasaulx, and in Berlin he studied Aristotle under Adolf Trendelenburg
before taking a doctorate in absentia at Tübingen in 1862. Brentano's
dissertation, *Von der mannigfachen Bedeutung des Seienden nach
Aristoteles* (Freiburg, 1862), argued against Eduard Zeller that for
Aristotle God had created mind *ex nihilo*. Following a brief stay at a
Dominican abbey in Graz, where he met Heinrich Denifle, Brentano
studied theology in Munich under his friend Ignaz Döllinger. In August, 1864, the budding philosopher was ordained priest, becoming a
docent in philosophy at Würzburg, where he published a second book

on Aristotle, *Die Psychologie des Aristoteles* (Mainz, 1867). Joining opposition to Pope Pius IX's proposed dogma of Papal Infallibility, Brentano drafted a cogent memorandum against it for Bishop von Ketteler in 1869.[2] Proclamation of the dogma in 1870 unsettled Brentano's faith because, as he said, after repudiating this newest article of faith, he could for the first time question dogmas that he had embraced since childhood. After three years of soul-searching, on April 11, 1873, Brentano left the priesthood and the church. Although his decision impelled Carl Stumpf and Anton Marty to do likewise, Brentano never ceased believing in God; his thought remained steeped in Christian values.

In January, 1874, Brentano accepted a call—arranged in part by Robert Zimmermann—to become a professor of philosophy at Vienna, where until 1880 he lectured to overflow audiences, among whom were Sigmund Freud and Tomáš Masaryk. Although Austrian law forbade ex-priests to marry, in 1880 Brentano announced his intention to marry a baptized Jewish patrician, Ida Lieben. Enforcing an antiquated rule, the university forced Brentano to resign his chair, whereupon he took up residence in Leipzig long enough to be wed there on September 16, 1880. Soon thereafter, he returned to Vienna as a docent in philosophy, holding that position until the death of his wife in 1894. However much the demotion rankled, aversion to Prussia and Protestantism precluded accepting a better post in Germany. Brentano continued to lavish time and advice on students, inviting the more gifted to dinner at his home on Friday evenings, as well as to his summer house on the Wolfgangsee. Unable to tolerate Vienna after his wife had died, during December, 1894, Brentano published five articles in the *Neue Freie Presse,* flaying official ingratitude.[3] From 1896 to 1915 he dwelt in Florence, plagued by a worsening eye ailment which an operation at Vienna in 1903 failed to cure. In 1897 he married again, this time a Viennese woman with Italian citizenship; after Italy's entry into the World War, the couple settled at Zürich. During his last years of nearly complete blindness, his wife read to him, enabling him to correspond with friends and pupils such as Anton Marty and Oskar Kraus. It was in letters to Kraus that Brentano formulated a critique of his own middle period. He died of appendicitis in March, 1917.

Brentano pursued the widest range of interests and hobbies. Playing chess with all-consuming passion, he lost games through fanciful experimentation. An avid gymnast and swimmer, he frequently swam the Danube, and in addition to being an enthusiatic cook and carpenter, he repeatedly tried writing poetry. Fondness for riddles led him to publish his favorites in *Neue Rätsel* (Vienna, 1878; 2d ed., 1909).[4] Although the answers were not disclosed, at Brentano's request the publisher agreed to send them to anyone who would enclose a small contribution for charity. Brentano also investigated optical illusions.[5] His friends included many of the keenest minds in Vienna, among them Theodor Meynert, Theodor Gomperz, Marie von Ebner-Eschenbach, Ferdinand von Saar, and Josef Breuer. Like Anton Bruckner, Brentano was indifferent to dress and food; priestlike he sat through meals intent upon theorizing. Brentano's otherworldliness—as well as his marriage—occasioned a novella by Adolf von Wilbrandt (1837–1911). In "Der Gast vom Abendstern," published in the two-volume *Novellen aus der Heimat* (Breslau, 1882), this director of the Burgtheater portrayed Brentano as a visitor from the plant Venus, whose longing to return there was thwarted by his wife.

In twenty-odd books, Brentano made decisive contributions to exegesis of Aristotle, to empirical psychology, to epistemology, and to ethics. He exerted greatest influence by reviving Aristotle's concept of mental act.[6] In *Psychologie vom empirischen Standpunkt* (Vienna, 1874; 2d ed., Leipzig, 1924), Brentano divided all mental phenomena into three classes of acts *(Seelentätigkeiten)*. First, a presentation *(Vorstellung)* occurs whenever anything is present to consciousness. Here Brentano revived the scholastic term intentionality *(Intentionalität)* to denote the act whereby a mind intends an object. Although this object may be either real or imagined, the act of intending it imparts to it mental existence. Citing Herbart, Brentano insisted that presentation underlies all psychic experience.

As a second category, judgments *(Urteile)* assert or deny the existence of an object presented. Upon this concept, Brentano built several innovations in logic. He declared that all categorical propositions are at bottom existential propositions. A categorical statement such as "All men are mortal" he transposed into the existential statement, "There is no immortal man." Even an axiom in geometry has only a negative character: when we say that "All triangles have 180 degrees," we mean that "There is no triangle that does not have 180 degrees." Brentano further postulated that every existential proposition resolves into two propositions. When we declare that "This flower is yellow," we are saying first, "This flower is," and second "It is yellow." Whereas the first proposition affirms the existence or nonexistence of the subject, the second asserts the existence or nonexistence of certain properties, or predicates. Thus when the axiom "All triangles have 180 degrees" is transposed into its double negative form, it affirms not that triangles exist but that their properties exist. During his middle years, Brentano believed that every object intended by the mind enjoys mental existence, so that contradictory properties such as those of Meinong's golden mountain exist in the mind, albeit not in the external world.

As his third basic category, Brentano posited phenomena of love and hate *(Phänomene der Liebe und des Hasses)*. Any object presented may be regarded with love or with hate. In this act Brentano insisted that will and feeling become indistinguishable.

These doctrines bore fruit above all in empirical psychology. The notion of intentionality was applied to perception by Brentano's Bavarian-born friend Carl Stumpf (1848–1936), who held that every psychic act refers to an object outside itself. Through research on how the mind relates to intended objects Stumpf stimulated his students to develop Gestalt psychology. Brentano, on the other hand, never abandoned psychologism in logic. In construing judgment to be a type of psychic act, he repudiated Bolzano's doctrine of propositions-in-themselves. Instead of enjoying extramental existence, propositions possessed for Brentano exclusively mental existence. Both Meinong and Husserl rejected this view, reviving Bolzano's Platonic conception.

During his later period, Brentano revised his earlier conception of mental existence. Now he argued that only concretely existing objects can be intended by the mind, branding as fictions concepts like being and nonbeing. When the mind thinks of an irreal object like a centaur, what it intends is not—*pace* early Brentano—the properties of a centaur, but the mind of a concrete person thinking about a centaur. Quarreling with the semantics of his loyal student Anton Marty, the later Brentano asserted that connectives in language are mere fictions, comparable to imaginary numbers; their presence in a sentence does not deter the sentence from referring exclusively to concrete things. Oskar Kraus, to whom Brentano wrote these views, admitted ruefully how difficult it is to systematize them. Pressing this thesis in rebuttal against Alfred Kastil and his student Franziska Mayer-Hillebrand, Jan Srzednicki has contended that Brentano invariably philosophized ad hoc, never aspiring to construct a system. It would seem more plausible to conclude that he excogitated several successive systems, as did his disciples Husserl and Ehrenfels.

Less controversy surrounds Brentano's ethical theory. In a lecture during January, 1889, before the Vienna Law Society, he formulated his ethics in reply to those of the jurist Rudolf von Jhering. *Vom Ursprung sittlicher Erkenntnis* (Leipzig, 1889) breathes the pure air of intuitionist ethics. During the year in which G. E. Moore published *Principia Ethica* (1903), that author called Brentano's work "a far better discussion of the most fundamental principles of Ethics than any other with which I am acquainted."[7] Brentano propounded an axiological ethics, centering on the theory of value *(Werttheorie)*, as distinct from the neo-Kantian philosophy of values *(Wertphilosophie)*. Brentano assigned values to the third class of experience: phenomena of love and hate. His ethical maxim paraphrases Bolzano:

> To promote as far as possible the good throughout this great whole . . . is manifestly the right end in life, toward which every act is to be directed. . . .[8]

This "great whole" Brentano defined to include "not merely the self, but also the family, the town, the state, the whole present world of life, even distant future times."[9] This principle of summation of the good *(Summierung des Guten)* recapitulates, said Brentano, the practical wisdom of the golden rule as well as of Kant's categorical imperative and even of Bentham's calculus of pleasures. To know that a thing is good is to assert that love toward that thing is right; similarly to say that a thing is bad to say that hatred of that thing would be right. These views were shared by G. E. Moore, who also endorsed Brentano's opinion that, in the former's words:

> All truths of the form "This is good in itself" are logically independent of any truth about what exists.

> All such ethical truths are true, *whatever the nature of the world may be.*[10]

This lofty conception of ethics echoed Bohemian Reform Catholicism. Like Bolzano, Brentano disputed Kant's deontological ethics as well as Bentham's utilitarian calculus. For both Catholics, the good is that which one can love unconditionally: it must serve the interests of the whole of the universe and should be loved without regard to attainability. In exalting the good of the whole, Brentano strongly influenced Christian von Ehrenfels.

Brentano's ethics of the whole stemmed from unwavering faith in the Providence of God. Even after he had left the church, he continued to pursue Catholic apologetics, without ever—as is sometimes reported —being attracted by Protestantism. For twenty years Brentano lectured on proofs for the existence of God, concluding that indubitably there exists an eternal, creating, and sustaining principle, which he called understanding *(Verstand)*. Although he acknowledged that doubt remains as to whether this principle is infinitely perfect and whether it is unitary, Brentano—the ex-priest—was convinced that it manifests both these qualities.[11] He corresponded at length with another of his students, a German priest Hermann Schell (1850–1906), who as a

professor at Würzburg taught that God is eternal activity, a doctrine
that the Vatican condemned in 1897.[12] Brentano voiced belief in Providence and in life after death in a poem that he had sent to Schell
two years earlier:

> Gott voll Liebe, Quell der Kraft,
> Dann auch wird Dein Reich mir kommen,
> Wenn des Pilgers Knie erschlafft,
> Wenn des Schiffers Stern verglommen.
>
> Immer wird Dein Wort erfüllt,
> Ob ich fordre, ob verzichte;
> Doch ich träum' Dein selig Bild,
> Und mich drängts nach Deinem Lichte.
>
> Und jed' Körnlein meiner Hand
> Und jed' Steinlein, ich vertraue;
> Senkt sich in Dein fruchtbar Land,
> Fügt sich Deinem ew'gen Baue.[13]

* ◆ *

> God, full of love, well of strength,
> Thy Kingdom will come even to me,
> When the pilgrim's knee slackens,
> When the sailor's star has faded.
>
> Thy Word is always fulfilled,
> Whether I demand it or resign myself;
> Still I dream Thy blessed image,
> And I am driven toward Thy light.
>
> And every grain in my hand,
> And every pebble, I avow,
> Sinks into Thy fertile land,
> And fits into Thy eternal frame.

No treatise could summarize so eloquently the faith of Bohemian Reform Catholicism.

As befits adherence to Aristotle, Brentano deemed post-Kantian
idealism a period of decline, dismissing the idealists' cult of originality
as adolescent. In 1895 he formulated a schema of how philosophy had
developed, arguing that it has traversed three cycles of four stages

from Thales to the post-Kantians. During each cycle an initial stage of investigation *(Forschung)* has given way to successive stages of degeneration which he labeled application *(Ausbildung)*, skepticism *(Skepsis)*, and mysticism *(Mystik)*. He periodized the three cycles of antiquity, the Middle Ages, and modernity as follows:[14]

Phase	Ancient	Medieval	Modern
Investigation	Thales to Aristotle	Thomas Aquinas	Bacon to Locke
Application	Stoics, Epicureans	Duns Scotus	The Enlightenment
Skepticism	Skeptics, Eclectics	William of Occam	Hume
Mysticism	Neoplatonists, Neo-Pythagoreans	Lullus, Cusanus	German Idealism

The very opposite of a therapeutic nihilist, Brentano hoped to stem decline by reviving the perennial philosophy of investigation, epitomized by Anaxagoras, Aristotle, Aquinas, and Locke. In 1905 he composed a long poem praising Anaxagoras (499–428 B.C.) as the father of philosophy.[15]

Unwavering dedication to the search for truth as well as willingness to befriend young colleagues, won for Brentano the respect of scholars as diverse as Meinong, Husserl, Ehrenfels, Marty, Kraus, Stumpf, Twardowski, and Masaryk. With them he conducted philosophical dialogue on the highest level, revivifying every question he touched. Of all the branches of philosophy, aesthetics alone left him cold. Rather than found a monolithic school like that of Herbart, Brentano stimulated students to provoke innovations in himself and in one another, as well as to train a second generation of *Enkelschüler*, which included Alois Höfler (1853–1922), Alfred Kastil (1874–1950), Hugo Bergmann (1883–), and Emil Utitz (1883–1957). Although each followed his own bent, these men carried the torch for Brentano by demanding rigorous analysis and by disseminating the concept of intentionality. Through his students, Brentano shattered the grip of Herbartianism on Austrian philosophy.

ALEXIUS MEINONG:
FROM BRENTANO HALFWAY TO BOLZANO

Alexius Meinong (1853–1920) was the first of Brentano's students to become known in England, due largely to the interest of Bertrand

Russell.[16] Born in Lemberg of a Catholic noble family, Meinong studied under Brentano from 1875 to 1878, writing studies of Hume which earned him a doctorate and habilitation. His entire career from 1882 to 1920 he spent as a professor of philosophy at Graz, founding in 1894 Austria's first laboratory of empirical psychology and training numerous disciples. The so-called Graz School of experimental psychology formed around him and such students as Alois Höfler, Stephan Witasek (1870–1915), Vittorio Benussi (1878–1927), and Ernst Mally (1879–1944). He was an amateur musician and composer like Herbart and Boltzmann, and he conducted lengthy correspondence with such friends as Tomáš Masaryk, Friedrich Jodl, and Edmund Husserl.

Meinong paid no attention to his surroundings while executing meticulous analyses in logic and psychology. Starting from Brentano's notion of intentionality, which Meinong rechristened directedness (*Gerichtetsein*), he forged his own theory of objects. In *Über Annahmen* (Leipzig, 1902), Meinong assailed Twardowski's assertion—itself derived from criticism of Bolzano—that ideas such as a golden mountain can have no objects because their content unites incompatible attributes.[17] To clarify the problem of nonexistent objects, Meinong borrowed Ehrenfels' distinction between Gestalt qualities and their foundation (*Fundament*). This foundation Meinong rechristened a founding content (*fundierender Inhalt*) or object of a lower order (*Inferiora*). The Gestalt quality he called, after Ehrenfels, a founded content (*fundierter Inhalt*) or object of a higher order (*Superiora*). Objects of lower order can exist, Meinong held, by themselves, whereas objects of a higher order must have those of a lower object to accompany them. These two objects together form a complex. The gist of Meinong's theory of objects was to assert that although such complexes can be affirmed or denied by the mind, they can never be presented to the mind. This act of affirming or denying complexes can proceed in one of two modes: in an assumption (*Annahme*) a complex is affirmed or denied by supposition, that is, without conviction; in a judgment (*Urteil*) the element of conviction is added. Thus Meinong held that the mind can assume and/or judge the existence of a golden mountain without having a presentation of one. Presentation (*Vorstellung*) he reserved, like Brentano, for existent objects. Objects whose contradictory attributes make their existence impossible cannot be presented, yet they can be thought.

In his theory of objects (*Gegenstandstheorie*), Meinong used Brentano's threefold distinction between a mental act, its content, and the object intended in the act. He carried over Brentano's notion that categorical propositions may affirm the existence of properties, which

Meinong called *Sosein*, without thereby affirming the existence of the object, which Meinong called its *Sein*. Objects that do not exist in space and time are said by Meinong to subsist (*bestehen*). Thus a golden mountain can subsist, but not exist. Moreover, even objects that do exist have attached to them others that merely subsist, as when we speak of the being (*Sein*) of horses. Such abstract entities, which the later Brentano rejected as fictions, Meinong classified as objects that subsist. Russell too found this unsatisfactory; discarding *Sosein*, he held that every statement either affirms or denies *Sein*.

Meinong insisted that the law of contradiction pertains exclusively to existent objects, since objects possessing contradictory properties may in thought subsist side-by-side. These *entia rationis*, which he called objectives (*das Gegenständliche*), go some distance toward Bolzano's propositions-in-themselves. With Bolzano, he held that any object or proposition, whether contradictory or not, can exist in the mind; he did not share Bolzano's view that all such propositions enjoy extramental existence outside of space and time. Against the later Brentano, Meinong enlarged the realm of mental objects. In applying these ideas to ethics, Meinong held that most ethical values subsist but do not exist.

Meinong's terminology dismays the modern reader; he transferred the vocabulary of chemistry to the psyche, speaking of elements, constituents, and moments in a way similar to Mach. To a generation trained on Wittgenstein and Husserl, Meinong's terms seem outdated; we feel less need to vindicate the autonomy of mind against the monism of chemists and physicists. Most of what is valuable in Meinong's distinction between act, content, and object was exploited to the full by Husserl. It fell to this other disciple of Brentano to elaborate a science of mental objects which would win lasting adherence.

EDMUND HUSSERL'S PHENOMENOLOGY:
A SYNTHESIS OF BRENTANO AND BOLZANO

Many disciples of Edmund Husserl (1859–1938) consider Brentano merely as a precursor of their mentor, who himself revered Brentano as the man who had guided him into philosophy.[18] Born in Prossnitz, Moravia, of Jewish parents, Husserl studied from 1876 to 1881 at Leipzig, Berlin, and Vienna under the mathematicians Karl Theodor Weierstrass and Leopold Kronecker. Upon recommendation of his friend Tomáš Masaryk, he returned to Vienna from 1884 to 1886 to hear Brentano. It was Masaryk who persuaded Husserl to convert to Protestantism. At a time when Husserl was still wavering—as Bolzano once had—between philosophy and mathematics, Brentano's lectures persuaded the young mathematician that philosophy merited serious endeavor. With a beginner's fascination, Husserl heard Brentano lecture to law students on ethics, to advanced students on psychology, and to seminars on logic, where the master analyzed Bolzano.

Later Husserl was among the few invited to visit Brentano's home after seminar meetings, and in June, 1886, he enjoyed the signal honor of being Brentano's house guest on the Wolfgangsee. Like many others, the young mathematician-turned-philosopher felt profoundly grateful for Brentano's generosity of time and spirit. His gratitude notwithstanding, Husserl knew that he could never espouse Brentano's psychologism, so that after 1886 their friendship began to cool. During the early 1890's Husserl did visit Brentano, calling upon him again at Florence in 1908. In 1919 Husserl confessed how much he venerated Brentano, having emulated his sense of mission as well as his demand for clarity and logical rigor. Husserl's insistence that but for Brentano he would never have written a word of philosophy is born out by the dedication of his first philosophical work, *Die Philosophie der Arithmetik: Psychologische und logische Untersuchungen* (Halle, 1891). The inscription ran: "To my teacher Franz Brentano: In heart-felt Gratitude" *(In inniger Dankbarkeit).*

Like his fellow Austrian-born philosophers Emil Lask, Johannes Volkelt, and Richard Hönigswald, Husserl pursued his mature career entirely in Germany, teaching at Halle (1887–1901), Göttingen (1901–1916), and Freiburg (1916–1929). With rare singlemindedness, he cultivated a vision of an entirely objective "presuppositionless" philosophy, advancing quickly beyond Brentano and Meinong to a view of logic akin to that of Leibniz and Bolzano. In his first major treatise, the two-volume *Logische Untersuchungen* (Halle, 1900–1901), he attacked the subjective logic of empiricists like J. S. Mill and Herbert Spencer, as well as Ernst Mach's principle of economy. Their psychologism, Husserl argued, abolishes the objectivity of logical structures. Husserl separated psychology from logic by pressing the reductio ad absurdum that results if axioms of logic are held to derive from experience. The law of contradiction itself would have to be discarded whenever men ceased to believe it. On the contrary, says Husserl, this law will remain valid even if no man ever believes it. However much thinkers may distort the notion of God's existence, this proposition remains either absolutely true or absolutely untrue. By denying the very possibility of objective truth, psychologism overstates its case and degenerates into skepticism.

In the *Logische Untersuchungen,* Husserl displayed debts to Brentano, to Frege, and to Leibniz. He distinguished the formal logic of propositions from formal ontology, by which he meant the theory of objects in Meinong's sense. The ex-mathematician affirmed the givenness of mental objects, going beyond Brentano to assert their objective character. Brentano's use of intentionality smacked to Husserl of psychologism. Although Husserl criticized Mach's psychological studies as one-sided, the younger man derived stimulus from corresponding with the physicist.[19] Besides citing Bolzano favorably, Husserl praised Herbart for doctrines that the latter had borrowed from Leibniz so as to refute Kant. In a final section, Husserl constructed a "phenomenological explanation of knowledge," based on Leibniz's *mathesis universalis.*

During lectures at Göttingen between 1901 and 1913 Husserl elaborated his logic into the transcendental phenomenology outlined in *Ideen zu einer reinen Phänomenologie und phänomenologischen Philosophie* (Halle, 1913). Here Husserl announced his great discovery. He had juxtaposed Bolzano's propositions-in-themselves to the early Brentano's notion of intentionality, propounding a dichotomy between what he called noema and noesis. Both of these elements, Husserl averred, are present in every act of consciousness. Noema is Bolzano's timeless proposition-in-itself, which is valid whether or not anyone thinks it, while noesis is Brentano's act whereby the mind intends an object. According to Husserl, what the mind intends in an act of noesis is nothing other than a noema. By venturing to study how the mind intends timeless truths, Husserl opened two complementary paths for examining consciousness: the phenomenologist may scrutinize either the noetic act or its noematic content. In the latter procedure, any proposition that the mind intends can be construed as a noema, valid in itself and protected (or "bracketed") from comparison with external reality. At the same time, each noema yields data about the mind's acts of consciousness. Instead of examining—as in empirical psychology—how the mind records external facts, the phenomenologist inspects its inmost structure.

Husserl shrouded his technique of introspection in esoteric terminology. Consciousness he defined as a correlation between the psychological act of noesis and the atemporal entity intended, to wit, noema. An indefinite number of noetic acts can correspond to a single noema, just as several noemata may be intended in a single act. Husserl further distinguished a perceived object from a perceptual noema, which is that object *as* it is intended in each noetic act of perception. This threefold distinction between object perceived, act of intending (noesis), and the content intended (noema) recapitulated Brentano's trichotomy, which Meinong had also used. A single external object, Husserl added, may occasion many perceptual noemata, as that object is considered from successive points of view. For the phenomenologist, each of these perceptual noemata can be studied as an entity in itself. Husserl next differentiated several modes of givenness whereby noemata may occur in consciousness. A noema of perception may glide into a noema of memory and thence into a noema of reflection. Such noemata comprise a noematic nucleus, where an object's common characteristics are envisioned at different levels of the mind. Throughout, Husserl asserted that consciousness entails an inescapable duality between temporal act and atemporal content. Like Anton Günther, he extolled Descartes for upholding dualism between external world and mind.

Husserl elaborated these and other concepts in massive detail, leaving at the Husserl-Archive in Louvain forty thousand pages of manuscript, many of which have yet to be studied. He pursued his mission with unswerving devotion, convinced that transcendental phenomenology alone can supply a science of mind to salvage modern culture. Like Brentano he yearned to reinstate *philosophia perennis;* even more than Brentano he lived sheltered from daily cares, immersed in a small circle of students at Göttingen and Freiburg. Although abstruse terminology helped restrict his following, Alexander Pfänder, Roman Ingarden, Felix Kaufmann, and Martin Heidegger fashioned his ideas into systems of their own. Max Scheler was influenced by reading Husserl, and Heidegger's many students, such as Jean-Paul Sartre and Karl Löwith, have disseminated the tradition. Roman Catholics have exploited the concept of noema in order to investigate how eternal truths lodge in the mind.

Husserl was so consumed by an inner vision that it seems irrelevant to trace elements in his thought to social conditions in Austria. He was the twentieth century's most uncompromising opponent of incursions by sociology and psychology into philosophy. Withal, he came from a background similar to that of such Jewish sociologists of knowledge as Lukács and Mannheim, as well as such Jewish psychologizers as Wilhelm Jerusalem and Rudolf Eisler. The influence of the mathematician Weierstrass, as well as of Brentano, was decisive in steering Husserl away from that type of thinking. He stands rather with other Austrian followers of Bolzano, such as Melchior Palágyi and Emil Lask. Both the Hungarian Palágyi and the Galician Jew Lask displayed more interest than Husserl in using propositions-in-themselves to reconstruct past thought. Husserl was so caught up in the timeless that he all but ignored history.

THE FORGOTTEN VERSATILITY
OF CHRISTIAN VON EHRENFELS

Next to Husserl, Brentano's most original student—and unlike Husserl utterly neglected by scholars—was Christian Freiherr von Ehrenfels (1859–1932).[20] Although he shone as a composer, dramatist, eugenicist, cosmologist, and theorist of ethics, it is almost exclusively as the father of Gestalt psychology that Ehrenfels is remembered. Born near Vienna, the eldest son of an Austrian nobleman and a French mother, Ehrenfels attended not gymnasium but an Oberrealschule. Spending one year at the Hochschule für Bodenkultur in Vienna, he followed in the footsteps of his grandfather Joseph Michael von Ehrenfels (1767–1843), who had reformed methods of sheep-raising and of apiculture with zeal such as his grandson would bring to eugenics. In October, 1882, Christian transferred his title and rights as heir to a younger brother Bernhard, leaving himself free for literary activity. Christian had been studying counterpoint and harmony under Bruckner, whose other-worldly dedication helped to kindle Ehrenfels' own. So great was Ehrenfels' reverence for Wagner that in 1882 he traveled on foot from Vienna to Bayreuth to hear the premiere of *Parsifal*. During the 1880's Ehrenfels wrote choral dramas for which he sought a composer in vain. Having taken a doctorate at Graz under Meinong in 1885, three years later he earned habilitation under Brentano at Vienna. He married Emma von Hartmann in 1894, and after some years of writing plays and essays, the restless theorist accepted in 1897 a professorship of philosophy at Prague, where he taught until 1929. Exceedingly popular as a lecturer, Ehrenfels broke precedent by conversing with students after class. Every year he offered lectures on Wagner in addition to courses in epistemology and ethics.[21]

Ehrenfels wrote his most famous work, "Über Gestalt-Qualitäten" (1890) while still an independent scholar.[22] In it he argued that we perceive melodies by virtue of a form-quality *(Gestalt-Qualität)*, which inheres in the whole and is more real than individual parts. Ehrenfels took his point of departure from Ernst Mach's *Beiträge zur Analyse der Empfindungen* (Jena, 1886), where the physicist had argued that in music and geometry we perceive what he called tone-forms *(Tonge-stalten)* and space-forms *(Raumgestalten)*. Mach had noted that one can vary the color or size of a circle without detracting from its circularity, that is, its space-form. To clarify this insight, Ehrenfels applied Brentano's doctrine of intentionality: the mind intends Gestalt qualities, supplying them to interpret the foundation *(Fundament)* of data actually perceived. It was Ehrenfels' distinction between foundation and Gestalt quality which Meinong developed into a dichotomy between objects of a lower and of a higher order.

Ehrenfels summarized a lifetime of reflection on form-qualities in an article that he dictated to his wife a few weeks before he died. A form-quality is "that perceived something which is more and other than the mere sum of its constituent parts, although they are essential to its existence."[23] When we listen to a melody, the individual notes are retained in the memory to form a base *(Fundament)*, on which the mind erects a "founded content" *(fundierter Inhalt)* or Gestalt. Although this unifying idea can emerge only in the presence of its base, Ehrenfels held that the mind itself supplies the founded content, which is not actually part of the base. The Gestalt psychologists Wertheimer and Köhler contended conversely that each Gestalt quality is given inextricably with the base, so as to be merely perceived by the mind, as Mach had originally imagined.

Ehrenfels expanded his theory to include a psychology of learning. He differentiated temporal Gestalt qualities such as melodies, motion, and color sequences from nontemporal ones such as musical harmony, spatial structure, and color harmony. Mnemonic devices such as jingles and caricatures embody Gestalt qualities, which the mind retains more easily than their isolated constituents. Since each Gestalt quality furnishes a pattern that the mind can relate to other wholes, intellect functions by interweaving Gestalt qualities, so as to encompass a maximum of data simultaneously. Creative thinking advances by generating constantly broader Gestalt qualities, which impart order to an ever-increasing range of experience.

Within the same year as Ehrenfels, Husserl had arrived at a nearly identical concept, which he called, perhaps less felicitously, figural moment *(das figurale Moment)*. In *Die Philosophie der Arithmetik*, he emphasized the

> especially powerful stimulus which is exercised upon the
> isolating perception by every sort of series, class, or system
> as well as by every configuration based on relations of
> distance and direction.[24]

Husserl remarked that he had coined his term a year before he read Ehrenfels' "penetrating" study, which reached him only as his book was going to press.

The concept of Gestalt quality won world renown not through Ehrenfels or Husserl but through students of Brentano's disciple Carl Stumpf. About 1910 at Berlin, Prague-born Max Wertheimer (1880–1943) developed a Gestalt theory of perception that inspired Wolfgang Köhler and Kurt Koffka. Their fame should not obscure the fact that the concept of Gestalt was devised by the Austrians Mach and Ehrenfels and refined by Wertheimer. It epitomized the preference of Austrian thinkers for interpreting phenomena as a whole. Ehrenfels himself became so preoccupied by ethics, social reform, and cosmology that he scarcely noticed the currency that his concept gained among empirical psychologists.

In psychology, Ehrenfels rejected Brentano's view that feeling *(Gefühl)* and desire *(Begehren)* belong to a common class of love and hate. Desire and feeling, replied Ehrenfels, each may exist without the other, and are as distinct as sensation and feeling.[25] In his two-volume *System der Werttheorie* (Leipzig, 1897–1898), Ehrenfels built this psychology of desire into a systematic axiology, which combined Meinong's theory of objects with Carl Menger's economic theory of value. Whereas Meinong held that an object acquires value because it pleases us, Ehrenfels contended that the things we most value cannot exist, for example perfect justice and complete knowledge.[26] These ideals we cherish not because they please us, but because we yearn to possess them, however vainly. For Ehrenfels as for Menger, value is measured by correlating the strength of desire with the availability of the thing desired. Although the *Werttheorie* provoked wide discussion, it is one of Ehrenfels' least original works. It gave no hint of the radical program of eugenics which its author was soon to espouse.

In more than twenty articles published from 1903 on,[27] Ehrenfels advocated polygamy as a panacea against the degeneration caused by industrialism. Because technology prolongs life for the unfit no less than for the fit, it thwarts natural selection of the most hardy. Large cities breed diseases, like syphilis that denatures heredity, as well as alcoholism that debases parenthood. Women scorn motherhood, indulging in pursuit of pleasure instead of caring for infants. As Gemeinschaft virtues vanished, social diseases would so weaken offspring, Ehrenfels predicted, that after one or two generations mortality rates would resume an upward swing. The sole preventive, Ehrenfels insisted, was to cultivate polygamy, so that the fittest men might conceive children by a variety of robust women. He urged that Europe emulate the Mongols and Muslims in exploiting polygamy by virile men. There being a larger number of suitable mothers than fathers,

Ehrenfels proposed establishing homes where women could rear children in a kind of kibbutz without men. In 1904 Ehrenfels defended against certain neo-Lamarckians Darwin's theory of evolution through selection of minute variations.[28] The eclipse of Darwin's theory he attributed to scientists' preference for detailed work that precluded synthesis. He chided Lamarckians for stubbornly hoping that human nature somehow would change after it had remained unaltered for thousands of years. Max Nordau he dismissed as a witty but ineffectual critic of degeneration. Applying Darwin's theory to eugenics, Ehrenfels urged the ablest men to pass on their useful variations so as to offset leveling (nivellistisch) tendencies.

In Sexualethik (Wiesbaden, 1907), Ehrenfels argued that procreation was being neglected in favor of self-indulgence. It was folly, the philosopher declared, to outlaw prostitution without sanctioning other outlets for sexual desire; only divorce and polygamy could supplant brothels. Although he cited with approval Freud's concepts of sublimation and of screen-images,[29] Ehrenfels desired to excoriate prevailing mores rather than to cure neuroses. Unlike Freud, Ehrenfels espoused sex education for women, ignoring the fact that polygamy entails their subjugation. During December, 1908, the Prague professor delivered two papers before the Vienna Psychoanalytic Society, one criticizing Fritz Wittels' advocacy of free love and the other espousing polygamy. He warned that without such reform the "Mongol" race would doom superior individuals to extinction.[30] As might be expected, the proposal for polygamy dismayed Freudians; the notion was deplored even by periodicals that consented to publish it. Undeterred, Ehrenfels wrote a drama about sexual reform, Die Sternenbraut, which played successfully in Prague until the author became infatuated with one of the actresses. In that city Ehrenfels further discredited himself by denouncing anti-Semitism. Hailing Jews as progenitors of excellence, about 1910 he declared at a university meeting that he had had a Jewish ancestor.[31]

Alarmed as he was over the declining caliber of the race, Ehrenfels was outraged by World War One. War caused counterselection among young men, killing the bravest while sparing the unfit.[32] To assuage his despair, he composed the Kosmogonie (Jena, 1916), which tailored the Leibnizian vision to a Marcionist cosmology. In it Ehrenfels elevated into a metaphysical principle the eugenic premise that men must intervene to forestall degeneration: unless man labors to maximize Gestalt, disorder may engulf the universe. Hailing human intellect as God's partner in a cosmic duel between Gestalt and entropy, Ehrenfels, like Schelling and Teilhard de Chardin, viewed man as cocreator with

God. So crucial was man's role in directing evolution that if he should falter, God's edifice of Gestalt might collapse. Convinced, like Teilhard, that disaster could and would be deterred, Ehrenfels predicted that through technology man soon would effect a quantum leap in the inner coherence of the world.[33] Thus within a Gnostic framework, Ehrenfels renewed Leibnizian faith in the triumph of reason. Although he may have been influenced by Brentano's concept of the Creator, Ehrenfels differed from his teacher in rejecting God's omnipotence. In the eyes of Hugo Bergmann and Felix Weltsch, Ehrenfels' cosmology seemed to defy the disintegration caused by World War One. They overlooked the fact that although Ehrenfels himself eschewed the Marcionist despair of Kafka or Paul Adler, his metaphysics differed little from theirs. An inscrutable power of destruction brooded over their world as over his, with no doctrine of Providence to safeguard the outcome.

Ehrenfels' gnosticism never reached the mystical intensity of the Moravian-born Eugen Heinrich Schmitt (1851–1916). A private scholar at Budapest, Vienna, and Berlin, Schmitt sought, under the influence of Leo Tolstoi, to indoctrinate a Gnostic elite. In his two-volume study, *Die Gnosis: Grundlagen der Weltanschauung einer edleren Kultur* (Jena, 1903–1907), Schmitt advocated a Christian pantheism designed to sway the balance between God and Satan. Both Schmitt and Ehrenfels rank as precursors of Hans Jonas, Hans Joachim Schoeps, Eric Voegelin, and Denis de Rougemont, all of whom have revived the concept of cosmic civil war to explain the catastrophes of our age. With the exception of Jonas, all these men studied at Prague or Vienna: Schoeps helped Brod to edit Kafka, Voegelin was a student of Hans Kelsen during the early 1920's, and de Rougemont studied at Vienna a few years later. Ehrenfels' anticipation of their hypotheses has been all but forgotten.

After completing the *Kosmogonie* in 1916, Ehrenfels succumbed for almost four years to severe depression, which he attempted to allay by studying music and mathematics. He hit upon the mental exercise of constructing ascending series of integers, in which elements of each series were generated by adding elements in the series next above, as follows:

$$1 \qquad 3 \qquad 5 \qquad 7 \qquad 9$$
$$4 \qquad 8 \qquad 12 \qquad 16$$

After two years of toying with such sequences, Ehrenfels formulated in

1919 a pattern that he believed would yield the long-sought law of prime numbers. After another two years of lecturing and writing on the subject, he published *Das Primzahlgesetz entwickelt und darge- stellt auf Grund der Gestalttheorie* (Leipzig, 1922). Although its argu- mentation was too fanciful to convince mathematicians, the essay of- fered some of its author's maturest reflections on Gestalt qualities. Fully recovered from despair, he heralded his discovery as a victory of light over darkness, a token of greater triumphs to come. These hopes for mankind he stated in *Die Religion der Zukunft* (1929), continuing to praise the study of "essential entities" such as integers and musical notes as the only effective balm against earthly woes.

Of the many Austrian thinkers in our century whom scholars have ignored, Ehrenfels may well have been the most original. He recog- nized how technology and social upheaval threatened the contempla- tive ideal of Bohemian Reform Catholicism. For him, Brentano's goal of maximizing the good of the whole necessitated drastic changes in sexual ethics if God was to be saved from disaster. Although he ex- changed the Aristotelian notion of static harmony for a Heraclitean vision of cosmic struggle, Ehrenfels retained Leibniz' conviction that in the end reason would prevail. By resort to Gnostic cosmology, Ehren- fels endeavored to prolong the Leibnizian world view in a world being industrialized and proletarianized. This scion of aristocracy combatted degeneracy by projecting onto the cosmos a vision of noblesse oblige: all men of quality owe it to God to fight on His side against impending chaos. A fervent Darwinist, Ehrenfels discerned a life-and-death strug- gle in every act of procreation, succumbing to that worship of mother- hood which racism entails. Inhabiting a society rent by strife, he viewed the cosmos itself as reflecting a contest between rich and poor, educated and uneducated, German and Czech. However resolutely Ehrenfels labored to avert calamity, not even he foresaw the disaster that was to come.

As a social reformer, this aristocrat stood in the company of such Bohemian-born philanthropists as Coudenhove-Kalergi, Suttner, and Popper-Lynkeus. In his career as a professor, he embodied the inde- pendence of spirit that had animated Bolzano and Brentano. Both through what he created and what he suffered, Ehrenfels provided Catholic Bohemia with one of its most gifted—and most poignant— spokesmen.

Last Exponents of
the Leibnizian Tradition

JOSEF POPPER-LYNKEUS:
ENLIGHTENMENT OPTIMISM IN A BOHEMIAN INVENTOR

BETWEEN 1870 and 1938 several thinkers unconnected to Brentano renewed the Leibnizian tradition. Perhaps the most idiosyncratic was the Jewish inventor, Josef Popper (1838–1921), who dwelt at Vienna from 1858 until his death.[1] Born and raised in the ghetto of Kolin, Popper studied engineering in Prague from 1854 to 1858 before going to Vienna as an official of the railroads. In 1867 he invented a steam valve, the proceeds of which enabled him to retire in 1898 and write independently. A lifelong bachelor, on his deathbed he married his companion of many years so that she might inherit his wealth. He was a close friend of Ernst Mach as well as of Schnitzler, Bahr, and Einstein. His disciples included the feuilletonist Fritz Wittels.

In 1878 Popper proclaimed the first of many utopian proposals in *Das Recht zu leben und die Pflicht zu sterben* (Dresden, 1878; 3d ed., 1903). Sketching a rational society modeled on Voltaire's credo, Popper urged that military service give way to universal alimentary duty *(Nährpflicht)*. Every citizen would serve a term in a nutrition army, which would provide food and shelter gratis to all. Money would function only to purchase luxury goods, which entrepreneurs might manufacture after completing alimentary duty. Popper proposed overturning penal law. Lawbreakers would be subjected to public ridicule instead of serving prison sentences. Popper expected that massive publicity of misdeeds would dissuade miscreants from repeating offenses, and they would be imprisoned only if nothing less could prevent recidivism. A freethinker, Popper propounded a substitute religion rooted in a sense of nature *(Natursinn)*, which entailed reverence for the good of the whole:

> One must awaken the feeling that each man belongs with
> everything else, a direct awareness of unity; each man should
> learn to feel at home in the whole.[2]

Popper advocated secularization of religion, insisting that modern life
requires relinquishing any single cluster of symbols like those of
Christianity. Deeming Spinoza's concept of nature too static, he extolled Beethoven's evocation of nature as infinite and growing.

Popper admired Voltaire as the complete man. In *Voltaire: Eine
Charakteranalyse* (Dresden, 1905), he praised the *philosophe's* capacity
to orchestrate so many interests and reforms. Although Voltaire had
attained supremacy in no field, he had shone in all. Surmounting a
world of specialists and moral cripples, the Frenchman had epitomized
manysidedness and compassion. He deserved, said Popper, a cenotaph,
which the entire globe ought to finance; a band of students should have
the honor of guarding it. It was hoped that such a memorial would
impel others to eradicate evils about which Voltaire had warned.

Popper's proposals culminated in the eight hundred pages of *Die
allgemeine Nährpflicht als Lösung der sozialen Frage* (Dresden,
1912). The nutrition army would guarantee survival to all without
enslaving anyone. Endorsing Edward Bellamy's *Equality* (New York,
1897), Popper urged a program of confiscating private property without indemnity and then restoring some of it in order to produce luxuries. Because food and shelter would abound, spouses need no longer
quarrel; they could pursue art and science instead. Dreading overpopulation, he demanded that abortion or infanticide be used to curb
prolific parents if ever food should be short. Reviving the naiveté of a
Condorcet, Popper believed that an alimentary army could lift ancestral burdens of mankind. His scheme never won serious support, although its blend of capitalism with socialism resembled more moderate
proposals by Anton Menger, Rudolf Goldscheid, and Gustav Ratzenhofer.

Since 1865 Popper had jotted down daydreams and nocturnal fantasies, which after retiring he suddenly decided to publish under the
title *Phantasien eines Realisten* (Dresden, 1899). The first edition of
this two-volume work bore the pseudonym Lynkeus, a name that
Popper may have borrowed from the watchman in Goethe's *Faust*,
Part Two, Act Five. Obliged to behold a conflagration that he cannot
stem, Goethe's Lynkeus first serenades the cosmos and then laments
man's ephemerality. Saul Rosenzweig has speculated that the sobriquet
alludes to the Order of the Golden Fleece, which Philip the Good of
Burgundy had founded in the fifteenth century and which had become the most prestigious lay order of the Habsburg Empire.

Because one of the eighty-odd pieces, "Gärende Kraft eines Geheimnisses," concerned incest between mother and son, culminating in
the murder of a priest, *Phantasien* was confiscated at Vienna in 1900.
A threat of prosecution only aided its success, for by 1921 *Phantasien*
had gone through twenty-one printings; to flaunt his pseudonym, the
author began calling himself Popper-Lynkeus.

Phantasien is best known for analogies with Freud's *Traumdeutung*
(1900), which Fritz Wittels pointed out to Freud in the early 1920's.
Although Freud declined an invitation to meet Popper, he respected
Popper's work, freely acknowledging affinities with him.[3] One ten-page
feuilleton in *Phantasien*, "Träumen als Wachen," echoed a premise of the
Traumdeutung that dreams reflect unconscious impulses through a
discernible structure. The protagonist explains how dreams distill
memories, usually those of being in harmony with the universe or of
guilt toward persons one has injured. Besides asserting that no one
can ever dream nonsense, because "it is always the same man whether
he wakes or dreams," Popper used the sketch to announce his own
version of the golden rule: whenever angry at a friend or relative, one
should imagine how grieved one would feel at his or her decease.
Although Popper lacked any notion of dreams as wish-fulfillment,
several times he dramatized the power of sexual fantasy. In "Ehe-
bruchsszene," a stranger obsessed by female infidelity stabs a blind
man's wife whose kindly glance he suspects is an invitation to adultery;
while in the hallucinatory "Nach der Trauung," a fiancé becomes obsessed by visions of his wife's finger boring into his chest. In a scene
reminiscent of Sacher-Masoch, "König Salomo als Maus" depicts King
Solomon as a lover trembling before a sadistic temptress, who per-
suades him to become a mouse and to jump into her mouth.

Similarities between Popper and Freud, however, should not be exaggerated. The theme of "Gärende Kraft eines Geheimnisses" seems
less maternal incest than anticlericalism. In order to initiate her son, a
Florentine widow sleeps with him, bearing a daughter, whose paternity
becomes a topic of gossip. So as to steel herself against divulging the
secret, the widow confesses it to a friar at Savonarola's monastery, and
when the friar refuses to hear her out, she stabs him to death—through
the ear. After spies have ferreted out the motive, Savonarola has
mother and son burned at the stake, leaving a solitary voice to object
that incest does not concern the state—Machiavelli. In this philosophical tale worthy of Voltaire, Popper wished to decry clerical abuses
rather than to probe motives for incest. In a longer dialogue, "Nach der
Predigt," also set at Florence in 1493, Popper had Leonardo, Michelangelo, Botticelli, and Machiavelli debate a sermon by Savonarola. As

they rehearse anticlerical arguments, Leonardo flays the Inquisition for having mocked the commandment to love one's neighbor. Leonardo also sympathizes profoundly with the Virgin Mary, while Machiavelli wishes that laity had arraigned bishops who ordered heretics killed. In other sketches, Popper was preoccupied with intactness, describing in "Grenzen der Liebe" how a repellant hand destroyed a lover's sense of his beloved's beauty. In "Der Todesstunde," Popper preached that the whole life, not the moment of death, embodies what we live for. In "Die Stadt der Liebe," bells ring at the moment of childbirth rather than at the time of death, and there is a cemetery set apart for lovers.

Although Popper was unusually concerned with the subconscious, his interest in dreams never led him to formulate a systematic psychology. Instead, his fantasies reiterate such Voltairean themes as anticlericalism, respect for human life, and hatred of coercion. Popper elaborated a priori schemes of social improvement, convinced that problems could and would be solved. Popper's benevolence prevented him from assailing therapeutic nihilists. He hoped betterment would come of its own accord.

OTHMAR SPANN:
VIRTUOSO OF CORPORATIST THOUGHT

One of the most maligned of Austrian theorists was the sociologist-philosopher, Othmar Spann (1878–1950).[4] Apart from a few students, his Catholic vision of society has found scant favor. The son of a small businessman who lived near Vienna, Spann studied at Realgymnasium there before attending universities at Vienna, Zürich, Bern, and Tübingen, where he earned a doctorate in 1903. After working for some years at a research institute in Frankfurt, he received his habilitation in 1908. From 1909 to 1919 he served as a professor of political economy at Brünn, where he succeeded fellow exponent of holistic economics, Vienna-born Friedrich von Gottl-Ottlilienfeld (1868–1958). After being wounded during World War One, from 1919 to 1938 Spann taught at the University of Vienna. In 1936, S.S. leader Reinhard Heydrich tried unsuccessfully to recruit Spann and his followers as Nazi propagandists. As soon as the Catholic foundation of Spann's thought became obvious, he was deprived of his professorship in 1938 and briefly imprisoned. From 1945 to 1950 he lived in retirement in the Burgenland, falsely branded a Nazi-sympathizer.

As mentioned previously, it was Spann who elevated Karl Pribram's distinction between individualism and universalism into a full-fledged social philosophy. In reviving Adam Müller's (1779–1829) conception of Gemeinschaft society, he asserted the Baroque-Biedermeier faith of Bolzano and Herbart in a social order built upon eternal law. In a similar vein, poems by his Franconian-born wife Erika Spann-Rhein-isch (1880–) celebrate the mysticism of Angelus Silesius and Para-celsus.

Spann analyzed the relation of the individual to society in terms of what he called pairing (Gezweiung), a concept that he modeled on Müller's notion of polarity (Polarität). Spann recalled that around 1900 Müller was so little known that only by accident did he in 1907 stumble upon the three volumes of Elemente der Staatskunst: Öffent-liche Vorlesungen (Berlin, 1809–1810).[5] In affirming the priority of the family, Müller had argued—while sketching a Catholic nature philoso-phy comparable to Schelling's—that the pairing of man and woman furnishes the basis of society. For Müller, other key dualities included youth and age, as well as man and God. Similarly, Spann argued that mental life arises from interaction of pairings such as mother and child, teacher and student, artist and audience. Because neither member can play his role without the other, a pair transcends either of its parts. However indispensable, each part is inferior to the whole.

Spann's universalism consists in assessing all phenomena from the vantage of the whole rather than that of its constituents. Reviving an argument dear both to Catholic apologetics and to Hegel, Spann in-sisted that universalism does not demean individualism in the way that individualism ignores the whole; rather universalism incorporates the perspective of the individual into a larger framework. Individualism, said Spann, jettisons the proposition that individuals flourish only in community. Like Herbart—and Max Adler—Spann held that each mind grows by responding to what others evoke in it. Far from being self-sufficient, each mind is a torch that must be lit from outside itself.

Spann began to emphasize the distinction between part and whole after studying statistics on illegitimate births at Frankfurt in 1905. Applying Rickert's distinction between causal analysis in natural science and the holistic-genetic method of history, Spann found that illegitimacy acquires an entirely different meaning depending on whether one traces its causes in the behavior of individuals, such as adultery, or weighs its consequences for society as a whole, to wit disinheritance and criminal tendencies in the children.[6] Just as Anton Menger argued that the bourgeoisie seeks to perpetuate laws penaliz-ing illegitimacy, Spann contended that focusing on causes may mask consequences. Individualistic social science cannot fathom the wholes that pervade society.

In keeping with Bohemian Reform Catholicism, Spann sought to reconstruct past social thought by resort to eternal categories. For him, the most fundamental of these is the polarity of universalism versus individualism. Unfortunately, it is not clear whether it was Spann or Karl Pribram who suggested these terms. Whereas in 1905 Spann differentiated deduction, or study of fundamentals *(Grundsätze)* from induction or empiricism, in 1911 he discussed universalism versus individualism without mentioning Pribram's article of 1908 which had expounded the latter terms.[7] Coining terms reminiscent of Buber and Ebner, Spann saluted idealism as the philosophy congenial to universalism because it recognizes a "Higher than thou" *(Über Dir)*, whereas empiricism, ally of individualism, denies any hierarchy of entities surmounting the individual.[8] Expositing a deductive system similar to that of Aristotle and Aquinas, Spann construed the whole as a final cause from which subtotalities derive purpose. Social science can infer knowledge of subtotalities not from experiment, but only from some higher totality. The structure of an economic system, for example, must be deduced from the structure of the society it serves. Flouting rules of empirical sociology, Spann's social science propounds norms on the ground that no one can explain how something works without first having understood what it seeks to be. Function follows *telos.*

For all his eagerness to turn social science on its head, Spann grounded his thought in theology. In *Geschichtsphilosophie* (Jena, 1932), which was dedicated to the memory of Schelling and Novalis, Spann celebrated their mysticism together with that of Augustine. Contending that creation affords the central concept of social life, Spann offered a traditional Catholic classification of three aspects of creation: first, God's initial creation of the universe and of man; second, God's ongoing creation known as Providence; and third, man's capacity of co-creation infused through inspiration *(Eingebung)*. The whole is paramount: each creature derives meaning by relating to the entirety. Spann climaxed his affirmation of Providence with a sublime vision:

> In the Creation God wills Himself, and therefore the world can will only God. That is, the mystical core of all history and of pairing discloses that we have worked not only for ourselves but for the whole, and for God, the Lord of the Harvest.[9]

Radiating the faith of Leibniz and Bolzano, Spann rebutted the Marcionism of Prague, convinced that God defies reproach. Providence holds sway, benevolent and omnipotent.

Almost without exception, Socialists have labeled Spann a Fascist. In an article of 1936, the usually judicious Karl Polanyi stigmatized Spann as a Fascist Hegel, who lacked the revolutionary dynamic inherent in the German.[10] By failing to distinguish *is* from *ought*, Spann made himself a fellow traveler of fascism. In portraying a holistic society more all-enveloping than Hegel's ever was, Spann had modeled society, said Polanyi, not on a person but on a corpse. The universalist envisioned a totally reified society, repugnant to liberal and Socialist alike. Having jettisoned all individualism—a verdict in which Polanyi erred—Spann thereby scuttled the doctrine of Christian individualism that personality possesses infinite value. Whereas, the critic concluded, Spann ought to have assailed atheist individualism as preached by Max Stirner or Friedrich Nietzsche, the universalist had cast his net too wide, ensnaring his own allies.

Spann's protestations notwithstanding, Polanyi recognized that if hard pressed Spann would sacrifice individualism to the totality. This travesty could occur because Spann scarcely heeded practical consequences of his philosophy. He labored so diligently to classify doctrines, that he overlooked what was unfolding around him. Universalism, which Spann intended to be descriptive rather than prescriptive, offered willy-nilly a model of totalitarian society. Small wonder that Heydrich, no less than Polanyi, regarded Spann as a potential Nazi. Although Spann would have preferred to inhabit the kind of Gemeinschaft society romanticized by Adam Müller, slowly he recognized the difference between Müller's Biedermeier idyll and Hitler's police state. However culpable his delay may have been, Spann shared political naiveté with countless other professors in Germany and Austria, for whom studying the history of ideas had obfuscated political reality.

Spann renewed the tradition of holistic thought which had animated Bohemian Reform Catholicism. As heir of Leibniz, Bolzano, and the Herbartians, he revived a vision that other Austrian thinkers such as Mach, Neurath, and Carl Menger had worked to supplant. As a historian of ideas, Spann wielded astonishing breadth of learning with rare dialectical skill. His scholarship cut deeper than Ehrlich's, while ranging wider than Kelsen's or Schumpeter's. As stubbornly as they, he refrained from prescribing remedies for specific problems, so that perched above the fray he seemed a bugbear to all combatants. If Pribram expounded the dichotomy between Gemeinschaft and Gesellschaft from an individualistic point of view, Spann surveyed it even more magisterially from the opposite standpoint. Although his social science falters in interpreting present or future, it is a powerful tool for elucidating past thought. As earnestly as anyone in the twentieth century, Spann empathized with the Biedermeier mentality, revitalizing its encyclopedism, its faith in Providence, its love of the past, and its indifference to political vicissitudes. Had he lived a century earlier, Spann would have been honored as a sage; a prodigy born too late, he deserves acclaim for having restored a tradition all but lost.

THE DEATH THROES OF
LEIBNIZIAN METAPHYSICS: HERMANN BROCH

The Jewish novelist Hermann Broch (1886–1951) was also an exponent of the renewed Leibnizian philosophy. In essays, many of them published posthumously, this lonely thinker revealed himself as a metaphysician of considerable rigor, who used Platonic categories in order to diagnose the spiritual ills of modernity. The phrase "gay apocalypse" *(fröhliche Apokalypse)* is one of many oxymorons generated by Broch's interplay of irreconcilable opposites.[11]

Born in Vienna, the son of a wealthy textile manufacturer who had come from Olmütz in northern Moravia, from 1908 to 1927 Broch managed the family business. As a student at the Technische Hochschule, he admired the writings of Otto Weininger, and he resented as keenly as did Ludwig Wittgenstein the upper bourgeois circles in which both moved. In 1908 Broch converted to Catholicism, probably to please his wife. Thereafter he bewailed the cleavage of empirical science from speculative philosophy for which he blamed Mach and Boltzmann. Having resolved in 1928 to live as an independent writer, he embarked for three years on study of mathematics, philosophy, and psychology in order to train himself to discourse on what he called the psychology of the masses *(Massenpsychologie)*. In 1938, after a brief imprisonment, he emigrated to the United States, where at a killing pace he churned out novels and treatises.

One of the most resolute of twentieth-century Platonists, Broch carried dualism almost to the point of Marcionism. In the essay "Leben ohne platonische Idee" (1932),[12] he excogitated Platonic dichotomies to delineate the modern predicament. His basic polarity was that between matter and spirit: matter, he specified, is an irrational force that impels heroes, while spirit is a rational force that guides the church. The hero, said Broch, seeks to implement with blood that dominion over the earth which the church once exercised in a spiritual, that is, Platonic, way. Once society has ceased to believe in a Platonic order of ideas, nothing can prevent people from worshiping a hero. In the realm of ideas, the desacralized hero finds a counterpart in the intellectual, who, like Julien Benda's *clerc*, wants so keenly to shed binding laws that he embraces heresy. For Broch, every secular intellectual is a heretic, just as every heró is a renegade against Platonic order.

Having stipulated these definitions, Broch disclosed how secular dictatorship parodies and replaces the church's universal dominion of the spirit. Because religion seeks above all to overcome death, the hero too must confront and conquer death. This he does by annihilating weaker persons so as to endow survivors with greater freedom. A dictator exercises demagogic charm by proclaiming at once a desire to liberate his people and constant readiness to face death. Dealing in death becomes a dictator's trademark whereby he dupes secularized men into annointing him with charisma formerly enjoyed by the church. The intellectual, once he has jettisoned the Platonic world, stands helpless before the blandishments of this merchant in death. Heedlessly the intellectual rallies to the dictator's side, as together they set out to conquer the world.

Scarcely veiled allusions to Hitler abound in this essay of 1932, which owes its originality to unflinching use of stipulated definitions. These Broch applied to society with the rigor of a metaphysician. Using dichotomies as crisp as those of Weininger, Broch seemed to mock the delight that thinkers like Buber and Kelsen took in polar opposites. Having anatomized the cosmos into two principles that no legerdemain can compromise, he berated the modern world for having spurned the higher of the two. Broch permitted no third form to mediate his opposites: spirit and matter, order and anarchy, love and sexuality, community and mass are cleft from all eternity. Through unswerving demand for vanished perfection, Broch echoed Nietzsche whose readiness to improvise key terms he also shared. The Viennese Platonist spun improvisations, which in form resemble those of the early Lukács.

By repudiating the modern world, Broch conceptualized a despair similar to that of Albert Ehrenstein and Karl Kraus. His pessimism further resembled that of Schopenhauer's disciple, the North German characterologist, Julius Bahnsen (1830–1881), who saw man as impaled on a Hobson's choice between activity and contemplation.[13] Although only together can these opposites satisfy man, fate, sighed Bahnsen, requires each individual to choose one or the other. Although Broch himself elected first the active and later the contemplative life, he could never forgive the majority of his contemporaries for having deified the active life. Broch deemed a combination of action and contemplation indispensable but impossible. The result was a *reductio ad absurdum:* Platonic metaphysics had degenerated into therapeutic nihilism. Viewing himself as the last of his kind, the quixotic Broch wrote himself to death, struggling to convince an elite how loss of transcendence had impoverished them. His theorizing did nothing either to assuage his own despondency or to salvage the world he mourned. A self-fulfilling prophecy, his Platonic metaphysics cast a deathly glow on what little remained of the Leibnizian vision.

22

Aristocrats as Philanthropists

BERTHA VON SUTTNER:
APOSTLE OF PEACE

As IF TO perpetuate Reform Catholicism, a few members of Bohemia's nobility sponsored social movements even after 1900. None did so more ardently or graciously than Bertha von Suttner (1843–1914).[1] It was she who persuaded her friend Alfred Nobel (1833–1896) to endow the Nobel Peace Prize, of which she became the fifth recipient in 1905. Born in Prague just after her father's death, Countess Kinsky grew up in aristocratic leisure until indigence forced her to pursue a career, at first unsuccessfully as a singer and then more successfully as a music teacher. In 1873 she took a position in the Vienna home of Baron von Suttner, where she fell in love with the son of the house, Arthur. Because his parents opposed the marriage, she took refuge at Paris in 1875, working as private secretary to Nobel.

In 1876 she and her beloved eloped from Vienna to the Russian Caucasus, where Bertha was appalled by the suffering of Russian soldiers during the Russo-Turkish War of 1877-1878. She converted her home at Tiflis into a hospital for the wounded and resolved to devote the remainder of her life to preventing war. Upon returning to Vienna in 1885, she began to write pacifistic novels, of which *Die Waffen Nieder! Eine Lebensgeschichte* (Dresden, 1889), became a best seller. In this naturalistic narrative of the wars of 1866 and 1870, she described her own experience at Tiflis, dramatizing the anguish of women whose husbands and sons die or get mutilated on the battlefield. In 1890 she founded the Austrian Peace Society, and from 1892 to 1899 she edited, together with a Jewish bookdealer Alfred Fried (1864–1921), a journal entitled *Die Waffen Nieder!*. In a gesture unprecedented for a woman during the 1890's, she had printed on her calling card the fact that she had written the book of this title. During the 1890's her movement won endorsement from such writers as Mór

Jókai and Peter Rosegger, as well as from the anticlerical philosophers Bartholomäus von Carneri and Josef Popper-Lynkeus. Hungarian intellectuals took an especially active role.

In 1891 Bertha's husband led in founding the Vienna branch of the Union for Defence Against Anti-Semitism *(Verein zur Abwehr des Antisemitismus)*. Other adherents of the gentile "Anti-Anti's" included Marie von Ebner Eschenbach, Theodor Billroth, and Johann Strauss. Although dispirited by the death of her husband in 1902, Suttner continued to write and lecture tirelessly in the cause of peace. She was laboring to prepare a Peace Congress scheduled to meet at Vienna in August, 1914, when death overtook her—one week before the shooting at Sarajevo.

Baroness von Suttner was remarkable not only for indefatigable energy but also for a prescient analysis of how technology was altering warfare. In 1899 she described total war with uncanny accuracy, predicting advances in technology similar to those that Mór Jókai had foreseen in his *Novel of the Coming Century* (1872). The war of the future would be total, she wrote, because it was no longer mere armies but entire nations that fought. Hundreds of thousands would perish, only to be replaced by others: "Army, reserve, militia—the aged, children, women—one after the other is slaughtered; what still lives becomes the prey of famine, of the infallible pestilence . . ."[2] Campaigns would be waged using long-range cannons, manned air balloons, submarines with torpedos, mines, and sabotage against trains and factories. Territory would not merely be captured; it would be devastated.

To promote peace, Suttner strove to enlist support of women. She cited an episode from the eve of the Warsaw uprising of 1863 when at a party of the elite, the men had agreed that rebellion was utterly futile. When they informed their wives that they had decided to cancel plans for insurgency, the women reviled them as unworthy of Polish manhood. If these women had not nurtured false ideals of military glory, Suttner argued, Poland could have averted the bloodbath of 1863.[3] Like those who campaigned to eliminate dueling, Suttner believed that a shift of women's approval from soldiers to men of peace could deter future wars. After 1900, she feared above all a universal war that could destroy civilization. Although the Hague Peace Conference, convened by Tsar Nicholas II from May 18 to July 29, 1899, had raised hopes, these were dashed by the Boer War.[4] The Permanent Court of Arbitration established at the conference hardly sufficed to stem the galloping arms race. Thereafter Suttner redoubled efforts to rally support for peace.

Determined to prove that an individual could influence events, Baroness von Suttner radiated the opposite of therapeutic nihilism. In debate before the Pacifist Club of the University of Vienna, she disputed a contention by Wilhelm Stekel that no single person could alter history.[5] Although convinced of the utility of her efforts, she respected men like Ludwig Gumplowicz whose belief in inevitability of conflict contradicted her own. Like another Viennese philanthropist, Hans Wilczek (1837–1922), she confined campaigns to extrapolitical forums; only rarely did she emulate Theodor Herzl in trying to sway monarchs. Through selfless dedication and a spirit of noblesse oblige, she endeavored to offset the Phaeacianism of her countrymen, demonstrating to what extent a citizen could overcome inertia and indifference.

RICHARD COUDENHOVE-KALERGI:
POLITICAL ECUMENIST

Another continuator of Bohemian noblesse oblige has been Richard Nikolaus Coudenhove-Kalergi (1894–), who, since the early 1920's, has led the Pan-Europe movement. His father, Heinrich Coudenhove-Kalergi (1859–1906), who had married a Japanese woman, led a life of unusual variety and fulfillment, serving first in the diplomatic corps and then residing on his estate in southwest Bohemia. A world traveler who spoke sixteen languages, the elder Coudenhove-Kalergi believed in travel as the only means of prolonging life. While touring, he said, one gained so many new impressions that each day one lived more fully than one could at home. Unlike the footloose Count Adalbert Sternberg, Coudenhove-Kalergi rejoiced in his estate, whose joys his son has described:

> Such a life combined health with security, dignity, wealth, leisure, and independence, giving ample opportunity to do much good to a whole region and, at the same time, govern a tiny kingdom of one's own without political responsibilities. Close contact with nature, with plants and animals, together with all the elements of real culture made a beautiful, artistic and easy way of life.[6]

Although the Coudenhove-Kalergi family numbered ancestors from Crete and Brabant by way of Russia and Paris, it epitomized values of Bohemian Reform Catholicism: altruism, piety, and oneness with nature. These qualities animated Heinrich Coudenhove-Kalergi's treatise,

Das Wesen des Antisemitismus (Berlin, 1901), which interpreted anti-Semitism as a product of religious rather than economic hatred. Having opened the book with a fifteen-page poem celebrating Enoch, the author closed by confessing that once he too had been an anti-Semite. After surveying Jewish history, he branded every sort of anti-Judaism unchristian. At a time when some Bohemian nobles were fanning anti-Semitism, Coudenhove-Kalergi recanted earlier sympathy with it, displaying the irenicism that would distinguish his son.

Richard Nikolaus Coudenhove-Kalergi was born in Tokyo.[7] In 1896 the family returned to their Bohemian estate, where the sons grew up between Czech and Sudeten-German populations, a few miles from Bavaria. Not only did Richard's mother have to struggle to learn Western ways, but the death of her husband in 1906 required her to guide her sons' education. Having grown up among advocates of Pan-Slavism and Pan-Germanism, Coudenhove-Kalergi viewed World War One as a collision between these imperialist ideologies. Imbued with the cosmopolitanism of his father and aided by his wife, the actress Ida Roland (1881–1951), in 1923 he founded at Vienna the Pan-Europe movement, which drew inspiration from Alfred Fried's study of the Pan-American Union. In *Paneuropa* (Vienna, 1924), Coudenhove-Kalergi argued that because the World War had abolished Europe's hegemony, World Powers would supersede Great Powers. England already enjoyed global authority thanks to her colonies, as did Russia by controlling the Eurasian landmass. Japan's emergence as a World Power soon would liberate Asia from European dominance, so that China too could assume privileged status. In 1924 the leading World Power was the United States, which must decide to abet or impede unification of Europe. To forestall war, Coudenhove-Kalergi envisioned five constellations of power: Pan-Europe would link continental countries with French possessions in Africa; Pan-America would consist of North and South America; the British Empire would circle the globe; Russia would span Eurasia; while Japan and China would control most of the Pacific. The only hope for a Europe devastated by war was to federate along lines that Aurel Popovici and others had proposed for Austria-Hungary. Pan-Europe would encompass a more flexible Austria-Hungary, one capable of competing with other World Powers. English would serve as world language, spoken by everyone in addition to his native tongue. An adept of geopolitics, Coudenhove-Kalergi repulsed utopians who wished to disseminate Esperanto, a language which a Jewish eye doctor from Warsaw, Ludwik Lazar Zamenhof (1859–1917), had published in 1887.

Coudenhove-Kalergi urged that capitalism and communism cross-fertilize each other just as the Protestant Reformation had spurred the Catholic church to regenerate itself. More hopefully than Friedrich von Wieser, he predicted that individualism and socialism would learn to cooperate instead of compete. A foretaste of this cooperation he discerned in industrial technology, whose mass production makes inventors the surest benefactors of the masses.[8] He lauded America's mass production as a greater step toward well-being than Russia's communism could provide. Technology also offers the first effective means of controlling nature and of stemming overpopulation. Technology makes it imperative that men be educated to assist one another, now that famine and warfare have been outdated. At a time when many Austrians were decrying how mechanized warfare had defaced the earth, Coudenhove-Kalergi praised the potential for good in technology.

Coudenhove-Kalergi combined during the early 1920's what was soundest in prophecies of expressionism with the ecumenism of his father. The result was a vision, at once prescient and premature, which anticipated many issues of the next fifty years. Just as Bertha von Suttner had foreseen the horrors of World War One without being able to forestall it, so Coudenhove-Kalergi forecast the prostration of Europe between Russia and the United States. During the 1950's when hopes for European federation came nearest to fruition, once again the opportunity was lost. Unabashed and anything but cynical, Coudenhove-Kalergi, like Alexis de Tocqueville and József Eötvös, displayed the foresight that an aristocrat above the battle can bring to political analysis. Rooted in the past while desiring a better future, he illuminated this hapless century with optimism from an earlier era.

23

Social Darwinists
as Subverters of
the Leibnizian Tradition

AMONG THE nearly forgotten theorists of the Habsburg Empire were several Social Darwinists who anticipated later trends in sociology. Two of them, Ludwig Gumplowicz and Gustav Ratzenhofer, gained wide hearing in the United States, while a third, Houston Stewart Chamberlain, won notoriety. All three evinced concern for the good of society as a whole; their secular parody of Bohemian Reform Catholicism would be put into practice by totalitarianism.

Descended from a family of rabbis, Ludwig Gumplowicz (1838–1909) was born and educated in the strife-torn city of Krakow. In 1862 he took a law degree there after several years of study at Vienna.[1] As an attorney in Krakow, he defended an anti-Habsburg revolutionary, having befriended in 1863 insurgents rebelling against Russian Poland. In 1866 Gumplowicz was denied a habilitation by the Krakow Faculty of Law on the grounds that his Polish patriotism precluded scholarly objectivity. The frustrated lawyer turned to journalism, founding the Polish paper *Kraj (Fatherland)* to assail Goluchowski's pro-Habsburg clericalism. While editing the paper from 1869 to 1874, Gumplowicz was unable to win the Polish and Jewish middle class to the cause of anticlerical nationalism. An embittered failure at age thirty-six, he took the advice of a former teacher, Gustav Demelius, to apply for a teaching post at Graz, which he won in 1876 with the dissertation *Rasse und Staat*. At about this time he converted to Protestantism.

As a docent and then a professor at Graz, Gumplowicz followed closely events in Galicia, besides reading with passion poets of Young Germany such as Heine and Gutzkow. Gumplowicz inspired his son Maximilian Ernst Gumplowicz (1864–1897) to become a docent of Polish literature at Vienna. In 1897 the son was jailed for traducing the state, which young Maximilian in an extension of his father's theory had called "a legally organized band of robbers." Convinced like Weininger that he could never rectify social wrongs, young Gumplowicz killed himself in prison. Although this blow shattered the older man, he found energy to edit his son's papers on the Khazar origin of Polish Jews, as well as to pour forth his own writings. As we have mentioned, the son's suicide had no bearing on Gumplowicz's own, which he committed together with his invalid wife in August, 1909, to forestall death by cancer of the tongue.

Rasse und Staat, retitled in a revised edition *Der Rassenkampf* (Innsbruck, 1883; 2d ed., 1909), earned Gumplowicz a reputation as *le terrible Autrichien.* He argued that every state had originated in a struggle between a conquering and a conquered race. By race he meant not an ethnic group in Gobineau's sense but any group or class, be it racial, national, or economic, which struggled for mastery over another. The competing nationalities in which Austria-Hungary abounded were all races. To explain this Hobbesian strife, Gumplowicz postulated a polygenetic theory of the origin of man. He held that across the earth a number of tribes had emerged independently of one another. Whenever one of these tribes migrated, it would conquer another, founding a state whose victims underwent first slavery and then serfdom. Gradually as conqueror and conquered developed common bonds of language, economic interest, and family, the two tribes would fuse into a nation. Descendants of the original two tribes would be differentiated into an upper class and a lower class, ruled by a single law.

Gumplowicz devised his theory of rule by conquest in order to rationalize failure as a nationalist in Galicia. He incorporated into sociology two myths current among Polish nobles. First was the legend that the three races of Poland descended from the sons of Noah: the aristocracy from Jephtha, Slav peasants from Ham, and German Jews from Shem. A second theory held that the aristocracy descended from Norman conquerors, while peasants derived from autochthonous Slavs. By exploiting oral traditions that equated class with race and rule with conquest, Gumplowicz could explain the refusal of Polish peasants and Jews to back a nationalist movement that they associated with aristocrats.

Frustration as an agitator made Gumplowicz into a therapeutic nihilist. In contrast to József Eötvös, who held a similar view about the would-be imperialism of every nationality, Gumplowicz believed that little could be done to alleviate strife in Austria-Hungary. He belittled reform proposals like those of Karl Renner, Otto Bauer, and Aurel Popovici, warning that:

> Human "freedom" is but the freedom of the captive lion to run to and fro in his cage and to follow the menagerie, cage and all, hither and thither, through city and country.[2]

Like most Galician Poles, Gumplowicz abhorred Russia. In *Sociologie und Politik* (Leipzig, 1892), he vilified the Asian hordes massing against Europe. He proposed that France and Germany form an alliance to isolate Russia from her buffer states by wooing Finland, Poland, Romania, and Bulgaria.

Gumplowicz has acquired an undeserved reputation as a racist. In spurning Gobineau's distinction between healthy and degenerate races, Gumplowicz repudiated use of war as a eugenic device. He resolved Marx's theory of economic conflict into struggle for rule, not wealth. His doctrine of statecraft postulated a double standard of morality, established by segregating public from private law. Among states, Hobbesian morality prevails—for them force acknowledges no higher authority—while for individuals there stands a constitutional framework of private rights, which each state grants its citizens in order to maximize prosperity.

As a professor of law, Gumplowicz was among the first to introduce systematic sociology to Austria. His theory of the origin of government has been adopted by such German sociologists as Franz Oppenheimer, Alfred Weber, and Alexander von Rüstow, as well as by the historian Eduard Meyer. Gumplowicz shared the sociologism of Durkheim, holding that what thinks and acts in a man is not individuality but collectivity. Arguing that sociology studies the "mutual relations and reciprocal effects of unlike social groups," Gumplowicz contended that

> we can never conceive of man as an isolated being; for he never can exist in isolation.[3]

Opposing the individualism of Carl Menger's economics and of the Austro-Marxists, Gumplowicz defended sociology as a science of group behavior that must be a contemplative, not a policy-making discipline.

As if to ignore the therapeutic nihilism inherent in his sociology, Gumplowicz was in private life a high-minded idealist, buoyant in spirit and singularly devoted to his invalid wife. Gumplowicz respected the opinions of those who impugned him. In 1896 he wrote to Bertha von Suttner that although he could not endorse her "beautiful idea" of ending war, he wanted her to persevere, oblivious to criticism such as his own.[4] Gumplowicz explained his ebullience by redefining optimism and pessimism:

> The pessimist in world-philosophy is usually an optimist in life. The troublous course of the world does not surprise him, he expects nothing better; he knows that the world is evil, that it cannot be otherwise. . . . The case is different with the optimist in world-philosophy. Convinced that things might be better if man will only better himself, . . . he experiences constantly new disappointments and falls from one despair into another. The optimist in world-philosophy usually presents to us in life the picture called up by the word "pessimist."[5]

Here Gumplowicz displayed a fascination with latent meanings worthy of Viennese impressionism, while in delineating the despondent optimist, he might have had his son in mind. Applying the above distinction to haves and have-nots, Gumplowicz explained that propertied classes believe that eternal law requires some to thrive while others starve. These pessimists revere the past. Nonpropertied classes tend to be optimists in world philosophy, who worship a beautiful future in order to shun the present. Besides foreshadowing Lukács' notion of reification, Gumplowicz anticipated Mannheim's later distinction between the past-oriented ideology of conservatives and the future-building utopia of revolutionaries.

In championing monistic method, Gumplowicz ranks as one of the founders of sociology. With a faith in unchanging laws worthy of Bernard Bolzano or Robert Zimmermann, Gumplowicz solaced himself by unmasking hypocrisy in a world rent by strife. Few Social Darwinists have been so resigned and few therapeutic nihilists so serene as this Pole who turned from agitation to contemplation. Fervor that had once trumpeted Polish nationalism now assailed both reformist and conservative social theory. Quite inaccurately scholars have imputed to Gumplowicz anti-Semitic racism comparable to that of Wagner or Chamberlain. No one tried so hard to rescue Gumplowicz from this slander as did his disciple Gustav Ratzenhofer.

GUSTAV RATZENHOFER:
SOCIOLOGY AS A POLICY SCIENCE

Gustav Ratzenhofer (1842–1904) is remembered chiefly for having influenced the Chicago Social Darwinist Albion W. Small. Many dismiss Ratzenhofer as an epigone of Gumplowicz, with whom he corresponded and who reviewed his books extremely favorably.[6] In actuality, Ratzenhofer elaborated a sociology of considerable systematic rigor and originality. The son of a clockmaker in Vienna, he rose through the ranks to become an army officer in 1864, closing a distinguished career as head of the Military High Court at Vienna from 1898 to 1901. In 1893 after nearly two decades of independent study, he published a three-volume work, *Wesen und Zweck der Politik als Teil der Soziologie und Grundlage der Staatswissenschaft* (Leipzig, 1893; repr. Aalen, 1967). This he followed with a spate of articles and books, of which the most important was *Positive Ethik: Die Verwirklichung des Sittlich-sollenden* (Leipzig, 1901). In October, 1904, Ratzenhofer died on shipboard en route home from the St. Louis Congress of Arts and Sciences. In a résumé of his sociology drafted for that congress, he characterized the United States as a land "whose future centers about the solution of the race-problem."[7]

Ratzenhofer's sociology matured from an analysis of social interest into a comprehensive portrayal of capitalistic society. Unlike Gumplowicz, Ratzenhofer strove to make sociology a policy science: it should become doctor to the body social. The goal of such a science would be to synthesize results of research in economics, politics, and social welfare into a program of reform. Such a synthesis would rest on what Ratzenhofer called positive monism, by which he meant Gumplowicz' doctrine that society, being part of nature, obeys unalterable laws. Past human development ought to be scrutinized as basis for forecasting the future, just as a tactician studies previous battles in order to anticipate future ones. Ratzenhofer insisted that force would persist in settling disputes, despite efforts by "women of both sexes" to supplant it.

Ratzenhofer endorsed Gumplowicz' theory that states originated through subjugation of settled laborers by roving marauders. To elucidate subsequent development, he proposed a polarity that anticipated the lifework of Pribram and Spann: society grows by dint of conflict between individualism and socialism. Gradually the communalism of vanquished settlers blends with the individualism of their conquerors to produce feudalism. Later capitalism fosters an anarchic spirit that undermines the family and degrades labor. Paralleling Karl von Vogelsang, Ratzenhofer believed that eventually capitalism would give way to an era of settledness *(Sesshaftigkeit)*, in which class strife would yield to cooperation between workers and owners. This ideal stage would vivify socialism with the energy of individualism, a symbiosis that Ratzenhofer hoped to germinate by replacing religion with positive monism. In his posthumous *Sociologie: Positive Lehre von den menschlichen Wechselbeziehungen* (Leipzig, 1907), the sociologist expounded a future-oriented policy science that transmuted Gumplowicz' therapeutic nihilism into constructive social science. Voicing moderate anti-Semitism, Ratzenhofer called for total assimilation of Jews so that they might accelerate progress. While remarking that Jews make first-rate officers, judges, and bureaucrats, Ratzenhofer warned that employment as journalists or attorneys aggravates their racial faults.[8]

Like many other refractory thinkers in Austria, Ratzenhofer has been forgotten by compatriots. At a time when dueling was still *de rigueur*, it was bad form for an officer to write social philosophy. In quest of synthesis, he provoked too many quarrels with conservatives, liberals, and Socialists to be welcomed by any of them. Ratzenhofer did not live to confront World War One or to explicate the racist mythologies that it made popular. Had he lived into the 1920's, Ratzenhofer might have gained a following among Socialists at Vienna who were striving to fuse socialism with individualism. Even then his perch above the fray would probably have made him more a spectator of failure than an architect of recovery. Only after 1945 would he have discerned any indication that scholars and statesmen were at last exploiting sociology as a guide to reform.

HOUSTON STEWART CHAMBERLAIN IN VIENNA: ADVOCATE OF RACIAL PURITY

From 1889 to 1909 there lived at Vienna the renegade son of a British admiral, Houston Stewart Chamberlain (1855–1927).[9] It was during these twenty years of immersion in Austrian culture that the Englishman wrote his major works—entirely in German. In contrast with Gumplowicz and Ratzenhofer, Chamberlain was not a sociologist but a publicist for Germanic superiority. The sociologists' dialectic of conqueror and conquered became for him a struggle between Teutons and non-Teutons, which he hoped would end not in mixing of races but in their purification. Born near Portsmouth, the Protestant Chamberlain was tutored in German by the theologian Otto Kuntze. After ten years of study at Geneva and Dresden, he came to Vienna to pursue plant physiology under the Jewish scholar Julius von Wiesner (1838–1916). When work at the microscope proved too nerve-racking, Chamberlain turned to popularizing ideas of Richard Wagner, whom he had met in 1882 and whose widow Cosima had become a close friend in 1888. In two books on Wagner published in 1892 and 1895, the Englishman displayed exceptional erudition, highlighted by clear writing and vitiated by Pan-Germanism.

Thanks to the success of his two-volume *Die Grundlagen des neunzehnten Jahrhunderts* (Vienna, 1899), in 1901 Chamberlain became a friend of the German Emperor Wilhelm, who sensed in the Englishman a kindred spirit capable of appreciating the emperor's vision. Chamberlain had systematized the ideas of Count de Gobineau, Wagner, and Nietzsche into an instrument of both high learning and destructiveness. After 1900, he gravitated toward disaffected German intellectuals like Paul de Lagarde and Moeller van den Bruck. Having divorced his half-Jewish wife Anna Horst after nearly thirty years of marriage, in 1908 he married Eva Wagner, the composer's daughter, moving a year later to Bayreuth and becoming a German citizen in 1916. About 1912 Chamberlain suffered accidental poisoning from quicksilver, which confined him to bed for the rest of his life. Throughout his career, he showed marked symptoms of manic-depressive neurosis, as periods of ecstasy gave way to nervous collapse.

Chamberlain's most famous, if not his most persuasive, book was *Die Grundlagen des neunzehnten Jahrhunderts*, which he wrote during nineteen feverish months in 1897 and 1898. He dedicated it to his friend and former teacher, von Wiesner, who was then rector of the University of Vienna. Like Spengler after him, Chamberlain was fascinated by the morphology of plants, an interest that both men derived from Goethe. In studying plant physiology, Chamberlain indulged a predilection for individuals and species that exhibited purity of form. A fancier of dogs, the Englishman held an animal-breeder's opinion of race: thoroughbreds alone possess pedigree. Like another admirer of Wagner, Christian von Ehrenfels, Chamberlain employed the word Gestalt to designate the integrating principle of form. He and Ehrenfels both lamented a leveling of human excellence, which Chamberlain, more dogmatically than Ehrenfels, attributed to interbreeding of races.

Chamberlain's studies in biology sharpened his knack for constructing comparisons and contrasts; again like Spengler, he delighted in startling juxtapositions. In *Immanuel Kant: Die Persönlichkeit als*

Einführung in das Werk (Munich, 1905), he contrasted the great philosopher with Goethe, Leonardo, Descartes, Bruno, and Plato. Other vagaries notwithstanding, Chamberlain executed comparisons in intellectual history with unusual skill. In the *Grundlagen*, he compared systematically what the Greeks, Romans, Teutons, and Jews have contributed to civilization. The Greeks created art and philosophy, the Romans state and law, the Germans the possibility of freedom, while the Jews practiced usury and exploitation. Modern Jews Chamberlain despised as offspring of interbreeding between ancient Semites and several later peoples. The Englishman's anti-Semitism echoed that prevalent at Vienna. Having married a half-Jewess, he could extoll individual Jews while declaring Judaism to be a menace to civilization. However amusing in a single individual, the slyness of a thousand Jakobs can destroy a community of the unsuspecting.[10] Reviling Jewish usury, Chamberlain projected onto the Old Testament the calumnies of Vienna's economic anti-Semites. Unwittingly Chamberlain parodied Lueger's dictum, "Who is a Jew is for me to decide," when he averred that David and Christ had been Aryans while Moses and Paul had been Jews.

Unlike Gumplowicz, Chamberlain deplored conflict or any other contact between races. He wanted to see each race left to develop in isolation, without the intermarrying that great empires such as the Roman or Habsburg promoted. He might have been speaking of Austria-Hungary when he wrote:

> [This is the tragedy of European history] . . . that the inherited culture of antiquity . . . was not transmitted to us by a definite people, but by a nationless mixture without physiognomy, . . . in which Mongrels held the whip-hand, namely, . . . by the raceless chaos of the decaying Roman Empire.[11]

Chamberlain's contempt for imperial policies of racial mixing was no doubt reinforced by the hysteria of German deputies who during the Badeni debates of 1897 recoiled at the prospect of being lumped with Czechs. Chamberlain assailed socialism on grounds that it too abetted racial mixing.

In championing the Teutons *(Germanen)*, whom he defined to include not only the Germans, French, and English, but all anticlericals, Chamberlain echoed the pan-Germanism of Georg von Schönerer, whose admiration for the Reformation he shared. Chamberlain denounced the Roman Catholic church which as heir to the raceless Roman Empire had impeded differentiation of races. He prized Catholic culture, nevertheless, as a heritage that every Protestant should know. In an article that he contributed in 1902 to *Die Fackel*—a periodical that he read regularly—Chamberlain argued that Catholicism and Protestantism were feuding brothers, who had more to gain by cross-fertilizing than by vilifying each other.[12]

A scholarly parallel to Chamberlain is afforded by the Galician-born art historian Josef Strzygowski (1862–1941), who pursued the artifacts of Aryan art into Central Asia. Strzygowski expounded a polarity between Aryan influences and southern, Rome-centered influences, which smacks of Chamberlain. The Englishman exerted direct influence on Hermann Keyserling (1880–1946), who took a doctorate in geology at Vienna in 1902. Keyserling's predilection for typologies and his celebration of creativity echo Chamberlain's sounder attainments.[13] Even more fruitful was Chamberlain's friendship with the Moravian-born essayist, Rudolf Kassner (1873–1959).[14] This renewer of Reform Catholicism esteemed the *Grundlagen* as an antidote to contemporary formlessness. Partially crippled since infancy, Kassner extended Chamberlain's polarities by depicting moral impulses as the outcome of clashing opposites. He constructed a science of physiognomy into a last monument of Leibnizian syncretism.

Far more invidious—and somewhat unfair to Chamberlain—is the parallel between his demand for racial purity and the Aryan cult of Adolf Josef Lanz (1874–1954). This repugnant figure, who called himself Jörg Lanz von Liebenfels, was rediscovered after 1945 by Wilfred Daim.[15] Born at Vienna the son of a teacher, Lanz studied from 1893 to 1899 as a Cisterican novice at Stift Heiligenkreuz near Mayerling before becoming an independent writer. As early as 1903 he marshaled algebraic symbols and enormously wide reading to prove that, in the words of the Rig-Veda, "The earth belongs to the Aryan."[16] From 1905 to 1931 he published at Vienna a journal, *Ostara*, whose readers included Kraus,[17] Strindberg, Lord Kitchener, and Hitler. In 1909 the latter visited Lanz to request some missing back numbers. Lanz proposed reestablishing the Knights Templars as an order of Aryans; to mark their proposed seat atop Burg Werfenstein in Upper Austria, he unfurled on December 25, 1907 a flag bearing a swastika.

The name "Ostara" Lanz took from a Germanic goddess of dawn and spring mentioned by Bede and Jacob Grimm. In his *Theozoologie oder die Kunde von den Sodoms-Äfflinge und dem Götterelektron* (Vienna, 1905), this monomaniac portrayed a future society in which racial purity would prevail. As if to mock Christian von Ehrenfels' program of polygamy, Lanz urged that a blond heroic race be raised in secret by cloistered mothers. In school Aryans would learn a master religion, being trained to use sterilization and castration in order to exterminate impure races. These lower races Lanz dubbed *Tschandalen* after a low Hindu caste disparaged by Nietzsche. Lanz delighted in comparing them to apes. His Gnostic vision posited a struggle to the death between Aryans and Tschandalen, with triumph assured to the blond, blue-eyed elite.

In Austria, Lanz's cult remained a joke, a kind of caricature of Schönerer's German-Nationalists as well as of Richard von Kralik's *Gralbund*. So long as Lanz's sinister proposals were confined to Austria, they could remain one among other harmless eccentricities. But as soon as Hitler transplanted them to Germany, the fantasies of Lanz, and to a lesser extent those of Chamberlain, threatened civilization.

At first glance, Bohemian Reform Catholicism seems remote from the therapeutic nihilism of Gumplowicz or the racism of Chamberlain. These Social Darwinists, albeit unwittingly, espoused a secular faith that caricatured the confidence felt by Bolzano or Spann in God's Providence. Whereas Reform Catholics held that God guides human conflict for the good of all, Social Darwinists affirmed similar purposefulness without invoking God. Within every society, a single group must hold sway in order to elicit the best energies of the whole. Wielding the supremacy of a humanized Providence, an elite may rule through disillusioned cunning, as in Gumplowicz, or by rational planning, as in Ratzenhofer, or by virtue of pure breeding, as in Chamberlain. These publicists justified their proposals by distorting arguments dear to Reform Catholics.

Not every disenchanted Leibnizian embraced politics. The Marcionists of Prague shunned activism, preferring to excogitate visions of world destruction or to contemplate distant redemption. When transferred to politics, however, Manichaean discontent wrought havoc. In hope of rescuing a beleaguered society, racists advocated ostracizing or even exterminating the peoples who threatened it. Lanz's phantasmagoria of a duel to the death between Tschandalen and Aryans climaxed decades of protest against the racial diversity of the Habsburg Empire. Arrayed against such fanaticism, the serenity of reformers such as Popper-Lynkeus, Suttner, and Coudenhove-Kalergi proved futile. Their devotion to the good of the whole would be parodied— and overwhelmed—by totalitarianism.

Part Five

THE HUNGARIAN CULT OF ILLUSION

Wenn man ein Seher ist,
braucht man kein Beobachter sein.

A seer has no need to be an observer.

—MARIE VON EBNER-ESCHENBACH

24

Institutions and
Intellectuals in Hungary

POLITICAL AND SOCIAL STRUCTURE

In contrast with the Czechs, who after 1850 disdained to write German, many Magyars disseminated their views through treatises composed in German. Some of these Hungarians have contributed decisively to modern thought, especially in exploring the interaction between society and thinkers. The next four chapters will apply to major Hungarian theorists the discipline that I call the sociology of thinkers. In order to explain why Hungarians should have pioneered this discipline, it is necessary to examine how intellectuals interacted with institutions in the "other half" of Austria-Hungary.

Two events overshadowed the history of Hungary during the nineteenth century: one was the unsuccessful revolt of 1848–1849 against Habsburg rule and the other was the awkward compromise *(Ausgleich)*, whereby in 1867 Hungary and Austria became partners. Planned by Ferenc Deák (1803–1876) and Gyula Andrássy (1823–1890) to appease demands for self-rule and granted by Franz Joseph as a last resort, the compromise established not one or two, but three governing bodies. These were: first, the royal *(königlich)* kingdom of Hungary; second, the imperial-royal *(kaiserlich-königlich* or *k. k.)* domain of the Austrian crownlands; and third, the three imperial-and-royal *(kaiserlich und königlich* or *k. u. k.)* ministries run jointly by Austria and Hungary. The joint ministries directed foreign affairs, the military, and the finances connected therewith. The Austro-Hungarian army bore in its title the letters *k. u. k.*, while the universities of Austria were labeled *k. k.*, and those of Hungary merely *k.* The ubiquity of these abbreviations inspired Robert Musil to coin *Kakanien* as a label for the empire that, he quipped, had succumbed for lack of a name.[1]

Even more bewildering than the nomenclature was the administration of this Dual Monarchy.[2] The two states were so thoroughly separated that a resident of one had to change citizenship before he could vote in elections of the other. Hungary flew its own green, white, and red flag of 1848, while the army paraded the black and yellow colors of the Habsburg dynasty. Finances centered in Vienna, where until 1897 a common bank issued currency for both realms. Thereafter, Hungary enjoyed partnership in issuing currency. The three common ministries were supervised by delegations, one from the Austrian and one from the Hungarian Parliament, which like international commissions met separately to vote the budget and determine policy. Every ten years the Ausgleich had to be renegotiated like any other treaty. Each parliament appointed a deputation to barter over the proportion of the common expenses each country would contribute. In 1897 and 1907 renewal of the financial treaty fomented a crisis, as Hungary demanded other concessions in return for ratifying the compromise. Until 1897 Hungary contributed a share (Präzipuum) of 31.4 percent, paying 34.4 percent thereafter. Transactions between the two states were snarled in bureaucracy. If police in Galicia wished to extradite a bandit who had crossed the border, punctilio required them to deal not with Hungarian border guards whom they saw every day but with Vienna.[3] There officials would translate a report from German into Magyar before dispatching it to Budapest for relay to the Hungarian side of the border.

On February 17, 1867, the Constitution of 1848 was restored in Hungary, and on June 8, Franz Joseph was crowned Apostolic King of Hungary. The term apostolic, which Catholic publicists flaunted, descended from Saint Stephen, who had led his people into the Catholic faith in the year 1000. As king, Franz Joseph exercised a priori veto over all legislation submitted to the Hungarian Parliament; every bill required his approval in advance. The Hungarian franchise remained one of the most restrictive in Europe. In 1874 the property qualification was raised so that instead of 6.7 percent only 5.9 percent of the population could vote. The ruling gentry opposed every attempt to enact universal suffrage.

Under Andrássy and Kálmán Tisza (1830–1902), Hungary furnished the chief stumbling block to every sort of reform in Austria as well as at home. Magyar aristocrats like Andrássy, Kálnoky, and Kállay directed the joint ministries at a time when Austrian nobles were abandoning politics. Hungarian leaders warned the Austrians not to inaugurate federalism in the western half of the empire, lest the subject peoples of Hungary be incited to rebel. Although Budapest granted subservient autonomy to Croatia, which had been demanded by Bishop Josef Georg Strossmayer (1815–1905), this was done so that

Magyars could rule the rest of the realm unhindered. Franz Joseph was the only official in Vienna who retained any legal authority in Hungary. Only rarely did he brandish power, as when during 1905 and 1906 he threatened to introduce universal suffrage by decree. Although this threat persuaded Hungarians to accede once more to the Ausgleich, such an ultimatum could not be risked again for fear that Hungary would secede.

By 1900 secession of Hungary seemed no idle fear. Up to 1890 the country had been dominated by Kálmán Tisza, whose Liberal party cooperated with Taaffe to preserve the status quo. Thereafter, a separatist coalition fanned Magyar nationalism, led by the son of Lajos Kossuth (1802–1894), Ferenc Kossuth (1841–1914), by Gyula Andrássy the younger (1860–1929), and by Dezsö Bánffy, who sponsored the anticlerical laws of 1894. The Independence party demanded the right of Hungarian officers to command in Magyar, and they threatened separate tariffs to protect Hungarian agriculture. Elated by the separation of Norway from Sweden, which Sweden granted in 1905, Magyar Separatists insisted that their country was already independent in all but name. They predicted that the Dual Monarchy would split upon the death of Franz Joseph.[4] In 1907 they joined in the refusal to accept universal suffrage. Separatists found their leading opponent in István Tisza (1861–1918), son of Kálmán, who after 1912 deployed a parliamentary guard to curb obstructionists in the Assembly. As prime minister from 1903 to 1905 and again from 1913 to 1917, this austere Calvinist showed his hostility to Franz Ferdinand. On October 31, 1918, Tisza was assassinated by three soldiers who blamed him for the outcome of the war.

The unusual constitution of Hungary reflected a peculiar social structure. Perhaps half the Magyars who were not peasants or servants could claim a title of nobility, so that in 1848 1 out of 14 persons in Hungary was classified as a nobleman (nobilis), as contrasted with 1 of 353 in Austria and 1 of 828 in Bohemia.[5] In 1867 466,000 Magyar nobles lived in Hungary in addition to 80,000 non-Magyar nobles in Transylvania. During the 1920's one out of five Hungarians claimed to be a nobleman and one of seventy an aristocrat. The nobility inherited its privileges from the Golden Bull of 1222, which King Andrew II (1205–1235) had conceded to the lesser nobility led by his own son Béla IV (1235–1270). This "constitution" exempted the gentry and clergy from taxation as well as from arbitrary imprisonment and confiscation, while allowing them an annual assembly. With some modifications, these provisions remained in force until the Laws of April, 1848; because the latter were not fully enforced, nobles retained most privileges down to 1944.

The vast majority of the nobility were merely freemen, belonging
to the class of lesser nobility or gentry, who derived from the medieval
servientes regis. Very few nobles belonged to the class of magnates,
who constituted the aristocracy of Hungary and attended the upper
house of the diet. A proper name ending in the suffix *i* or, still more
refined, *y*, both of which denoted place of origin, bore the same significance as the German "von" and the French "de." Further to distinguish shades of difference in rank, the Hungarian language offered
as many as fifteen formulas of address for lofty personages.[6] These
gradations adhered to the schematism of ranks and titles, which the
state published every year between the 1780's and 1944. Hoping that
bearers of newly granted titles would show greater subservience than
aristocrats of venerable lineage, Horthy created new nobles. To the
four basic titles of "Excellency," "Dignity," "Greatness," and "Authority," the regent added a fifth, "Valiant."[7] Even after 1930, both the
middle and upper classes considered it demeaning for a freeman to
perform menial tasks such as carrying a shopping bag in public; domestic servants peopled every household. As a further sign of feudal
customs, dueling persisted down to 1944.

More even than the class structure or the limited franchise, what
delayed Hungary's democratization was ownership of huge estates.
The largest had been amassed as the Turks receded by families like
the Esterházy and the Károlyi, who owned hundreds of thousands of
acres, farmed by tenants and administered by bailiffs. Although most
latifundia disappeared in 1919, to this day the Esterházy family owns
much of the Burgenland, which Hungary ceded to Austria in 1920.
Although in 1850 Alexander Bach had liberated the peasants of Hungary, in contrast to Joseph II's reform in Austria and Bohemia, Bach
deprived the peasants of land, leaving farmers abjectly dependent on
magnates and gentry. The peasants' sullen acquiescense belied the
claim of the gentry to speak in their tenants' interest. Jacqueries occurred frequently, reviving the anti-Habsburg tradition of Lajos Kossuth
as well as of the Kurucz rebellions around 1700. The word Kurucz
derived from the Latin word for cross, *crux*, recalling that in 1514 a
peasants' crusade against the Turks had turned against the landlords.

Up to 1867 and even beyond, magnates and gentry enforced their
will through the official known as the *táblabiró*, or county magistrate.
Chosen from the gentry, he exercised on their behalf a multitude of
offices that József Eötvös described in 1845:

All complaints of the people pass through his hands: all decrees of the powers that be are promulgated and administered

by him. The district justice [táblabiró] regulates the rivers, makes roads, and constructs bridges. He is the representative of the poor, the inspector of the schools; he is lord chief forester whenever a wolf happens to make its appearance; he is "protomedicus" in case of an epidemic; he is justice of the peace, the king's advocate in criminal cases, commissioner of the police, of war, of hospitals; in short, he is all in all.[8]

Owing to the powers of the táblabiró, counties were ruled throughout the nineteenth century by a clique of magnates and gentry. In 1898 a so-called Slave Law empowered owners of large estates to use corporal punishment against striking agricultural workers and to recruit press gangs at harvest time, practices that continued after 1920. Small wonder that peasants emigrated from Hungary in ever-increasing numbers. Between 1890 and 1910 about one and one-half million citizens of Hungary landed in the United States; 340,000 Austro-Hungarians arrived during 1907 alone.[9]

The wealth and prestige of the Roman Catholic church provided another obstacle to modernization. Although the Counter-Reformation had never stamped out Calvinism or Lutheranism, by 1900 the church held in Hungary the largest estates it possessed anywhere in Europe. As late as 1910 the church directed two-thirds of the schools. Whereas the hierarchy defended Magyarization, Pope Leo XIII spoke out against the oppression of the Slovaks and the Ruthenes. Because the church abetted Magyarization, anticlerical sentiment never reached the fever pitch of Bismarck's *Kulturkampf*. In 1894–1895 civil marriage became obligatory and priests were forbidden to baptize the children of mixed marriages against the will of one parent.[10] Even more conspicuously than in Austria, the Roman Catholic church upheld the state, rejoicing in its Apostolic King and staging on August 20 the annual St. Stephen's Day Procession, which resembled an outdoor mass. By 1900 this provided the sole occasion on which the nobility wore the national costume, marching behind the clergy in cavalry boots, braided breeches, fur-trimmed capes, and plumed hats.

Despite intense patriotism, Hungarians entered World War One with less enthusiasm than any other principal belligerent.[11] Having urged a peaceful settlement with Serbia in July, 1914, they blamed Vienna for having provoked a conflict in which Hungary could gain nothing and lose much. Once Tisza had closed the borders, food remained plentiful throughout the war, and the Hungarian Parliament remained in session, offering a platform for separatists and pacifists. In this uncensored atmosphere Mihály Károlyi launched peace proposals, and numerous Socialist and Communist radicals published journals. Because an ample food supply made it unnecessary for the victorious Allies to provision Budapest, during the winter of 1918–1919 the Hungarians followed their own devices, making feasible in Budapest what could not occur in Vienna: a Bolshevik coup.

Hungarian misgivings toward the war found poignant expression in memoirs that Aladár Kuncz (1886–1931) published as *Black Monastery* (Budapest, 1931; New York, 1934). Having been a tourist in Paris when the war broke out, this young gymnasium teacher from Klausenburg was interned by the French as a potential spy. A onetime Francophile, he spent five years in prison, mostly at the Black Monastery on the island of Noirmoutier, where treatment grew ever more barbarous and appeals hopeless. If the captives protested—wrongly as it turned out—that in Hungary no French citizen had been arrested or even detained, the guards might withhold food, mail, or exercise. The image that most prewar Hungarians had entertained of France as a liberal country belied the cruelty meted out to these innocent victims, who remained too underfed to spy and too demoralized to retaliate. When Kuncz returned to Hungary in late 1919, he encountered a populace suddenly more impoverished and depressed than any he had known in prison. World War One had turned Hungary into something bleaker than the Black Monastery: people now lived without hope.

In 1919 Hungary demonstrated her ambivalent stance between past and future by evolving within four-and-one-half months from the liberal regime of Károlyi to the bolshevism of Kun to the semi-Fascist monarchism of Admiral Horthy. No other country in Europe ran such a gamut between extremes, and next to Russia none so alarmed the peacemakers at Versailles, who trembled that Kun's coup would ignite Communist rebellions elsewhere. Mihály Károlyi (1875–1955), a critic of Franz Joseph and of the limited franchise, had established himself as a national leader during the wartime sessions of Parliament. On October 31, 1918, he was appointed premier, proclaiming seventeen days later a republic, of which he was elected president on January 11, 1919. He insisted later that if universal suffrage had been introduced in 1907 his republic could have survived. Instead Béla Kun (1886–1939) forced Károlyi to resign on March 21, 1919, eventually removing all moderate Socialists from the government. Although the 133 days of bolshevism unleashed a civil war, there were relatively few purges and even an air of levity.[12] Counterrevolution triumphed when on August 1, 1919, Kun fled to Vienna, as Romanian troops marched toward Budapest to invest Admiral Miklós Horthy (1868–1957) as regent. The first two of these chiefs of state possessed characteristics that would have precluded most men from political leadership. Károlyi suffered from a cleft palate and a limp which had kept him out of army service, and which may have helped turn him into a compulsive gambler. Kun was extremely ugly, with a pallid complexion and great pointed ears; his enemies compared him to a toad. Horthy afforded a different sort of anomaly: having been naval aide-de-camp to Franz Joseph from 1909 to 1914, he restored the preciosity of the Habsburg court. As regent, he became, as one wit put it, admiral without a sea in a kingdom without a king.

From 1920 to 1944 the regent made Hungary the most deformed and least reformed of Habsburg successor states, presiding over that rarest of twentieth-century polities, a monarchist restoration. As prime minister from 1921 to 1931, István Bethlen (1874–1947) curbed his Fascist rival Gyula Gömbös (1886–1936) by relying upon the land-owning gentry. The Catholic historian Gyula Szekfü (1883–1955) hailed Bethlen as a latter-day Széchenyi guiding a neo-Baroque regime.[13] In foreign policy, the Regency renounced all responsibility for World War One, arguing that the Hungarian cabinet had emphatically opposed war with Serbia in July, 1914. For twenty-five years Magyar rulers dreamed of reconquering Slovakia and Transylvania. Encircled by members of the Little Entente, irredentist Hungary had little choice but to ally first with Mussolini and later with Hitler. Disenchantment at Nazi domination impelled many intellectuals, including Szekfü, to espouse Marxism even before the liberation of 1945.

The most repugnant feature of Horthy's first decade was the White Terror of 1920.[14] With a vengeance reminiscent of General Haynau's bloody assizes of 1849, torture was used indiscriminately, public whipping was reinstated, political murders were concealed, and Jews who had arrived as refugees since 1914 were expelled. Jews who had no passports were put in internment camps, devoid of adequate food and sanitation. Anti-Semitism mounted partly because Kun's regime had employed a preponderance of Jews and partly because a weakened economy made wealthy Jews anathema. In order to deprive Jews of a livelihood, all cinema and tobacconist licenses were revoked and redistributed to gentiles. A *numerus clausus* of 6 percent—this represented the supposed proportion of Jews in the population—reduced university enrollment by one-half. Although strikes were again prohibited, no measures could rehabilitate industries such as furniture-making, which operated at one-fifth of its prewar level, because it lacked timber from Slovakia and Transylvania. As late as 1930 horses and horse-drawn carriages abounded in the streets of Budapest, disguising the demise of the *belle époque*. To exploit the national pride of the Magyars, Horthy and Bethlen launched a saturation campaign of propaganda. Streetcars blazoned the creed of postwar Hungary:

> I believe in one God. I believe in one Fatherland. I believe in one divine hour coming. I believe in the resurrection of Hungary. Amen.[15]

Similarly every house door bore a small metal plate with the words, "Nem, nem soha," "No, No, Never,"—never will we submit to the degradation of our country. Instead, the quixotic Hungarians submitted to degradation from Horthy, who abused in his countrymen the recalcitrant patriotism that earlier had inspired more worthy achievements. Although the regent misused the Hungarians' power of imagination in order to sustain a semifeudal regime, Magyar capacity to dream while under duress continued to stimulate originality in thought.

BUDAPEST: A MODERNIZING CITY
IN A SEMIFEUDAL NATION

Despite the backwardness of its environs, after 1870 Budapest rapidly became one of the most modern cities in Europe. Whereas previously Hungary had lacked a genuine cultural center, the twin cities of Buda and Pest joined in 1873 to provide a cultural and economic forum for a prospering nation. Between 1870 and 1910 the population of Budapest tripled to 800,000, growing at a rate nine times faster than that of the nation as a whole,[16] Spread over eighty square miles, by the 1890's the Hungarian metropolis occupied the largest area of any municipality on the Continent. An unwieldly city council of four hundred members supervised rebuilding the twin cities. In 1870 stone quais were laid along the Danube to regulate its flow and to provide a fashionable promenade, which in 1896 was crowned by the Parliament. At the same time, the Margaret Island, which had been a hunting ground for Archduke Joseph (1833–1905), was opened by him to the public. Son of the Palatine of the same name, he maintained the island as a pleasure park until the city acquired it in 1908. In 1872 a radial avenue, later named Andrássy Street, was designed to be the most beautiful boulevard in Europe. Running straight for two miles, it connected the Inner City with the Town Park (Városliget), the Prater of Budapest. Andrássy Street grew wider as it neared the Town Park: the first third permitted buildings abutting on the street, the second third allowed narrow front gardens of uniform dimensions, while the final third featured villas set at a prescribed distance from the street. An underground subway built by Swiss engineers on Andrássy Street for the Exposition of 1896 was considered the finest in Europe—it was also the first—and was studied by designers of the New York subways. As early as 1889, Budapest had adopted electric streetcars. During the same year a zone system of railway fares promoted commuting into Budapest from as far as 150 miles away.

The city prospered on the grain trade; Budapest provided the grain mill center of Europe, second in the world only to Minneapolis-St. Paul. Hungarian mills had pioneered steel rollers that produced extra-fine flour needed for pastry. Budapest also manufactured leathergoods, dyes, bricks, wagons, and ships, commodities whose production doubled between 1898 and 1910. Budapest was the largest city in Europe to have mineral springs inside city limits; the bottled water sold all over the Continent. In order to finance upkeep of highways, the government harvested fruit trees planted along them. Many towns had an orchard tended by the parish priest and the schoolmaster, who profited from fruit sold at Budapest.

Few outsiders noticed the modernity of Budapest until the Millenial Exposition of 1896. Planned by Gabriel Baross in 1892 and carried out under the aegis of Finance Minister Béla Lukács (1847–1901), permanent buildings were erected for the exposition in the Town Park. In an orgy of self-congratulation, the exposition displayed none but products manufactured in Hungary. When citizens learned that chandeliers in the newly opened Parliament came from Vienna, these were at once replaced by chandeliers of native manufacture. Magyar exuberance proved so infectious that some visitors wondered whether Hungary might not soon overtake Austria. An American observer compared resurgent Hungary to a cuckoo that had grown fat in the nest of lethargic Austria.[17]

Behind the luxurious facade lurked dangers from the past. During the winter of 1892–1893, cholera took five hundred lives. This epidemic was caused by drinking the unfiltered water of the Danube into which sewage had been dumped untreated. Housing was slow to improve. In 1891 two-thirds of all dwellings were of one story, and three-fifths consisted of only one room. Many people lived in dank cellars until mortality statistics collected by József Körösi (1844–1906) led to prohibition of cellar dwellings. Cramped street-level homes became so damp during summer that hardly anyone stayed at home; watering carts aggravated the dampness by spraying dusty streets while soaking passersby. Restaurants, coffeehouses, and public baths teemed with crowds noisier than those at Vienna.

In large measure it was assimilated Jews who turned Budapest from a trading center into an industrial and financial metropolis. Until Béla Kun's regime, a marriage of convenience linked the Magyar gentry and the Jews, who filled the commercial and professional ranks that the nobility disdained. Jews adopted Magyar names, even before anti-clerical laws of April, 1893, granted them full legal equality with other citizens. About 1910, one-quarter of the population of Budapest was Jewish, including two-fifths of 6,700 lawyers, three-fifths of 2,000 doctors, and two-fifths of 1,200 journalists.[18] While championing Hungary's growth, many Jews spoke German in their homes, adding a cosmopolitan leaven to an otherwise xenophobic city.

Although around 1900 Hungary offered a haven for Jews, twenty years earlier the country had endured a flurry of anti-Semitism. Fraudulent accusations of ritual murder discredited for several decades the anti-Semitic party of Géza von Istóczy (1842–1915).[19] On April 1, 1882, a fourteen-year-old Calvinist girl named Eszter Solymosi disappeared near the home of József Scharf, sexton of the Jewish synagogue at Tisza-Eszlár in southern Hungary. Her mother accused Scharf of having murdered the girl in order to get Christian blood for matzoh. A local magistrate, who had learned of ritual murder from August Rohling's Der Talmudjude (1871), forced Scharf's fourteen-year-old son to "confess" participation in the crime. A year later, a trial of Nyíregyháza exonerated the accused while exposing a conspiracy to convict them. Owing to enormous publicity, the Tisza-Eszlár case became Europe's best known judicial persecution of Jews prior to the Dreyfus affair.

The conspiracy of 1882, more concerted than that at Polna in Bohemia seventeen years later, served to recall that Budapest lay in a semi-Oriental country. In 1900, one-half the population of Hungary remained illiterate, and the hospitality about which Hungarians boasted resembled open-handed generosity of feudal lords during centuries when travel had been arduous and risky. More conspicuously than Vienna, Budapest seemed a city on a borderland, poised between East and West, between feudalism and modernity.

A GIFT FOR WISH-FULFILLMENT (DÉLIBÁB)

During Hungary's struggle against Habsburg rule, literature reinforced political renaissance. Even more than in Russia, intellectuals strove to uplift the masses, and between 1848 and 1860 it was writers alone who sustained the Magyars' sense of nationhood. Although rebirth of Hungarian as a literary language came simultaneously with that of Czech, Magyar writers quickly outstripped the Germans of their country, whereas Bohemia began to founder in strife between ruling Germans and fractious Czechs.

Until the late eighteenth century, Hungary had been governed in Latin. The nobility spoke French or German in addition to Latin, leaving peasants and servants to converse in Magyar. In May, 1784, Joseph II substituted German for Latin as the language of administration. Insisting that an enlightened country could be governed only in a living language, the doctrinaire emperor directed all officials to learn German within three years. Magyars were so outraged that they revived their ancestral tongue. The efficacy of their renaissance is shown in the fact that whereas Herder in volume 4 of *Ideen zur Philosophie der Geschichte der Menschheit* (1791) predicted that Magyars together with their language would disappear, two years later in volume 1 of his *Briefe zu Beförderung der Humanität* (Riga, 1793), he saluted the Magyars' struggle to preserve their native tongue.[20] In 1792 Magyar became a required subject at school, except in Croatia, and in 1805 the lower house of the diet was permitted to debate in Magyar as well as in Latin. Petitions addressed to royal officials in Magyar had to be answered in that language.

A symbolic turning point in the rebirth of the language came in October, 1825, when István Széchenyi (1791–1860) addressed the upper house of the diet in what the magnates still regarded as the language of peasants.[21] A month later, the great reformer offered one year's income from his estates to help found a Hungarian Academy of Sciences, with the result that the academy was soon oversubscribed. Magyarization was next trumpeted by the fiery journalist Lajos Kossuth, who deemed dissemination of Magyar the most effective weapon to foil tyranny from Vienna and rivalry from Slavs. Between 1832 and 1844, Magyar was established as the official language of Hungary; by 1836 it had become obligatory in courts of law; in 1840 government offices had to communicate with each other in Magyar; and in 1844 the language was required in the diet and within all offices. Starting in that year, laws were promulgated in Hungarian, and it became the language of instruction in all schools except in Croatia, Slavonia, and among Germans in Transylvania. The language triumphed so completely that after the defeat of 1849 Hungarians used linguistic autonomy to frustrate their Austrian rulers. During the 1850's, Alexander Bach commissioned thousands of German-speaking officials to throttle

Hungary. Instead, failure to collect taxes from people of alien speech brought the Habsburg Empire near bankruptcy, necessitating the constitutional reforms of the 1860's.

After 1867, Magyarization brought mixed blessings. In 1879 Croats and Germans were no longer exempted from learning Magyar. In 1891 attendance at kindergarten became compulsory for all nationalities so as to help non-Magyars learn what was to them a foreign language. In that year every locality received a Magyar name, and citizens were encouraged to adopt Magyar surnames. Ignoring hardships imposed ·on Slovaks, Romanians, Germans, and Croats, Franz Joseph endorsed Magyarization in hope of strengthening his realm. Although as king of Hungary he visited the realm sometimes three or four times a year, he never shared his wife's adoration for that country. During later years, she conversed by preference in Magyar, reflecting the predilections of Budapest, where even Wagner was performed in translation. If one wished to speak German, in the capital it was customary first to say "please" in Hungarian; otherwise a German sentence would be answered in Magyar. In the countryside such touchiness gave way to a custom of greeting each acquaintance in his native tongue. Because everyone knew pleasantries in four or five languages, it was possible, as Emil Reich recounted, to begin a sentence in Latin, to continue it in Hungarian, and to finish it in Slovak or German. While nobles spoke French without accent, peasant families exchanged children so that Magyars and Germans could assimilate each other's language.

The abolition of German as an official language sparked a countermovement, especially after German-speaking professors at the University of Budapest were ousted in 1872. German intellectuals began to extol the heyday before 1740 when Hungarian Protestants had flocked to German universities. A leading spokesman of the beleaguered minority, Edmund Steinacker (1839–1929), was forced from Parliament in 1892 for assailing Magyarization.[22] While growing up in Budapest, Theodor Herzl identified so strongly with German culture that he wrote a poem celebrating Bismarck's *Kulturkampf*, and after age twenty he refused to speak Hungarian.[23] Greater dispassion motivated philologists like Gustav Heinrich (1845–1922) and the Realschule-teacher Johann Heinrich Schwicker (1839–1902), who surveyed relations between German and Hungarian literature. A later spokesman was Jakob Bleyer (1874–1933), who served in the lower house from 1926 to 1933, opposing the anti-German policies of Horthy. It was Bleyer who inspired the Vienna-born historian Fritz Valjavec (1909–1960) to study the diffusion of German culture throughout southeastern Europe.

Magyarization represented a great triumph for the national spirit. It intensified a national trait that Hungarians call *délibáb*, which means literally *fata morgana*. We shall use the term to designate a propensity for wish-fulfillment, a tendency that Ferenczi called magic thinking. Readiness to see the world through rose-colored glasses induced Magyars to exaggerate their grandeur, while they ignored the misery of subject peoples. Délibáb inclined political thinkers like Kossuth, Lukács, and Theodor Hertzka to celebrate present conditions as if utopia had arrived. In military life, magic thinking abetted a kind of quixotic impatience, which rendered soldiers magnificent on attack but often too fickle to persist in defense. Among the bourgeoisie, a cult of illusion intensified desire to acquire the latest technological wonders: elevators, subways, and up-to-date bridges veiled backward social structure. Capacity for dreaming has made Magyars superlative advocates, ever ready to defend Hungary as an exception among nations.

In part, magic thinking is encouraged by the Magyar language.[24] Its several hundred prefixes and suffixes so abound in shades of meaning that speakers lose track of denotations. Because some affixes have no fixed usage, writers can with impunity coin words of indeterminate meaning. The language does not discipline its users to scrutinize reality. Linguistic flexibility also prompts improvisation: Hungarians have excelled at telling tall tales and at disregarding empirical obstacles. According to Béni Kállay, imperial finance minister during the 1880's and 1890's, opulence of vocabulary and readiness of invention make Magyar better suited for translating Oriental languages than are the overly cerebral French or German.[25] Denis de Rougemont recalled watching Hungarians become so intoxicated by the rhythm of speech that they strove less to convey a meaning than to vent a mood.[26]

All of these qualities epitomize the most inventive and at one time the most beloved of Hungarian writers, Móricz Jókai (1825–1904).[27] Almost forgotten today, Mór Jókai published during a period of sixty years nearly 100 novels, comprising 350 volumes—an output that places him among the most prolific of European novelists. The son of a pious Calvinist lawyer in Komorn, Jókai studied with Petöfi in the Calvinist boarding school at Pápa before becoming an apprentice lawyer in Pressburg. After publishing a drama in 1842 and failing in an ambition to become a painter, at age twenty he moved to Pest where Vörösmarty hailed his ability. After publishing his first novel in 1846 and editing a journal with Petöfi in 1847, on March 15, 1848, Jókai and his friend organized a demonstration of students to support Kossuth's call to rebellion. After seventeen months of futile struggle, Jókai narrowly escaped a death sentence thanks to bribes paid by his wife, the leading

Hungarian actress of her day, Róza Laborfalvi (1819–1886). In 1850 the fugitive emerged from months of skulking in swamps and mountains to begin a series of novels that would rekindle the dreams of his countrymen. To signify allegiance to the populace he had dropped the aristocratic *y* from his name in 1848, changing it from Jókay to Jókai.

During the 1850's, he wrote some of his best works, winning a new audience among Hungarians anxious to escape the tyranny of Bach's regime. His first great success was *A Country Nabob* (1853), which described the eccentricities of an elderly magnate during the 1820's. Its sequel *Zoltán Karpathy* (1854) carried the tale into the Széchenyi Reform era, dramatizing the founding of the National Theater in 1837 and the Pest flood of 1838. The novels won such acclaim that readers traveled to the capital just to behold the house where the author lived. In the *Day of Wrath* (1856), Jokai recounted the misery of peasants during the cholera epidemic of 1831, describing superstitions and passions of the countryside in unforgettable detail. One of his boldest plots enlivens *The New Landowner* (1863), whose protagonist is modeled on the Austrian General Julius Haynau (1786–1853), known as the "Butcher of Brescia." After slaughtering Hungarian rebels during the White Terror of 1849, the general settled among them as a benevolent landlord.

In addition to becoming a sculptor and painter of note, Jókai was one of the most resourceful of all storytellers, planning each novel down to the smallest detail and then churning out as many as thirty thousand words a day. Although he excelled at evoking local color, Jókai's characterizations tended to be black-and-white, and his comic gift, while all-pervasive, often lapsed into blandness. Long after naturalism and even impressionism had reshaped the novel elsewhere in Europe, this Hungarian was writing picaresque tales based on Dickens, Hugo, and Dumas *père*. Droller than Hugo and a finer stylist than Dumas, Jókai succeeded best at describing events from his own century. His historical novels, which exuded sympathy for the Turks and for his own Calvinist ancestors, breathe an atmosphere of utopia. In them, and to some extent in all his works, Jókai suffused the world with délibáb, enchanting youth much as Schiller delighted young Germans. After Jules Verne had quickened his interest in technology, Jókai showed uncanny prescience in *The Novel of the Coming Century* (1872). Here he foretold how Hungary would weather a world war fought with aircraft, while Imperial Russia would disintegrate beneath Socialist rule.

Unlike his Austrian confreres, Grillparzer and Stifter, who agonized for lack of a political vocation, Jókai became a national hero. From

1861 to 1896 he served as deputy in the lower chamber; thereafter he was appointed to the upper house. A favorite of Crown Prince Rudolf as well as of Empress Elisabeth, he upheld the Compromise of 1867, labeling the Separatists of the 1890's hotheads. Although absorption in politics made some of his later works slapdash, his short stories remained exemplary. The novella *Saffi* (1884), shortly thereafter retitled *The Gypsy Baron*, furnished the basis for Strauss's operetta of 1885. Jókai was so popular that in 1896 a de luxe fiftieth jubilee edition of his novels was oversubscribed. Every county in Hungary sent the author a memorial album, and painters donated canvases to signify their homage. While tending roses at his villa in the suburb of Schwabenberg, for thirty years Jókai could claim to be the best known personage in Budapest, a genuine culture-hero. Never was any Austrian writer so honored as this Hungarian, who had sustained national self-confidence during years of oppression. More than anyone else, Jókai taught his countrymen to love literature, so that even the fastidious Endre Ady (1877–1919) could proclaim in 1904, "The country which has had a Jókai can never fall back to the level of Afghanistan."[28]

Jókai edited several newspapers in addition to serving in Parliament. Although in 1863 audacity as a journalist landed him in prison—where he sculpted while serving one month of a year's sentence—the novelist never ceased flaunting national pride. By uniting the roles of author and national hero, Jókai embodied a peculiarly Hungarian phenomenon. In contrast to Austrians, Hungarians expected writers to participate in politics and to be feted for it. Spared the hate-love that the Viennese public inflicted on its favorites, after 1850 Hungarian writers basked in the approval of their countrymen, and none more so than Jókai. He was perhaps the finest example in nineteenth-century letters of a writer whose creativity reinforced wishes of his readers. Thanks in part to him, the alienated authors of Young Vienna or of Baudelaire's Paris were inconceivable in Budapest. As we shall see, intimacy between writer and public in Hungary helped inspire Lukács and Mannheim to pioneer the sociology of knowledge.

The list of Hungarian writers who exhorted their countrymen is long. Next to Jókai, the most popular was the poet Sándor Petőfi (1823–1849), whose fiery folk songs helped ignite the Revolution of 1848. In his novel *The Village Notary* (1845), József Eötvös (1813–1871) exposed the venality of village officials with humor worthy of Jókai. The Transylvanian-born Zsigmond Kemény (1814–1875) wrote novels whose fatalism resembles that of Thomas Hardy. By portraying the nation's past in heroic colors, the epic poet János Arany (1817–1882) became the first author in Hungary to earn a living entirely through sale of his works. Even the pessimist Imre Madách (1823–1864), an admirer of Hogarth, used the character of Miltiades in his *Tragedy of Man* (1862) to personify the frustrated heroism of the 1850's. In ballads and epics, Mihály Vörösmarty (1800–1855) exalted the patriotic aspirations of the pre-March period. No Hungarian writer displayed the aversion to politics of Goethe, Keller, or Stifter. The apolitical German *Bildungsroman* was unthinkable in Hungary.

Besides Jókai, two other writers were members of the diet. Ferenc Kölcsey (1790–1838), who introduced the literary ballad into Magyar around 1820, made ardent nationalistic speeches during the 1830's. József Eötvös so excelled as a political theorist that his two-volume *The Influence of the Ruling Ideas of the Nineteenth Century on the State* (Budapest, 1851–1854) bears comparison with de Tocqueville's *L'Ancien régime* (Paris, 1856). Both of these aristocratic statesmen argued that liberty is incompatible with equality. The Hungarian stressed nationalism as a third ruling idea of the century, unmasking Slav nationalism as a disguised imperialism that only a centralized constitutional monarchy could check.

Painting and music reflected the same nationalistic fervor as literature. The painters Bertalan Székely von Adámos (1835–1910) and Mihály Munkácsy (1844–1900) celebrated the history and folklore of Hungary. A friend of Makart, Székely depicted historical scenes, such as the death of Lajos II at Mohács, with dramatic intensity rivaling that of Jókai or Petőfi.[29] In music, a national school surrounded Ferenc Erkel (1810–1893), conductor at the National Theater, and Mihály Mosonyi (1814–1870), who wrote a funeral symphony for Széchenyi. Their cultivation of Hungarian folk music had been stimulated by the triumphal visit of Franz Liszt to Budapest in January, 1840. They were undeterred when in 1859 Liszt stated that Hungarian music derived entirely from gypsy airs.

As in nineteenth-century Russia, literary critics helped to politicize literature. József Bajza (1804–1854), Ferenc Toldy (1805–1875), and Pál Gyulai (1826–1909) exhorted their countrymen to self-improvement, as did Belinsky, Chernyshevsky, and Dobrolyubov in Russia. The three writers who in 1837 founded the journal *Athenaeum*, Vörösmarty, Bajza, and Toldy, demanded that literature exalt the nation; they condemned cosmopolitan themes as treachery to Hungary. Although Gyulai chided Jókai for implausible plots and wooden characters, the critic was no less a nationalist, admiring Arany's combination of formal perfection with patriotic themes. Hungarian critics differed from those elsewhere by addressing themselves not to the reader but to the writer, instructing him how to cultivate national spirit.[30] Critics enjoyed monopoly power by virtue of the fact that Budapest housed nearly all the nation's publishers, literary societies, and many of the readers, leaving Klausenburg a poor second. Around 1900 more than two hundred newspapers and periodicals in Magyar were published in Budapest. Although the city never produced a German-language literature comparable to that of Prague, forty-odd German periodicals weathered the upsurge of Magyarization.

After 1900, the political involvement of writers degenerated into a feud between imitators of Jókai and cosmopolitans like Endre Ady, who wished to enrich Hungarian letters through influences from France and Germany. Objecting that epigones of Jókai had debased nationalism into xenophobia, in 1908 admirers of Ady founded the journal *Nyugat (West)* to oppose the nationalists' *Kelet (East)*.[31] Financed by Lajos Hatvany (1880–1961) and staffed largely by Jews, *Nyugat* was edited by Hugó Veigelsberg (1869–1949), who took as his pen name Ignotus, a pseudonym that Széchenyi had used in 1859 to publish a critique of Bach's regime. Georg Lukács printed essays in *Nyugat,* before cosmopolitanism impelled him to study in Germany. The writer who became best known abroad, the Jew Ferenc Molnár (1878–1952), infused délibáb into operetta-like plays such as *Liliom* (1909). He represented a late blooming of Jókai's irrepressible fantasy. A later master of délibáb has been the Calvinist physician László Németh (1901–), who through forty years has voiced unwavering faith in the mission of the Magyars. His recent novel, *Compassion* (Budapest, 1965; German trans., Stuttgart, 1968), evokes the Budapest of 1922.

Still another flowering of Hungarian improvisation occurred in an unduly neglected English-language essayist of Hungarian birth, Emil Reich (1854–1910). A Catholic born at Preschau in Slovakia, Reich studied at Prague, Budapest, and Vienna before dwelling in the United States from 1884 to 1889. After a sojourn in Paris, from 1897 to 1910 he settled in London as a writer and lecturer. Flaunting a brilliant feuilletonistic style, in numerous books and articles he extolled Hungarian imperialism as a wave of the future, which would benefit southeastern Europe in the way that Rome and Great Britain had uplifted their colonies. He regretted that Hungary had not become the Prussia of the Habsburg Empire.[32] Reich characterized Zionism as an aberration arising from Jews' lack of national feeling. Incapable of the chauvinism that spurred gentile Hungarians, rootless Jews invited economic anti-Semitism.[33] Preoccupied by power politics and national character, Reich used the term "geo-politics" as early as 1908, eight years before the Swedish sociologist Rudolf Kjellén (1864–1922) made it famous.[34] His sympathy for imperialism notwithstanding, Reich minted brilliant aperçus, which frequently offer deeper insight into politics than those of another feuilletonistic historian, Egon Friedell. Through a prolix yet striking style, Reich exemplified the penchant for improvisation which he believed characterized all Hungarian literature. Coining the term *parlature* for the oratorical flair of Hungarians, Reich followed Jenö Péterfy in interpreting Jókai as a master of improvisation. That novelist seemed a creator who like Franz Liszt overflowed with fecundity, seldom deserting the peaks of exaltation.[35] In his own essays, Reich proved to be a spellbinder, whose rhapsodies on historical themes illustrate the atmosphere of délibáb which pervaded Hungarian life.[36]

In some measure, Magyar chauvinism compensated for the isolation inevitable for speakers of a non-Indo-European language, which foreigners rarely learned. On the one hand, Hungarians cultivated an exuberant pride in their ancestors, exuding self-satisfaction. An Irish violinist, Walter Sharkey, detected this quality in Hungarian musicians:

> No other race could rival the Hungarian in rhythm, because no other race had such relaxation. And he ascribed their relaxation to their inborn consciousness of aristocracy, of having achieved not in themselves but in their forbears that which entitled them to freedom from the tension of their still-striving neighbors to the west.[37]

This inherited sense of achievement abetted improvisation. Freed from necessity to prove oneself, a Magyar could indulge fantasy with impunity. On the other hand, an innate sense of superiority goaded Hungarians who lived abroad to vindicate the brilliance of their countrymen. Because Magyar literature and culture were all but unknown, Hungarians abroad had to start from scratch if they wished to demonstrate the accomplishments of their nation. As Count Zays put it in the 1880's:

> The Magyar loves his country and his nationality better than humanity, better than liberty, better than himself, better even than God and his eternal salvation.[38]

Although expressed above with improvisatory exaggeration, ability to put a cause ahead of self has animated exiles like Georg Lukács, Karl Mannheim, Arnold Hauser, the Polanyi brothers, Franz Alexander, and David Rapoport. The fact that all these men were Jewish only intensified their diligence. In natural science, similar dedication has distinguished Theodor von Kármán, John von Neumann, Leo Szilard, Eugene Wigner, Peter Goldmark, and Edward Teller. Accustomed to indulge flights of fancy as well as to labor for a higher goal, these Hungarian Jews pioneered innumerable technological marvels. Nationalism combined with love of improvisation provided ideal incentive for inventors.[39] In their own way, they expressed the same devotion to country which led Géza Róheim to request that he be buried in a Hungarian flag.

PREINDUSTRIAL NATIONALITIES
UNDER THE MAGYAR YOKE

The same Magyar nationalism that stimulated innovative thought caused subject nationalities to be oppressed. Romanians, Slovaks, Ruthenians, Serbs, and Croats experienced only the seamy side of Hungarian pride. Although numerous Austrians, among them Karl Lueger and Franz Ferdinand, denounced Magyar tyranny, it received widest publicity from a Scotsman, Robert W. Seton-Watson (1879–1951).[40] He divulged malfeasance whereby the party in power rigged elections: there existed about one hundred so-called safe districts, mostly in non-Magyar regions where fewer than fifteen hundred persons voted. "Mamelukes" planted here prevented non-Magyars from reaching the polls by declaring bridges unsafe or by announcing an epidemic of animal disease, so that voters had to walk great distances. Because there was no secret ballot, police easily frightened would-be voters from the polling place, virtually disenfranchising Romanians and Slovaks.[41]

Scandal was aggravated by the fact that Hungarian officials systematically violated the Law of Nationalities, which József Eötvös had drafted in 1868. Although this law guaranteed every person the right to be taught at school and to be tried in court using his own language, in practice courts and schools employed nothing but Magyar. Compulsory attendance at kindergartens did not suffice to erase the language handicap of non-Magyars, with the result that subject nationalities could not educate a middle class. A bare handful of Romanians learned sufficient Magyar to attend gymnasium and even fewer entered university. In Transylvania all judges, lawyers, and jurors were Magyars, even where one Romanian was suing another. A plaintiff who spoke no Magyar was required to hire both a translator and an interpreter if he wished to transact even the simplest official business.

To protest violations of the Law of Nationalities, in 1892 a uniate priest led a deputation of three hundred Romanian intellectuals and peasants to petition Franz Joseph. Not only were they refused an audience with the emperor, but after they had published a manifesto of their grievances, they were prosecuted at Klausenburg for "incitement against Magyar nationality," to wit, advocating secession. For having attempted to exercise a constitutional right, the five leaders landed in jail for terms of two-and-one-half to five years; as usual, authorities in Vienna declined to intervene.[42] It was in vain hope of rectifying such injustices that in 1906 the Romanian Aurel Popovici (1863–1917) proposed a federal system for dividing Austria-Hungary into fifteen nations.

In 1869 the Serbs and Croatians who had safeguarded the southern military frontier since 1690 were consigned to Hungarian rule. Franz Joseph rewarded 170 years of loyalty by abrogating the *Privilegia* with which Leopold I had guaranteed autonomy. The inventor Michael Pupin (1858–1935) recalled how grievously this betrayal shocked the Croats, coming just three years after they had won the battle of Custozza and twenty years after they had helped vanquish Kossuth.

> I remember my father saying to me one day, "Thou shalt never be a soldier in the emperor's army. The emperor has broken his word; the emperor is a traitor in the eyes of the military frontiersmen. We depise the man who is not true to his word." . . . this treacherous act of the Austrian emperor in 1869 was the beginning of the end of the Austrian Empire. . . . The love of the people for the country in which they lived began to languish and finally died.[43]

After the military frontier had been merged into Croatia, this semi-independent province became so restive that in April, 1912, Hungary suspended its constitution and placed the land under a dictator, Cuvaj.[44] Once again Austrian authorities refused to intervene in what was deemed a purely Magyar affair. In return for Hungarian support of Austrian immobility, Austrians condoned Magyar oppression.

The most colorful region of Hungary was Transylvania, which surpassed even Bukovina in preserving Oriental traits. After 1848, the rift between Romanians and Magyars had become irreparable. In that year Austrian agents had provoked Romanian peasants to rise against their masters; Magyar nobles were buried alive and had their tongues cut out, leaving bitterness that precluded all sympathy for the subject race.[45] The region constituted a vast ethnographic museum, seething with legends of vampires and werewolves. Peasants believed that any person killed by the illegitimate child of two illegitimate parents would become a vampire *(nosferatu)*. In order to exorcise such a spirit, it was necessary either to drive a stake through the corpse, to shoot a bullet through the coffin, to stuff the mouth with garlic, or else to burn the heart. These rituals took place in every Romanian village.[46] On one occasion, peasants mistook a French botanist stooping on a hillside for a wolf. When he stood erect, they took him for a werewolf who had changed shape; he eluded assault only because a wagon happened along.[47] It was superstitions such as these which Bram Stoker exploited in his novel *Dracula* (London, 1897), whose title is taken from the Romanian word *dracul* for devil. Mór Jókai dramatized similar beliefs in his Transylvanian tale, *Poor Plutocrats* (1860).

Even more backward than the Romanians were the Ruthenians of Upper Hungary. This mountainous region, which fell to Czechoslovakia in 1919 under the name Sub-Carpathian Ruthenia before becoming part of the Soviet Union in 1945, was exploited by Hungarian magnates as a vast hunting preserve. There Ruthenian peasants inhabited clay huts without chimneys, victimized into a state of starvation and alcoholism.[48] Some fasted as often as 250 days per year, while venerating medicine men and wonder-rabbis.

Another Carpathian enclave contained the Hungarian Szeklers, a Magyar tribe that had preserved folkways long since abandoned by dwellers of the plains.[49] It was among Szeklers that after 1905 Béla Bartók collected Hungarian folksongs that had disappeared elsewhere. These enabled him to prove that Hungarian music was not exclusively of gypsy origin as Franz Liszt had supposed. Still another minority consisted of German or Saxon colonists, who had settled Transylvania during the sixteenth century. Concentrated in the southeast, they retained sixteenth-century folkways, at the same time introducing modern industry and finance, and making Klausenburg a financial center. When they lost autonomy in 1876, they became another oppressed minority, joining the Germans of Budapest to denounce Magyarization.

Gypsies occupied a special place among minorities in Hungary.[50] Upon their appearance in 1417, they were welcomed as blacksmiths in an economy shifting from pastoral to agricultural. They owed their cohesiveness to their origin as a caste of musicians in India—the Doms —for whom birth constituted an indelible mark of identity. Up to 1750 they were respected as Christian refugees from the Turks, until their resistance to settlement under Maria Theresa and Joseph II made them pariahs. After a Hungarian linguist István Vályi had discovered in 1763 similarity between Hindi and the gypsy language Romany, the language was studied by among others Archduke Joseph (1833–1905), who in 1888 published a grammar of Romany written in Hungarian. Gypsies retained a number of taboos, among them a prohibition against the slaughter of horses and a dread of corpses. Dying gypsies were abandoned to expire in the open air; midwives and women in childbirth were also considered impure. Because they despised manual labor, gypsies excelled as thieves, working in teams whose loyalty baffled police. Gypsies also possessed an extraordinary sense of direction, rivaling American Indians in skill at tracking.[51]

Since the seventeenth century, gypsy musicians entertained Hungarian magnates, and the leader *(primás)* of a band that served high nobles enjoyed enormous prestige among his fellows. Gypsy orchestras played without using scores—many of the musicians could not even read music. They excelled at improvisation and cultivated a tradition that honored the violinist János Bihari (1764–1827) as the "gypsy Beethoven." The improvisatory skill of gypsy musicians has been described by an American observer:

> an orchestra is playing impetuously, almost uncivilized in its abandon. Violins are held in all sorts of positions. The bowing seems strangely athletic, almost savage. The tempo, full of sudden surprises, is apparently controlled only—and evidently arbitrarily—by the leader's whim.[52]

In its preference for the minor mode, for ornamented melody, and for complex rhythm, gypsy music recalls the music of India.

Steadfastly refusing to assimilate Western civilization, gypsies maintained the most particularistic society within Austria-Hungary. In Budapest, Vienna, and even Prague, they reminded capitalists and bureaucrats of age-old mores that belittled industrialism and Roman law. Regarded by the populace as a necessary evil, gypsies resembled rural Jews by parading exotic dress and language while suffering a similar reputation for craftiness. Jews, of course, were far more industrious, prospering both at agriculture and finance, and they flocked to cities, which the gypsies shunned. Whereas urban Jews became the most industrialized and most intellectual of Austria-Hungary's nationalities, gypsies remained at the opposite extreme. Although their cohesiveness withstood every attempt at Westernization and Magyarization, they too fell victim to Hitler. Together with everyone else in the Danube Basin, gypsies would have benefited after World War One if successor states could have forgotten Magyar oppression enough to cooperate in resisting Germany.

25

Utopians from Hungary

THE IMPROVISATORY GENIUS
OF THEODOR HERZL

POLITICAL ACTIVISM inspired several Budapest-born publicists to earn
fame after departing Hungary. Two of them, Theodor Herzl and his
friend Theodor Hertzka, pursued careers at Vienna, while a third, Max
Nordau, wrote at Paris. Passion for politics differentiated these Hungarian Jews from their Austrian counterparts.

Born in Budapest the son of an energetic and pious merchant,
Theodor Herzl (1860–1904) grew up feeling in a minority on two counts,
as a Jew and as a German.[1] While in gymnasium he wrote a poem
lauding Luther as champion of Germany, and as a student of law at
Vienna from 1878 to 1883, he participated with Hermann Bahr and
Heinrich Friedjung in a German-National student group about which
he planned to write a novel. While practicing law in Vienna, in 1884 he
began to contribute feuilletons first to the *Wiener Allgemeine Zeitung*
and then to the *Neue Freie Presse*. The handsome young journalist
also wrote comedies, which won less acclaim than his brilliantly improvised feuilletons. He married in July, 1889, and in October, 1891, he
became Paris correspondent of the *Neue Freie Presse*, arriving there in
time to witness a tide of economic anti-Semitism unleashed by the
Panama Scandal. In 1894 he was appalled to see France cementing an
alliance with Russia at the very moment when pogroms were decimat-
ing Ukrainian Jewry. The indifference of Western Jews to religious and
economic anti-Semitism incited Herzl in 1895 to draft his proposal for
a Jewish state. Following publication of *Der Judenstaat: Versuch
einer modernen Lösung der Judenfrage* (Vienna, 1896), the journalist
transformed himself from a Viennese aesthete into an engagé Hungarian intellectual, pitting himself against businessmen, politicians, and
monarchs in order to fulfill his dream.

Herzl's proposal was simple. Through diplomatic concert, the states
of Europe should grant to a Jewish stock company sovereignty over a

portion of the colonial territory at their disposal. Jewish management would turn this state into a refuge for any European Jews who wished to escape either pogroms or assimilation. Imbued with a political rather than a religious conception of Judaism, Herzl hoped that the sultan would allow Western Jews to settle Palestine. If not, Herzl was willing, as many of his followers were not, to accept a tract in Argentina or central Africa. Settlements for Russian Jews had been begun in Palestine by the Jewish Colonization Association that a Munich-born banker Moritz de Hirsch (1831–1896) had founded in 1891. It was to Hirsch that Herzl first unfolded his scheme. The term Zionism had been coined in May, 1890, by a Vienna-born journalist Nathan Birnbaum (1864–1937) in his journal *Selbst-Emancipation,* which endorsed Hirsch's initiative of buying land in Palestine.

From 1896 until his death in 1904, Herzl organized six world congresses of Jewry. He entreated the sultan, the German emperor, the king of Italy, and the pope, tirelessly lobbying for his program. Although he did not expect to witness its fulfillment, he never doubted that eventually European states would see the wisdom of encouraging restive Jews to emigrate. Although the *Neue Freie Presse* under the baptized Jew Moritz Benedikt forbade the word Zionism to appear in its columns, the paper employed Herzl as feuilleton editor from 1896 to 1904, a post that Kraus had turned down. Herzl used this position to further the career of Arthur Schnitzler and to give a literary start to Stefan Zweig. No less than Kraus and Freud, Herzl nurtured hate-love toward Vienna. He once told Stefan Zweig, "Everything which I know I learned abroad. Only there can one learn to think across distances."[2] Herzl was derided by Karl Kraus in a pamphlet *Eine Krone für Zion* (Vienna, 1898) and by other urbanized Viennese, who scoffed at sending Ringstrasse-dandies to till the desert of Palestine. Orthodox Jews decried Zionism as a blasphemy that usurped the function of the Messiah. Despite lampoons, Herzl's movement flourished. At the time of Herzl's death, the Zionist bank in London, the Jewish Colonial Trust, boasted 135,000 shareholders, then the largest number financing any enterprise in the world. His funeral on July 7, 1904, was attended by as many as 10,000 Jews, who trekked from all over Europe to honor their fallen leader. As we have mentioned, somehow a rumor started that Herzl had died a suicide, whereas in reality he had died of pneumonia, a few minutes after bidding farewell to his wife and mother.

Herzl toiled above all to aid Eastern Jews. At the First Zionist Congress in Basel from August 29 to 31, 1897, a seventy-man delegation of Russian Jews had awed him. As the last ghetto Jews, they retained,

Herzl believed, a sense of national unity unsullied by assimilation. He romanticized rural Jews of Bohemia and Galicia, such as Leopold Kompert and Karl Emil Franzos described. He foresaw that in a Jewish state Russian Jews would have to open land and build farms before Western industry could begin. Despite the prominence of Russian Jews in the movement, Herzl retained German as its official language.

Herzl interpreted anti-Semitism toward Western Jews as being economic in origin. Through centuries of ghetto-living, Jews had so mastered commercial skills that after emancipation they could compete at once with the gentile middle class. In this struggle, a Jew often used fair means and foul, fearing that if he failed he would sink into a proletariat but knowing that if he succeeded he could acquire wealth impregnable to confiscation. All Jews suffered because some preened as financial leaders while others fomented revolution. Reviled by both right and left, not even assimilated Jews could elude the stigma of race, as Herzl had dramatized in a pre-Zionist play, *Das neue Ghetto* (Vienna, 1898). By founding a Jewish state, Herzl hoped to spare others the dilemma of choosing either to join the radical left or to cultivate self-hatred. However much he had smarted under assimilation, Herzl remained at bottom a conservative. His esteem for rural Jews entailed abhorrence of revolution:

> that a highly conservative people, like the Jews, have always been driven into the ranks of revolutionists, is the most lamentable feature in the tragedy of our race.[3]

Unlike some other Zionists, Herzl claimed no special virtue or talent for the Jewish race. He deemed the bulk of his people unperceptive and unimaginative, notably urban Jews who belittled his dreams as the wish-fulfillment of an *ingénu*.

Why did Herzl choose to abandon his desk—to which he longed to return—in order to lead what he called an experiment in the psychology of the masses?[4] At least three traditions within Austro-Hungarian intellectual life converged in Herzl. First, he was a utopian in the manner of Hungarian nationalists, resembling other Budapest-born Jews like Hertzka and Nordau, whom he equaled in moral fervor and surpassed in skill as an organizer. As intellectuals born in Hungary, these publicists took it for granted that a writer should agitate. Fortifying Herzl's zeal was a Hungarian gift for improvisation. Exuding délibáb, he undertook gambits that rivaled episodes out of Jókai, as he strove to enlist in common cause the pope and the king of Italy or to interview the emperor of Germany at Istanbul. Although he regarded Hungary —together with England—as one of two havens for assimilated Jews in Europe, boyhood as a German and a Jew in Budapest had schooled him to think first in terms of nationality. Incited by Magyars to yearn for national identity, he identified himself initially with the Germans of Austria and later with the Jews.

Second, Herzl utilized techniques of mass movements which he had learned from the German-National club at the University of Vienna. He sought for Jews the kind of autonomy that Georg von Schönerer had been demanding for Austria's Germans. At Zionist congresses, Herzl improvised the sort of inflammatory rhetoric with which Schönerer and Lueger courted followers. Although Herzl wrote for the favorite newspaper of Vienna's assimilated Jews, he repudiated their do-nothing liberalism; likewise he impugned federalistic proposals by Austro-Marxists, who regarded Jews not as a nationality but as a religion. A scion of Budapest, Herzl wanted Jews to become a full-fledged nation like the Magyars, albeit without oppressing other peoples.

Third, Herzl represented a kind of Josephinist conservative, who sought to bolster the status quo by persuading monarchs that Jewish revolutionaries should emigrate. Imbued with faith in bureaucracy and concern for the whole of society such as marked Austrian Catholic philosophers, Herzl envisioned a conservative revolution that would remove agitators for change. Once rid of troublesome Jews, Christian Europe could achieve equilibrium. As mentioned previously. Herzl deemed the Jews a conservative people, and he offered to help other conservatives like the German emperor and the pope to safeguard their values. However quixotic this policy may seem, it accorded with the Josephinist practice of protecting stability by banishing troublemakers. Herzl may have reinforced his trust in monarchs after witnessing Franz Joseph yield to the Hungarians in 1867 and to supporters of Lueger in 1897. The emperor's willingness to compromise, however tardily, may have encouraged Herzl to expect that less stubborn monarchs would hasten to forestall unrest.

As a cosmopolitan, Herzl transcended the Habsburg Empire. Having gestated his program in Paris, he maneuvered on a European-wide, even a worldwide scale. He traversed the Near East and Russia, visiting any capital that promised to further his goal. Because socialism threatened to seduce potential followers, he labored to differentiate his movement from it. Although during the 1880's Herzl had pandered to Viennese Phaeacianism, by 1895 he had shed any trace of therapeutic nihilism. In the manner of Karl Lueger, he sympathized deeply with suffering masses, enduring both obloquy and adulation for their sake. By uniting the best qualities of the Hungarian and the Jew, Herzl scandalized the Viennese.

THEODOR HERTZKA:
A UTOPIAN SOCIALIST OF THE 1890'S

A second Budapest-born utopian active in Vienna, the journalist Theodor Hertzka (1845–1924) gained far less renown than Herzl.[5] Having absorbed the political activism of Hungarian intellectuals, Hertzka studied at Vienna where for a time he joined Carl Menger's school of economics. During the 1870's he served as economics editor of the *Neue Freie Presse*, and from 1886 to 1901 he edited the Vienna weekly *Zeitschrift für Staats- und Volkswirtschaft*, where he advocated free trade and cooperative ownership of land. Like Popper-Lynkeus he prided himself on daring to propound simple solutions: during the early 1890's, he urged resolving the bimetallic crisis by minting coins from an alloy of nine parts silver to one part gold.

Hertzka won fame through a futuristic novel, *Freiland: Ein soziales Zukunftsbild* (Leipzig, 1890). It described how a group of educated Europeans colonize an International Free Society among Masai in the mountains of Kenya until after several generations the Society has girdled the globe. Hertzka's key proposal was to forbid rent and interest: land and capital would be furnished free of charge to entrepreneurs, who would compete for modest profit once they need no longer fear bankruptcy through usury. Although no one would own any of the free land or capital, all would share the common supply. Echoing Karl von Vogelsang and Anton Menger, Hertzka taught that economic growth was lagging because workers received too little income to consume what they manufactured. By abolishing interest, Hertzka aimed to lower prices without scuttling individualism. *Freiland* reflected debate on the status of women by arguing that women devote themselves to attracting men chiefly because lack of legal rights precludes taking pride in their own achievements. Like Auguste Comte, Hertzka wanted to exclude women from competition with men so that they could care for children, the sick, and the aged. In his effort to combine individualism with socialism, Hertzka hailed Francis Bacon as the clearest and soberest of modern thinkers. Hertzka's chief disciple was a Berlin-born Jewish physician Franz Oppenheimer (1864–1943), who built a sociology around communal ownership of land.

To implement his utopia, Hertzka envisioned a Darwinian struggle between good and bad social systems, insisting that through natural selection better systems would supersede worse. For a time during the 1890's this faith proved contagious, as Freeland associations sprouted all over Europe. In 1893 an Australian, William Lane, established a Freeland Community of trade unionists in Paraguay, which failed when the teetotaler Lane expelled members for breaking a pledge of total abstinence. A year later a small colony in Kenya, led by Julius Wilhelm, fared no better. In *Entrückt in die Zukunft: Sozialpolitischer Roman* (Berlin, 1895), Hertzka ceased advocating Freeland in order to portray the world two hundred years hence in the manner of Bellamy's *Looking Backward* (1888). The utopian economist foresaw economic abundance, aviation, independence of wives and children, and other amenities to which Freeland communities had aspired.

Like Theodor Herzl, Hertzka brought to Vienna the faith of a Hungarian intellectual that writers belong in politics. Indulgence in délibáb visions was quintessentially utopian, prone to produce premature enterprises such as the Freeland colonies. To parry a similar accusation against Zionism, Herzl in the preface to the *Judenstaat* differentiated his own proposal from that of Hertzka. *Freiland*, said Herzl, epitomized a utopia because there existed no pressing evil for it to relieve, whereas a Jewish state would liquidate a grievance. Although Herzl surely underestimated the urgency of the social' question, he was right that Hertzka's plan stood no better chance of success than did the schemes of Popper-Lynkeus.

MAX NORDAU: DISILLUSIONED UTOPIAN TURNED ASSAILANT OF DEGENERACY

A third Jewish utopian from Budapest, Max Nordau (1849–1923), is remembered chiefly as a lieutenant of Herzl.[6] The son of a rabbi named Südfeld, Nordau received a doctorate in medicine at Budapest in 1876, before moving his practice to Paris four years later. There he won fame for a series of feuilletonistic treatises that indicted industrial civilization for causing degeneration. Nordau met Herzl in 1895, ten years later succeeding him as leader of political Zionism while spending the rest of his life in Paris. Endowed by age thirty-five with snow-white hair framing black eyes and a black beard, he resembled a Hebrew prophet.

Although more disenchanted than either Hertzka or Herzl, Nordau became by far the more popular writer. In *Die konventionellen Lügen der Kulturmenschheit* (Leipzig, 1883), which went through ten editions within a year, Nordau restated in flamboyant rhetoric the outcry of the French Enlightenment against traditional institutions such as church, monarchy, aristocracy, and marriage. To counteract duplicity, he advocated a natural ethics based on Ludwig Feuerbach's notion of solidarity; someday, Nordau believed, the word "humanity" would cease to be an abstraction, designating instead a feeling of brotherhood shared by all men.

Nordau won added fame by assailing fin-de-siècle morals in the two-volume *Entartung* (Berlin, 1892–1893). Extending research begun by the criminologist Cesare Lombroso (1836–1909), Nordau branded contemporary art as degenerate *(entartet)*. Invoking Darwin's theory of useful variations, Nordau postulated that a genius advances life, while a degenerate person regresses. Nordau repudiated Lombroso's thesis that genius entails neurosis. Genius is progressive and unique, whereas degeneracy is atavistic and self-multiplying. In modern times, regressiveness is rampaging. In place of Enlightenment ideals of brotherhood and self-sacrifice, Nordau discerned among the upper classes and intellectuals a cult of mysticism, celebrated by Verlaine, Tolstoy, and Maeterlinck. In the diabolist Baudelaire, the aesthete Oscar Wilde, and the sadist Friedrich Nietzsche, the Hungarian diagnosed egomania, while love of filth mars the naturalistic works of Zola and Gerhart Hauptmann. With imperturbable self-confidence, Nordau endorsed Hanslick's critique of Wagner, whom he dubbed a masochist; he dismissed Pre-Raphaelites and Ruskin as mystics; he disparaged Tolstoy's asceticism as a revival of the Skoptsi sect; and he contrasted Baudelaire's cult of the prostitute with the chaste emotions of Goethe's *Hermann und Dorothea* (1798). Puvis de Chavannes displays degeneracy by painting dull shades as if he were color-blind.

Despite admiration for the Enlightenment, Nordau's roots lay in preindustrial Hungary. Extolling the fellow-feeling of particularistic society, Nordau contended that in Paris and Berlin desire for self-gratification is loosening bonds of brotherhood. Like the benign anarchist Peter Kropotkin, the Hungarian implored industrializing society to restore virtues inherent in nature.[7] Nordau explained that contemporary regressiveness results from wear-and-tear exerted on leaders by railroads, steamships, telephones, telegraphs, and factories.[8] Modern degeneracy spreads faster than that of Imperial Rome because the earlier epidemic had infected primarily the lower classes, whereas today corruption begins at the top and filters downward.

Nordau experienced all the frustrations of a utopian. Seeing his délibáb fantasies obstructed, he evolved from excogitating utopias to

denigrating modernity. With arrogance surpassing that of Otto Weininger, Nordau informed critics of *Entartung* that from nineteen out of
twenty of them he could learn nothing whatever. To refute the taunt
that he himself was degenerate, the Hungarian accused reviewers of
having repudiated standards for the sake of posting a rhetorical victory.[9] Utter lack of humor exacerbated his smugness; when Sigmund
Freud called on Nordau in 1885 or 1886, the psychiatrist found the
older man unbearably vain.[10] Nordau distinguished himself among
feuilletonists by behaving with deadly seriousness.

Throughout his jeremiads, Nordau espoused the Hungarian conviction that a writer's main business is to edify. Advocates of *l'art pour
l'art* he branded as immoral. Instead of elevating life, naturalists belittle it, pandering to readers' selfish illusions. Rebutting the objection
that he imputed to an author traits of his characters, Nordau pontificated that this procedure is justified when all of a writer's creations
reflect vices such as found in Ibsen or Baudelaire. In declaring that an
immoralist "has written thus because he could not write otherwise. His
books are confessions,"[11] Nordau applied to artists of all nations a
standard that prevailed in Hungary. Nordau expected every writer to
emulate Jókai and Eötvös by exhorting citizens to serve their country.

As a Zionist, Nordau's exaltation inspired clairvoyance. The Dreyfus
Affair alarmed him even more gravely than it did Herzl. During 1898
he fully expected Frenchmen to begin murdering Jews, although he
discerned an obstacle to another St. Bartholomew's Massacre in the
fact Jews look like Southern Frenchmen. Not even a degenerate
country could require men to wear badges identifying their race.[12]
Nordau cited articles of 1898 in *L'Osservatore Romano*, which vilified
Jews for having fled the ghetto to spread the pestilence of liberal
thought. In a decaying age, the Roman Catholic church desired to
annihilate Jews as eagerly as did republican France. Nordau was one
of very few who during the Dreyfus Affair envisioned something of
the Armageddon that was to come forty years later.

26

Sociology of Knowledge
A Hungarian Truism

GEORG LUKÁCS' DIALECTIC
OF FORM VERSUS LIFE

FEW THINKERS have tried so hard to conceal continuity between their early career and their later thought as Georg Lukács (1885–1971). One result of Lukács' hate-love for his pre-Marxist youth has been to obscure the fact that he virtually created the sociology of literature and profoundly influenced the sociology of knowledge. A second consequence is that anyone who undertakes to interpret his thought must to some extent contradict Lukács' own interpretation of it.[1]

Georg Lukács was the son of Josef von Lukács (d. ca. 1924), director of the General Hungarian Kreditbank. So far as I can learn, the family was not related either to Béla Lukács (1847–1901), the finance minister who helped organize the Millenial Exposition of 1896, or to László Lukács (1850–1932), who served as prime minister during 1913. Georg von Lukács, as he called himself until 1918, grew up in one of those assimilated upper-bourgeois Jewish families of Budapest which spoke German at home and enjoyed high social prestige. In 1913 and again in 1922, none other than Thomas Mann was a guest in the home of Lukács' father.[2] Having first studied law, in 1906 Georg von Lukács took a doctorate in literature at Budapest under Fechnerian aesthetician Zsolt Beöthy (1844–1922). As early as 1902 while still in gymnasium, he had contributed to the journal *Magyar Szalon* drama reviews modeled on those of the Berlin impressionist Alfred Kerr (1867–1948). In 1904 he was one of three cofounders of the Thalia Theater at Budapest, which performed Ibsen, Strindberg, and Chekhov in imitation of Otto Brahm's Free Stage at Berlin and of André-Léonard Antoine's naturalistic Théâtre libre in Paris. In 1908 Lukács' revised dissertation in Hungarian, in two volumes, *The Development of Mod-*

ern Drama (Budapest, 1911) won the coveted prize of the conservative Kisfaludy Society. In 1908 he also helped to found the journal *Nyugat*, in which between 1908 and 1910 he published a dozen essays. During 1909–1910 he studied at Berlin under Georg Simmel, whom in 1918 he characterized as a transitional figure—an impressionist and pluralist whose experiments in sociology had marked a necessary stage in Lukács' own development.[3]

During 1910 Lukács traveled through Italy and France, while corresponding with the dramatist Paul Ernst (1866–1933). The winter of 1911–1912 he spent at Florence prior to settling in Heidelberg between 1912 to 1915 to study under Max Weber and the Galician-born Jew, Emil Lask (1875–1915). There Lukács' friends included Friedrich Gundolf, Ernst Bloch and surprisingly, Stefan George. He was a frequent guest in the home of Max Weber, whose widow Marianne remembered Lukács as a courteous, intense conversationalist who could hold his own in any company. She added that he professed belief that just then a cosmic conflict between Lucifer and God was coming to a climax, which would either rescue or destroy mankind. For his habilitation, Lukács was writing a treatise on aesthetics, which Max Weber, Emil Lask, and Ernst Bloch followed with interest. In 1917 portions of it were published in *Logos*.[4] He also worked on a volume on Dostoevski, the introduction to which was published in 1916 as *Die Theorie des Romans*. In that year he served briefly as a censor in Budapest, having been declared unfit for active duty.

After two years of traveling between Budapest and Heidelberg, in late 1917 he settled in Budapest to join Karl Mannheim's Free School of the Humanities. Under the personal influence of his syndicalist colleague in the Free School, Ervin Szabó (1877–1918), in December 1918 Lukács joined the newly founded Communist party of Hungary.[5] From that time on he dropped the von from his name. During Béla Kun's Bolshevik Republic, Lukács served as assistant commissar for culture, writing many essays and broadsides. In September, 1919, he fled to Vienna where after a brief imprisonment he lived until 1929. As a delegate in 1920 to the World Congress of the Communist International at Moscow, he had occasion to meet Lenin. In January, 1922, the Hungarian met Thomas Mann briefly in Vienna, an encounter that apparently prompted Mann to model the Communist Jesuit Naphta in *Der Zauberberg* (1924) partly on Lukács.[6]

From 1919 to 1924 Lukács vied with Béla Kun, who had fled to Moscow, for leadership of the Hungarian Communist party in exile. The nine essays he wrote between March 1919, and December, 1922, which were published in *Geschichte und Klassenbewusstsein: Studien*

über marxistische Dialektik (Berlin, 1923; repr. Neuwied, 1968) unleashed such a scandal among orthodox Leninists that he was removed
from the Central Committee, deprived of editorship of the Vienna-
based *Kommunismus,* and vilified as a Hegelian deviationist. After his
marriage at Vienna to Gertrud Bortstieber, Lukács lived in the home
of his wife, a victim of extreme poverty.[7] For three months in 1929, he
sojourned illegally in Hungary before going to Berlin. He spent 1930–
1931 working at the Marx-Engels Institute in Moscow, where Nikolai
Ryazanov was editing newly discovered manuscripts of the young
Marx. During the next two years he worked among Marxist literati in
Berlin before fleeing to Moscow. In 1933 he broke a self-imposed
silence about criticisms of *Geschichte und Klassenbewusstsein* to denounce the influence of Simmel, Weber, and Dilthey on his youthful
work.[8] In Moscow he wrote *Der junge Hegel* (completed in 1938;
Zürich, 1948), as well as many essays on novels of the nineteenth
century and on Thomas Mann. In 1945 he returned to Budapest, where
he remained, except for a brief period of exile in 1956–1957, while publishing more than ever before.

I shall argue that unmistakable continuity runs from Lukács' essays
of 1908 through *Geschichte und Klassenbewusstsein* down to his
exegesis of German thought during the 1930's and beyond. Already in
essays on Kassner and Novalis, written at age twenty-three, he articu-
lated the central problem of his thought: the relation of form to life.
How do objective categories of reason interact with form-defying
impulses of the soul and of society? Throughout his career, Lukács has
been fascinated by a single basic polarity, positing a dichotomy between, on the one hand, ideas, independent of experience a la Bolzano
and Lask, and on the other hand, experience devoid of ideas a la
Nietzsche and Dilthey. On one side he has ranged form, thinking self,
metaphysical stance, dreams—incarnations of Lask's categories and
Bolzano's propositions-in-themselves; on the other side have come life,
soul, uniqueness, external reality, society—disparate manifestations of
Nietzsche's blind will-to-power and Dilthey's unreasoning *Erlebnis.*
Having postulated that every writer must come to terms with relations
between these two realms, all his life Lukács has classified writers
according to how they do this.

In *Die Seele und die Formen* (Hungarian ed., Budapest, 1910; expanded German ed., Berlin, 1911), Lukács published ten essays, written between 1908 and 1910, each of which analyzes relations between
form and life. Because of the rhapsodic style of *Die Seele und die
Formen,* reminiscent of Rudolf Kassner, it will be useful to consider
first interplay between form and life, self and society in *Die Theorie*

des Romans.[9] This clearest of Lukács' early works was written during 1914–1915 out of dismay at the enthusiasm with which most German intellectuals had greeted World War One.

In *Die Theorie des Romans,* Lukács distinguished two ways in which novelists have portrayed the incommensurability between self (or hero) and environment (or society) in the period since 1600, when the world first discovered its abandonment by God. Certain writers, whom Lukács called abstract idealists, constrict the self within its own dreams where it can escape the complexity of the external world. This approach gives rise to the world-fleeing heroes of Cervantes' *Don Quixote,* Schiller's *Don Carlos,* Kleist's *Michael Kohlhaas* and, paradoxically, Balzac's entire human comedy. A second approach, which Lukács labeled the romanticism of disillusionment, expands and glorifies the self so that it appears grander than its environment. Flaubert in *L'Éducation sentimentale* (1869) described the education of such a self, as it nurtures its own superior sensitivity. Environment is belittled, self glorified, a procedure that Lukács discerned also in Turgenev and Tolstoi.

As against these two approaches that separate self and life to the detriment of life, Lukács praised the *Bildungsroman,* above all Goethe's *Wilhelm Meisters Lehrjahre* (1795–96). Goethe's hero seeks to reconcile his dreams with his environment by transforming both himself and society to match his ideals. Throughout, Lukács insisted that each writer's choice of approach is a matter not of personal preference but rather an expression of objective world-historical forces. In keeping with this Hegelian premise, *Die Theorie des Romans* postulated a dialectical movement from self *(für sich)* to external reality *(an sich)* to Goethe's synthesis of the two *(an und für sich).* This dialectic can founder in conflict, deforming either the self through abstract idealism or society through the romanticism of disillusionment. Far preferable is Goethe's resolution of conflict through mutual improvement of self by environment and environment by self. Dostoevski offered a new mode of synthesis, in which a sacrificial self introjects the conflict so as to transform both itself and society.

The same Hegelian triad underlies the ten essays of *Die Seele und die Formen.* Using slightly different vocabulary, Lukács dissected various inadequate modes of relation between form (or reason) and life (or soul). Only in tragedy can the two be reconciled. Kierkegaard wants to subjugate life to form and, as shown in his relation to Regine Olsen, founders in the attempt. Among romantic poets who sought to escape from life into form, only Novalis enriches himself thereby. Stefan George makes a no less futile flight into pure form. These men parallel the abstract idealist of the 1916 essay: in order to flee an unbearable external reality they deprive the self. The disillusionment-romantics of 1916 find their counterpart in the bourgeois realist Theodor Storm, whose quest for harmony between life and form merely impoverishes life. By portraying only the prosaic side of life and creating no characters of overwhelming passion, he renders external reality innocuous. A writer who falls between the two types is the French idyllic novelist Charles-Louis Philippe (1874–1909), whose characters endure lives of quiet desperation in petit-bourgeois poverty. They are so sunk in their environment that they cannot dream of escaping it. Enjoying neither their poverty (life) nor their dreams (form) they vacillate between self-abasement and self-aggrandizement. The same indecisiveness is found in a spokesman of Young Vienna, Richard Beer-Hofmann, whose impressionistic tales elevate an accident of external life into an inevitability for the self. Laurence Sterne offers another mixed case, in which an impressionist, who prefers life, battles a classicist, who prefers form.

In two pivotal essays, Lukács elaborated a dichotomy between Platonist and poet which Rudolf Kassner had introduced in 1900. The Hungarian classified his predecessor as a Platonist who lives in perpetual yearning for perfection of form, which he knows he cannot find amid life. To the Platonist is juxtaposed the critic, a role into which Lukács in the opening essay casts himself. The critic studies art not from the standpoint of the artist, who inevitably exaggerates his own uniqueness, but from the standpoint of the philosopher, who is privileged to see in art, form united with life. Hegelian that he is, the critic believes that in art, form and life seek to be reconciled. His first allegiance, however, is to form, whose conflicts and accommodations with life he examines. In the final essay on metaphysics of tragedy, such a critic asserts that form and life can achieve synthesis only in tragedy: here Lukács instanced works by his friend Paul Ernst to illustrate the ancient—and Hegelian—ideal of tragedy. The tragic hero recognizes his fate as his own responsibility. Once he has felt his guilt as his own act, he can knowingly shape external events so as to triumph over fortuity. By accepting punishment, the hero internalizes the laws of the external world; he alone reconciles form to life.

In both *Die Seele und die Formen* and *Die Theorie des Romans*, Lukács presumed to impute to literary characters metaphysical positions. A work as complex as *Don Quixote* or *Wilhelm Meister* he analyzed according to the metaphysical stance of its author, which is deduced from that of the characters. Writers as diverse as Kierkegaard and Theodor Storm he pigeonholed with sovereign ease. Even before

Lukács had studied under Weber and Lask, he was forcing works of literature to fit a schema of ideal types. In 1962 he reported that Wilhelm Dilthey's *Das Erlebnis und die Dichtung* (Leipzig, 1905) had exerted a decisive influence in encouraging him thus to apply typologies to literature.[10] So pervasive was Lukács' enthusiasm for polar opposites, however, that propensity to use them must have predated even Dilthey's influence. What a godsend the quasi-Hegelian categories of Emil Lask and of Max Weber must have seemed to Lukács upon arriving at Heidelberg in 1912. His virtuosity at manipulating polar opposites had at last met its match.

Around 1908, Lukács' basic polarity was simply form versus soul. By 1916 this had taken on the Hegelian guise of form versus society. His fascination with conflict between mind and society reflected that attitude of political involvement characteristic of Hungarian writers. As we have emphasized, since the 1830's Magyar novelists and poets had become guardians of the national conscience. Besides taking an active role in politics, Petöfi, Jókai, and their associates used art to edify national life. They assumed, *pace* Lukács, that form and life, intellect and society do cooperate. They took for granted the synthesis that Lukács found only in tragedy and in Goethe. Lukács' supreme originality lies, therefore, not in having recognized the ubiquity of polarity between writer and society—most Hungarian writers did that —but in applying it to non-Hungarian literature. By invoking Kierkegaard's skepticism, Lukács challenged the shibboleth of his country's literary life. Upon examination, most non-Hungarian literature turns out to celebrate not harmony of mind and society but its very opposite. Western heroes, unlike those of Jókai, retreat into an impoverished inner world of form, as in Cervantes or Schiller, or else they belittle external life in the manner of Flaubert and Turgenev.

No doubt it was naive of Hungarian writers to depict exclusively characters who live as deeply immersed in their society as those of Eötvös or Jókai. Within a society torn by national conflicts, this vision could be nothing but another product of délibáb, that talent for wish-fulfillment from which Lukács himself is anything but free. The early Lukács managed, however, to convert his countrymen's self-deception into a powerful tool of literary analysis. By turning on its head the category of political involvement which seemed self-evident to fellow Hungarian literati, he unmasked in other literatures discord between self and society. What Hungarians refused to see in their nation, Lukács found to prevail elsewhere. Several years before he had reached this insight, Lukács participated in founding the journal *Nyugat*, which sought to disseminate Western, especially French, literary trends in

Hungary. By a curious symmetry, Lukács later reversed the process by disseminating Hungarian platitudes to the rest of Europe.

Nowhere is Lukács' debt to Hungarian literary pieties so explicit as in the "Sociology of Modern Drama" which he wrote in 1909 as the Introduction to his *The Development of Modern Drama* (Budapest, 1911).[11] Scholars who argue that Hegel and Marx first drew Lukács' attention to the phenomenon of social class will be surprised to learn how closely this work anticipates Marxist aesthetics. In it he explains how intimate theater arose in order to provide the cultured elite a refuge from urban masses. In modern drama it is not passions, as in the Greeks, but ideologies that collide, exemplifying the competition of individuals in capitalist society. The individualism of the cultured bourgeois has emerged as a weapon in his struggle to supplant the medieval guild economy. Instead of the reason-defying passions of ancient tragedy, drama now unmasks the rational calculations of bourgeois *arrivistes*. The frustration that Hebbel and Ibsen inflict upon their heroes reveals a breakdown of the individualism that the eighteenth century had glorified.

The "Sociology of Modern Drama" is richer in concrete analysis than is *Die Seele und die Formen*. It is perhaps the first work to analyze in detail the way in which the social class of theatergoers influences the theme of drama. In keeping with Lukács' basic polarity, the dichotomy between dramatist and audience corresponds to that between form and life. A dramatist must choose that form, or metaphysical stance, which will woo an audience by reflecting its prejudices. A popular dramatist must share the shortcomings of his audience, while one who chooses an esoteric form faces isolation from life.

This notion of symbiosis between author and audience predated Lukács' Marxism by at least nine years. It reappeared in a little-known dialogue, "Von der Armut am Geiste" (1912), which amply reflects that Manichaean dualism of which Marianne Weber spoke.[12] In this dialogue, Lukács propounded an existentialist ethic of self-sacrifice and poverty of spirit reminiscent of Dostoevski. A young poet, who suffers moral qualms not unlike those of Otto Weininger, discourses on his own inauthenticity to the sister of his beloved, who has just committed suicide. He excoriates himself for lacking the clairvoyant goodness of a St. Francis or a Prince Myshkin, that gift of divining the needs of others which could have saved his friend. Branding the routine of bourgeois society as a round of mechanical duties devoid of morality, the poet salutes poverty of spirit as the highest ethic. One must hold oneself ever ready to undertake a godsent mission that will bind together a scattered life. God alone can awaken a commitment that by imposing form on life redeems the chaos of external reality.

In this most existential—and Christian—of his writings, Lukács hails the Sermon on the Mount, Plotinus, Dostoevski, and Kierkegaard. He praises Prince Myshkin, Alyosha Karamazov, and Kierkegaard's Abraham as "Gnostics of the deed" who recognize and accept the disproportion between their own higher ethic and ordinary life. Lukács' poet berates lukewarm persons who cannot emulate this elite in poverty of spirit. The poet himself commits suicide, leaving open on his desk the Revelations of Saint John the Divine at 3:15–16, where the angel reproaches the Church of Laodicea for sheltering those who burn neither hot nor cold.

This almost forgotten work lends some weight to Lucien Goldmann's thesis that Lukács in his essay on tragedy in *Die Seele und die Formen* anticipated twentieth-century existentialism.[13] Goldmann overstates his case, however, when he says that it was Lukács who hailed death as guarantor of authenticity. As we know, during the 1890's writers of Young Vienna like Schnitzler and Beer-Hofmann had revived the Baroque vision of death as limit and liberator, and Rudolf Kassner had preceded the Hungarian in calling attention to Kierkegaard.[14] Lukács' innovation lay rather in exploiting the political monomania of Hungarian writers to assess non-Hungarian literature. In due course, Lukács' search for authenticity and for a new caste of servants of mankind impelled him to take political action through the Communist party. The party was to furnish that phalanx of saints who in poverty of spirit would assail the Laodiceans of a bourgeois world. The Manichaean vision of his 1912 dialogue anticipated the ascetic faith of Lukács the Marxist.

Even as a Marxist, he continued to unmask discord between form and life. In the essays "Klassenbewusstsein" (March, 1920) and "Die Verdinglichung und das Bewusstsein des Proletariats" (undated),[15] he used this polarity to differentiate the mentality of the bourgeoisie, epitomized by Kantian philosophy, from that of the proletariat, as described by Marx and Lenin. Like heroes of Schiller, the bourgeoisie is crippled by abstract idealism into recoiling from external reality. Instead of recognizing that social arrangements consist of relations between men, the bourgeoisie views society as though it were bound by immutable laws, as dehumanized as the natural laws of physics. By imagining society to be incapable of change, the middle classes reify social relations, regarding society literally as a thing, impervious to human initiative. In its Quixote world of abstract ideals, the bourgeoisie abdicates all attempt to change society. Lukács saw Kant as the archspokesman of this mentality. Without mentioning Max Adler, he criticized the German Marxist Heinrich Cunow (1862–1936) for reviving the ethics of Kant. Everything of value in Kant may be found, said Lukács, subsumed into Hegel's critique of him, upon which Marx built.

In contrast to the bourgeoisie, the proletariat represents potential synthesis of form and life. It has learned to understand external reality through the discipline of capitalist oppression, and its aspiration for freedom through form is guided by the Communist party. The party elite provides form, the proletariat life, and the revolution seeks to synthesize these into a new order of society, where just as in Goethe's *Wilhelm Meister* form and life at last will harmonize. Lukács believed —in a fit of délibáb—that this synthesis had come to pass. Given such a utopia, he felt justified, as assistant commissar of culture during 1919, in imposing his own ascetic morality on the nation and in silencing reactionary writers who threatened it and in banning alcoholic beverages that might obfuscate awareness of it.[16] In this new state, social arrangements would incarnate ideals. Social order would correspond to the higher purpose for which form had destined it, so that individuals need no longer retreat into abstract idealism or romantic disillusionment. The harmony between writer and society which Petöfi had envisioned and Jókai had assumed was now reality.

In characterizing the new society, Lukács imputed to the proletariat a unique ability to grasp the totality of experience. Economic interest has stripped the bourgeoisie of ability to understand more than a fragment of the whole; what it can grasp it makes into unchangeable, oppressive laws. Through its degradation, the proletariat has learned to see social relations whole, demanding that theory match practice. Although the proletariat despises the self-serving ideologies of the middle classes, it must recognize that these too comprise part of reality. The proletariat has no right to expunge the bourgeoisie; rather middle-class individualism must be incorporated *(aufgehoben)* in a new society if the latter is to embrace the whole of experience.

The wholeness, which supplies the proletariat its raison d'être, will be fulfilled through revolution instigated by the party elite. Although Lukács repudiated Rosa Luxemburg's call for spontaneous revolution, he agreed with her that after a revolution Marxism will have outlived its usefulness. Marxism is a weapon forged by the class-consciousness of the proletariat to destroy class-society. But because the proletariat is itself a product of the old order, its class-consciousness must disappear in the utopia to come. Dialectical materialism is not eternal truth but merely an instrument used by the Communist party to help the proletariat synthesize form with life. Already helpless to elucidate precapitalist society, as a by-product of capitalism Marxism will vanish in postcapitalist society. It was for this self-denying heresy that Lukács incurred ostracism as a revisionist and anti-Leninist; he accepted chastisement with perfect poverty of spirit, never counterattacking and eventually recanting.

Morris Watnick and others have shown that Lukács' instrumental view of Marxism influenced Karl Mannheim. Superannuated by its own success, Marxism can contain only a relative measure of truth; it embodies the onesidedness of what Mannheim called a utopia. The instrumentalism that cost Lukács his orthodoxy derived from his commitment to the polarity between form and life. This polarity obliged him to recognize that both form and life advance valid claims, which genuine synthesis must incorporate. Neither form nor life can be permitted to throttle the other, as in Schiller's abdication from life or Turgenev's aggrandizement of form. Because form and life each must unfold according to laws of its own, Marxism as form cannot dictate what life should become. Such life-defying Marxism would degenerate into just another abstract idealism. In *Geschichte und Klassenbewusstsein*, Lukács labored in vain to save Communist society from being reified by its own builders.

Lukács' deviationism derived from adherence to the basic conviction of his youth: life and form are hostile brothers, neither of which should be permitted to quash its rival. Ever since Cervantes pioneered the novel, literature has burgeoned with attempts by either life or form to negate the other. Because Marxism alone recognizes evils of the external world, notably of capitalism, followers of Marx enjoy a unique opportunity to sponsor a society where form and life will coincide. The defect in Lukács' panacea is that he restricted to a party elite the dignity of representing form. In order not to impede the future synthesis for which he yearned, Lukács abased himself before the will of the party, even when it flouted his own respect for life. With the impatience of a utopian, he worshiped in the party that awesome power of objective truth which he had earlier reproached in the Platonism of Kassner. As spokesman of form, the party radiates a majesty not unlike that of Bolzano's proposition-in-itself: whatever it decrees is valid, whether or not any individual pays heed.

After Hitler had seized power, Lukács found fresh pretext for welcoming Bolshevik discipline. Amid the annihilation of reason in Western Europe, Lukács hailed Russia as the outpost of Western values. Stalin's Russia was nursing the synthesis of form and life against the day when she might export its remnants back to Europe. At Moscow during the 1930's, Lukács drafted that indictment of his own youth which he published in *Die Zerstörung der Vernunft* (East Berlin, 1954). In it he vilified the very men who had encouraged him to elaborate his polarity between life and form, reinterpreting Dilthey, Simmel, and Weber—not to mention his onetime friends Gundolf and George— as apostles of schism between form and life. By celebrating life, they isolated it from control by form, foreshadowing Hitler's cult of force. His own pre-1918 convictions Lukács disavowed as another piece of abstract idealism.

At once contrived and disarmingly frank, this self-criticism conceals basic facts. In works like *Die Seele und die Formen*, Lukács flaunted sympathy with abstract idealists, while a few years later in *Die Theorie des Romans* he relished certain disillusionment-romantics. Nevertheless, there persists through these works a preference for synthesis of form and life, as embodied in classical tragedy or *Wilhelm Meisters Lehrjahre*. When Lukács converted to Marxism in 1918, he merely projected into politics a yearning for synthesis which had captivated him for more than a decade. At least initially Marxism promised not caesura but consummation.

If we ask what pervades Lukács' tergiversations since 1908, it is that Hungarian gift of wish-fulfillment called délibáb; he can minimize abuses by recognizing in the here-and-now traits of a hoped-for future. Whether in glorifying the elite of 1912 who achieve poverty of spirit or in fawning before leaders of the Communist party, Lukács has excelled at giving to every situation its saving grace. Lukács typifies his national tradition more vigorously than either he or his critics like to admit.

THE EMERGENCE OF KARL MANNHEIM'S PAN-RELATIVISM UNDER THE STAR OF LUKÁCS

The theorizing of Karl Mannheim (1893–1947) is intimately related to that of Lukács. Although many scholars hail Mannheim as the founder of sociology of knowledge *(Wissenssoziologie)*, his chief insights were adapted from his older colleague. Born in Budapest of middle-class Jewish parents—his father was Hungarian and his mother German— Mannheim studied there under Béla Zalay, at Berlin under Georg Simmel, and at Heidelberg under Lask and Rickert.[17] In 1917 and 1918 he was leader of the Budapest Free School of the Humanities, which recruited Socialist intellectuals to teach working men. Under the title of *Lélek és Kultura [Soul and Culture]* (Budapest, 1918), Mannheim edited a collection of essays by his colleagues. In his introduction,[18] Mannheim celebrated Lukács' notion that form can be a means of escaping the limitations of one's environment. Unlike Lukács and the other faculty members, he specifically rejected the use of sociology for understanding thought.

In 1919 Mannheim departed Budapest, disappointed by Béla Kun's regime, but chastened into acknowledging the utility of sociology. From 1919 to 1924 he studied at Heidelberg under Alfred Weber; besides hearing lectures by Heidegger and Emil Lederer, he read works of Husserl and Scheler. After taking a habilitation under Weber in 1924, Mannheim served as a docent in Heidelberg from 1925 to 1929; as professor of sociology at Frankfurt from 1929 to 1933, he succeeded Franz Oppenheimer. In 1933 he moved to London, where he embarked upon a second career in social planning and reform of education. From 1933 to 1941 he taught at the London School of Economics and from 1941 to 1947 at the Institute of Education of the University of London. He died in 1947 as he was about to take office as director of the European branch of UNESCO.

Mannheim's transition from anti-Marxist formalism to a semi-Marxist sociologism can be traced best by following the influence exerted upon him by Lukács. As we have seen, the latter turned on its head the Hungarian tradition of solidarity between writer and audience. By 1917, Mannheim had learned from Lukács to recognize the cleft between form and life as the fundamental problem of modern thought. Although in *Soul and Culture* Mannheim could see nothing but discord between mind and external reality, he was already preoccupied by the relation between the two poles. Nearly all his colleagues at the Free School of the Humanities went on, like him, to explore this preeminently Hungarian problem. Frigyes Antal became a student of Max Dvořák, Béla Balázs pioneered the sociology of cinema, Arnold Hauser wrote a sociology of art history, Ervin Szabó had already studied Petöfi's role in the Revolution of 1848, while Béla Bartók and Zoltán Kodály were collecting Hungarian folk songs, thereby helping to inspire Populist writers like Gyula Illyés (1902–).

As an indication of his change of mind, Mannheim wrote in 1920 a laudatory review of Lukács' *Die Theorie des Romans*.[19] Without examining the book in detail, he praised Lukács for using ideal types to relate the world view of writers to that of their society. Laboring under such disparate influences as those of the pre-Marxist Lukács, Alfred Weber, and Max Scheler, Mannheim could not sift out his own position until after *Geschichte und Klassenbewusstsein* had appeared. Although he adopted with alacrity Lukács' Marxist sociology of classes, Mannheim transformed the latter's identification of truth with the

Communist party into a tool for interpreting all social thought. Mannheim postulated that every social philosophy must play the instrumental role that Lukács reserved for Marxism. Every body of social
thought is a device used by a social class, ostensibly to better society
but in reality to abet its own interests. Limited by conditions of its
own age, every social program must distort truth in order to further
the interests of its class. Lukács' heretical contention that Marxism
itself would wither away holds true, declared Mannheim, of all social
thought. In *Ideologie und Utopie* (Bonn, 1929), Mannheim distinguished between ideologies, which strive to revive or preserve the past,
and utopias, which seek to transform the future according to some
blueprint. Neither of these outlooks can transcend those limitations
that Lukács diagnosed in Marxism and Mannheim recognized in all
social philosophies.

By espousing pan-relativism, Mannheim departed decisively from
his mentor. Truth Lukács regarded as a dialectical relation between
form and life; these opposite poles refine and transform each other
until they achieve reconciliation in a classless society. For a brief
period, the party elite of communism can claim to monopolize truth
because it understands, however fleetingly, the relation between its
own program (form) and life. Soon, however, truth will migrate to
lodge in the citizenry of the classless society. Mannheim never harbored such a dialectical notion of truth. Rather he defined truth by
the standard of neo-Kantian empiricism: individual sciences should
specialize in elaborating hypotheses to explain the facts of their narrow domain. There can exist no overarching schema to unify facts
from all domains. Thus no party can claim, however briefly, to monopolize truth. Instead, social thinkers should piece together those insights
from specialized sciences that promise to improve social conditions. By
its very nature, such an eclectic social theory cannot be absolute. In
place of Lukács' Communist elite, Mannheim extolled the intelligentsia
as the group best equipped to formulate social goals. Displaying unusual sensitivity to the diverse needs of society, Mannheim echoed
John Stuart Mill's insistence on heeding every argument of every
opponent. This pan-relativism, which he called relationism, spurred
Mannheim constantly to revise his principles, especially after he settled
in England.

One of the most trenchant critics of the pre-1933 Mannheim was
Vienna-born Ernst Grünwald (1912–1933), who as a twenty-year-old
student at Vienna compiled a historical critique of the sociology of
knowledge.[20] Had he not been killed in a mountaineering accident the
following year—he was then working on a phenomenology of language

—Grünwald might have become a leading sociologist of knowledge. In his richly documented *Das Problem der Soziologie des Wissens* (Vienna, 1934; repr., Hildesheim, 1967), he refuted Mannheim's relationism on the grounds that its premise is self-contradictory. Relationism posits that no proposition concerning society can be true absolutely because it must reflect the limitations of its own society. This premise itself, however, constitutes such a proposition about society, and therefore it too cannot be true absolutely because it must reflect its social origin. Thus the brash young scholar hoisted Mannheim's sociology of knowledge on the petard of pan-relativism. As Werner Stark points out, however, Mannheim's premise is a proposition not about society, but about the abiding nature of man. As such, it may claim validity independent of shifting social conditions.[21] Despite youthful excesses, Grünwald's book provides a useful survey of the history of sociology of knowledge, furnishing excellent analyses of Lukács, Max Adler, Max Weber, and several dozen others.

Grünwald did not inquire what social conditions may have prompted the pre-1933 Mannheim to regard every proposition about society as politically motivated. To a degree, pan-relativism reflected the partisanship of political debate in Austria-Hungary after 1900, when nationalists marshaled the loftiest absolutes to defend mutually exclusive programs. This internecine struggle of nationalities, which fascinated Ludwig Gumplowicz, eventually destroyed the empire, abolishing the framework that had given meaning to the strivings of each party. By exposing the dependence of each partisan on the whole, the collapse of 1918 "relativized" every political platform that Austria-Hungary had launched. No less important was indebtedness of Lukács and Mannheim to the traditional political involvement of Hungarian intellectuals. As we have seen, *l'art pour l'art* never took root among Hungarian thinkers, for whom it remained second nature to deem literature an extension of politics. Stimulated by Lukács, Mannheim broadened this premise so as to construe not just literature but philosophy as a vehicle of politics. As a third debt to their homeland, both Lukács and Mannheim unleashed that creative energy so conspicuous among Hungarian Jews in exile. Their diligence never flagged, as if they felt impelled to vindicate to foreigners the otherwise neglected genius of their countrymen.

It is regrettable that Mannheim should be remembered chiefly for *Ideologie und Utopie*, for after 1933 he began to replace pan-relativism with Anglo-Saxon zeal for piecemeal reform. Instead of distrusting all utopias, the later Mannheim endorsed Max Weber's plea that intellectuals forge a value-free social science to guide emerging mass society.

Like Otto Neurath, Mannheim esteemed education as the chief tool for transforming elites of Europe into a cadre of technocrats. These two men shared encyclopedic interests as well as a commitment to bettering society through science, and each died before he could add a hoped-for capstone to his career. Whereas Neurath sought to unify the language of science, Mannheim wanted to awaken the intelligentsia to its unprecedented responsibilities. If Mannheim and Neurath could ever have collaborated, they might have made a monumental contribution, laying a foundation for a comprehensive sociology of ideas. As it is, Neurath deserves to be honored as a universal man whose inventions we all use, while Mannheim seems a kind of tempered Lukács who popularized Hungarian truisms in Great Britain and the United States.

27

Hungarian Psychoanalysts
and Film Critics

SÁNDOR FERENCZI AND LIPOT SZONDI:
DEVOTEES OF DÉLIBÁB

AMONG FREUD's faithful adherents, Sándor Ferenczi (1873–1933)
basked in special affection.[1] He was the only disciple with whom Freud
discussed his own health. After earning a doctorate in medicine at
Vienna in 1894, Ferenczi settled in his native Budapest to practice
medicine by using hypnosis. In 1907 he wrote to Freud before meeting
him the next year and undergoing analysis almost at once. After accompanying Freud to the United States, he won to the movement a
bevy of Hungarians. At the Budapest Congress of September, 1918,
Freud mistakenly hailed Hungary as the most promising forum for
psychoanalysis.[2] The son of Polish Jews living in Budapest, Ferenczi, in
1913, expounded the phenomenon of magical thinking whereby ego
seeks to evade reality.[3] Contending that children evolve through four
stages of magical thinking—in other words délibáb—Ferenczi held that
an adult's desire to wield omnipotence through magical gestures entails regression. The Hungarian analyzed his countrymen's will-of-the-
wisp thinking as a narcissistic impulse to control or escape reality.

In *Thalassa: Versuch einer Genitaltheorie* (Vienna, 1922), Ferenczi
speculated about origins of human genitals. The womb perpetuates
primeval slime in which life began, so that for the fetus birth means
ascending from an aquatic to a terrestrial existence. Sexual intercourse
fulfills desire to wallow and even drown in primordial mud. These
hypotheses, which Ferenczi devised while on army duty during 1914
and 1915, foreshadowed not only Rank's theory of a birth trauma, but
also Freud's notion of a death wish. Both men adopted the Hungarian's
premise that ontogeny recapitulates phylogeny, a doctrine that underlay what Ferenczi called bioanalysis. Thanks to a fecund imagination,

Ferenczi incurred the destiny of Biedermeier inventors like Josef Ressel: at first ignored, his discoveries eventually were duplicated and then attributed to the rediscoverer.

Hungarian fantasy inspired an even more startling hypothesis in the lifework of Lipot Szondi (1893–).[4] If Alfred Adler adapted psychoanalysis to Gesellschaft society, Szondi expounded its relevance for Gemeinschaft society.

Born in Budapest of Orthodox Jewish parents, during the 1930's Szondi tempered early adherence to Freud while tracing genealogies of misfits and geniuses. Working with criminals, epileptics, and neurotics for a Hungarian commission, he devised a test in which a person is shown eight photographs; one each of a homosexual, sadist, epileptic, hysteric, catatonic, paranoic, depressive, and manic. By noting which photograph most attracts and which most revulses a subject, Szondi charted the relative strength of the eight drives corresponding to the pictures. After testing thousands of Hungarians, Szondi founded a discipline that he called fate-analysis (anankology), which examines how drives influence decision-making.

Having observed that healthy persons often marry sickly ones, Szondi advanced an ancestor-theory of marital choice. Attraction in love results, he asserted, from shared recessive genes; repressed ancestral traits act as nature's matchmaker. No other love exists than that between gene relatives, that is, persons who have inherited common traits from common ancestors. Grounding Freud's Oedipus complex in genetics, Szondi argued that although all love entails incest, civilization replaces blood incest with gene incest. Among primitives, marriage taboos forbid marriage between descendents of common grandparents and great-grandparents. In urban society, individuals who do not mature from loving a sibling or a parent to a gene relative incur neurosis or else regress to perverted or criminal behavior. After publishing in 1938 a study of marital choice,[5] Szondi perfected his test to measure how eight drives transmit inherited impulses. Through statistical analysis of thousands of couples, he endeavored to place study of love, or erology, among the exact sciences.

Szondi emigrated from Budapest to Zürich in 1945—the journey being interrupted by brief internment at Belsen. He enlarged his theory to elucidate other kinds of choices. Equating choice with fate, he declared this phenomenon, like character, to be a projection of the unconscious. All selection, whether of a spouse, profession, friends, or neurosis springs from inherited proclivities, especially those carried by recessive genes. In a world cleft between man and woman, mind and nature, God and man, Szondi hailed ego as mediator; it subverts none of these realms while striving to coordinate them all. The Hungarian revived Goethe's notion that ego is an Archimedean point where opposites meet; the ego of man provides the node of the universe.

Through statistical research, Szondi strove to substantiate a conviction rooted in Hungarian consciousness, that the dead hand of the past rules the present. Genes would fulfill Burke's dictum that society constitutes a contract between the living, the dead, and those yet unborn. By insisting that each life unleashes a duel between dominant and recessive genes, Szondi propounded a dualism similar to that of Christian von Ehrenfels. Szondi's stress on ancestors renewed a theme of Austrian drama: Grillparzer had dramatized an ancestral curse in *Die Ahnfrau* (1818), where an unavenged "poor soul" haunts descendants, while in *Der böse Geist Lumpazivagabundus* (1835), Nestroy depicted rustics whom heredity destines to degenerate. By dreading vampires and demons, Transylvanian peasants cultivated other legends of tyranny beyond the grave.

With measured pessimism, Szondi challenged progressivism. To rebut Alfred Adler's faith in the self-made man of capitalism, Szondi exhibited hereditary misfits from peasant society. Against Marxists and other utopians, Szondi averred that psychotherapy can merely facilitate choice among a few options permitted by genes. The Hungarian berated existentialists for ignoring the straitjacket within which genes confine us. While he agreed with Sartre that a person may choose illness or even death, this "choice," said Szondi, is determined largely by heredity. Having garnered wisdom from inhabiting Gemeinschaft, Szondi applied to Gesellschaft a truism that village idiots cannot be socialized. Rational social order will founder so long as offspring remain blighted by double recessive genes. However much Szondi may have indulged in délibáb, correlations that he detected between heredity and deviance in Horthy's Hungary demand attention. Even geneticists, a group scarcely known for optimism, have overlooked Szondi's findings. Without embracing therapeutic nihilism, this Hungarian unearthed stumbling blocks to well-being which reformers have ignored without refuting.

CINEMA AS THE ART-FORM OF
MAGIC THINKING AND OF IMPRESSIONISM

The qualities of activism and fantasy which differentiated Hungarians from Austrians extended beyond psychoanalysis to ways in which intellectuals evaluated cinema. Whereas Austrians deplored this technological art, Hungarians saluted it. On the negative side, Franz Kafka joined a cinema club at Prague, only to find motion pictures disquieting:

> Cinema disrupts looking The speed of the movements and the rapid change of images force people constantly to overlook. Sight does not master the images; rather they master sight, overflowing the consciousness. Cinema means putting a uniform over the eye, which until now had been unclothed.[6]

Given Kafka's phantasmagoric imagination, he may have viewed in cinema a rival that could manipulate surrealistic images more vividly than he.

Egon Friedell turned from youthful enthusiasm for film into one of its most acidulous critics. About 1912 in Berlin, this Viennese impressionist had hailed silent film as the art of the age.[7] Through sketchiness, abruptness, and lacunae, it reproduces the shifting perspectives dear to modern sensibility—that is, to impressionism. By 1930 Friedell berated cinema as the quintessence of all that he abhorred in the postwar world. Bracketing it with aviation, gas warfare, radium, and atomic theory, he fulminated that these gadgets glorify motion while dispelling serenity. Like the radio, film isolates artist from audience, abolishing the feeling of uniqueness that makes theater live. Lamenting lost privacy, Friedell wrote:

> The human voice has won ubiquity, the human gesture eternity, but at the price of the soul. It is building the Tower of Babel. . . . Already radio broadcasts concerts of nightingales and speeches by the pope. That is the decline of the West.[8]

Combining neo-Biedermeier nostalgia with impressionistic alertness to novelty, Friedell denounced the new medium for toppling his world.

Joseph Roth waxed even more lachrymose, as he applied to motion pictures his special blend of preference for the old with awareness of the new. In the novel *Der Antichrist* (Amsterdam, 1934), the narrator recalls having witnessed during his youth an itinerant cinema, which regaled villagers with scenes of a nude Cleopatra preceding newsreels of the Russo-Japanese War. Roth excoriated the cinema huckster for exploiting shadows of dying soldiers to whet bloodlust in his clientele.[9] Having first titillated the libido, this capitalist purloined the soldiers' shadows in order further to debase his audience. He substituted a fake miracle of "living shadows" for genuine miracle, completing the task of antichrist and exposing Hollywood as a modern Hades.

Hungarians reacted more judiciously to motion pictures. In September, 1913, Georg Lukács sketched in the *Frankfurter Zeitung* an aesthetics of cinema. He contended that although film can never supplant theater, the new medium enjoys an integrity of its own.[10] In the art of building suspense, cinema surpasses the stage, reinvigorating the legerdemain of Poe, Hoffmann, and Arnim by embellishing the ordinary. Henceforth the stage should be reserved for tragedy and high comedy, leaving motion pictures to purvey a world in which, like an amusement park, everything is possible. By abrogating the rule of causes, motives, and fate, cinema projects fantasies that can never reproduce inner life. Even while depriving man of his soul, that is of his power of speech, silent pictures have restored him his body.

Lukács anticipated the views of another Hungarian Jew, Béla Balázs (1884–1949), who in 1924 published the first analysis of cinema to be widely read. Born in Szeged, Balázs reworked folktales into novels and plays, while writing librettos for one-act operas such as Bartók's *Bluebeard's Castle* (1911) and *The Wooden Prince* (1916). Lukács led those who defended this revival of fairy tales and magic.[11] Already a Marxist, during 1917 and 1918 Balázs taught at Karl Mannheim's Free School of the Humanities, offering a seminar on Hungarian lyric poets. Because he had supported Béla Kun, in 1919 Balázs fled to Vienna, where, inspired by Alexander Korda, he pursued studies of cinema. Besides writing several screenplays, he pioneered dramaturgy of cinema in *Der sichtbare Mensch oder die Kultur des Films* (Vienna, 1924). In 1930 he revised the book to encompass talking pictures under the title *Der Geist des Films* (Halle, 1930). After spending the Hitler years in Moscow, Balázs published a capstone to his aesthetic in *Der Film: Werden und Wesen einer Kunst* (Vienna, 1949).

In 1924 Balázs urged that cinema be welcomed into the Parliament of Arts. His dramaturgy he intended to enlighten cineastes and public alike, exulting that on a single day no fewer than three hundred thousand spectators might attend the two hundred movie houses of Vienna.[12] Balázs expected film to counteract an overly literary culture by teaching men to communicate with their bodies. He extolled the dance of Ruth St. Denis, pantomime, and art nouveau for rendering man visible at last. By disseminating a vocabulary of gestures, motion pictures would institute a workable international language. As a Marxist, Balázs applauded film for exalting workaday objects familiar to the working classes. Regrettably film-making remains in the hands of big business, which through the device of the detective celebrates worship of money. Mystery films elevate the detective into a Saint George of capitalism, who defends private property against burglars coveting the Holy Grail of lucre. Such films fascinate members of the lower middle class, who envy the license of criminals to flout respectability. Deploring sumptuous sets that glorify homes of the rich, Balázs sighed that decoration has banished genuine values.

Already in 1924, Balázs showed insight into techniques of filmmaking. Close-ups, he argued, are unique to cinema, demarcating it from other media. Through intimate rendering of minutiae, close-ups captivate children, who more readily than adults focus on detail. Interspersed through a film, close-ups convey unprecedented emphases, thereby disclosing a director's sensibility. Cinema can stir awe at sheer immensity, evoking as in no other medium the grandeur of sea, storm, or desert. The Hungarian hailed what he called impressionism in film, which consists in depicting events exclusively through the eyes of a protagonist; by witnessing only what impinges on an actor, an audience identifies totally with him.

Whereas Lukács and Friedell deplored the absence of live actors, Balázs welcomed it. Differentiating the text of a play from its performance, he lamented that theatergoers mistakenly compare an actor's execution of a role with its written version. Happily, in cinema there exists no written version to impose extraneous standards. Not the scenarist, but the director and stars are the poets who improvise drama in this art of surfaces where text fades into mime. Thanks to film, at long last visages can fulfill the premise of eighteenth-century physiognomists that outer features reflect inner being: beauty of face connotes beauty of character while hideous features signify malice.

Whereas *Der sichtbare Mensch* extolled silent film, six years later in *Der Geist des Films* Balázs saluted talking pictures. After 1945, he espoused an intermediate position, holding that silent and talking pictures constitute separate art-forms. He reiterated his conviction of 1924 that absence of sound intensifies visual poetry. In his attempt to delineate the language of cinema, Balázs paralleled philosophers of language such as Mauthner and Wittgenstein. Like them he regretted constrictions of speech, and together with Buber and Ebner, he exhorted men to confront each other more candidly than print allows. Whereas Balázs deemed gesture the best egress from solipsism, Buber and Ebner prized dialogue. A devotee of folklore, Balázs dubbed film a modern fairy tale that appeases man's deepest instincts, just as Hanns Sachs extolled motion pictures for reproducing the state of dreaming to which all art aspires. By dispensing fantasies, cinema provides the most popular art of the century. Cinema is popular, Balázs warned, in the sense that a populace is molded by it, not it by the populace. Already in 1924, Balázs glimpsed sinister purposes that would debase the new art.

A more comprehensive sociology of cinema issued from a colleague of Balázs at the Budapest Free School of the Humanities, Arnold Hauser (1892–), who lectured there on dilettantism. Born in Temesvár, Hauser studied under Georg Simmel and Max Weber, as well as Henri Bergson and Gustave Lanson at Paris, before pursuing art history in Italy under the influence of Max Dvořák. At Berlin from 1921 to 1924, he studied under Ernst Troeltsch and Werner Sombart, equipping himself for a grandiose synthesis that he offered in his two-volume *A Social History of Art* (London, 1951). Preeminent at delineating post-1830 movements, this quasi-Marxist treatise culminates in an analysis of cinema which Hauser elaborated at Vienna between 1924 and 1938.[13]

Hauser interprets cinema as the art form of the machine suited to conveying insights pioneered by Viennese impressionism. Motion pictures epitomize impressionism by capturing the experience of speed which provoked fickleness in urban intellectuals. Just as Altenberg had sketched strangers entering and leaving a coffeehouse, a camera chronicles comings and goings. By juxtaposing scenes distant in space and time, cinema makes isolated events simultaneous, just as in interior monologue, Schnitzler conflated disjointed memories. More vividly even than psychoanalysis, motion pictures portray "continuous crossing and intersection of two different lines of the plot." Hauser likens this technique to expressionist dramas—such as Paul Adler's—which depict events separate in space and time as "emerging simultaneously in vision."[14] Cinema spatializes time; it glorifies what is contemporary by intensifying preoccupation with the passing moment. Whereas medieval Christians brooded about the future—life after death—and romantics about the past, technology forces twentieth-century men to worship the present. Change comes so rapidly that only in a fleeting "now" can man repose. Comparable enthusiasm for film montage animated Broch, who besides writing film plays, coordinated simultaneous events in the three volumes of *Die Schlafwandler* (Zürich, 1931–1932) and *Der Tod des Vergil* (New York, 1945).[15]

In explicating Viennese impressionism, Hauser reveals himself as one of its last exponents. Anything but feuilletonistic, Hauser rivals Friedell in scope and audacity while surpassing him in acumen. Having absorbed many-sided training, notably from Dvořák and Weber, Hauser interprets Western history using premises reminiscent of Mannheim. As Hungarian intellectuals, both men recognized how intimately thought interacts with society, each factor at once multiplying and foreclosing options for the other. In a comment that fits Hungary better than any other nation, Hauser posits:

> there is always a conscious or unconscious practical purpose,
> a manifest or latent propagandistic tendency in the works
> of art.[16]

As if délibáb ruled the world, Hauser contends that men distort reality
in order to discern whatever they want to see. Because thought entails
wish-fulfillment, truth can only be partial and misleading, vindicating
the perspectivism dear to impressionists. Such a world view univer-
salizes distortion:

> The idea that men spend their lives concealed from them-
> selves and others, that the truth of human knowledge is at
> best truth from a certain point of view, that reality only makes
> itself known to us in ever-changing and never generally valid
> forms, is nothing but Impressionistic thinking.[17]

Hauser enriches the shifting perspectives of Schnitzler and Freud
with Hungarian passion for politics and Marxist awareness that no
one can isolate himself from a group. To reconcile Marxism with
impressionism, Hauser postulates incessant change, so that

> every factor is in a state of motion and subject to constant
> change of meaning, in which there is nothing static, nothing
> timelessly valid. . . .[18]

To be consistent, impressionism must embrace the timeless and ephemeral. That is what Alexius Meinong and Edmund Husserl essayed in
philosophy; Martin Buber and Ferdinand Ebner in theology; Hans
Kelsen and Othmar Spann in social theory; not to mention Robert
Musil and Hermann Broch in fiction. It is a paradox of the Gay
Apocalypse that certain thinkers who purported to despise impressionism inadvertently espoused its tenets. For them, there exists no experience too lowly or too lofty to banish from the record of man.
Greedy for the new, yet alert to the old, impressionists cultivated a
Protean sensitivity that enabled them to interiorize every doctrine of
every age.

Although sectarians may impugn openness to multiplicity as puerile,
it offers the safest guide to the past, especially when amplified by an
impressionist's flair for detecting hidden structures. In order to envision
the entire past as contiguous to the present, the historian must trans-
mute prejudices into perspectives and biases into tools. Neither idealism nor positivism, universalism nor nominalism, Gemeinschaft nor

Gesellschaft alone suffices. In order to understand the past on its own terms, each specialist must relive the preconceptions of each age before integrating them with abiding premises. Only capacity to coordinate surfaces with structure can accomplish this feat.

Since 1945 Hauser has propounded a vision of mankind's growth, at once all-encompassing and uniquely his own. His distillation of Western culture mirrors the paradox of impressionism—and of creativity— that what is most universal is also most personal. Coordinating breadth and depth, Hauser demonstrates how magnificently the Habsburg Empire equipped scholars to appraise innovation. Whether in assailing or acclaiming modernity, Austrians and Hungarians have probed most deeply into it.

Part Six

SOOTHSAYERS
OF
MODERNITY

Die Ambrosia der früheren Jahrhunderte
ist das tägliche Brot der späteren.

The ambrosia of earlier centuries
is the daily bread of later ones.

—MARIE VON EBNER-ESCHENBACH

28

The Gay Apocalypse

CRITICS OF TECHNOLOGY

AUSTRIAN WRITERS have been perhaps the most trenchant foes of
modernity. Their critique derives from Biedermeier attitudes; nostalgia,
love of spectacle, fondness for the countryside, delight in minutiae, and
passivity toward bureaucracy have characterized nearly every Austrian
intellectual since 1800. The debacle of 1848 reinforced these predilections, just when natural science was winning respect as a mode of
contemplative life. After 1870 prolonged economic dislocation frightened Austria's lower middle classes, while nouveaux riches cultivated
Biedermeier tastes. It was their offspring who during the 1890's transformed aestheticism into impressionism. The next generation was
blighted by World War One, as dismemberment both of the empire
and of too many young men redoubled nostalgia. After 1918 Austrian
intellectuals were saying about their country's defeat what Karl Kraus
had written concerning the sinking of the *Titanic,* that this was God's
revenge *ex machina* on worshipers of the machine.[1]

Even after the war, most Viennese continued to regard their city as
the navel of the earth. Blending city and country, nestled below vine-
covered hills, and bathed by a mighty river, Vienna seemed to have
eluded many of the curses of metropolitan life. The fulminations of
Kraus aside, it was primarily in Prague that disenchantment with
cities festered. In *Barbara, oder die Frömmigkeit,* Werfel likened the
exodus of peasants toward the city to a great flight, an escape from
community into the anonymity of the crowd. Bohemian-born Alfred
Kubin (1877–1959), best known for surrealistic drawings, wrote an
antiutopia, *Die andere Seite: Ein phantastischer Roman* (Munich,
1909), which portrayed an industrial city as a madhouse ruled by an
unseen tyrant.[2] Ehrenfels blamed the city for increasing alcoholism,
syphilis, and neglect of children, as technology prevented natural

selection from killing the unfit. The Moravian-born Jew Jakob Julius David (1859–1906) deplored the deprivations of rural students who languished at Vienna. Among the Viennese, Herzl wanted Jews to return to the soil, freed from necessity to flaunt urban values. Kokoschka detested the amassing of people in cities too small for them, while in "Vorstadt im Föhn" Salzburg-born Trakl pictured blood from slaughterhouses besmirching a suburb. In poems like "Die Teilnahmslosen" and "Die Dinge und Wir," Alfons Petzold complained that factories manufacture men into machines; instead of rejoicing in God's handiwork, laborers cower before their tools.

The degeneration that these Cassandras decried alarmed nearly everyone after World War One. In *Schriftsteller und totalitäre Welt* (Bern, 1967), Wolfgang Rothe has delineated how the war engendered what he calls a totalitarian world, in which the individual was overpowered by a war machine. As if to travesty Neurath's desire to prolong war economy into peacetime, total war necessitated total government in order to coordinate resources. Instead of being a means of policy as in Clausewitz, war became a substitute for policy. Language began to reflect a military ethos of command and conquest, embodying what Ebner would call ego-isolation. Prostitution and drug traffic expanded to appease soldiers, who beheld angelic faces adorning propaganda posters.[3] The duplicity that previously had afflicted Austria permeated the rest of Europe. In Rothe's totalitarian or totalized world, the environment was mobilized so as to suffocate individuality by exacting conformity to a self-deified bureaucracy. In a prison world, Jews felt acutely helpless, epitomizing the alienation of author from public which already pervaded most of Europe and which war brought to Hungary as well. Rothe discerns denunciation of bureaucracy in novels by Musil, Kafka, and Broch, and in verse by Rilke and Hofmannsthal. Recognizing that civilization was tottering, these seers contrasted the anarchy of impulses which had followed the war with forebodings of disaster which had preceded it.

Musil depicted a totalized world by evoking the inertia of Vienna during 1913 in his three-volume *Der Mann ohne Eigenschaften* (Berlin and Lausanne, 1930–1943). The protagonist Ulrich is a "man of possibilities" who, like aesthetes of Young Vienna, prefers contemplating what might be to affecting what is. In accord with his principle of insufficient reason, Ulrich can never discover why any given actuality ought to exist rather than some other. Too diffident either to abet or hinder the cabals and crimes that surround him, Ulrich solaces himself in Marcionistic love for his sister. Like Broch, Ebner, and Rank, Musil blamed rationality for thwarting self-fulfillment:

The inner sterility, the monstrous combination of expertise

The Hungarian author could not have known that Austrian officials

at details with indifference toward the whole, the terrible
abandonment of men in a desert of particulars, his unprecedented restlessness, malice, and apathy, the avarice, coldness,
and violence of our era, all these are alleged to result solely
from the losses which a logically precise thought has inflicted
upon the soul![4]

Musil yearned for a Gemeinschaft society, where Leibnizian attention
to the whole might resume.

Austria spawned many indictments of war. We have already mentioned the apocalyptic visions of Prague-born Paul Adler. Another
pessimist, Albert Ehrenstein vilified a God who could permit such
havoc, asking, "What is God without man?" and concluding "Less than
man without God."[5] In frenetic prophecies like "Stimme über Barbaropa" and "Ich bin des Lebens und des Todes müde," Ehrenstein
reviled war, calling heaven to witness the carnage that was defiling
earth. In *Die Kapuzinergruft* (1938), Roth opined that the World War
deserved that name because everyone had lost his world. By destroying
private life, the war accelerated appetites: young men who had dreaded getting married and having children hastened to do so in August,
1914, so that they could die purposefully. They marched into battle
elated, lest they live to resume domestic boredom.[6] In *Die vierzig
Tage des Musa Dagh* (Vienna, 1933), Werfel described the fascism
of a Turkish dictator who displaced and imprisoned Armenians in
order to perpetuate wartime power. In a widely performed drama,
Wunder um Verdun (Berlin, 1931), Vienna-born Hans von Chlumberg
(1897–1930) shocked audiences by having battlefield dead rise up to
salute the twentieth anniversary of World War One. While tourists
dally in military cemeteries and statesmen laud the dead, the rein-
carnated soldiers repudiate a world whose hypocrisy their deaths had
helped to save.[7]

Among antiwar writings, Aladár Kuncz's neglected masterpiece,
Black Monastery (1931), exposed totalitarianism among French officials. The shock of having France invaded elicited draconian measures
against innocent tourists. For nearly five years, Kuncz and over five
thousand other Germans and Austro-Hungarians languished in antique
prisons, where sadistic guards harassed them. Desperate to invest his
ordeal with purpose, Kuncz anticipated Heidegger and Sartre by discovering that when tradition disintegrates each man must forge his
own values. No one has described the birth of a totalitarian world so
poignantly as Kuncz.

were abusing interned aliens even more despicably. During August, 1914, Poles and Serbs of all ages were abducted from tourist spas and imprisoned without a word to their families. In camps like those at Gran or at Thalerhof near Graz, upper-class ladies from Poland were compelled to bathe naked before jeering soldiers, while Slavic priests cleaned latrines.[8] Guards delighted in beating British civilians who could not pay bribes for the privilege of residing under house arrest. As in the case of Kuncz's ordeal, such terrorism has been largely forgotten.

The most outspoken of Austria's antimilitarists was Karl Kraus who, after denouncing the war throughout its duration, compiled out of newspaper clippings his *Die letzten Tage der Menschheit*. In the Grumbler *(Nörgler)*, Kraus voiced Thersites-like contempt for all belligerents, while in the Optimist he satirized Austrian ability to justify any conduct by expounding all sides of a question. Excoriating especially the press service—directed by Roda Roda—and profiteers, Kraus memorialized the insanity of the times. He blamed himself for having abetted mass suicide by chronicling it. Constructed like a newsreel by splicing excerpts from the press, his collage anticipated semidocumentary novels of the new factuality *(neue Sachlichkeit)*.

The war brought an apocalypse of industrialism, fulfilling what Kraus had proclaimed in 1908:

> We were complex enough to build the machine, but we are too primitive to make it serve us. We dispatch world-traffic on narrow-gauge brain-tracks.[9]

Disconsolate anti-mechanism was voiced by Werfel, who implored Christians to restore Gemeinschaft society in order to quench the *auto-da-fé* of technology:

> The state, war, science are an endless chain of vampyric snares, which must be soaked with blood in order to acquire the visage of life.[10]

The notion that machines are bloodthirsty received classic formulation from Gustav Meyrink (1868–1932) in his three-volume *Des deutschen Spiessers Wunderhorn: Gesammelte Novellen* (Munich, 1903–1908). Born in Vienna, the son of a Swabian politician and a German actress whose name Meyer he made his own, Meyrink worked at Prague as a bank clerk before becoming in 1903 a regular contributor to *Simplicissimus*. In prewar novellas he depicted every sort of demented scientist, proliferating images of world destruction and dehumanization with Marcionist perversity. A master of suspense in the manner of E. T. A. Hoffmann and Edgar Allan Poe, Meyrink spun phantasmagorias. In "Die Pflanzen des Dr. Cinderella," Meyrink envisioned a plant consisting of human eyes nestled on a network of blood vessels. In "Das Präparat," two friends discover that the body of a murdered companion has been fashioned into a functioning automaton by a Persian professor. In "Dr. Lederer," a scientist devises a projector that can shoot pictures into the heavens, one of which causes a pregnant woman to bear a child resembling a portrait projected the night of his birth. In "Die schwarze Kugel," two Hindus exhibit a black sphere that unleashes a negative being, sucking the entire universe into a void. Evoking naturalistic detail, Meyrink makes improbable horrors seem routine. In the novel *Der Golem* (Leipzig, 1915), he revived the legend of Rabbi Löw (ca. 1525–1609), an adviser of Rudolf II, who had built an automaton of clay which terrorized the streets of Prague. Through ghoulish figures, Meyrink denounced as black magic a science that eviscerates the human body and denatures the cosmos.

Some of Meyrink's fantasies came true as a result of industrial pollution. In 1930 Joseph Roth visited a landscape west of Leipzig which ammonia factories at Leuna had denuded, depopulating the village of Rundstedt and killing vegetation. Roth likened the man-made devastation to that of a battlefield:

> I walked through the dying nature; it was like visiting a sick-bed, no, like a funeral procession. And the dying patient was already a corpse and his own cemetery at once. . . . Here mold is healthier than life, decay is fruitful and slays health, the stench kills the fragrance, and the howling mutes song.[11]

In this apocalypse, factory fumes have ravaged nature in order to enrich a few. Perhaps the bleakest despair of all was voiced by Kokoschka, who in 1945 pontificated from London:

> We do not mind the stench of the funeral pyre of our world. Since Humanism is dead, man is soulless, he no longer cares whether he lives or dies. The march of industrial civilization will be marked by utter ruin and destruction, like the path of the hordes which once invaded Europe. There will be no portrait left of modern man because he has lost face and is turning back towards the jungle.[12]

Flaunting therapeutic nihilism, Kokoschka, no less than Roth and

Kraus, anathematized a world that seemed to crush every value man had ever cherished. Already before World War One, duplicity and rapacity in Austria had revulsed young intellectuals. That cataclysm revolted them, making the prewar era seem an idyll that had spawned a posthuman age. The Gay Apocalypse had turned into a nightmare.

DUPLICITY SPURS CREATIVITY

Throughout the years described in this book, Austrians, as distinct from Hungarians, suffered feelings of inferiority. As Arthur Schnitzler wrote to his sister-in-law in December, 1914, the phrase "really Austrian" *(echt österreichisch)* connoted disapproval, while to call something "really German" was to praise it as "noble, strong, and beautiful."[13] In Austria as well as abroad, qualities that distinguished the Habsburg Empire from more Westernized nations were censured—Schlamperei, Protektion, particularism, and aestheticism—while the constructive side of these traits—tolerance, magnanimity, independence, and creativity—went unsung. Foreigners and Austrians alike have emphasized faults to the exclusion of virtues; in the words of Vienna-born Ernst Stein (1901–1968), they have interpreted

> Grace as shallowness and melancholy as a pose; surplus in moods as a lack of principles; apparent facility at creating as superficiality; an incomparable gift for *aperçus* as minor form; irresistible atmosphere as local color, but aspiring to what is European as presumption—a merry bed of contradictions which has embittered the life of many a great man.[14]

These paradoxes engendered attitudes that we have labeled hate-love, ambivalence, and duplicity. When Freud declared that neurosis arises in hate-love for one's parents, he was diagnosing the Austrian attitude toward country and self as well. Ambivalence could culminate in self-hatred, as when Nestroy boasted, "I believe the worst of everyone, including myself, and I have seldom been wrong."[15] Most acute in Jews, self-hatred could goad its victim to creativity or cripple him with self-pity. Duplicity flourished amid institutions whose workings blatantly contradicted their facade. The emperor, whose portrait hung as a model of rectitude in every classroom, infringed common decency by badgering family and subordinates. He affronted his son, neglected his wife, harassed his successor's consort, and duped loyal servants. Outdated institutions like press censorship were administered so slackly as to caricature them. Other moldering regulations were ignored, reminding citizens how capricious bureaucracy could be. Unchastity was blinked at in parish priests, and common-law marriages multiplied because only non-Catholics could divorce. While brothels catered to every class, university professors in 1900 pronounced a mural of nudes too lewd to deck their Aula. In 1879 a gigantic public festival celebrated the twenty-fifth aniversary of an unhappy marriage. The parade was staged by an egomaniac whose nudes could win acclaim because they adorned historical settings. Within a bureaucracy where business transpired in secret, everyone suspected intervention from above and speculated about the "personal," to wit, the sexual. Playacting was part of every transaction; each party knew how to regard another's cordiality as a ruse. As Robert Musil put it:

> In this country a man always acted . . . differently from how
> he thought, or thought differently from how he acted.[16]

Max Nordau extended the cleft between pretense and reality into a critique of the "conventional lies of mankind," while Joseph Roth decried a mendacious morality that declaimed lofty principles while exculpating all and sundry. Roth suggested that Franz Joseph had deliberately misled courtiers by gilding the tawdriness of their stratagems with royal impassivity.[17] In *Professor Bernhardi*, Schnitzler portrayed a physician who in order to act ethically flouted Austrian conventions; he landed in jail. Elsewhere Schnitzler dubbed the Habsburg Empire the abode of social insincerity:

> Here as nowhere else there existed harsh conflict without a
> trace of hatred and a kind of tender love without need for
> faithfulness. Between political opponents there existed or developed ludicrous personal sympathies, while party-comrades
> insulted, slandered, and betrayed each other.[18]

Small wonder that here impressionism, with its gift for descrying latent meaning behind every surface, blossomed into a world view. In Vienna, experts at dissimulation, such as Bahr and Altenberg, professed to find no fixity beneath a flux of sensations, while positivists, such as Freud and Mach, ferreted out natural laws behind a welter of detail. Still others, like Schnitzler and Schaukal, exhumed the Baroque cult of death in order to vivify life. In Bohemia duplicity alternately confirmed and disrupted the Leibnizian vision. Insofar as dissimulation portended a beneficent, albeit hidden, order, a secretive state might betoken that order, with bureaucracy playing God. Yet no sooner had faith in official benevolence collapsed, as in Prague after 1880, than arbitrary rule incited thinkers to invoke the malevolent creator envisioned by Marcion. Law seemed an oppressor and obedience to it complicity in world destruction.

No group personified the Janus-head of Habsburg institutions so conspicuously as the Jews. One reason why Jews flourished in Austria was that centuries in the ghetto had accustomed them to unmask and exploit self-deception in others. Thriving on marginal conditions, they seized opportunity without having to feel dishonored if thwarted. As if dissembling from themselves, Jewish writers hid behind pseudonyms, among them Nordau, Altenberg, Friedell, Roda Roda, Salten, Rank, and Wittels, not to mention the youthful Hofmannsthal. Eager to vindicate themselves, some Jews like Freud, Kraus, Weininger, and Wittgenstein became disillusionists, tearing the veil from time-honored conventions, while others like Popper-Lynkeus, Hertzka, Herzl, and Buber, resorted to utopias. Jewish fecundity had the tragic consequence of aggravating gentile envy and fear, even as anti-Semite and insecure Jew together looked toward Germany as a bulwark against Slavdom. It was an irony worthy of Habsburg contrivance that the Jews, whom Austrian Germans insulted, should have revered German culture. Through outspokenness and doggedness, the Jew became a Doppelgänger of the anti-Semite, flaunting qualities that the latter wished to extirpate in himself.

Duplicity in public life promoted creativity in private. In order to cushion abrasive contact between nationalities, Austrians cultivated a courtliness that mollified hostility. Living cheek-by-jowl, educated Germans, Czechs, Magyars, Poles, Italians, and Jews consorted with Romanians, Slovaks, Serbs, Croats, and Ruthenians, most of whom lacked formal education. A British geneticist, C. D. Darlington, has emphasized that outstandingly creative individuals tend to come from marriages between persons of widely disparate ancestry. By promoting fresh genetic combinations, outbreeding propagates both geniuses and misfits. During the late nineteenth century, the Habsburg Empire harbored the world's most diverse gene pool, where interbreeding of races flourished. According to Darlington, interracial populations tend to beget individuals of exceptional talent, as well as persons of substandard ability who prey upon social services.[19] Both of these consequences abounded in Franz Joseph's empire.

In the cultural sphere, Béla Bartók has shown how the propinquity of so many people provoked new permutations of familiar elements. To explain the extraordinary efflorescence of folk melody within the Habsburg Empire, Bartók analyzed what he called crossing and re-

crossing of motifs. A Hungarian folk melody would be borrowed by
Slovaks, altered by them, and then reclaimed by Magyars, who would
shape it into still a third tune.[20] A similar process of crossing and
recrossing enriched vocabulary, gestures, cuisine, clothing, music, folklore, and mores, helping inhabitants of both city and country to accommodate multiplicity. Intermingling with half-foreign fellow citizens,
nearly every Austrian developed a detachment that Walter Brecht
called a

> veritable romantic irony, the almost uncanny ability to see
> and understand at once all fifty-two sides of a question, and
> their opposite just as easily.[21]

Impelled to integrative thinking by daily encounters with disparate
peoples, Austrians refined the art of dialogue, becoming in the words of
Anton Wildgans, "connoisseurs of men" (Menschenkenner), who exercised tolerance and courtesy in order that society might endure.[22]

Exposure to overwhelming diversity engendered negative capability,
tempting men like Hermann Bahr to be all things to all men. Chame-
leon-like, he tried so hard to assimilate everything alien—nihil huma-
num alienum puto—that he ended upholding nothing except flux. Yet
there was dignity—and profound Christianity—in his declaration, "I
have always loved my enemies,"[23] as there was in the pronouncement
of Bertha von Suttner, "I like to let opponents, especially such distinguished opponents, speak out."[24] Heeding every adversary, the anti-
dogmatists of Austria, created thought both penetrating and all-embracing. More imaginatively than anyone else, they combined open-
mindedness with rigor. Robert Musil may have been right when he
wrote:

> Yes, maybe Kakanien was, despite much which speaks to the
> contrary, a country for geniuses; and probably that is another
> reason why it succumbed.[25]

Masters of both surfaces and depths, thinkers from Austria-Hungary
devised the premises upon which our self-knowledge is built.

AUSTRIA'S INTELLECTUAL ACHIEVEMENT

Which of the innovators chronicled in this book, one may wonder, have
most decisively influenced posterity? First place undoubtedly must go
to Freud. No other thinker of the twentieth century, Austrian or other-

wise, has so impregnated contemporary consciousness, permeating every facet of economic, social, and intellectual life. The ubiquity of psychoanalysis rests largely on the fact that today's most widely held world view is positivism, tinctured with impressionism. The extent to which after 1945 it was Austrians who disseminated this world view must remain for others to explore. A second movement claiming innumerable adherents is Buber's philosophy of dialogue: like psychoanalysis it reconciles positivism with impressionism by differentiating levels of the psyche.

Third, reverence for fantasy has sustained Austrian literature. Defying the philistinism of both bureaucracy and the masses, novelists as disparate as Kafka, Musil, and Roth have proclaimed the sovereignty of imagination. In repudiating technology and barbarization, Marcionists and therapeutic nihilists denounced totalitarian behavior with futile prescience. In contrast to French or American writers, Austrian authors devoted vastly more energy to diagnosis than to cure.

In addition to formulating visions that have come to constitute our self-awareness, Austrians launched major innovations in nearly all fields of thought. In philosophy, logical positivism and linguistic analysis spread from Vienna to every English-speaking university. Brentano opened new perspectives in epistemology, psychology, and ethics, while Husserl's phenomenology has become a discipline unto itself. In legal theory, Kelsen's positivism reformulated problems of his field, while in economic theory, Menger and his students collaborated in founding marginal analysis. In social theory, Lukács and Mannheim instituted the discipline that the latter called sociology of knowledge. As refined by subsequent researchers, it promotes a detachment invaluable for mollifying dissidents who claim exemption from any established order. Hungarian theorists have taught us that no program for changing society can escape being contaminated by that society. Like psychoanalysis, sociology of knowledge strengthens relativism with systematic rigor.

Hardly any Austrian utopians have seen their dreams fulfilled. To be sure, Herzl's Jewish state and Mayreder's balanced sexuality have become facts of life, as has Loos's crusade against ornament. Most of the other visions seem as quixotic as ever—whether Popper-Lynkeus' program for eradicating poverty, Suttner's dream of peace, or Coudenhove-Kalergi's scheme for uniting Europe. Together with embittered perfectionists such as Weininger and Broch, these visionaries have received scant applause from a world that worships efficacity.

Although it may be too early to assess everything that thinkers of Austria bequeathed us, clearly their talent for integrative thinking is dying out. For twenty years, no country has produced a philosopher or social theorist to rival in innovative power Freud, Husserl, Wittgenstein, Kelsen, or Neurath. Although, all things considered, most Europeans and Americans may be better off than were their ancestors fifty years ago, anyone who has savored Austrian creative thought must find its loss irreparable. Intellectual life today lacks the discoveries and sweeping visions that enthralled readers around 1900 or even 1930. In an Alexandrian age, when droves of workers are processing insights garnered two or more generations ago, what an astonishing number of these insights emerged within the Habsburg Empire or its successor states! In the United States and Great Britain, professionals have consigned psychoanalysis to the physicians whom Freud impugned; they have relegated philosophy to engineers-in-words; and they have scattered shreds of Neurath's universal genius among sociologists, city planners, philosophers of science, economic historians, and graphic designers. By dispersing the Jews of Vienna and Prague, the Nazis dismembered that community whose members almost single-handedly had integrated thought.

Lest we succumb to neo-Biedermeier nostalgia, let us concede that few intellectuals today would desire to resurrect Vienna, Prague, or Budapest as they existed at the turn of the century. Technical wizardry has so bemused us that we scorn the amenities that it all but abolished: local color, eccentricity, noblesse oblige, and tradition. By reaping the fruits of uniformity, we have withered those of particularism, so that at least in philosophy and social theory we are expending intellectual capital accumulated while the two orders still mingled. Granted that an interim of reworking concepts can profit us, what sort of thinkers will provide new insights twenty years from now? Scrutiny of the last twenty years offers scant hope for a renaissance in theorizing. To be sure, thanks to a few Austrians sprinkled across North America and Great Britain, integrative thinking has not quite vanished. Since 1945, Arnold Hauser, Michael Polanyi, Friedrich von Hayek, Ludwig von Bertalanffy, Karl Popper, and Ernst Gombrich have crowned their careers with wide-ranging syntheses.[26] Although today their scope and perspicacity dazzle us, fifty years ago their work might have seemed almost routine.

If we may for a moment indulge in wish-fulfillment, we can discern in recent works by Polanyi, Hayek, Bertalanffy, and Ehrenzweig the silhouette of a future society, which carries into a technologized world qualities that energized Austrian thought. Each in his own way, these utopians call for new creativity grounded in individualism and tolerance. By demanding that ego and id be liberated from outdated edicts of superego, they preach receptivity to inner experience. Earlier, their plea for spontaneity had been voiced by Schlick, Buber, Ebner, and Rank, the Austrians who most explicitly anticipated tenets of today's youth. For millions, creativity has become an ego ideal, rendering every dogma suspect and elevating self-fulfillment into arbiter supreme. Yet it would be fatuous to equate the youth revolution of the late 1960's with the Gay Apocalypse. Young people today lack the rigor, sense of continuity, and *savoir faire* that enabled Austrians to discover structure beneath multiplicity. Such deficiencies make it ironic that today's youth is seeking what these men and women had found: capacity to see life whole and courage to follow one's deepest impulses.

It remains to be seen whether a global civilization can approximate conditions that once made Austria a beacon of modernity within a drifting world. Now that mutability has become our daily bread, no one has more to teach us than these connoisseurs of metamorphosis. Yet in at least one respect, we ought not to emulate the Habsburg Empire. More than most creative ages, the Gay Apocalypse regarded itself as marking an end rather than a beginning. Indeed Karl Kraus or Stefan Zweig would be astonished to learn that civilization has survived at all, and if we have foiled their expectation, it is no thanks to therapeutic nihilism such as theirs. By heeding more constructive voices, we may yet have time to invalidate their despair. Taken by itself, however, the Gay Apocalypse teaches that time effaces more than it sustains.

Notes

Abbreviations

ADB   *Allgemeine Deutsche Biographie,* 56 vols. (Leipzig, 1875–1912).

AJP   *American Journal of Psychology* (Ithaca, N.Y.; Austin, Tex., 1887–).

AJS   *American Journal of Sociology* (Chicago, 1895–).

ASWSP   *Archiv für Sozialwissenschaften und Sozialpolitik,* 69 vols. (Berlin, Tübingen, Leipzig, 1883–1933).

DVLG   *Deutsche Vierteljahresschrift für Literaturwissenschaft und Geistesgeschichte* (Halle, Stuttgart, 1923–).

EP   *Encyclopedia of Philosophy,* ed. Paul Edwards, 8 vols. (New York, 1967).

GW   Gesammelte Werke

IESS   *International Encyclopedia of the Social Sciences,* ed. David L. Sills, 17 vols. (New York, 1968).

IJP   *International Journal of Psycho-Analysis* (London, 1920–).

JAPA   *Journal of the American Psychoanalytic Association* (New York, 1953–).

JCEA   *Journal of Central European Affairs* (Boulder, Colo., 1941–1964).

JCH   *Journal of Contemporary History* (London, 1966–).

JMH   *Journal of Modern History* (Chicago, 1929–).

Jones   Ernest Jones, *Life and Work of Sigmund Freud,* 3 vols. (London, 1953–1957; 2d ed., vols. 1 and 2, 1956–1958). [page references are to the British edition].

KML   *Kindlers Malerei Lexikon,* 5 vols. (Zürich, 1964–1968).

MIOGF   *Mitteilungen des Instituts für Österreichische Geschichtsforschung* (Vienna, 1880–).

NOB   *Neue Österreichische Biographie* (Vienna, 1923–).

PSQ   *Political Science Quarterly* (New York, 1886–).

SEER   *Slavonic and East European Review* (London, 1922–).

SKAW-Wien   *Sitzungsberichte der Kaiserlichen Akademie der Wissenchaften* (Vienna, 1850–).

YLBI   *Yearbook of the Leo Baeck Institute of Jews from Germany* (London, 1958–).

ZAAK   *Zeitschrift für Aesthetik und allgemeine Kunstwissenschaft,* 37 vols. (Stuttgart, 1905–1943).

ZfphF   *Zeitschrift für philosophische Forschung* (Wurzbach, 1946–).

Notes

INTRODUCTION

1. A cogent appraisal of methodological disputes since 1900 appears in Jost Hermand, *Synthetisches Interpretieren: Zur Methodik der Literaturwissenschaft* (Munich, 1968). For controversies within the history of philosophy see John Passmore, "Philosophy, Historiography of," *EP*, 6 (1967), 226-230; Lutz Geldsetzer, *Die Philosophie der Philosophiegeschichte im 19. Jahrhundert: Zur Wissenschaftstheorie der Philosophiegeschichtsschreibung und –betrachtung* (Meisenheim am Glan, 1968).
2. A searching analysis of secularization is David L. Edwards, *Religion and Change* (London, 1969), esp. pp. 109-157 on the psychology of unbelief.
3. For an assessment of gains versus risks in combining synoptic with monographic analysis see Siegfried Kracauer, *History: The Last Things Before the Last* (New York, 1969), pp. 104-138.
4. On recent trends in the study of engagé intellectuals see: J. P. Nettl, "Ideas, Intellectuals, and Structures of Dissent," in Philip Rieff, ed., *On Intellectuals: Theoretical Studies, Case Studies* (Garden City, N. Y., 1969), pp. 53-122.
5. See Werner Stark, *The Sociology of Knowledge: An Essay in Aid of a Deeper Understanding of the History of Ideas* (London, 1958).
6. Two scholars of seventeenth-century British political theory advocate cross-fertilization between internal history of ideas and the sociology of thinkers. See John Dunn, "The Identity of the History of Ideas," *Philosophy*, 18 (1968), 85-104; Quentin Skinner, "Meaning and Understanding in the History of Ideas," *History and Theory*, 8 (1969), 3-53.
7. For further reasons why Americans find German thought impenetrable see Kurt Lewin, "Some Social-psychological Differences Between the United States and Germany" [1936], in *Resolving Social Conflicts: Selected Papers on Group Dynamics* (New York, 1948), pp. 3-33. This analysis delineates pre-1938 Austrians as aptly as pre-1933 Germans.

CHAPTER 1

1. On the evolution of the term Austria see Erich Zöllner, "Formen und Wandlungen des Österreichbegriffes," in Hugo Hantsch, Erich Voegelin, and Franco Valsecchi, eds., *Historica: Studien zum geschichtlichen Denken und Forschen* (Vienna, 1965), pp. 63-89. A synopsis of attempts by Austrian historians to circumscribe their subject appears in Heinrich Ritter von Srbik, *Geist und Geschichte vom deutschen Humanismus bis zur Gegenwart* (Salzburg, 1951), 2:80-121.
2. On the Counter-Reformation in Austria see Robert A. Kann, *The Problem of Restoration: A Study in Comparative Political History* (Berkeley and Los Angeles, 1968), pp. 231-278 [contains excellent bibliography].
3. On the Habsburg struggle against the Turks see Erwin Hanslick, *Österreich: Erde und Geist* (Vienna, 1917); Clemens Graf zu Brandis, *Die historische Mission Österreichs in Europa* (Zürich, 1946); John Stoye, *The Siege of Vienna*

(London, 1964); Lavender Cassels, *The Struggle for the Ottoman Empire, 1717-1740* (London, 1966).

4. On Austrian Baroque see Heinrich Ritter von Srbik, "Abenteurer am Hofe Kaiser Leopold I (Alchimie, Technik und Merkantilismus)," *Archiv für Kulturgeschichte,* 8 (1910) 52-71; Hermann Bahr, "Vorbarock" and "Barock," in *Summula* (Leipzig, 1921), pp. 167-177; André Tibal, *L'Autrichien: Essai sur la formation d'une individualité nationale (du XVI au XVIII siècle)* (Paris, 1936); Oswald Redlich, *Weltmacht des Barock: Österreich in der Zeit Leopolds I* (Vienna, 1938; 4th ed., 1961); Hans Kohn, "AEIOU: Some Reflections on the Meaning and Mission of Austria," *JMH* 11 (1939), 513-527; Ann Tizia Leitich, *Vienna Gloriosa: Weltstadt des Barock* (Vienna, 1947); Friedrich Heer, *Land im Strom der Zeit: Österreich gestern, heute, morgen* (Vienna, 1958); Anna Coreth, *Pietas Austriaca: Ursprung und Entwicklung barocker Frömmigkeit in Österreich* (Vienna, 1959); Therese Schüssel, *Kultur des Barock in Österreich,* 2nd ed. (Graz, 1960).

5. On Baroque mentality see René Wellek, "The Concept of Baroque in Literary Scholarship," *Journal of Aesthetics and Art Criticism,* 5 (1946), 77-109; Richard Alewyn, ed., *Deutsche Barockforschung: Dokumentation einer Epoche* (Cologne, 1965) [reprints twenty-four articles].

6. Anna Coreth, *Pietas,* pp. 17-35.

7. *Ibid.*, pp. 43-69.

8. Oskar Kokoschka, "An Approach to the Baroque Art of Czechoslovakia," *Burlington Magazine,* 81 (Nov., 1942), 263-268.

9. On the concept of Josephinism see Wenzel Lustkandl, *Die josephinischen Ideen und ihr Erfolg* (Vienna, 1881); Fritz Valjavec, *Der Josephinismus: Zur geistigen Entwicklung Österreichs im 18. und 19. Jahrhundert* (Brünn, 1944); Ferdinand Maas, S. J., *Der Josephinismus: Quellen zu seiner Geschichte in Österreich 1760-1850: Amtliche Dokumente aus dem Wiener Haus-, Hof-, und Staatsarchiv,* 5 vols. (Vienna, 1951-1961); Roger Bauer, "Le Josephisme," *Critique,* 14 (1958), 622-639; Herbert Rieser, *Der Geist des Josephinismus: Der Kampf der Kirche um ihre Freiheit* (Vienna, 1964); Zöllner, "Bemerkungen zum Problem der Beziehungen zwischen Aufklärung und Josephinismus," in *Österreich und Europa: Festgabe für Hugo Hantsch* (Graz, 1965), pp. 203-219; Klaus Epstein, *The Genesis of German Conservatism* (Princeton, 1966), pp. 158-175, 394-413. See also the works by Eduard Winter cited in chap. 19, n. 2.

10. Heinrich Benedikt, "Der Josephinismus vor Joseph II," in *Österreich und Europa,* pp. 183-201. On Maria Theresa's reforms see Constance Lily Morris, *Maria Theresia: The Last Conservative* (New York, 1937); Edith Murr Link, *The Emancipation of the Austrian Peasant, 1740-1798* (New York, 1949); William E. Wright, *Serf, Seigneur, and Sovereign: Agrarian Reform in Eighteenth Century Bohemia* (Minneapolis, 1966); Herman Freudenberger, "State Intervention as an Obstacle to Economic Growth in the Habsburg Monarchy," *Journal of Economic History,* 27 (1967), 493-509; Henry E. Strakosch, *State Absolutism and the Rule of Law: The Struggle for Codification of Civil Law in Austria 1753-1811* (Sydney, 1968) [penetrating].

11. See Robert Zimmermann, "Von Ayrenhoff bis Grillparzer: Zur Geschichte des Dramas in Österreich" [1864], in *Studien und Kritiken zur Philosophie und Aesthetik* (Vienna, 1870), 2:1-73 [exceptionally informative]. On Sonnenfels see Louise Sommer, *Die österreichische Kameralisten in dogmengeschichtlicher Darstellung* (Vienna, 1925; repr. Aalen, 1967), 2:319-444; Kann, *A Study in*

Austrian Intellectual History: From Late Baroque to Romanticism (New York, 1960), pp. 146-258.

12. On responses to censorship see Walter C. Langsam, "Emperor Francis II and the Austrian Jacobins, 1792-1796," *American Historical Review*, 50 (1945), 471-490; Ernst Wangermann, *From Joseph II to the Jacobin Trials: Government Policy and Public Opinion in the Habsburg Dominions in the Period of the French Revolution* (London, 1959) [mildly Marxist]; Denis Silagi, *Jakobiner in der Habsburger Monarchie: Ein Beitrag zur Geschichte des aufgeklärten Absolutismus in Österreich* (Vienna, 1962); Leslie Bodi, "Enlightened Despotism and Literature of the Enlightenment," *German Life and Letters*, 22 (1968-1969), 324-333.

13. See Josef Redlich, *Das österreichische Staats- und Reichsproblem: Geschichtliche Darstellung der inneren Politik der habsburgischen Monarchie von 1848 bis zum Untergang des Reiches*, 2 vols. (Leipzig, 1920), 1:1-88; Viktor Bibl, *Der Zerfall Österreichs*, 2 vols. (Vienna, 1922-1924); Srbik, *Metternich: Der Staatsmann und der Mensch*, 3 vols. (Munich, 1925-1954); R. John Rath, *The Viennese Revolution of 1848* (Austin, 1957); Otto Brunner, "Staat und Gesellschaft im vormärzlichen Österreich," in Werner Conze, ed., *Staat und Gesellschaft im deutschen Vormärz, 1815-1848* (Stuttgart, 1962), pp. 39-78 [incisive].

14. See Carl Julius Weber, *Deutschland oder Briefe eines in Deutschland reisenden Deutschen* [1826-1828], 2d ed. (Stuttgart, 1834), 2:156-690, esp. 194-203 on political conditions; Heinrich Laube, *Reise durch das Biedermeier* [1834-1837] (Hamburg, 1965), pp. 227-279; Frances M. Trollope, *Vienna and the Austrians*, 2 vols. (London, 1838); "Travellers in Austria and Hungary," *The Quarterly Review*, 65 (1839-40), 234-272.

15. On the concept of Biedermeier see Günther Weydt, "Literarisches Biedermeier: die überindividuellen Ordnungen," *DVLG*, 13 (1935), 44-58; Paul Kluckhohn, "Biedermeier als literarische Epochenzeichnung," *DVLG*, 13 (1935), 1-43; Clemens Heselhaus, "Wiederherstellung: Restauratio-Restitutio-Regeneratio," *DVLG*, 25 (1951), 54-81; Friedrich Sengle, "Voraussetzungen und Erscheinungsformen der deutschen Restaurationsliteratur," *DVLG*, 30 (1956), 268-294. Critiques of the concept Biedermeier as a literary category appear in Jost Hermand, *Die literarische Formenwelt des Biedermeier* (Giessen, 1958); Willi Flemming, "Die Problematik der Bezeichnung 'Biedermeier,'" *Germanisch-Romanische Monatsschrift*, 8 (1958), 379-388.

16. On Austrian Biedermeier see Wilhelm Bietak, *Das Lebensgefühl des "Biedermeier" in der österreichischen Dichtung* (Vienna, 1931); Bietak, "Zwischen Romantik, Jungem Deutschland und Realismus: Eine Literatur- und Problemschau vom Standpunkt der Biedermeierforschung," *DVLG*, 13 (1935), 163-206; Bietak, "Probleme der Biedermeierdichtung," in *Beiträge zum Grillparzer- und Stifterbild* (Graz, 1965) pp. 5-20; Bauer, *"La réalité: Royaume de Dieu": Études sur l'originalité du théâtre viennois dans la premiére partie du 19ème siècle* (Munich, 1965) [exceptionally well-documented]; Rio Preisner, *Johann Nepomuk Nestroy: Der Schöpfer der tragischen Posse* (Munich, 1968), esp. pp. 11-66 [a model of Marxist literary analysis]. On poets who resisted Biedermeier passivity see Antal Mádl, *Politische Dichtung in Österreich (1830-1848)* (Budapest, 1969).

17. On the use of polar opposites in classifying societies see Horace M. Miner, "Community-Society Continua," *IESS*, 3 (1968), 174-180; Rudolf Heberle, "Tönnies, Ferdinand," *IESS*, 16 (1968), 98-103; Jürgen Habermas, "Technik

und Wissenschaft als 'Ideologie'?" *Man and World*, 1 (1968), 483-523, esp. 491-495.

18. Walter Brecht, "Österreichische Geistesform und österreichische Dichtung," *DVLG*, 9 (1931), 607-627, esp. 622-623. For a contrast between Prussian and Austrian institutions, see Otto Hintze, "Der österreichische und preussische Beamtenstand im 17. und 18. Jahrhundert," *Historische Zeitschrift*, 86 (1901), 401-444.

19. Hugo von Hofmannsthal, "Preusse und Österreicher: Ein Schema" [1917], in *Ausgewählte Werke* (Frankfurt, 1957), 2:615-617. See also Hofmannsthal, "Österreich im Spiegel seiner Dichtung" [1916], *ibid.*, pp. 593-605.

20. Erich Kahler, *The Jews Among the Nations* (New York, 1967), p. 10. Perhaps the best history of the Jews since 1800 is Ismar Elbogen, *A Century of Jewish Life* (Philadelphia, 1944). On Jews in Austria see Josef Fraenkel, ed., *The Jews of Austria: Essays on their Life, History and Destruction* (London, 1967). Indispensable reference works are Siegmund Kaznelson, ed., *Juden im deutschen Kulturbereich: Ein Sammelwerk*, 3d ed. (Berlin, 1964); John F. Oppenheimer, ed., *Lexikon des Judentums* (Gütersloh, 1967).

21. See Ben Halpern, "The Jewish Consensus," *Jewish Frontier*, 29 (Sept., 1962), 9-13; Raphael Loewe, "Defining Judaism: Some Ground-Clearing," *Jewish Journal of Sociology*, 7 (1965-1966), 153-175. On varieties of assimilation see Kurt Stillschweig, "Jewish Assimilation as an Object of Legislation," *Historia Judaica*, 8 (1946), 1-18; Jacob Neusner, "From Theology to Ideology: The Transmutation of Judaism in Modern Times," in Kalman H. Silvert, ed. *Churches and States: The Religious Institution and Modernization* (New York, 1967), pp. 13-48 [extremely perceptive].

22. Immanuel Velikovsky, "Can a Newly Acquired Language Become the Speech of the Unconscious? Word-Plays in the Dreams of Hebrew-Thinking Persons," *Psychoanalytic Review*, 21 (1934), 329-335. See also Mark Zborowski, "The Place of Book-Learning in Traditional Jewish Culture," in Margaret Mead and Martha Wolfenstein, eds., *Childhood in Contemporary Cultures* (Chicago, 1955), pp. 118-141. For an analysis of "latent Mandarinism" in Jewish learning, see Neusner, "Judaism in the History of Religions," *History and Theory*, Beiheft 8 (1968), pp. 31-45, esp. 40-41.

23. Wilhelm Stekel, *Autobiography: The Life Story of a Pioneer Psychoanalyst* (New York, 1950), p. 131.

24. Hermann Broch, *Massenpsychologie: Schriften aus dem Nachlass* (Zürich, 1959), pp. 196-201.

25. Salcia Landmann, ed., *Jüdische Witze* (Munich, 1963), p. 133. On self-degradation in Jewish jokes see Theodor Reik, *Jewish Wit* (New York, 1962), pp. 219-226.

26. Freud discusses jokes about *Schnorrer* in *Der Witz und seine Beziehungen zum Unbewussten* in *GW*, 6 (London, 1940), 123-124.

27. Emil Reich, *Plato as an Introduction to Modern Criticism of Life* (London, 1906), pp. 116, 120-121. The fixation of Jewish mothers on infancy is confirmed in Martha Wolfenstein, "Two Types of Jewish Mothers," in Mead and Wolfenstein, eds., *Childhood*, pp. 424-440.

28. On the *Shtetl*, see Solomon A. Birnbaum, "The Cultural Structure of East Ashkenazic Jewry," *SEER*, 24 (1946-47), 73-92; Mark Zborowski and Elizabeth Herzog, *Life is With People: The Jewish Little-Town of Eastern Europe* (New York, 1952). On Jews in Galicia see Gottfried Schramm, "Die Ostjuden als

soziales Problem des 19. Jahrhunderts," in Heinz Maus, ed., *Gesellschaft, Recht und Politik* (Neuwied, 1968), pp. 353-380.

29. For example, Leopold Kompert, "Schlemihl," in *Aus dem Ghetto* (Leipzig, 1848); Karl Emil Franzos, "Schiller in Barnow" in *Die Juden von Barnow: Novellen* (Stuttgart, 1877). Joseph Roth continued this tradition in *Radetzkymarsch* (Berlin, 1932) and *Die Kapuzinergruft* (Bilthoven, 1938.)

30. See Stefan Zweig. *Die Welt von Gestern: Erinnerungen eines Europäers* (Stockholm, 1942), pp. 38-39. On the Jews of Vienna see Sigmund Mayer, *Die Wiener Juden: Kommerz, Kultur, Politik 1700-1900* (Vienna, 1916); Hans Tietze, *Die Juden Wiens: Geschichte, Wirtschaft, Kultur* (Leipzig, 1933); Max Grunwald, *Vienna* (Philadelphia, 1936); Hugo Gold, *Geschichte der Juden in Wein: Ein Gedenkbuch* (Tel Aviv, 1966).

31. Stanislaw Andreski, "An Economic Theory of Antisemitism," in *Elements of Comparative Sociology* (London, 1964), pp. 291-310. See also Peter G. J. Pulzer, *The Rise of Political Antisemitism in Germany and Austria* (New York, 1964); Dirk van Arkel, *Antisemitism in Austria* (Leiden, 1966). A neglected compendium of anti-Semitic motifs is Eduard Fuchs, *Die Juden in der Karikatur: Ein Beitrag zur Kulturgeschichte* (Munich, 1921), esp. pp. 195-205 on Austrian satirists.

32. See Otto Fenichel, "Psychoanalysis of Antisemitism" [1937], *American Imago,* 1^2 (1939-40), 24-39; Bruno Bettelheim, "The Dynamism of Anti-Semitism in Gentile and Jew," *Journal of Abnormal and Social Psychology*, 42 (1947), 153-168; Rudolph M. Loewenstein, *Christians and Jews: A Psychoanalytic Study* (New York, 1951) [penetrating; by a friend of Hanns Sachs].

33. On Rohling see Gotthard Deutsch, "Rohling, August," *Jewish Encyclopedia* (New York, 1912), 10:442; Joseph Samuel Bloch, *My Reminiscences* (Vienna, 1923), pp. 61-135.

34. Quoted in Ernst Rychnovsky, "The Struggle Against the Ritual Murder Superstition," in *Thomas G. Masaryk and the Jews: A Collection of Essays* (New York, 1941), p. 150. On the Polna affair see also T. G. Masaryk, *Die Bedeutung des Polnaer Verbrechens für den Ritualmordaberglaube* (Berlin, 1900); Arthur Nussbaum, *Der Polnaer Ritualmordprozess: Eine kriminalpsychologische Untersuchung auf aktenmässiger Grundlage* (Berlin, 1906); Nussbaum, "The 'Ritual Murder' Trial of Polna," *Historia Judaica*, 9 (1950), 57-74; František Červinka, "The Hilsner Affair," *YLBI*, 13 (1968), 142-157.

CHAPTER 2

1. See Peter Feldl, *Das verspielte Reich: Die letzten Tage Österreich-Ungarns* (Vienna, 1968). For hypotheses about how the empire might have survived, see Hans Kohn, "Was the Collapse Inevitable?" *Austrian History Yearbook,* 3.3 (1967), 250-263; Joachim Remak, "The Healthy Invalid: How Doomed the Habsburg Empire?" *JMH*, 41 (1969), 127-143.

2. Max Graf, *Legend of a Music City* (New York, 1945), p. 65.

3. Robert Waelder, "Historical Fiction," *JAPA*, 11 (1963), 629.

4. Max Brod, *Streitbares Leben, 1884-1968*, 2d ed. (Munich, 1969), p. 219.

5. Two recent works offer searching analyses of Franz Joseph's reign: Heinrich Benedikt, *Die Monarchie des Hauses Österreich: Ein historisches Essay* (Munich, 1968); C. A. Macartney, *The Habsburg Empire, 1790-1918* (London, 1969), pp. 322-833 [superb on Hungary, weak on Bohemia; scants intellectual

history]. A useful digest of pre-1945 scholarship is Anatol Murad, *Franz Joseph I of Austria and His Empire* (New York, 1968).

6. Eduard Hanslick, "Aus meinem Leben," *Deutsche Rundschau*, 80 (1894), 35. See also Móriz Jókai, "Denkrede auf Kronprinz Rudolf," *Ungarische Revue*, 9 (1889), 385-406.

7. See Julius Szeps, ed., *Kronprinz Rudolf: Politische Briefe an einen Freund 1882-1889* (Vienna, 1922).

8. Berta Szeps, *My Life and History* (New York, 1939), pp. 20-151, esp. 146-151. A fundamental reassessment appears in Fritz Judtmann, *Mayerling ohne Mythos: Ein Tatsachenbericht* (Vienna, 1968).

9. Berta Szeps, *My Life and History*, pp. 147-148.

10. *Ibid.*, p. 22-23, 151.

11. Josef Redlich, *Schicksalsjahre Österreichs 1908–1919: Das politische Tagebuch Josef Redlichs*, 2 vols. (Graz, 1953,) 1:235.

12. Paul Nikitsch-Boulles, *Vor dem Sturm: Erinnerungen an Erzherzog Thronfolger Franz Ferdinand* (Berlin, 1925), pp. 217-225 [by the Archduke's private secretary]; Theodor von Sosnosky, *Franz Ferdinand der Erzherzog-Thronfolger: Ein Lebensbild* (Munich, 1927), pp. 226-229.

13. "Ich bin ein Pechvogel." Albert Schäffle, *Aus meinem Leben* (Berlin, 1905), 2:70.

14. On the two societies Comte Paul Vasili, *La Société de Vienne* (Paris, 1885); A. S. Levetus, *Imperial Vienna: An Account of Its History, Traditions, and Arts* (London, 1905), pp. 364-398; Nora Fugger, *The Glory of the Habsburgs: Memoirs* (New York, 1932), chaps. 1-4.

15. Martin Freud, *Sigmund Freud: Man and Father* (New York, 1958), p. 29.

16. Virginio Gayda, *Modern Austria: Her Racial and Social Problems* (London, 1915), p. 201.

17. Mór Jókai, *Black Diamonds* [1870] (New York, 1896), p. 241.

18. The speech of February 17, 1888, is quoted in Robert Arthaber, "Engelbert Pernerstorfer," *NOB*, 2 (1925), pp. 105-106. See also Oscar Jászi, *The Dissolution of the Habsburg Monarchy* (Chicago, 1929; repr. 1961), p. 237. On Otto see Erich Graf von ʹKielmansegg, *Kaiserhaus, Staatsmänner und Politiker* (Vienna, 1966), pp. 130-142.

19. R. H. Bruce Lockhart, *Retreat from Glory* (London, 1934), pp. 60-61. See also Fred Hennings, *Solange er lebt: Aus dem Wien der Jahrhundertwende* (Vienna, 1968), pp. 41-43.

20. Lockhart, *Retreat from Glory*, p. 184. See also Willi Frischauer, *The Grand Hotels of Europe* (New York, 1965), pp. 118-138.

21. Graf, *Legend*, pp. 69-70.

22. Hanns Sachs, *Freud: Master and Friend* (Cambridge, Mass., 1946), p. 27.

23. Olga Schnitzler, *Spiegelbild der Freundschaft* (Salzburg, 1962), p. 27.

24. Fugger, *The Glory of the Habsburgs*, pp. 284-285.

25. Wolf von Schierbrand, *Austria-Hungary: Polyglot Empire* (New York, 1917), pp. 173-175.

CHAPTER 3

1. See Alexander Spitzmüller, ". . . und hat auch Ursach', es zu lieben" (Vienna, 1955), esp. pp. 174-198 on Franz Joseph.

2. See Ernst Lothar, *Das Wunder des Überlebens: Erinnerungen und Ergebnisse* (Vienna, 1961), pp. 27-28. For literary portraits of lesser officials see Marie von Ebner-Eschenbach, "Ein Spätgeborener" [1875]; Franz Werfel, *Der Tod des Kleinbürgers* (Vienna, 1927).

3. See Alexander Spitzmüller, "Emil Steinbach," *NOB*, 2 (1925), 48-62.

4. On social legislation see Ludwig Brügel, *Soziale Gesetzgebung in Österreich von 1848 bis 1918: Eine geschichtliche Darstellung* (Vienna, 1919). On earlier conditions see René Lavollée, *Les classes ouvrières en Europe: Études sur leur situation matérielle et morale* (Paris, 1884), 2:297-353.

5. On the Reichsrat see Gustav Kolmer, *Parlament und Verfassung in Österreich*, 8 vols. (Vienna, 1902-1914) [covers 1848 to 1904]; on ministries see Alois von Czedik, *Zur Geschichte der k.k. österreichischen Ministerien 1861 bis 1916: nach den Erinnerungen*, 4 vols. (Vienna, 1917-1920).

6. Mark Twain, "Stirring Times in Austria," *Harper's Magazine*, 96 (1898), 530-540; for a sequel see Twain, "Concerning the Jews," *ibid.*, 99 (1899), 527-535. See also Berthold Sutter, *Die badenischen Sprachenverordnungen von 1897*, 2 vols. (Graz, 1965), 2:106-108. For comparisons with other Parliaments see Georg Jellinek, "Parliamentary Obstruction," *PSQ*, 19 (1904), 579-588; Brita Skottsberg, *Der österreichische Parlamentarismus* (Göteborg, 1940) [covers 1848 to 1938].

7. Freud, *Die Traumdeutung*, 8th ed. *GW*, 2/3 (London, 1942), p. 275.

8. See Frank Pentland Chambers, *The War Behind the War, 1914-1918* (New York, 1939), pp. 179-186; Arthur J. May, *The Passing of the Hapsburg Monarchy 1914-1918*, 2 vols. (Philadelphia, 1966).

9. Archibald Colquhoun and Ethel Colquhoun, *The Whirlpool of Europe: Austria-Hungary and the Habsburgs* (London, 1907), p. 210. For other examples see E. B. Lanin, "Count Taaffe and Austrian Politics," *Contemporary Review*, 63 (1893), 279-304, esp. 297n.

10. Maria Hornor Lansdale, *Vienna and the Viennese* (Philadelphia, 1902), p. 358.

11. Karl Kraus, "Aus dem dunkelsten Österreich" [1906], in *Sittlichkeit und Kriminalität* [1908] (Frankfurt, 1966), pp. 203-207.

12. Kraus, "Der Hexenprozess von Leoben" [1904], *ibid.*, pp. 83-97.

13. Kraus, "Der Fall Riehl" [1906], and "Die Ära nach dem Prozess Riehl" [1907], *ibid.*, pp. 180-199 and 207-215.

14. See William A. Jenks, *Austria under the Iron Ring 1879-1893* (Charlottesville, Va., 1965), pp. 141-157.

15. On the Friedjung trial see Karl Kraus, "Prozess Friedjung [1909], in *Untergang der Welt durch schwarze Magie* [1922], in *Werke*, 8 (Munich, 1960), 23-40; Herman Bahr, "Prozess Friedjung," *Neue Rundschau*, 21 (1910), 240-250; Virginio Gayda, *Modern Austria* (London, 1915), pp. 289-291; Henry Wickham Steed, *Through Thirty Years, 1892-1922: A Personal Narrative*, 2 vols. (Garden City, 1924), 1:308-314. On the official agencies for leaking stories see Kurt Paupié, *Handbuch der österreichischen Pressegeschichte. II. Die zentralen pressepolitischen Einrichtungen des Staates* (Vienna, 1966).

16. On techniques of censorship see J. M. Vincent, "Politics and History at Vienna," *The Nation*. 53 (Nov., 1891), 443-445; Eugene Limedorfer, "Great Newspapers of Continental Europe. IV. Austrian and Hungarian Newspapers," *The Bookman*, 11 (1900), 149-157. On wartime censorship see Paupié, *Handbuch*, 2: 148-173.

17. Berta Szeps, *My Life and History* (New York, 1939), pp. 62-63. Kurt Paupié, *Moritz Szeps: Werk, Persönlichkeit und Beziehungen zum Kaiserhaus* (1949) was not available to me.

18. For a survey of the press see Paupié, *Handbuch*, vol. 1 (1960). See also Adam Wandruszka, *Geschichte einer Zeitung: Das Schicksal der "Presse" und der "Neuen Freie Presse" von 1848 biz zur zweiten Republik* (Vienna, 1958).

19. The fullest account of military life is Alfons Danzer, *Unter den Fahnen: Die Völker Österreich-Ungarns in Waffen* (Vienna, 1889). See also Franz Neubauer, *Die Gendarmerie in Österreich 1849-1924* (Vienna, 1924); Herbert V. Patera, *Unter Österreichs Fahnen: Ein Buch vom österreichischen Soldaten* (Graz, 1960); Ludwig Jedlicka, *Unser Heer: 300 Jahre österreichisches Soldatentum in Krieg und Frieden* (Vienna, 1963) [concentrates on post-1914]; Friedrich Wallisch, *Servus, Herr Oberst* (Graz, 1965). Georg Auffarth, *Inhalt und Form: Das Buch vom Offizier* (Vienna, 1910), was not available to me.

20. Emil Reich, "The Crisis in Hungary," *Contemporary Review*, 88 (1905), 642-645.

21. "Ein Offizier ist ein jämmerliches Wesen, jeder beneidet den Gleichgestellten, tyrannisiert den Untergebenen und fürchtet sich von dem Höheren, und je höher er selbst ist, desto mehr fürchtet er sich." Freud, *Briefe 1873-1939*, 2d ed. (Frankfurt, 1968), p. 226 [letter of Sept. 1, 1886].

22. Wilhelm Stekel, *Autobiography: The Life Story of a Pioneer Psychoanalyst* (New York, 1950), p. 82.

23. Gayda, *Modern Austria*, pp. 248-249.

24. Richard Alewyn, *Über Hugo von Hofmannsthal*, 3d ed. (Göttingen, 1963), pp. 78-79.

25. See Hans Kohn, *Living in a World Revolution: My Encounters with History* (New York, 1964), pp. 86-87.

26. See R. Cl. Bachofen von Echt, "The Duel in Germany and Austria," *Nineteenth Century*, 53 (1903), 678-685. This summarizes Gustav Hergsell, *Duellkodex* (Vienna, 1891).

27. See Alfonso de Bourbon, "Efforts to Abolish the Duel," *North American Review*, 175 (1902), 194-200; Bourbon, "The Fight Against Duelling in Europe," *Fortnightly Review*, 90 (1908), 169-184.

28. See Schnitzler's *Freiwild* (1896), as well as his comments about the compulsion to duel quoted in Reinhard Urbach, *Arthur Schnitzler* (Velber, 1968), pp. 47-48. See also Ferdinand von Saar, *Leutnant Burda* [1887], in *Das erzählerische Werk*, 3 vols. (Vienna, 1959), 1:307-374.

29. Lansdale, *Vienna*, pp. 203-204.

30. On Redl see Adalbert Graf von Sternberg, *Warum Österreich zugrunde gehen musste*, 4th ed. (Vienna, 1927), pp. 117-129; Robert B. Asprey, *The Panther's Feast* (New York, 1959) [well-researched, semifictionalized account]; Egon Erwin Kisch, *Wie ich erfuhr, dass Redl ein Spion war: Zwölf Reportagen* (East Berlin, 1961); Kisch, *Der rasende Reporter: Klassische Reportagen* (Hamburg, 1961), pp. 255-298.

31. See Moritz Auffenberg-Komarów, *Aus Österreichs Höhe und Niedergang: Eine Lebensschilderung* (Munich, 1921); Sternberg, *Warum*, pp. 130-138.

32. On the Roman Catholic church in Austria-Hungary see Ernst Viktor Zenker, *Kirche und Staat mit besonderer Rücksichtigung der Verhältnisse in Österreich* (Vienna, 1909); Joseph A. Wodka, *Kirche in Österreich: Wegweiser durch ihre Geschichte* (Vienna, 1959) [thorough]; F. M. M. Steiner, "Church and State in

Austria," *Dublin Review*, 233 (1959), 107-121; Erika Weinzierl-Fischer, *Die österreichischen Konkordate von 1855 und 1933* (Munich, 1960); Herbert Rieser, *Der Geist des Josephinismus: Der Kampf der Kirche um ihre Freiheit* (Vienna, 1964); Severin R. von Lama, *Am tiefsten Quell: Mystik in Österreich* (Vienna, 1964; Gerhard Silberbauer, *Österreichs Katholiken und die Arbeiterfrage* (Graz, 1966); Erika Weinzierl-Fischer and Ferdinand Klostermann, eds., *Kirche in Österreich 1918-1965*, 2 vols. (Vienna, 1966).

33. T. G. Masaryk, *Der Selbstmord als sociale Massenerscheinung der modernen Civilisation* (Vienna, 1881), p. 197.

34. Julius Braunthal, *In Search of the Millenium* (London, 1945), p. 50.

35. Wallisch, *Es hat mich sehr gefreut* (Graz, 1967), p. 115.

36. On Vogelsang see Hans Rizzi, "Karl Freiherr von Vogelsang," *NOB*, 2 (1925), 186-195; Wiard Klopp, *Leben und Wirken des Sozialpolitikers Karl Freiherrn von Vogelsang: nach den Quellen gearbeitet* (Vienna, 1930) [very thorough; by Vogelsang's son-in-law]; Marcel Saner, *Freiherr Karl von Vogelsangs Gesellschafts- und Wirtschaftslehre* (Freiburg i.d. S., 1939) [excellent bibliography]; Richard Charmatz, "Karl von Vogelsang," in *Lebensbilder aus der Geschichte Österreichs* (Vienna, 1947), pp. 112-123; Johann Christoph Allmayer-Beck, *Vogelsang: Vom Feudalismus zur Volksbewegung* (Vienna, 1952); Alfred Diamant, *Austrian Catholics and the First Republic: Democracy, Capitalism, and the Social Order, 1918-1934* (Princeton, 1960), pp. 42-63; Silberbauer, *Österreichs Katholiken*, pp. 61-119.

37. See Klopp, *Leben und Wirken*, pp. 398-457; Lillian Parker Wallace, *Leo XIII and the Rise of Socialism* (Durham, N.C., 1966), pp. 254-268.

38. Wolf von Schierbrand, *Austria-Hungary: Polyglot Empire* (New York, 1917), pp. 318-319.

39. S. I. de Zuylen de Nyevelt, "Austria: Its Society, Politics, and Religion," *Living Age*, 192 (1892), 8.

40. John H. Gray, "Religious Freedom in Austria," *The Nation*, 53 (July 23, 1891), 68.

41. "Ich hoffe, dass wir auch jene Universitäten zurückerobern, die unsere Kirche gegründet hatte." Quoted in Wodka, *Kirche in Österreich*, p. 352. On the Wahrmund Case see also Friedrich Jodl, "Der Klerikalismus und die Universitäten" [1908], in *Vom Lebenswege* (Stuttgart, 1917), 2:458-477; Hugo Haan, "Gustav Marchet," *NOB*, 2 (1925), 150-151; Paul Molisch, *Politische Geschichte der deutschen Hochschulen in Österreich von 1848 bis 1918*, 2d ed. (Vienna, 1939), pp. 166-176.

42. See Josef Samuel Bloch, *Erinnerungen aus meinem Leben*, vol. 2 (Vienna, 1922) [concerns a libel suit against Deckert].

43. See Konrad Deubler, *Tagebücher und Briefe*, ed. Arnold Dodel-Port, 2 vols. (Leipzig, 1886).

44. Gayda, *Modern Austria*, p. 213.

45. On Protestanism in Austria see Georg Loesche, *Die Geschichte des Protestantismus im vormaligen und im neuen Österreich* (Vienna, 1902; 3d ed., 1930); Karl Völker, *Die Entwicklung des Protestantismus in Österreich* (Leipzig, 1917); Grete Mecenseffy, *Geschichte des Protestantismus in Österreich* (Graz, 1956); Franz Lau, "Los-von-Rom-Bewegung," *Die Religion in Geschichte und Gegenwart*, 3d ed., 4 (1960), 452-455.

46. See Friedrich Engel-Janosi, *Österreich und der Vatikan, 1846-1918* (Graz, 1960), 2:2-47.

47. Braunthal, *In Search of the Millenium*, p. 49.
48. Leopold Rosenmayr, "The Sociology of Religious Phenomena in Germany and Austria since Max Weber," *American Catholic Sociological Review*, 15 (1954), 145-146.
49. On Lueger see "A Great Burgomaster and His Work," *Dublin Review*, 143 (1908), 321-345; P. J. Connolly, "Karl Lueger," *Studies* [Dublin], 3 (1914), 280-291; 4 (1915), 226-249; Rudolf Kuppe, *Karl Lueger und seine Zeit* (Vienna, 1933); Kurt Skalnik, *Dr. Karl Lueger: Der Mann zwischen den Zeiten* (Vienna, 1954); Heinrich Schnee, *Karl Lueger: Leben und Wirken eines grossen Sozial- und Kommunalpolitikers* (Berlin, 1960) [excellent bibliography]; Erich Graf von Kielmansegg, *Kaiserhaus, Staatsmänner und Politiker* (Vienna, 1966), pp. 365-407.
50. On Felder see Cajetan Felder, *Erinnerungen eines Wiener Bürgermeisters* (Vienna, 1964); Karl Glossy, "Kajetan Felder," *NOB*, 4 (1927), 206-224.
51. Artur Schnabel, *My Life and Music* (London, 1961), pp. 19-20.
52. *Ibid.*, p. 30. On the calculatedness of Lueger's anti-Semitism see Arthur Schnitzler, *Jugend in Wien* (Vienna, 1968), pp. 146-147.
53. The clearest account is Salomon Frankfurter, *Österreichs Bildungswesen: Die Volks-, Bürger- und Mittelschulen* (Vienna, 1920). See also Emanuel Hannak, "Die Schule," in *Wien 1848–1888* (Vienna, 1888), 2:1-128: Hannak, *The Training of Teachers in Austria* (New York, 1889); Gustav Strakosch-Grassman, *Geschichte des österreichischen Unterrichtswesens* (Vienna, 1905). On school reforms of the 1920's see Robert Dottrens, *L'éducation nouvelle en Autriche* (Neuchâtel, 1927); Beryl Parker, *The Austrian Educational Institutes* (Vienna, 1931).
54. See Richard Meister, *Entwicklung und Reformen des österreichischen Studienwesens. Teil I. Abhandlung. Teil II. Dokumente*, SKAW-Wien, Phil-Hist. Klasse, 239/1 (1962), 1-275 and 1-281 [covers 1554 to 1960]; Hans Lentze, *Die Universitätsreform des Ministers Graf Leo Thun-Hohenstein*, ibid., 239/2 (1962), 1-372 [exhaustive; contains a superb bibliography].
55. C. P. Oberndorf, ed., "The Autobiography of Josef Breuer," *IJP*, 34 (1953), 65. On the transition at the Akademisches Gymnasium see also Moritz Benedikt, *Aus meinem Leben: Erinnerungen und Erörterungen* (Vienna, 1906), pp. 15-35.
56. See Kisch, *Die Abenteuer in Prag* (Vienna, 1920), pp. 54-59; Kohn, *Living in a World Revolution*, pp. 39-43 [perceptive evaluation of gymnasium training].
57. Freud, "Zur Psychologie des Gymnasiasten" [1914], in *GW*, 10 (London, 1946), 204-207, esp. 207.
58. See Fritz Mauthner, *Prager Jugendjahre: Erinnerungen* [1918] (Frankfurt, 1969), pp. 110-117; Schnitzler, *Jugend in Wien*, p. 81. On priests as teachers see also Franz Blei, "Erzählung einer Jugend" [1930], in *Schriften in Auswahl* (Munich, 1960), pp. 45-56.
59. Freud, *Die Traumdeutung*, 8th ed. in *GW*, 2/3 (London, 1942), 280-282. Freud recounted his own Matura experience in a letter of June 16, 1873. See Ernest L. Freud, ed. "Some Early Unpublished Letters of Freud," *IJP*, 50 (1969), 419-427, esp. 425-426.
60. Jodl, "Was leistet das humanistische Gymnasium für die allgemeine Bildung?" [1898], in *Vom Lebenswege* (Stuttgart, 1917), 2:542-574, esp. 560, 564. On the deterioration of gymnasien around 1900 see Bruno Kisch, *Wanderungen und Wandlungen: Die Geschichte eines Arztes im 20. Jahrhundert* (Cologne, 1966), pp. 61-63. For a more optimistic assessment, which lists the Latin and Greek

classics studied, see August Scheindler, "Pro Gymnasio: Ein Beitrag zur Kenntnis des gegenwärtigen Zustand des österreichischen Gymnasiums," in *Festgabe zum 100jährigen Jubiläum des Schottengymnasiums* (Vienna, 1907), pp. 261-299, esp. 269-274.

61. H. S. Chamberlain, "Der voraussetzungslose Mommsen," *Die Fackel,* Nr. 87 (Dec. 1, 1901), p. 8.

62. I have followed the version in Jones, 1:374 rather than that in Kurt Eissler, "Challenges to Freud's Honesty," in *Medical Orthodoxy and the Future of Psychoanalysis* (New York, 1965), pp. 516-525 [with excellent bibliography]. Although Freud specified otherwise, Eissler contends that it was Elise Gomperz who donated a painting, albeit not by Böcklin. See Freud's two letters to Mrs. Gomperz in Freud, *Briefe 1873-1939,* pp. 256-258 [letters of Nov. 25, 1901 and December 8, 1901] and his letter to Fliess, *ibid.,* pp. 259-261 [letter of March 11, 1902].

63. See Meister, *Geschichte der Akademie der Wissenschaften in Wien 1847-1947* (Vienna, 1947).

64. Lothar, *Das Wunder des Überlebens,* p. 22.

65. *Ibid.*

66. Oskar Kraus, "Oskar Kraus," in Raymund Schmidt, ed., *Die Philosophie der Gegenwart in Selbstdarstellungen,* 7 (Leipzig, 1929), 165.

67. See Charles Franklin Thwing, *Universities of the World* (New York, 1911), p. 150.

68. Szeps, *My Life and History,* p. 166.

69. On student politics see Molisch, *Politische Geschichte;* J. McGrath, "Student Radicalism in Vienna," JCH, 2³ (1967), 183-201.

70. On student dueling see Karl Hans Strobl, *Die Vaclavbude: Prager Studentenroman* (Berlin, 1902); Kisch, *Die Abenteuer in Prag,* pp. 137-149; Stekel, *Autobiography,* pp. 70-71.

71. Felix Braun, *Das Licht der Welt: Geschichte eines Versuches, als Dichter zu leben* [1949] (Vienna, 1962), pp. 235-237.

72. Arthur Koestler, *Arrow in the Blue: An Autobiography* (New York, 1952), p. 59.

73. See Stephan Bauer, "Ludo Moritz Hartman," NOB, 3 (1926), 197-209.

74. Szeps, *My Life and History,* pp. 167-168.

75. The most complete list of Austrian inventors is found in Ludwig Reiter, *Österreichische Staats- und Kulturgeschichte* (Klagenfurt, 1947). See also *Geboren in Österreich,* 2d ed., 2 vols. (Vienna, 1969).

76. Graphic accounts occur in Ellis Ashmead-Bartlett, *The Tragedy of Central Europe* (London, 1923); C. A. Macartney, *The Social Revolution in Austria* (Cambridge, 1926); G. E. R. Gedye, *Heirs to the Habsburgs* (London, 1932); Anna Eisenmenger, *Blockade: The Diary of an Austrian Middle-Class Woman, 1914-1924* (New York, 1932); Willi Frischauer, *Twilight in Vienna: The Capital without a Country* (Boston, 1938) [fictionalized memoirs]; Malcolm Bullock, *Austria 1918-1938: A Study in Failure* (London, 1939); Franz Borkenau, *Austria and After* (London, 1939); Karl Ausch, *Als die Banken fielen: Zur Soziologie der politischen Korruption* (Vienna, 1968).

77. Ashmead-Bartlett, *The Tragedy,* p. 36.

78. See Guido Zernatto, *Die Wahrheit über Österreich* (New York, 1938), pp. 47-49. For a less emotional account see Karl R. Stadler, *The Birth of the Austrian Republic 1918-1921* (Leyden, 1966), pp. 39-44.

79. O. de L., "Austrian Factors," *Contemporary Review,* 122 (1922), 426-434.
80. See Charles O. Hardy, *The Housing Program of the City of Vienna* (Washington, D.C., 1934); Ernst Karl Winter, "Housing and Resettlement in Vienna," *National Municipal Review,* 26 (1937), 397-402.
81. For critiques of post-1945 Austria see Otto Schulmeister, *Die Zukunft Österreichs* (Vienna, 1967); Barbara Coudenhove-Kalergi, "Eine Nation aus Gespenstern?" *Neues Forum,* 14 (1967), 747-749; William T. Bluhm, "Nation-Building: The Case of Austria," *Polity,* 1 (1968), 149-177.

CHAPTER 4

1. "Das Gesindel lebt sich aus und wir entbehren. . . . So geht unser Bestreben mehr dahin, Leid von uns abzuhalten, als uns Genuss zu verschaffen. . . . Sie haben auch mehr Gemeingefühl als wir, es ist nur in ihnen lebhaft, dass sie einer das Leben des andern fortsetzen, während jedem von uns mit seinem Tod die Welt erlischt." Freud, *Briefe 1873-1939,* 2d ed. (Frankfurt, 1968), pp. 56-57 [letter of Aug. 29, 1883]. For a translation see Jones, 1:208-209.
2. Karl Pribram, *Conflicting Patterns of Thought* (Washington, D.C., 1949), p. 131.
3. See Pribram, "Die Weltanschauungen der Völker und ihre Politik," *ASWSP,* 44 (1917-18), 161-197; Pribram "Deutscher Nationalismus und deutscher Sozialismus," *ASWSP,* 49 (1922), 298-376; Pribram, "Nominalismus und Begriffsrealismus in der Nationalökonomie," *Schmollers Jahrbuch,* 55 (1931), 1-42; Pribram, "Prolegomena to a History of Economic Reasoning," *Quarterly Journal of Economics,* 45 (1951), 1-37; Pribram, "Patterns of Economic Reasoning," *American Economic Review,* 43 (1953), 243-258.
4. Pribram, "Patterns," p. 257.
5. On Carl Menger see James Bonar, "The Austrian Economists and Their Theory of Value," *Quarterly Journal of Economics,* 3 (1888-89), 1-31; Joseph Schumpeter, "Carl Menger," *Zeitschrift für Volkswirtschaft und Sozialpolitik,* 1 N.F. (1921), pp. 197-206; Oskar Engländer, "Karl Mengers Grundsätze der Volkswirtschaftslehre," *Schmollers Jahrbuch,* 51 (1927), 371-401; Friedrich A. Hayek, "Carl Menger," in *The Collected Works of Carl Menger* (London, 1934), 1:v-xxxviii; Hayek, "Menger, Carl," *IESS,* 10 (1968), 124-127; George J. Stigler, "The Economics of Carl Menger," *Journal of Political Economy,* 45 (1937), 229-250; Felix Somary, *Erinnerungen aus meinem Leben,* 2d ed. (Zürich, 1959), pp. 30-36.
6. On the *Methodenstreit* see Eugen von Böhm-Bawerk, "The Historical versus the Deductive Method in Political Economy," *Annals of the American Academy of Political and Social Science,* 1 (1891), 244-271; Böhm-Bawerk, "The Austrian Economists," *ibid.,* 1 (1891), 361-384; Ludwig Mises, "Soziologie und Geschichte: Epilog zum Methodenstreit in der Nationalökonomie," *ASWSP,* 61 (1929), 465-512; Gerhard Ritzel, *Schmoller versus Menger: Eine Analyse des Methodenstreits im Hinblick auf den Historismus in der Nationalökonomie* (Frankfurt, 1950) [contains excellent bibliography].
7. Oskar Kraus, "Die aristotelische Werttheorie in ihren Beziehungen zu den Lehren der modernen Psychologenschule," *Zeitschrift für die gesamte Staatswissenschaft,* 61 (1905), 573-592.
8. On Wieser see Friedrich von Hayek, "Friedrich von Wieser," *Jahrbücher für Nationalökonomie und Statistik,* 125 (1926), 513-530; Hayek, "Wieser, Friedrich von," *IESS,* 16 (1968), 549-550; Adolf Menzel, *Friedrich Wieser als*

Soziolog (Vienna, 1927); Oskar Morgenstern, "Friedrich von Wieser, 1851-1926," *American Economic Review*, 17 (1928), 669-674; Hans Mayer, "Friedrich von Wieser," *NOB*, 6 (1929), 180-198; George J. Stigler, *Production and Distribution Theories: The Formative Period* (New York, 1941), pp. 158-178; T. W. Hutchison, *A Review of Economic Doctrines 1870-1929* (Oxford, 1953), pp. 153-164; R. S. Howey, *The Rise of the Marginal Utility School 1870-1889* (Lawrence, Kans., 1960), pp. 143-154.

9. Friedrich von Wieser, *Social Economics* [1914] (New York, 1926), p. 5.

10. *Ibid.*, p. 4.

11. On Schumpeter see Gottfried Haberler, "Joseph Alois Schumpeter 1883-1950," *Quarterly Journal of Economics*, 44 (1950), 333-372 [repr. in Harris, below]; Seymour E. Harris, ed., *Schumpeter: Social Scientist* (Cambridge, Mass., 1951) [contains twenty essays on Schumpeter]; Morgenstern, "Joseph A. Schumpeter 1883-1950," *Economic Journal*, 61 (1951), 197-202; Martin Kessler, "The Synthetic Vision of Joseph Schumpeter," *Review of Politics*, 23 (1961), 334-355; Wolfgang F. Stolper, "Schumpeter, Joseph A.," *IESS*, 14 (1968), 67-72; Gottfried Eisermann, "Joseph Schumpeter als Soziologe," in *Bedeutende Soziologen* (Stuttgart, 1968), pp. 53-73.

12. Haberler, "Joseph Alois Schumpeter," p. 369.

13. "Aber das kann niemand verkennen, was das damalige Österreich unter für den Fernstehenden kaum glaublichen Schwierigkeiten im einzelnen auf allen Gebieten des öffentlichen Lebens geleistet hat, wie gründlich und erfolgreich damals auf allen Gebieten öffentlicher Verwaltung die Vorbedingungen für einen lebenskräftigen und leistungsfähigen Staat geschaffen wurden. In der Summe dieser Leistungen war die finanzpolitische die wichtigste." Schumpeter, "Eugen von Böhm-Bawerk," *NOB*, 2 (1925), 64.

14. See Emil Kauder, "Intellectual and Political Roots of the Older Austrian School," *Zeitschrift für Nationalökonomie*, 17 (1957), 411-425.

CHAPTER 5

1. The clearest introduction is John Henry Merryman, *The Civil Law Tradition: An Introduction to the Legal Systems of Western Europe and Latin America* (Stanford, 1969). On the prerogatives of judges see James Wilford Garner, "The Judiciary of the German Empire," *PSQ*, 17 (1902), 490-514; 18 (1903), 512-530; John P. Dawson, *The Oracles of the Law* (Ann Arbor, 1968), pp. 432-506 [analyses criteria in decisions used by German courts since 1789]. On legal training see Hans Lentze, "Austrian Law Schools and Legal History," in Morris D. Forkosch, ed., *Essays in Legal History in Honor of Felix Frankfurter* (Indianapolis, 1966), pp. 159-174.

2. See Rupert Emerson, *State and Sovereignty in Modern Germany* (New Haven, 1928), pp. 59-62.

3. On Ehrlich see Max Rheinstein, "Sociology of Law," *Ethics*, 48 (1937-38), 232-239; George Gurvitch, *Sociology of Law* (London, 1947), pp. 116-122; P. H. Partridge, "Ehrlich's Sociology of Law," in Geoffrey Sawer, ed., *Studies in the Sociology of Law* (Canberra, 1961), pp. 1-29 [perceptive]; Sawer, *Law in Society* (Oxford, 1965), pp. 174-177; Manfred Rehbinder, *Die Begründung der Rechtssoziologie durch Eugen Ehrlich* (Berlin, 1967); N. S. Timasheff, "Ehrlich, Eugen," *IESS*, 4 (1968), 540-542.

4. Translated as *Fundamental Principles of the Sociology of Law* (Cambridge,

Mass., 1936); summarized in Ehrlich, "The Sociology of Law," *Harvard Law Review*, 36 (1922-23), 130-145. See also Ehrlich, *Recht und Leben: Gesammelte Schriften zur Rechtstatsachenforschung und zur Freirechtslehre*, ed. Manfred Rehbinder (Berlin, 1967).

5. On Anton Menger see Ehrlich, "Anton Menger," *Süddeutsche Monatshefte*, 3 (1906), 285-318; Karl Grünberg, "Anton Menger," *Biographisches Jahrbuch und deutscher Nekrolog*, 11 (1908), 3-22; Grünberg, "Anton Menger," *Zeitschrift für Volkswirtschaft und Sozialpolitik*, 18 (1909), 29-78; Julius Kraft, "Anton Menger als Methodiker der Rechtstheorie," *Archiv für die Geschichte des Sozialismus*, 12 (1926), 182-198.

6. On Gross see Waldemar Kaempffert, "The Crime-Master and How He Works," *McClure's Magazine*, 43 (June, 1914), 99-111, 114; Roland Grassberger, "Hans Gross," *Journal of Criminal Law, Criminology, and Police Science*, 47 (1956-57), 397-405; Erich Döhring, "Hans Gross," *Neue Deutsche Biographie*, 7 (1966), 139-141. For a critique of Gross's interpretation of the Polna case see Arthur Nussbaum, "The 'Ritual Murder' Trial of Polna," *Historia Judaica*, 9 (1950), 57-74, esp. 64-72.

7. See Joseph Gollomb, *Master Man Hunters* (New York, 1926), pp. 252-315; Victor Wallace Germains, *Austria of Today: With a Special Chapter on the Austrian Police* (London, 1932), pp. 189-215.

8. For a biography of Kelsen see: Rudolf Aladár Métall, *Hans Kelsen: Sein Leben und Werk: Autorisierte Biographie* (Vienna, 1968) [contains exhaustive bibliography]. On his thought see Erich Voegelin, "Kelsen's Pure Theory of Law," *PSQ*, 42 (1927), 268-276; Isaac Husik, "The Legal Philosophy of Hans Kelsen," *Journal of Social Philosophy*, 3 (1937-38), 297-324. A comprehensive anthology is Hans Klecatsky, René Marcic, and Herbert Schambeck, eds., *Die Wiener rechtstheoretische Schule: Schriften von Hans Kelsen, Adolf Merkl, Alfred Verdross*, 2 vols. (Vienna, 1968).

9. On Kelsen's constitution see Mary MacDonald, *The Republic of Austria: A Study in the Failure of Democratic Government* (London, 1946); Winfried R. Dallmayr, "Background and Development of the Austrian Constitutional Court," *JCEA*, 21 (1961-62), 403-433, esp. 409-429.

10. See K. M. Bergbohm, *Jurisprudenz und Rechtsphilosophie: Kritische Abhandlungen* (Leipzig, 1892), p. 279.

11. See Julius Stone, *The Province and Function of Law: Law as Logic, Justice, and Social Control: A Study in Jurisprudence* (Cambridge, Mass., 1950), pp. 91-114.

12. Hans Kelsen, "The Pure Theory of Law: Its Methods and Fundamental Concepts," *Law Quarterly Review*, 50 (1934), 483.

13. See Kelsen, *Sozialismus und Staat: Eine Untersuchung der politischen Theorie des Marxismus* (Leipzig, 1920; 3d ed., Vienna, 1965), pp. 170-174.

14. Kelsen, "Die platonische Gerechtigkeit" *Kantstudien*, 38 (1933), 91-117; trans. as "Platonic Justice," *Ethics*, 48 (1937), 367-400.

15. Kelsen, "Die platonische Liebe," *Imago*, 19 (1933), 34-98 and 225-255; trans. in part as "Platonic Love," *American Imago*, 3¹⁻² (1942-46), 3-110. See also Kelsen, "The Soul and the Law," *Review of Religion*, 1 (1937), 337-360; Kelsen, "The Philosophy of Aristotle and the Hellenic-Macedonian Policy," *Ethics*, 48 (1937), 1-64.

16. See Kelsen, "Absolutism and Relativism in Philosophy and Politics," *American Political Science Review*, 42 (1948), 906-914.

CHAPTER 6

1. On Austro-Marxism see Ludwig Brügel, *Geschichte der österreichischen Sozialdemokratie*, vols. 3-5 (Vienna, 1922-1925); Paul Michael Zulehner, *Kirche und Austromarxismus: Eine Studie zur Problematik Kirche-Staat-Gesellschaft* (Vienna, 1967); Norbert Leser, *Zwischen Reformismus und Bolschewismus: Der Austromarxismus als Theorie und Praxis* (Vienna, 1968) [comprehensive].

2. On Viktor Adler see Stefan Grossmann, *Ich war begeistert: Eine Lebensgeschichte* (Berlin, 1931), pp. 92-105, 255-267; Julius Braunthal, *In Search of the Millenium* (London, 1945); Braunthal, *Victor und Friedrich Adler: Zwei Generationen Arbeiterbewegung* (Vienna, 1965); Wanda Lanzer and Ernst K. Herlitza, eds., *Victor Adler im Spiegel seiner Zeitgenossen* (Vienna, 1968).

3. Jones, 1:48, 215-216. See also William J. McGrath, "Student Radicalism in Vienna," *JCH*, 2³ (1967), 183-201.

4. "Abgesehen von Frankreich und England hat Österreich vielleicht in ganz Europa die freisinnigsten Gesetze, so sehr, dass es einer Republik ähnelt, die statt eines Präsidenten eine Majestät an der Spitze hat." Quoted in Heinrich Benedikt, *Die Monarchie des Hauses Österreich* (Munich, 1968), p. 181.

5. See Edmund Silberner, *Sozialisten zur Judenfrage* (Bonn, 1963), pp. 231-247; "The Jewish Background of Victor and Friedrich Adler," *YLBI*, 10 (1965), 266-276.

6. See Friedrich Adler, *Vor dem Ausnahmegericht* (Berlin, 1919; repr., Vienna, 1967). On Schuhmeier see Helga Schmidt and Felix Czeike, *Franz Schuhmeier* (Vienna, 1964).

7. On refugees at Vienna during the 1920's, see Victor Serge, *Memoirs of a Revolutionary 1901-1941* (New York, 1963), pp. 175-192.

8. On Bauer see Richard Charmatz, "Der Theoretiker und Praktiker des Marxismus: Dr. Otto Bauer," in *Lebensbilder aus der Geschichte Österreichs* (Vienna, 1947), pp. 219-240; Braunthal, "Otto Bauer: Ein Lebensbild," in Bauer, *Eine Auswahl aus seinem Lebenswerk* (Vienna, 1961), pp. 9-101; Viktor Reimann, *Zu Gross für Österreich: Seipel und Bauer im Kampf um die erste Republik* (Vienna, 1968), pp. 253-380. Bauer's speeches between 1919 and 1934 appear in Heinz Fischer, ed., *Zum Wort Gemeldet: Otto Bauer* (Vienna, 1968).

9. Braunthal, *In Search of the Millenium*, p. 73.

10. On Bauer as foreign minister see Alfred D. Low, "The First Austrian Republic and Soviet Hungary," *JCEA*, 20 (1960-61), 174-203.

11. Repr. in Bauer, *Eine Auswahl*, pp. 102-139.

12. On Seipel see Barbara Ward, "Ignaz Seipel and the Anschluss," *Dublin Review*, 203 (1938), 33-50; Reimann, *Zu Gross für Österreich*, pp. 41-252 [likens Seipel to Metternich in stature and policy].

13. On these reforms see Karl Pribram, "Die Sozialpolitik im neuen Österreich," *ASWSP*, 48 (1921-22), 615-680; Felix Czeike, *Wirtschafts- und Sozialpolitik der Gemeinde Wien in der ersten Republik, 1919-1934*, 2 vols. (Vienna, 1958-1959).

14. On the Socialist underground see Joseph Buttinger, *Am Beispiel Österreichs: Ein geschichtlicher Beitrag zur Krise der sozialistischen Bewegung* (Cologne, 1953).

15. On Renner see Karl Renner, *An der Wende zweier Zeiten (Lebenserinnerungen)* (Vienna, 1946) [covers only to 1895]; Robert A. Kann, "Karl Renner,"

JMH, 23 (1951), 243-249; Frederick Hertz, "Karl Renner: Statesman and Political Thinker," *Contemporary Review*, 179 (1951), 142-145; Otto Weinberger, "Karl Renner als Soziolog," *Zeitschrift für die gesamte Staatswissenschaft*, 109 (1953), 726-736; Jacques Hannak, *Karl Renner und seine Zeit: Versuch einer Biographie* (Vienna, 1965) [extremely thorough].

16. On Fischhof see Charmatz, *Adolf Fischhof: Das Lebensbild eines österreichischen Politikers* (Stuttgart, 1910); Kann, *The Multinational Empire* (New York, 1950), 2:143-157; Werner J. Cahnman, "Adolf Fischhof and his German Followers," *YLBI*, 4 (1959), 111-139.

17. The text is reprinted in Klaus Berchtold, ed., *Österreichische Parteiprogramme 1868-1966* (Munich, 1967), pp. 144-145. On Renner's federalism see Rudolf Schlesinger, *Federalism in Central and Eastern Europe* (New York, 1945), pp. 213-218, 237-240; A. G. Kogon, "The Social Democrats and the Conflict of Nationalities in the Habsburg Monarchy," *JMH*, 21 (1949), 204-217; Kann, *The Multinational Empire*, 2:157-167; Rudolf Wierer, *Der Föderalismus im Donauraum* (Graz, 1960), pp. 106-110.

18. A second edition was entitled *Die Rechtsinstitute des Privatrechts und die soziale Funktion: Ein Beitrag zur Kritik des bürgerlichen Rechts* (Vienna, 1929; repr., Stuttgart, 1965). See Wolfgang Friedmann, *Legal Theory*, 4th ed. (London, 1960), pp. 328-331.

19. Malcolm Bullock, *Austria 1918-1938: A Study in Failure* (London, 1939), pp. 136-137.

20. On Max Adler see Oskar Blum, "Max Adlers Neugestaltung des Marxismus," *Archiv für die Geschichte des Sozialismus*, 8 (1919), 177-247; Emil Franzel, "Das Werk Max Adlers," *Der Kampf*, 4 (1937), 291-297; Constanze Glaser, "Max Adler," *Philosophia*, 2 (1937), 290-292; Norbert Leser, "Austro-Marxism: A Reappraisal," *JCH*, 1² (1966), 130-132; Peter Heintel, *System und Ideologie: Der Austromarxismus im Spiegel der Philosophie Max Adlers* (Munich, 1966) [highly technical]; Heintel, "Austromarxismus und Religion," *Neues Forum*, 14 (1967), 140-143, 236-239.

21. See Max Adler, *Soziologie des Marxismus*, vols. 2 and 3 (Vienna, 1964).

22. On the Vienna empiricists see Paul F. Lazarsfeld, "An Episode in the History of Social Research: A Memoir," in Donald Fleming and Bernard Bailyn, eds., *The Intellectual Migration: Europe and America, 1930-1960* (Cambridge, Mass., 1969), pp. 270-337, esp. 272-291.

23. See Adler, "Die Stellung von Marx und Engels zum Materialismus" [1930], in *Soziologie des Marxismus*, 1:79-86. See also Adler, "Marxismus ist nicht Materialismus" [1913], *Neues Forum*, 14 (1967), 485-488.

24. Adler, "Die sozialistische Idee der Befreiung bei Karl Marx," in *Marxstudien*, 4 (Vienna, 1918), vi-xxiv, esp. xii-xx. Adler's source was Franz Mehring, ed., *Gesammelte Schriften von Marx und Engels, 1841-1850*, 3 vols. (Stuttgart, 1902), which included Marx's dissertation of 1841.

25. Alasdair MacIntyre, "Marxist Mask and Romantic Face: Lukács on Thomas Mann," *Encounter*, 24 (April, 1965), 68.

CHAPTER 7

1. C. A. Macartney, *The Social Revolution in Austria* (Cambridge, 1926), p. 207. On Viennese mores and art around 1900, see Otto Friedländer, *Letzter Glanz der Märchenstadt: Das war Wien um 1900* [1948]. (Vienna, 1969); Willy

Haas, *Die belle Epoque* (Munich, 1967) [compares Vienna with Paris, Munich, Berlin, and London]. Both works contain lavish illustrations. A choice anthology with rare photographs is Jost Perfahl, ed., *Wien Chronik*, 3d ed. (Salzburg, 1969).

2. See Georg Jellinek, "Die deutsche Philosophie in Österreich" [1874], in *Ausgewählte Schriften und Reden*, 2 vols. (Berlin, 1911), 1:61-62.

3. Arthur Koestler, *Arrow in the Blue: An Autobiography* (New York, 1952), p. 44.

4. Hanns Sachs, *Freud: Master and Friend* (Cambridge, Mass., 1946), p. 23.

5. Martin Freud, *Sigmund Freud: Man and Father* (New York, 1958), pp. 24-25.

6. The fullest account of these mores is A. S. Levetus, *Imperial Vienna: An Account of Its History, Traditions, and Arts* (London, 1905), pp. 364-398.

7. Hans Wilczek, *Gentleman of Vienna: Reminiscences* (New York, 1934), p. 23.

8. Stefan Zweig, *Die Welt von Gestern* (Stockholm, 1942), pp. 98-102. On other prewar aberrations see Magnus Hirschfeld, *Sittengeschichte des Weltkrieges*, 2 vols. (Leipzig, 1930; 2d ed., Hanau, 1966), 1:1-26.

9. For case histories see Arthur Schnitzler, *Jugend in Wien* (Vienna, 1968), pp. 109-116, 175-176; Franz Blei, "Erzählung einer Jugend" [1930], in *Schriften in Auswahl* (Munich, 1960), pp. 125-140. A sprightly typology of Viennese women appears in Ludwig Hirschfeld, *Das Buch von Wien* (Munich, 1927), pp. 238-255.

10. Martin Freud, *Sigmund Freud*, pp. 169-170.

11. Lou Andreas-Salomé, *Lebensrückblick: Grundriss einiger Lebenserinnerungen* (Zürich, 1951), p. 132. On Richard Beer-Hofmann's decisive influence on Lou see Rudolph Binion, *Frau Lou: Nietzsche's Wayward Disciple* (Princeton, 1968), pp. 190-207, esp. 207 [describes Lou's sojourn at Vienna 1895-1896].

12. On Mizzi Veith see Richard Waldegg and Rudolf Till, *Sittengeschichte von Wien*, 4th ed. (Stuttgart, 1965), pp. 413-415. For a reaction to these customs by an upper middle-class Viennese girl, aged twelve to fourteen, see Hermine von Hug-Helmuth, ed., *Tagebuch eines halbwüchsigen Mädchens* (Vienna, 1919) [extremely revealing].

13. On the Viennese coffeehouse see Alfred Polgar, "Theorie des 'Café Central,'" in *An den Rand Geschrieben* (Berlin, 1926), pp. 85-91, repr. in *Fensterplatz* (Hamburg, 1959), pp. 7-12; Ludwig Hirschfeld, "Kaffeehauskultur," in *Das Buch von Wien*, pp. 31-48, esp. 45-48; Alfred Peters, "Das Wiener Café," *Kölner Vierteljahrshefte für Soziologie*, 9 (1930-31), 192-195; Phyllis Bottome, *Alfred Adler: A Biography* (New York, 1939), pp. 45-46; Gustav Gugitz, *Das Wiener Kaffeehaus: Ein Stück Kultur- und Lokalgeschichte* (Vienna, 1940) [covers 1683 to 1848]; Herta Singer, *Im Wiener Kaffeehaus* (Vienna, 1959) [anecdotal]; Emil Franzel, "Das Café," in *Sehnsucht nach den alten Gassen* (Vienna, 1964), pp. 13-15; Claudio Magris, *Der habsburgische Mythos in der österreichischen Literatur* (Salzburg, 1966), pp. 187-190.

14. For reminiscences of the Café Griensteidl see Felix Salten, "Aus den Anfängen: Erinnerungsskizzen," *Jahrbuch deutscher Bibliophilen und Literaturfreunde*, 18/19 (1932-33), 31-46.

15. See Johannes Urzidil, "Vermächtnis eines Jünglings," in *Prager Triptychon* (Munich, 1960), pp. 185-186.

16. On Bahr see Hermann Bahr, *Zur Überwindung des Naturalismus: Theoretische Schriften 1887-1904* (Stuttgart, 1968): Bahr, *Selbstbildnis* (Berlin, 1923);

Heinz Kindermann, *Hermann Bahr: Ein Leben für das europäische Theater* (Graz, 1954).

17. Peter Altenberg, "So wurde ich" [1912], in Walther Killy, ed., *20. Jahrhundert: Texte und Zeugnisse 1880-1933* (Munich, 1967), pp. 280-281. See also Altenberg, *Auswahl aus seinen Büchern*, ed. Karl Kraus (Vienna, 1932; repr. Zürich, 1963). On Altenberg see Randolph J. Klawiter, "Peter Altenberg and das junge Wien," *Modern Austrian Literature*, 1 (Winter, 1968), 1-55 [contains exhaustive bibliography]. Schnitzler's posthumous drama, *Das Wort* (Frankfurt, 1966), impugns Altenberg's levity. See Reinhard Urbach, " 'Schwätzer sind Verbrecher': Bemerkungen zu Schnitzlers Dramenfragment 'Das Wort,' " *Literatur und Kritik*, 3 (1968), 292-304.

18. See J. P. Stern, *Re-Interpretations* (New York, 1964), p. 54; Karl Wache, *Jahrmarkt der Wiener Literatur* (Vienna, 1966), pp. 103-114. An exhaustive history and typology of feuilletons appears in Wilmont Haacke, *Handbuch des Feuilletons*, 3 vols. (Emsdetten, 1951-1953). This version lacks the anti-Semitic outbursts that mar Haacke's otherwise identical *Feuilletonkunde: Das Feuilleton als literarische und journalistische Gattung*, 2 vols. (Leipzig, 1943-1944).

19. See Friedrich Schlögl, *Wiener Blut: Kleine Culturbilder aus dem Volksleben der alten Kaiserstadt an der Donau* (Vienna, 1875); Ferdinand Kürnberger, *Feuilletons*, ed. Karl Riha (Frankfurt, 1967), esp. pp. 141-178 on linguistic improprieties in the press.

20. These articles are collected in Daniel Spitzer, *Wiener Spaziergänge*, 7 vols. (Vienna, 1879-1894, repr. 1968). A sampling appears in Daniel Spitzer, *Hereinspaziert ins alte Wien* (Herrenalb, 1967).

21. See Vinzenz Chiavacci,. *Aus dem Kleinleben der Grossstadt: Wiener Genrebilder* (Vienna, 1884). Eduard Pötzl contributed several essays to the compendium, *Wienerstadt: Lebensbilder aus der Gegenwart* (Vienna, 1895) [offers vivid portrayal of daily life].

22. Repr. in Kraus, *Untergang der Welt durch schwarze Magie* [1922], *Werke*, 8 (Munich, 1960), 188-214.

23. Joseph Roth, "Feuilleton" [July, 1921], in Killy, *20. Jahrhundert*, pp. 274-276.

24. Roda Roda, "Der alte Österreicher," in *Das grosse Roda Roda Buch* (Berlin 1933), pp. 384-391.

25. On Friedell see Polgar, "Der grosse Dilettant: Zu Egon Friedells 'Kulturgeschichte der Neuzeit': Der Mann und das Werk," *Der Monat*, 2 (1949-50), 410-419; Hilde Spiel, "Egon Friedell," in *Welt im Widerschein: Essays* (Munich, 1960), pp. 255-263; Walther Schneider, "Einführung," in Friedell, *Aphorismen und Briefe* (Munich, 1961), pp. 9-20.

26. A friend of Friedell, Hanns Sassmann (1882-1944) narrated the history of Austria with similar flair in *Das Reich der Träumer: Eine Kulturgeschichte Österreichs vom Urzustand bis zur Repulik* (Berlin, 1932). A visitor to Vienna during the early 1930's, John Gunther adopted the style of the feuilleton in *Inside Europe* (New York, 1936).

27. See Freud, *Aus den Anfängen der Psychoanalyse 1887-1902* (London, 1950), pp. 276-277 [letter of June 12, 1900]; Jones, 1:388. For an analysis of the dream in question (Irma's injection) see Freud, *Die Traumdeutung*, 8th ed. in *GW*, 2/3 (London, 1942), pp. 110-126, 298-310.

28. See Henry Schnitzler, "Gay Vienna: Myth and Reality," *Journal of the History of Ideas*, 15 (1954), 94-118 [by the son of Arthur Schnitzler]. On the Burg-

theater see Rudolph Lothar, ed., *Das Wiener Burgtheater: Ein Wahrzeichen österreichischer Kunst und Kultur* (Vienna, 1934).

29. Zweig, *Die Welt von Gestern*, p. 33.

30. *Ibid.*, p. 31. On theater mania see also Germaine Goblot, "Les parents de Karl Kraus," *Études germaniques*, 5 (1950), 43-53 [penetrating].

31. "Ich sage mir oft, ich sage mir täglich: Nein, man kann in Wien nicht mehr leben, fort! Hier sind nicht zwölf Menschen, die halbwegs europäisch empfinden. Und hinter ihnen ist gleich nichts; das Chaos. Aber dann malt Klimt ein neues Bild. Dann macht Roller den Tristan oder den Fidelio neu, Mahler dirigiert, die Mildenburg singt. Und ich sage mir dann: Ich könnte doch nirgends leben als in Wien, wirklich leben, was mir Leben ist." Bahr, "Dekorationen," *Neue Rundschau*, 16 (1905), 162.

32. "Er [Nestroy] kann nichts mehr tun, als das Wienerische mit dem damals noch sehr fremd, 'geschraubt' klingenden Hochdeutsch zu konfrontieren und auf solche Art seine komischen Wirkungen aus einer Sprachspannung zu erzielen, die wahrhaft *genial* ist, weil sie ihre Wurzeln eben in der Sprache hat." Josef Weinheber, *Briefe* in *Sämtliche Werke*, 5 (Salzburg, 1956), 199 [letter to Will Vesper of Dec. 31, 1938]. A useful lexicon of Austrian dialect is Jakob Ebner, *Wie sagt man in Österreich? Wörterbuch der österreichischen Besonderheiten* (Mannheim, 1969) [abounds in citations from Austrian literature].

33. "[W]ir haben eine sehr hohe dichterische Sprache und sehr liebliche und ausdrucksstarke Volksdialekte. . . . Woran es uns mangelt, das ist die mittlere Sprache, nicht zu hoch, nicht zu niedrig, in der sich die Geselligkeit der Volksglieder untereinander auswirkt." Hofmannsthal, "Wert und Ehre deutscher Sprache" [1927], in *Ausgewählte Werke* (Frankfurt, 1957), 2:751.

34. The keenest analysis is by Prague-born J. P. Stern in "Vienna 1900," *The Listener*, 67 (Feb., 1962), 291-295; Stern, *Re-Interpretations: Seven Studies in Nineteenth Century German Literature* (New York, 1964), pp. 51-61; Stern, "Introduction," Arthur Schnitzler, *Liebelei, Leutnant Gustl, Die letzten Masken* (Cambridge, 1966), pp. 1-44, esp. 34-35.

CHAPTER 8

1. See Victor Zuckerkandl, *Vom musikalischen Denken: Begegnung von Ton und Wort* (Zürich, 1964), pp. 248-251.

2. Quoted in English in Henry Schnitzler, " 'Gay Vienna': Myth and Reality," *Journal of the History of Ideas*, 15 (1954), 112-113. See Laube, *Reise durch das Biedermeier* (Hamburg, 1965), pp. 248-250.

3. On Johann Strauss junior see Ernst Decsey, "Johann Strauss," *NOB*, 2 (1925), 154-163; Hans Weigel, "Johann Strauss oder die Stunde der Operette," in *Flucht vor der Grösse: Beiträge zur Erkenntnis und Selbsterkenntnis Österreichs* (Vienna, 1960), pp. 209-282. A perceptive chronicle of Viennese operetta is Bernard Grun, *Die leichte Muse: Kulturgeschichte der Operette*, 2d ed. (Munich, 1961) [by a colleague of Lehár].

4. Berta Szeps, *My Life and History* (New York, 1939), p. 164.

5. See H. L. Mencken, George Jean Nathan, and Willard Huntington Wright, *Europe after 8:15* (New York, 1914), pp. 35-70; Ludwig Hirschfeld, *Das Buch von Wien* (Munich, 1927), pp. 131-141.

6. For a reaction to the World Exposition of 1873 see Anna Freud Bernays, "My

Brother Sigmund Freud," *American Mercury*, 51 (1940), 338. See also "Vienna at Exhibition Time," *Blackwood's Magazine*, 114 (1873), 442-458.

7. See Artur Schnabel, *My Life and Music* (London, 1961), pp. 8-42, esp. 9 and 24. Effusive recollections of this musical milieu pervade Ethel Newcomb, *Leschetizky as I Knew Him* (New York, 1921; repr. 1967).

8. On Hanslick see Eduard Hanslick, *Aus meinem Leben*, 2 vols. (Berlin, 1894); Max Graf, *Composer and Critic* (New York, 1946), pp. 244-251; Weigel, "Eduard Hanslick: Eine Ehrenrettung," *Neues Forum*, 13 (1966), 413-418; Carl Dahlhaus, "Eduard Hanslick und der musikalische Formbegriff," *Die Musikforschung*, 20 (1967), 145-153; Robert W. Hall, "On Hanslick's Supposed Formalism in Music," *Journal of Aesthetics and Art Criticism*, 25 (1967), 433-436. Stewart Deas, *In Defense of Hanslick* (London, 1940) was not available to me.

9. Morse Peckham, *Beyond the Tragic Vision: The Quest for Identity in the Nineteenth Century* (New York, 1962), pp. 278-284. Hanslick summed up his estimate of Viennese music in "Musik," in *Wien 1848-1888* (Vienna, 1888), 2:301-342.

10. Suzanne K. Langer, *Philosophy in a New Key* (Cambridge, Mass. 1942; repr. New York, 1948), p. 193.

11. On Adler see Guido Adler, *Wollen und Wirken: Aus dem Leben eines Musikhistorikers* (Vienna, 1935); Adler, "Style Criticism," *The Musical Quarterly*, 20 (April, 1934), 172-176.

12. On Bruckner see Erich Kinast, "Immanuel Kant, Anton Bruckner: Das Psychogramm des Philosophen und des Künstlers," *Deutsche Psychologie*, 4 (1926), 305-374, esp. 345-368, 372-374 [contains choice bibliography]; Graf, "Anton Bruckner's Catholicism," *Commonweal*, 36 (1942), 486-488; Graf, *Legend of a Musical City* (New York, 1945), pp. 142-152; Max Auer, *Anton Bruckner: Sein Leben und Sein Werk*, 6th ed. (Vienna, 1949; repr. 1965).

13. Max Brod, *Streitbares Leben, 1884-1968*, 2d ed. (Munich, 1969), pp. 214-218. For other anecdotes see Decsey, *Musik war sein Leben* (Vienna, 1962), pp. 33-36, 80-83.

14. On Wolf see Hugo Wolf, *Briefe an Melanie Köchert* (Tutzing, 1964); Decsey, *Hugo Wolf*, 4 vols. (Leipzig, 1903); Ernest Newman, *Hugo Wolf* (London, 1907); Hermann Bahr, *Selbstbildnis* (Berlin, 1923), pp. 153-155; Stefan Grossmann, *Ich war begeistert* (Berlin, 1931), pp. 162-165; Graf, *Legend of a Musical City*, pp. 134-141; Frank Walker, *Hugo Wolf: A Biography* (London, 1952; 2d ed. 1968) [exhaustive].

15. "Meine Werke, meine Musik muss er lieben und schätzen, für die muss er sich über alles interessieren—meine Person ist dabei ganz Nebensache." Rosa Mayreder, "Erinnerungen an Hugo Wolf" [1928], in *Die Krise der Väterlichkeit* (Graz, 1963), p. 58.

16. On Mahler see Bahr, "Mahler" [1914], in *Essays: Kulturprofil der Jahrhundertwende* (Vienna, 1962), pp. 275-282 [likens Mahler to the violinist Pisani portrayed in Edward Bulwer-Lytton's *Zanoni* (1842)]; Bruno Walter, *Gustav Mahler* [1936] (New York, 1941); Alma Mahler-Werfel, *Gustav Mahler: Erinnerungen und Briefe* (Amsterdam, 1940); Mahler-Werfel, *Mein Leben* (Frankfurt, 1960); Donald Mitchell, *Gustav Mahler: The Early Years* (London, 1958); Neville Cardus, *Gustav Mahler: His Mind and His Music*, 2 vols. (London, 1965–); Arnold Schönberg et al., *Über Gustav Mahler* (Tübingen, 1966); William E. Mooney, "Gustav Mahler: A Note on Life and Death in

Music," *Psychoanalytic Quarterly*, 37 (1968), 80-102; Kurt Blaukopf, *Gustav Mahler, oder der Zeitgenosse der Zukunft* (Vienna, 1969).

17. See John L. Kuehn, "Encounter at Leyden: Mahler Consults Sigmund Freud," *Psychoanalytic Review*, 52 (1965), 345-365; also Jones, 2:88-89. On Mahler's attitude toward death see Graf, *Modern Music* (New York, 1946), pp. 89-101; Graf, *From Beethoven to Shostakovitch: The Psychology of the Composing Process* (New York, 1947), pp. 130-137.

18. Mahler-Werfel, *Gustav Mahler*, pp. 89-90.

19. Kurt List, "Mahler: Father of Modern Music," *Commentary*, 10 (1950), 42-48.

20. A useful anthology of Schönberg's essays and verse is Arnold Schönberg, *Schöpferische Konfessionen*, ed. Willi Reich (Zürich, 1964). On Schönberg see Laurence Gilman, "Irrubrical Schönberg and His Extraordinary Music," *North American Review*, 199 (1914), 452-457; Graf, *Modern Music*, pp. 168-196; Rene Leibowitz, *Schoenberg and His School: The Contemporary Stage of the Language of Music* (New York, 1949); Peter Gradenwitz, "Gustav Mahler and Arnold Schoenberg," *YLBI*, 5 (1960), 262-284; Hans Heinz Stuckenschmidt, *Arnold Schönberg* [1951] (London, 1964); Willi Reich, *Arnold Schönberg oder der konservative Revolutionär* (Vienna, 1968). For recollections about Schönberg's disciples see Theodor Adorno, "Erinnerung," in Adorno, *Berg: Der Meister des kleinsten Übergangs* (Vienna, 1968), pp. 15-42. A penetrating stylistic analysis is Will Hofmann, "Expressionismus. III. Stilbestimmung des musikalischen Expressionismus," *Die Musik in Geschichte und Gegenwart*, 3 (Kassel, 1954), 1658-1673.

21. Schönberg, "Offener Brief," *Die Fackel*, Nr. 272-273 (Feb. 15, 1909), pp. 34-35.

22. "Aber wenn wir die Teile auseinandergenommen haben, sind wir meist nicht mehr imstande, sie wieder genau zusammenzusetzen, und haben verloren, was wir vorher schon besessen hatten: das Ganze mit allen Details und seiner Seele." Schönberg, "Rede in Prag [1913], in Schönberg, et al., *Über Gustav Mahler*, pp. 12-13.

23. Anton Ehrenzweig, *The Hidden Order of Art* (London, 1967), pp. 253-256.

CHAPTER 9

1. On Makart see Friedrich Pollak, "Makart, Hans M.," *ADB*, 52 (1906), 158-164; "Hans Makart," *NOB*, 6 (1929), 15-43; Emil Pirchan, *Hans Makart* (Leipzig, 1942; 2d ed. 1954); Ann Tizia Leitich, *Verklungenes Wien: Vom Biedermeier zur Jahrhundertwende* (Vienna, 1942), pp. 99-107; Hermann Uhde-Bernays, "Hans Makart," in *Mittler und Meister: Aufsätze und Studien* (Munich, 1948), pp. 224-234 [highly informative]; Ernst Köller, "Makart und seine Zeit," *Das Kunstwerk*, 8 (Feb., 1954), 16-17; Paul Lindau, "Ein Atelierbesuch bei Hans Makart" [1874], in *Bildende Kunst*, 7 (1959), 418-420; Daniel Spitzer, *Hereinspaziert ins alte Wien* [1865-1891] (Herrenalb, 1967), pp. 138-143, 173-177, 328; Gerd Tolzien, "Makart, Hans," *KML*, 4 (1967), 255-258.

2. See Leitich, *Die Wienerin* (Stuttgart, 1939), pp. 207-210.

3. For a contemporary account see Karl Ziak, ed., *Unvergängliches Wien* (Vienna, 1964), p. 356.

4. On Romako (pronounced RoMAko) see Fritz Novotny, *Der Maler Anton Romako 1832-1889* (Vienna, 1954); J. Muschik, "Anton Romako: ein Maler

zwischen den Zeiten," *Das Kunstwerk*, 18 (March, 1965), 16-21; Rudolf Bachleitner, "Romako, Anton," *KML*, 5 (1968), 114-117.

5. On Klimt see Hermann Bahr, "Klimt" [1913], in *Essays: Kulturprofil der Jahrhundertwende* (Vienna, 1962), pp. 287-291; Hans Tietze, "Gustav Klimt," *NOB*, 3 (1926), 82-89; Hans Ankwicz von Kleehoven, "Gustav Klimt (1862-1918)," *Das Kunstwerk*, 8 (Feb., 1954), 32-43; Pirchan, *Gustav Klimt*, 2d ed. (Vienna, 1956); Alfred Werner, "The World of Gustav Klimt," *Arts*, 33 (April, 1959), 25-31; Werner, "The Women of Klimt and Schiele," *The Reporter*, 32 (Feb. 25, 1965), 44-48; Tolzien, "Klimt, Gustav," *KML*, 3 (1966), 657-688; Fritz Novotny and Johannes Dobai, *Gustav Klimt* (Salzburg, 1967); Richard Hamann and Jost Hermand, *Stilkunst um 1900* (East Berlin, 1967), pp. 220-222, 334-340.

6. On Schiele see James Thrall Soby, "Two Masters of Expressionism," *Saturday Review*, 40 (March 2, 1957), 28-29; Werner, "Schiele and Austrian Expressionism," *Arts*, 35 (Oct., 1960), 46-51; Geno Baro, "Schiele's Mannerism," *Arts*, 39 (Jan., 1965), 70-72; Thomas M. Messer, *Gustav Klimt and Egon Schiele* (New York, 1965); Wolfgang Fischer, "Egon Schiele and the Spirit of Vienna before 1918," *The Connoisseur Yearbook*, (1965), pp. 101-106 [useful comparisons with composers]; Fischer, "Schiele, Egon," *KML*, 5 (1968), 239-241; Otto Kallir, *Egon Schiele: Oeuvre-Katalog der Gemälde* (Vienna, 1966); Siegfried Freiberg, *'Ihr werdet sehen . . .': Ein Egon Schiele-Roman* (Vienna, 1967); Horst Denkler, "Malerei mit Wörtern: Zu Egon Schieles poetischen Schriften," in Renate von Heydebrand and Klaus Günther Jost, eds., *Wissenschaft als Dialog: Studien zur Literatur und Kunst seit der Jahrhundertwende* (Stuttgart, 1969), pp. 271-288. Egon Schiele, *Briefe und Prosa*, ed. Arthur Roessler (Vienna, 1921) was not available to me.

7. Otto Benesch, "Egon Schiele. 2. The Artist," *Studio International*, 168 (1964), 173.

8. Wladyslaw Tatarkiewicz, "Abstract Art and Philosophy," *British Journal of Aesthetics*, 2 (1961-62), 227-238, esp. 232-233.

9. On Kokoschka see Oskar Kokoschka, "Aus der Jugendbiographie," in *Schriften 1907-1955* (Munich, 1956; repr. Frankfurt, 1964), pp. 11-41: Edith Hoffmann, *Kokoschka: Life and Work* (London, 1947) [exceptionally informative]; Hans Maria Wingler, *Oskar Kokoschka: Das Werk des Malers* (Salzburg, 1956); Wingler, "Kokoschka, Oskar," *KML*, 3 (1966), 715-730; Werner, "Kokoschka's Baroque Expressionism," *Arts*, 33 (Sept., 1959), 43-47; Josef Paul Hodin, *The Dilemma of Being Modern: Essays on Art and Literature* (New York, 1959), pp. 67-75; Hodin, ed., *Bekenntnis zu Kokoschka: Erinnerungen und Deutungen* (Berlin, 1963); Hodin, *Oskar Kokoschka: The Artist and His Time: A Biographical Study* (London, 1966); Alma Mahler-Werfel, *Mein Leben* (Frankfurt, 1960).

10. Quoted in Hodin, *The Dilemma of Being Modern*, p. 69.

11. On the growth of Vienna see Frederick R. Farrow, "The Recent Development of Vienna," *Transactions of the Royal Institute of British Architects*, 4 (1887-1888), 82-87; Fred Hennings, *Ringstrassensymphonie*, 3 vols. (Vienna, 1963-1964); Karl Ziak, ed., *Unvergängliches Wien: Ein Gang durch die Geschichte von der Urzeit bis zur Gegenwart* (Vienna, 1964), pp. 329-337; George R. Collins and Christiane Collins, *Camillo Sitte and the Birth of Modern City Planning* (New York, 1965), pp. 34-44, 126-131; Hans Bobek and Elisabeth

Lichtenberger, *Wien: Bauliche Gestalt und Entwicklung seit der Mitte des 19. Jahrhunderts* (Graz, 1966). On individual buildings see Richard Groner and Felix Czeike, *Wien wie es war: Ein Nachschlagewerk für Freunde des alten und neuen Wien*, 5th ed. (Vienna, 1965); Gerhardt Kapner, *Die Denkmäler der Wiener Ringstrasse* (Vienna, 1969). See also Friedrich Javorsky, *Lexikon der Wiener Strassennamen* (Vienna, 1964).

12. For photographs of Ringstrasse Vienna see Paul Kortz, *Wien am Anfang des XX. Jahrhunderts: Ein Führer in technischer und künstlerischer Richtung*, vol. 2 (Vienna, 1906); Karl Mayreder, *Wien und Umgebung*, 6th ed. (Vienna, 1911); Herbert Zippe, *Bildband zur Geschichte Österreichs* (Innsbruck, 1967); Franz Hubmann, *Die gute alte Zeit: Alte Photographien aus Wien* (Salzburg, 1968) [superb pictures of passersby]; Fred Hennings, *Solange er lebt*, projected in 5 vols. (Vienna, 1968–).

13. See Rudolf Eitelberger von Edelsberg, "Heinrich Ferstel und die Votivkirche" [1878], in *Gesammelte kunsthistorische Schriften*, (Vienna, 1879), 1:271-348.

14. On Van der Nüll see *ibid.*, pp. 228-270.

15. On Sitte see Elbert Peets, "Famous Town Planners: Camillo Sitte," *Town Planning Review*, 12 (1926-27), 249-259; Heinrich Sitte, "Camillo Sitte 1843-1903," *NOB*, 6 (1929), 132-149; Collins and Collins, *Camillo Sitte*.

16. On Wagner see Joseph August Lux, *Otto Wagner: Eine Monographie* (Munich, 1914); Dagobert Frey, "Otto Wagner," *NOB*, 1 (1923), 178-187; Pirchan, *Otto Wagner: Der Grosse Baukünstler* (Vienna, 1956) [by a pupil of Wagner]; Hamann and Hermand, *Stilkunst um 1900*, pp. 329-334.

17. These plans are reproduced in Otto Antonia Graf, *Otto Wagner: Das Werk des Wiener Architekten, 1841-1918* (Darmstadt, 1963); Heinz Geretsegger and Max Peintner, *Otto Wagner 1841-1918: Unbegrenzte Groszstadt, Beginn der modernen Architektur* (Salzburg, 1964).

18. On Loos see Hansjörg Graf, "Adolf Loos: Ein früher Designer," *Neue Rundschau*, 75 (1964), 513-518; Ludwig Münz and Gustav Künstler, *Adolf Loos: Pioneer of Modern Architecture* (New York, 1966); Willy Haas, *Die belle Epoque* (Munich, 1967), pp. 323-335; Elsie Altmann Loos, *Adolf Loos der Mensch* (Vienna, 1968) [highly informative; by Loos's third wife]. Lina Loos, *Das Buch ohne Titel: Erlebte Geschichten* (Vienna, 1948) [by Loos's first wife] was not available to me.

19. Reprinted in Adolf Loos, *Sämtliche Schriften*, ed. Franz Glück, vol. 1 (Vienna, 1962), which also contains *Trotzdem* (Vienna, 1931), a collection of essays written 1903 to 1931.

20. Reprinted in Münz and Künstler, *Adolf Loos*, p. 230.

21. On the Vienna School of Art History see Julius von Schlosser, "Die Wiener Schule der Kunstgeschichte: Rückblick auf ein Säkulum deutscher Gelehrtenarbeit in Österreich," *MIOGF*, Ergänzungsband, 13 (1934), 145-226; Udo Kultermann, *Geschichte der Kunstgeschichte: Der Weg einer Wissenschaft* (Vienna, 1966), pp. 278-302.

22. On Eitelberger see Hubert Janitschek, "Rudolf Eitelberger," *Repertorium für Kunstwissenschaft*, 8 (1885), 398-404; J. Folnesics, "Eitelberger, Rudolf E. von Edelberg," *ADB*, 55 (1910), 734-738; Taras von Borodajkewycz, "Aus der Frühzeit der Wiener Schule der Kunstgeschichte: Rudolf Eitelberger und Leo Thun," *Festschrift Hans Sedlmayr* (Munich, 1962), pp. 321-348.

23. On Thausing see Anton Springer, "Moriz Thausing," *Repertorium für Kunst-*

wissenschaft, 8 (1885), 142-147; Theodor von Frimmel, "Thausing, Moritz Th.," *ADB*, 37 (1894), 660-664.

24. See Edgar Wind, *Art and Anarchy* (New York), pp. 32-51, 138-151.

25. On Wickhoff see Gustav Glück, "Franz Wickhoff," *Repertorium für Kunstwissenschaft*, 32 (1909), 386-390; Schlosser, "Franz Wickhoff," *NOB*, 8 (1935), 190-198.

26. On Riegl see Erwin Panofsky, "Der Begriff des Kunstwollens," *ZAAK*, 14 (1920), 321-339; Wind, "Zur Systematik der künstlerischen Probleme," *ZAAK*, 18 (1925), 438-486; Hans Sedlmayr, "Einleitung," in Riegl, *Gesammelte Aufsätze* (Augsburg, 1929), pp. xi-xxxiv; Tietze, "Alois Riegl," *NOB*, 8 (1935), 142-149; Géza Révész, *Psychology and the Art of the Blind* (London, 1950), pp. 207-213; Otto Pächt, "Art Historians and Art Critics. VI. Alois Riegl," *Burlington Magazine*, 105 (1963), 188-193.

27. Wind, *Art and Anarchy*, p. 23.

28. On Dvořák see Dagobert Frey, "Max Dvořák's Stellung in der Kunstgeschichte," *Jahrbuch für Kunstgeschichte*, 1 (1922), 1-21; Josef Weingartner, "Max Dvořák und die kunsthistorische Wiener Schule," *Hochland*, 21 (1924), 345-351; Benesch, "Max Dvořák: Ein Versuch zur Geschichte der historischen Geisteswissenschaften," *Repertorium für Kunstgeschichte*, 44 (1924), 159-197; Benesch, "Max Dvořák (1874-1921)," *NOB*, 10 (1957), 189-198; Ludwig von Bertalanffy, Review of Max Dvořák, *Kunstgeschichte als Geistesgeschichte* (Vienna, 1923), in *ZAAK*, 20 (1926), 375-381; Sedlmayr, "Kunstgeschichte als Geistesgeschichte," *Wort und Wahrheit*, 4 (1949), 264-277; J. Neumann, "Das Werk Max Dvořáks und die Gegenwart," *Acta historiae artium*, 8 (1962), 177-213; Karl Maria Swoboda, "Preface," in Dvořák *Idealism and Naturalism in Gothic Art* [1918] (Notre Dame, 1967), pp. xix-xxx.

29. On Schlosser see "Johannes Schlosser," in Johannes Jahn, ed., *Die Kunstwissenschaft der Gegenwart in Selbstdarstellungen* (Leipzig, 1924), pp. 95-134. Sedlmayr, "Julius Ritter von Schlosser," *MIOGF*, 52 (1938), 513-519; Ernst Gombrich, "Obituary: Julius von Schlosser," *Burlington Magazine*, 74 (1939), 98-99. On Strzygowski see "Josef Strzygowski," in Jahn, ed., *Die Kunstwissenschaft*, pp. 157-181; Bertalanffy, Review of Strzygowski, *Krisis der Geisteswissenschaften* (1923), in *ZAAK*, 22 (1928), 213-226.

30. See Sedlmayr, *Verlust der Mitte: Die bildende Kunst des 19. und 20. Jahrhunderts als Symptom und Symbol der Zeit* (Salzburg, 1948). On Sedlmayr see Meyer Schapiro, "The New Viennese School," *The Art Bulletin*, 18 (1936), 258-266.

31. Marie Luise Kaschnitz describes her husband in "Biographie des Verfassers," in Guido Kaschnitz von Weinberg, *Ausgewählte Schriften* (Berlin, 1965), 1:228-239. On parallels between Kaschnitz von Weinberg and Claude Lévi-Strauss see Sheldon Nodelman, "Structural Analysis in Art and Archaeology," *Yale French Studies*, Nr. 36-37 (1966), 89-103.

32. Translated as *Idealism and Naturalism in Gothic Art* (Notre Dame, 1967).

33. Reprinted in Dvořák, *Kunstgeschichte als Geistesgeschichte* pp. 259-276. See also Dvořák, "Vorwort," in Oskar Kokoschka, *Variationen über ein Thema* (Vienna, 1921).

34. Perhaps the most promising attempt at an integrative history of culture is Jean Gebser, *Ursprung und Gegenwart*, 2 vols. (Stuttgart, 1949-1953; 2d ed., 1966).

CHAPTER 10

1. On Mayreder see Rosa Mayreder, *Das Haus in der Landskrongasse: Jugender-innerungen* (Vienna, 1948); Käthe Braun-Prager, *Rosa Mayreder* (Vienna, 1955); Braun-Prager, "Einleitung," in Meyreder, *Krise der Väterlichkeit* (Graz, 1963), pp. 5-26 [by a sister of Felix Braun].

2. Mayreder, *A Survey of the Woman Problem* (London, 1912), p. 139.

3. Jones, 1:114.

4. Mayreder, "Geschlecht und Kultur," *Annalen der Natur- und Kulturphiloso-phie*, 12 (1913), 289-306.

5. F. M. Colby, Review of Mayreder, *A Survey of the Woman Problem*, in *North American Review*, 198 (1913), 875.

6. On Weininger see Karl Kraus, *Die Fackel*, Nr. 144 (Oct. 17, 1903), pp. 1-3, 15-22; Emil Lucka, *Otto Weininger: Sein Werk und seine Persönlichkeit* (Vienna, 1905); Hermann Swoboda, *Otto Weiningers Tod* (Leipzig, 1910; 2d ed., 1923); Carl Dallago, *Otto Weininger und sein Werk* (Innsbruck, 1912); Hans Kohn, "Das kulturelle Problem des modernen Westjuden," *Der Jude*, 5 (1920-21), 287-291; Kohn, "Notes on the Life and Work of Arthur Schnitzler and Otto Weininger," *YLBI*, 6 (1961), 152-169; Oskar Baum, "Otto Wein-inger," in Gustav Krojanker, ed., *Juden in der deutschen Literatur* (Berlin, 1922), pp. 121-138; Theodor Lessing, *Der jüdische Selbsthass* (Berlin, 1930), pp. 80-100; David Abrahamsen, *The Mind and Death of a Genius* (New York, 1946) [indispensable but overly detailed]; Abrahamsen, "Otto Weininger and Bisexuality: A Psychoanalytical Study," *American Journal of Psychotherapy*, 1 (1947), 25-44; Abrahamsen, "The Mind and Death of a Genius: Shadows of the Past," *Psychoanalytic Review*, 34 (1947), 336-356; Werner Kraft, *Karl Kraus: Zum Verständnis seines Werkes* (Salzburg, 1956), pp. 73-94; Mar-garete Susman, "Otto Weininger: Ein Moralist als Verneiner" [1954], in *Vom Geheimnis der Freiheit: Gesammelte Aufsätze 1914-1964*, ed. Manfred Schlös-ser (Darmstadt, 1965), pp. 155-169; Manfred Durzak, *Hermann Broch: Der Dichter und seine Zeit* (Stuttgart, 1968), pp. 11-23.

7. See Margarete Jodl, *Friedrich Jodl: Sein Leben und Wirken, dargestellt nach Tagebüchern und Briefen* (Stuttgart, 1920), pp. 183-184. See also Stefan Zweig, "Vorbeigehen an einem unauffälligen Menschen: Otto Weininger," in *Europäisches Erbe* (Frankfurt, 1960), pp. 223-226.

8. Abrahamsen, "Otto Weininger and Bisexuality," p. 40-41; Abrahamsen, *The Mind and Death of a Genius*, pp. 54-55.

9. Sigmund Freud, *Briefe 1873-1939*, 2d ed. (Frankfurt, 1968), pp. 265-266. See Jones, 2:14-15; Vincent Brome, *Freud and His Early Circle* (New York, 1968), pp. 1-13.

10. Heinz Politzer, *Franz Kafka: Parable and Paradox* (Ithaca, 1962), pp. 197-200.

11. Ferdinand Ebner, *Schriften* (Munich, 1963), 1:49-50, 295-296.

12. Alfred Werner, "Schiele and Austrian Expressionism," *Arts*, 35 (Oct., 1960), 49.

13. Otto Weininger, *Geschlecht und Charakter: Eine prinzipielle Untersuchung*, 5th ed. (Vienna, 1905), pp. 409-452, esp. 423 and 439. Günter Grass inter-polated some of these passages into the novel *Hundejahre* (Neuwied, 1963), pp. 37-38, 202-203, 220-223, 236. See Wesley V. Blomster, "The Documenta-

tion of a Novel: Otto Weininger and 'Hundejahre' by Günter Grass," *Monatshefte*, 61 (1969), 122-138.

14. See Lessing, *Der jüdische Selbsthass*, pp. 101-131; Friedrich Heer, *Der Glaube des Adolf Hitler: Anatomie einer politischen Religiosität* (Munich, 1968), pp. 167-168.

15. Abrahamsen, *The Mind and Death of a Genius*, p. 55.

16. German text and English translation taken from *ibid.*, p. 21. For other poems by Weininger, see *ibid.*, pp. 62-63, 84; Kraft, *Karl Kraus*, p. 93.

CHAPTER 11

1. "Da der Tod (genau zu nehmen) der wahre Endzweck unsers Lebens ist, so habe ich mich seit ein paar Jahren mit diesem wahren, besten Freunde des Menschen so bekannt gemacht, dass sein Bild nicht alleine nichts Schreckendes mehr für mich hat, sondern recht viel Beruhigendes und Tröstendes. Und ich danke meinem Gott, dass er mir das Glück gegönnt hat, mir die Gelegenheit (Sie verstehen mich) zu verschaffen, ihn als den Schlüssel zu unserer wahren Glückseligkeit kennen zu lernen. Ich lege mich nie zu Bette, ohne zu bedenken, dass ich vielleicht, so jung als ich bin, den andern Tag nicht mehr sein werde, und es wird doch kein Mensch von allen, die mich kennen, sagen können, dass ich im Umgange mürrisch oder traurig wäre, und für diese Glückseligkeit danke ich alle Tage meinem Schöpfer und wünsche sie vom Herzen jedem meiner Mitmenschen." Albert Leitzmann, ed., *Wolfgang Amadeus Mozarts Leben in seinen Briefen und Berichten der Zeitgenossen* (Leipzig, n.d.), pp. 414-415. The translation appears in Wolfgang Amadeus Mozart, *The Letters of Mozart and His Family, Chronologically Arranged*, ed. Emily Anderson (London, 1938), 3:1351.

2. "Ich habe den Tod lieb. Nicht als Erlöser; denn ich leide nicht am Leben. Nein, aber als Erfüller. Er wird mir alles bringen, was noch fehlt. Dann geht die Saat meines Lebens erst auf. Er nimmt mir nichts und gibt mir noch so viel . . . [Ich erwarte den Tod] mit einer bangen Freude, wie wir als Kinder das Christkindl erwarteten; wir sassen im Finstern, aber durch die Türspalte drang ein Strahl lieben Lichts." Hermann Bahr, "Selbstinventur," *Neue Rundschau*, 23 (1912), 1303.

3. "Neben dem wahrhaft religiösen Menschen und neben dem Dichter steht immer der Tod, ein Mahner, das Leben mit letzterreichbarem Sinn zu erfüllen, auf dass es nicht umsonst gelebt sei." Hermann Broch, "James Joyce und die Gegenwart" [1936], in *Dichten und Erkennen: Essays* (Zürich, 1955), 1:205.

4. Hugo von Hofmannsthal, "Maria Theresia" [1917], in *Ausgewählte Werke* (Frankfurt, 1957), 2:612.

5. Stefan Zweig, *Die Welt von Gestern: Erinnerungen eines Europäers* (Stockholm, 1942), p. 34. See also Herbert Eisenreich, "Die schöne Leich: Von der Lust des Wieners am Sterben," *Forum*, 10 (1963), 140-142.

6. Richard N. Coudenhove-Kalergi, *An Idea Conquers the World* (London, 1953), p. 32.

7. See Harman Grisewood, "The Gigantic Fetish: A Study of Comte's Religious Peculiarity," *Dublin Review*, 225 (1951), 89-97.

8. On the origin of royal funerals see Michael de Ferdinandy, "Die Rolle des Königs: Die theatralische Bedeutung des spanischen Hofzeremoniells," *Der Monat*, 19 (May, 1967), 48-49.

9. Berta Szeps, *My Life and History* (New York, 1939), pp. 98-101.

10. Ferdinand Kürnberger, "Ein Aphorismus zur Denkmal-Pest unserer Zeit" [1872], in *Literarische Herzenssachen: Reflexionen und Kritiken* (Vienna, 1877), pp. 311-319.

11. Arnold Hauser, *The Social History of Art* (London, 1951), 2:871.

12. *Ibid.*, 2:873. On the rendition of ephemerality in French impressionist painting see Werner Hofmann, *Grundlagen der modernen Kunst: Eine Einführung in ihre symbolischen Formen* (Stuttgart, 1966), pp. 179-190. For an interpretation of art nouveau (*Jugendstil*) as a European-wide world view similar to impressionism see Hans H. Hofstätter, *Geschichte der europäischen Jugendstilmalerei*, 2d ed. (Cologne, 1965), pp. 13-45, 216-231. The most ambitious typology of impressionism appears in Richard Hamann and Jost Hermand, *Impressionismus* (East Berlin, 1960). A simplistic but stimulating typology is found in Luise Thon, *Die Sprache des deutschen Impressionismus: Ein Beitrag zur Erfassung ihrer Wesenszüge* (Munich, 1928). The earliest attempt at synthesis was Hamann, *Der Impressionismus in Leben und Kunst* (Cologne, 1907).

13. "Ist nicht der Tod im Leben, ist er nicht mitten drin, sitzt in uns, um uns, haucht uns an und ist unser Freund und Gefährte? . . . Alle Menschen leben im grossen Schatten des Todes, der von Gott ist und ihnen vertraut sein soll wie der Duft ihrer Blumen vor dem Fenster, wie der Hauch ihres Mundes." Richard Schaukal, *Grossmutter: Ein Buch vom Leben und Tod: Gespräche mit einer Verstorbenen* (Stuttgart, 1906), p. 18.

14. Schaukal, "Erfindungen an der Bahre," in *Um die Jahrhundertwende* (Munich, ca. 1965), pp. 178-179. See also "Vom Tod zu Tod," *ibid.*, pp. 218-227.

15. Albert Ehrenstein, *Gedichte und Prosa*, ed. Karl Otten (Neuwied, 1961), pp. 354-375. *Tubutsch* is reprinted *ibid.*, pp. 277-310. On Ehrenstein's debt to impressionism see Fritz Martini, "Albert Ehrenstein," in Wolfgang Rothe, ed., *Expressionismus als Literatur: Gesammelte Studien* (Bern, 1969), pp. 690-706. On Ehrenstein as an existentialist in the manner of Sartre's *Nausée* see Gabriel Beck, *Die erzählende Prosa Albert Ehrensteins (1886-1950): Interpretation und Versuch einer literarhistorischen Einordnung* (Freiburg/Schweiz, 1969) [comprehensive].

16. On Beer-Hofmann see Solomon Liptzin, *Richard Beer-Hofmann* (New York, 1936); Erich Kahler, "Richard Beer-Hofmann 1866-1945," *Commentary*, 1 (April, 1946), 43-50; Otto Oberholzer, *Richard Beer-Hofmann: Werk und Weltbild des Dichters* (Bern, 1947).

17. "Alles, was wuchs, brauchte viel Zeit zum Wachsen; und alles, was unterging, brauchte lange Zeit, um vergessen zu werden." Roth, *Radetzkymarsch* [1932] (Cologne, 1967), p. 142. On impressionism in Roth see Józef Wittlin, "Erinnerungen an Joseph Roth," in Hermann Linden, ed., *Joseph Roth: Leben und Werk—Ein Gedächtnisbuch* (Cologne, 1949), pp. 48-58 [highly informative]; Hansjürgen Böning, *Joseph Roths 'Radetzkymarsch': Thematik, Struktur, Sprache* (Munich, 1968), pp. 182-190 [contains exhaustive bibliography].

18. On Svevo see Edouard Roditi, "Novelist-Philosophers. I. Italo Svevo," *Horizon*, 10 (1944), 342-359; Renato Poggioli, "Introduction" in Svevo, *Confessions of Zeno* (New York, 1947), pp. 1-8; Piero Rismondo, "Der Fall Italo Svevo," *Wort und Wahrheit*, 14 (1959), 418-426 [sees Svevo as *sui generis*, neither Italian nor Austrian]. On Svevo's debt to Austria-Hungary see Claudio Magris, *Der habsburgische Mythos* (Salzburg, 1966), pp. 204 and 310, n. 43.

19. Arthur Schnitzler, *Jugend in Wien: Eine Autobiographie* (Vienna, 1968), p. 127. On Schnitzler see Françoise Derré, *L'Oeuvre d'Arthur Schnitzler: Imagerie Viennoise et problèmes humains* (Paris, 1966) [exhaustive]; J. P. Stern, "Introduction" in Schnitzler, *Liebelei, Leutnant Gustl, Die letzten Masken* (Cambridge, 1966), pp. 1-44 [extremely penetrating]. On Schnitzler's preoccupation with death see Solomon Liptzin, *Arthur Schnitzler,* (New York, 1932), pp. 1-23.

20. Hauser, *Social History of Art,* 2:908.

21. Quoted in George Sylvester Viereck, *Glimpses of the Great* (London, 1931), p. 331.

22. *Ibid.,* p. 332.

23. Ernst Bertram, "Über den Wiener Roman," *Mitteilungen der literarhistorischen Gesellschaft, Bonn,* 4 (1919), 3-44, esp. 3-10.

24. Other contemporaries who stressed Protean changeability as a trait of impressionism were Bahr, *Dialog vom Tragischen* [1904], repr. in Bahr, *Zur Überwindung des Naturalismus* (Stuttgart, 1968), pp. 183-188; Arthur Schurig, "Hugo von Hofmannsthal," *Deutsche Rundschau,* 134 (1908) 101-115. See also Herbert Cysarz, "Alt-Österreichs letzte Dichtung (1890-1914)," *Preussische Jahrbücher,* 214 (1928), 32-51.

25. Quoted in Viereck, *Glimpses,* p. 341. For a well-argued Marxist view of how Schnitzler's impressionism reflects upper-middle-class attitudes see Anna Stroka, "Der Impressionismus in Arthur Schnitzlers 'Anatol' und seine gesellschaftlichen und ideologischen Voraussetzungen," *Germanica Wratislaviensia* [Breslau], 12 (1967-68), 97-111.

26. An indispensable compendium of pathographies is Wilhelm Lange-Eichbaum and Wolfram Kurth, *Genie, Irrsinn und Ruhm: Genie-Mythos und Pathographie des Genies,* 6th ed. (Munich, 1967) [contains massive bibliography]. Also useful is Walter Muschg, *Tragische Literaturgeschichte,* 3d ed. (Bern, 1957). On suicide see T. G. Masaryk, *Der Selbstmord als sociale Massenerscheinung der modernen Civilisation* (Vienna, 1881) [contains excellent statistics]; Jack D. Douglas, *The Social Meanings of Suicide* (Princeton, 1967) [comprehensive]. On suicides in Austria see Siegfried Rosenfeld, "Der Selbstmord im k. und k. österreichischen Heere: Eine statistische Studie," *Deutsche Worte,* 13 (1893), 449-515; Bratassević, "Die Selbstmorde in Wien während der Jahre 1854-1894," *Statistische Monatsschrift,* 21 (1895), 255-278.

27. Alois Höfler, "Ludwig Boltzmann als Mensch und Philosoph," *Süddeutsche Monatshefte,* 3 (1906), 421.

28. Friedrich Wallisch, *Es hat mich sehr gefreut* (Graz, 1967), pp. 13-15.

29. See Freud, *Briefe 1873-1939,* 2d ed., (Frankfurt, 1968), pp. 65-72 [letter of Sept. 16, 1883]. Cf. Jones, 1:187.

30. On Steiner see Theodor Lessing, *Der jüdische Selbsthass* (Berlin, 1930), pp. 132-151.

31. See Ludwig von Ficker, *Denkzettel und Danksagungen: Aufsätze, Reden* (Munich, 1967), pp. 204-206.

32. Paul Friedmann, ed., *On Suicide: With Particular Reference to Suicide Among Young Students* [1910] (New York, 1967), p. 87. See also David Ernst Oppenheim, "Suicide in Childhood," in Nunberg and Federn, eds., *Minutes of the Vienna Psychoanalytic Society* (New York, 1967), 2:481-497 [session of April 20, 1910]. This discussion is renewed in thirteen articles in *Zeitschrift für psychoanalytische Pädagogik,* 3 (1928-29), 333-442.

33. See Freud's statement in Friedmann, ed., *On Suicide*, p. 140. Freud solved the riddle in "Trauer und Melancholie" [1917], *GW*, 10 (London, 1946), 438-439, by arguing that when during melancholia the self withdraws all libido from the environment, it comes to regard itself as a thing.
34. All previous studies of Tausk, including the facts regarding his birthplace and year of birth, are superseded by Paul Roazen, *Brother Animal: The Story of Freud and Tausk* (New York, 1969), esp. pp. 122-160 on the suicide. Three papers written by Tausk during 1915 and 1916 are translated under Roazen's editorship in *Psychoanalytic Quarterly*, 38 (1969), 354-431.
35. On Juhász see Joseph Reményi, *Hungarian Writers and Literature* (New Brunswick, N. J., 1964), pp. 279-283.
36. Alma Mahler-Werfel, *Mein Leben* (Frankfurt, 1960), pp. 194-195.
37. See Arthur Stern, "Stefan Zweig und sein Freitod: Eine psychologisch-psychiatrische Betrachtung: Zum 25. Todestage," *Zeitschrift für die Geschichte der Juden*, 4 (1967), 247-256.
38. See Fritz Novotny, *Der Maler Anton Romako 1832-1889* (Vienna, 1954), p. 68.
39. See Wilhelm Kosch and Eugen Kuri, *Biographisches Staatshandbuch: Lexikon der Politik, Presse und Publizistik*, 2 vols. (Bern, 1963), 1:518; Richard Bamberger and Franz Maier-Bruck, eds., *Österreich-Lexikon*, 2 vols. (Vienna, 1966), 1:499.
40. Karl Polanyi, "Hamlet," *Yale Review*, 43 (1954), 339.

CHAPTER 12

1. On Mach's life see Ernst Mach, *The Analysis of Sensations* [1900] (New York, 1959), pp. 30-31; Paul Carus, "Professor Mach and His Work," *The Monist*, 21 (1911), 19-42; Hans Henning, *Ernst Mach als Philosoph, Physiker und Psycholog: Eine Monographie* (Leipzig, 1915); Robert Bouvier, *La pensée d'Ernst Mach: Essai de biographie intellectuelle et critique* (Paris, 1923); Anton Lampa, "Ernst Mach," *NOB*, 1 (1923), 93-102; Fr. Herneck, "Ernst Mach: Eine bisher unveröffentlichte Autobiographie," *Physikalische Blätter*, 14 (1958), 385-390; Thomas S. Szasz, "Introduction," in Mach, *Analysis*, pp. v-xxxi; K. D. Heller, *Ernst Mach: Wegbereiter der modernen Physik* (Vienna, 1964); Joachim Thiele, "Zur Wirkungsgeschichte der Schriften Ernst Machs," *ZfphF*, 20 (1966), 118-130; Thiele, "Briefe deutscher Philosophen an Ernst Mach," *Synthese*, 18 (1968), 285-301. Maria Mach, *Erinnerungen einer Erzieherin* (Vienna, 1912) [memoirs by Mach's sister] was not available to me. For bibliography see Thiele, "Ernst Mach-Bibliographie," *Centaurus*, 8 (1963), 189-237 [lists 417 titles by Mach and 99 on him]. Since 1957 Mach's *Nachlass* has reposed in the Ernst-Mach-Institut at Freiburg.
2. Quoted in Philipp Frank, *Between Physics and Philosophy* (Cambridge, Mass., 1941), p. 211.
3. See Ernst Mach and P. Salcher, "Photographische Fixirung der durch Projectile in der Luft eingeleiteten Vorgänge," *SKAW-Wien*, Math.-Naturw. Klasse, 95.II (1887), 764-780; Mach and Salcher, "Über die in Pola and Meppen angestellten ballistisch-photographischen Versuche," *ibid.*, 98. IIa (1889), 41-50.
4. On Mach's philosophy of science see Julius Baumann, "Über Ernst Mach's philosophische Ansichten," *Archiv für systematische Philosophie*, 4 (1898), 44-64; Carus, "Professor Mach's Philosophy," *The Monist*, 16 (1906), 331-356;

Frank, *Modern Science and its Philosophy*, (Cambridge, Mass., 1949). pp. 6-21, 53-89; Richard von Mises, *Positivism: A Study in Human Understanding* [1938] (Cambridge, Mass., 1951), pp. 80-90; Mario Bunge, "Mach's Critique of Newtonian Mechanics," *American Journal of Physics*, 34 (1966), 585-596; Peter Alexander, "Mach, Ernst," *EP*, 5 (1967), 115-119; Robert S. Cohen, "Ernst Mach: Physics, Perception, and the Philosophy of Science," *Synthese*, 18 (1968), 132-170 [followed by five other articles in a symposium on Mach].

5. See Gerald Holton, "Mach, Einstein, and the Search for Reality," *Daedalus*, 97 (1967-68), 636-673; Francis Seaman, "Mach's Rejection of Atomism," *Journal of the History of Ideas*, 29 (1968), 381-393.

6. Johann Wolfgang von Goethe, *Maximen und Reflexionen*, Nr. 499, in *Werke* (Hamburg, 1953), 12:434. The English version is quoted in Frank, *Modern Science*, p. 63.

7. Mach, "On the Part Played by Accident in Invention and Discovery," *The Monist*, 6 (1895-96), 161-175.

8. Summarized in E. B. Titchener, "Mach's 'Lectures on Psychophysics,' " *AJP*, 33 (1922), 213-222.

9. The second edition was retitled *Die Analyse der Empfindungen und das Verhältnis des Psychischen zum Physischen* (Jena, 1900; 9th ed., 1922); translated as *The Analysis of Sensations* [1900] (New York, 1959). Mach summarized his position in "Psychic and Organic Life," *The Monist*, 23 (1913), 1-15.

10. See Mach, "On Sensations of Orientation," *The Monist*, 8 (1897-98), 79-96; Mach, "On Physiological as Distinguished from Geometrical Space," *The Monist*, 11 (1900-1901), 321-338.

11. See Hermann Bahr, *Dialog vom Tragischen* [1904], repr. in Bahr, *Zur Überwindung des Naturalismus* (Stuttgart, 1968), pp. 183-198, esp. 198. See also Bahr, "Mach" [1916], in *Bilderbuch* (Vienna, 1921), pp. 35-41.

12. Gotthart Wunberg, *Der frühe Hofmannsthal: Schizophrenie als dichterische Struktur* (Stuttgart, 1965), p. 37. On Mach see *ibid.*, pp. 30-40.

13. See Richard Hamann, *Der Impressionismus in Leben und Kunst* (Cologne, 1907), pp. 113-125; Hamann and Hermand, *Impressionismus* (East Berlin, 1966), pp. 111-112, 207-211; Egon Friedell, *Kulturgeschichte der Neuzeit* [1927-1931] (Munich, 1965), pp. 1333-1339, 1385-1389.

14. See Mach, *Analysis*, p. 386.

15. See Rudolf M. Holzapfel, *Panideal: Das Seelenleben und seine soziale Neugestaltung* (Leipzig, 1901) [with a foreword by Mach]; Richard Hönigswald, *Zur Kritik der Mach'schen Philosophie* (Berlin, 1903); Emil Lucka, "Das Erkenntnisproblem und Machs 'Analyse der Empfindungen': Eine kritische Studie," *Kantstudien*, 8 (1903), 396-447; Robert Musil, *Beiträge zur Beurteilung der Lehren Machs* (Berlin, 1908) [doctoral dissertation under Carl Stumpf]. On Musil's fusion of positivism with impressionism see Renate von Heydebrand, *Die Reflexionen Ulrichs in Robert Musils Roman, 'Der Mann ohne Eigenschaften,'* (Münster, 1966).

16. Mach, *Analysis*, pp. 174-176.

17. See Cohen, "Ernst Mach," pp. 162-166; Gustav Wetter, *Dialectical Materialism: A Historical and Systematic Survey of Philosophy in the Soviet Union* (New York, 1963), pp. 92-100, 145, 405.

18. Friedrich Adler, *Ernst Machs Überwindung des mechanischen Materialismus* (Vienna, 1918).

19. On Boltzmann see Alois Höfler, "Ludwig Boltzmann als Mensch und Philo-

soph," *Süddeutsche Monatshefte*, 3 (1906), 418-422; Lampa, "Ludwig von Boltzmann," *Biographisches Jahrbuch und deutscher Nekrolog*, 11 (1908), 96-104; Wilhelm Ostwald, *Grosse Männer* (Leipzig, 1909), pp. 401-407; Gustav Jäger, "Ludwig Boltzmann," *NOB*, 2 (1925), 117-137; Engelbert Broda, *Ludwig Boltzmann: Mensch, Physiker, Philosoph* (Vienna, 1955); René Dugas, *La théorie physique au sens de Boltzmann et ses prolongements modernes* (Neuchâtel, 1959); Paul K. Feyerabend, "Boltzmann, Ludwig," *EP*, 1 (1967), 334-337.

20. Ludwig Boltzmann, "On the Necessity of Atomic Theories in Physics," *The Monist*, 12 (1901-1902), 65-79.

21. On Schlick see Viktor Kraft, "Moritz Schlick," *Philosophia*, 1 (1936), 323-330; Friedrich Waismann, "Vorwort," in Schlick, *Gesammelte Aufsätze, 1926-1936* (Vienna, 1938), pp. vi-xxxi: Herbert Feigl, "Moritz Schlick," *Erkenntnis*, 7 (1939), 393-419; David Rynin, "Schlick, Moritz," *IESS*, 14 (1968), 52-56.

22. On the Vienna Circle see Otto Neurath, *Le développement du Cercle de Vienne et l'avenir de l'empirisme logique* (Paris, 1935); Julius Rudolph Weinberg, *An Examination of Logical Positivism* (London, 1936; 2d ed., Patterson, N. J., 1960); Roy Wood Sellars, "Positivism in Contemporary Philosophical Thought," *American Sociological Review*, 4 (1939), 34-41; Frank, *Between Physics and Philosophy*; Frank, *Modern Science*, pp. 1-50; Mises, *Positivism*; Ingeborg Bachmann, "Ludwig Wittgenstein: Zu einem Kapitel der jüngsten Philosophiegeschichte" [1953], in *Gedichte, Erzählungen, Hörspiel, Essays* (Munich, 1964), pp. 277-288; A. J. Ayer, "The Vienna Circle," in Gilbert Ryle, ed., *The Revolution in Philosophy* (London, 1956), pp. 70-87; Ayer, "Editor's Introduction," in *Logical Positivism* (Glencoe, Ill., 1959), pp. 3-28; James Opie Urmson, *Philosophical Analysis: Its Development Between the Two World Wars* (Oxford, 1956); Waismann, *Wittgenstein und der Wiener Kreis: Aus dem Nachlass*, ed. B. F. McGuiness (Oxford, 1967) [contains minutes of discussions 1929-1932]; H. L. Mulder, "Wissenschaftliche Weltauffassung: Der Wiener Kreis," *Journal of the History of Philosophy*, 6 (1968), 386-390 [highly informative].

23. In Albert E. Blumberg and Herbert Feigl, "Logical Positivism: A New Movement in European Philosophy," *Journal of Philosophy*, 28 (1931), 281-296. Feigl has written a superb synopsis of the movement in Herbert Feigl, "The Wiener Kreis in America," in Donald Fleming and Bernard Bailyn, eds., *The Intellectual Migration: Europe and America, 1930-1960* (Cambridge, Mass., 1969), pp. 630-673.

24. Moritz Schlick, *Problems of Ethics* [1930] (New York, 1939), p. 139.

25. *Ibid.*, p. 158.

26. "Brauchen wir eine Lebensregel, so sei es diese, 'Bewahre den Geist der Jugend.' Denn er ist der Sinn des Lebens." Schlick, *Vom Sinn des Lebens* (Berlin, 1927), p. 354.

27. Emil Utitz, "Zur Philosophie der Jugend," *Kantstudien*, 35 (1930), 450-465.

28. Schlick, *Aphorismen*, ed. Blanche Hardy Schlick (Vienna, 1962), pp. 13-14.

29. On Wilhelm Neurath see Hermann R. von Schullen zu Schrattenhofen, "Wilhelm Neurath," *Jahrbücher für Nationalökonomie*, 79 (1902), 161-166; Schullern, "Neurath, Wilhelm," *Biographisches Jahrbuch und deutscher Nekrolog*, 6 (1904), 274-278. Oncken, "Neurath als volkswirtschaftlicher Theoretiker," *Schweizerische Blätter für Wirtschafts- und Sozialpolitik*, 11 (1903), 617-627, was not available to me.

30. On Otto Neurath see Otto Neurath, "Unified Science and its Encyclopedia,"

Philosophy of Science, 4 (1937), 265-277, esp. 273-277; Waldemar Kaempffert, "Facts March On with Neurath," *Survey Graphic,* 28 (1939), 538-540; Kaempffert, "Appreciation of an Elephant," *Survey Graphic,* 35 (1946), 46-49; Horace M. Kallen, "Postscript: Otto Neurath," *Philosophy and Phenomenological Research,* 6 (1946), 529-533; Cohen, "Neurath, Otto," *EP,* 5 (1967), 477-479.

31. See Neurath, *Ludwig Hermann Wolframs Leben,* 2 vols. (Berlin, 1906) [exceedingly learned].

32. Neurath, "Die konfessionelle Struktur Osteuropas und des näheren Orients und ihre politisch-nationale Bedeutung," *ASWSP,* 39 (1914), 482-524; Neurath, "Die konfessionelle Struktur Österreich-Ungarns und die orientalische Frage," *Weltwirtschaftliches Archiv,* 3 (1914), 108-138.

33. See Neurath, "Nationalökonomie und Wertlehre: Eine systematische Untersuchung," *Zeitschrift für Volkswirtschaft, Sozialpolitik und Verwaltung,* 20 (1911), 52-114; Neurath, "Probleme der Kriegswirtschaftslehre," *Zeitschrift für die gesamte Staatswissenschaft,* 69 (1913), 438-501.

34. Neurath, "Beiträge zur Geschichte der Opera servilia," *ASWSP,* 41 (1916), 438-465 [abounds in Greek and Latin citations].

35. See Ernst Niekisch, *Gewagtes Leben: Begegnungen und Begebnisse* (Cologne, 1958), pp. 53-57; Ernst Karl Winter,"The Rise and Fall of Austrian Labor," *Social Research,* 6 (1939), 323. Neurath, *Bayerische Sozialisierungserfahrungen* (Vienna, 1920) was not available to me.

36. See Neurath, "Museums of the Future," *Survey Graphic,* 22 (1933), 458-463, 479, 484-486; Neurath, *International Picture Language: The First Rules of Isotype* (London, 1936); Neurath, *Modern Man in the Making* (New York, 1939); Neurath, "Visual Education: The Isotype System of Visual Education," *Sociological Review,* 38 (1946), 55-57.

37. Quoted in Kaempffert, "Appreciation," p. 47.

38. See Neurath, "Protocol Sentences" [1932], in Ayer, ed., *Logical Positivism,* pp. 199-208; Weinberg, *Examination of Logical Positivism,* pp. 275-280.

39. See Neurath, "Sociology and Physicalism," [1932] in Ayer, ed., *Logical Positivism,* pp. 282-317; and Neurath, "Universal Jargon and Terminology," *Proceedings of the Aristotelian Society,* 41 (1940-41), 127-148.

CHAPTER 13

1. "Ich fürchte, wir werden Gott nicht los, weil wir noch an die Grammatik glauben. . . ." Friedrich Nietzsche, "Die 'Vernunft' in der Philosophie," *Götzendämmerung, oder Wie man mit dem Hammer philosophiert* (1889), Sect. 5.

2. On Mauthner see Fritz Mauthner, *Prager Jugendjahre: Erinnerungen* [1918] (Frankfurt, 1969); Mauthner, "Fritz Mauthner," in Raymund Schmidt, ed., *Die Philosophie der Gegenwart in Selbstdarstellungen* (Leipzig, 1922), 3:121-144; Max Krieg, *Fritz Mauthner's Kritik der Sprache: Eine Revolution in der Philosophie* (Munich, 1914); Walter Eisen, "Fritz Mauthner," *Kantstudien,* 29 (1924), 321-324; Alois Rzach, "Fritz Mauthner," *NOB,* 3 (1926), 144-151; Theodor Kappstein, *Fritz Mauthner: Der Mann und Sein Werk* (Berlin, 1926); Gershon Weiler, "On Fritz Mauthner's Critique of Language," *Mind,* 67 (1958), 80-87; Weiler, "Fritz Mauthner: A Study in Jewish Self-Rejection," *YLBI,* 8 (1963), 136-148; Weiler, "Fritz Mauthner as an Historian," *History and Theory,* 4 (1964), 57-71; Weiler, "Mauthner, Fritz," *EP,* 5 (1967), 221-

224; Joachim Thiele, "Zur 'Kritik der Sprache': Briefe von Fritz Mauthner an Ernst Mach," *Muttersprache*, 76 (1966), 78-85.

3. On Landauer see Max Brod, *Streitbares Leben* (Munich, 1960), pp. 89-91; Wolf Kalz, *Gustav Landauer: Kultursozialist und Anarchist* (Meisenheim, 1967); Werner Kraft, "Ludwig Wittgenstein und Karl Kraus" [1961], in *Rebellen des Geistes* (Stuttgart, 1968), pp. 109-111.

4. Weiler, "On Fritz Mauthner's Critique," p. 82.

5. George Sylvester Viereck, *Glimpses of the Great* (London, 1930), p. 341.

6. On Hofmannsthal's crisis see Gotthart Wunberg, *Der frühe Hofmannsthal: Schizophrenie als dichterische Struktur* (Stuttgart, 1965), pp. 106-117; Richard Brinkmann, "Hofmannsthal und die Sprache," *DVLG*, 35 (1961), 69-95; Manfred Hoppe, *Literatentum, Magie und Mystik im Frühwerk Hugo von Hofmannsthals* (Berlin, 1968), esp. pp. 75-95.

7. On Stöhr see Prof. Dr. Hoffmann [of Vienna], "Sprachliche Logik und Mathematik," *Archiv für systematische Philosophie*, 19 (1913), 43-49; Felix M. Cleve, *The Giants of Pre-Socratic Philosophy: An Attempt to Reconstruct Their Thoughts*, 2 vols., (The Hague, 1965), pp. xxix-xxxviii, 35-134, 453-544 [the dedication reads in part: "To Adolf Stöhr (1855-1921), whose philosophy, as Ernst Mach predicted, 'will be understood and admired in 200 years.' "]; Franz Austeda, "Stöhr, Adolf," *EP*, 8 (1967), 18-19.

8. Stöhr's *Algebra der Grammatik* (Leipzig, 1898) was not available to me. On it see Ernst Mach, *The Analysis of Sensations* [1900] (New York, 1959), pp. 227-230, 303, 318.

9. "Die Psychologie ist in der unangenehmen Nötigung, sich bei der Bennenung und Behandlung ihres Gegenstandes einer bildlichen Sprache zu bedienen, die für solche Zwecke nicht geworden ist. Die Sprache ist ursprünglich ein Ausdruck für Tun und Erleiden." Stöhr, *Psychologie* (Vienna, 1917), p. 12.

10. "In der Tat ist die Geschichte der Logik und ein grosser Teil der Geschichte der Philosophie die Geschichte des Ringens mit der Glossomorphie und den Metaphern; die Geschichte des Kampfes des werdenden Denkens mit dem herrschenden Reden." Stöhr, *Lehrbuch der Logik in psychologisierender Darstellung* (Vienna, 1910), p. 409.

11. Cleve, *Giants of Pre-Socratic Philosophy*, p. 543.

12. Stöhr, *Heraklit* (Vienna, 1920).

13. See Ferdinand Ebner, *Schriften* (Munich, 1963), 1:582-583, 805-806, 1068.

14. On Wahle see Friedrich Flinker, *Über Wirklichkeit und Logik: Eine kritische Darlegung der Lehre Richard Wahles* (Cernauti, 1924); Sophus Hochfeld, *Die Philosophie Richard Wahles und Johannes Rehmkes Grundwissenschaft* (Potsdam, 1926); Austeda, "Wahle, Richard," *EP*, 8 (1967), 275-276.

15. See Jones, 1:123-127, 179, and Arthur Schnitzler, *Jugend in Wien* (Vienna, 1968), p. 96.

16. Wahle, "Über die geometrische Methode des Spinoza," *SKAW-Wien*, Phil-Hist. Klasse, 116 (1888), 431-452; Wahle, "Die Glückseligkeitslehre der 'Ethik' des Spinoza," *ibid.*, 119 (1889), Heft 11, pp. 1-44.

17. Wahle, *Entstehung der Charaktere* (Munich 1928), pp. 47-58.

18. "Man muss sagen, Kant hat die Erkenntnistheorie in desolatem Zustande vollkommener Konfusion zurückgelassen." "So haben wir die Lehren Herbarts ziemlich eingehend betrachtet—ein Bündel interessanter Fehler; und er war noch einer der besten Männer!" "In der Philosophie sind offensichtlich alle

möglichen Kategorien erschöpft und nunmehr kann jeder über den Agnostizismus hinwegsehende und hinweggehende Versuch leicht als Unsinn erkannt werden." Wahle, *Die Tragikomödie der Weisheit* (Vienna, 1915), pp. 364, 373, 406.

19. "dass das volle Wort von dem leeren nicht unterschieden wird, und dass sich in der Form des Abstrakten jede Ungenauigkeit, Fehlerhaftigkeit, Lüge und jede listige Phrase breitmachen kann." *Ibid.*, p. 414.

20. On Kraus's life see Leopold Liegler, *Karl Kraus und sein Werk* (Vienna, 1920); Heinrich Fischer, "The Other Austria and Karl Kraus," in Hans José Rehfisch, ed., *In Tyrannos: Four Centuries of Struggle Against Tyranny in Germany* (London, 1944), pp. 311-328; Béla Menczer, "Karl Kraus and the Struggle Against the Modern Gnostics," *Dublin Review*, 224 (Oct.-Dec., 1950), 32-52; Sigismund von Radecki, *Wie ich glaube* (Cologne, 1953), pp. 11-44 [vivid memoirs by a friend]; Kraft, *Karl Kraus: Beiträge zum Verständnis seines Werkes* (Salzburg, 1956); Hans Mayer, "Karl Kraus und die Nachwelt," *Sinn und Form*, 9 (1957), 934-949; Willy Haas, *Die literarische Welt: Erinnerungen* (Munich, 1960), pp. 22-27 [trenchant]; Caroline Kohn, *Karl Kraus* (Stuttgart, 1966); Wilma Abeles Iggers, *Karl Kraus: A Viennese Critic of the Twentieth Century* (The Hague, 1967); Frank Field, *The Last Days of Mankind: Karl Kraus and His Vienna* (London, 1967); Hans Weigel, *Karl Kraus oder die Macht der Ohnmacht: Versuch eines Motivenberichts zur Erhellung eines vielfachen Lebenswerkes* (Vienna, 1968) [chronological catena of excerpts]; Fritz J. Raddatz, "Der blinde Seher: Überlegungen zu Karl Kraus," *Merkur*, 22 (1968), 517-532. An indispensable tool is Friedrich Jenaczek, *Zeittafeln zur 'Fackel': Themen, Ziele, Probleme* (Munich, 1965).

21. ". . . weil ich, in meiner unfreien Sprachauffassung befangen, die sozusagen eine prästabilierte Harmonie der Sprachen und der Sphären annimmt, die Kunst zwar oberhalb des Verstandes erlebe, aber nicht unterhalb." Karl Kraus, "Ein neuer Mann," *Die Fackel*, Nr. 546-550 (July, 1920), p. 50. On Kraus's view of language see Walter Benjamin, "Karl Kraus" [1931], in *Schriften* (Frankfurt, 1955), 2:159-195; Lucien Goldmann, "Un grand polémiste: Karl Kraus" [1945], in *Recherches dialectiques*, 2d ed. (Paris, 1959), pp. 229-235; Erich Heller, *The Disinherited Mind: Essays in Modern German Literature and Thought* (London, 1952), pp. 183-201; J. P. Stern, "Karl Kraus's Vision of Language," *Modern Language Review*, 61 (1966), 71-84 [penetrating].

22. "An vieles, was ich erst erlebe, kann ich mich schon erinnern." Quoted in Kraft, *Karl Kraus*, p. 84.

23. Kraus, *Worte in Versen, Werke*, 7 (Munich, 1959), 236-237.

24. Haas, *Die literarische Welt*, pp. 23-26. For an even more damaging portrait see Fritz Wittels, "The 'Fackel'-Neurosis," in Hermann Nunberg and Ernst Federn, eds., *Minutes of the Vienna Psychoanalytic Society*. (New York, 1967), 2:383-393 [paper of Jan. 12, 1910]. Wittels followed with a sardonic *roman à clef* on Kraus, *Ezechiel der Zugereiste* (Berlin, 1910).

25. On Ludwig Wittgenstein's life see Ludwig Hänsel, "Ludwig Wittgenstein," *Wissenschaft und Weltbild*, 4 (1951), 274-277 [knew Wittgenstein as a prisoner of war in Italy]; Georg Henrik von Wright, "Biographical Sketch" [1955], in Norman Malcolm, *Ludwig Wittgenstein: A Memoir* (London, 1958), pp. 1-22; Paul Engelmann, *Letters from Ludwig Wittgenstein with a Memoir*, ed. B. F. McGuiness (Oxford, 1967); Ludwig von Ficker, "Rilke und der unbekannte Freund," in *Denkzettel und Danksagungen: Aufsätze, Reden*

(Munich, 1967), pp. 199-221; Stephen Toulmin, "Ludwig Wittgenstein," *Encounter*, 32 (Jan., 1969), 58-71.

26. On Karl Wittgenstein see Georg Günther, "Karl Wittgenstein und seine Bedeutung für den Aufbau und die Entwicklung der österreichischen Volkswirtschaft," *NOB*, 4 (1927), 156-163.

27. "Überhaupt hat der Fortschritt das an sich, dass er viel grösser ausschaut, als er wirklich ist." Used as an epigraph in Ludwig Wittgenstein, *Philosophical Investigations* (Oxford, 1953), p. viii.

28. Engelmann, *Letters*, p. 123.

29. Ficker, *Denkzettel*, pp. 201-204. See also Wittgenstein, *Briefe an Ludwig von Ficker* (Salzburg, 1969), for twenty-nine letters written to Ficker between 1914 and 1919.

30. See Wittgenstein's letter of March 31, 1917, in Engelmann, *Letters*, p. 4.

31. See Wittgenstein's letter of Nov. 16, 1914 in Ficker, *Denkzettel*, p. 205.

32. Engelmann, *Letters*, p. 80.

33. On Wittgenstein's philosophy see Wolfgang Stegmüller, *Hauptströmungen der Gegenwartsphilosophie*, 3d ed., (Stuttgart, 1965), pp. 526-696, 713-715; Malcolm, "Wittgenstein, Ludwig Josef Johann," *EP*, 8 (1967), 327-340 [with extensive bibliography]; K. T. Fann, ed., *Ludwig Wittgenstein: The Man and His Philosophy* (New York, 1967) [an anthology of thirty articles]; Arne Naess, *Four Modern Philosophers: Carnap, Wittgenstein, Heidegger, Sartre* (Chicago, 1968), pp. 67-171.

34. Wittgenstein, *Tractatus Logico-Philosophicus* (London, 1922), pp. 1-2.

35. *Ibid.*, p. 146.

36. It was finally published as Waismann, *The Principles of Linguistic Philosophy*, ed. R. Harré (London, 1965); on Wittgenstein see Waismann, *Principles*, pp. 307-320. For a letter from Wittgenstein to Waismann in early July, 1929, see H. L. Mulder, "Wissenschaftliche Weltauffassung: Der Wiener Kreis," *Journal of the History of Philosophy*, 6 (1968), 389-390. On Waismann see Stuart Hampshire, "Friedrich Waismann 1896-1959," *Proceedings of the British Academy*, 46 (1960), 309-317; Rudolf Carnap, "Autobiography" [1963], repr. in Fann, ed., *Ludwig Wittgenstein*, pp. 36-37; and B. F. McGuiness, "Vorwort des Herausgebers," in Waismann, *Wittgenstein und der Wiener Kreis: Aus dem Nachlass*, (Oxford, 1967), pp. 11-31.

37. One of these is reprinted in Wittgenstein, "Lecture on Ethics" [1929 or 1930], *Philosophical Review*, 74 (1965), 1-12. See also Wittgenstein, *Preliminary Studies for the 'Philosophical Investigations' Generally Known as the Blue and Brown Books* [1933-1935] (Oxford, 1958); G. E. Moore, "Wittgenstein's Lectures in 1930-33," *Mind*, 63 (1954), 1-15, 289-316; 64 (1955), 1-27.

38. Kraus, "Zur Sprachlehre," *Die Fackel*, Nr. 572-576 (June, 1921), p. 1. In an otherwise excellent analysis Werner Kraft mistakenly reports the date of publication as being July, 1920. See Kraft, "Ludwig Wittgenstein und Karl Kraus" [1961], in *Rebellen des Geistes* (Stuttgart, 1968), pp. 102-134, esp. 120.

39. Paul Feyerabend, "Herbert Feigl: A Biographical Sketch," in *Mind, Matter, and Method: Essays in Philosophy and Science in Honor of Herbert Feigl* (Minneapolis, 1966), p. 8.

40. Charles Parsons, "Mathematics, Foundations of," *EP*, 5 (1967), 204. A useful introduction is Arend Heyting, *Intuitionism: An Introduction*, 2d ed. (Amsterdam, 1966), pp. 1-12.

41. See S. Morris Engel, "Schopenhauer's Impact on Wittgenstein," *Journal of the History of Philosophy*, 7 (1969), 285-302. For parallels to Nietzsche see Erich Heller, "Ludwig Wittgenstein: Unphilosophical Notes," *Encounter*, 13 (Sept., 1959), 40-48.
42. Hampshire, "Friedrich Waismann," p. 316.
43. See Hänsel, "Ludwig Wittgenstein," p. 276.
44. Wolfe Mays, "Recollections of Wittgenstein," in Fann, ed., *Ludwig Wittgenstein*, p. 83.
45. Engelmann, *Letters*, pp. 92-93.
46. Rush Rhees, "Conversations on Freud," in Cyril Barrett, ed., *Ludwig Wittgenstein: Lectures and Conversations on Aesthetics, Psychology and Religious Belief* (Berkeley and Los Angeles, 1967), pp. 41-52.

CHAPTER 14

1. On Buber see Martin Buber, "Autobiographical Fragments," in Paul Arthur Schilpp and Maurice Friedman, eds., *The Philosophy of Martin Buber* (La Salle, Ill., 1967), pp. 3-39; Hans Kohn, *Martin Buber: Sein Werk und seine Zeit: Ein Beitrag zur Geistesgeschichte Mitteleuropas 1880-1930* [1930], 3d ed. (Cologne, 1961); Bernhard Caspar, *Das dialogische Denken: Eine Untersuchung der religionsphilosophischen Bedeutung Franz Rosenzweigs, Ferdinand Ebners und Martin Bubers* (Freiburg, 1967), pp. 17-68, 270-381.
2. On the Hasidic dynasty at Sadagora see Lucy S. Dawidowicz, ed., *The Golden Tradition: Jewish Life and Thought in Eastern Europe* (Boston, 1967), pp. 195-200.
3. See Franz Rosenzweig, *Der Stern der Erlösung* (Frankfurt, 1921). On Rosenzweig see Samuel Hugo Bergmann, *Faith and Reason: An Introduction to Modern Jewish Thought* (New York, 1961), pp. 55-80.
4. On Ebner see Ferdinand Ebner, *Schriften*, vol. 2 (Munich, 1963), 551-1105 [diaries and autobiography]; vol. 3 (Munich, 1965) [letters of 1912-1931]; Josef Rauscher, "Von Mauthner zu Ebner: Sprachkritik und Sprachwirklichkeit," *Hochland*, 22 (1924-25), 86-94; Rauscher, "Ferdinand Ebner," *Hochland*, 30 (1933), 86-89; Theodor Steinbüchel, *Der Umbruch des Denkens: Die Frage nach der christlichen Existenz erläutert an Ferdinand Ebners Menschdeutung* (Regensburg, 1936; repr. Darmstadt, 1966); Ludwig von Ficker, "Erinnerung an Ferdinand Ebner" [1950], in *Denkzettel und Danksagungen: Aufsätze, Reden* (Munich, 1967), pp. 170-181, 339-343; Robert Braun, "Ferdinand Ebner und sein Vater," *Hochland*, 44 (1952), 525-533; Theodor Schleiermacher, "Ich und Du: Grundzüge der Anthropologie Ferdinand Ebners," *Kerygma und Dogma*, 3 (1957), 208-219; Paul Bormann, "Das Wort und die geistigen Realitäten: Zur Phänomenologie der Sprache und des Gesprächs," *Theologie und Glaube*, 49 (1959), 401-422; Eugen Thurnher, "Sprache, Denken, Sein: Zu Ferdinand Ebners Philosophie des Wortes," *Literaturwissenschaftliches Jahrbuch*, 1 (1960), 227-236; Franz Seyr, "Biographisches Nachwort," in Ebner, *Schriften*, 2:1109-1154; Caspar, *Das dialogische Denken*, pp. 198-269.
5. "dass es [das Wort] das 'Vehikel' des Verhältnisses zwischen dem Ich und dem Du sei, das heisst im letzten Grunde: des Verhältnisses zwischen dem Menschen und Gott. In diesem Verhältnis aber hat der Mensch sein geistiges Leben." Ebner, *Schriften*, 3:226 [letter of Aug. 11, 1918 to Luise Karpischek].

6. On Ebner's relation to Buber, Feuerbach, and Stöhr, see Ebner, "Versuch eines Ausblicks in die Zukunft" in *Schriften,* 1:805-819. *Das Wort und die geistigen Realitäten* is reprinted, *Schriften,* 1:75-342. On Ebner's affinity with the "Thou" rhetoric of expressionist drama see Wolfgang Rothe, "Der Mensch vor Gott: Expressionismus und Theologie," in Rothe, ed., *Expressionismus als Literatur: Gesammelte Schriften* (Bern, 1969), pp. 37-66, esp. 45-50.

CHAPTER 15

1. Freud's own accounts are found in Freud, "Zur Geschichte der psychoanalytischen Bewegung" [1914], in *GW,* 10 (London, 1946), 44-113; "Selbstdarstellung" [1925], in *GW,* 14 (London, 1948), 33-96. The indispensable source is Jones [Jones (1879-1958) first met Freud in April, 1908]. Reuben Fine, *Freud: A Critical Re-Evaluation of His Theories* (New York, 1962), contains a useful bibliography. For other bibliographies see Alexander Grinstein, ed., *Index of Psychoanalytic Writings,* 9 vols. (New York, 1956-1965); Norman Kiell, *Psychoanalysis, Psychology and Literature: A Bibliography* (Madison, 1963); George Mora, "The History of Psychiatry: A Cultural and Bibliographical Survey," *Psychoanalytic Review,* 52 (1965), 298-328. On terminology see Lewis W. Brandt, "Some Notes on Freudian Terminology," *JAPA,* 9 (1961), 331-339 [excellent analysis of German terms]; Jean Laplanche and J.-B. Pontalis, *Vocabulaire de la psychanalyse,* ed., Daniel Lagache (Paris, 1967) [traces changes in Freud's use of terms]; Ludwig Edelberg, *Encyclopedia of Psychoanalysis* (New York, 1968); Charles Rycroft, *A Critical Dictionary of Psychoanalysis* (London, 1968). Lilla Veszy-Wagner's Concordance *(Gesamtregister)* to Freud's writings in *GW,* 18 (Frankfurt, 1968), is a model of its kind.
2. Among the most revealing memoirs are Anna Freud Bernays, "My Brother Sigmund Freud," *American Mercury,* 51 (1940), 335-342; Ernst Simmel, "Sigmund Freud: The Man and His Work," *Psychoanalytic Quarterly,* 9 (1940), 163-176; Max Graf, "Reminiscences of Professor Sigmund Freud," *Psychoanalytic Quarterly,* 11 (1942), 465-476; Hanns Sachs, *Freud: Master and Friend* (Cambridge, Mass., 1946); Martin Freud, *Sigmund Freud: Man and Father* (New York, 1958); Martin Freud, "Who Was Freud?" in Josef Fraenkel, ed., *The Jews of Austria: Essays on Their Life, History and Destruction* (London, 1967), pp. 197-211 [by Freud's son]. On Freud's mother see Judith Bernays Heller, "Freud's Mother and Father: A Memoir," *Commentary,* 21 (1956), 418-421 [by Freud's niece].
3. Bernays, "My Brother Sigmund Freud," p. 341.
4. On Freud's ambivalence toward travel see John E. Gedo, "Freud's Self-Analysis and His Scientific Ideas," *American Imago,* 25 (1968-69), 99-118.
5. Max Eastman, *Great Companions: Critical Memoirs of Some Famous Friends* (London, 1959), pp. 129-131. Cf. Jones, 2:67.
6. Jones, 3:97. On Freud's cancer see Jones, 3:94-101, 497-521.
7. On the Medical Faculty of Vienna see Max Neuburger, "British Medicine and the Old Vienna Medical School," *Bulletin of the History of Medicine,* 12 (1942), 486-528; Hortense Koller Becker, "Carl Koller and Cocaine," *Psychoanalytic Quarterly,* 32 (1962), 309-373, esp. 311-317; Esmond R. Long, *A History of Pathology,* 2d ed. (New York, 1965), pp. 102-113; Erna Lesky, *Die Wiener medizinische Schule* (Graz, 1965) [exceptionally thorough].

8. See Fritz Valjavec, *Geschichte der abendländischen Aufklärung* (Vienna, 1961), pp. 210-218.

9. Quoted in Vincent Yardley Bowditch, *Life and Correspondence of Henry Ingersoll Bowditch* (Boston, 1902), 1:315-316. On Rokitansky see Carl von Rokitansky, *Selbstbiographie und Antrittsrede* [1876 and 1844], ed. Erna Lesky (Vienna, 1960); Theodor Meynert, "Karl Rokitansky: Ein Nachruf" [1878], in *Sammlung von populär-wissenschaftlichen Vorträgen über den Bau und die Leistungen des Gehirns* (Vienna, 1892), pp. 69-82; Lesky, "Carl von Rokitansky (1804-1878)," *NOB*, 12 (1957), 38-51.

10. See Adolf Kussmaul, *Jugenderinnerungen eines alten Arztes*, 3d ed. (Stuttgart, 1899), pp. 363-383, esp. 382-383 for the poem. See also Heinrich Buess, "Zur Frage des therapeutischen Nihilismus im 19. Jahrhundert," *Schweizerische Medizinische Wochenschrift*, 87 (1957), 444-447.

11. The French disillusionist Louis-Ferdinand Céline (1894-1961) began his literary career with a dissertation on Semmelweis: Louis-Ferdinand Céline, *La vie et l'oeuvre de Philippe-Ignace Semmelweis* (Paris, 1924; 5th ed., 1952). A more sober account appears in Lesky, *Wiener medizinische Schule*, pp. 210-219.

12. Fritz Wittels, "Freud's Scientific Cradle," *American Journal of Psychiatry*, 100 (1943-44), 525.

13. For a graphic account see C. O'Conor-Eccles, "The Hospital Where the Plague Broke Out," *Nineteenth Century*, 46 (1899), 591-602. On conditions in other Viennese hospitals see A. S. Levetus, *Imperial Vienna* (London, 1905), pp. 355-363; Arthur Schnitzler, *Jugend in Wien* (Vienna, 1968), pp. 199-204.

14. O'Conor-Eccles, "Hospital Where Plague Broke Out," p. 594.

15. Wittels, "Freud's Scientific Cradle," p. 527.

16. On Brücke see Ernst Theodor Brücke, "Ernst W. Brücke (1819-1892)," *NOB*, 5 (1928), 66-73 [by Brücke's grandson]; Brücke, *Ernst Brücke* (Vienna, 1928) [lists 140 works by Brücke]; Siegfried Bernfeld, "Freud's Earliest Theories and the School of Helmholtz," *Psychoanalytic Quarterly*, 13 (1944), 341-362, esp. 348-358; Bernfeld, "Freud's Scientific Beginnings," in *American Imago*, 6 (1949), 163-188; Jones, 1:40-70; Robert R. Holt, "Two Influences on Freud's Scientific Thought: A Fragment of Intellectual Biography," in Robert W. White, ed., *The Study of Lives* (New York, 1965), pp. 364-387; Peter Amacher, *Freud's Neurological Education and Its Influence on Psychoanalytic Theory* (New York, 1965), pp. 9-20.

17. See Ernst W. Brücke, *Die Physiologie der Farben für die Zwecke der Kunstgewerbe* (Leipzig, 1866; 2d ed., 1887). See also Brücke, *Die Darstellung der Bewegung durch die bildenden Künste* (1881); Brücke, *Nacht und Morgen des Michelangelo* (1890).

18. See Brücke, *Grundzüge der Physiologie und Systematik der Sprachlaute für Linguisten und Taubstummenlehrer* (Vienna, 1856; 2d ed., 1876); Brücke, *Neue Methode der phonetischen Transkription* (1863).

19. On Meynert see Dora Stockert-Meynert, *Theodor Meynert und seine Zeit: Zur Geistesgeschichte Österreichs in der zweiten Hälfte des 19. Jahrhunderts* (Vienna, 1930) [by Meynert's daughter]; Maria Dorer, *Historische Grundlagen der Psychoanalyse* (Leipzig, 1932), pp. 128-143, 148-152; James W. Papez, "Theodor Meynert (1833-1892)," in Webb Haymaker, ed., *The Founders of Neurology* (Springfield, Ill., 1953) pp. 64-67; Amacher, *Freud's Neurological*

Education, pp. 21-41; Lesky, *Wiener medizinische Schule,* pp. 373-405. Meynert's verse was published in *Gedichte* (1905).

20. For Freud's opinion of Leidesdorf see Freud, *Briefe 1873-1939,* 2d ed. (Frankfurt, 1968), pp. 153-156 [letter of June 8, 1885 in which Leidesdorf is the unnamed professor].

21. Schnitzler, *Jugend in Wien,* p. 265.

22. Meynert, *Psychiatry,* trans. Barney Sachs (New York, 1885), p. 5.

23. Jones, 1:72.

24. *Ibid.,* p. 309. See also Heinz Hartmann, "The Development of the Ego Concept in Freud's work" [1956], in Hartmann, *Essays on Ego Psychology* (New York, 1964), pp. 268-296.

25. On Freud's cocaine experiments see Jones, 1:86-108; Bernfeld, "Freud's Studies on Cocaine, 1884-1887," *JAPA,* 1 (1953), 581-613; Hortense Koller Becker, "Carl Koller," pp. 309-373; Alexander Schusdek, "Freud on Cocaine," *Psychoanalytic Quarterly* 34 (1965), 406-412.

26. "Sie wissen, ich war immer einer der schönsten Fälle von männlicher Hysterie." Freud, *Traumdeutung,* 8th ed. (London, 1942), p. 439. See also Freud, *Aus den Anfängen der Psychoanalyse* (London, 1950), pp. 56-57 [letter of Aug. 29, 1888 to Fliess on Meynert's dogmatism]; Freud, *Briefe,* pp. 40-42, 105-106 [letters of Oct. 5, 1882, and Feb. 14, 1884, to Martha Bernays on Meynert's kindness].

27. On Krafft-Ebing see Berta Szeps, *My Life and History* (New York, 1939), pp. 124, 164-166; Ernst van den Haag, "Introduction," in Richard Krafft-Ebing, *Psychopathia Sexualis: A Medico-Forensic Study* [1886] (New York, 1965), pp. 7-19.

28. On Sacher-Masoch see Thérèse Bentzon, "Un Romancier galicien: M. Sacher-Masoch," *Revue des deux mondes,* 220 (Dec., 1875), 816-837; W. H. C., "Leopold Sacher-Masoch," *The Bookman,* 2 (1896), 401-404; Carl Felix von Schlichtegroll, *Sacher-Masoch und der Masochismus: Literarhistorische und kulturhistorische Studie* (Dresden, 1901); Richard M. Meyer, "Sacher-Masoch, Leopold von," *ADB,* 53 (1907), 681-682; R. Latzke, "Die Realisten: Leopold von Sacher-Masoch," in Eduard Castle, ed., *Geschichte der deutschen Literatur in Österreich-Ungarn* (Vienna, 1936), 1:955-973 [exceptionally judicious]; Reinhard Federmann, *Sacher-Masoch oder die Selbstvernichtung* (Graz, 1961); James Cleugh, *The First Masochist: A Biography of Leopold von Sacher-Masoch (1836-1895)* (London, 1967) [to be used with caution]. Laurenz Müllner, "Sacher-Masoch's *Vermächtnis Kains,*" in *Literatur- und Kunsthistorische Studien* (Vienna, 1895), pp. 32-45 was not available to me.

29. See Friedrich Hebbel, *Tagebücher,* in *Werke* (Munich, 1967), 5:270 [entry of Jan. 11, 1860]. Marie von Ebner-Eschenbach dramatized the events of 1846 in the tale *Jakob Szela* (1883). A memoir by Sacher-Masoch's father was not available to me: Sacher, *Polnische Revolutionen: Erinnerungen aus Galizien* (Prague, 1863).

30. Max Nordau, *Degeneration* (London, 1895), pp. 413-414.

31. Krafft-Ebing, *Psychopathia sexualis,* p. 31.

32. *Ibid.,* p. 30.

33. Szeps, *My Life and History,* p. 165.

34. Published as "Zur Ätiologie der Hysterie" [1896], in *GW,* 1 (London, 1952), 423-459.

35. Freud, *Aus den Anfängen der Psychoanalyse* (London, 1950), pp. 186-189 [letter of Sept. 21, 1897]. See Jones, 1:289-292; Leo Sadow et al., "The Process of Hypothesis Change in Three Early Psychoanalytic Concepts," *JAPA,* 16 (1968), 245-273, esp. 251-259.
36. On Breuer see Freud, "Obituary Notice: Josef Breuer," *IJP,* 6 (1925), 459-460; Hans Horst Meyer, "Josef Breuer 1842-1925," *NOB,* 5 (1928), 30-47; C. P. Oberndorf, "The Autobiography of Josef Breuer," *IJP,* 34 (1953), 64-67; John Sullivan, "From Breuer to Freud," *Psychoanalytic Review,* 46³ (1959), 69-90; Jones, 1:243-294; Erwin H. Ackerknecht, "Josef Breuer," *NOB,* 15 (1963), 126-130; Robert A. Kann, ed., *Marie von Ebner-Eschenbach-Dr. Josef Breuer: Ein Briefwechsel, 1889-1916* (Vienna, 1969).
37. See Josef Breuer, "Krankengeschichten: Beobachtung I: Frl. Anna O. . . ." in Breuer and Freud, *Studien über Hysterie* (Vienna, 1895), pp. 15-37. On her later life see Dora Edinger, "Bertha Pappenheim (1859-1936): A German Jewish Feminist," *Jewish Social Studies,* 20 (1958), 180-186; Edinger, "Einleitung," in Bertha Pappenheim, *Leben und Schriften* (Frankfurt, 1963), pp. 9-27; Jones, 1:245-248, 277.
38. See Pappenheim, *Sisyphus-Arbeit: Reisebriefe aus den Jahren 1911 und 1912* (Leipzig, 1924) [discusses the Balkans, Palestine, Galicia, and Russia].
39. Another exponent of hypnotism, the Hungarian Jew Moritz Benedikt (1835-1920), specified in *Hypnotismus und Magnetismus* (1889) that repression of sexual desire causes neurosis. On Benedikt see Moritz Benedikt, *Aus meinem Leben: Erinnerungen und Erörterungen* (Vienna, 1906); Dorer, *Historische Grundlagen,* p. 125, and Jones, 1:276-277.
40. The letter is published in *Gesnerus,* 14 (1957), 169-171 and translated in Paul F. Cranefield, "Joseph Breuer's Evaluation of His Contribution to Psychoanalysis," *IJP,* 39 (1958), 319-322.
41. George H. Pollock, "The Possible Significance of Childhood Object Loss in the Josef Breuer-Bertha Pappenheim (Anna O.)-Sigmund Freud Relationship," *JAPA,* 16 (1968), 711-739. On additional differences of method between Breuer and Freud see Nathan Schlessinger et al., "The Scientific Style of Breuer and Freud in the Origins of Psychoanalysis," *JAPA,* 15 (1967), 404-422.
42. On Fliess see Ernst Kris, "Einleitung," in Freud, *Aus den Anfängen der Psychoanalyse* (London, 1950), pp. 9-48; Schusdek, "Freud's 'Seduction Theory': A Reconstruction," *Journal of the History of the Behavioral Sciences,* 2 (1966), 159-166; Walter A. Stewart, *Psychoanalysis: The First Ten Years* (New York, 1967); Jones, 1:316-383.
43. For a sample of Fliess's virtuosity at manipulating numbers, see Wilhelm Fliess, "Der Ablauf des Lebens und seine Kritiker," *Annalen der Naturphilosophie,* 10 (1911), 314-350.
44. The *Entwurf* is published in Freud, *Aus den Anfängen der Psychoanalyse* (London, 1950), pp. 297-384, and summarized in Karl H. Pribram, "The Neuropsychology of Sigmund Freud," in A. J. Bachrach, ed., *Experimental Foundations of Clinical Psychology* (New York, 1962), pp. 442-468.

CHAPTER 16

1. Jones, 1:322-323.
2. "Ich habe wie Sie eine unbändige Zuneigung zu Wien und Österreich, obschon ich, vielleicht nicht wie Sie, seine Abgründe kenne." Ernst Lothar, *Das*

Wunder des Überlebens: Erinnerungen und Ergebnisse (Vienna, 1961), p. 37.

3. "Österreich-Ungarn ist nicht mehr. Anderswo möchte ich nich leben. Emigration kommt für mich nicht in Frage. Ich werde mit dem Torso weiterleben und mir einbilden, dass es das Ganze ist." *Ibid.*, p. 37.

4. "der Hysterische leide grösstenteils an Reminiszensen." Freud and Breuer, *Studien über Hysterie* (1895), in *GW*, 1 (London, 1952), 86.

5. See the case of "Fräulein Elisabeth von R...." *ibid.*, pp. 196-251, esp. 222-224, 227. For an analysis of the case-history "Katharina . . ." (1895) as though it were a novella see Ludwig Rohner, *Der deutsche Essay: Materialien zur Geschichte und Ästhetik einer literarischen Gattung* (Neuwied, 1966), pp. 228-239.

6. Two scintillating articles on Freud's affinity with Habsburg society are Zevedei Barbu, "The Historical Pattern of Psycho-analysis," *British Journal of Sociology*, 3 (1952), 64-76, and Alfred Schick, "The Cultural Background of Adler's and Freud's Work," *American Journal of Psychotherapy*, 18 (1964), 7-24. A revised version of the latter is Schick, "The Vienna of Sigmund Freud," *Psychoanalytic Review*, 55 (1968-69), 529-551.

7. On political overtones in Freud's dreams see Immanuel Velikovsky, "The Dreams Freud Dreamed," *Psychoanalytic Review*, 28 (1941), 487-511; Alexander Grinstein, *On Sigmund Freud's Dreams* (Detroit, 1968) [traces literary allusions in nineteen dreams of 1895-1899].

8. Friedrich Hacker, "Psychologia Austriaca: Der österreichische Anteil an die Lehre Sigmund Freuds," *Forum*, 5 (1958), 54-56. For a psychoanalysis of bureaucracy see Fedor Vergin, *Das unbewusste Europa: Psychoanalyse der europäischen Politik* (Vienna, 1931), pp. 29-54. On Franz Joseph and his post-1918 heritage see Vergin, *Unbewusste Europa*, pp. 78-83, 161-170, 245-254.

9. Freud, "Zur Geschichte der psychoanalytischen Bewegung" [1914], in *GW*, 10 (London, 1946), 51-52.

10. See Max Eastman, *Heroes I have Known* (New York, 1942), p. 264. For photographs of Freud's flat see *Du*, 11 (Oct., 1951), 27-36; Joost A. M. Meerloo, "Freud, the Creative Scientist: Reflections upon Some Pictures of Sigmund Freud," *Psychoanalytic Review*, 44 (1957), 220-224. Most of the books in Freud's personal library are listed in Nolan D. C. Lewis and Carney Landis, "Freud's Library," *Psychoanalytic Review*, 44 (1957), 327-354 [lists 814 titles now in the possession of the New York Psychiatric Institute].

11. Eastman, *Great Companions: Critical Memoirs of Some Famous Friends* (London, 1959), p. 129.

12. Jones, 2:439. On Tarock see also Jones, 1:362; 2:428.

13. Mór Jókai, *Black Diamonds* [1870] (New York, 1896), p. 173.

14. Hermann Bahr, *Selbstbildnis* (Berlin, 1923), p. 210. For a fanciful view of Tarock see Fritz von Herzmanovsky-Orlando, *Maskenspiel der Genien, Werke*, 2 (Munich, 1958), pp. 21-23 [concerns a state called Tarockanien whose constitution is based on rules of the game].

15. See Victor A. Oswald, Jr. and Veronica Pinter Mindess, "Schnitzler's 'Fräulein Else' and the Psychoanalytic Theory of Neuroses," *Germanic Review*, 26 (1951), 279-288; Frederick J. Beharriell, "Schnitzler's Anticipation of Freud's Dream Theory," *Monatshefte für deutschen Unterricht*, 45 (1953), 81-89; Beharriell, "Freud's Double: Arthur Schnitzler," *JAPA*, 10 (1962), 722-730; Herbert I. Kupper and Hilda S. Rollmann-Branch, "Freud and Schnitzler—(Doppelgänger)," *JAPA*, 7 (1959), 109-126; Heinz Politzer, "Diagnose und

Dichtung: Zum Werk Arthur Schnitzlers," in *Das Schweigen der Sirenen: Studien zur deutschen und österreichischen Literatur* (Stuttgart, 1968), pp. 110-141; Robert O. Weiss, "The Psychoses in the Works of Arthur Schnitzler," *German Quarterly*, 41 (1968), 377-400 [classifies "psychotic" symptoms manifested by characters in thirty of Schnitzler's works].

16. Freud, "Bruchstück einer Hysterie-Analyse" [1905], in *GW*, 5 (London, 1942), 203n. See Freud's letter of May 8, 1906 to Schnitzler in Freud, *Briefe 1873-1939*, 2d ed. (Frankfurt, 1968), pp. 266-267. For early appreciations by Freud's followers see Theodor Reik, *Arthur Schnitzler als Psycholog* (Munich, 1913); Hanns Sachs, "Die Motivgestaltung bei Schnitzler," *Imago*, 2 (1913), 302-318.

17. "So habe ich den Eindruck gewonnen, dass Sie durch Intuition—eigentlich aber infolge feiner Selbstwahrnehmung—alles das wissen, was ich in mühseliger Arbeit in anderen Menschen aufgedeckt habe." Freud, *Briefe*, p. 357 [letter of May 14, 1922].

18. George Sylvester Viereck, *Glimpses of the Great* (London, 1930), p. 333.

19. "Die neue [Psychologie] wird ihre [der Gefühle] ersten Elemente suchen, die Anfänge in den Finsternissen der Seele, bevor sie noch an dem klaren Tag herausschlagen, diesen ganzen langwierigen, umständlichen, wirr verschlungenen Prozess der Gefühle, der ihre komplizierten Thatsachen am Ende in simplen Schlüssen über die Schwelle des Bewusstseins wirft." Bahr, *Die Überwindung des Naturalismus* [1891], in *Zur Überwindung des Naturalismus* (Stuttgart, 1968), p. 57.

20. On Freud's taste in novels see Peter Bruckner, "Sigmund Freuds Privatlektüre," *Psyche*, 15 (March, 1962), 881-901; 16 (July, 1962), 721-743; 16 (March, 1963), 881-895.

21. Nunberg and Federn, eds., *Minutes of the Vienna Psychoanalytic Society* (New York, 1962), 1:239 [paper of Nov. 13, 1907].

22. See Avicenna [Fritz Wittels,] "Die Lustseuche," *Die Fackel*, Nr. 238 (Dec. 16, 1907), pp. 1-24, esp. 9-10.

23. Repr. in Oskar Panizza, *Das Liebeskonzil und andere Schriften* (Neuwied, 1964), pp. 69-136.

24. See Ernst Kris, *Psychoanalytical Explorations in Art* (New York, 1952); Ernst Gombrich, *Art and Illusion: A Study in the Psychology of Pictorial Representation* (New York, 1960); Gombrich, "Psycho-Analysis and the History of Art" [1954], in *Meditations on a Hobby Horse and Other Essays on the Theory of Art* (London, 1963), pp. 30-44; Gombrich, "The Use of Art for the Study of Symbols," *American Psychologist*, 20 (1965), 34-50; Gombrich, "Freud's Aesthetics," *Encounter*, 26 (Jan., 1966), 30-40.

25. "zu einem Verfahren der schichtweisen Ausräumung des pathogenen psychischen Materials, welches wir gerne mit der Technik der Ausgrabung einer verschütteten Stadt zu vergleichen pflegten." Freud and Breuer, *Studien über Hysterie*, p. 201 [this passage is by Freud].

26. The term "Oedipus complex" was first used in Freud, "Beiträge zur Psychologie des Liebeslebens. I. Über einen besonderen Typus der Objektwahl beim Manne" [1910], in *GW*, 8 (London, 1943), 73. As early as October 15, 1897, Freud had written to Fliess that Sophocles' *Oedipus the King* captivates audiences because each hearer shudders to see his own infantile dream of incest unfold on stage. See Freud, *Aus den Anfängen der Psychoanalyse* (London, 1950), p. 193.

27. On Freud and the Greeks see Bernice S. Engle, "Melampus and Freud," *Psychoanalytic Quarterly*, 11 (1942), 83-86; Garfield Tourney, "Empedocles and Freud, Heraclitus and Jung," *Bulletin of the History of Medicine*, 30 (1956), 109-123; Tourney, "Freud and the Greeks," *Journal of the History of the Behavioral Sciences*, 1 (1965), 67-85; Walther Riese, "The Pre-Freudian Origins of Psychoanalysis," *Science and Psychoanalysis*, 1 (1958), 29-72, esp. 43-47 on Hippocrates; Mark D. Altschule, "Greek Revival," in *Roots of Modern Psychiatry: Essays in the History of Psychiatry* (New York, 1965), pp. 188-204.

28. Freud, *Die Traumdeutung*, 8th ed., in *GW*, 2/3 (London, 1942), 202-203, 198-199.

29. Freud, *Briefe*, pp. 27-32, esp. 30-31 [letter of July 23, 1882].

30. See Lewis W. Brandt, "Freud and Schiller," *Psychoanalytic Review*, 46⁴ (1959), 97-101.

31. David Bakan, *Sigmund Freud and the Jewish Mystical Tradition* (New York, 1958), esp. pp. 271-301.

32. Ernst Simon, "Sigmund Freud, the Jew," *YLBI*, 2 (1957), 270-305, esp. 290-292.

33. Manès Sperber, "Freud and His Psychoanalysis" [1954], in *The Achilles Heel* (Garden City, N. Y., 1960), pp. 146-171, esp. 165-171 [favors Alfred Adler].

34. Quoted in Max Graf, "Reminiscences of Professor Sigmund Freud," *Psychoanalytic Quarterly*, 11 (1942), 473.

35. Freud, "On Being of the B'nai B'rith: An Address to the Society of Vienna," *Commentary*, 1 (March, 1946), 23-24. A useful narrative of Freud's grapplings with Judaism is Earl A. Grollman, *Judaism in Sigmund Freud's World* (New York, 1965).

36. Freud dissects a number of Jewish jokes in *Der Witz und seine Beziehungen zum Unbewussten* [1905] in *GW*, 6 (London, 1940), 86-87, 123-124, 159. Freud's style is analyzed in Walter Schönau, *Sigmund Freuds Prosa: Literarische Elemente seines Stils* (Stuttgart, 1968) [stresses the influence of Lessing].

37. Jacques Lacan, "L'Instance de la lettre dans l'inconscient ou la raison depuis Freud" [1957], in *Écrits* (Paris, 1966), pp. 493-528, esp. 509-514. For another structuralist view of Freud's preoccupation with writing see Jacques Derrida, "Freud et la scène de l'écriture" [1966], in *L'Écriture et la différence* (Paris, 1967), pp. 293-340. A scintillating introduction to the entire structuralist movement appears in Anthony Wilden, "Lacan and the Discourse of the Other," in Jacques Lacan, *The Language of the Self: The Function of Language in Psychoanalysis* (Baltimore, 1968), pp. 159-311. See also Jan Miel, "Jacques Lacan and the Structure of the Unconscious," *Yale French Studies*, Nr. 36-37 (1966), 104-111.

38. P. C. Gordon Walker, "History and Psychology," *Sociological Review*, 37 (1945), 37-49, esp. 48.

39. Suzanne C. Bernfeld, "Freud and Archaeology," *American Imago*, 8 (1951), 107-128, esp. 119.

40. "unser Unbewusstes ist gegen die Vorstellung des eigenen Todes ebenso unzugänglich, gegen den Fremden ebenso mordlustig, gegen die geliebte Person ebenso zwiespältig (ambivalent) wie der Mensch der Urzeit." Freud, "Zeitgemässes über Krieg und Tod," in *GW*, 10 (London, 1946), 354.

41. See Georg Groddeck, *Über das Es* [1920] in *Psychoanalytische Schriften zur*

Psychosomatik (Wiesbaden, 1966), pp. 46-76. On Groddeck see Lawrence Durrell, "Studies in Genius. VI. Groddeck," *Horizon,* 17 (1948), 384-403; Egenolf Roeder von Diersburg, "Georg Groddeck's Philosophie des Es," *ZfphF,* 15 (1961), 131-138; Carl and Sylva Grossman, *The Wild Analyst: The Life and Work of George Groddeck* (New York, 1967) [overly laudatory].

42. "Es denkt: aber dass dies 'es' gerade jenes alte berühmte 'Ich' sei, ist, milde geredet, nur eine Annahme, eine Behauptung, vor allem keine 'unmittelbare Gewissheit.' " Nietzsche, *Jenseits von Gut und Bös: Vorspiel einer Philosophie der Zukunft* (1886), pt. 1, sect. 17. On Freud's references to Nietzsche see Bruce Mazlish, "Freud and Nietzsche," *Psychoanalytic Review,* 55 (1968-69), 360-375.

43. Franz Alexander, "The Need for Punishment and the Death Instinct," *IJP,* 10 (1929), 269.

44. See Wilhelm Reich, *Character Analysis,* 3d ed. (New York, 1949). On Reich see Philip Rieff, "The World of Wilhelm Reich," *Commentary,* 38 (Sept., 1964), 50-58; Paul Edwards, "Reich, Wilhelm," *EP,* 7 (1967), 104-115 [sympathetic]; Mary Higgins and Chester M. Raphael, eds., *Reich Speaks of Freud: Wilhelm Reich Discusses His Work and Relationship With Sigmund Freud* (New York, 1967) [this interview of 1952 reveals more about Reich than about Freud]; Paul A. Robinson, *The Freudian Left: Reich, Róheim, Marcuse* (New York, 1969), pp. 9-73; Ilse Ollendorf Reich, *Wilhelm Reich: A Personal Biography* (New York, 1969) [a candid memoir by Reich's third wife].

45. For earlier versions see Anton Ehrenzweig, "Unconscious Form-Creation in Art," *British Journal of Medical Psychology,* 20 (1948), 185-214; 22 (1949), 88-109; Ehrenzweig, "The Origin of the Scientific and the Heroic Urge: The Guilt of Prometheus," *IJP,* 30² (1949), 108-123; Ehrenzweig, *The Psycho-Analysis of Artistic Vision and Hearing: An Introduction to a Theory of Unconscious Perception* (London, 1953; 2d ed., New York, 1965); Ehrenzweig, "The Mastering of Creative Anxiety," in *Art and Artist* (Berkeley and Los Angeles, 1956), pp. 33-52; Ehrenzweig, "The Creative Surrender: A Comment on 'Joanna Field's' Book *An Experiment in Leisure,*" *American Imago,* 14 (1957), 193-210; Ehrenzweig, "A New Psychoanalytical Approach to Aesthetics," *British Journal of Aesthetics,* 2 (1961-62), 301-317. On Ehrenzweig see "Anton Ehrenzweig," *Studio International,* 173 (1967), 8.

46. Ehrenzweig, *The Hidden Order of Art: A Study in the Psychology of Artistic Imagination* (London, 1967), pp. 186, 197-205 [relates Goethe's *Faust* to Mozart's *The Magic Flute*].

47. Freud, "Das Unheimliche," [1919] in *GW,* 12 (London, 1947), p. 247. Ehrenzweig, *The Hidden Order,* pp. 194-195.

48. See Ilse Bry and Alfred H. Rifkin, "Freud and the History of Ideas: Primary Sources 1886-1910," *Science and Psychoanalysis,* 5 (New York, 1962), 6-36, esp. 28.

49. Freud assessed the scope of his movement in: Freud, "Das Interesse an der Psychoanalyse" [1913], in *GW,* 8 (London, 1943), 390-420.

50. "Psychoanalyse ist jene Geisteskrankheit, für deren Therapie sie sich hält." Karl Kraus, *Nachts* [1918], in *Beim Wort genommen* in *Werke,* 3 (Munich, 1955), p. 351. Wittels' pathography appears in Wittels, "Die Fackel-Neurosis," in Nunberg and Federn, *Minutes,* 2:382-393 [session of Jan. 12, 1910].

51. "Das Unterbewusstsein scheint nach den neuesten Forschungen so eine Art

Ghetto der Gedanken zu sein. Viele haben jetzt Heimweh." Kraus, *Nachts* in *Werke*, 3:349.

52. "Psychologie ist der Omnibus, der ein Luftschiff begleitet," *ibid.*, p. 349. For other aphorisms belittling Freud see *ibid.*, pp. 346-355. See also Kraus, "Die Psychoanalen," in *Worte in Versen*, *Werke*, 7 (Munich, 1959), 412-416.
53. Egon Friedell, *Kulturgeschichte der Neuzeit* [1927-1931] (Munich, 1965), pp. 1517-1533, esp. 1522.
54. On the early reception of psychoanalysis, see J. H. Schultz, "Psychoanalyse: Die Breuer-Freudschen Lehren, ihre Entwicklung und Aufnahme," *Zeitschrift für angewandte Psychologie*, 2 (1908-09), 440-497 [lists 172 titles including book reviews]. See also Wladimir G. Eliasberg, "Early Criticisms of Freud's Psychoanalysis: the Conscious versus the Unconscious," *Psychoanalytic Review*, 41 (1954), 347-353.
55. Alexander, *The Western Mind in Transition: An Eyewitness Story* (New York, 1960), pp. 56-57.

CHAPTER 17

1. The soundest surveys of Freud's disciples are Dieter Wyss, *Die tiefenpsychologischen Schulen von den Anfängen bis zur Gegenwart*, 2d ed. (Göttingen, 1966); Franz Alexander and Sheldon T. Selesnick, *The History of Psychiatry: An Evaluation of Psychiatric Thought and Practice from Prehistoric Times to the Present* (New York, 1966); Franz Alexander, Samuel Eisenstein, and Martin Grotjahn, eds., *Psychoanalytic Pioneers* (New York, 1966) [biographies of forty-one followers of Freud]; Vincent Brome, *Freud and His Early Circle* (New York, 1968).
2. See Max Graf, "Reminiscences of Professor Sigmund Freud," *Psychoanalytic Quarterly*, 11 (1943), 471-475.
3. See Wilhelm Stekel, "In Memoriam Herbert Silberer," *Fortschrittliche Sexualwissenschaft und Psychoanalyse*, 1 (1924), 408-420, esp. 415.
4. See Freud, "Über die weibliche Sexualität" [1931], in *GW*, 14 (London, 1948), 515-537.
5. Robert R. Holt, "Freud's Cognitive Style," *American Imago*, 22 (1965), 163-179, esp. 167.
6. For samples of Sadger's and Stekel's early work see Herman Nunberg and Ernst Federn, eds., *Minutes of the Vienna Psychoanalytic Society*, vols. 1 and 2 (New York, 1962-1967); vol. 3 is in preparation. Of special interest are Sadger's psychoanalysis of Lenau, *ibid.*, 1:62-69 [Nov. 28, 1906]; Stekel's analysis of Grillparzer, *ibid.*, 2:2-12 [Oct. 14, 1908]. On Stekel see Fritz Wittels, Review of Stekel, *The Interpretation of Dreams* (1944) in *Psychoanalytic Quarterly*, 14 (1945), 540-544.
7. See Herbert Silberer, *Problems of Mysticism and its Symbolism* (New York, 1917). On Silberer see Stekel, "In Memoriam Herbert Silberer," 408-420.
8. Repr. in Eduard Hitschmann, *Great Men: Psychoanalytical Studies* (New York, 1956) [lists Hitschmann's writings].
9. For a revised version see Graf, *From Beethoven to Shostakovich: The Psychology of the Composing Process* (New York, 1947). See also Graf, "Methodology of the Psychology of Poets," in Nunberg and Federn, *Minutes*, 1:259-269 [paper of Dec. 11, 1907]. On Graf see André Michel, *L'École freudienne devant la musique* (Paris, 1965), pp. 21-30, 447-477.

10. See Wittels, *Sigmund Freud: His Personality, His Teaching and His School* (London, 1924; rev. ed., New York, 1931); Wittels, "Revision of a Biography," *AJP*, 45 (1933), 745-749.

11. See Wittels "The Position of the Psychopath in the Psycho-Analytic System," *IJP*, 19 (1938), 471-488; Wittels, "Collective Defense Mechanisms Against Homosexuality," *Psychoanalytic Review*, 31 (1944), 19-33; Wittels, "Economic and Psychological Historiography," *AJS*, 51 (1945-46), 527-532; Wittels, "Heinrich von Kleist—Prussian Junker and Creative Genius: A Study in Bisexuality," *American Imago*, 11 (1954), 11-31. Wittels contributed seven papers to Nunberg and Federn, *Minutes*, including his psychoanalysis of Karl Kraus, *Minutes*, 2:382-393. On Wittels see Philip R. Lehmann, "Fritz Wittels," *Psychoanalytic Quarterly*, 20 (1951), 96-104 [lists eighty-two items by Wittels].

12. On Sachs see Hanns Sachs, *Freud: Master and Friend* (Cambridge, Mass., 1946); Ernest Jones, "Hanns Sachs," *IJP*, 27 (1946), 168-169; Felix Deutsch, "Hanns Sachs 1881-1947," *American Imago*, 4² (1946-47), 3-14; Rudolph M. Loewenstein, "In Memoriam: Hanns Sachs 1881-1947," *Psychoanalytic Quarterly*, 16 (1947), 151-156 [lists seventy-eight writings by Sachs].

13. See Sachs, *Gemeinsame Tagträume* (Vienna, 1924); Sachs, "What Would Have Happened If . . .", *American Imago*, 3⁴ (1942-46), 61-66.

14. Sachs, "The Delay of the Machine Age," *Psychoanalytic Quarterly*, 2 (1933), 404-423. On narcissism see Freud, "Zur Einführung des Narzissmus" [1914], in *GW*, 10 (London, 1946) 139-170.

15. Sachs, "Mission of the Movies," *Life and Letters Today*, 26 (1940), 261-268, esp. 266. Similar themes pervade Angelo Montani and Giulio Pietranera, "First Contribution to the Psycho-Analysis and Aesthetics of Motion-Picture" *(sic)* [1938], *Psychoanalytic Review*, 33 (1946), 177-196.

16. On Adler see Egon Friedell, "Exkurs über den Wert der Krankheit" [1927], in *Kulturgeschichte der Neuzeit* (Munich, 1965), pp. 68-82; Hertha Orgler, *Alfred Adler: The Man and His Work: Triumph over the Inferiority Complex* (London, 1939; 3d ed., 1963) [uncritical]; Phyllis Bottome, *Alfred Adler: Apostle of Freedom*-(London, 1939) [fulsome]; Lewis Way, *Adler's Place in Psychology: An Exposition of Individual Psychology* (New York, 1950; 2d ed., 1962); Heinz L. Ansbacher and Rowena R. Ansbacher, eds., *The Individual Psychology of Alfred Adler: A Systematic Presentation in Selections from His Writings* (New York, 1956; repr., 1964); Helene Papanek and Ernst Papanek, "Individual Psychology Today," *American Journal of Psychotherapy*, 15 (1961), 4-26 [excellent bibliography]; Carl Furtmüller, "Biographical Essay" [1946], in Alfred Adler, *Superiority and Social Interest: A Collection of Later Writings* (Evanston, Ill., 1964), pp. 311-393; Paul Rom, *Alfred Adler und die wissenschaftliche Menschenkenntnis* (Frankfurt, 1966); Brome, *Freud and His Early Circle* pp. 48-61, 212-218.

17. See Alfred Adler, "On the Psychology of Marxism," in Nunberg and Federn, *Minutes*, 2:172-178, esp. 174 [paper of March 10, 1909].

18. On Rank see: Ernest Jones, "Otto Rank," *IJP*, 21 (1940), 112-113; Fay Berger Karpf, *The Psychology and Psychotherapy of Otto Rank: An Historical and Comparative Introduction* (New York, 1953); Ira Progoff, *The Death and Rebirth of Psychology* (New York, 1956), pp. 188-253 [compares Rank with Adler and Jung]; Jesse Taft, *Otto Rank: A Biographical Study Based on Notebooks, Collected Writings, Therapeutic Achievements and Personal Asso-*

ciations (New York, 1958); Jack Jones, "Otto Rank: A Forgotten Heresy," *Commentary*, 30 (1960), 219-229 [perceptive]; Jones, "Rank, Otto," *IEES*, 13 (1968), 314-319; Anaïs Nin, *The Diary of Anaïs Nin, 1931-1934* (New York, 1966), pp. 269-300; Brome, *Freud and His Early Circle*, pp. 164-194.

19. For excerpts from his diaries of 1903 to 1905 see Taft, *Otto Rank*, pp. 3-52.
20. Otto Rank, *Beyond Psychology* (Camden, N. J., 1941), p. 289.
21. *Ibid.*, p. 16.
22. *Ibid.*, p. 290.
23. *Ibid.*, pp. 287-288.

CHAPTER 18

1. Useful histories of Bohemia and Moravia are Ernest Denis, *La Bohême depuis la Montagne-Blanche*, 2 vols. (Paris, 1903) [magisterial, pro-Czech]; Bertold Bretholz, *Geschichte Böhmens und Mährens*, 4 vols. (Reichenberg, 1921-1924); R. W. Seton-Watson, *A History of the Czechs and Slovaks* (London, 1943; repr. Hamden, Conn., 1965); Hermann Münch, *Böhmische Tragödie: Das Schicksal Mitteleuropas im Lichte der tschechischen Frage* (Braunschweig, 1949); Helmut Preidel, ed., *Die Deutschen in Böhmen und Mähren: Ein historischer Rückblick*, 2d ed. (Gräfelfing, 1952) [contains fourteen papers, many unduly nostalgic]; Karl Bosl, ed., *Handbuch der Geschichte der böhmischen Länder*, 4 vols. (Stuttgart, 1966-) [exhaustive]; Stanley Z. Pech, *The Czech Revolution of 1848* (Chapel Hill, N. C., 1969). Theories of Czech nationality are outlined in Eugen Lemberg, "Der Staat im Denken des tschechischen Volkes," *Jahrbücher für Geschichte Osteuropas*, 3 (1938), 357-394. On the language quarrel see Raimund Friedrich Kaindl, *Der Völkerkampf und Sprachenstreit in Böhmen im Spiegel der zeitgenössischen Quellen* (Vienna, 1927); Theodor Veiter, "Die Sudetenländer," in Karl Gottfried Hugelmann, ed., *Das Nationalitätenrecht des alten Österreich* (Vienna, 1934), pp. 289-428. On the role of Jews in the language quarrel see Guido Kisch, "Linguistic Conditions Among Czechoslovak Jewry: A Legal-Historical Study," *Historia Judaica*, 8 (1946), 19-32.
2. Madelaine R. Brown, "Arnold Pick (1851-1924)," in Webb Haymaker, ed., *The Founders of Neurology* (Springfield, Ill., 1953), p. 202.
3. Emilie de Laveleye, "Würzburg and Vienna: Scraps of a Diary," *Living Age*, 164 (1884), 122. For further controversies concerning Czech schools see Walter Goldinger, "The Nationality Question in Austrian Education," *Austrian History Yearbook*, 3.3 (1967), 136-156.
4. See Berthold Sutter, *Die badenischen Sprachenverordnungen von 1897: Ihre Genesis und ihre Auswirkungen vornehmlich auf die innerösterreichischen Alpenländer*, 2 vols. (Graz, 1960-1965).
5. M. J. Landa, "Bohemia and the War," *Contemporary Review*, 108 (1915), 100-104.
6. See Horst Glassl, *Der mährische Ausgleich* (Munich, 1967). On Moravia see Lillian Schacherl, *Mähren: Land der friedlichen Widersprüche* (Munich, 1968). On two neglected novelists of Moravian society see Peter Goldammer, "Jakob Julius David: Ein vergessener Dichter," *Weimarer Beiträge*, 5 (1959), 323-368; Karel Krejčí, *Oskar Jellinek: Leben und Werk* (Brünn, 1967).
7. On the German language in Prague see Fritz Mauthner, *Prager Jugendjahre: Erinnerungen* [1918] (Frankfurt, 1969) pp. 30-34, 48-50; Rainer Maria Rilke,

Briefe (Wiesbaden, 1950), 1:473; Peter Demetz, "The Czech Themes of R.
M. Rilke," *German Life and Letters*, 6 (1952-53), 35-49; Demetz, "Noch
Einmal: Prager Deutsch," *Literatur und Kritik*, 1 (Sept., 1966), 58-59; Willy
Haas, *Die literarische Welt: Erinnerungen* (Munich, 1960), pp. 10-11; Jo-
hannes Urzidil, *Da geht Kafka*, 2d ed. (Munich, 1966), p. 12; Pavel Trost,
"Und wiederum: Prager Deutsch," *Literatur und Kritik*, 1 (Dec., 1966), 107-
108 [disputes Urzidil and Demetz]; Emil Skala, "Das Prager Deutsch," in
Eduard Goldstücker, ed., *Weltfreunde: Konferenz über die Prager deutsche
Literatur* (Prague, 1967), pp. 119-125.

8. See Andrew G. Whiteside, *Austrian National Socialism Before 1918* (The
   Hague, 1962), pp. 87-111, esp. 105-108 [contains excellent bibliography];
   Othmar Feyl, "Sozialdemokratischer Revisionismus und Reformismus und die
   Anfänge des 'Nationalen Sozialismus' in Böhmen vor Hitler," in *Ost und West
   in der Geschichte des Denkens und der kulturellen Beziehungen* [Eduard
   Winter Festschrift] (East Berlin, 1966), pp. 700-714. See also Virginio
   Gayda, *Modern Austria* (London, 1915), pp. 326-337; Erik R. v. Kuehnelt-
   Leddihn, *Freiheit oder Gleichheit? Die Schicksalsfrage des Abendlandes* (Salz-
   burg, 1953), pp. 371-384, 571-578.

9. J. M. Wilson, "Remediable Defects in Our Conception of Elementary Edu-
   cation," *Contemporary Review*, 100 (1911), 49-59. See also Gayda, *Modern
   Austria*, pp. 68-69; Stanley B. Winters, "The Young Czech Party (1874-1914):
   An Appraisal," *Slavic Review*, 28 (1969), 426-444.

10. For evocations of Prague see Jan Neruda, *Kleinseitner Geschichten* [1878], ed.
    Josef Mühlberger (Munich, 1965); Johanna Baronin Herzogenberg, *Prag* (Mu-
    nich, 1966); Traugott Krischke, ed., *Einladung nach Prag* (Munich, 1966)
    [an anthology]; Demetz, "Die traurige altberühmte Stadt," *Die Zeit*, Nr. 13
    (April 2, 1968), p. 10.

11. See Ignát Herrmann, Jos. Teige, and Zickmund Winter, *Das Prager Ghetto*
    (Prague, 1903) [contains striking photographs]. On the underworld of the
    ghetto see Egon Erwin Kisch, *Die Abenteuer in Prag* (Vienna, 1920); Kisch,
    Prager Pitaval (Berlin, 1931).

12. See the reminiscences of Ernst Mach's daughter in K. D. Heller, *Ernst Mach:
    Wegbereiter der modernen Physik* (Vienna, 1964), pp. 16-17.

13. See "Flood at Prague," *Harper's Weekly*, 34 (1890), 799.

14. On intellectuals in Prague see Karl Kraus, "Elysisches," in *Worte in Versen*,
    Werke, 7 (Munich, 1959), 77-78; Demetz, *René Rilkes Prager Jahre* (Düssel-
    dorf, 1953), esp. pp. 89-112 on relations between Czechs and Germans; Haas,
    Die literarische Welt, pp. 9-76 [esp. on Werfel]; Max Brod, *Der Prager Kreis*
    (Stuttgart, 1966); Brod, *Streitbares Leben, 1884-1968*, 2d ed. (Munich, 1969);
    Urzidil, *Prager Triptychon* (Munich, 1960); Urzidil, *Da geht Kafka*; Hans
    Kohn, *Living in a World Revolution* (New York, 1964), pp. 1-89; Gustav
    Janouch, *Franz Kafka und seine Welt* (Vienna, 1965); Janouch, *Jaroslav
    Hašek* (Bern, 1967); Goldstücker, *Weltfreunde*.

15. Repr. in Karl Otten, ed., *Prosa jüdischer Dichter* (Stuttgart, 1959), pp. 153-
    201, 355-447. On Adler see *Prosa jüdischer Dichter*, pp. 625-628. Other useful
    anthologies of German writers at Prague are Oskar Wiener, ed., *Deutsche
    Dichter aus Prag* (Vienna, 1919); Rüdiger Engerth, ed., *Im Schatten des
    Hradschin: Kafka und sein Kreis* (Graz, 1965).

16. See Haas, "Der junge Max Brod: Persönliche Erinnerungen," *Tribüne*, 3
    (1964), 1075-1080; Paul Raabe, "Der junge Max Brod und der Indifferentis-

mus," in Goldstücker, *Weltfreunde,* pp. 253-269; Berndt W. Wessling, *Max Brod: Ein Portrait* (Stuttgart, 1969).

17. "Denn, ach! ich bin müde der uralten Regeln und Gesetze, aller Ursachen und Gründe und bete um Wunder unter Posaunenschlag und unter Donner und Blitz!" Paul Kornfeld, "Gebet um Wunder" [1920], repr. in Karl Otten, ed., *Schofar: Lieder und Legenden jüdischer Dichter* (Neuwied, 1962), p. 224. On Kornfeld see Manon Maren-Grisebach, "Paul Kornfeld," in Wolfgang Rothe, ed., *Expressionismus als Literatur* (Bern, 1969), pp. 519-530.

18. Kohn, *Living in a World Revolution,* pp. 33-34. See also Bruno Kisch, *Wanderungen und Wandlungen* (Cologne, 1966), pp. 48-49. The Moravian-born Catholic Rudolf Kassner wrote glowingly of his nurse in *Die Zweite Fahrt: Erinnerungen* (Zürich, 1946), pp. 26-37.

19. Sigmund Freud, *Aus den Anfängen der Psychoanalyse 1887-1902* (London, 1950), pp. 189-193 [letters of Oct. 3 and 15, 1897]. See Suzanne C. Bernfeld, "Freud and Archaeology," *American Imago,* 8 (1951), 107-128, esp. 115-123; Renée Gicklhorn, "The Freiberg Period of the Freud Family," *Journal of the History of Medicine and Allied Sciences,* 24 (1969), 37-43.

20. "In Barbara könnte man eine Frau des zwölften oder dreizehnten Jahrhunderts erblicken. Für Ferdinand wenigstens ist sie auf Goldgrund gemalt. Noch heute dünkt es ihn, dass selbst das Animalische seiner frühen Kindheit von Heiligung durchdrungen war." Franz Werfel, *Barbara, oder die Frömmigkeit* (Vienna, 1929), p. 82. On Werfel's theology see Adolf D. Klarmann, "Franz Werfel," in Rothe, *Expressionismus als Literatur,* pp. 410-425.

21. Haas, *Die literarische Welt,* pp. 38-40.

CHAPTER 19

1. "J'ay trouvé que la pluspart des Sectes ont raison dans une bonne partie de ce qu'elles avancent, mais non pas tant en ce qu'elles nient." Leibniz, letter to Nicolas Remond of Jan. 10, 1714 in *Die philosophischen Schriften,* ed. C. J. Gerhardt (Berlin, 1887; repr., Hildesheim, 1960), 3:607. A superlative account of Leibniz's thought appears in Lewis White Beck, *Early German Philosophy: Kant and His Predecessors* (Cambridge, Mass., 1969), pp. 196-240. On Leibniz in Austria see Robert Mühler, "Ontologie und Monadologie in der österreichischen Literatur des 19. Jahrhunderts," in Joseph Stummvoll, ed., *Die österreichische Nationalbibliothek: Festschrift Josef Bick* (Vienna, 1948), pp. 488-504.

2. On Bolzano see Eduard Winter, *Der Bolzanoprozess: Dokumente zur Geschichte der Prager Karlsuniversität im Vormärz* (Brünn, 1934); Winter, *Der Josefinismus und seine Geschichte: Beiträge zur Geistesgeschichte Österreichs 1740-1848* (Brünn, 1943); Winter, *Der böhmische Vormärz in Briefen B. Bolzano's an F. Příhonský (1824-1848)* (East Berlin, 1956); Winter, *Besnard Bolzano: Ein Denker und Erzieher im österreichischen Vormärz* (Graz, 1967). After resigning from the priesthood, Bohemian-born Eduard Winter (1896-) has lived in East Germany since World War Two.

3. See Winter, ed., *Wissenschaft und Religion im Vormärz: Der Briefwechsel Bernard Bolzanos mit Michael Josef Fesl 1822-1848* (East Berlin, 1965). On Fiebrich see Wilhelm Zeil, "Vinzenz Fiebrich—ein vergessener Bolzanist in Wien," in *Ost und West in der Geschichte des Denkens und der kulturellen Beziehungen* [Eduard Winter Festschrift] (East Berlin, 1966), pp. 540-548. A

useful abridgment of the *Wissenschaftslehre* is Bolzano, *Grundlegung der Logik: Ausgewählte Paragraphen aus der "Wissenschaftslehre, Band I und II,"* ed. Friedrich Kambartel (Hamburg, 1963).

4. See Bolzano, *Über das Verhältnis der beiden Volksstämme in Böhmen: Drei Vorträge im Jahre 1816 an der Hochschule zu Prag gehalten* (Vienna, 1849), esp. pp. 20-21, 45-47. See also Helmut Diwald, "Bernard Bolzano und der Bohemismus," in Diwald, ed., *Lebendiger Geist: Hans-Joachim Schoeps zum 50. Geburtstag* (Leiden, 1959), pp. 91-115.

5. On Lambert see Robert Zimmermann, "Lambert der Vorgänger Kants: Ein Beitrag zur Vorgeschichte der Kritik der reinen Vernunft," *Denkschriften der philosophisch-historischen Klasse*, Kaiserliche Akademie der Wissenschaften, 29 (Vienna, 1879), 1-74, esp. p. 20; Beck, *Early German Philosophy*, pp. 402-412.

6. Arnold Kowalewski, "Bolzano als Kronzeuge im Streit um die Religions-philosophie des Als Ob," *Annalen der Philosophie*, 3 (1923), 427-453.

7. "Wähle von allen dir möglichen Handlungen immer diejenige, die, alle Folgen erwogen, das Wohl des Ganzen, gleichviel in welchen Teilen, am meisten befördert." Cited in Winter, "Bernard Bolzano (1781-1848)," *NOB*, 16 (1965), 177.

8. Bolzano, *Von dem besten Staat* (Prague, 1932). On Bolzano's utopia see Franz Stephan Schindler, "Bolzano als Sozialpolitiker," *Deutsche Arbeit*, 8 (1908-09), 683-699; Arthur Salz, "Bernhard Bolzano's Utopie 'Vom besten Staat,'" *ASWSP*, 31 (1910), 498-519; Cyrill Horáček, "Bernhard Bolzano und seine Utopie, 'Vom Besten Staat,'" *Archiv für die Geschichte des Sozialismus*, 2 (1911-12), 68-97.

9. See Edmund Husserl, *Logische Untersuchungen* (Halle, 1901), 2:225-227; Melchior Palágyi, *Kant und Bolzano: Eine kritische Parallele* (Halle, 1902); Hugo Bergmann, *Das philosophische Werk Bernard Bolzanos, mit Benutzung ungedruckter Quellen kritisch untersucht* (Halle, 1909).

10. On Reform Catholicism see Christoph Thienen-Adlerflycht, *Graf Leo Thun im Vormärz: Grundlagen des böhmischen Konservatismus im Kaisertum Österreich* (Graz, 1967) [highly perceptive with an exceptionally fine bibliography]; Matthias Murko, *Deutsche Einflüsse auf die Anfänge der böhmischen Romantik* (Graz, 1897); Eugen Lemberg, *Grundlagen des nationalen Erwachens in Böhmen: Geistesgeschichtliche Studie am Lebensgang Joseph Georg Meinerts (1773-1844)* (Reichenberg, 1932); Johannes Urzidil, *Goethe in Böhmen*, 3d ed. (Zürich, 1965); Winter, *Romantismus, Restauration und Frühliberalismus im österreichischen Vormärz* (Vienna, 1968). See also works on Bolzano in n. 2 above.

11. See Oskar Kraus, "The Special Outlook and Tasks of German Philosophy in Bohemia," *SEER*, 13 (1934-1935), 345-349. Leonhardi's *Der Philosophenkongress als Versöhnungsrat* (1869) was not available to me.

12. On Günther see Ernst Karl Winter, "Anton Günther: Ein Beitrag zur Romantikforschung," *Zeitschrift für die gesamte Staatswissenschaft*, 88 (1930), 281-333; Joseph Pritz, *Glauben und Wissen bei Anton Günther: Eine Einführung in sein Leben und Werk mit einer Auswahl seiner Schriften* (Vienna, 1963); Roger Bauer, *Der Idealismus und seine Gegner in Österreich* (Heidelberg, 1966), pp. 80-104.

13. On Herbart's development see Zimmermann, "Perioden in Herbart's philoso-

phischem Geistesgang: Eine biographische Studie," *SKAW-Wien*, Phil.-Hist. Klasse, 83 (1876), 179-234; G. F. Stout, "The Herbartian Psychology," *Mind*, 13 (1888), 321-338, 473-498; Charles de Garmo, *Herbart and the Herbartians* (New York, 1896); Benjamin B. Wolman, "The Historical Role of Johann Friedrich Herbart," in Wolman, ed., *Historical Roots of Contemporary Psychology* (New York, 1968), pp. 29-46.

14. See Zimmermann, "Über den Einfluss der Tonlehre auf Herbart's Philosophie," *SKAW-Wien*, Phil-Hist. Klasse, 73 (1873), 33-74.

15. See Wilhelm Jerusalem, "Robert Hamerlings 'Atomistik des Willens' " [1891], in *Gedanken und Denker: Gesammelte Aufsätze* (Vienna, 1905), pp. 113-121.

16. Zimmermann, *Anthroposophie* (Vienna, 1882), p. ix.

17. See C. S. Barach, *Kleine philosophische Schriften* (Vienna, 1878). On Barach see Ernst Topitsch, "Kant in Österreich," in *Philosophie der Wirklichkeit: Festschrift zum 80. Geburtstag Robert Reiningers* (Vienna, 1949), pp. 250-253; Johannes Volkelt, "Mein philosophischer Entwicklungsgang," in Raymund Schmidt, ed., *Die Philosophie der Gegenwart in Selbstdarstellungen*, 2d ed. (Leipzig, 1923), 1:216.

18. Augustin Smetana, *Geschichte eines Excommunicirten: Eine Selbstbiographie*, ed. Alfred Meissner (Leipzig, 1863).

19. On Zimmermann's relation to Bolzano, see Winter, ed., *Der böhmische Vormärz*, pp. 8-9, 65-66, 183-290. On Zimmermann's development see Bernhard Münz, "Zimmermann, Robert von," *ADB*, 45 (1900), 294-299; Friedrich Jodl, "Robert Zimmermann" [1899], in *Vom Lebenswege: Gesammelte Vorträge und Aufsätze* (Stuttgart, 1916), 1:433-440; Bernard Bosanquet, *A History of Aesthetic*, 2d ed. (London, 1904; repr., New York, 1957), pp. 373-381; Bauer, *Der Idealismus*, pp. 71-76. For a critique see Otto Flügel, "Zimmermann's metaphysische Ansichten," *Zeitschrift für exakte Philosophie*, 12 (1883), 266-316.

20. Quoted in Eduard Hanslick, *Aus meinem Leben*, 2d ed. (Berlin, 1894), 1:17.

21. Zimmermann, "Continental Literature: Germany," in *Athenaeum*. From 1870 to 1886 this appeared in the final issue for Dec.; from 1887 to 1898 it was published in the first issue for July. Arminius Vámbéry contributed articles on Hungary to the same series.

22. Rudolf Steiner, *Mein Lebensgang* (Dornach, 1925), pp. 35-36.

23. See Robert Vischer, "Über das optische Formgefühl: Ein Beitrag zur Aesthetik" [1872], in *Drei Schriften zum ästhetischen Formproblem* (Halle, 1927), pp. 1-44, esp. 22 on *Einfühlung*. On Zimmermann's critique see *Drei Schriften*, p. 45n. On Robert Vischer see Hermann Glockner, "Robert Vischer und die Krisis der Geisteswissenschaften im letzten Drittel des neunzehnten Jahrhunderts: Ein Beitrag zur Geschichte des Irrationalitätsproblems," *Logos*, 14 (1925), 297-343; 15 (1926), 47-102.

24. See Lionello Venturi, "Robert Zimmermann et les origines de la science de l'art," in *Deuxième Congrès international d'esthétique et de science de l'art* (Paris, 1937), 2:35-38.

25. Zimmermann, *Über den Antheil Wiens an der deutschen Philosophie: Inaugurationsrede* (Vienna, 1886); Zimmermann, "Philosophie und Philosophen in Österreich," *Österreichisch-Ungarische Revue*, 6 (1889), 177-198, 259-272. Zimmermann reviewed forty years of Viennese literature and scholarship in "Wissenschaft und Literatur," in *Wien 1848-1888* (Vienna, 1888), 2:129-196.

CHAPTER 20

1. On Brentano's development see Oskar Kraus, *Franz Brentano: Zur Kenntnis seines Lebens und seiner Lehre mit Beiträgen von Carl Stumpf und Edmund Husserl* (Munich, 1919); Kraus, "Einleitung des Herausgebers," in Franz Brentano, *Psychologie vom empirischen Standpunkt*, 2d ed. (Leipzig, 1924; repr. Hamburg, 1955), 1:xvii-xcviii; Kraus, "Franz Brentano," *NOB*, 3 (1926), 102-118; Emil Utitz, "Franz Brentano," *Kantstudien*, 22 (1918), 217-242; Utitz, "Erinnerungen an Franz Brentano" [1938], *ZfphF*, 13 (1959), 102-110; Mario Puglisi, "Franz Brentano: A Biographical Sketch," *AJP*, 35 (1924), 414-419; Franziska Mayer-Hillebrand, "Rückblick auf die bisherigen Bestrebungen zur Erhaltung und Verbreitung von Franz Brentanos philosophischen Lehren und kurze Darstellung dieser Lehren," *ZfphF*, 17 (1963,) 146-169 [thorough bibliography of secondary works]; Hugo Bergmann, "Franz Brentano," *Revue internationale de philosophie*, 20 (1966), 349-372 [this Brentano-issue contains eight other articles].

2. Repr. in Ludwig Lenhart, "Das Franz Brentano-Gutachten über die päpstliche Infallibilität," *Archiv für mittelrheinische Kirchengeschichte*, 7 (1955), 295-334.

3. Repr. in Brentano, *Meine letzten Wünsche für Österreich* (Stuttgart, 1895).

4. Republished as Brentano, *Aenigmatias*, 5th ed. (Bern, 1962).

5. See Brentano, "Über ein optisches Paradoxon," *Zeitschrift für Psychologie*, 3 (1892), 349-358; 5 (1893), 61-82.

6. Jan Srzednicki, *Franz Brentano's Analysis of Truth* (The Hague, 1965); see also Gustav Bergmann, *Realism: A Critique of Brentano and Meinong* (Madison, Wisc., 1967); John J. Sullivan, "Franz Brentano and the Problems of Intentionality," in Wolman, ed., *Historical Roots of Contemporary Psychology* (New York, 1968), pp. 248-274 [useful introduction]. For writings of the later Brentano see his *Wahrheit und Evidenz*, ed. Oskar Kraus (Leipzig, 1930), and *Versuch über die Erkenntnis aus seinem Nachlass*, ed. Alfred Kastil (Leipzig, 1925).

7. G. E. Moore, Review of Brentano, *The Origin of the Knowledge of Right and Wrong* [1902], in *International Journal of Ethics*, 14 (1903), 115.

8. "Das Gute in diesem weiten Ganzen nach Möglichkeit zu fördern, das ist offenbar der richtige Lebenszweck, zu welchem jede Handlung geordnet werden soll. . . ." Brentano, *Vom Ursprung sittlicher Erkenntnis* (Leipzig, 1889), p. 28.

9. "Nicht allein das eigene Selbst: die Familie, die Stadt, der Staat, die ganze gegenwärtige irdische Lebewelt, ja die Zeiten ferner Zukunft. . . ." *Ibid.*, pp. 27-28.

10. G. E. Moore, *Origin of the Knowledge*, p. 116. See also Howard O. Eaton, "The Validity of Axiological Ethics," *Ethics*, 43 (1933), 253-268.

11. Brentano, *Vom Dasein Gottes*, ed. Alfred Kastil (Leipzig, 1929), esp. pp. 436-445.

12. See Eduard Winter, *Franz Brentanos Ringen um eine neue Gottessicht: Nach dem unveröffentlichten Briefwechsel Franz Brentano-Hermann Schell* (Brünn, 1941). For Brentano's critique of Schell, see Brentano, *Die Lehre Jesu und ihre bleibende Bedeutung*, ed. Alfred Kastil (Leipzig, 1922).

13. Letter of Oct. 30, 1895, cited in Winter, *Franz Brentanos Ringen*, p. 20.

14. Cited in Eaton, *The Austrian Philosophy of Values* (Norman, Okla., 1930), p. 26. For a critique see Branislav Petronievics, "Kritische Bemerkungen zu

Brentano's 'Die vier Phasen der Philosophie,' " *Philosophia*, 3 (1938), 179-187; for Brentano's hope of renewal see Brentano, *Über die Zukunft der Philosophie* [1893], ed. Oskar Kraus (Leipzig, 1929), pp. 7-81.

15. Portions are quoted in Utitz, "Erinnerungen an Franz Brentano," pp. 109-110.

16. On Meinong see "A. Meinong," in Raymund Schmidt, ed., *Die Philosophie der Gegenwart in Selbstdarstellungen*, 2d ed. (Leipzig, 1923), 1:101-160; Bertrand Russell, "Meinong's Theory of Complexes and Assumptions," *Mind*, 13 (1904), 204-219, 336-354, 509-524; Eaton, *The Austrian Philosophy;* J. N. Findlay, *Meinong's Theory of Objects and Values* (Oxford, 1933; 2d ed., 1963); Rudolf Kindinger, ed., *Philosophenbriefe: Aus der wissenschaftlichen Korrespondenz von Alexius Meinong* (Graz, 1965); Rudolf Haller, "Meinongs Gegenstandstheorie und Ontologie," *Journal of the History of Philosophy*, 4 (1966), 313-324; Bergmann, *Realism*, pp. 335-441; Reinhardt Grossmann, "Non-Existent Objects: Recent Work on Brentano and Meinong," *American Philosophical Quarterly*, 6 (1969), 17-32. On Meinong's students see Karl Wolf, "Die Grazer Schule: Gegenstandstheorie und Wertlehre," *Wissenschaft und Weltbild*, 21² (June-Sept., 1968), 31-56. Meinong's complete works are being published as *Gesamtausgabe*, ed. Haller and Kindinger, 7 vols. (Graz, 1968–).

17. On the Polish school of logic which Twardowski founded see Z. A. Jordan, *Philosophy and Ideology* (Dordrecht, 1963), pp. 5-75; Henryk Skolimowski, *Polish Analytical Philosophy: A Survey and A Comparison with British Analytical Philosophy* (London, 1967).

18. See Edmund Husserl, "Erinnerungen an Franz Brentano," in Kraus, ed., *Franz Brentano*, pp. 153-167. On Husserl see Herbert Spiegelberg, *The Phenomenological Movement: A Historical Introduction*, 2 vols., 2d ed. (The Hague, 1965); Joseph J. Kockelmans, *A First Introduction to Husserl's Phenomenology* (Pittsburgh, 1967). Both contain massive bibliographies. One of the clearest expositions is Aron Gurwitsch, "Husserl's Theory of the Intentionality of Consciousness in Historical Perspective," in Edward N. Lee and Maurice Mandelbaum, eds., *Phenomenology and Existentialism* (Baltimore, 1967), pp. 25-58.

19. See Hermann Lübbe, "Positivismus und Phänomenologie (Mach und Husserl)," in Helmut Höfling, ed., *Beiträge zu Philosophie und Wissenschaft: Hermann Szilasi zum 70. Geburtstag* (Munich, 1960), pp. 161-184, esp. 181-182; Joachim Thiele, "Ein Brief Edmund Husserls an Ernst Mach," *ZfphF*, 19 (1965), 134-138 [concerns letter of June 18, 1901].

20. On Ehrenfels see Max Brod, "Christian von Ehrenfels zum Gedenken," *Kantstudien*, 37 (1932), 313-314; Brod, *Streitbares Leben, 1884-1968*, 2d ed. (Munich, 1969), pp. 209-218; Eaton, *The Austrian Philosophy of Values;* Imma Bodmershof [daughter of Ehrenfels], "Christian von Ehrenfels," in Ferdinand Weinhandl, ed., *Gestalthaftes Sehen: Ergebnisse und Aufgaben der Morphologie* (Darmstadt, 1960), pp. 427-435.

21. See Christian von Ehrenfels, *Richard Wagner und seine Apostaten: Ein Beitrag zur Jahrhundertfeier* (Vienna, 1913); Ehrenfels, *Allegorische Dramen für musikalische Composition gedichtet* (Vienna, 1895) [contains eight librettos].

22. Ehrenfels, "Über Gestaltqualitäten" [1890], in Weinhandl, ed., *Gestalthaftes Sehen*, pp. 11-43.

23. Ehrenfels, "On Gestalt-Qualities" [1932], *Psychological Review*, 44 (1937), 521.

24. "Einen besonders kräftigen Reiz üben auf das isolierende Bemerken alle Arten

von Reihen, Ordnungen, Systeme und alle aus Abstands- und Richtungs-
relationen aufgebauten Configurationen. . . ." Husserl, *Die Philosophie der
Arithmetik* (Halle, 1891), p. 236.

25. Ehrenfels, "Über Fühlen und Wollen: Eine psychologische Studie," *SKAW-
Wien*, Phil-Hist. Klass, 114 (1887), 523-634.

26. Ehrenfels, "The Ethical Theory of Value," *International Journal of Ethics*, 6
(1896), 371-384. On Ehrenfels' quarrel with Meinong, see John Stuart Mac-
kenzie, "Notes on the Theory of Value," *Mind*, 4 (1895), 424-449.

27. Ehrenfels, "Die aufsteigende Entwicklung der Menschen," *Politisch-Anthropologische Revue*, 2 (1903-04), 45-59; Ehrenfels, "Entwicklungsmoral," *ibid.*,
2 (1903-04), 214-226; Ehrenfels, "Sexuales Ober- und Unterbewusstsein,"
ibid., 2 (1903-04), 456-476 [uses Theodor Meynert's concept of the unconscious, not Freud's]; Ehrenfels, "Monogamische Entwicklungsaussichten," *ibid.*,
2 (1903-04), 706-718; Ehrenfels, "Die sexuale Reform," *ibid.*, 2 (1903-04),
970-993; Ehrenfels, "Das Mütterheim," *ibid.*, 5 (1906-07), 221-239; Ehrenfels,
"Grundbegriffe der Ethik," *Grenzfragen des Nerven- und Seelenlebens*, Nr.
55 (1907), pp. 1-30; Ehrenfels, "Die konstitutive Verderblichkeit der Mono-
gamie und die Unentbehrlichkeit einer Sexualreform," *Archiv für Rassen- und
Gesellschaftsbiologie*, 4 (1907), 615-651, 803-830; 5 (1908), 97-112.

28. Ehrenfels, "Beiträge zur Selektionstheorie," *Annalen der Naturwissenschaft*, 3
(1904), 71-95.

29. Ehrenfels, *Sexualethik* (Wiesbaden, 1907), pp. 31 and 71.

30. Ehrenfels, Review of *Die sexuelle Not* by Fritz Wittels in Herman Nunberg
and Ernst Federn, eds., *Minutes of the Vienna Psychoanalytic Society* (New
York, 1967), 2:82-92 [paper of Dec. 16, 1908]; Ehrenfels, "A Program for
Breeding Reform," *ibid.*, pp. 93-100 [paper of Dec. 23, 1908].

31. For these unflattering points see Brod, *Streitbares Leben*, pp. 211, 214. *Die
Sternenbraut* was published in Ehrenfels, *Die Stürmer: Drei Chordramen*
(Prague, 1912).

32. Ehrenfels, "Biologische Friedensrüstungen," *Archiv für Rassen und Gesellschaftsbiologie*, 11 (1914-15), 580-613.

33. Ehrenfels, *Cosmogony* [1916] (New York, 1948), pp. 196-210.

CHAPTER 21

1. On Popper-Lynkeus see Josef Popper-Lynkeus, *Selbstbiographie* (Leipzig,
1917; 2d ed., 1924); Adolf Gelber, *Josef Popper-Lynkeus: Sein Leben und
Sein Wirken* (Vienna, 1923); Wilhelm Kromphardt, "Die Lösung der Magen-
frage durch Josef Popper," *Schmollers Jahrbuch*, 49 (1925), 563-587; Richard
von Mises, "Josef Popper-Lynkeus," *NOB*, 7 (1931), 206-217; Saul Rosenzweig, "The Idiocultural Dimension of Psychotherapy: Pre- and Post-History
of the Relations Between Sigmund Freud and Popper-Lynkeus," *Psychoanalysis and the Social Sciences*, 5 (1958), 9-50; Paul Edwards, "Popper-
Lynkeus, Josef," *EP*, 6 (1967), 401-407. Fritz Wittels, *Die Vernichtung der
Not* (Vienna, 1922) was no available to me.

2. "Man muss das Gefühl der Zusammengehörigkeit des Menschen mit allem
Anderen, das unmittelbare Bewusstsein der Einheit erwecken; der Mensch soll
sich in dem All heimisch fühlen lernen." Popper-Lynkeus, *Das Recht zu leben
und die Pflicht zu sterben*, 3d ed. (Dresden, 1903), p. 111.

3. See Freud, "Josef Popper-Lynkeus und die Theorie des Traumes" [1923], in

GW, 13 (London, 1940), 357-359; Freud, "Meine Berührung mit Josef Popper-Lynkeus" [1932], in *GW*, 16 (London, 1950), 261-266. See also A. A. Brill, "Translator's Prologue to Josef Popper-Lynkeus, 'Dreaming like Waking,' " *Psychoanalytic Review*, 34 (1947), 184-188; Wittels, "Freud's Connection with Popper-Lynkeus," *Psychoanalytic Review*, 34 (1947), 492-497.

4. On Spann see Fritz Sander, "Othmar Spann's 'Überwindung' der individualistischen Gesellschaftsauffassung," *ASWSP*, 53 (1924-25), 11-80; Barth Landheer, "Othmar Spann's Social Theories," *Journal of Political Economy*, 39 (1931), 239-248; Engelbert Gutwenger, S. J., "Die Religionsphilosophie von Othmar Spann und ihre metaphysische Voraussetzungen," *Zeitschrift für katholische Theologie*, 70 (1948), 456-476; Wilhelm Andreae, "Unitas Multiplex: Der Aufbau der Soziologie nach Othmar Spann," *Jahrbücher für Nationalökonomie und Statistik*, 162 (1950), 401-420; Frederick D. Rodeck, "Othmar Spann," *American Sociological Review*, 15 (1950), 803; Hans Riehl, ed., *Othmar Spann: Das philosophische Werk im Auszug* (Vienna, 1950); Johann Fischl, *Geschichte der Philosophie* (Graz, 1954), 5: 41-44; Rolf Amtmann, *Die Geisteslehre Othmar Spanns* (Graz, 1960); Alfred Diamant, *Austrian Catholics and the First Republic* (Princeton, 1960), pp. 131-140, 229-240; Josef Barwitsch, "Von Marx über Nietzsche zu Othmar Spann," *ZfphF*, 19 (1965), 692-702. *Die Zeitschrift für Ganzheitsforschung* (Vienna, 1957–), edited by Walter Heinrich, is sponsoring a complete edition of Spann's works in twenty-two volumes (Graz, 1963–).

5. Othmar Spann, "Preface to the Sixteenth Edition," in *The History of Economics* (New York, 1930), p. 11. On Spann's interpretation of Müller see Otto Weinberger, "Das neue Schrifttum über Adam Müller," *ASWSP*, 51 (1924), 808-816.

6. Spann, *Untersuchung über die uneheliche Bevölkerung von Frankfurt a.M.* (Dresden, 1905); Spann, "Zur Logik der socialwissenschaftlichen Begriffbildung," in *Festgabe für Friedrich Julius Neumann* (Tübingen, 1905), pp. 161-178.

7. Spann, *Die Haupttheorien der Volkswirtschaftslehre auf lehrgeschichtlichen Grundlage* (Vienna, 1911); Karl Pribram, "Die Idee des Gleichgewichts in der älteren Nationalökonomie," *Zeitschrift für Volkswirtschaft, Socialpolitik und Verwaltung*, 17 (1908), 1-28.

8. Spann, *Der Schöpfungsgang des Geistes: Die Wiederherstellung des Idealismus auf den allen Gebieten der Philosophie* (Jena, 1928), pp. xv-xx.

9. "Gott will in der Schöpfung sich selbst und daher kann auch die Welt nur Gott wollen. Das ist, der mystische Kern aller Geschichte und an der Gezweiung zeigt sich, dass wir nicht nur für uns, sondern für das Ganze gewirkt haben und für Gott dem Herrn der Ernte." Spann, *Geschichtsphilosophie* (Jena, 1932), p. 448.

10. Karl Polanyi, "The Essence of Fascism," in John Lewis, ed., *Christianity and the Social Revolution* (New York, 1936), pp. 359-394, esp. 359-376. For a more balanced view of Spann's participation in politics see Herman Lebovics, *Social Conservatism and the Middle Classes in Germany, 1914-1933* (Princeton, 1969), pp. 109-138, 233-236.

11. On Broch as metaphysician see Wolfgang Rothe, "Hermann Broch als politischer Denker," *Zeitschrift für Politik*, 5 (1958), 329-341; Rothe, "Der junge Broch," *Neue Deutsche Hefte*, 7 (1960), 780-797; Rothe, *Schriftsteller und totalitäre Welt* (Bern, 1966), pp. 160-204; Manfred Durzak, *Hermann Broch:*

Der Dichter und seine Zeit (Stuttgart, 1968). The phrase *"fröhliche Apoka-lypse"* occurs in Hermann Broch, *Hofmannsthal und seine Zeit: Eine Studie* [1955] (Munich, 1964), p. 49 [written 1947 to 1949].

12. Repr. in Broch, *Die unbekannte Grösse und frühe Schriften mit den Briefen an Willa Muir* (Zürich, 1961), pp. 276-282.

13. See Harry Slochower, "Julius Bahnsen: Philosopher of Heroic Despair, 1830-1881," *Philosophical Review*, 41 (1932), 368-384; Heinz-Joachim Heydorn, *Julius Bahnsen: Eine Untersuchung zur Vorgeschichte der modernen Existenz* (Göttingen, 1952).

CHAPTER 22

1. On Suttner see Bertha von Suttner, *Memoiren* (Stuttgart, 1909; repr., Bremen, 1965); Caroline Elisabeth Playne, *Bertha von Suttner and the Struggle to Avert the World War* (London, 1936) [fulsome praise]; Irwin Abrams, "Bertha von Suttner and the Nobel Peace Prize," *JCEA*, 22 (1962-63), 286-307; Alois Hoffmann, "Bertha von Suttner: Zum 50. Todestag der österreichischen Schriftstellerin," *Philologica Pragensia*, 7 (1964), 244-256.

2. Suttner, "Universal Peace: From a Woman's Standpoint," *North American Review*, 169 (1899), 55. See also her anonymous *Das Maschinenzeitalter: Zukunftsvorlesungen über unsere Zeit* (Zürich, 1890).

3. Suttner, "Universal Peace," p. 52.

4. See Suttner, "The Present Status and Prospects of the Peace Movement," *North American Review*, 171 (1900), 653-663.

5. Wilhelm Stekel, *Autobiography: The Life Story of a Pioneer Psychoanalyst* (New York, 1950), p. 62.

6. Richard N. Coudenhove-Kalergi, *An Idea Conquers the World* (London, 1953), p. 25. For a similar picture of life among the Bohemian nobility see Karl Anton Rohan, *Heimat Europa: Erinnerungen und Erfahrungen* (Düsseldorf, 1954), pp. 13-18.

7. On Richard Coudenhove-Kalergi see Coudenhove-Kalergi, *Idea Conquers;* Coudenhove-Kalergi, *Paneuropa 1922 bis 1966* (Vienna, 1966).

8. See Coudenhove-Kalergi, "Forecasts," *Living Age*, 315 (1922), 503-506; Coudenhove-Kalergi, "Ethics and Technics," *Living Age*, 316 (1923), 138-140.

CHAPTER 23

1. On Gumplowicz see Lester F. Ward, "Evolution of Social Structures," *AJS*, 10 (1904-1905), 589-605; Ward, "Ludwig Gumplowicz," *AJS*, 15 (1909-1910), 410-413; I. Kochanowski, "Ludwig Gumplowicz," *AJS*, 15 (1909-1910), 405-409; Harry Elmer Barnes, "The Struggle of Races and Social Groups as a Factor in the Development of Political and Social Institutions," *Journal of Race Development*, 9 (1918-1919), 300-310; Barnes, "Gumplowicz, Ludwig," *IESS*, 6 (1968), 203-205; James P. Lichtenberger, *Development of Social Theory* (New York, 1923), pp. 432-453; Bernhard Zebrowski, *Ludwig Gum-plowicz: Eine Bio-Bibliographie* (Berlin, 1926) [contains an exhaustive bibliography of works by and on Gumplowicz]; William M. McGovern, *From Luther to Hitler: The History of Fascist-Nazi Philosophy* (Cambridge, Mass., 1941), pp. 474-485; Gottfried Salomon-Delatour, *Moderne Staatslehren* (Neu-

wied, 1965), pp. 631-641. A judicious Marxist critique of Gumplowicz appears in Werner Sellnow, *Gesellschaft - Staat - Recht: Zur Kritik der bürgerlichen Ideologien über die Entstehung von Gesellschaft, Staat und Recht* (East Berlin, 1963), pp. 436-456.

2. Ludwig Gumplowicz, *The Outlines of Sociology* [1885] (Philadelphia, 1899), pp. 190-191. See also Gumplowicz, *Das Recht der Nationalitäten und Sprachen in Österreich-Ungarn* (Innsbruck, 1879).

3. Gumplowicz, *Outlines of Sociology*, pp. 195, 218. On the economic determination of thought see *ibid.*, pp. 163-168.

4. Quoted in Bertha von Suttner, *Memoiren* [1909] (Bremen, 1965), pp. 300-302.

5. Gumplowicz, "An Austrian Appreciation of Lester F. Ward," *AJS*, 10 (1905), 643-644.

6. On Ratzenhofer see Ludwig Gumplowicz, Review of Ratzenhofer, *Wesen und Zweck der Politik* (1893), in *Annals of the American Academy of Political and Social Science*, 5 (1894-95), 128-136; Gumplowicz, *Geschichte der Staatstheorien* (Innsbruck, 1905), pp. 446-491, 567-568; Gumplowicz, Review of Ratzenhofer, *Soziologie* (1907), in *AJS*, 14 (1908), 101-111; Rudolf Holzapfel, "Wesen und Methoden der sozialen Psychologie," *Archiv für systematische Philosophie*, 9 (1903), 38-48; Otto Gramzow, *Gustav Ratzenhofer und seine Philosophie* (Berlin, 1904); Albion W. Small, *General Sociology: An Exposition of the Main Development in Sociology from Spencer to Ratzenhofer* (Chicago, 1905), pp. 183-396; Small, "Ratzenhofer's Sociology," *AJS*, 13 (1908), 433-438; Arthur F. Bentley, "Simmel, Durkheim, and Ratzenhofer," *AJS*, 32 (1926), 250-256; Lichtenberger, *Development of Social Theory*, pp. 453-465.

7. Gustav Ratzenhofer, "Problems of Sociology," *AJS*, 10 (1904), 184.

8. Ratzenhofer, *Soziologie: Positive Lehre von den menschlichen Wechselbeziehungen* (Leipzig, 1907), pp. 135, 179-180.

9. The best work in English on Chamberlain is Jean Réal, "The Religious Conception of Race: Houston Stewart Chamberlain and Germanic Christianity," in Jacques Rueff, ed., *The Third Reich* (London, 1955), pp. 243-287. See also Carl Becker, Review of H. S. Chamberlain, *Foundations of the Nineteenth Century*, in *The Dial*, 50 (1911), 387-391; Anna Horst Chamberlain, *Meine Erinnerungen an Houston Stewart Chamberlain* (Munich, 1923); Otto Graf zu Stolberg-Wernigerode, "Houston S. Chamberlain," *Neue Deutsche Biographie*, (1957), 3:187-190; E. J. Young, *Gobineau und der Rassismus: Eine Kritik der anthropologischen Geschichtstheorie* (Meisenheim am Glan, 1968), pp. 242-269 [stresses the influence on Chamberlain of Vacher de Lapouge]. Chamberlain's autobiography, *Lebenswege meines Denkens*, 2d ed. (Munich, 1922) was not available to me.

10. Houston Stewart Chamberlain, "Ein Brief über Heinrich Heine" [Nov. 23, 1906], repr. in Walther Killy, ed., *20. Jahrhundert: Texte und Zeugnisse 1880-1933* (Munich, 1967), pp. 1119-1122, esp. 1119 [argues that to ascribe Heine's libertinism to his Jewishness would exculpate Heine].

11. Chamberlain, *Foundations of the Nineteenth Century* (New York, 1910), 1:299.

12. Chamberlain, " 'Katholische' Universitäten," *Die Fackel*, Nr. 92 (Jan., 1902), pp. 1-32. For a second piece in *Die Fackel*, see Chamberlain, "Der voraussetzungslose Mommsen," *ibid.*, Nr. 87 (Dec. 1, 1901), pp. 1-13.

13. Arnold Keyserling (1922–) continues his father's work at Vienna. His *Geschichte der Denkstile* (Vienna, 1968) formulates an exhaustive typology of Western thinkers.

14. See Rudolf Kassner, "Erinnerung an Houston St. Chamberlain," *Europäische Revue*, 5 (April, 1929), 22-30; Kassner, "Erziehung," in *Buch der Erinnerung* [1938], 2d ed. (Erlenbach-Zürich, 1954), pp. 125-131 [both highly revealing]. On Kassner see A. Cl. Kensik and D. Bodmer, eds., *Rudolf Kassner zum 80. Geburtstag: Gedenkbuch* (Erlenbach-Zürich, 1953). Kassner's works are being republished in *Sämtliche Werke*, 6 vols. (Pfullingen, 1969–).

15. See Wilfried Daim, *Der Mann der Hitler die Ideen gab: Von den religiösen Verirrungen eines Sektierers zum Rassenwahn des Diktators* (Munich, 1958). On Lanz see also Hellmut Andics, *Der ewige Jude: Ursachen und Geschichte des Antisemitismus* (Vienna, 1965), pp. 250-257; Richard Hamann and Jost Hermand, *Stilkunst um 1900* (East Berlin, 1967), pp. 65-72; Friedrich Heer, *Der Glaube des Adolf Hitler* (Munich, 1968), pp. 126, 165-169, 709-718.

16. J. Lanz-Liebenfels, "Die Urgeschichte der Kunst," *Politisch-Anthropologische Revue*, 2 (1903-04), 134-156, esp. 154.

17. On Lanz's vindication of Kraus as a "blond Jew," see Karl Kraus, "Er ist doch e Jud" [Oct., 1913], repr. in *Untergang der Welt durch schwarze Magie* [1922], *Werke*, 8 (Munich, 1960), 331-338, esp. 336-337.

CHAPTER 24

1. Robert Musil, *Der Mann ohne Eigenschaften* [1930-1943] (Hamburg, 1952), pp. 31-35.

2. The clearest account is Ifor L. Evans, "Economic Aspects of Dualism in Austria-Hungary," *SEER*, 6 (1927), 529-542. See also Theodor Mayer, ed., *Der österreichisch-ungarische Ausgleich von 1867: Seine Grundlagen und Auswirkungen* (Munich, 1968); Leslie C. Tihany, "The Austro-Hungarian Compromise, 1867-1918: A Half Century of Diagnosis, Fifty Years of Post-Mortem," *Central European History*, 2 (1969), 114-138 [thorough bibliography].

3. E. B. Lanin, "Count Taaffe and Austrian Politics," *Contemporary Review*, 63 (1893), 300n.

4. For samples of Separatist opinion see Albert Apponyi, "The Army Question in Austria and Hungary," *Monthly Review*, 16 (1904), 1-37; Ferenc Kossuth, "The Hungarian Crisis: Its Causes and Effects," *The National Review*, 45 (1905), 251-261.

5. Priscilla Robertson, *Revolutions of 1848: A Social History* (Princeton, 1952), p. 262. On social classes before 1800 see Béla K. Király, *Hungary in the Late Eighteenth Century: The Decline of Enlightened Despotism* (New York, 1969), pp. 15-73. On the nobility of the 1860's see Arthur J. Patterson, "The Electoral Laws of Hungary," *Fortnightly Review*, 5 (1866), 1-14; Patterson, "Country Life in Hungary before the Elections," *Fortnightly Review*, 5 (1866), 705-717; Patterson, "A Hungarian Election," *Fortnightly Review*, 6 (1866), 129-150. For a Marxist view see Péter Hanák, "Skizzen über die ungarische Gesellschaft am Anfang des 20. Jahrhunderts," *Acta Historica* [Budapest], 10 (1964), 1-45.

6. See Maurus Jókai, "Das magyarische Volk," in *Die österreichisch-ungarische Monarchie in Wort und Bild: Ungarn* (Vienna, 1888), 1:282-358, esp. 299 [an

excellent account of Hungarian mores]; Oscar Jászi, *The Dissolution of the Habsburg Monarchy* (Chicago, 1929; repr., 1961), pp. 220-247.

7. See John Kosa, "Hungarian Society in the Time of the Regency (1920-1944)," *JCEA*, 16 (1956), 253-265.

8. József Eötvös, *The Village Notary* [1845] (London, 1850), 1:14.

9. See Arthur J. May, *The Habsburg Monarchy 1867-1914* (Cambridge, Mass., 1951), p. 235-238. For a detailed account see Otto Neurath, "Zum österreichischen Auswanderungsgesetzentwurf," *Zeitschrift für Volkswirtschaft, Sozialpolitik und Verwaltung*, 23 (1914), 297-378.

10. See Moritz Csáky, *Der Kulturkampf in Ungarn: Die kirchenpolitische Gesetzgebung der Jahre 1894-95* (Graz, 1967). On the Hungarian church see William Juhasz, "The Development of Catholicism in Hungary in Modern Times," in Joseph N. Moody, ed., *Church and Society: Catholic Social and Political Thought and Movements 1789-1950* (New York, 1953), pp. 659-719.

11. See Norman Stone, "Hungary and the Crisis of July 1914," *JCH*, 1³ (1966), 153-170.

12. On the events of 1919 see Wilhelm Boehm, *Im Kreuzfeuer zweier Revolutionen* (Munich, 1924); Stephan Bonsal, *Unfinished Business* (New York, 1944); Ferenc Tibor Zsuppán, "The Early Activities of the Hungarian Communist Party, 1918-1919," *SEER*, 43 (1964-1965), 314-334; Rudolf L. Tökés, *Béla Kun and the Hungarian Soviet Republic* (New York, 1967).

13. See Gyula Szekfü, "Der ungarische Character" [1940], in Julius von Farkas, ed., *Ungarns Geschichte und Kultur in Dokumenten* (Wiesbaden, 1955), pp. 189-196. On Szekfü see St. Barta, "Julius Szekfü 60 Jahre alt," *Ungarische Jahrbücher*, 23 (1943), 282-286. A balanced view of the Horthy regime appears in J. Erös, "Hungary," in S. J. Woolf, ed., *European Fascism* (London, 1968), pp. 111-145.

14. See Dorothy Thompson, "Amazing Hungary," *Contemporary Review*, 120 (1921), 329-336; Jászi, *Revolution and Counter-Revolution in Hungary* (London, 1924), pp. 160-176. Jakob Kraus, *Martyrium: Ein jüdisches Jahrbuch* (Vienna, 1922) was not available to me.

15. George A. Birmingham, *A Wayfarer in Hungary* (London, 1925), pp. 67-68.

16. On the growth of Budapest see Albert Shaw, *Municipal Governments in Continental Europe* (New York, 1895), pp. 435-468; Schuyler M. Meyer, "Impressions of Budapest," *Architectural Record*, 26 (1909), 428-447 [contains excellent photographs]; Béla Borsos et al., *Budapest* (Budapest, 1959) [superbly illustrated]; Pál Granasztói, "An Architect's View of Budapest," *New Hungarian Quarterly*, 6 (Autumn, 1965), 201-213. On economic development see V. Sándor, "Die grossindustrielle Entwicklung in Ungarn, 1867-1900," *Acta Historica* [Budapest], 3 (1954-1956), 139-237; Iván T. Berend and György Ránki, "Economic Factors in Nationalism: The Example of Hungary at the Beginning of the Twentieth Century," *Austrian History Yearbook*, 3.3 (1967), 163-186.

17. E. Irenaeus Stevenson, "The Cuckoo and the Sparrow: The Hungarian Millenial and its Significance," *Outlook* 54 (1896), 504-506.

18. See Vernon Duckworth Barker, "Foundations of Magyar Society," *SEER*, 11 (1932), 393-395; Robert A. Kann, "Hungarian Jewry During Austria-Hungary's Constitutional Period," *Jewish Social Studies*, 7 (1945), 357-386; E. R. Kutas, "Judaism, Zionism, and Anti-Semitism in Hungary," *JCEA*, 8 (1948-49), 377-389; Bernard Klein, "Hungarian Politics and the Jewish Question in

the Inter-War Period," *Jewish Social Studies*, 28 (1966), 79-98.

19. See Charles H. H. Wright, "The Jews and the Malicious Charge of Human Sacrifice," *Nineteenth Century*, 14 (1883), 753-778; Paul Nathan, *Der Prozess von Tisza-Eszlár: Ein antisemitisches Kulturbild* (Berlin, 1892). Károly Eötvös, *Der grosse Prozess* (1884) [by the attorney for the defense] was not available to me. A Hungarian edition (1968) of Eötvös' memoir is summarized in Péter Hanák, "Acquittal—But No Happy Ending," *New Hungarian Quarterly*, 10 (Winter, 1969), 119-125. Arnold Zweig dramatized the case in *Die Sendung Semaels: Jüdische Tragödie in fünf Aufzügen* [1914-1918]; repr., in Zweig, *Dramen*, (East Berlin, 1963), pp. 67-152. Vienna-born Rudolf Brunngraber (1901-1960) narrated the events in a novel, *Prozess auf Tod und Leben* (Vienna, 1948); repr. as *Pogrom* (1956).

20. See Gyula Szekfü, "Le Hongrois: Langue d'état," in *État et Nation* (Paris, 1945), pp. 11-103, esp. 27-28, 31-34. Johann Gottfried Herder, *Ideen zur Philosophie der Geschichte der Menschheit* [1784-1791], Book 16 (Darmstadt, 1965), p. 429; Herder, "Gespräch über dem Tode des Kaiser Josephs II" [1793], in *Briefe zu Beförderung der Humanität*, 1, *Sämtliche Werke* 17 (Berlin, 1881), 47-63, esp. 58-59.

21. On Széchenyi see George Barany, *Stephen Széchenyi and the Awakening of Hungarian Nationalism, 1791-1841* (Princeton, 1968).

22. On the German minority see Edmund Steinacker, *Lebenserinnerungen* (Munich, 1937); E. V. Windisch, "Die Entstehung der Voraussetzungen für die deutsche Nationalitätenbewegung in Ungarn in der zweiten Hälfte des 19. Jahrhunderts," *Acta Historica* [Budapest], 11 (1965), 3-55 [comprehensive].

23. Leon Kellner, *Theodor Herzls Lehrjahre 1860-1895* (Vienna, 1920), pp. 17-18.

24. A searching analysis of the language is Géza Barczi, "The Hungarian Language," *New Hungarian Quarterly*, 4 (Jan., 1963), 52-62.

25. Cited in Emilie de Laveleye, "Würzburg and Vienna: Scraps from a Diary," *Living Age*, 164 (1884), 126.

26. Denis de Rougemont, "Le Paysan du Danube" [1929], in *Journal d'une époque (1926-1946)* (Paris, 1968), p. 49.

27. The fullest accounts of Hungarian literature in other languages are Johann Heinrich Schwicker, *Geschichte der ungarischen Literatur* (Leipzig, 1889), 944 pp.; Joseph Reményi, *Hungarian Writers and Literature: Modern Novelists, Critics, and Poets* (New Brunswick, N. J., 1964). On Jókai see Jókai, "My Literary Recollections," *The Forum*, 19 (1895), 667-680; Jókai, *Eyes like the Sea* [1890] (New York, 1894) [an autobiographical novel describing the 1840's]; John Bell Henneman, "Nestor of Hungarian Letters," *Sewanee Review*, 4 (1896), 189-211; R. Nisbet Bain, "Maurus Jókai: The Man and His Work," *Living Age*, 231 (1901), 185-194; H. W. V. Temperley, "Maurus Jókai and the Historical Novel," *Contemporary Review*, 86 (1904), 107-115; Alexander Hevesi, "Maurus Jókai: The Greatest Novelist of Hungary," *SEER*, 8 (1929-30), 356-367; Francis Magyar, "Jókai's Reception in England and America," *American Slavic and East European Review*, 17 (1958), 332-345; Miklós Nagy, "Jókais Romanbaukunst," *Acta Litteraria* [Budapest], 7 (1965), 103-144 [thorough].

28. Quoted in Zoltán Horváth, *Die Jahrhundertwende in Ungarn* (Neuwied, 1966), p. 180.

29. See I. Kirimi-Kisdégi, "Székely von Ádámos, Bertalan," *KML*, 5 (1968), 464-465; A. Ryszkiewicz, "Munkácsy Mihály," *KML*, 4 (1967), 547-549. On

Hungarian painting see Antal Kampis, *The History of Art in Hungary* (Budapest, 1966).

30. See George F. Cushing, "Problems of Hungarian Literary Criticism," *SEER*, 40 (1961-1962), 341-345; the reply, Péter Nagy, "Problems of Hungarian Criticism: Some Remarks on George F. Cushing's Study," *New Hungarian Quarterly*, 4 (July, 1963), 132-135.

31. See Ludwig Hatvany, "Das alte und das junge Ungarn," *Neue Rundschau*, 21 (1910), 383-400.

32. Reich's works on Austria-Hungary include Emil Reich, "Hungary at the Close of Her First Millenium," *Nineteenth Century*, 39 (1896), 837-849; Reich, "Austria-Hungary and the Ausgleich," *Nineteenth Century*, 43 (1898), 466-480; Reich, *Hungarian Literature: An Historical and Critical Survey* (London, 1898); Reich, "Austria and Hungary in the Nineteenth Century," in F. A. Kirkpatrick, ed., *Lectures on the History of the Nineteenth Century* (Cambridge, 1902); Reich, "The 'Partition' of Austria-Hungary," *International Quarterly*, 7 (1903), 45-58; Reich, "The Crisis in Hungary," *Contemporary Review*, 88 (1905), 516-525, 635-648; Reich, "The Crisis in the Near East: I. The Austro-Hungarian Case," *Nineteenth Century*, 64 (1908), 705-718. The Hungarian Emil Reich is not to be confused with Moravian-born philosopher Emil Reich (1864-1937), who taught at the University of Vienna from 1890 to 1933.

33. See Reich, "Jew-Baiting on the Continent," *Nineteenth Century*, 40 (1896), 422-438; Reich, "Zionism," *ibid.*, 42 (1897), 260-274.

34. See Reich, *General History of the Western Nations from 5000 B.C. to 1900* (London, 1908), 1:35-42.

35. Reich, *Hungarian Literature*, pp. 228-239.

36. See Reich, *Plato as an Introduction to Modern Criticism of Life* (London, 1906); Reich, *Woman Through the Ages*, 2 vols. (London, 1906); Reich, *Success in Life* (New York, 1907).

37. Clara Laughlin, *So You're Going to Germany and Austria* (Boston, 1930), p. 507.

38. Quoted in de Laveleye, "Würzburg and Vienna," p. 126.

39. For a different view, based on interviews with Wigner and Teller, see Laura Fermi, *Illustrious Immigrants: The Intellectual Migration from Europe 1930-41* (Chicago, 1968), pp. 53-59.

40. See Scotus Viator [R. W. Seton-Watson], *Racial Problems in Hungary* (London, 1908); Seton-Watson, "Hungary and the Southern Slavs," *Contemporary Review*, 101 (1912), 820-830.

41. Seton-Watson, *Corruption and Reform in Hungary: A Study of Electoral Practice* (London, 1911). See also C. J. C. Street, *Hungary and Democracy* (London, 1923), pp. 33-91. A recent Marxist indictment is Z. Horváth, "The Rise of Nationalism and the Nationality Problem in Hungary in the Last Decades of Dualism," *Acta Historica* [Budapest], 9 (1963), 1-37.

42. Suum Cuique, "Hungarian Tyranny and Roumanian Suffering," *Contemporary Review*, 106 (1914), 766-774.

43. Michael Pupin, *From Immigrant to Inventor*, (New York, 1922; repr., 1960), p. 9. On customs of the Banat see pp. 3-22.

44. Seton-Watson, "Austria-Hungary as a Balkan Power," *Contemporary Review*, 102 (1912), 801-806.

45. Emily Gerard, "Transylvanian Peoples," *Living Age*, 173 (1887), 131-142.

46. Gerard, "Transylvanian Superstitions," *Nineteenth Century*, 18 (1885), 130-149, esp. 142.

47. *Ibid.*, p. 143.

48. See Oscar Jászi, "The Problem of Sub-Carpathian Ruthenia," in R. J. Kerner, ed., *Czechoslovakia* (Berkeley and Los Angeles, 1945), pp. 193-215 (esp. 197-199).

49. On the Szeklers see Linda Dégh, *Folktales and Society: Story-Telling in a Hungarian Peasant Community* [1962] (Bloomington, Ind., 1969).

50. On Hungarian gypsies see Erasmus Schwab, *Land und Leute in Ungarn* (Leipzig, 1865), pp. 369-408; Victor Tissot, *Voyage au pays des Tsiganes (La Hongrie inconnue)* (Paris, 1880); Erdmann Doane Beynon, "The Gypsy in a Non-Gypsy Economy," *AJS*, 42 (1936-37), 358-370; Paul Graf Pálffy von Erdöd, *Abschied von Vorgestern und Gestern* (Stuttgart, 1961), pp. 213-233.

51. Hans Gross, *Handbuch für Untersuchungsrichter als System der Kriminalistik*, 6th ed. (Munich, 1914), 1:502-530.

52. Elbert F. Baldwin, "Twin City of the Magyars," *Outlook*, 81 (1905), 515.

CHAPTER 25

1. On Herzl see Theodor Herzl, *Tagebücher 1895-1904*, 3 vols. (Berlin, 1922-1923); Herzl, *Gesammelte Zionistische Werke*, 5 vols. (Tel Aviv, 1934-1935); Sidney Whitman, "Theodor Herzl," *Contemporary Review*, 86 (1904), 371-376; Leon Kellner, *Theodor Herzls Lehrjahre 1860-1895* (Vienna, 1920); Stefan Zweig, *Begegnungen mit Menschen, Büchern, Städten* (Vienna, 1937), pp. 93-100; Saul Raphael Landau, *Sturm und Drang im Zionismus: Rückblick eines Zionisten: Vor, Mit und Um Theodor Herzl* (Vienna, ca. 1937); Alex Bein, *Theodore Herzl: A Biography* [1934] (Philadelphia, 1941); Hannah Arendt, "The Jewish State: Fifty Years After," *Commentary*, 1 (May, 1946), 1-8; Israel Cohen, *Theodore Herzl: Founder of Political Zionism* (New York, 1959).

2. "Alles, was ich weiss, habe ich im Ausland gelernt. Nur dort gewöhnt man sich, in Distanzen zu denken." Quoted in Zweig, *Begegnungen*, p. 98.

3. Herzl, "Zionist Congress," *Contemporary Review*, 72 (1897), 597-598.

4. *Ibid.*, p. 596. On precursors of political Zionism see Ismar Elbogen, *A Century of Jewish Life* (Philadelphia, 1944), pp. 224-308; Norman Bentwich and John M. Shaftesley, "Forerunners of Zionism in the Victorian Era," in John M. Shaftesley, ed., *Remember the Days: Essays on Anglo-Jewish History Presented to Cecil Roth* (London, 1966), pp. 207-239.

5. On Hertzka see Jeremiah W. Jenks, Review of Hertzka, *Freiland*, in *PSQ*, 5 (1890), 706-708; C. Godfrey Gümpel, "A Possible Solution of the Social Question," *Westminster Review*, 138 (1892), 270-285; Edward Salmon, "Sidelights on Socialism: Experiments by Colonisation," *Fortnightly Review*, 63 (1895), 260-266; G. D. H. Cole, *A History of Socialist Thought*, vol. 3:2 (London, 1956), pp. 559-565; Gottfried Heindl, "Freiland," *Literatur und Kritik*, 1 (March, 1967), 110-115.

6. On Nordau see Vernon Lee, "Deterioration of Soul," *Fortnightly Review*, 65 (1896), 928-943; Anna and Maxa Nordau, *Max Nordau: A Biography* (New York, 1943) [an encomium by his wife and daughter].

7. Max Nordau, "Philosophy and Morals of War," *North American Review*, 169 (1899), 792.

8. Nordau, "A Reply to My Critics," *Century*, 50 (1895), 549.
9. *Ibid.*, p. 546.
10. Jones, 1:205.
11. Nordau, "A Reply to My Critics," p. 550.
12. See Robert H. Sherard, "Dr. Nordau on the Jews and Their Fears," *Review of Reviews*, 17 (1898), 315-317.

CHAPTER 26

1. The best introduction to post-1918 Lukács is Morris Watnick, "Georg Lukács: An Intellectual Biography, I-IV," *Soviet Survey*, Nrs. 24-26, 28 (1958-1959), pp. 60-66, 51-57, 61-68, 75-81. For a condensed version see Watnick, "Relativism and Class Consciousness: George Lukács," in Leopold Labedz, ed., *Revisionism: Essays on the History of Marxist Ideas* (New York, 1962), pp. 142-165. The best survey of pre-1918 Lukács is Zoltán Kenyeres, "Beginn der Laufbahn G. Lukács' und sein Weg zum Marxismus," *Acta Litteraria* [Budapest], 7 (1965), 361-375, which examines his Hungarian writings. Stimulating but highly technical is Peter Ludz, "Vorwort," in Georg Lukács, *Schriften zur Literatursoziologie* (Neuwied, 1961; 3d ed., 1968), pp. 11-68. More down-to-earth is Ludz, "Der Begriff der 'demokratischen Diktatur' in der politischen Philosophie von Georg Lukács," in Lukács, *Schriften zur Ideologie und Politik*, ed. Peter Ludz (Neuwied, 1967), pp. xvii-lv. See also Ludz, "Georg Lukács: Biographische Daten," *Schriften zur Ideologie*, pp. 709-718. On parallels between Lukács and the Hegelian aesthetic of Friedrich Theodor Vischer see Horst Althaus, *George Lukács oder Bürgerlichleit als Vorschule einer marxistischen Aesthetik* (Bern, 1962). Provocative but unreliable is Victor Zitta, *Georg Lukács' Marxism: Alienation, Dialectics, Revolution: A Study in Utopia and Ideology*. An indispensable tool is Jürgen Hartmann, "Chronologische Bibliographie der Werke von Georg Lukács," in Frank Benseler, ed., *Festschrift zum achtzigsten Geburtstag von Georg Lukács* (Neuwied, 1965), pp. 625-696.
2. Thomas Mann, "Brief an Dr. Seipel," *Werke*, 11 (Frankfurt, 1960), 780-782 [a letter of about 1928 requesting that Lukács not be deported from Austria]. On Mann's contact with other Hungarian intellectuals see Pál Réz, "Thomas Mann and Hungary: His Correspondence with Hungarian Friends," *New Hungarian Quarterly*, 2 (July, 1961), 84-99.
3. Lukács, "Georg Simmel: Ein Nachruf" [1918], in Kurt Gassen and M. Landmann, eds., *Buch des Dankes an Georg Simmel: Briefe, Erinnerungen, Bibliographie* (Berlin, 1958), pp. 171-176.
4. Lukács, "Die Subjekt-Objekt Beziehung in der Aesthetik," *Logos*, 8 (1917), 1-39. This difficult text, which records debts to Kant, Hegel, and Husserl, should be read in conjunction with Lukács, "Emil Lask: Ein Nachruf," *Kantstudien*, 22 (1917), 349-370. On Lukács and Weber, see Marianne Weber, *Max Weber: Ein Lebensbild* (Tübingen, 1926), pp. 473-476. For Lukács' dismissal of his own "neo-romanticism," see Lukács, "Vorwort" [dated July, 1962], in *Die Theorie des Romans*, 2d ed. (Neuwied, 1963), pp. 5-18, and "Vorwort," *Aesthetik* vol. 1:1 (Neuwied, 1963), p. 31.
5. See Erwin Szabó, "Aus den Parteien- und Klassenkämpfen in der ungarischen Revolution von 1848," *Archiv für die Geschichte des Sozialismus*, 8 (1919), 258-307. On Szabó see Lukács, "Taktik und Ethik" [1919], in *Schriften zur Ideologie und Politik*, p. 32; Oskar Jászi, "Erwin Szabó und sein Werk: Ein

Wort der Erinnerung," *Archiv für die Geschichte des Sozialismus*, 10 (1922); 22-37; Zoltán Horváth, *Die Jahrhundertwende in Ungarn* (Neuwied, 1966), pp. 354-361. On *Nyugat*, see Horváth, *Jahrhundertwende*, pp. 386-412. For Lukács' later assessment of pre-1918 Hungarian literature see Lukács, "The Importance and Influence of Ady," *New Hungarian Quarterly*, 10 (Autumn, 1969), 56-63.

6. See Karl Kerényi, "Zauberberg-Figuren: Ein biographischer Versuch," in *Tessiner Schreibtisch: Mythologisches, Urmythologisches* (Stuttgart, 1963), pp. 125-141; Alasdair MacIntyre, "Marxist Mask and Romantic Face: Lukács on Thomas Mann," *Encounter*, 24 (April, 1965), 64-72. In *Der Zauberberg*, Mann has Naphta take lodgings with a family named Lukaçek.

7. For reminiscences of Lukács in Vienna see Victor Serge, *Memoirs of a Revolutionary 1901-1941* (London, 1963), pp. 185-192.

8. Lukács, "Mein Weg zu Marx" [1933], in *Schriften zur Ideologie und Politik*, pp. 323-329. For a less embattled account of his first years as a Marxist see Lukács, "Vorwort" [March, 1967], in *Frühschriften II* (Neuwied, 1968), pp. 11-41.

9. Lukács, "Die Theorie des Romans: Ein geschichts-philosophischer Versuch über die Formen der grossen Epik," in *ZAAK*, 11 (1916), 225-271, 390-431 (repr., Berlin, 1920); 2d ed. (Neuwied, 1963).

10. Lukács, "Vorwort," *Die Theorie des Romans*, p. 7.

11. The German version is: Lukács, "Zur Soziologie des modernen Dramas," *ASWSP*, 38 (1914), 303-345, 662-706.

12. Lukács, "Von der Armut am Geiste: Ein Gespräch und ein Brief," *Neue Blätter*, 2^{5-6} (1912), 67-92.

13. Lucien Goldmann, "Georg Lukács: L'essayiste," *Revue d'esthétique*, 3 (1950), 82-95; Goldmann, *Le dieu caché: Étude sur la vision tragique dans les Pensées de Pascal et dans le théâtre de Racine* (Paris, 1955); Goldmann, "Introduction aux premiers écrits de Georges Lukács," *Temps modernes*, 18 (1962), 254-280.

14. Rudolf Kassner, "Sören Kierkegaard: Aphorismen," *Neue Rundschau*, 17 (1906), 513-543. A conception of death as molder (*Gestalter*) of life appears in Georg Simmel, "Zur Metaphysik des Todes," *Logos*, 1 1910), 57-80.

15. For fifteen atricles of 1919 to 1922 see Lukács, *Frühschriften II*, pp. 43-159.

16. On Lukács as Commissar, see Rudolf L. Tökés, *Béla Kun and the Hugarian Soviet Republic* (New York, 1967), pp. 149, 152-154, 254-255.

17. On Mannheim see Albert Salomon, "Karl Mannheim 1893-1947," *Social Research*, 14 (1947), 350-364; Leopold Wiese, "Karl Mannheim," *Kölner Zeitschrift für Soziologie*, 1 (1948-49), 98-100; Helmut R. Wagner, "The Scope of Mannheim's Thinking," *Social Research*, 20 (1953), 100-109; Gunther W. Remmling, "Karl Mannheim: Revision of an Intellectual Portrait," *Social Forces*, 40 1961-62), 23-30; Kurt H. Wolff, "Karl Mannheim in seinen Abhandlungen bis 1933," in Mannheim, *Wissenssoziologie: Auswahl aus dem Werk* (Neuwied, 1964), pp. 11-65, 691-710; David Kettler, "Sociology of Knowledge and Moral Philosophy: The Place of Traditional Problems in the Formation of Mannheim's Thought," *PSQ*, 82 (1967), 399-426; Remmling, *Wissenssoziologie und Gesellschaftsplanung: Das Werk Karl Mannheims* (Dortmund, 1968) [with exhaustive bibliography].

18. A German translation appears in Mannheim, *Wissenssoziologie* (Neuwied, 1964), pp. 66-84.

19. Repr. *ibid.*, pp. 85-90; originally published in *Logos*, 9 (1920-21), 50-53.
20. On Grünwald see Walther Eckstein, "Vorwort," in Grünwald, *Das Problem der Soziologie des Wissens: Versuch einer kritischen Darstellung der wissenssoziologischen Theorien* (Vienna, 1934; repr., Hildesheim, 1967); Wolff, "Ernst Grünwald and the Sociology of Knowledge: A Collective Venture in Interpretation," *Journal of the History of the Behavioral Sciences*, I (1965), 152-164; Hermann Kramer, *Ursachen der Meinungsverschiedenheiten in der Philosophie* (Berlin, 1967), pp. 143-147.
21. Werner Stark, *The Sociology of Knowledge* (London, 1958), p. 195.

CHAPTER 27

1. On Ferenczi see Sandor Lorand, "Sándor Ferenczi," in Franz Alexander, Samuel Eisenstein, and Martin Grotjahn, eds., *Psychoanalytic Pioneers* (New York, 1966), pp. 14-35; Frank Auld, Jr., "Ferenczi, Sándor," *IESS*, 5 (1968), 367-369.
2. Jones, 3:8.
3. See Sándor Ferenczi, "Stages in the Development of the Sense of Reality" [1913], in *First Contributions to Psycho-Analysis* [1916] (London, 1952), pp. 213-239.
4. On Szondi see Michael Balint, "On Szondi's 'Schicksalsanalyse' and "Triebdiagnostik,'" *IJP*, 29 (1948), 240-249; "Test by Portraits," *Life Magazine*, 24 (March 22, 1948), 67-69; Susan Deri, *Introduction to the Szondi Test: Theory and Practice* (New York, 1949); Roy Schafer, Review of Deri, *Szondi Test*, in *Journal of Abnormal and Social Psychology*, 45 (1950), 184–188; L. J. Borstelmann and W. G. Klopfer, "The Szondi Test: A Review and Critical Examination," *Psychological Bulletin*, 50 (1953), 112-132; Wilhelm Hinterleithner, "Menschenbild und Machtübertragung: Eine Würdigung der Psychologie L. Szondis," *Wissenschaft und Weltbild*, 11 (1958), 39-47; Armin Beeli, "Der Beitrag der Schicksalsanalyse Szondis," in Wilhelm Bitter, ed., *Psychotherapie und religiöse Erfahrung* (Stuttgart, 1965), pp. 157-176 [penetrating]. H. Ellenberger, "Das menschliche Schicksal als wissenschaftliches Problem: Zur Einführung in die Schicksalsanalyse von Szondi," *Psyche*, 4 (1950-51), 576-610 was not available to me.
5. See Lipot Szondi, "Contributions to 'Fate Analysis': An Attempt at a Theory of Choice in Love," *Acta Psychologica*, 3 (1937), 1-80. Szondi summarized his later views in "Mensch und Schicksal: Elemente einer dialektischen Schicksalswissenschaft (Anakologie)," *Wissenschaft und Weltbild*, 7 (1954), 15-34.
6. "Das Kino stört das Schauen. Die Raschheit der Bewegungen und der schnelle Wechsel der Bilder zwingen den Menschen zu einem ständigen Überraschen. Der Blick bemächtigt sich nicht der Bilder, sondern diese bemächtigen sich des Blickes. Sie überschwemmen das Bewusstsein. Das Kino bedeutet eine Uniformierung des Auges, das bis jetzt unbekleidet war." Quoted in Gustav Janouch, *Gespräche mit Kafka* (Frankfurt, 1951), p. 93. See also Wolfgang Jahn, "Kafka und die Anfänge des Kinos," *Jahrbuch der deutschen Schillergesellschaft*, 6 (1962), 353-368. Kafka's friend Max Brod contributed a screenplay to Kurt Pinthus, ed., *Das Kinobuch: Kinostücke* [1914] (Zürich, 1963), pp. 71-75.
7. Egon Friedell, "Kunst und Kino" [ca. 1912], in *Wozu das Theater? Essays, Satiren, Humoresken* (Munich, 1965), pp. 99-107.

8. "Die menschliche Stimme hat Allgegenwart, die menschliche Gebärde Ewigkeit erlangt, aber um den Preis der Seele. Es ist der Turmbau zu Babel. . . . Es werden durch Rundfunk bereits Nachtigallenkonzerte und Papstreden übertragen. Das is der Untergang des Abendlandes." Friedell, *Kulturgeschichte der Neuzeit* [1927-1931] (Munich, 1965), p. 1513.

9. Joseph Roth, *Der Antichrist* [1934], in *Romane, Erzählungen, Aufsätze* (Cologne, 1964), pp. 625-632. On Roth's view of cinema see Fritz Hackert, *Kulturpessimismus und Erzählform: Studien zu Joseph Roths Leben und Werk* (Bern, 1967), pp. 16-21.

10. Georg Lukács, "Gedanken zu einer Ästhetik des Kinos" [1913], in *Schriften zur Literatursoziologie*, 3d ed. (Neuwied, 1968), pp. 75-80. See also Guido Aristarco, "Lukács' Beiträge zu Film und Filmkritik," in Frank Benseler, ed., *Festschrift zum achtzigsten Geburtstag von Georg Lukács* (Neuwied, 1965), pp. 588-604.

11. See Zoltán Kenyeres, "Beginn der Laufbahn G. Lukács und sein Weg zum Marxismus," *Acta Litteraria* [Budapest], 7 (1965), 370-371. On Balázs see Robert Musil, "Ansätze zu neuer Ästhetik: Bemergungen über eine Dramaturgie des Films (Béla Balázs: *Der sichtbare Mensch*)," [1925] in Musil, *Tagebücher, Aphorismen, Essays und Reden* (Hamburg, 1955), pp. 667-683; Ervin Gyertyán, "Béla Balázs and the Film," *New Hungarian Quarterly*, 2 (July, 1961), 189-194.

12. Béla Balázs, *Der sichtbare Mensch oder die Kultur des Films* (Vienna, 1924), pp. 11-12. For astonishing statistics on movie attendance in Great Britain during the 1920's, see A. J. P. Taylor, *English History 1914-1945* (Oxford, 1965), pp. 314-315.

13. Arnold Hauser, *A Social History of Art* (London, 1951), 2:939-959. See also Hauser, *The Philosophy of Art History* (New York, 1959), pp. 357-365, 396-399.

14. Hauser, "Conceptions of Time in Modern Art and Science," *Partisan Review*, 23 (1956), 332.

15. See Manfred Durzak, "Hermann Broch und der Film," *Der Monat*, 18 (May, 1966), 68-75. For other Austrians who admire cinema see Hans Winge, "Die Intellektuellen und der Film," *Forum*, 5 (1948), 421-422.

16. Hauser, "The New Outlook," *Art News*, 51 (June, 1952), 45.

17. Hauser, "Conceptions of Time," p. 327.

18. Hauser, *A Social History of Art*, 2:661. For a critique of Hauser see Ernst Gombrich, "The Social History of Art" [1953], in *Meditations on a Hobby Horse and Other Essays on the Theory of Art* (London, 1963), pp. 86-94.

CHAPTER 28

1. Karl Kraus, "Grosser Sieg der Technik" [1912], in *Untergang der Welt durch schwarze Magie* [1922], repr. in *Werke*, 8 (Munich, 1960), 51.

2. For a contemporary appraisal see Felix Poppenberg, "Apokalypse," *Neue Rundschau*, 21 (1910), 413-418 [compares Kubin's novel with Valery Bryusov's *The Republic of the Southern Cross*].

3. The indispensable compendium on sexual mores is Magnus Hirschfeld, *Sittengeschichte des Weltkrieges*, 2 vols. (Leipzig, 1930; 2d ed., Hanau, 1966) [contains rare illustrations]. A choice anthology of German and Austrian responses to the war is Ernst Johann, ed., *Innenansicht eines Krieges: Bilder-*

Briefe - Dokumente, 1914-1918 (Frankfurt, 1968) [presents about 500 excerpts in chronological sequence]. On battlefield experiences see William K. Pfeiler, *War and the German Mind: The Testimony of Men of Fiction Who Fought at the Front* (New York, 1941).

4. "Die innere Dürre, die ungeheuerliche Mischung von Schärfe im Einzelnen und Gleichgültigkeit im Ganzen, das ungeheure Verlassensein des Menschen in einer Wüste von Einzelheiten, seine Unruhe, Bosheit, Herzensgleichgültigkeit ohnegleichen, Geldsucht, Kälte und Gewalttätigkeit, wie sie unsre Zeit kennzeichnen, sollen nach diesen Berichten einzig und allein die Folge der Verluste sein, die ein logisch scharfes Denken der Seele zufügt!" Robert Musil, *Der Mann ohne Eigenschaften* (Hamburg, 1952), p. 40. Musil surveyed postwar intellectual disarray in Musil, "Das hilflose Europa oder Reise vom Hundertsten ins Tausendste" [1922], in *Tagebücher, Aphorismen, Essays und Reden* (Hamburg, 1955), pp. 622-640.
5. Albert Ehrenstein, *Gedichte und Prosa*, ed. Karl Otten (Neuwied, 1961), pp. 23-24.
6. Joseph Roth, *Die Kapuzinergruft* [1938] (Munich, 1967), pp. 44, 46, 51-52.
7. See Elisabeth Pablé, "Der vergessene Welterfolg: Hans von Chlumberg," *Literatur und Kritik*, Nr. 36-37 (1969), pp. 382-395.
8. "Horrors of Austrian Prisons: Inhuman Treatment of Civilian Women and Men at Internment Camps," *New York Times Current History Magazine*, 8:2 (1918), 97-99 [by a correspondent of the London *Telegraph*].
9. "Wir waren kompliziert genug, die Maschine zu bauen, und wir sind zu primitiv, uns ihr bedienen zu lassen. Wir treiben einen Weltverkehr auf schmalspurigen Gehirnbahnen." Kraus, "Apokalypse" [1908], in *Werke*, 8 (Munich, 1960), 11.
10. "Der Staat, der Krieg, die Wissenschaft, eine unendliche Kette vampyrischer Attrapen, die mit Blut getränkt werden müssen, um das Antlitz des Lebens zu bekommen." Franz Werfel, "Die christliche Sendung," *Neue Rundschau*, 38 (1917), 99. For later works denouncing technology, see Joachim G. Leithauser, "Im Gruselkabinett der Technik: Kritische Bemerkungen zur Mode des romantischen Pessimismus," *Der Monat*, 3 (1950-51), 474-486. For an anthology of Austrian reactions to warfare see Albert Massiczek and Erica Wantoch, eds., *Weltkrieg, Weltfriede: 161 österreichische Autoren in einer Anthologie* (Vienna, 1967), esp. pp. 45-136.
11. "Und ich ging zu Fuss durch die sterbende Natur, es war wie ein Krankenbesuch, nein, wie ein Leichenzug. Und der Sterbende war schon eine Leiche und sein eigener Friedhof zugleich. . . . Der Moder ist hier gesünder als das Leben, die Fäulnis ist fruchtbar und mordet die Gesundheit, der Gestank tötet den Duft und das Geheul betäubt den Gesang . . ." Roth, "Reisebrief aus Merseburg" [1930], in Walter Killy, ed., *Zeichen der Zeit. IV. Verwandlung der Wirklichkeit* (Frankfurt, 1958), p. 236. Another Austrian bemoaned the desolation at Leuna in Hans Natonek, "Germany's City of Robots," *Living Age*, 339 (1930-31), 48-51.
12. Quoted in Josef Paul Hodin, *The Dilemma of Being Modern* (New York, 1959), p. 69.
13. Arthur Schnitzler, "Briefe zur Politik," *Neues Forum*, 15 (1968), 678 [letter of Dec. 22, 1914 to Elisabeth Steinrück].
14. "die Anmut als Seichtheit und die Melancholie als Pose; den Überschuss an Stimmungen als Mangel an Grundsätzen; die scheinbare Leichtigkeit des

Schaffens als Oberflächlichkeit; die unvergleichliche Gabe des Aperçus als Kleine Form; die unwiderstehliche Atmosphäre als Lokalkolorit, aber den Griff ins Europäische als Überhebung–ein fideles Nest von Widersprüchen, die manchem Grossen das Leben verbittert haben." Ernst Stein, "Mit Schiele hat sich die Nachwelt blamiert," *Die Zeit,* Nr. 15 (April 16, 1968), p. 11.

15. "Ich glaub' von jedem Menschen das Schlechteste, selbst von mir, und ich hab' mich selten getäuscht." Quoted in Otto Schulmeister, *Die Zukunft Österreichs* (Vienna, 1967), p. 81.

16. "Man handelte in diesem Land . . . immer anders, als man dachte, oder dachte anders, als man handelte." Musil, *Der Mann,* p. 34. Already in 1913 Musil denounced Austrian politics as a sham. See Musil, "Politik in Österreich," [1913] *Tagebücher,* pp. 589-592.

17. Roth, *Radetzkymarsch* [1932] (Cologne, 1967), pp. 237, 272.

18. "Hier wie nirgends anderswo gebe es wüsten Streit ohne Spur von Hass und eine Art von zärtlicher Liebe, ohne das Bedürfnis der Treue. Zwischen politischen Gegnern existierten oder entwickelten sich lächerliche persönliche Sympathien; Parteifreunde hingegen beschimpften, verleumdeten, verrieten einander." Schnitzler, *Der Weg ins Freie* [1908] (Berlin, 1918), p. 414.

19. C. D. Darlington, *The Evolution of Man and Society* (London, 1969), pp. 678-679. Darlington interprets the consequences of Habsburg inbreeding, *ibid.,* pp. 521-526.

20. Béla Bartók, "Race Purity in Music," *Horizon,* 10 (1944), 405.

21. "geradezu seine 'romantische' Ironie, die fast unheimliche Fähigkeit alle 52 Seiten einer Sache auf einmal zu sehen und zu verstehen, aber auch ebensogut ihr Gegenteil." Walter Brecht, Österreichische Geistesform und österreichische Dichtung," *DVLG,* 9 (1931), 624.

22. Anton Wildgans, *Rede über Österreich* (Vienna, 1930), p. 27.

23. "Ich habe stets meine Feinde geliebt." Hermann Bahr, "Selbstinventur," *Neue Rundschau,* 23 (1912), 1297.

24. "weil ich die Gegner, besonders so vornehme Gegner, gerne zu Worte kommen lasse." Bertha von Suttner, *Memoiren* [1909] (Bremen, 1965), p. 302.

25. "Ja, es war, trotz vielem, was dagegen spricht, Kakanien vielleicht doch ein Land für Genies; und wahrscheinlich ist es daran auch zugrunde gegangen." Musil, *Der Mann,* p. 35.

26. See Michael Polanyi, *Personal Knowledge: Towards a Post-Critical Philosophy* (Chicago, 1958; 2d ed., 1962); Friedrich von Hayek, *The Sensory Order: An Inquiry into the Foundations of Theoretical Psychology* (Chicago, 1952); Ludwig von Bertalanffy, *Robots, Men, and Minds: Psychology in the Modern World* (New York, 1967); Bertalanffy, *General System Theory: Foundations, Development, Applications* (New York, 1968).

Bibliography

Bibliography

BIBLIOGRAPHY

The purpose of this bibliography is to further research on the political, social, and especially the intellectual history of the Habsburg Empire and its successor states. In order to stress general works on the period since 1800, journal articles have been largely omitted. Works on Hungary are listed separately to emphasize their availability. The compilation of memoirs, it is hoped, will stimulate use of these often neglected sources. Monographs on particular thinkers which appear in the notes are not listed in the bibliography. Works published in English, German, and French through 1969 are included. The bibliography is arranged as follows:

PART ONE Political and Social History
      A. Political and Social History of Austria
      B. Political and Social History of Hungary
      C. Memoirs on Austria-Hungary

PART TWO Intellectual History Since 1800
      A. Reference Works in Intellectual History
      B. Surveys of Austrian Thought and Literature
      C. Surveys of Hungarian Thought and Literature
      D. Surveys of Philosophy in Austria
      E. Surveys of Social Theory in Austria
      F. Surveys of Fine Arts in Austria

PART ONE: POLITICAL AND SOCIAL HISTORY SINCE 1800

A. POLITICAL AND SOCIAL HISTORY OF AUSTRIA

Andics, Hellmut. *Der Staat den keiner wollte: Österreich 1918-1938.* Vienna: Verlag Herder, 1962. 2d ed. 1964.

Arkel, Dirk van. *Antisemitism in Austria.* Leiden, 1966 [thorough].

Auerbach, Bertrand. *Les Races et les nationalités en Autriche-Hongrie.* Paris, 1898. 2d ed. 1917.

Bauer, Otto. *Die österreichische Revolution.* Vienna, 1923. Repr. 1965.

Benedikt, Heinrich, ed. *Geschichte der Republik Österreich.* Munich, 1954.

———. *Die wirtschaftliche Entwicklung in der Franz-Joseph-Zeit.* Vienna: Verlag Herold, 1958.

———. *Die Monarchie des Hauses Österreich: Ein historisches Essay.* Munich: R. Oldenbourg Verlag, 1968 [penetrating].

Berchtold, Klaus, ed. *Österreichische Parteiprogramme 1868-1966.* Munich: R. Oldenbourg Verlag, 1967 [useful introduction, pp. 11-105].

Bernatzik, Edmund. *Der österreichischen Verfassungsgesetze.* Leipzig, 1906.

Bibl, Viktor. *Die Zerfall Österreichs.* 2 vols. Vienna, 1922-1924.

Böhm, Wilhelm. *Konservative Umbaupläne im alten Österreich: Gestaltungsprobleme des Völkerreiches.* Vienna: Europa Verlag, 1967.

Bosl, Karl, ed. *Handbuch der Geschichte der böhmischen Länder.* 4 vols. Stuttgart: Anton Hiersemann, 1966-1969 [masterful compendium with exhaustive bibliographies].

Brügel, Ludwig. *Soziale Gesetzgebung in Österreich von 1848 bis 1919: Eine geschichtliche Darstellung.* Vienna, 1919.

——. *Geschichte der österreichischen Sozialdemokratie.* 5 vols. Vienna, 1922-1925.

Bullock, Malcolm. *Austria 1918-1938: A Study in Failure.* London, 1939.

Charmatz, Richard. *Geschichte der auswärtigen Politik Österreichs im 19. Jahrhundert.* 2 vols. 2d ed. Leipzig, 1918.

——. *Lebensbilder aus der Geschichte Österreichs.* Vienna, 1947.

Colquhoun, Archibald Ross, and Ethel Colquhoun. *The Whirlpool of Europe: Austria-Hungary and the Habsburgs.* London, 1907 [abounds in anecdotes].

Czedik, Alois von. *Zur Geschichte der k.k. österreichischen Ministerien 1861 bis 1916 nach den Erinnerungen.* 4 vols. Vienna, 1917-1920.

Czeike, Felix. *Wirtschafts- und Sozialpolitik der Gemeinde Wien in der ersten Republik 1919-1934.* 2 vols. Vienna: Verlag für Jugend und Volk, 1958-1959.

Danzer, Alfons. *Unter den Fahnen: Die Völker Österreich-Ungarns in Waffen.* Vienna, 1889 [evokes military life].

Denis, Ernest. *La Bohême depuis la Montagne-Blanche.* 2 vols. Paris, 1903 [exhaustive, pro-Czech].

Diamant, Alfred. *Austrian Catholics and the First Republic: Democracy, Capitalism, and the Social Order, 1918-1934.* Princeton: Princeton University Press, 1960.

Drage, Geoffrey. *Austria-Hungary.* London, 1909 [bluntly factual].

Feldl, Peter. *Das verspielte Reich: Die letzten Tage Österreich-Ungarns.* Vienna: Paul Zsolnay Verlag, 1968.

Franz, Georg. *Liberalismus: Die deutschliberale Bewegung in der habsburgischen Monarchie.* Munich: Callwey, 1955.

Funder, Friedrich. *Als Österreich den Sturm bestand: Aus der ersten in die zweite Republik.* 3d ed. Vienna: Verlag Herold, 1957.

Gayda, Virginio. *Modern Austria: Her Racial and Social Problems with a Study of Italia Irredenta* [1913]. London, 1915 [favors the Italians and Czechs].

Geyde, G. E. R. *Heirs to the Habsburgs.* London: Arrowsmith, 1932.

Glassl, Horst. *Der mährische Ausgleich.* Munich: Fides Gesellschaft, 1967.

Gulick, Charles A. *From Habsburg to Hitler.* 2 vols. Berkeley and Los Angeles: University of California Press, 1948.

Guttry, Alexander von. *Galizien: Land und Leute.* Munich, 1916.

Hantsch, Hugo. *Die Nationalitätenfrage im alten Österreich: Das Problem der konstruktiven Reichsgestaltung.* Vienna: Verlag Herold, 1953.

——. *Die Geschichte Österreichs.* Vol. 1. 4th ed. Graz: Verlag Styria, 1959. Vol. 2. 3d ed. 1962.

——. *Leopold Graf Berchtold: Grandseigneur und Staatsmann.* 2 vols. Graz: Verlag Styria, 1963.

Hellbling, Ernst C. *Österreichische Verfassungs- und Verwaltungsgeschichte Ein Lehrbuch für Studierende.* Vienna: Springer-Verlag, 1956.

Hugelmann, Karl Gottfried, ed. *Das Nationalitätenrecht des alten Österreich.* Vienna: Wilhelm Braumüller, 1934 [indispensable handbook frequently with German-National bias].

Jászi, Oscar. *The Dissolution of the Habsburg Monarchy.* Chicago: University of Chicago Press 1929. Repr. 1961 [informative critique of institutions].

Jenks, William A. *Austria Under the Iron Ring 1879-1893.* Charlottsville, Va.: University Press of Virginia, 1965.

Kann, Robert A. *The Multinational Empire: Nationalism and National Reform in the Habsburg Monarchy 1848-1918.* 2 vols. New York: Columbia University Press, 1950. Repr. New York, Octagon Books, 1964.

Kleinwaechter, Friedrich F. G. *Der Untergang der österreichisch-ungarischen Monarchie.* Leipzig, 1920.

Kolmer, Gustav. *Parliament und Verfassung in Österreich.* 8 vols. Vienna, 1902-1914.

Lansdale, Maria Hornor. *Vienna and the Viennese.* Philadelphia, 1902 [informative on mores].

Levetus, A. S. *Imperial Vienna: An Account of Its History, Traditions, and Arts.* London, 1905.

Macartney, C. A. *The Social Revolution in Austria.* Cambridge: The University Press, 1926.

———. *The Habsburg Empire, 1790-1918.* London: Macmillan, 1969 [magisterial].

Massiczek, Albert, and Hermann Sagl. *Zeit an der Wand: Österreichs Vergangenheit 1848-1965 in den wichtigsten Anschlägen und Plakaten.* Vienna: Europa Verlag, 1967 [reproduces 160 posters].

May, Arthur J. *The Hapsburg Monarchy 1867-1914.* Cambridge, Mass.: Harvard University Press, 1951 [indispensable].

———. *The Passing of the Hapsburg Monarchy 1914-1918.* 2 vols. Philadelphia: University of Pennsylvania Press, 1966.

Mayer, Franz Martin, Raimund Friedrich Kaindl, and Hans Pirchegger. *Geschichte und Kulturleben Österreichs.* Ed. Anton Adalbert Klein. Vol. 3. 5th ed. Vienna: Wilhelm Braumüller, 1965.

Molisch, Paul. *Geschichte der deutschnationalen Bewegung in Österreich: Von ihren Anfängen bis zum Zerfall der Monarchie.* Jena: Gustav Fischer, 1926.

———. *Politische Geschichte der deutschen Hochschulen in Österreich von 1848 bis 1918.* 2d ed. Vienna: Wilhelm Braumüller, 1939.

Münch, Hermann. *Böhmische Tragödie: Das Schicksal Mitteleuropas im Lichte der tschechischen Frage.* Baunschweig: Georg Westermann Verlag, 1949 [highly informative].

Murad, Anatol. *Franz Joseph I. of Austria and His Empire.* New York: Twayne, 1968 [concise].

Die österreichisch-ungarische Monarchie in Wort und Bild. 24 vols. Vienna, 1886-1902.

Palmer, Francis H. E. *Austro-Hungarian Life in Town and Country.* New York, 1903.

Pech, Stanley Z. *The Czech Revolution of 1848.* Chapel Hill: University of ·North Carolina Press, 1969.

Preradovich, Nikolaus von. *Die Führengsschichten in Österreich und Preussen (1804-1918): Mit einem Ausblick bis zum Jahre 1945.* Wiesbaden: Steiner, 1955. 2d ed. 1966.

Pribram, Alfred Francis. *Austrian Foreign Policy, 1908-1918.* London, 1923.

Pulzer, Peter G. J. *The Rise of Political Anti-Semitism in Germany and Austria.* New York: John Wiley, 1964 [less balanced than Arkel].

Redlich, Josef. *Das österreichische Staats- und Reichsproblem: Geschichtliche Darstellung der inneren Politik der habsburgischen Monarchie von 1848 bis zum Untergang des Reiches.* 2 vols. Leipzig: P. Reinhold, 1920-1926.

――. *Emperor Franz Joseph of Austria: A Biography.* New York: Macmillan, 1929.

Robertson, Priscilla. *Revolutions of 1848: A Social History.* Princeton: Princeton University Press, 1952. Repr. New York: Harper and Row, 1960. Pp. 187-307.

Schierbrand, Wolf von. *Austria-Hungary: Polyglot Empire.* New York, 1917 [revealing on life at court].

Seton-Watson, R. W. *A History of the Czechs and Slovaks.* London, 1943. Repr. Hamden, Conn.: Archon Books, 1965.

Shepherd, Gordon. *The Austrian Odyssey.* London: Macmillan, 1957.

Silberbauer, Gerhard. *Österreichs Katholiken und die Arbeiterfrage.* Graz: Verlag Styria, 1966.

Srbik, Heinrich Ritter von. *Metternich: Der Staatsmann und der Mensch.* 3 vols. Munich: Verlag F. Bruckmann, 1925-1954.

――. *Deutsche Einheit: Idee und Wirklichkeit vom heiligen Reich bis Königgrätz.* 4 vols. Munich, 1935-1942. Repr. Darmstadt: Wissenschaftliche Buchgesellschaft, 1963.

Steed, Henry Wickham. *The Hapsburg Monarchy.* 2d ed. London, 1914 [exceptionally well-informed].

Strakosch-Grassmann, Gustav. *Geschichte des österreichischen Unterrichtswesens.* Vienna, 1905.

Sutter, Berthold. *Die badenischen Sprachenverordnungen von 1897: Ihre Genesis und ihre Ausweichungen vornehmlich auf die innerösterreichischen Alpenländer.* 2 vols. Graz: Verlag Hermann Böhlaus Nachfolger, 1960-1965.

Taylor, A. J. P. *The Habsburg Monarchy 1809-1918: A History of the Austrian Empire and Austria-Hungary.* London: Hamish Hamilton, 1948. Repr. New York: Harper and Row, 1965.

Thomson, S. Harrison. *Czechoslovakia in European History.* Princeton: Princeton University Press, 1943. 2d ed. 1953.

Vasili, Comte Paul. *La Société de Vienne.* Paris, 1885 [useful survey].

Waldegg, Richard, and Rudolf Till. *Sittengeschichte von Wien.* 4th ed. Stuttgart: Weltspiegel Verlag, 1965 [stresses the demimonde].

Walter, Friedrich. *Die österreichische Zentralverwaltung.* Vols. 2 and 3. Vienna: Holzhausen, 1950-1964 [continues the opus of Thomas Fellner up to 1867].

Wandruszka, Adam. *Das Haus Habsburg: Die Geschichte einer europäischen Dynastie.* Stuttgart: Friedrich Vorwerk Verlag, 1956. 2d ed. 1959.

――. *Geschichte einer Zeitung: Das Schicksal der 'Presse' und der 'Neuen Freien Presse' von 1848 bis zur zweiten Republik.* Vienna: Neue Wiener Presse, 1958.

――. "Österreich-Ungarn vom ungarischen Ausgleich bis zum Ende der Monarchie (1867-1918)." In Theodor Schieder, ed. *Handbuch der europäischen Geschichte.* Vol. 6. Stuttgart: Union Verlag, 1968. Pp. 353-399.

Whiteside, Andrew Gladding. *Austrian National Socialism before 1918.* The Hague: Martinus Nijhoff, 1962.

――. "Austria." In Hans Rogger and Eugen Weber, eds. *The European Right: A Historical Profile.* Berkeley and Los Angeles: University of California Press, 1966. Pp. 308-363.

Wien 1848-1888. 2 vols. Vienna, 1888 [surveys cultural institutions].

Wierer, Rudolf. *Der Föderalismus im Donauraum.* Graz: Verlag Hermann Böhlaus Nachfolger, 1960.

Wiskemann, Elizabeth. *Czechs and Germans: A Study of the Struggle in the Historic Provinces of Bohemia and Moravia.* London: Oxford University Press, 1938; 2d ed. London: Macmillan, 1967.

Wodka, Josef. *Kirche in Österreich: Wegweiser durch ihre Geschichte.* Vienna: Verlag Herder, 1959 [comprehensive].

Zeman, Z. A. B. *The Break-Up of the Habsburg Empire 1914-1918: A Study in National and Social Revolution.* London: Oxford University Press, 1961.

Zenker, Ernst Viktor. *Kirche und Staat mit besonderer Rücksichtigung der Verhältnisse in Österreich.* Vienna, 1909 [insightful].

Zöllner, Erich. *Geschichte Österreichs: Von den Anfängen bis zur Gegenwart.* Munich: R. Oldenbourg Verlag, 1966 [judicious].

B.   POLITICAL AND SOCIAL HISTORY OF HUNGARY

Baranyai, Zoltán, ed. *Ungarn: Das Antlitz einer Nation.* Budapest: Königlich-Ungarische Universitäts-Bücherei, 1940.

Bertha, Sándor de. *La Hongrie moderne de 1849 à 1901: Étude historique.* Paris, 1901 [narrative of politics].

Bibliographia Hungariae: Verzeichnis der 1861-1921 erschienenen, Ungarn betreffenden Schriften in nichtungarischen Sprache. 4 vols. Berlin, 1923-1929 [exhaustive].

Birmingham, George A. *A Wayfarer in Hungary.* London, 1925 [perceptive on mores].

Boehm, Wilhelm. *Im Kreuzfeuer zweier Revolutionen.* Munich, 1924 [concerns 1918-1920].

Bogyay, Thomas von. *Grundzüge der Geschichte Ungarns.* Darmstadt: Wissenschaftliche Buchgesellschaft, 1967.

Borsos, Béla, Alajos Sódor, and Mihály Zádor. *Budapest.* Budapest: Müszaki Könyvkiadó, 1959 [superbly illustrated].

Braham, Randolph. *The Hungarian Jewish Catastrophe: A Selected and Annotated Bibliography.* New York: YIVO Institute for Jewish Research, 1962.

———, ed. *Hungarian-Jewish Studies.* New York: World Federation of Hungarian Jews, 1966.

Bucsay, Mihály. *Geschichte des Protestanismus in Ungarn.* Stuttgart: Evangelischer Verlag, 1959.

A Companion to Hungarian Studies. Budapest: Society of the Hungarian Quarterly, 1943.

Csáky, Moritz. *Der Kulturkampf in Ungarn: Die kirchenpolitische Gesetzgebung der Jahre 1894/95.* Graz: Hermann Böhlaus Nachf., 1967.

Csuday, Jenö. *Die Geschichte der Ungarn,* 2 vols. 2d ed. Berlin, 1899.

Cushing, G. F. "Hungary." In Doreen Warriner, ed. *Contrasts in Emerging Societies: Readings in the Social and Economic History of South-Eastern Europe in the Nineteenth Century.* Bloomington: Indiana University Press, 1965. Pp. 29-113 [presents choice documents].

Deák, István. "Hungary." In Hans Rogger and Eugen Weber, eds. *The European Right: A Historical Profile.* Berkeley and Los Angeles: University of California Press. Pp. 364-407.

Diner-Dénes, Joseph. *La Hongrie: Oligarchie, Nation, Peuple.* Paris, 1927.

Domanovszky, Sándor. *Die Geschichte Ungarns.* Munich, 1923.

Engelmann, Nikolaus. *Die banater Schwaben: Auf Vorposten des Abendlandes.* Freilassing: Pannonia, 1966.

Erdei, Ferenc, ed. *Information Hungary.* Oxford, 1968 [Marxist].

Eszlary, Charles d'. *Histoire des Institutions publiques hongroises.* 3 vols. (5 projected) Paris: Marcel, 1959– [vol. 3 covers 1600 to 1848].

Gonnard, René. *La Hongrie au XXe siècle: Étude économique et sociale.* Paris, 1908 [stresses agriculture].

Görlich, Ernst Joseph. *Ungarn.* Nürnberg: Glock und Lutz, 1965.

Gubernatis, Angelo de. *La Hongrie politique et sociale.* Florence, 1885 [perceptive on social classes].

Hatvany, Lajos. *Das verwundete Land.* Leipzig, 1921 [covers 1918-1920].

Horváth, Michael. *Fünfundzwanzig Jahre aus der Geschichte Ungarns 1823-1848.* 2 vols. Leipzig, 1867.

Jászi, Oscar. *Revolution and Counter-Revolution in Hungary.* London: P. S. King, 1924.

Jekelfalussy, Joseph de, ed. *The Millenium of Hungary and Its People.* Budapest, 1897 [compendium of articles on political, social, and intellectual life].

Jókai, Maurus. "Das magyarische Volk." In *Die österreichisch-ungarische Monarchie in Wort und Bild: Ungarn.* Vol. 1. Vienna, 1888. Pp. 282-358 [insightful].

Kain, Albert, ed. *Ungarn.* Stuttgart, 1911 [contains superb photographs].

Király, Béla K. *Hungary in the Late Eigteenth Century: The Decline of Enlightened Despotism.* New York: Columbia University Press, 1969 [excellent analysis of social classes].

Knatchbull-Hugessen, Cecil M. *The Political Evolution of the Hungarian Nation.* 2 vols. London, 1908 [vol. 2 covers the period from 1848 to 1908 thoroughly].

Kosa, John. "Hungarian Society in the Time of the Regency (1920-1944)," *Journal of Central European Affairs,* 16 (1956), 253-265.

Macartney, C. A. *Hungary.* London: E. Benn, 1934.

———. *Hungary and Her Successors: The Treaty of Trianon and Its Consequences 1919-1937.* London: Oxford University Press, 1937.

———. *October Fifteenth: A History of Modern Hungary 1929-1945.* 2 vols. Edinburgh: The University Press, 1956-1957. 2d ed. 1961.

———. *Hungary: A Short History.* Edinburgh: The University Press, 1962.

Mailáth, Johann Graf. *Geschichte der Magyaren,* 5 vols. 2d ed. Regensburg, 1852 [vol. 4 covers from 1740 to 1848; vol. 5 covers 1848].

Marczali, Henrik. *Ungarische Verfassungsgeschichte.* Tübingen, 1910.

———. *Ungarisches Verfassungsrecht.* Tübingen, 1911 [concise].

Marko, Árpád von. *Ungarisches Soldatentum.* Budapest, 1942 [describes military exploits to 1860].

Paikert, G. C. *The Danube Swabians: German Populations in Hungary, Rumania and Yugoslavia and Hitler's Impact on Their Patterns.* The Hague: Martinus Nijhoff, 1967.

Patterson, Arthur J. *The Magyars: Their Country and Institutions.* 2 vols. London, 1869.

Sándor, Vilmos, and Péter Hanák, eds. *Studien zur Geschichte der österreichisch-*

ungarischen Monarchie. Budapest: Akadémiai Kiadó, 1961 [twenty articles mostly on economic history].

Sayous, Édouard. *Histoire générale des Hongrois.* 2 vols. Paris, 1876. 2d ed. 1900.

Schwab, Erasmus. *Land und Leute in Ungarn.* Leipzig, 1865.

Schwicker, Johann Heinrich. *Die Deutschen in Ungarn und Siebenbürgen.* Vienna, 1881.

Seton-Watson, R. W. [Scotus Viator]. *Racial Problems in Hungary.* London, 1908.

———. *Corruption and Reform in Hungary: A Study of Electoral Practice.* London, 1911 [with eyewitness accounts of elections in ten counties].

———. "The Era of Reform in Hungary," *Slavic Review,* 2 (1942-43), 145-166 [covers 1780-1848].

Sosnosky, Theodor von. *Die Politik im Habsburgerreich: Randglossen zur Zeitgeschichte.* 2 vols. Berlin, 1911-1913.

Steinacker, Harold. *Austro-Hungarica: Ausgewählte Aufsätze und Vorträge zur Geschichte Ungarns und der österreichisch-ungarischen Monarchie.* Munich: R. Oldenbourg Verlag, 1963.

Street, C. J. C. *Hungary and Democracy.* London: T. Fischer Unwin, 1923 [polemical].

Szekfü, Gyula. *Der Staat Ungarn.* Stuttgart, 1918.

———. *État et Nation.* Paris: Presses Universitaires de France, 1945 [extremely useful].

Teleki, Pál. *The Evolution of Hungary and Its Place in European History.* New York, 1923.

Tökés, Rudolf L. *Béla Kun and the Hungarian Soviet Republic: The Origins and Role of the Communist Party of Hungary in the Revolutions of 1918-1919.* New York: Frederick Praeger, 1967 [judicious].

Yolland, Arthur B. *Hungary.* London, 1917 [useful appendices].

C. Memoirs on Austria-Hungary

Alexander, Franz. *The Western Mind in Transition: An Eyewitness Story.* New York: Random House, 1960 [by a Hungarian psychoanalyst].

Andreas-Salomé, Lou. *In der Schule bei Freud: Tagebuch eines Jahres 1912-1913.* Munich: Kindler Verlag, 1958.

Apponyi, Albert. *The Memoirs of Count Apponyi.* New York: Macmillan, 1935.

Auffenberg-Komarrów, Moritz. *Aus Österreichs Höhe und Niedergang: Eine Lebensschilderung.* Munich, 1921.

Bahr, Hermann. *Selbstbildnis.* Berlin, 1923.

Baum, Vicki. *Es war alles ganz anders: Erinnerungen.* Berlin: Verlag Ullstein, 1962 [perceptive on Vienna, 1888-1916].

Benedikt, Moritz. *Aus meinem Leben: Erinnerungen und Erörterungen.* Vienna, 1906 [by a physician at Vienna].

Berger, Alfred von. *Autobiographische Schriften.* Vienna, 1913. Biederstein Verlag, 1960. Pp. 1-143.

Bloch, Josef Samuel. *Erinnerungen aus meinem Leben.* 2 vols. Vienna, 1922 [de-
Blei, Franz. "Erzählung einer Jugend" [1930]. In *Schriften in Auswahl.* Munich: scribes campaigns against anti-Semitism 1880-1895].

Bonsal, Stephen. *Heyday in a Vanished World.* New York: Norton, 1937.

——. *Unfinished Business.* New York: Doubleday, 1944.

Brandl, Franz. *Kaiser, Politiker und Menschen.* Leipzig: Günther, 1936 [revelations by a police official].

Braun, Felix. *Das Licht der Welt: Geschichte eines Versuches, als Dichter zu leben.* Vienna: Herder Verlag, 1949. Repr. 1962.

Braunthal, Julius. *In Search of the Millenium.* London: Victor Gollancz, 1945.

Brod, Max. *Der Prager Kreis.* Stuttgart: W. Kohlhammer Verlag, 1966.

——. *Streitbares Leben, 1884-1968.* 2d ed. Munich: F. A. Herbig, 1969.

Brunn, Fritz. *Memoirs of a Doctor of the Old and New Worlds.* New York: Crambruck Press, 1969.

Cormons, Ernest U. *Schicksale und Schatten: Eine österreichische Autobiographie.* Salzburg: Otto Müller Verlag, 1951 [covers 1882-1916].

Coudenhove-Kalergi, Richard N. *An Idea Conquers the World.* London: Hutchinson, 1953.

Deutsch, Julius. *Ein weiter Weg: Lebenserinnerungen.* Vienna: Amalthea-Verlag, 1960.

Ehrhart, Robert. *Im Dienste des alten Österreich.* Vienna: Bergland Verlag, 1958 [covers 1893-1918].

Eisenmenger, Anna. *Blockade: The Diary of an Austrian Middle-Class Woman, 1914-1924.* New York: Long and Smith, 1932.

Felder, Cajetan. *Erinnerungen eines Wiener Bürgermeisters.* Vienna: Forum Verlag, 1964 [covers 1814 to about 1890].

Fiechtner, Helmut A., ed. *Hugo von Hofmannsthal: Der Dichter im Spiegel der Freunde.* Vienna: Humboldt Verlag, 1949. Repr. Bern: Francke Verlag, 1965 [contains forty reminiscences].

Fischer, Ernst. *Erinnerungen und Reflexionen.* Reinbek: Rowohlt, 1969.

Fugger, Princess Nora. *The Glory of the Habsburgs: Memoirs.* New York: Dial, 1932 [evokes the court of Franz Joseph].

Funder, Friedrich. *Vom Gestern ins Heute: Aus dem Kaiserreich in die Republik.* Vienna: Verlag Herold, 1952 [describes the Christian Socialists, 1892 to 1922].

Grossmann, Stefan. *Ich war begeistert: Eine Lebensgeschichte.* Berlin: Fischer, 1931 [by a Social Democrat].

Haas, Willy. *Die literarische Welt: Erinnerungen.* Munich: Paul List Verlag, 1960 [evokes Prague].

Hebbel, Friedrich. *Tagebücher.* In *Werke.* Vols. 4 and 5. Munich: Carl Hanser Verlag, 1967 [dwelt in Vienna 1845 to 1863].

Herder, Charlotte. *. . . schaut durch ein farbiges Glas auf die aschfarbene Welt: Kindheit und Jugend im alten Prag.* Freiburg: Herder Verlag, 1953 [the daughter of Otto Willmann describes Prague 1872 to 1902].

Horthy, Admiral Nicholas. *Memoirs.* London: Hutchinson, 1956.

Hug-Helmuth, Hermine von, ed. *Tagebuch eines halbwüchsigen Mädchens.* Vienna, 1919 [diary of an upper-middle-class Viennese girl at gymnasium].

Károlyi, Michael. *Fighting the World: The Struggle for Peace.* London: Kegan, Paul, 1924.

——. *Memoirs: Faith Without Illusion.* London: Jonathan Cape, 1956.

Károlyi-Andrássy, Catherine. *A Life Together: Memoirs.* London: Allen and Unwin, 1966.

Kassner, Rudolf. *Die zweite Fahrt: Erinnerungen.* Erlenbach-Zürich: Eugen Rentsch Verlag, 1946.

————. *Buch der Erinnerung* [1938]. 2d ed. Erlenbach-Zürich: Eugen Rentsch Verlag, 1954. Pp. 1-142 [describes Vienna from 1892 to about 1910].

Kautsky, Karl. *Erinnerungen und Erörterungen.* The Hague: Mouton, 1960 [describes Prague and Vienna to about 1880].

Kielmansegg, Erich Graf von. *Kaiserhaus, Staatsmänner und Politiker: Aufzeichnungen.* Vienna and Munich: R. Oldenbourg Verlag, 1966.

Kisch, Bruno. *Wanderungen und Wandlungen: Die Geschichte eines Arztes im 20. Jahrhundert.* Cologne: Greven Verlag, 1966 [concerns Prague].

Koestler, Arthur. *Arrow in the Blue: An Autobiography.* Vol. 1. New York: Macmillan, 1952.

Kohn, Hans. *Living in A World Revolution: My Encounters With History.* New York: Trident Press, 1964.

Lorenz, Adolf. *My Life and Work: The Search for a Missing Glove.* New York: Scribner's, 1936 [by the father of Konrad Lorenz; evokes Viennese medical practice between 1875 and 1935].

Lothar, Ernst. *Das Wunder Überlebens: Erinnerungen und Ergebnisse,* Vienna: Paul Zsolnay Verlag, 1961.

Mahler-Werfel, Alma. *Mein Leben.* Frankfurt: S. Fischer Verlag, 1960.

Mauthner, Fritz. *Prager Jugendjahre: Erinnerungen* [1918]. Frankfurt: S. Fischer Verlag, 1969.

Mayer, Sigmund. *Ein jüdischer Kaufmann, 1831 bis 1911: Lebenserinnerungen.* Leipzig, 1911.

Mayreder, Rosa. *Das Haus in der Landskrongasse: Jugenderinnerungen.* Vienna: Mensa, 1948.

Menczel, Philipp. *Trügerische Lösungen: Erlebnisse und Betrachtungen eines Österreichers.* Stuttgart: Deutsche Verlags-Anstalt, 1932 [describes Bukovina to 1919].

Pálffy von Erdöd, Paul Graf. *Abschied von Vorgestern und Gestern.* Stuttgart: Schuler, 1961.

Petzold, Alfons. *Das rauhe Leben: Der Roman eines Menschen.* Berlin: Ullstein Verlag, 1920 [describes the Viennese proletariat 1882-1920].

Pupin, Michael. *From Immigrant to Inventor.* New York: Scribner's, 1922. Repr. 1960 [on the Banat].

Redlich, Josef. *Schicksalsjahre Österreichs 1908-1919: Das politische Tagebuch Josef Redlichs.* 2 vols. Graz: Verlag Hermann Böhlaus Nachfolger, 1953-1954.

Renner, Karl. *An der Wende zweier Zeiten (Lebenserinnerungen).* Vienna: Danubia, 1946 [covers to 1895].

Rohan, Karl Anton. *Heimat Europa: Erinnerungen und Erfahrungen.* Düsseldorf: Diederich, 1954 [on Bohemian nobility].

Schnabel, Artur. *My Life and Music.* London: Longmans, 1961.

Schnitzler, Arthur. *Jugend in Wien: Eine Autobiographie.* Vienna: Verlag Fritz Molden, 1968 [covers to 1889; written 1915-1920].

Sieghart, Rudolf. *Die letzten Jahrzehnte einer Grossmacht: Menschen, Völker, Probleme des Habsburger-Reichs.* Berlin: Ullstein Verlag, 1932.

Slomka, Jan. *From Serfdom to Self-Government: Memoirs of a Polish Village Mayor, 1842-1927.* London: Minerva, 1941 [describes peasant life in East Galicia].

Somary, Felix. *Erinnerungen aus meinem Leben.* 2d ed. Zürich: Manesse Verlag, 1959.

484 BIBLIOGRAPHY

Spiel, Hilde. *Rückkehr nach Wien: Tagebuch 1946*. Munich: Nymphenburger Verlag, 1968.

Spitzmüller, Alexander. *". . . und hat auch Ursach,' es zu lieben."* Vienna: Frick, 1955.

Steed, Henry Wickham. *Through Thirty Years 1892-1922: A Personal Narrative*. 2 vols. Garden City, N. Y.: Doubleday, 1924.

Stekel, Wilhelm. *Autobiography: The Life Story of a Pioneer Psychoanalyst*. New York: Liveright, 1950.

Sternberg, Adalbert Graf von. *Warum Österreich zugrunde gehen musste*. 4th ed. Vienna: Tagesfragen, 1927.

Suttner, Bertha von. *Memoiren* [Stuttgart, 1909]. Bremen: Carl Schünemann Verlag, 1965.

Szeps, Berta. *My Life and History*. New York: Alfred A. Knopf, 1939 [highly informative].

Uhl, Friedrich. *Aus meinem Leben*. Stuttgart, 1908.

Wechsberg, Joseph. *Sweet and Sour*. Boston: Houghton Mifflin, 1948.

Wilczek, Hans. *Gentleman of Vienna: Reminiscences*. New York: Reynal and Hitchcock, 1934 [evokes the upper aristocracy from 1840 to 1920].

Winter, Josefine. *Fünfzig Jahre eines Wiener Hauses*. Vienna: Wilhelm Braumüller, 1927 [describes Jewish patrician families between 1875 and 1925].

Zweig, Stefan. *Die Welt von Gestern: Erinnerungen eines Europäers*. Stockholm: Bermann-Fischer Verlag, 1942 [indispensable].

PART TWO: INTELLECTUAL HISTORY SINCE 1800

A. REFERENCE WORKS IN INTELLECTUAL HISTORY
[all are of fundamental importance]

Allgemeine Deutsche Biographie. 56 vols. Leipzig, 1875-1912.

Bamberger, Richard, and Franz Maier-Bruck, eds. *Österreich-Lexikon*. 2 vols. Vienna: Österreichischer Bundesverlag, 1966.

Bernsdorf, Wilhelm, ed. *Internationales Soziologenlexikon*. Stuttgart: Ferdinand Enke Verlag, 1959.

Bettelheim, Anton et al., eds. *Neue Österreichische Biographie, 1815-1918*. Vienna: Amalthea-Verlag, 1923–.

Brockhaus Enzyklopädie [projected in 20 vols.]. Wiesbaden: F. A. Brockhaus, 1966–.

Der Grosse Brockhaus. 12 vols. 16th ed. Wiesbaden: F. A. Brockhaus, 1954-1957.

Edwards, Paul, ed. *The Encyclopedia of Philosophy*. 8 vols. New York: Macmillan and Free Press, 1967.

Eisenberg, Ludwig. *Das geistige Wien: Künstler- und Schriftsteller-Lexikon*. 2 vols. Vienna, 1893.

Fleming, Donald, and Bernard Bailyn, eds. *The Intellectual Migration: Europe and America, 1930-1960*. Cambridge, Mass.: Harvard University Press, 1969 [contains fourteen synoptic articles plus a glossary of three hundred notable emigrés].

Galling, Kurt, ed. *Die Religion in Geschichte und Gegenwart: Handwörterbuch für Theologie and Religionswissenschaft.* 7 vols. 3d ed. Tübingen: J. C. B. Mohr, 1957-1965 [Protestant].

Giebisch, Hans, and Gustav Gugitz. *Bio-bibliographisches Literaturlexikon Österreichs von der Anfängen bis zur Gegenwart.* Vienna: Brüder Hollinek, 1964.

Groner, Richard, and Felix Czeike. *Wien wie es war. Ein Nachschlagewerk für Freunde des alten und neuen Wien,* 5th ed. Vienna: Verlag Fritz Molden, 1965.

Herlitz, Georg, and Bruno Kirschner, eds. *Jüdisches Lexikon: Ein enzyklopädisches Handbuch des jüdischen Wissens.* 5 vols. Berlin: Jüdischer Verlag, 1927-1930.

Hofer, Josef, and Karl Rahner, eds. *Lexikon für Theologie und Kirche.* 11 vols. 2d ed. Freiburg: Verlag Herder, 1957-1965 [Roman Catholic].

Kaznelson, Sigmund, ed. *Juden im deutschen Kulturbereich: Ein Sammelwerk.* 3d ed. Berlin: Jüdischer Verlag, 1962.

Klusacek, Christine. *Österreichs Wissenschaftler und Künstler unter dem NS-Regime.* Vienna: Europa Verlag, 1966.

Knoll, Fritz. *Österreichische Naturforscher, Ärzte und Techniker.* Vienna: Gesellschaft für Natur und Technik, 1957 [omits many major figures].

Kosch, Wilhelm. *Deutsches Literatur-Lexikon: Biographisches und Bibliographisches Handbuch.* 4 vols. 2d ed. Bern: Francke Verlag, 1949-1958.

Kosch, Wilhelm, and Eugen Kuri. *Biographisches Staatshandbuch: Lexikon der Politik, Presse und Publizistik.* 2 vols. Bern: Francke Verlag, 1963 [volume 2 abounds in errors].

Kunisch, Hermann, ed. *Handbuch der deutschen Gegenwartsliteratur.* Munich: Nymphenburger Verlagshandlung, 1965.

Landmann, Isaac, ed. *The Universal Jewish Encyclopedia.* 10 vols. New York: Universal Jewish Encyclopedia, 1939-1943.

Lange-Eichbaum, Wilhelm, and Wolfram Kurth. *Genie, Irrsinn und Ruhm: Genie-Mythus und Pathographie des Genies.* 6th ed. Munich: Ernst Reinhardt Verlag, 1967.

Lenhoff, Eugen, and Oskar Posner. *Internationales Freimaurerlexikon.* Vienna: Amalthea-Verlag, 1932. Repr. 1966.

Neue Deutsche Biographie. Berlin: Duncker und Humblot, 1953–.

New Catholic Encyclopedia. 15 vols. New York: McGraw-Hill, 1967.

Oppenheimer, John F., ed. *Lexikon des Judentums.* Gütersloh: C. Bertelsmann Verlag, 1967.

Paupié, Kurt. *Handbuch der Österreichischen Pressegeschichte.* 2 vols. Vienna: Wilhelm Braumüller, 1960-1966.

Santifaller, Leo., ed. *Österreichisches Biographisches Lexikon 1815-1950* [projected in 6 vols.]. Graz: Verlag Hermann Böhlaus Nachf., 1957–.

Schuder, Werner, ed. *Kürschners Deutscher Gelehrtenkalender 1966.* 2 vols. 10th ed. Berlin: Walter de Gruyter, 1966.

Seligman, Edwin R. A., ed. *Encyclopaedia of the Social Sciences.* 15 vols. New York: Macmillan, 1930-1935.

Sills, David L., ed. *International Encyclopedia of the Social Sciences.* 17 vols. New York: Macmillan and Free Press, 1968.

Singer, Isidore, ed. *The Jewish Encyclopedia.* 12 vols. New York, 1901-1906.

Teichl, Robert, ed. *Österreicher der Gegenwart: Lexikon schöpferischer und schaffender Zeitgenossen.* Vienna: Österreichische Staatsdruckerei, 1951.

Williams, Trevor I., ed. *A Biographical Dictionary of Scientists.* London: Adam and Charles Black, 1969.

Wilpert, Gero von, ed. *Lexikon der Weltliteratur: Biographisch-bibliographiscnes Handwörterbuch nach Autoren und anonymen Werken.* Stuttgart: Alfred Kröner Verlag, 1963.

Wilpert, Gero von, and Adolf Gühring, eds. *Erstausgaben deutscher Dichtung: Eine Bibliographi zur dutschen Literatur 1600-1960.* Stuttgart: Alfred Kröner Verlag, 1967.

Wininger, Salomon, ed. *Grosse Jüdische Nationalbiographie.* 7 vols. Czernowitz: Orient, 1925-1936.

Wurzbach, Constant von, ed. *Biographisches Lexikon des Kaiserthums Österreich.* 60 vols. Vienna, 1856-1891. Repr. New York: Johnson Reprint, 1966.

Ziak, Karl, ed. *Unvergängliches Wien: Ein Gang durch die Geschichte von der Urzeit bis zur Gegenwart.* Vienna: Europa-Verlag and Forum-Verlag, 1964.

Ziegenfuss, Werner, and Gertrud Jung, eds. *Philosophen-Lexikon: Handwörterbuch der Philosophie nach Personen.* 2 vols. Berlin: Walter de Gruyter, 1949-1950.

Zischka, Gert A. *Allgemeines Gelehrten-Lexikon: Biographisches Handwörterbuch zur Geschichte der Wissenschaften.* Stuttgart: Alfred Kröner Verlag, 1961.

B.   Surveys of Austrian Thought and Literature

Adel, Kurt. *Geist und Wirklichkeit: Vom Werden der österreichischen Dichtung.* Vienna: Österreichische Verlagsanstalt, 1967 [encyclopedic and judicious].

Bauer, Roger. *"La réalité: Royaume de Dieu": Études sur l'originalité du théâtre viennois dans la première partie du 19ème siecle.* Munich: Hueber, 1965.

Beck, Gabriel. *Die erzählende Prosa Albert Ehrensteins (1886-1950): Interpretation und Versuch einer literarhistorischen Einordnung.* Freiburg/Schweiz: Universitätsverlag, 1969 [pp. 9-36 offer a discerning appraisal of Expressionism].

Bertram, Ernst, "Über den Wiener Roman," *Mitteilungen der literarhistorischen Gesellschaft* [Bonn], 4 (1909), 3-44.

Bianquis, Geneviève. *La poésie autrichienne: De Hofmannsthal à Rilke.* Paris: Presses Universitaires de France, 1926.

Bietak, Wilhelm. *Das Lebensgefühl des "Biedermeier" in der österreichischen Dichtung.* Vienna: Wilhelm Braumüller, 1931.

Blauhut, Robert. *Österreichische Novellistik des 20. Jahrhunderts.* Vienna: Wilhelm Braumüller, 1966 [succinct].

Brecht, Walter. "Österreichische Geistesform und österreichische Dichtung: Nach einem Vortrag," *Deutsche Vierteljahresschrift für Literaturwissenschaft und Geistesgeschichte,* 9 (1931), 607-627.

Breicha, Otto, and Gerhard Fritsch, eds. *Finale und Auftakt: Wien 1898-1914.* Salzburg: Otto Müller Verlag, 1964.

———. *Aufforderung zum Misstrauen.* Salzburg: Residenz Verlag, 1967 [anthology on the arts since 1945].

Castle, Eduard, ed. *Geschichte der deutschen Literatur in Österreich-Ungarn im Zeitalter Franz Josephs I.* 2 vols. Vienna: Fromme, 1936-1937 [indispensable, esp. on minor figures].

Derré, Françoise. *L'Oeuvre d'Arthur Schnitzler: Imagerie Viennoise et problèmes humains.* Paris: Didier, 1966 [combines literary and social history].

Fermi, Laura. *Illustrious Immigrants: The Intellectual Migration from Europe 1930-41.* Chicago: University of Chicago Press, 1968 [esp. pp. 3-11, 32-59].

Fischer, Ernst. *Die Entstehung des österreichischen Volkscharacters*. Vienna: Verlag Neues Österreich, 1945.

———. *Von Grillparzer zu Kafka: Sechs Essays*. Vienna: Globus-Verlag, 1962 [provocative on Grillparzer, Lenau, Nestroy, Kraus, Musil, and Kafka].

Fraenkel, Josef, ed. *The Jews of Austria: Essays on Their Life, History and Destruction*. London: Vallentine-Mitchell, 1967 [thirty-four essays].

Fuchs, Albert. *Moderne österreichische Dichter: Essays*. Vienna: Globus-Verlag, 1946.

———. *Geistige Strömungen in Österreich, 1867 bis 1918*. Vienna: Globus-Verlag, 1949 [informative on social thought, weak on philosophy].

Hackert, Fritz. *Kulturpessimismus und Erzählform: Studien zu Joseph Roths Leben und Werk*. Bern: Verlag Herbert Lang, 1967 [esp. pp. 1-62 on Viennese Impressionism].

Hauser, Arnold. *The Social History of Art*. Vol. 2. London: Routledge and Kegan Paul, 1951. Pp. 869-978, esp. 908, 919-924.

Heer, Friedrich. *Land im Strom der Zeit: Österreich gestern, heute, morgen*. Vienna: Herold Verlag, 1958.

———. *Der Glaube des Adolf Hitler: Anatomie einer politischen Religiosität*. Munich: Bechtle Verlag, 1968.

Krojanker, Gustav, ed. *Juden in der deutschen Literatur: Essays über zeitgenössische Schriftsteller*. Berlin, 1922 [of twenty-four essays thirteen deal with Austrian Jews].

Lessing, Theodor. *Der jüdische Selbsthass*. Berlin: Jüdischer Verlag, 1930 [three of the six case studies concern Weininger, Arthur Trebitsch, and Max Steiner].

Magris, Claudio. *Der habsburgische Mythos in der österreichischen Literatur* [1963]. Salzburg: Otto Müller Verlag, 1966 [provocative critique of pro-Habsburg nostalgia].

Mertens, Heinz. *Unheldenhafte und heldenhafte Menschen bei den Wiener Dichtern um 1900*. Bonn, 1929 [typology of Viennese impressionists].

Nadler, Josef. *Literaturgeschichte Österreichs*. Linz: Österreichischer Verlag, 1948. 2d ed. Salzburg: Otto Müller Verlag, 1951.

Politzer, Heinz. *Das Schweigen der Sirenen: Studien zur deutschen und österreichischen Literatur*. Stuttgart: J. B. Metzler, 1968. Pp. 42-206 [eight essays on Austrian writers].

Preisner, Rio. *Johann Nepomuk Nestroy: Der Schöpfer der tragischen Posse*. Munich: Carl Hanser Verlag, 1968 [a discriminating Marxist analysis].

Reiter, Ludwig. *Österreichische Staats- und Kulturgeschichte*. Klagenfurt: Jörgl, 1947 [a year-by-year chronology; exceptionally thorough on inventors].

Rothe, Wolfgang. *Schriftsteller und totalitäre Welt*. Bern: Francke Verlag, 1966 [incisive on Musil, Kafka, Broch, and the impact of World War One].

———, ed. *Expressionismus als Literatur: Gesammelte Studien*. Bern: Francke Verlag, 1969.

Schmidt, Adalbert. *Dichtung und Dichter Österreichs im 19. und 20. Jahrhundert*. 2 vols. Salzburg: Verlag das Bergland-Buch, 1964.

Schnitzler, Henry. "Austria." In Barrett H. Clark and George Freedley, eds. *A History of Modern Drama*. New York: Appleton-Century, 1947. Pp. 124-159 [discriminating].

————. "Gay Vienna: Myth and Reality," *Journal of the History of Ideas*, 15 (1954), 94-118.

Schorske, Carl E. "Politics and the Psyche in *fin de siècle* Vienna: Schnitzler and Hofmannsthal," *American Historical Review*, 66 (1960-61), 930-946 [first of a series on the decline of bourgeois liberalism in Vienna].

————. "The Transformation of the Garden: Ideal and Society in Austrian Literature," *American Historical Review*, 72 (1966-67), 1283-1320 [on Stifter, Saar, Andrian-Werburg, Hofmannsthal, Kokoschka].

————. "Politics in a New Key: An Austrian Triptych," *Journal of Modern History*, 39 (1967-68) 343-386 [on Schönerer, Lueger, Herzl].

————. "Interviews with Historians: Carl E. Schorske," *Colloquium*, Nr. 7 (Fall, 1968), pp. 22-31 [provocative on Viennese architects, Freud, and Austrian religiosity].

Schulmeister, Otto, ed. *Spectrum Austriae*. Vienna: Verlag Herder, 1957 [excellent articles on literature, art, and cultural attitudes].

————. *Die Zukunft Österreichs*. Vienna: Verlag Fritz Molden, 1967 [penetrating on Austria's post-1945 attitudes toward her past].

Soergel, Albert, and Curt Hohoff. *Dichtung und Dichter der Zeit: Vom Naturalismus bis zur Gegenwart*. 2 vols. Düsseldorf: August Bagel Verlag, 1964 [useful survey].

Stern, Joseph Peter. "Vienna 1900," *The Listener*, 67 (February, 1962), 291-295.

————. *Re-Interpretations: Seven Studies in Nineteenth Century German Literature*. New York: Basic Books, 1964 [pp. 42-77, esp. 51-61 on Viennese aestheticism].

————. "Introduction." In Arthur Schnitzler. *Liebelei, Leutnant Gustl, Die letzten Masken*. Cambridge: Cambridge University Press, 1966 [pp. 1-44, superb on Viennese attitudes and parlance].

Wunberg, Gotthart. *Der frühe Hofmannsthal: Schizophrenie als dichterische Struktur*. Stuttgart: W. Kohlhammer Verlag, 1965 [esp. pp. 11-40 on Bahr, Mach, and Viennese impressionism].

Zohn, Harry. *Wiener Juden in der deutschen Literatur: Essays*. Tel Aviv: Olamenu, 1964.

C. SURVEYS OF HUNGARIAN THOUGHT AND LITERATURE

Alexander, Bernhard. "Wissenschaftliches Leben, Literatur, bildende Künste." In Albert von Berzeviczy, ed. *Ungarn*. Leipzig, 1918. Pp. 408-459.

Alvarez, Alfred. "Hungary." In *Under Pressure: The Writer in Society: Eastern Europe and the U.S.A.* Baltimore: Penguin Books, 1965. Pp. 32-49 [based on interviews of 1962].

————. "Introduction." In *Hungarian Short Stories* London: Oxford University Press, 1967. Pp. ix-xvi [provocative].

Andritsch, Johann, ed. *Ungarische Geisteswelt von der Landnahme bis Babits*. Baden-Baden: Holle Verlag, 1960 [excellent bibliography].

Báczy, Johann. "Die ungarische Literatur." In *Die österreichisch-ungarische Monarchie in Wort und Bild: Ungarn*. Vol. 3. Vienna, 1893. Pp. 245-342.

Cushing, George Frederick. "Introductory Essay." In *Hungarian Prose and Verse: A Selection with an Introductory Essay*. London: Athlone Press, 1956. Pp. i-xxxv.

——. "The Birth of National Literature in Hungary," *Slavonic and East European Review*, 38 (1959-60), 459-475.

——. "Problems of Hungarian Literary Criticism," *Slavonic and East European Review*, 40 (1961-1962), 341-355 [penetrating].

Duczynska, Ilona, and Karl Polanyi, eds. *The Plough and the Pen: Writings from Hungary 1930-1956*. London: Peter Owen, 1963.

Farkas, Julius von. *Die ungarische Romantik*. Berlin, 1931.

——. *Die Entwicklung der ungarischen Literatur*. Berlin, 1934.

——. *Der Freiheitskampf des ungarischen Geistes 1867-1914: Ein Kapitel aus der Geschichte der neueren ungarischen Literatur*. Berlin: Walter de Gruyter, 1940.

——. "Der ungarische Vormärz: Petöfis Zeitalter," *Ungarische Jahrbücher*, 23 (1943), 15-186.

——, ed. *Ungarns Geschichte und Kultur in Dokumenten*. Wiesbaden: Otto Harrassowitz, 1955.

Hankiss, János, and G. Juhász. *Panorama de la littérature hongroise contemporaine*. Paris, 1930 [covers 1867 to 1929].

Hatvany, Ludwig. "Das alte und das junge Ungarn," *Neue Rundschau*, 21 (1910), 383-400.

Horváth, Zoltán. *Die Jahrhundertwende in Ungarn: Geschichte der zweiten Reformgeneration (1896-1914)*. Neuwied: Luchterhand, 1966 [extremely useful].

Jones, D. Mervyn. *Five Hungarian Writers*. Oxford: At the Clarendon Press, 1966 [on Zrínyi, Mikes, Vörösmarty, Eötvös, Petöfi].

Juhasz, William. "The Development of Catholicism in Hungary in Modern Times." In Joseph N. Moody, ed. *Church and Society: Catholic Social and Political Thought and Movements 1789-1950*. New York: Arts, 1953. Pp. 659-719 [informative].

Kampis, Antal. *The History of Art in Hungary*. Budapest: Corvina Press, 1966.

Katona, Lajos, and Franz Szinnyei. *Geschichte der ungarischen Literatur*. Berlin, 1911. 2d ed. 1927 [brief].

Klaniczay, Tibor, József Szauder, and Miklós Szabolcsi. *History of Hungarian Literature*. Budapest: Corvina Press, 1964.

Klein, Karl Kurt. "Ungarn in der deutschen Dichtung." In Wolfgang Stammler, ed. *Deutsche Philologie im Aufriss*. Vol. 3. 2d ed. Berlin: Erich Schmidt Verlag, 1962. Pp. 551-564.

Kont, Ignác. *Geschichte der ungarischen Literatur*. Leipzig, 1906.

Krücken, Oskar, and Imre Parlagi. *Das geistige Ungarn: Biographisches Lexikon*. 2 vols. Vienna, 1918 [excellent on minor figures].

Reich, Emil. *Hungarian Literature: An Historical and Critical Survey*. Boston, 1898 [provocative].

Reményi, Joseph. *Hungarian Writers and Literature: Modern Novelists, Critics, and Poets*. New Brunswick, N. J.: Rutgers University Press, 1964 [indispensable for 1780 to the present].

Riedl, Frederick. *A History of Hungarian Literature*. New York, 1906.

Sayous, Édouard. *Histoire des hongrois et de leur littérature politique de 7901 à 1815*. Paris, 1872.

Schwicker, Johann Heinrich. *Geschichte der ungarischen Literatur*. Leipzig, 1889 [exceptionally thorough].

Sivirsky, Antal. *Die ungarische Literatur der Gegenwart.* Bern: Francke Verlag, 1962 [covers 1880 to 1960].

Sötér, István. *Aspects et parallélismes de la littérature hongroise.* Budapest: Akadémiai Kiadó, 1966 [sixteen essays].

Sötér, István, and Ottó Süpek, eds. *Littérature hongroise, littérature européenne: Études de la littérature comparée.* Budapest: Akadémiai Kiadó, 1964 [twenty-five essays].

Süle, Tibor. *Sozialdemokratie in Ungarn: Zur Rolle der Intelligenz in der Arbeiterbewegung, 1899-1910.* Graz: Hermann Böhlaus Nachf., 1967 [concentrates on Jászi and Ervin Szabó].

Szabolcsi, Miklós, ed. *Meilenstein: Drei Jahrzehnte im Spiegel der ungarischen Literatur.* Budapest: Corvina Press, 1965 [covers 1933 to 1963].

Tezla, Albert. *An Introductory Bibliography to the Study of Hungarian Literature.* Cambridge, Mass.: Harvard University Press, 1964 [remarkably thorough].

Ujfalvy, Charles Eugène. *La Hongrie: Son histoire, sa langue et sa littérature.* Paris, 1872.

Weber, Johann. *Eötvös und die ungarische Nationalitätenfrage.* Munich: R. Oldenbourg Verlag, 1966.

D.   Surveys of Philosophy in Austria

Bauer, Roger. *Der Idealismus und seine Gegner in Österreich.* Heidelberg: Carl Winter, 1966 [covers little known figures 1780-1860].

Bourke, Vernon J. *History of Ethics.* Garden City, N. Y.: Doubleday, 1968.

Brock, Werner. *An Introduction to Contemporary German Philosophy.* Cambridge: The University Press, 1935.

Edwards, Paul, ed. *The Encyclopedia of Philosophy.* 8 vols. New York: Macmillan and Free Press, 1967.

Enciclopedia filosofica. 4 vols. Venice and Rome, 1957.

Erdmann, Johann G. *Grundriss der Geschichte der Philosophie. II. Philosophie der Neuzeit.* 4th ed. Berlin, 1896 [covers from Descartes to Lotze].

Fischl, Johann. *Geschichte der Philosophie. V. Idealismus, Realismus und Existentialismus der Gegenwart.* Graz: Verlag Styria, 1954 [perceptive introduction].

Frank, Philipp. *Modern Science and Its Philosophy.* Cambridge, Mass.: Harvard University Press, 1949. Repr. New York: Collier Books, 1961 [on Mach and the Vienna Circle].

Gabriel, Leo, and Johann Mader, eds. "Philosophie in Österreich," *Wissenschaft und Weltbild,* 21:2 (June-Sept., 1968), 1-216 [twelve articles on Brentano, Meinong, Wittgenstein, Reininger, Ebner, et al.].

Glockner, Hermann. *Die europäische Philosophie von den Anfängen bis zur Gegenwart.* 2d ed. Stuttgart: Reclam, 1960 [one of the best surveys of Western philosophy].

Jellinek, Georg. "Die deutsche Philosophie in Österreich" [1874]. In *Ausgewählte Schriften und Reden.* Vol. 1. Berlin, 1911. Pp. 55-68.

Johnston, William M. "Syncretist Historians of Philosophy at Vienna, 1860-1930," *Journal of the History of Ideas,* 1971 [concerns Theodor Gomperz, Friedrich Jodl, Wilhelm Jerusalem, Rudolf Eisler].

———. "Neo-Idealists From Austria, 1870-1938," *Modern Austrian Literature,* 1971

BIBLIOGRAPHY 491

[concerns Johannes Volkelt, Robert Reininger, Melchior Palágyi, Emil Lask, Alois Riehl].

Kraus, Oskar. "The Special Outlook and Tasks of German Philosophy in Bohemia," *Slavonic and East European Review*, 13 (1934-35), 345-349.

Lütgert, Wilhelm. *Die Religion des deutschen Idealismus und ihr Ende.* 4 vols. Gütersloh: C. Bertelsmann, 1923-1930. Repr. Hildesheim: G. Olms, 1967 [masterful].

Meyer, Hans. *Geschichte der abendländischen Weltanschauung. V. Die Weltanschauung der Gegenwart.* 2d ed. Paderborn: Ferdinand Schöningh, 1966 [Thomistic; offers exceptionally comprehensive coverage since 1830].

Mühlher, Robert. "Ontologie und Monadologie in der österreichischen Literatur des 19. Jahrhunderts." In Joseph Stummvoll, ed. *Die österreichische Nationalbibliothek: Festschrift für Josef Bick.* Vienna: Bauer, 1948. Pp. 488-504 [fundamental].

Neurath, Otto. *Le développement du Cercle de Vienne et l'avenir de l'empirisme logique.* Paris: Hermann, 1935.

Oesterreich, Traugott Konstantin. *Die deutsche Philosophie des XIX. Jahrhunderts und der Gegenwart.* Vol. 4 of Friedrich Überweg's *Grundriss der Geschichte der Philosophie.* 12th ed. Berlin, 1923 [indispensable, especially for tracing affiliation between a teacher and his pupils].

Ortner, Max. "Kant in Österreich," *Jahrbuch der Grillparzer-Gesellschaft,* 14 (Vienna, 1904), 1-25 [covers 1780-1810].

Schmidt, Heinrich, and Georgi Schischkoff, eds. *Philosophisches Wörterbuch.* 17th ed. Stuttgart: Alfred Kröner Verlag, 1965.

Siegel, Carl. "Unterrichtsreform: Philosophie." In Eduard Castle, ed. *Geschichte der deutschen Literatur in Österreich-Ungarn im Zeitalter Franz Josephs I.* Vol. 1. Vienna: Fromme, 1936. Pp. 17-48 [indispensable].

Stegmüller, Wolfgang. *Hauptströmungen der Gegenwartsphilosophie: Eine kritische Einführung.* 3d ed. Stuttgart: Alfred Kröner Verlag, 1965 [on Brentano, Husserl, Reininger, Schlick, Carnap, Wittgenstein].

Topitsch, Ernst. "Kant in Österreich." In *Philosophie der Wirklichkeit: Festschrift zum 80. Geburtstag Robert Reiningers.* Vienna: A. Sexl, 1949. Pp. 236-253 [penetrating].

Winter, Eduard. *Der Josefinismus und seine Geschichte: Beiträge zur Geistesgeschichte Österreichs 1740-1848.* Brünn: Rudolf M. Rohrer Verlag, 1943 [encyclopedic].

———. *Romantismus, Restauration und Frühliberalismus im österreichischen Vormärz.* Vienna: Europa Verlag, 1968 [covers 1790-1848].

———. *Revolution, Neoabsolutismus und Liberalismus in der Donaumonarchie.* Vienna: Europa Verlag, 1969 [covers 1848-1868].

Ziegenfuss, Werner, and Gertrud Jung, eds. *Philosophen-Lexikon: Handwörterbuch der Philosophie nach Personen.* 2 vols. Berlin: Walter de Gruyter, 1949-1950 [incomparably useful, especially on minor figures].

Zimmermann, Robert. "Wissenschaft und Literatur." In *Wien 1848-1888.* Vol. 2. Vienna, 1888. Pp. 129-196.

———. "Philosophie und Philosophen in Österreich," *Österreichisch-Ungarische Revue,* 6 (1889), 177-198, 259-272 [extremely informative].

E. SURVEYS OF SOCIAL THEORY IN AUSTRIA

Alexander, Franz, and Sheldon T. Selesnick. *The History of Psychiatry: An Evaluation of Psychiatric Thought and Practice from Prehistoric Times to the Present.* New York: Harper and Row, 1966 [sometimes cavalier toward prepsychoanalytic figures].

Alexander, Franz, Samuel Eisenstein, and Martin Grotjahn, eds. *Psychoanalytic Pioneers.* New York: Basic Books, 1966 [articles on forty-one figures].

Bernatzik, Edmund. *Die österreichischen Verfassungsgesetze.* Leipzig, 1906.

Brügel, Ludwig. *Geschichte der österreichischen Sozialdemokratie.* 5 vols. Vienna: Franz Deuticke, 1922-1925.

Cole, G. D. H. *A History of Socialist Thought.* 5 vols. London: Macmillan, 1953-1960. Vol. 3:2 (1956), 519-565. Vol. 4:1 (1958), 213-257. Vol. 5 (1960), 150-169 concern Austro-Marxists.

Duschenes, Friedrich, Wenzel Ritter von Belsky, and Carl Baretta, eds. *Österreichisches Rechts-Lexikon: Praktisches Handwörterbuch des öffentlichen und privaten Rechts der in Reichsrathe vertretenen Königreiche und Länder.* 4 vols. Prague, 1894-1898.

Elster, Ludwig, Adolf Weber, and Friedrich Wieser. eds. *Handwörterbuch der Staatswissenschaften.* 8 vols. 4th ed. Jena: Gustav Fischer, 1923-1928.

Emerson, Rupert. *State and Sovereignty in Modern Germany.* New Haven: Yale University Press, 1928.

Friedmann, Wolfgang. *Legal Theory.* 4th ed. London: Stevens and Sons, 1960 [lucid].

Garner, James Wilford. "The Judiciary of the German Empire," *Political Science Quarterly,* 17 (1902), 490-514; 18 (1903), 512-530 [extremely useful].

Heyt, Friso D., and Laszlo A. Vaskovics. "Die gegenwärtige Situation der österreichischen Soziologie." In Gottfried Eisermann, ed. *Die gegenwärtige Situation der Soziologie.* Stuttgart: Ferdinand Enke Verlag, 1967. Pp. 97-140.

Howey, R. S. *The Rise of the Marginal Utility School 1870-1889.* Lawrence, Kans.: University of Kansas Press, 1960.

Hutchison, T. W. *A Review of Economic Doctrines 1870-1929.* Oxford: At the Clarendon Press, 1953 [exceptionally clear].

Kauder, Emil. *A History of Marginal Utility Theory.* Princeton, N. J.: Princeton University Press, 1965.

Lesky, Erna. *Die Wiener medizinische Schule im 19. Jahrhundert.* Graz: Verlag Hermann Böhlaus Nachf., 1965 [exhaustive].

Lowrie, Robert H. *The History of Ethnological Theory.* New York: Farrar and Rinehart, 1937. Repr. New York: Holt, Rinehart and Winston, 1966.

Merryman, John Henry. *The Civil Law Tradition: An Introduction to the Legal Systems of Western Europe and Latin America.* Stanford: Stanford University Press, 1969 [compares the Anglo-Saxon and continental legal systems].

Mischler, Ernst and Josef Ulbrich. *Österreichisches Staatswörterbuch: Handbuch des gesamten österreichischen öffentlichen Rechtes.* 4 vols. Vienna, 1905-1909 [lucid].

Pongratz, Ludwig J. *Problemgeschichte der Psychologie.* Bern: Francke Verlag, 1967.

Reble, Albert. *Geschichte der Pädagogik.* 8th ed. Stuttgart: Ernst Klett Verlag, 1965 [succinct].

Rosenmayr, Leopold, and Eva Köckeis, eds. *Sociology in Austria: History, Present Activities and Projects.* Graz: Hermann Böhlaus Nachf., 1966.

Salomon-Delatour, Gottfried. *Moderne Staatslehren.* Neuwied: Luchterhand, 1965 [one of the best histories of political theory].

Schumpeter, Joseph A. *History of Economic Analysis.* New York: Oxford University Press, 1954 [illuminates all fields of social theory].

Sellnow, Werner. *Gesellschaft - Staat - Recht: Zur Kritik der bürgerlichen Ideologien über die Entstehung von Gesellschaft, Staat und Recht (Von der bürgerlichen Aufklärung bis zum deutschen Positivismus des 19. Jahrhunderts).* East Berlin: Rütten und Loening, 1963 [a massively learned Marxist exposition of nineteenth-century sociology, legal theory, and ethnology].

Srbik, Heinrich Ritter von. *Geist und Geschichte vom deutschen Humanismus bis zur Gegenwart.* 2 vols. Munich: Verlag F. Bruckmann; Salzburg: Otto Müller Verlag, 1950-1951. Repr. 1964 [perhaps the most comprehensive history of historical writing; vol. 2, pp. 80-121 describes Austrian historians from 1800 to 1918].

Stark, Werner. *The Sociology of Knowledge: An Essay in Aid of a Deeper Understanding of the History of Ideas.* London: Routledge and Kegan Paul, 1958 [penetrating].

Stigler, George J. *Production and Distribution Theories: The Formative Period.* New York: Macmillan, 1941.

Verdross, Alfred. *Abendländische Rechtsphilosophie: Ihre Grundlagen und Hauptprobleme in geschichtlicher Schau.* 2d ed. Vienna: Springer-Verlag, 1963 [incisive].

Wyss, Dieter. *Die tiefenpsychologischen Schulen von den Anfängen bis zur Gegenwart: Entwicklung, Probleme, Krisen.* 2d ed. Göttingen: Vandenhoeck und Ruprecht, 1966 [comprehensive].

F. Surveys of Fine Arts in Austria

Feuchtmüller, Rupert, and Wilhelm Mrazek. *Kunst in Österreich 1860-1918.* Vienna: Forum Verlag, 1964.

Feuerstein, Günther, Herbert Hutter, Ernst Koller, and Wilhelm Mrazek. *Moderne Kunst in Österreich.* Vienna: Forum Verlag, 1965.

Grimschitz, Bruno. *The Old Vienna School of Painting.* Vienna: Kunstverlag Wolfrum, 1961 [superb plates].

———. *Austrian Painting from Biedermeier to Modern Times.* Vienna: Kunstverlag Wolfrum, 1963.

Hamann, Richard, and Jost Hermand. *Deutsche Kunst und Kultur von der Gründerzeit bis zum Expressionismus.* 4 vols. East Berlin: Akademie-Verlag, 1959-1967 [vol. 5 in preparation; magisterial synopsis of literature and fine arts].

Hevesi, Ludwig. *Österreichische Kunst im 19. Jahrhundert.* 2 vols. Leipzig, 1903 [indispensable on minor figures].

Hoffmann, Edith. *Kokoschka: Life and Work.* London: Faber and Faber, 1947 [elucidates all genres of Austrian art].

Hoffmann, Werner. *Das irdische Paradies: Kunst im 19. Jahrhundert.* Munich: Prestel-Verlag, 1960.

————. *Moderne Malerei in Österreich*. Vienna: Kunstverlag Wolfrum, 1965.

Kindlers Malerei Lexikon. 5 vols. Zürich: Kindler Verlag, 1964-1968.

Novotny, Fritz. *Painting and Sculpture in Europe 1780-1880*. Baltimore: Penguin Books, 1960 [stresses Germany].

Riehl, Hans. *Österreichische Malerei in Hauptwerken*. Vienna: Verlag Kremayr und Scheriau, 1957.

Schmidt, Gerhard. *Neue Malerei in Österreich*. Vienna: Verlag Brüder Rosenbaum, 1956.

Sotriffer, Kristian. *Modern Austrian Art: A Concise History*. London: Thames and Hudson, 1965 [incisive].

Uhl, Ottokar. *Moderne Architektur in Wien: Von Otto Wagner bis heute*. Vienna: Schroll Verlag, 1966.

Waissenberger, Robert. *Wien und die Kunst in unserem Jahrhundert*. Vienna: Verlag für Jugend und Volk, 1965 [brief].

Index

Index

Abel, Heinrich (1843–1926), 61
Abraham a Sancta Clara (1644–1709), 14
Ackeret, Jakob, 182
Adler, Alfred (1870–1937): analyzed, 255–258; and Austro–Marxists, 250; and Freud, 174, 177, 253; and Rank, 258, 259, 260; and Szondi, 381, 382; and Velikovsky, 24
Adler, Friedrich (1879–1960), 103, 186
Adler, Guido (1855–1941), 134, 152, 155
Adler, Max (1873–1937): analyzed, 109–111; friends of, 99, 101, 194; and Lukács, 372–373; as sociologist, 312, 378
Adler, Paul (1878–1946): and Ehrenfels, 306; and Hauser, 386; as Marcionist, 270–271, 273, 393
Adler, Raïssa Epstein, 256
Adler, Viktor (1852–1918): analyzed, 99–102; on Austria, 22, 46, 241; colleagues of, 103, 106; as a Jew, 27, 269
Ady, Endre (1877–1919), 349, 351
Aehrenthal, Aloys (1854–1912), 49
Alarcón, Pedro de, 156
Albert, Eduard (1841–1900), 226
Albrecht I, duke of Austria (c. 1255–1308)
Albrecht, archduke (1817–1895), 38
Alexander, Bernhard (1850–1927), 251
Alexander, Franz (1891–1964), 248, 251, 352
Alfonso, crown prince of Spain, 54
Alt, Rudolf von (1812–1905), 141, 289
Altenberg, Peter (1859–1919): Buber on, 215; described, 120; friends of, 123, 151, 206; as impressionist, 137, 169, 173, 386, 397, 398; writings of, 127, 139
Amerling, Friedrich von (1803–1887), 141
Anaxagoras, 296
Andersen, Hans Christian, 123
Andrássy, Gyula (1823–1890), 335, 336
Andrássy, Gyula (1860–1929), 337
Andreas-Salomé, Lou: friends of, 136, 178, 421; on women, 118, 272
Andreski, Stanislaw, 27
Andrew II, king of Hungary (1205–1235), 337
Andrian-Werburg, Leopold von (1875–1951), 145
Angelus, Silesius, 312
Anna O. *See* Pappenheim, Bertha

Anschütz, Gerhard, 95
Antal, Frigyes (1887–1954), 154, 376
Anti-Semitism, causes of, 27–28, 65–66, 359, 398
Antoine, André-Léonard, 365
Anzengruber, Ludwig (1839–1889), 59
Aquinas, Thomas: Brentano on, 296; Günther on, 280; and Herbart, 284; Pribram on, 77; and Spann, 313
Arany, János (1817–1882), 349–350
Aristotle: Brentano on, 80, 290–292, 295, 296; Ehrenfels on, 307; in gymnasium, 68; Péterfy on, 176; Wahle on, 202, 203; Weininger on, 160; and Zimmermann, 288
Arlt, Ferdinand von (1812–1887), 227
Arndt, Ernst Moritz, 188
Arnim, Achim von, 384
Arnim, Bettina von, 290
Auenbrugger, Leopold von (1722–1809), 224
Auersperg, Adolf (1821–1885): and Concordat, 56, 68; and Czechs, 106, 265; and Freud, 245; and Rudolf, 35
Auffenberg-Komarów, Moritz (1852–1928), 55
Augustine, 209, 213, 313
Austin, John, 96, 97
Avenarius, Richard, 182, 186, 202

Baader, Franz, 196
Babenberg family, 11
Bach, Alexander (1813–1893), 338, 345–346, 348, 351
Bach, Johann Sebastian, 217
Bacon, Francis, 77, 197, 296, 361
Badeni, Count Kasimir (1846–1909): and Freud, 47, 239; provoked debates, 37, 47, 106, 267, 330
Bahnsen, Julius, 316
Bahr, Hermann (1863–1934): on death, 166, 249; described, 119–120; and Ehrenzweig, 172; and Herzl, 357; as impressionist, 173, 174, 180, 243, 397, 399; Kraus on, 119, 206; on Mach, 185, 186; and Molnár, 30, 130; nostalgia of, 32, 63, 126; and Popper-Lynkeus, 308; and Redlich, 49–50; on Saar, 169; on Ta-

Bonitz, Hermann (1814–1888), 67, 284
Bortstieber, Gertrud, 367
Botticelli, Sandro, 310
Bowditch, Henry Ingersoll, 225
Brahm, Otto, 365
Brahms, Johannes (1833–1897): described, 134; friends of, 119, 134, 207, 227; and Richard Wagner, 132; Hugo Wolf on, 136; and Zimmermann, 289
Braunthal, Julius (1891–), 57, 103
Brecht, Walter (1876–1950), 22, 399
Brehm, Alfred, 134
Breitner, Hugo (1873–1946), 75
Brentano, Christian, 290
Brentano, Clemens Maria, 290
Brentano, Franz (1838–1917): analyzed, 290–296; on Bolzano, 277; and Breuer, 235; critics of, 190, 199, 202; and Ehrenfels, 302–307; as ex-priest, 60, 281; and Husserl, 253, 299–301; influence of, 1, 23, 77, 285, 400; and Mach, 186, 250; and Carl Menger, 80, 85; and Meinong, 297–298; and Zimmermann, 287–288
Brentano, Lujo, 193, 290
Breuer, Josef (1842–1925): analyzed, 235–237; friends of, 136, 226, 292; and Freud, 52, 239, 253, 257–258; at gymnasium, 67; and Mach, 184–185
Broch, Hermann (1886–1951): analyzed, 315–317; and Buber, 174, 215, 216, 220; on cinema, 386; on death, 166, 167; on Jews, 23, 25; on science, 185, 187, 188; on Vienna, 1, 27, 44, 121, 131, 392; and Weininger, 160, 400; and Wittgenstein, 212, 213
Brod, Max (1884–1968): and Landauer, 197; as Marcionist, 269, 270, 271, 306; on war, 31
Bronner, Ferdinand (1867–1948), 161
Brouwer, Jan, 211
Brown, Norman O., 248
Broz, Josip, 101
Brücke, Ernst Wilhelm (1819–1892): analyzed, 229–231; and Breuer, 235, 236; and Freud, 222, 244, 253, 261; in politics, 69–70; as polymath, 6, 147, 195
Brücke, Hans, 231
Bruckner, Anton (1824–1896): analyzed, 135; habits of, 44, 292; Hanslick on, 132, 133; and Schönberg, 139; as teacher, 134, 135, 137, 302; Hugo Wolf on, 136
Brunngraber, Rudolf (1901–1960), 464
Bruno, Giordano, 330
Bryusov, Valery, 470

Buber, Martin (1878–1965): analyzed, 214–217; and Broch, 174, 316; and Ebner, 217–220, 260, 385, 387; influence of, 1, 245, 273, 400, 402; as a Jew, 25, 26, 398; and Kornfeld, 271–272; and Landauer, 197; and Spann, 313
Buber, Salomon (1827–1906), 214
Büchner, Ludwig, 110
Bühler, Charlotte (1893–), 109
Bühler, Karl (1879–1963), 109
Bukharin, Nikolai, 85
Burke, Edmund, 382
Burstyn, Gunther (1879–1945), 55
Busch, Wilhelm, 212

Calderón de la Barca, Pedro, 22
Campbell, Joseph, 259
Canisius. Peter (1521–1597), 13
Carlyle, Thomas, 123
Carnap, Rudolf (1891–1970): and Neurath, 192, 195; and Vienna Circle, 189, 190; on Wittgenstein, 211
Carneri, Bartholomäus von (1821–1909), 319
Carus, Carl Gustav, 282
Céline, Louis-Ferdinand, 442
Cervantes, Miguel de: Dvořák on, 154; Freud on, 244; Lukács on, 368, 369, 370, 374
Chamberlain, Houston Stewart (1855–1927): analyzed, 328–332; and Gumplowicz, 323, 326; Mayreder on, 157; on Protektion, 69; and Weininger, 160, 161; and Wiesner, 70
Chamberlain, Joseph, 65
Charcot, Jean, 222, 231, 232, 240
Charlemagne, 42
Charles V, Holy Roman Emperor (1519–1556), 12, 142
Chekhov, Anton, 365
Chernyshevsky, Nikolai, 350
Chiavacci, Vinzenz (1847–1916), 121
Chlumberg, Hans von (1897–1930), 393
Chotek, Sophie (1868–1914), 36, 40
Chrobak, Rudolf (1843–1910), 226, 235, 240
Clam-Martinic, Heinrich (1826–1887), 265
Clarke, Samuel, 289
Clausewitz, Carl von, 392
Cleve, Felix (1890–), 199
Coch, Georg (1842–1890), 46
Cohen, Hermann, 96, 110
Columbus, Christopher, 244
Comenius, Jan (1592–1670), 280
Comte, Auguste, 167, 289, 361

Joseph II, Holy Roman Emperor (1765–1790): and bureaucracy, 45, 61, 89; described, 16–18; and hospitals, 223–234; and Hungary, 335, 338, 355
Joyce, James, 171, 172
József, Attila (1905–1937), 178
Juhász, Gyula (1883–1937), 178
Jung, Carl Gustav: and Freud, 174, 253, 255; and Rank, 260, 261
Jungmann, Josef (1773–1847), 266

Kafka, Franz (1883–1924): on bureaucracy, 50, 392; on cinema, 382–383; as Marcionist, 27, 198, 270, 271, 273; on women, 160, 272; writings of, 122, 306
Kahler, Erich (1885–1970), 24
Kainz, Josef (1858–1910), 125
Kalbeck, Max (1850–1921), 134
Kállay, Béni (1839–1903), 336, 347
Kálnoky, Gustav (1832–1898), 336
Kandinsky, Wassily, 146
Kant, Immanuel: Max Adler on, 109–111; Brentano on, 294, 295–296; and Herbart, 274, 281, 282, 284, 300; hostility to, 184, 202, 279, 285–286; influence of, 67, 91, 226, 275, 289, 330; Lukács on, 372–373; and neo-Kantians, 96–97, 251, 285, 377; and Weininger, 160, 161
Karl I, emperor of Austria (1916–1918), 28, 42, 101
Karl Ludwig, archduke (1833–1896), 36
Karl VI, Holy Roman Emperor (1711–1740), 14, 15
Kármán, Theodor von (1881–1963), 353
Karner, Joseph. See Renner, Karl
Károlyi, Mihály (1875–1955), 339–341
Károlyi family, 338
Karpischek, Luise, 217, 219
Kaschnitz von Weinberg, Guido (1890–1958), 154
Kassner Rudolf (1873–1959): and Chamberlain, 331; duality in, 174; Lukács on, 367, 369, 372, 374
Kastil, Alfred (1874–1950), 293, 296
Kauder, Emil, 86
Kaufmann, Felix (1895–1949), 189, 301
Kaunitz, Wenzel Anton Price (1711–1794), 15
Kautsky, Jan (1827–1896), 101
Kautsky, Karl (1854–1938), 101, 110
Kekulé, August, 187
Kéler, Sigismund von, 83
Keller, Gottfried, 212, 213, 350
Kelsen, Hans (1881–): analyzed, 95–98; constitution of, 74, 75; on dualism, 109,

191, 316; and Freud, 243; at gymnasium, 67; influence of, 248, 306, 400, 401; as a Jew, 23, 27, 269; and Rank, 258; and Spann, 314, 387
Kemény, Zsigmond (1814–1875), 349
Kern, Vinzenz von (1760–1829), 224
Kerr, Alfred, 365
Kettcler, Wilhelm Emmanuel von, 291
Keyserling, Arnold (1922–), 462
Keyserling, Hermann, 331
Kielmansegg, Erich von (1847–1923), 64, 70
Kienzl, Wilhelm (1857–1941), 108
Kierkegaard, Sören: and Ebner, 218, 219; Lukács on, 368, 369, 370, 371; in Prague, 119
Kinsky, Bertha von. See Suttner, Bertha von
Kirchhoff, Robert, 187
Kisch, Egon Erwin (1885–1948), 55, 68
Kitchener, Lord Herbert, 331
Kjellén, Rudolf, 351–352
Klages, Ludwig, 247
Klein, Johann (1788–1856), 226
Kleist, Heinrich, 52, 136, 368
Klimt, Ernst (1864–1892), 144
Klimt, Gustav (1862–1918): admirers of, 118, 126, 137, 152; analyzed, 144–146; as decorator, 139
Kluckhohn, Paul, 19
Knaus, 60
Knies, Karl, 81
Köchert, Melanie, 136
Kodály, Zoltán (1882–1967), 376
Koestler, Arthur (1905–), 71–72, 116
Koffka, Kurt, 304
Köhler, Wolfgang, 303, 304
Kohn, Hans (1891–1971), 68, 272
Kokoschka, Oskar (1886–): analyzed, 146–147; friends of, 137, 153, 170; and Romako, 143; and suicide, 179; on technology, 392, 395–396; in Vienna, 251
Kolbenheyer, Erwin Guide (1878–1962), 199
Kölcsey, Ferenc (1790–1838), 350
Koller, Alexander von (1813–1890), 265
Kompert, Leopold (1822–1886), 26, 359
Königstein, Leopold (1850–1924), 241
Korda, Alexander (1893–1956), 384
Kornfeld, Paul (1889–1942), 138, 270, 271–272, 273
Körösi, József (1844–1906), 343
Korsch, Karl, 111
Kossuth, Ferenc (1841–1914), 37, 51, 337
Kossuth, Lajos (1802–1894): and Franz

335; on Mach, 185–186; on sadism, 52–53
Mussolini, Benito, 341

Näcke, Paul, 245
Napoleon Bonaparte: and Austria, 12, 18, 39, 44; Bauer on, 102
Neill, A. S., 248
Neipperg, Adam, 39
Németh, László (1901–), 351
Nerval, Gérard de, 179
Nestroy, Johann (1801–1862): and Kraus, 203, 204, 213; and Offenbach, 129; satires by, 22, 117, 121, 122, 382, 396; and Wittgenstein, 208
Neumann, John von (1903–1957), 353
Neurath, Otto (1882–1945): analyzed, 192–195; and Mach, 184, 186; as Socialist, 75, 105, 223, 314, 379; versatility of, 6, 401; and Vienna Circle, 189, 190, 192, 211; on war, 392
Neurath, Wilhelm (1840–1901), 192–193, 194, 195
Newton, Isaac, 187
Nicholas I, tsar of Russia, 37
Nicholas II, tsar of Russia, 319
Niekisch, Ernst, 193
Nietzsche, Friedrich: and Broch, 316; Chamberlain on, 329; Ebner on, 218; insanity of, 142, 179, 233; and Kraus, 4, 206; on language, 196; Lanz on, 332; Lukács on, 367; Mahler on, 137; Mauthner on, 197; Nordau on, 363; and psychoanalysts, 247, 255, 258; Schlick on, 190, 192; and Spann, 314; and Hugo Wolf, 136
Nihilism, therapeutic, defined, 71, 223–229
Nikisch, Arthur (1855–1922), 137–138
Nobel, Alfred, 318
Nordau, Max (1849–1923): analyzed, 362–364; Ehrenfels on, 305; and Herzl, 1, 121, 359; as Hungarian, 193, 397, 398; on masochism, 234
Nothnagel, Hermann (1841–1905), 227
Novalis: Friedell on, 123; Lukács on, 367, 368; Spann on, 313

Obermayr, F., 156
Occam, William of, 103, 183, 296
O'Conor-Eccles, C., 228
Offenbach, Jacques, 129, 213
Olbrich, Josef Maria (1867–1908), 144
Olsen, Regine, 368
Oppenheimer, Franz, 325, 361, 376

Oppolzer, Johann von (1808–1871), 226, 227, 235
Ostwald, Wilhelm, 183, 187, 188
Otto, archduke (1865–1906), 41–42, 146
Otto I, Holy Roman Emperor (962–973), 11
Ottokar Premysl (ca. 1230–1278), 12

Pacelli, Cardinal Eugenio, 57
Paderewski, Ignacy, 132
Paine, Thomas, 96
Palacký, František (1798–1876): on Austroslavism, 266, 268, 269; and Renner, 107; and Stifter, 279
Palágyi, Melchior (1859–1924), 277, 301
Panizza, Oskar, 179, 244
Pappenheim, Bertha (1859–1936), 235–237
Paracelsus, 199, 241, 312
Parmenides, 200–201
Parsons, Talcott, 20, 22
Pascal, Blaise, 217
Pellico, Silvio (1789–1854), 19
Pernerstorfer, Engelbert (1850–1918): and Viktor Adler, 99, 100, 241; on hospitals, 47, 227–228; on Otto, 42
Pestalozzi, Johann Heinrich, 281, 293
Péterfy, Jenö (1850–1899), 176, 352
Petöfi, Sándor (1823–1849): as Hungarian, 350, 370, 373; and Jókai, 347, 349; Szabó on, 376
Petzold, Alfons (1882–1923), 102, 392
Petzval, Josef (1807–1891), 186
Pfänder, Alexander, 301
Pfizmaier, August (1808–1887), 21
Phaeacianism: defined, 115
Pherecydes, 202
Philippe, Charles-Louis, 369
Philip the Good of Burgundy, 309
Pick, Arnold (1851–1924), 267
Piloty, Karl Theodor von, 141
Pinsent, David, 208
Pistor, Fanny, 233
Pius VI, pope (1775–1799), 17
Pius IX, pope (1846–1878), 56, 280, 291
Planck, Max, 188
Plato: Chamberlain on, 330; Friedell on, 123; Kelsen on, 97; Mach on, 185; Péterfy on, 176; Weininger on, 160
Platonism: in Bolzano, 276, 293; in Broch, 315–317; in Eisler, 2; in Kassner, 369, 374; in Kraus, 205
Plotinus, 282, 372
Poe, Edgar Allan, 384, 395
Polanyi, Karl (1886–1964), 180, 314, 352
Polanyi, Michael (1891–), 180, 352, 401